SELECTED ANTITRUST CASES
Landmark Decisions

Selected Antitrust Cases
Landmark Decisions

IRWIN M. STELZER
President
National Economic Research Associates, Inc.
New York City

with the assistance of
HOWARD P. KITT
Vice President
National Economic Research Associates, Inc.

Sixth Edition   1981

RICHARD D. IRWIN, INC.   Homewood, Illinois   60430
Irwin-Dorsey Limited   Georgetown, Ontario   L7G 4B3

804813

ISBN 0-256-02339-5
Library of Congress Catalog Card No. 80-82099

Printed in the United States of America

1 2 3 4 5 6 7 8 9 0 K 8 7 6 5 4 3 2 1

Unambiguously
To Adam

Preface

The purpose of this sixth edition remains that of providing students of economics, government, and business administration with an opportunity to obtain an understanding of the manner in which economic theory is reflected in antitrust policy. Teachers in these fields are almost uniform in their agreement that there is no substitute for an actual reading of the case materials, in order to facilitate an understanding of the legal and economic issues raised by our antitrust laws, and to provide the student with interesting concrete problems. Students can rarely be required, however, to read lengthy court opinions in addition to a standard text. Consequently, we have compiled a list of the leading decisions in this area and edited them to manageable proportions, taking care, at the same time, to preserve all that is of lasting significance in the opinions. In every instance, the original language of the court has been retained; the deletions made were not permitted to interfere with the smooth flow of thought and language of these judicial opinions. Any footnotes added by the author are initialed.

A word about the selection of cases: only those which represent truly landmark opinions have been included. An attempt has been made to select cases so that the student will have both an understanding of the law as it now stands and a knowledge of the historical development of the attitude of the courts on the various legal-economic issues. In addition, I have continued to devote substantial space to dissenting opinions so that students can better understand the inherent complexities of the economic issues faced by the courts.

Although each section of the book is self-contained in the sense that it covers an issue or problem in its entirety, the various chapters are definitely interrelated. Thus, for example, Chapter 1 treats court attitudes toward overwhelming market power, while Chapter 2 deals with the legal and economic issues raised by direct price-fixing agreements. The cases in these portions of the book were also selected so that the student might easily compare court attitudes toward price-fixing agreements, on the one hand, and monopoly power on the other.

This book has now been revised five times since its initial appearance nearly 24 years ago. As in the past, the desire to keep costs at a level which would permit continued use of this book as a supplementary text had to be balanced against the need to add cases.

Although final responsibility for selection of materials remains mine, I am indebted to others for their advice. Alfred E. Kahn, then of Cornell University and now Advisor to the President on Inflation, provided the guidance to the structure of all previous editions and, therefore, to this one; without his assistance throughout my professional career I doubt very much whether I would have found the field as rewarding and stimulating as it has been. John Shenefield graciously provided detailed suggestions concerning materials to be included. Joel B. Dirlam, of the University of Rhode Island, was, as usual, extremely helpful. Howard P. Kitt, a vice president of our firm, alone edited a number of cases in this and earlier editions and made important contributions to the reorganization of the book. With each new addition, his proportionate role in this venture increases, to the point where his modesty will soon no longer be sufficient to prevent his designation as co-author. I would also like to acknowledge the efforts of Cynthia Barr and Doug Mann, who carefully proofread each new selection against the official published decisions.

Irwin M. Stelzer

Contents

PART THREE
MERGERS AND THE PROBLEMS THEY POSE

PART FOUR
TRADE PRACTICES

PART ONE

Monopolization and Direct Conspiracy

1

Monopolization

Traditionally, the antitrust laws have been applied to two types of combines—the so-called close-knit combinations, formed by trust, holding company, merger or consolidation, and the loose-knit confederation to be discussed in Chapter 2. The cases presented below trace the development of court attitudes from the adoption of the "rule of reason" in the *Standard Oil* decision of 1911. This doctrine required the courts to examine the circumstances surrounding the formation of a combination and the pattern of its business behavior to determine whether an intent to monopolize existed. This culminated in the proposition, set forth in the *United States Steel* case, that the law does not make mere size an offense. Some saw a retreat from this position in the *Alcoa* and *American Tobacco* decisions (see Chapter 4)—a move to what they hailed as a "New Sherman Act," under which the structure of an industry, rather than the behavior of firms in it, would be determinative. Whether these decisions did in fact mark the replacement of the rule of reason with a simple "size in bad" criterion is debatable. But it is generally agreed that these two cases greatly increased the ease with which the antitrust laws could be brought to bear against large firms. But the "rule of reason" survived, even if in modified form.

The *Shoe Machinery* case was an attempt to apply a rule of reason modified to account for the *Alcoa* decision. So, too, with the *Cellophane* case, which is of interest also because it represents an attempt by the judiciary to wrestle with the economist's concept of workable or effective competition. The *Grinnell* case represents a reaffirmation of the holding of *Alcoa*—that overwhelming monopoly power, consciously acquired, necessarily runs afoul of the Sherman Act. Thus, until the *CalComp* and *Berkey* decisions, included herein for the first time, things stood about where they had been for 50 years: size alone was not an offense, but its conscious acquisition and use could put it beyond the antitrust pale. These latest cases may represent a change, a reflection of a growing hesitancy on the part of courts to curb aggressive marketplace behavior by the large firms, on the grounds that such behavior constitutes "competition-on-the-merits." Actions once thought to constitute clearly unacceptable behavior by large firms seem no longer so easily proscribed, the courts apparently fearing that they would protect inefficient competitors if they limited the behavior of dominant firms too severely. It is unclear whether and to what degree this is colored by the fact that *Cal-Comp* and *Berkey* were private suits brought by aggrieved competitors in pursuit of, among other things, treble damages. Perhaps the outcome of the Government's pending monopolization proceedings against IBM and AT&T will provide a clearer picture.

Standard Oil Company of New Jersey v. United States
221 U.S. 1 (1911)

Note: MR. CHIEF JUSTICE WHITE delivered the opinion of the Court, the legal reasoning of which is abstracted below. The findings of fact, too lengthy to be set forth in detail here, were essentially as follows: Standard of Ohio, organized by John D. and William Rockefeller in 1870, had by 1872 acquired all but 3 or 4 of the 35 to 45 refineries in Cleveland. By obtaining preferential rates and large rebates from the railroads the combination was able to force competitors to join it or be driven out of business. As a result, the combine obtained control of 90 percent of the petroleum industry, a dominance which enabled it to fix the price of both crude and refined petroleum. In 1899 Standard Oil of New Jersey was established as a holding company to replace the Ohio trust. The new organization continued to obtain preferential treatment from railroads, engaged in several unfair practices against competing pipelines so as to obtain control of that means of transportation as well, engaged in local price cutting to suppress competition, set up bogus independents, engaged in industrial espionage, and earned enormous profits. The Court continued:

. . . *The text of the [Sherman A]ct and its meaning.*
. . . The debates . . . conclusively show . . . that the main cause which led to the legislation was the thought that it was required by the economic condition of the times; that is, the vast accumulation of wealth in the hands of corporations and individuals, the enormous development of corporate organization, the facility for combination which such organizations afforded, the fact that the facility was being used, and that combinations known as trusts were being multiplied, and the widespread impression that their power had been and would be exerted to oppress individuals and injure the public generally. . . .

There can be no doubt that the sole subject with which the first section deals is restraint of trade as therein contemplated, and that the attempt to monopolize and monopolization is the subject with which the second section is concerned. It is certain that those terms, at least in their rudimentary meaning, took their origin in the common law, and were also familiar in the law of this country prior to and at the time of the adoption of the act in question.

We shall endeavor then, first to seek their meaning . . . by making a very brief reference to the elementary and indisputable conceptions of both the English and American law on the subject prior to the passage of the Antitrust Act. . . .

Without going into detail, and but very briefly surveying the whole field, it may be with accuracy said that the dread of enhancement of prices and of other wrongs which it was thought would flow from the undue limitation on competitive conditions caused by contracts or other acts of individuals or corporations, led, as a matter of public policy, to the prohibition or treating as illegal all contracts or acts which were unreasonably restrictive of competitive conditions, either from the nature or character of the contract or act or where the surrounding circumstances were such as to justify the conclusion that they had not been entered into or performed with the legitimate purpose of reasonably forwarding personal interest and developing trade, but on the contrary were of such a character as to give rise to the inference or presumption that they had been entered into or done with the intent to do wrong to the general public and to limit the right of individuals, thus restraining the free flow of commerce and tending to bring about the evils, such as enhancement of prices, which were considered to be against public policy. It is equally true to say that the survey of the legislation in this country on this subject from the beginning will show, depending as it did, upon the economic conceptions which obtained at the time when the legislation was adopted or judicial decision was rendered, that contracts or acts were at one time deemed to be of such a character as to justify the inference of wrongful intent which were at another period thought not to be of that character. But this again, as we have seen, simply followed the line of development of the law of England.

Let us consider the language of the 1st and 2d sections, guided by the principle that where words are employed in a statute which had at the time a well-known meaning at common law or in the law of this country, they are presumed to have been used in that sense unless the context compels to the contrary.

As to the 1st section. . . . [A]s the contracts or acts embraced in the provision were not expressly defined, since the enumeration addressed itself simply to classes of acts, those classes being broad enough to embrace every conceivable contract or combination which could be made concerning trade or commerce or the subjects of such commerce, and thus caused any act done by any of the enumerated methods anywhere in the whole field of human activity to be illegal if in restraint of trade, it inevitably follows that the provision necessarily called for the exercise of judgment which required that some standard should be resorted to for the purpose of determining whether the prohibitions contained in the statute had or had not in any given case been violated. Thus not specifying but indubitably contemplating and requiring a standard, it follows that it was intended that the standard of reason which had been applied at the common law in this country in dealing with subjects of the character embraced by the statute, was intended to be the measure used for the purpose of determining whether in a given case a particular act had or had not brought about the wrong against which the statute provided.

And a consideration of the text of the 2d section serves to establish that it was intended to supplement the 1st, and to make sure that by no possible guise could the public policy embodied in the 1st section be frustrated or evaded. . . .

. . . In other words, having by the 1st section forbidden all means of monopolizing trade, that is, unduly restraining it by means of every contract, combination, etc., the 2d section seeks, if possible, to make the prohibitions of the act all the more complete and perfect by embracing all attempts to reach the end prohibited by the 1st section, that is, restraints of trade, by any attempt to monopolize, or monopolization thereof, even although the acts by which such results are attempted to be brought about or are brought about be not embraced within the general enumeration of the 1st section. And, of course, when the 2d section is thus harmonized with and made as it was intended to be the complement of the 1st, it becomes obvious that the criteria to be resorted to in any given case for the purpose of ascertaining whether violations of the section have been committed, is the rule of reason guided by the established law and by the plain duty to enforce the prohibitions of the act, and thus the public policy which its restrictions were obviously enacted to subserve. And it is worthy of observation, as we have previously remarked concerning the common law, that although the statute, by the comprehensiveness of the enumerations embodied in both the 1st and 2d sections, makes it certain that its purpose was to prevent undue restraints of every kind or nature, nevertheless by the omission of any direct prohibition against monopoly in the concrete it indicates a consciousness that the freedom of the individual right to contract when not unduly or improperly exercised was the most efficient means for the prevention of monopoly, since the operation of the centrifugal and centripetal forces resulting from the right to freely contract was the means by which monopoly would be inevitably prevented if no extraneous or sovereign power imposed it and no right to make unlawful contracts having a monopolistic tendency were permitted. In other words that freedom to contract was the essence of freedom from undue restraint on the right to contract. . . .

. . . *The contentions of the parties as to the meaning of the statute and the decisions of this court relied upon concerning those contentions.*

In substance, the propositions urged by the Government are reducible to this: That the language of the statute embraces every contract, combination, etc., in restraint of trade, and hence its text leaves no room for the exercise of judgment, but simply imposes the plain duty of applying its prohibitions to every case within its literal language. The error involved lies in assuming the matter to be decided. This is true because as the acts which may come under the classes stated in the 1st section and the restraint of trade to which that section applies are not specifically enumerated or defined, it is obvious that judgment must in every case be called into play in order to determine whether a particular act is embraced within the statutory classes, and whether if the act is within such classes its nature or effect causes it to be a restraint of trade within the intendment of the act. To hold to the contrary would require the conclusion either that every contract, act, or combination of any kind or nature, whether it operated a restraint on trade or not, was within the statute, and thus the statute would be destructive of all right to contract or agree or combine in any respect whatever as to subjects embraced in interstate trade or commerce, or if this conclusion were not reached, then the contention would require it to be held that as the statute did not define the things to which it related and excluded resort to the only means by which the acts to which it relates could be ascertained—the light of reason—the enforcement of the statute was impossible because of its uncertainty. The merely generic enumeration which the statute makes of the acts to which it refers and the absence of any definition of restraint of trade as used in the statute leaves room for but one conclusion, which is, that it was expressly designed not to unduly limit the application of the act by precise definition, but while clearly fixing a standard, that is, by defining the ulterior boundaries which could not be transgressed with impunity, to leave it to be determined by the light of reason, guided by the principles of law and the duty to apply and enforce the public policy embodied in the statute, in every given case whether any particular act or contract was within the contemplation of the statute.

But, it is said, persuasive as these views may be, they may not be here applied, because the previous decisions of this court have given to the statute a meaning which expressly excludes the construction which must result from the reasoning stated. The cases are *United States* v. *[Trans-Missouri] Freight Association* . . . and *United States* v. *Joint Traffic Association*. . . . Both the cases involved the legality of combinations or associations of railroads engaged in interstate commerce for the purpose of controlling the conduct of the parties to the association or combination in many particulars. The association or combination was assailed in each case as being in violation of the statute. It was held that they were. It is undoubted that in the opinion in each case general language was made use of, which, when separated from its context, would justify the conclusion that it was decided that reason could not be resorted to for the purpose of determining whether the acts complained of were within the statute. It is, however, also true that the nature and character of the contract or agreement in each case was fully referred to and suggestions as to their unreasonableness pointed out in order to indicate that they were within the prohibitions of the statute. As the cases cannot by any possible conception be treated as authoritative without the certitude that reason was resorted to for the purpose of deciding them, it follows as a matter of course that it must have been held by the light of reason, since the conclusion could not have been otherwise reached, that the assailed contracts or agreements were within the general enumeration of the statute, and that their operation and effect brought about the restraint of trade which the statute prohibited. This being inevitable, the deduction can in reason only be this: That in the cases relied upon it having been found that the acts complained of were within the statute and operated to produce the injuries which the statute forbade, that resort to reason was not permissible in order to allow that to be done which the statute prohibited. This being true, the rulings in the case relied upon when rightly appreciated were therefore this and nothing more: That as considering the contracts or agreements, their necessary effect and the character of the parties by whom they were made, they were clearly restraints of trade within the purview of the statute, they could not be taken out of that category by indulging in general reasoning as to the expediency or nonexpediency of having made the contracts or the wisdom or want of wisdom of the statute which prohibited their being made. That is to say, the cases but decided that the nature and character of the contracts, creating as they did, a conclusive presumption which brought them within the statute, such result was not to be disregarded by the substitution of a judicial appreciation of what the law ought to be for the plain judicial duty of enforcing the law as it was made.

But aside from reasoning it is true to say that the cases relied upon do not when rightly construed sustain the doctrine contended for, as established by all of the numerous decisions of this court which have applied and enforced the Anti-trust Act, since they all in the very nature of things, rest upon the premise that reason was the guide by which the provisions of the act were in every case interpreted. . . .

And in order not in the slightest degree to be wanting in frankness, we say that in so far, however, as by separating the general language used in the opinions in the *Freight Association* and *Joint Traffic* cases from the context and the subject and parties with which the cases were concerned, it may be conceived that the language referred to conflicts with the construction which we give the statute, they are necessarily now limited and qualified. . . .

. . . *The facts and the application of the statute to them.*

. . . Giving to the facts . . . the weight which it was deemed they were entitled to, in the light afforded by the proof of other cognate facts and circumstances, the court below held that the acts and dealings established by the proof operated to destroy the "potentiality of competition" which otherwise would have existed to such an extent as to cause the transfers of stock which were made to the New Jersey corporation and the control which resulted over the many and various subsidiary corporations to be a combination or conspiracy in restraint of trade in violation of the 1st section of the act, but also to be an attempt to monopolize and a monopolization bringing about a perennial violation of the 2d section.

We see no cause to doubt the correctness of these conclusions . . .

a.   Because the unification of power and control over petroleum and its products which was the inevitable result of the combining in the New Jersey corporation by the increase of its stock and the transfer to it of the stocks of so many other corporations, aggregating so vast a capital, gives rise, in and of itself, in the absence of countervailing circumstances, to say the least, to the *prima facie* presumption of intent and purpose to maintain the dominancy over the oil industry, not as a result of normal methods of industrial development, but by new means of combination which were resorted to in order that greater power might be added than would otherwise have arisen had normal methods been followed, the whole with the purpose of excluding others from the trade and thus centralizing in the combination a perpetual control of the movements of petroleum and its products in the channels of interstate commerce.

b.   Because the *prima facie* presumption of intent to restrain trade, to monopolize and to bring about monopolization . . . is made conclusive by considering, *1,* the conduct of the persons . . . instrumental in bringing about the extension of power . . . ; , *2,* . . . the proof as to what was done under those [trust] agreements . . . as well as by weighing the modes in which the power vested . . . has been exerted and the results which have arisen from it.

. . . [W]e think no disinterested mind can survey the period in question without being irresistibly driven to the conclusion that the very genius for commercial development and organization which it would seem was manifested from the beginning soon begot an intent and purpose to exclude others which was frequently manifested by acts and dealings wholly inconsistent with the theory that they were made with the single conception of advancing the development of business power by usual methods, but which on the contrary necessarily involved the intent to drive others from the field and to exclude them from their right to trade and thus accomplish the mastery which was the end in view. . . . The exercise of the power which resulted from that organization fortifies the foregoing conclusions, since the development which came, the acquisition here and there which ensued of every efficient means by which competition could have been asserted, the slow but resistless methods which followed by which means of transportation were absorbed and brought under control, the system of marketing which was adopted by which the country was divided into districts and the trade in each district in oil was turned over to a designated corporation within the combination and all others were excluded, all lead the mind up to a conviction of a purpose and intent which we think is so certain as practically to cause the subject not to be within the domain of reasonable contention. . . .

. . . *The remedy to be administered.*

It may be conceded that ordinarily where it was found that acts had been done in violation of the statute, adequate measure of relief would result from restraining the doing of such acts in the future. . . . But in a case like this, where the condition which has been brought about in violation of the statute, in and of itself, is not only a continued attempt to monopolize, but also a monopolization, the duty to enforce the statute requires the application of broader and more controlling remedies. . . .

In applying remedies for this purpose, however, the fact must not be overlooked that injury to the public by the prevention of an undue restraint on, or the monopolization of trade or commerce is the foundation upon which the prohibitions of the statute rest, and moreover that one of the fundamental purposes of the statute is to protect, not to destroy, rights of property. . . .

So far as the decree held that the ownership of the stock of the New Jersey corporation constituted a combination in violation of the 1st section and an attempt to create a monopoly or to monopolize under the 2d section and commanded the dissolution of the combination, the decree was clearly appropriate. . . .

Our conclusion is that the decree below was right and should be affirmed, except as to the minor matters concerning which we have indicated the decree should be modified. Our order will therefore be one of affirmance with directions, however, to modify the decree in accordance with this opinion. The court below to retain jurisdiction to the extent necessary to compel compliance in every respect with its decree.

And it is so ordered.

[MR. JUSTICE HARLAN concurred in part and dissented in part.]

United States v. *United States Steel Corporation*
251 U.S. 417 (1920)
MR. JUSTICE McKENNA delivered the opinion of the Court.

Suit against the Steel Corporation and certain other companies which it directs and controls by reason of the ownership of their stock, it and they being separately and collectively charged as violators of the Sherman Anti-trust Act.

It is prayed that it and they be dissolved because engaged in illegal restraint of trade and the exercise of monopoly.

Special charges of illegality and monopoly are made and special redresses and remedies are prayed, among others, that there be a prohibition of stock ownership and exercise of rights under such ownership, and that there shall be such orders and distribution of the stock and other properties as shall be in accordance with equity and good conscience and "shall effectuate the purpose of the Anti-trust Act." General relief is also prayed.

The Steel Corporation is a holding company only; the other companies are the operating ones, manufacturers in the iron and steel industry, 12 in number. There are, besides, other corporations and individuals more or less connected with the activities of the other defendants, that are alleged to be instruments or accomplices in their activities and offendings; and that these activities and offendings (speaking in general terms) extend from 1901 to 1911, when the bill was filed. . . .

The case was heard in the District Court by four judges. They agreed that the bill should be dismissed; they disagreed as to the reasons for it. . . . One opinion (written by Judge Buffington and concurred in by Judge McPherson) expressed the view that the Steel Corporation was not formed with the intention or purpose to monopolize or restrain trade, and did not have the motive or effect "to prejudice the public interest by unduly restricting competition or unduly obstructing the course of trade." The corporation, in the view of the opinion, was an evolution, a natural consummation of the tendencies of the industry on account of changing conditions. . . . And the concentration of powers (we are still representing the opinion) was only such as was deemed necessary, and immediately manifested itself in improved methods and products and in an increase of domestic and foreign trade. . . .

Not monopoly, therefore, was the purpose of the organization of the corporation but concentration of efforts with resultant economies and benefits. . . .

All considerations deemed pertinent were expressed and their influence was attempted to be assigned and, while conceding that the Steel Corporation after its formation in times of financial disturbance, entered into informal agreements or understandings with its competitors to maintain prices, they terminated with their occasions, and, as they had ceased to exist, the court was not justified in dissolving the corporation.

The other opinion (by Judge Woolley and concurred in by Judge Hunt . . .) was in some particulars, in antithesis to Judge Buffington's. The view was expressed that neither the Steel Corporation nor the preceding combinations, which were in a sense its antetypes, had the justification of industrial conditions, nor were they or it impelled by the necessity for integration, or compelled to unite in comprehensive enterprise because such had become a condition of success under the new order of things. On the contrary, that the organizers of the corporation and the preceding companies had illegal purpose from the very beginning, and the corporation became "a combination of combinations, by which, directly or indirectly, approximately 180 independent concerns were brought under one business control," which, measured by the amount of production, extended to 80 percent or 90 percent of the entire output of the country, and that its purpose was to secure great profits which were thought possible in the light of the history of its constituent combinations, and to accomplish permanently what those combinations had demonstrated could be accomplished temporarily, and thereby monopolize and restrain trade.

The organizers, however (we are still representing the opinion), underestimated the opposing conditions and at the very beginning the Corporation instead of relying upon its own power sought and obtained the assistance and the cooperation of its competitors (the independent companies). In other words, the view was expressed that the testimony did "not show that the corporation in and of itself ever possessed or exerted sufficient power when acting alone to control prices of the products of the industry." Its power was efficient only when in cooperation with its competitors, and hence it concerted with them in the expedients of pools, associations, trade meetings, and finally in a system of dinners inaugurated in 1907 by the president of the company, E. H. Gary, and called "the Gary Dinners." The dinners were congregations of producers and "were nothing but trade meetings," successors of the other means of associated action and control through such action. They were instituted first in "stress of panic," but, their potency being demonstrated, they were afterwards called to control prices "in periods of industrial calm." "They were pools without penalties" and more efficient in stabilizing prices. But it was the further declaration that "when joint action was either refused or withdrawn the Corporation's prices were controlled by competition."

The Corporation, it was said, did not at any time abuse the power or ascendancy it possessed. It resorted to none of the brutalities or tyrannies that the cases illustrate of other combinations. . . . It combined its power with that of its competitors. It did not have power in and of itself, and the control it exerted was only in and by association with its competitors. Its offense, therefore, such as it was, was not different from theirs and was distinguished from theirs "only in the leadership it assumed in promulgating and perfecting the policy." This leadership it gave up and it had ceased to offend against the law before this suit was brought. It was hence concluded that it should be distinguished from its organizers and that their intent and unsuccessful attempt should not be attributed to it, that it "in and of itself is not now and has never been a monopoly or a combination in restraint of trade," and a decree of dissolution should not be entered against it.

This summary of the opinions . . . indicates that the evidence admits of different deductions as to the genesis of the Corporation and the purpose of its organizers, but only of a single deduction as to the power it attained and could exercise. Both opinions were clear and confident that the power of the Corporation never did and does not now reach to monopoly, and their review of the evidence, and our independent examination of it, enables us to elect between their respective estimates of it, and we concur in the main with that of Judges Woolley and Hunt. And we add no comment except, it may be, that they underestimated the influence of the tendency and movement to integration, the appreciation of the necessity or value of the continuity of manufacture from the ore to the finished product. . . .

. . . In other words, our consideration should be of not what the Corporation had power to do or did, but what it has now power to do and is doing, and what judgment shall be now pronounced—whether its dissolution, as the Government prays, or the dismissal of the suit, as the Corporation insists?

The alternatives are perplexing—involve conflicting considerations, which, regarded in isolation, have diverse tendencies. . . . Monopoly . . . was not achieved, and competitors had to be persuaded by pools, associations, trade meetings, and through the social form of dinners, all of them, it may be, violations of the law, but transient in their purpose and effect. They were scattered through the years from 1901 (the year of the formation of the Corporation), until 1911, but, after instances of success and failure, were abandoned nine months before this suit was brought. There is no evidence that the abandonment was in prophecy of or dread of suit; and the illegal practices have not been resumed, nor is there any evidence of an intention to resume them, and certainly no "dangerous probability" of their resumption. . . .

What, then can now be urged against the Corporation? Can comparisons in other regards be made with its competitors and by such comparisons guilty or innocent existence be assigned it? It is greater in size and productive power than any of its competitors, equal or nearly equal to them all, but its power over prices was not and is not commensurate with its power to produce.

It is true there is some testimony tending to show that the Corporation had such power, but there was also testimony and a course of action tending strongly to the contrary. The conflict was by the judges of the District Court unanimously resolved against the existence of that power, and in doing so they but gave effect to the greater weight of the evidence. It is certain that no such power was exerted. On the contrary, the only attempt at a fixation of prices was, as already said, through an appeal to and confederation with competitors, and the record shows besides that when competition occurred it was not in pretense, and the Corporation, declined in productive powers—the competitors growing either against or in consequence of the competition. If against the competition we have an instance of movement against what the Government insists was an irresistible force; if in consequence of competition, we have an illustration of the adage that "competition is the life of trade" and is not easily repressed. The power of monopoly in the Corporation under either illustration is an untenable accusation. . . .

. . . [C]ompetitors, dealers, and customers of the Corporation testify in multitude that no adventitious interference was employed to either fix or maintain prices and that they were constant or varied according to natural conditions. Can this testimony be minimized or dismissed by inferring that, as intimated, it is an evidence of power not of weakness; and power exerted not only to suppress competition but to compel testimony, is the necessary inference, shading into perjury to deny its exertion? The situation is indeed singular, and we may wonder at it, wonder that the despotism of the Corporation, so baneful to the world in the representation of the Government, did not produce protesting victims.

But there are other paradoxes. . . . In one, competitors (the independents) are represented as oppressed by the superior power of the Corporation; in the other they are represented as ascending to opulence by imitating that power's prices, which they could not do if at disadvantage from the other conditions of competition; and yet confederated action is not asserted. If it were this suit would take on another cast. The competitors would cease to be the victims of the Corporation, and would become its accomplices. And there is no other alternative. The suggestion that lurks in the Government's contention that the acceptance of the Corporation's prices is the submission of impotence to irresistible power is, in view of the testimony of the competitors, untenable. They, as we have seen, deny restraint in any measure or illegal influence of any kind. The Government, therefore, is reduced to the assertion that the size of the Corporation, the power it may have, not the exertion of the power, is an abhorrence to the law, or, as the Government says, "the combination embodied in the Corporation unduly restrains competition by its *necessary effect* . . . , and therefore is unlawful regardless of purpose." . . . To assent to that, to what extremes should we be led? . . .

We have pointed out that there are several of the Government's contentions which are difficult to represent or measure, and, the one we are now considering, that is, the power is "unlawful regardless of purpose," is another of them. It seems to us that it has for its ultimate principle and justification that strength in any producer or seller is a menace to the public interest and illegal because there is potency in it for mischief. The regression is extreme, but short of it the government cannot stop. The fallacy it conveys is manifest. . . .

. . . The Corporation is undoubtedly of impressive size, and it takes an effort of resolution not to be affected by it or to exaggerate its influence. But we must adhere to the law and the law does not make mere size an offense or the existence of unexerted power an offense. It, we repeat, requires overt acts, and trusts to its prohibition of them and its power to repress or punish them. It does not compel competition, nor require all that is possible. . . .

. . . We have seen whatever there was of wrong intent could not be executed; whatever there was of evil effect was discontinued before this suit was brought, and this, we think, determines the decree. We say this in full realization of the requirements of the law. It is clear in its denunciation of monopolies and equally clear in its direction that the courts of the Nation shall prevent and restrain them (its language is "to prevent and restrain violations of" the act), but the command is necessarily submissive to the conditions which may exist and the usual powers of a court of equity to adapt its remedies to those conditions. In other words, it is not expected to enforce abstractions and do injury thereby, it may be, to the purpose of the law. It is this flexibility of discretion—indeed essential function—that makes its value in our jurisprudence—value in this case as in others. We do not mean to say that the law is not its own measure, and that it can be disregarded, but only that the appropriate relief in each instance is remitted to a court of equity to determine, not, and let us be explicit in this, to advance a policy contrary to that of the law, but in submission to the law and its policy, and in execution of both. And it is certainly a matter for consideration that there was no legal attack on the Corporation until 1911, 10 years after its formation and the commencement of its career. We do not, however speak of the delay simply as to its time—that there is estoppel in it because of its time—but on account of what was done during that time—the many millions of dollars spent, the development made, and the enterprises undertaken, the investments by the public that have been invited and are not to be ignored. And what of the foreign trade that has been developed and exists? . . .

The Government, however, tentatively presents a proposition which has some tangibility. It submits that certain of the subsidiary companies are so mechanically equipped and so officially directed as to be released and remitted to independent action and individual interests and the competition to which such interests prompt, without any disturbance to business. . . . They are fully integrated, it is said, possess their own supplies, facilities of transportation and distribution. They are subject to the Steel Corporation is, in effect, the declaration, in nothing but its control of their prices. We may say parenthetically that they are defendants in the suit and charged as offenders, and we have the strange circumstance of violators of the law being urged to be used as expedients of the law.

But let us see what guide to a procedure of dissolution of the corporation and the dispersion as well of its subsidiary companies, for they are asserted to be illegal combinations, is prayed. And the fact must not be overlooked or underestimated. The prayer of the Government calls for not only a disruption of present conditions, but the restoration of the conditions of 20 years ago, if not literally, substantially. . . .

In conclusion we are unable to see that the public interest will be served by yielding to the contention of the Government respecting the dissolution of the Company or the separation from it of some of its subsidiaries; and we do see in a contrary conclusion a risk of injury to the public interest, including a material disturbance of, and, it may be serious detriment to, the foreign trade. And in submission to the policy of the law and its fortifying prohibitions the public interest is of paramount regard.

We think, therefore, that the decree of the District Court should be affirmed.

So ordered.

MR. JUSTICE McREYNOLDS and MR. JUSTICE BRANDEIS took no part in the consideration or decision of the case.

MR. JUSTICE DAY, dissenting.

This record seems to me to leave no fair room for a doubt that the defendants, in the United States Steel Corporation and the several subsidiary corporations which make up that organization, were formed in violation of the Sherman Act. I am unable to accept the conclusion which directs a dismissal of the bill instead of following the well-settled practice, sanctioned by previous decisions of this court, requiring the dissolution of combinations made in direct violation of the law.

It appears to be thoroughly established that the formation of the corporations, here under consideration, constituted combinations between competitors, in violation of law, and intended to remove competition and to directly restrain trade. I agree with the conclusions of Judges Woolley and Hunt, expressed in the court below . . . that the combinations were not submissions to business conditions but were designed to control them for illegal purposes, regardless of other consequences, and "were made upon a scale that was huge and in a manner that was wild," and "properties were assembled and combined with less regard to their importance as integral parts of an integrated whole than to the advantages expected from the elimination of the competition which theretofore existed between them." Those judges found that the constituent companies of the United States Steel Corporation, nine in number, were themselves combinations of steel manufacturers, and the effect of the organization of these combinations was to give a control over the industry at least equal to that theretofore possessed by the constituent companies and their subsidiaries; that the Steel Corporation was a combination of combinations by which directly or indirectly 180 independent concerns were brought under one control. . . .

The enormous overcapitalization of companies and the appropriation of $100,000,000 in stock to promotion expenses were represented in the stock issues of the new organizations thus formed, and were the basis upon which large dividends have been declared from the profits of the business. This record shows that the power obtained by the corporation brought under its control large competing companies which were of themselves illegal combinations, and succeeded to their power; that some of the organizers of the Steel Corporation were parties to the preceding combinations, participated in their illegality, and by uniting them under a common direction intended to augment and perpetuate their power. It is the irresistible conclusion from these premises that great profits to be derived from unified control were the object of these organizations.

The contention must be rejected that the combination was an inevitable evolution of industrial tendencies compelling union of endeavor. . . .

For many years, as the record discloses, this unlawful organization exerted its power to control and maintain prices by pools, associations, trade meetings, and as the result of discussion and agreements at the so-called "Gary Dinners," where the assembled trade opponents secured cooperation and joint action through the machinery of special committees of competing concerns, and by prudent prevision took into account the possibility of defection, and the means of controlling and perpetuating that industrial harmony which arose from the control and maintenance of prices.

It inevitably follows that the corporation violated the law in its formation and by its immediate practices. The power, thus obtained from the combination of resources almost unlimited in the aggregation of competing organizations, had within its control the domination of the trade, and the ability to fix prices and restrain the free flow of commerce upon a scale heretofore unapproached in the history of corporate organization in this country.

These facts established, as it seems to me they are by the record, it follows that, if the Sherman Act is to be given efficacy, there must be a decree undoing so far as is possible that which has been achieved in open, notorious, and continued violation of its provisions.

I agree that the act offers no objection to the mere size of a corporation, nor to the continued exertion of its lawful power, when that size and power have been obtained by lawful means and developed by natural growth, although its resources, capital and strength may give to such corporation a dominating place in the business and industry with which it is concerned. It is entitled to maintain its size and the power that legitimately goes with it, provided no law has been transgressed in obtaining it. But I understand the reiterated decisions of this court construing the Sherman Act to hold that this power may not legally be derived from conspiracies, combinations, or contracts in restraint of trade. To permit this would be to practically annul the Sherman Law by judicial decree. This principle has been so often declared by the decisions that it is only necessary to refer to some of them. It is the scope of such combinations, and their power to suppress and stifle competition and create or tend to create monopolies, which, as we have declared so often as to make its reiteration monotonous, it was the purpose of the Sherman Act to condemn, including all combinations and conspiracies to restrain the free and natural flow of trade in the channels of interstate commerce. . . .

As I understand the conclusions of the court, affirming the decree directing dismissal of the bill, they amount to this: that these combinations, both the holding company and the subsidiaries which comprise it, although organized in plain violation and bold defiance of the provisions of the act, nevertheless are immune from a decree effectually ending the combinations and putting it out of their power to attain the unlawful purposes sought, because of some reasons of public policy requiring such conclusion. I know of no public policy which sanctions a violation of the law, nor of any inconvenience to trade, domestic or foreign, which should have the effect of placing combinations, which have been able thus to organize one of the greatest industries of the country in defiance of law, in an impregnable position above the control of the law forbidding such combinations. Such a conclusion does violence to the policy which the law was intended to enforce, runs counter to the decisions of the court, and necessarily results in a practical nullification of the act itself. . . .

Nor can I yield assent to the proposition that this combination has not acquired a dominant position in the trade which enables it to control prices and production when it sees fit to exert its power. Its total assets on December 31, 1913, were in excess of $1,800,000,000; its outstanding capital stock was $868,583,600; its surplus $151,798,428. Its cash on hand ordinarily was $75,000,000; this sum alone exceeded the total capitalization of any of its competitors, and with a single exception, the total capitalization and surplus of any one of them. That such an organization thus fortified and equipped could if it saw fit dominate the trade and control competition would seem to be a business proposition too plain to require extended argument to support it. Its resources, strength and comprehensive ownership of the means of production enable it to adopt measures to do again as it has done in the past, that is, to effectually dominate and control the steel business of the country. From the earliest decisions of this court it has been declared that it was the effective power of such organizations to control and restrain competition and the freedom of trade that Congress intended to limit and control. That the exercise of the power may be withheld, or exerted with forbearing benevolence, does not place such combinations beyond the authority of the statute which was intended to prohibit their formation, and when formed to deprive them of the power unlawfully attained.

It is said that a complete monopolization of the steel business was never attained by the offending combinations. To insist upon such result would be beyond the requirements of the statute and in most cases practicably impossible. . . .

It is affirmed that to grant the Government's request for a remand to the District Court for a decree of dissolution would not result in a change in the conditions of the steel trade. Such is not the theory of the Sherman Act. That act was framed in the belief that attempted or accomplished monopolization, or combinations which suppress free competition, were hurtful to the public interest, and that a restoration of competitive conditions would benefit the public. We have here a combination in control of one-half of the steel business of the country. If the plan were followed, as in the *American Tobacco* case, of remanding the case to the District Court, a decree might be framed restoring competitive conditions as far as practicable. . . . In my judgment the principles there laid down if followed now would make a very material difference in the steel industry. Instead of one dominating corporation, with scattered competitors, there would be competitive conditions throughout the whole trade which would carry into effect the policy of the law.

It seems to me that if this act is to be given effect, the bill, under the findings of fact made by the court, should not be dismissed, and the cause should be remanded to the District Court, where a plan of effective and final dissolution of the corporations should be enforced by a decree framed for that purpose.

MR. JUSTICE PITNEY and MR. JUSTICE CLARKE concur in this dissent.

United States v. Aluminum Company of America[1]
148 F.2d 416 (2d Cir. 1945)

Before L. HAND, SWAN, and AUGUSTUS N. HAND, Circuit Judges.

L. HAND, Circuit Judge.

. . . For convenience we have divided our discussion into four parts: (1) whether "Alcoa" monopolized the market in "virgin" aluminum ingot; (2) whether "Alcoa" was guilty of various unlawful practices, ancillary to the establishment of its monopoly; (3) whether [Aluminum] "Limited" and "Alcoa" were in an unlawful conspiracy; and whether, if not, "Limited" was guilty of a conspiracy with foreign producers; (4) what remedies are appropriate in the case of each defendant who may be found to have violated the Act.

I. "ALCOA'S" MONOPOLY OF "VIRGIN" INGOT

There are various ways of computing "Alcoa's" control of the aluminum market—as distinct from its production—depending upon what one

---

[1] Because the Supreme Court was unable to obtain a quorum to review the District Court's opinion in this case, it was sent to the Circuit Court of Appeals for final decision. IMS.

regards as competing in that market. The judge [in the District Court] figured its share—during the years 1929–1938, inclusive—as only about thirty-three percent; to do so he included "secondary," and excluded that part of "Alcoa's" own production which it fabricated and did not therefore sell as ingot. If, on the other hand, "Alcoa's" total production, fabricated and sold, be included, and balanced against the sum of imported "virgin" and "secondary," its share of the market was in the neighborhood of sixty-four percent for that period. The percentage we have already mentioned—over ninety—results only if we both include all "Alcoa's" production and exclude "secondary." That percentage is enough to constitute a monopoly; it is doubtful whether sixty or sixty-four percent would be enough; and certainly thirty-three percent is not. Hence it is necessary to settle what we shall treat as competing in the ingot market. That part of its production which "Alcoa" itself fabricates, does not of course ever reach the market as ingot; and we recognize that it is only when a restriction of production either inevitably affects prices, or is intended to do so, that it violates Section 1 of the Act. . . . However, even though we were to assume that a monopoly is unlawful under Section 2 only in case it controls prices, the ingot fabricated by "Alcoa," necessarily had a direct effect upon the ingot market. All ingot—with trifling exceptions—is used to fabricate intermediate, or end, products; and therefore all intermediate, or end, products which "Alcoa" fabricates and sells, pro tanto reduce the demand for ingot itself. . . . We cannot therefore agree that the computation of the percentage of "Alcoa's" control over the ingot market should not include the whole of its ingot production.

As to "secondary," . . . we can say nothing more definite than that, although "secondary" does not compete at all in some uses, (whether because of "sales resistance" only, or because of actual metallurgical inferiority), for most purposes it competes upon a substantial equality with "virgin." On these facts the judge found that "every pound of secondary or scrap aluminum which is sold in commerce displaces a pound of virgin aluminum which otherwise would, or might have been, sold." We agree: so far as "secondary" supplies the demand of such fabricators as will accept it, it increases the amount of "virgin" which must seek sale elsewhere; and it therefore results that the supply of that part of the demand which will accept only "virgin" becomes greater in proportion as "secondary" drives away "virgin" from the demand which will accept "secondary." (This is indeed the same argument which we used a moment ago to include in the supply that part of "virgin" which "Alcoa" fabricates; it is not apparent to us why the judge did not think it applicable to that item as well.) At any given moment therefore "secondary" competes with "virgin" in the ingot market; further, it can, and probably does, set a limit or "ceiling" beyond which the price of "virgin" cannot go, for the cost of its production will in the end depend only upon the expense of scavenging and reconditioning. It might seem for this reason that in estimating "Alcoa's" control over the ingot market, we ought to include the supply of "secondary," as the judge did. Indeed, it may be thought a paradox to say that anyone has the monopoly of a market in which at all times he must meet a competition that limits his price. We shall show that it is not.

In the case of a monopoly of any commodity which does not disappear in use and which can be salvaged, the supply seeking sale at any moment will be made up of two components: (1) the part which the putative monopolist can immediately produce and sell; and (2) the part which has been, or can be, reclaimed out of what he has produced and sold in the past. By hypothesis he presently controls the first of these components; the second he has controlled in the past, although he no longer does. During the period when he did control the second, if he was aware of his interest, he was guided, not alone by its effect at that time upon the market, but by his knowledge that some part of it was likely to be reclaimed and seek the future market. That consideration will to some extent always affect his production until he decides to abandon the business, or for some other reason ceases to be concerned with the future market. Thus, in the case at bar "Alcoa" always knew that the future supply of ingot would be made up in part of what it produced at the time, and, if it was as far-sighted as it proclaims itself, that consideration must have had its share in determining how much to produce. How accurately it could forecast the effect of present production upon the future market is another matter. Experience, no doubt, would help; but it makes no difference that it had to guess; it is enought that it had an inducement to make the best guess it could, and that it would regulate that part of the future supply, so far as it should turn out to have guessed right. The competition of "secondary" must therefore be disregarded, as soon as we consider the position of "Alcoa" over a period of years; it was as much within "Alcoa's" control as was the production of the "virgin" from which it had been derived. . . .

We conclude therefore that "Alcoa's" control over the ingot market must be reckoned at over ninety percent; that being the proportion which its production bears to imported "virgin" ingot. . . .

. . . Was this a monopoly within the meaning of Section 2? The judge found that, over the whole half century of its existence, "Alcoa's" profits upon capital invested, after payment of income taxes, had been only about ten percent, and, although the plaintiff puts this figure a little higher, the difference is negligible. . . . This assumed, it would be hard to say that "Alcoa" had made exorbitant profits on ingot, if it is proper to allocate the profit upon the whole business proportionately among all its products—ingot, and fabrications from ingot. A profit of ten percent in such an industry, dependent, in part at any rate, upon continued tariff protection, and subject to the vicissitudes of new demands, to the obsolescence of plant and process—which can never be accurately gauged in advance—to the chance that substitutes may at any moment be discovered which will reduce the demand, and to the other hazards which attend all industry; a profit of ten percent, so conditioned, could hardly be considered extortionate.

There are however, two answers to any such excuse; and the first is that the profit on ingot was not necessarily the same as the profit of the business as a whole, and that we have no means of allocating its proper share to ingot. . . . But the whole issue is irrelevant anyway, for it is no excuse for "monopolizing" a market that the monopoly has not been used to extract from the consumer more than a "fair" profit. The Act has wider purposes. Indeed, even though we disregarded all but economic considerations, it would by no means follow that such concentration of producing power is to be desired, when it has not been used extortionately. Many people believe that possession of unchallenged economic power deadens initiative, discourages thrift and depresses energy; that immunity from competition is a narcotic, and rivalry is a stimulant, to industrial progress; that the spur of constant stress is necessary to counteract an inevitable disposition to let well enough alone. Such people believe that competitors, versed in the craft as no consumer can be, will be quick to detect opportunities for saving and new shifts in production, and be eager to profit by them. In any event the mere fact that a producer, having command of the domestic market, has not been able to make more than a "fair" profit, is no evidence that a "fair" profit could not have been made at lower prices. . . . True, it might have been thought adequate to condemn only those monopolies which could not show that they had exercised the highest possible ingenuity, had adopted every possible economy, had anticipated every conceivable improvement, stimulated every possible demand. No doubt, that would be one way of dealing with the matter, although it would imply constant scrutiny and constant supervision, such as courts are unable to provide. Be that as it may, that was not the way that Congress chose; it did not condone "good trusts" and condemn "bad" ones; it forbade all. Moreover, in so doing it was not necessarily actuated by economic motives alone. It is possible, because of its indirect social or moral effect, to prefer a system of small producers, each dependent for his success upon his own skill and character, to one in which the great mass of those engaged must accept the direction of a few. These considerations, which we have suggested only as possible purposes of the Act, we think the decisions prove to have been in fact its purposes.

It is settled, at least as to Section 1, that there are some contracts restricting competition which are unlawful, no matter how beneficient they may be; no industrial exigency will justify them; they are absolutely forbidden. . . . Starting, however, with the authoritative premise that all contracts fixing prices are unconditionally prohibited, the only possible difference between them and a monopoly is that while a monopoly necessarily involves an equal, or even greater, power to fix prices, its mere existence might be thought not to constitute an exercise of that power. That distinction is nevertheless purely formal; it would be valid only so long as the monopoly remained wholly inert; it would disappear as soon as the monopoly began to operate; for, when it did—that is, as soon as it began to sell at all—it must sell at some price and the only price at which it could sell is a price which it itself fixed. Thereafter the power and its exercise must needs coalesce. Indeed it would be absurd to condemn such contracts unconditionally, and not to extend the condemnation to monopolies; for the contracts are only steps toward that entire control which monopoly confers: they are really partial monopolies.

But we are not left to deductive reasoning. Although in many settings it may be proper to weigh the extent and effect of restrictions in a contract against its industrial or commercial advantages, this is never to be done when the contract is made with intent to set up a monopoly. . . . Perhaps, it has been idle to labor the point at length; there can be no doubt that the vice of restrictive contracts and of monopoly is really one, it is the denial to commerce of the supposed protection of competition. To repeat, if the earlier stages are proscribed, when they are parts of a plan, the mere projecting of which condemns them unconditionally, the realization of the plan itself must also be proscribed.

We have been speaking only of the economic reasons which forbid monopoly; but, as we have already implied, there are others, based upon the belief that great industrial consolidations are inherently undesirable, regardless of their economic results. . . . Throughout the history of these [antitrust] statutes it has been constantly assumed that one of their purposes was to perpetuate and preserve, for its own sake and in spite of possible cost, an organization of industry in small units which can effectively compete with each other. We hold that "Alcoa's" monopoly of ingot was of the kind covered by Section 2.

It does not follow because "Alcoa" had such a monopoly, that it "monopolized" the ingot market: it may not have achieved monopoly; monopoly may have been thrust upon it. If it had been a combination of existing smelters which united the whole industry and controlled the production of all aluminum ingot, it would certainly have "monopolized" the market. . . . We may start therefore with the premise that to have combined ninety percent of the producers of ingot would have been to "monopolize" the ingot market; and, so far as concerns the public interest, it can make no difference whether an existing competition is put an end to, or whether prospective competition is prevented. . . . Nevertheless, it is unquestionably true that from the very outset the courts have at least kept in reserve the possibility that the origin of a monopoly may be critical in determining its legality. . . . This notion has usually been expressed by saying that size does not determine guilt; that there must be some "exclusion" of competitors; that the growth must be something else than "natural" or "normal"; that there must be a "wrongful intent," or some other specific intent; or that some "unduly" coercive means must be used. At times there has been emphasis upon the use of the active verb, "monopolize," as the judge noted in the case at bar. . . . What engendered these compunctions is reasonably plain; persons may unwittingly find themselves in possession of a monopoly, automatically so to say: that is, without having intended either to put an end to existing competition, or to prevent competition from arising when none had existed; they may become monopolists by force of accident. . . . A single producer may be the survivor out of a group of active competitors, merely by virtue of his superior skill, foresight and industry. . . . The successful competitor, having been urged to compete, must not be turned upon when he wins. . . .

It would completely misconstrue "Alcoa's" position in 1940 to hold that it was the passive beneficiary of a monopoly, following upon an involuntary elimination of competitors by automatically operative economic forces. . . . This increase and this continued and undisturbed control did not fall undesigned into "Alcoa's" lap; obviously it could not have done so. It could only have resulted, as it did result, from a persistent determination to maintain the control, with which it found itself vested in 1912. There were at least one or two abortive attempts to enter the industry, but "Alcoa" effectively anticipated and forestalled all competition, and succeeded in holding the field alone. True, it stimulated demand and opened new uses for the metal, but not without making sure that it could supply what it had evoked. . . . It was not inevitable that it should always anticipate increases in the demand for ingot and be prepared to supply them. Nothing compelled it to keep doubling and redoubling its capacity before others entered the field. It insists that it never excluded competitors; but we can think of no more effective exclusion than progressively to embrace each new opportunity as it opened, and to face every newcomer with new capacity already geared into a great organization, having the advantage of experience, trade connections and the elite of personnel. Only in case we interpret "exclusion" as limited to manoeuvres not honestly industrial, but actuated solely by a desire to prevent competition, can such a course, indefatigably pursued, be deemed not "exclusionary." So to limit it would in our judgment emasculate the Act; would permit just such consolidations as it was designed to prevent. . . .

We disregard any question of "intent." . . . By far the greatest part of the fabulous record piled up in the case at bar, was concerned with proving such an intent. The plaintiff was seeking to show that many transactions, neutral on their face, were not in fact necessary to the development of "Alcoa's" business, and had no motive except to exclude others and perpetuate its hold upon the ingot market. Upon that effort success depended in case the plaintiff failed to satisfy the court that it was unnecessary under Section 2 to convict "Alcoa" of practices unlawful of themselves. The plaintiff has so satisfied us, and the issue of intent ceases to have any importance. . . . In order to fall within Section 2, the monopolist must have both the power to monopolize, and the intent to monopolize. . . .[N]o monopolist monopolizes unconscious of what he is doing. So here, "Alcoa" meant to keep, and did keep, that complete and exclusive hold upon the ingot market with which it started. That was to "monopolize" that market, however innocently it otherwise proceeded. So far as the judgment held that it was not within Section 2, it must be reversed. . . .

II.   "ALCOA'S" UNLAWFUL PRACTICES

[Since it was found that Alcoa had monopolized the ingot market, the question of its unlawful practices would, according to the Court, be moot. But war-wrought changes in the ingot market made consideration of these charges necessary to the proper framing of a decree.]

. . . In spite of the prolixity of the evidence, the challenged practices can be divided into three classes: . . .

(a)   "Pre-emption" of Bauxite and Water-Power

The plaintiff attempted to prove, and asserts that it did prove, that "Alcoa" bought up bauxite deposits . . . in excess of its needs, and under circumstances which showed that the purchases were not for the purpose of securing an adequate future supply, but only in order to seize upon any available supply and so assure its monopoly. The very statement of this charge shows that it depends upon "Alcoa's" intent, for, if the purchases provided for the future needs of the business, or for what "Alcoa" honestly believed were its future needs, they were innocent. . . . The judge . . . overruled all the plaintiff's contentions . . . [and] we should be unwarranted in declaring these findings "clearly erroneous." . . .

(b)   Suppression of Competitors Seeking to Invade the Ingot Market

[Alcoa's purchases of various potential competitors were treated by the court in the same manner as its purchases of bauxite and water-power sites, i.e., the finding of the lower court that these acquisitions did not evidence an intent to suppress competition was upheld.] . . .

(c)   "Alcoa's" Domination of the Fabricating Fields

The last of "Alcoa's" supposedly unlawful practices was its infiltration into, and manipulation of, some of the markets for fabricated goods. These were three kinds: (1) buying an interest in the Aluminum Castings Company, and Aluminum Manufactures, Inc.; (2) the "Price Squeeze"; (3) the "Piston Patent Pool."

(1) "Castings" were one of the earliest uses of aluminum. . . . Five of these [casting producers] combined in . . . [1909] to form the Aluminum Castings Company, of whose shares "Alcoa" received fifty percent in exchange for advances made. . . .

The Aluminum Goods Manufacturing Company makes cooking and

other utensils out of aluminum. . . . At the trial thirty-one percent of the shares were held by "Alcoa" and its officers. . . . [T]here is nothing to support the conclusion that here was a practice or manoeuvre merely to suppress or exclude competitors. . . .

(2) The "Price Squeeze." The plaintiff describes as the "Price Squeeze" a practice by which, it says, "Alcoa" intended to put out of business the manufacturers of aluminum "sheet" who were its competitors; for "Alcoa" was itself a large—in fact much the largest—maker of that product. . . .

The plaintiff's theory is that "Alcoa" consistently sold ingot at so high a price that the "sheet rollers," who were forced to buy from it, could not pay the expenses of "rolling" the "sheet."

. . . [W]e think that the plaintiff made out a prima facie case that "Alcoa" had been holding ingot at a price higher than a "fair price," and had reduced the price only because of pressure [resulting from a Department of Justice investigation into the complaints of several "sheet" makers]. If that was not so, it should have rebutted the inference.

In spite of this evidence the judge found that in these years [1925–1932] "Alcoa" had not intended to monopolize the "sheet" market; or to exclude others; or to fix discriminatory prices, or prices of any kind; or to sell below the cost of production, measuring ingot price as part of the cost. . . . That is indeed hard to believe. . . . That it was unlawful to set the price of "sheet" so low and hold the price of ingot so high, seems to us unquestionable, provided, as we have held, that on this record the price of ingot must be regarded as higher than a "fair price." True, this was only a consequence of "Alcoa's" control over the price of ingot, and perhaps it ought not to be considered as a separate wrong; moreover, we do not use it as part of the reasoning by which we conclude that the monopoly was unlawful. But it was at least an unlawful exercise of "Alcoa's" power after it had been put on notice by the "sheet rollers'" complaints; and this is true, even though we assent to the judge's finding that it was not part of an attempt to monopolize the "sheet" market. . . .

(3) The Piston Patent Situation. The plaintiff charges "Alcoa" with three kinds of misuses of patents: (1) an unlawful limitation of the production of licensees of its own patents; (2) accepting a license agreement from another patentee that unlawfully limited its own production; (3) using its own patents to force the purchase of ingot upon licensees. [The Court held that in two instances the evidence was not sufficient to establish unlawfulness, while in the third, expiration of the patents involved made it unnecessary for the court to pass upon the agreement.]

III. "LIMITED"

[In this portion of its decision the Court found that cartel arrangements between Limited, a Canadian firm, and Alliance, a Swiss concern, affected imports into the United States and therefore violated the Sherman

Act. It was held, however, that "Alcoa" had not participated in the cartel, and therefore could not be held responsible for the import restrictions.]

IV. THE REMEDIES

Nearly five years have passed since the evidence was closed; during that time the aluminum industry . . . has been revolutionized by the nation's efforts in a great crisis. That alone would make it impossible to dispose of the action upon the basis of the record as we have it. . . .

. . . [I]t is impossible to say what will be "Alcoa's" position in the industry after the war. . . . Dissolution is not a penalty but a remedy; if the industry will not need it for its protection, it will be a disservice to break up an aggregation which has for so long demonstrated its efficiency. . . .

But there is another, and even more persuasive, reason why we should not now adjudge a dissolution of any kind. The Surplus Property Act of 1944 provides . . . [that the disposal agencies shall dispose of government properties in such a manner as] ". . . to give maximum aid in the reestablishment of a peacetime economy of free independent private enterprise"; [and] ". . . to discourage monopolistic practices and to strengthen and preserve the competitive position of small business concerns in an economy of free enterprise.". . . [If the disposal authorities fail to reestablish competitive conditions, it will then be necessary for the District Court to act.]

[An injunction was then issued against resumption of the "price squeeze," and "Limited" was enjoined from entering into any agreement covering imports into this country.]

Judgment reversed, and cause remanded for further proceedings not inconsistent with the foregoing.

United States v. United Shoe Machinery Corp.

110 F. Supp. 295 (D. Mass. 1953)
aff'd per curiam 347 U.S. 521 (1954)

WYZANSKI, District Judge.

. . . . .

December 15, 1947 the Government filed a complaint against United Shoe Machinery Corporation under Section 4 of the Sherman Act . . . in order to restrain alleged violations of Sections 1 and 2 of that Act. . . .

Stripped to its essentials, the 52-page complaint charged, *first,* that since 1912 United had been "monopolizing interstate trade and commerce in the shoe machinery industry of the United States." The *second* principal charge laid by the complaint was that United had been *(a)* "monopolizing the distribution in interstate commerce of numerous . . . shoe factory supplies" and *(b)* "attempting to monopolize the distribution in interstate commerce of . . . other such supplies." . . . *Third,* the complaint alleged United was "attempting to monopolize and monopolizing the manufacture and distribution in interstate commerce of tanning machinery used in the manufacture of shoe leather." . . .

In support of this three-pronged attack, directed to shoe machinery, shoe factory supplies, and tanning machinery, the Government set forth detailed allegations with respect to acquisitions, leases, patents, and a host of other aspects of United's business. . . .

After stating its changes, the Government prayed for an adjudication of United's violations of both Section 1 and Section 2 of the Sherman Act; an injunction against future violations; a cancellation of United's shoe machinery leases; a requirement that United offer for sale all machine types "manufactured and commercialized by it and be enjoined from leasing shoe machinery except upon terms . . . approved by the Court"; a requirement that, on such terms as the Court may deem appropriate, United make available to all applicants all patents and inventions relating to shoe machinery; an injunction against United manufacturing or distributing shoe factory supplies; a cancellation of exclusive contracts governing shoe factory supplies; and a divestiture of United's ownership of virtually all branches and subsidiaries concerned with shoe factory supplies or tanning machinery.

Defendant answered seasonably, denying all the significant allegations. . . .

A trial of prodigious length followed. . . .

In an anti-trust case a trial court's task is to reduce, as far as fairness permits, a complex record to its essentials, so that the parties, the Supreme Court, other courts, the bar, and the general public may understand the decree, and may recognize the premises on which that judgment rests. It is not the Court's duty to make a precise finding on every detail of four decades of an industry. It is not its duty to approach the issues as an historian, an archaeologist . . . , an economist, or even a master appointed to settle every factual dispute. A trial judge who undertakes such tasks will unnecessarily sacrifice the rights of litigants in other cases clamoring for attention. Moreover, he will encourage just that type of extravagant presentation which has come to plague the field of anti-trust law. Hence this opinion is to be construed as denying on the ground of immateriality every request not granted. . . .

III. OPINION ON ALLEGED VIOLATIONS

. . . . .

There are 18 major processes for the manufacturing of shoes by machine. Some machine types are used only in one process, but others are used in several; and the relationship of machine types to one another may be competitive or sequential. The approximately 1,460 shoe manufacturers themselves are highly competitive in many respects, including their choice of processes and other technological aspects of production. Their total demand for machine services, apart from those rendered by dry thread sewing machines in the upper-fitting room, constitutes an identifiable market which is a "part of the trade or commerce among the several States." Section 2 of the Sherman Act. . . .

United, the largest source of supply, is a corporation lineally descended from a combination of constituent companies, adjudged lawful by the Supreme Court of the United States in 1918. . . . It now has assets rising slightly over 100 million dollars and employment rolls around 6,000. In recent years it has earned before federal taxes 9 to 13.5 million dollars annually.

Supplying different aspects of that market are at least 10 other American manufacturers and some foreign manufacturers, whose products are admitted to the United States free of tariff duty. Almost all the operations performed in the 18 processes can be carried out without the use of any of United's machines, and (at least in foreign areas, where patents are no obstacle,) a complete shoe factory can be efficiently organized without a United machine.

Nonetheless, United at the present time is supplying over 75%, and probably 85% of the current demand in the American shoe machinery market, as heretofore defined. This is somewhat less than the share it was supplying in 1915. In the meantime, one important competitor, Compo Shoe Machinery Corporation, became the American innovator of the cement process of manufacture. In that sub-market Compo roughly equals United. . . .

United is the only machinery enterprise that produces a long line of machine types, and covers every major process. It is the only concern that has a research laboratory covering all aspects of the needs of shoe manufacturing; though Compo has a laboratory concentrating on the needs of those in the cement process. . . . Through its own research, United has developed inventions many of which are now patented. Roughly 95% of its 3,915 patents are attributable to the ideas of its own employees.

Although at the turn of the century, United's patents covered the fundamentals of shoe machinery manufacture, those fundamental patents have expired. Current patents cover for the most part only minor developments, so that it is possible to "invent around" them, to use the words of United's chief competitor. However, the aggregation of patents does to some extent block potential competition. It furnishes a trading advantage. It leads inventors to offer their ideas to United, on the general principle that new complicated machines embody numerous patents. And it serves as a hedge or insurance for United against unforeseen competitive developments.

In the last decade and a half, United has not acquired any significant patents, inventions, machines, or businesses from any outside source, and has rejected many offers made to it. Before then, while it acquired no going businesses, in a period of two decades it spent roughly $3,500,000 to purchase inventions and machines. Most of these were from moribund companies, though this was not true of the acquisitions underlying the significant Littleway process and the less significant heel seat fitting machines and patents, each of which was from an active enterprise and might have served as a nucleus of important, though, at least initially, not extensive competition.

In supplying its complicated machines to shoe manufacturers, United, like its more important American competitors, has followed the practice of never selling, but only leasing. Leasing has been traditional in the shoe machinery field since the Civil War. So far as this record indicates, there is virtually no expressed dissatisfaction from consumers respecting that system; and Compo, United's principal competitor, endorses and uses it. Under the system, entry into shoe manufacture has been easy. The rates charged for all customers have been uniform. The machines supplied have performed excellently. United has, without separate charge, promptly and efficiently supplied repair service and many kinds of other service useful to shoe manufacturers. These services have been particularly important, because in the shoe manufacturing industry a whole line of production can be adversely affected, and valuable time lost, if some of the important machines go out of function, and because machine breakdowns have serious labor and consumer repercussions. The cost to the average shoe manufacturer of its machines and services supplied to him has been less than 2% of the wholesale price of his shoes.

However, United's leases, in the context of the present shoe machinery market, have created barriers to the entry by competitors into the shoe machinery field.

First, the complex of obligations and rights accruing under United's leasing system in operation deter a shoe manufacturer from disposing of a United machine and acquiring a competitor's machine. . . . The lessee is now held closely to United by the combined effect of the 10-year term, the requirement that if he has work available he must use the machine to full capacity, and by the return charge which can in practice, through the right of deduction fund, be reduced to insignificance if he keeps this and other United machines to the end of the periods for which he leased them.

Second, when a lessee desires to replace a United machine, United gives him more favorable terms if the replacement is by another United machine than if it is by a competitive machine.

Third, United's practice of offering to repair, without separate charges, its leased machines, has had the effect that there are no independent service organizations to repair complicated machines. In turn, this has had the effect that the manufacturer of a complicated machine must either offer repair service with his machine, or must face the obstacle of marketing his machine to customers who know that repair service will be difficult to provide. . . .

Although maintaining the same nominal terms for each customer, United has followed, as between machine types, a discriminatory pricing policy. . . . [T]hese sharp and relatively durable differentials are traceable, at least in large part, to United's policy of fixing a higher rate of return where competition is of minor significance, and a lower rate of return where competition is of major significance. . . .

On the foregoing facts, the issue of law is whether defendant in its shoe machinery business has violated that provision of Section 2 of the Sherman Act. . . .

Yet, in these recent authorities[1] there are discernible at least three different, but cognate, approaches.

The approach which has the least sweeping implications really antedates the decision in *Aluminum*. But it deserves restatement. An enterprise has monopolized in violation of Section 2 of the Sherman Act if it has acquired or maintained a power to exclude others as a result of using an unreasonable "restraint of trade" in violation of Section 1 of the Sherman Act. . . .

A more inclusive approach was adopted by Mr. Justice Douglas in *United States* v. *Griffith*. . . . He stated that to prove a violation of Section 2 it was not always necessary to show a violation of Section 1. . . . And he concluded that an enterprise has monopolized in violation of Section 2 if it *(a)* has the power to exclude competition, and *(b)* has exercised it, or has the purpose to exercise it. . . . The least that this conclusion means is that it is a violation of Section 2 for one having effective control of the market to use, or plan to use, any exclusionary practice, even though it is not a technical restraint of trade. But the conclusion may go further.

Indeed the way in which Mr. Justice Douglas used the terms "monopoly power" and "effective market control," . . . and cited *Aluminum* suggests that he endorses a third and broader approach, which originated with Judge Hand. It will be recalled that Judge Hand said that one who has acquired an overwhelming share of the market "monopolizes" whenever he does business, . . . apparently even if there is no showing that his business involves any exclusionary practice. But, it will also be recalled that this doctrine is softened by Judge Hand's suggestion that the defendant may escape statutory liability if it bears the burden of proving that it owes its monopoly solely to superior skill. . . .

This Court finds it unnecessary to choose between the second and third approaches. For, taken as a whole, the evidence satisfies the tests laid

---

[1] *U.S.* v. *Aluminum Co. of America*, 148 F.2d 416 (1945); *American Tobacco Co.* v. *U.S.*, 328 U.S. 781 (1946); *U.S.* v. *Griffith*, 334 U.S. 100 (1948); *Schine Chain Theatres* v. *U.S.*, 334 U.S. 110 (1948); *U.S.* v. *Paramount Theatres*, 334 U.S. 131 (1948); *U.S.* v. *Columbia Steel Co.*, 334 U.S. 495 (1948). IMS.

down in both *Griffith* and *Aluminum*. The facts show that (1) defendant has, and exercises, such overwhelming strength in the shoe machinery market that it controls that market, (2) this strength excludes some potential, and limits some actual, competition, and (3) this strength is not attributable solely to defendant's ability, economies of scale, research, natural advantages, and adaptation to inevitable economic laws. . . .

To combat United's market control, a competitor must be prepared with knowledge of shoemaking, engineering skill, capacity to invent around patents, and financial resources sufficient to bear the expense of long developmental and experimental processes. The competitor must be prepared for consumers' resistance founded on their long-term, satisfactory relations with United, and on the cost to them of surrendering United's leases. Also, the competitor must be prepared to give, or point to the source of, repair and other services, and to the source of supplies for machine parts, expendable parts, and the like. Indeed, perhaps a competitor who aims at any large scale success must also be prepared to lease his machines. These considerations would all affect *potential* competition, and have not been without their effect on *actual* competition.

Not only does the evidence show United has control of the market, but also the evidence does not show that the control is due entirely to excusable causes. The three principal sources of United's power have been the original constitution of the company, the superiority of United's products and services, and the leasing system. The first two of these are plainly beyond reproach. . . .

But United's control does not rest solely on its original constitution, its ability, its research, or its economies of scale. There are other barriers to competition, and these barriers were erected by United's own business policies. Much of United's market power is traceable to the magnetic ties inherent in its system of leasing, and not selling, its more important machines. The lease-only system of distributing complicated machines has many "partnership" aspects, and it has exclusionary features such as the 10-year term, the full capacity clause, the return charges, and the failure to segregate service charges from machine charges. Moreover, the leasing system has aided United in maintaining a pricing system which discriminates between machine types.

In addition to the foregoing three principal sources of United's power, brief reference may be made to the fact that United has been somewhat aided in retaining control of the shoe machinery industry by its purchases in the secondhand market, by its acquisitions of patents, and, to a lesser extent, by its activities in selling to shoe factories supplies which United and others manufacture. . . .

. . . [T]hey are not practices which can be properly described as the inevitable consequences of ability, natural forces, or law. They represent something more than the use of accessible resources, the process of invention and innovation, and the employment of those techniques of employment, financing, production, and distribution, which a competitive society must foster. They are contracts, arrangements, and policies which, instead of encouraging competition based on pure merit, further the dominance of a particular firm. In this sense, they are unnatural barriers; they unnecessarily exclude actual and potential competition; they restrict a free market. While the law allows many enterprises to use such practices, the Sherman Act is now construed by superior courts to forbid the continuance of effective market control based in part upon such practices. Those courts hold that market control is inherently evil and constitutes a violation of Section 2 unless economically inevitable, or specifically authorized and regulated by law.

It is only fair to add that . . . United's power does not rest on predatory practices. Probably few monopolies could produce a record so free from any taint of that kind of wrongdoing. The violation with which United is now charged depends not on moral considerations, but on solely economic considerations. United is denied the right to exercise effective control of the market by business policies that are not the inevitable consequences of its capacities or its natural advantages. That those policies are not immoral is irrelevant. . . .

Moreover, . . . United has not proved that monopoly is economically compelled by the thinness of the shoe machinery market. It has not shown that no company could undertake to develop, manufacture, and distribute certain types of machines, unless it alone met the total demand for those types of machines.

Nor has United affirmatively proved that it has achieved spectacular results at amazing rates of speed, nor has it proved that comparable research results and comparable economies of production, distribution, and service could not be achieved as well by, say, three important shoe machinery firms, as by one. Compo with a much smaller organization indicates how much research can be done on a smaller scale. Yet since Compo is limited to the simpler cement process machines, too much reliance should not be placed on this comparison. Nonetheless, one point is worth recalling. Compo's inventors first found practical ways to introduce the cement process which United had considered and rejected. This experience illustrates the familiar truth that one of the dangers of extraordinary experience is that those who have it may fall into grooves created by their own expertness. They refuse to believe that hurdles which they have learned from experience are insurmountable, can in fact be overcome by fresh, independent minds.

So far, nothing in this opinion has been said of defendant's *intent* in regard to its power and practices in the shoe machinery market. This point can be readily disposed of by reference once more to *Aluminum*. . . . Defendant intended to engage in the leasing practices and pricing policies which maintained its market power. That is all the intent which the law requires when both the complaint and the judgment rest on a charge of "monopolizing," not merely "attempting to monopolize." Defendant having willed the means, has willed the end.

Next, come those issues relating to supplies. . . .

In certain of those supply fields . . . United has control of the market . . . [which] comes principally from United's power over the shoe machinery market. And for that reason the exercise of dominant power in those supply fields is unlawful. An enterprise that by monopolizing one field, secures dominant market power in another field, has monopolized the second field, in violation of Section 2 of the Sherman Act. . . .

IV. OPINION ON REMEDY

. . . . .

The Government's proposal that the Court dissolve United into three separate manufacturing companies is unrealistic. United conducts all machine manufacture at one plant in Beverly, with one set of jigs and tools, one foundry, one laboratory for machinery problems, one managerial staff, and one labor force. It takes no Solomon to see that this organism cannot be cut into three equal and viable parts. . . .

A petition for dissolution should reflect greater attention to practical problems and should involve supporting economic data and prophesies such as are presented in corporate reorganization and public utility dissolution cases. Moreover, the petition should involve a more formal commitment by the Attorney General, than is involved in the divergent proposals that his assistants have made in briefs and in oral arguments addressed to the Court.

On the whole, therefore, the suggested remedy of dissolution is rejected.

From the opinion on defendant's violations it follows that some form of relief regarding defendant's leases and leasing practices is proper and necessary. . . .

Although leasing should not now be abolished by judicial decree, the Court agrees with the Government that the leases should be purged of their restrictive features. In the decree filed herewith, the term of the lease is shortened, the full capacity clause is eliminated, the discriminatory commutative charges are removed, and United is required to segregate its charges for machines from its charges for repair service. . . .

The Court also agrees with the Government that if United chooses to continue to lease any machine type, it must offer that type of machine also for sale. . . . Insofar as United's machines are sold rather than leased, they will ultimately, in many cases, reach a secondhand market. From that market, United will face a type of substitute competition which will gradually weaken the prohibited market power which it now exercises. Moreover, from that market, or from United itself, a competitor of United can acquire a United machine in order to study it, to copy its unpatented features, and to experiment with improvements in, or alterations of, the machine. Thus, in another and more direct way, United's market power will be diminished. . . .

One other phase of the decree to which this opinion should expressly advert is the method of handling those subsidiaries and branches which produce supplies in fields which United has monopolized. The clearest examples are nails and tacks, and eyelets for the shoe machinery market. These are large scale monopolizations attributable to the machinery monopoly. And United should be divested of its business of manufacturing and distributing these particular supplies, because this is the kind of dissolution which can be carried out practically, and which will also reduce monopoly power in each of the affected supply fields. . . .

Note: Some ten years after this decision the Government petitioned the District Court to review the efficacy of the remedies it had prescribed. The District Court ruled that its power to modify the original decree was limited to cases involving "(1) a clear showing of (2) grievous wrong (3) evoked by new and unforeseen circumstances." On appeal, the Court, Mr. Justice Fortas writing its opinion, reversed, 391 U.S. 244 (1968), holding it to be established that "in a Section 2 case, upon appropriate findings of violation, it is the duty of the court to prescribe relief which will terminate the illegal monopoly, deny to the defendant the fruits of its statutory violation, and ensure that there remain no practices likely to result in monopolization in the future."

The District Court was directed to determine whether the relief it had granted had restored "workable competition in the market" and assured "the complete extirpation of the illegal monopoly."

Judge Wyzanski then accepted a consent decree under which United Shoe Machinery Corp. would divest itself of "particular shoe machine models, which models accounted for $8,500,000 in gross revenues to defendant from lease and sale of shoe machinery." This reduction in revenues, the parties estimated, "would be sufficient to reduce defendant's share of the shoe machinery market during the base year to no more than 33 percent."

In order to facilitate divestiture, the company agreed to assign any patent principally relating to the models divested (and their parts); to provide the purchaser with service for two years; to train the purchaser's personnel in such service; and, for ten years after the sale to provide replacement parts at "a reasonable price." In addition, United agreed to compulsory licensing, for about a decade, under substantially all of its shoe machine and product patents.

United States v. E. I. duPont de Nemours and Company

351 U.S. 377 (1956)

MR. JUSTICE REED delivered the opinion of the Court.

The United States brought this civil action under Section 4 of the Sherman Act. . . . The complaint, filed December 13, 1947, . . . charged duPont with monopolizing, attempting to monopolize and conspiracy to monopolize interstate commerce in cellophane and cellulosic caps and bands in violation of Section 2 of the Sherman Act. Relief by injunction was sought against defendant and its officers, forbidding monopolizing or attempting to monopolize interstate trade in cellophane. The prayer also sought action to dissipate the effect of the monopolization by divestiture or other steps. . . . [J]udgment was entered for duPont on all issues.[1]

The Government's direct appeal here . . . "attacks only the ruling that duPont has not monopolized trade in cellophane." At issue for determination is only this alleged violation by duPont of Section 2. . . .

During the period that is relevant to this action, duPont produced almost 75% of the cellophane sold in the United States, and cellophane constituted less than 20% of all "flexible packaging material" sales. . . .

The Government contends that, by so dominating cellophane production, duPont monopolized a "part of the trade or commerce" in violation of Section 2. Respondent agrees that cellophane is a product which constitutes "a 'part' of commerce within the meaning of Section 2." . . . But it contends that the prohibition of Section 2 against monopolization is not violated because it does not have the power to control the price of cellophane or to exclude competitors from the market in which cellophane is sold. The court below found that the "relevant market for determining the extent of duPont's market control is the market for flexible packaging materials," and that competition from those other materials prevented duPont from possessing monopoly powers in its sales of cellophane. . . .

The Government . . . argues that the market for other wrappings is distinct from the market for cellophane and that the competition afforded cellophane by other wrappings is not strong enough to be considered in determining whether duPont has monopoly powers. Market delimitation is necessary under duPont's theory to determine whether an alleged monopolist violates Section 2. The ultimate consideration in such a determination is whether the defendants control the price and competition in the market for such part of trade or commerce as they are charged with monopolizing. Every manufacturer is the sole producer of the particular

---

[1] *United States* v. *E. I. duPont de Nemours & Co.*, 118 F. Supp. 41. The opinion occupies 192 pages of the volume. The Findings of Fact, 854 in number, cover 140 pages. . . . [Citations to the lower court's findings have been omitted. IMS.]

commodity it makes but its control in the above sense of the relevant market depends upon the availability of alternative commodities for buyers: *i.e.,* whether there is cross-elasticity of demand between cellophane and the other wrappings. This interchangeability is largely gauged by the purchase of competing products for similar uses considering the price, characteristics and adaptability of the competing commodities. The court below found that the flexible wrappings afforded such alternatives. This Court must determine whether the trial court erred in its estimate of the competition afforded cellophane by other materials. . . .

Two additional questions were raised in the record and decided by the court below. That court found, that even if duPont did possess monopoly power over sales of cellophane, it was not subject to Sherman Act prosecution, because (1) the acquisition of that power was protected by patents, and (2) that power was acquired solely through duPont's business expertness. It was thrust upon duPont. . . .

Since the Government specifically excludes attempts and conspiracies to monopolize from consideration, a conclusion that duPont has no monopoly power would obviate examination of these last two issues.

I. FACTUAL BACKGROUND

. . . In the early 1900s Jacques Brandenberger, a Swiss chemist, [inadvertently discovered the first "cellophane."] . . . This first "cellophane" was thick, hard, and not perfectly transparent, but Brandenberger apparently foresaw commercial possibilities in his discovery. . . . He obtained patents to cover . . . his process.

. . . [H]owever, . . . the disclosures of these early patents were not sufficient to make possible the manufacture of commercial cellophane. . . .

In 1917 Brandenberger assigned his patents to La Cellophane Societe Anonyme and joined that organization. . . .

In 1923 duPont organized with La Cellophane an American company for the manufacture of plain cellophane. The undisputed findings are that:

> . . . La Cellophane . . . granted duPont Cellophane Company the exclusive right to make and sell in North and Central America under La Cellophane's secret processes for cellophane manufacture. DuPont Cellophane Company granted to La Cellophane exclusive rights for the rest of the world under any cellophane patents or processes duPont Cellophane Company might develop. . . .

Subsequently duPont and La Cellophane licensed several foreign companies, allowing them to manufacture and vend cellophane in limited areas. . . . Technical exchange agreements with these companies were entered into at the same time. However, in 1940, duPont notified these foreign companies that sales might be made in any country, and by 1948 all the technical exchange agreements were canceled.

Sylvania, an American affiliate of a Belgian producer of cellophane, not covered by the license agreements above referred to, began the manufacture of cellophane in the United States in 1930. Litigation between the French and Belgian companies resulted in a settlement whereby La Cellophane came to have a stock interest in Sylvania, contrary to the La Cellophane-duPont agreement. This resulted in adjustments as compensation for the intrusion into United States of La Cellophane that extended duPont's limited territory. . . . Since 1934 Sylvania has produced about 25% of United States cellophane.

An important factor in the growth of cellophane . . . was the perfection of moistureproof cellophane, a superior product of duPont research and patented by that company through a 1927 application. . . .

In 1931 Sylvania began the manufacture of moistureproof cellophane under its own patents. After negotiations over patent rights, duPont in 1933 licensed Sylvania to manufacture and sell moistureproof cellophane produced under the duPont patents at a royalty of 2% of sales. These licenses, with the plain cellophane licenses from the Belgian Company, made Sylvania a full cellophane competitor, limited on moistureproof sales by the terms of the licenses to 20% of the combined sales of the two companies of that type by the payment of a prohibitive royalty on the excess. . . . There was never an excess production. The limiting clause was dropped on January 1, 1945, and Sylvania was acquired in 1946 by the American Viscose Corporation with assets of over $200,000,000.

Between 1928 and 1950, duPont's sales of plain cellophane increased from $3,131,608 to $9,330,776. Moistureproof sales increased from $603,222 to $89,850,416, although prices were continuously reduced. . . . It could not be said that this immense increase in use was solely or even largely attributable to the superior quality of cellophane or to the technique or business acumen of duPont, though doubtless those factors were important. The growth was a part of the expansion of the commodity-packaging habits of business, a by-product of general efficient competitive merchandising to meet modern demands. The profits, which were large, apparently arose from this trend in marketing, the development of the industrial use of chemical research and production of synthetics, rather than from elimination of other producers from the relevant market. . . .

II. THE SHERMAN ACT AND THE COURTS

The Sherman Act has received long and careful application by this Court to achieve for the Nation the freedom of enterprise from monopoly or restraint envisaged by the Congress that passed the Act in 1890. Because the Act is couched in broad terms, it is adaptable to the changing types of commercial production and distribution that have evolved since its passage. . . . It was said in *Standard Oil Co.* v. *United States*, . . . that fear of the power of rapid accumulations of individual and corporate wealth from the trade and industry of a developing national economy caused its passage. . . . While the economic picture has changed, large aggregations of private capital, with power attributes, continue. Mergers go forward. Industries such as steel, automobiles, tires, chemicals, have only a few production organizations. A considerable size is often essential for efficient operation. . . .

Judicial construction of antitrust legislation has generally been left unchanged by Congress. This is true of the Rule of Reason. While it is fair to say that the Rule is imprecise, its application in Sherman Act litigation, as directed against enhancement of price or throttling of competition, has given a workable content to antitrust legislation. . . . It was judicially declared a proper interpretation of the Sherman Act in 1911. . . . This Court has not receded from its position on the Rule. There is not, we think, any inconsistency between it and the development of the judicial theory that agreements as to maintenance of prices or division of territory are in themselves a violation of the Sherman Act. It is logical that some agreements and practices are invalid *per se*, while others are illegal only as applied to particular situations. . . .

. . . It is true that Congress has made exceptions to the generality of monopoly prohibitions. . . . But those exceptions express legislative determination of the national economy's need of reasonable limitations on cutthroat competition or prohibition of monopoly. "[W]here exceptions are made, Congress should make them." *United States* v. *Line Material Co.*, 333 U.S. 287, 310. . . . We therefore turn to Section 2 . . . to determine whether duPont has violated that section by its dominance in the manufacture of cellophane in the before-stated circumstances.

III. THE SHERMAN ACT,
SECTION 2—MONOPOLIZATION

The only statutory language of Section 2 pertinent on this review is: "Every person who shall monopolize . . . shall be deemed guilty. . . ." . . . Our cases determine that a party has monopoly power if it has, over "any part of the trade or commerce among the several States," a power of controlling prices or unreasonably restricting competition. . . .

Senator Hoar, in discussing Section 2, pointed out that monopoly involved something more than extraordinary commercial success, "that it involved something like the use of means which made it impossible for other persons to engage in fair competition." This exception to the Sherman Act prohibitions of monopoly power is perhaps the monopoly "thrust upon" one of *United States* v. *Aluminum Co. of America,* 148 F.2d 416, 429. . . .

If cellophane is the "market" that duPont is found to dominate, it may be assumed it does have monopoly power over that "market." Monopoly power is the power to control prices or exclude competition. It seems apparent that duPont's power to set the price of cellophane has only been limited by the competition afforded by other flexible packaging materials. Moreover, it may be practically impossible for anyone to commence manufacturing cellophane without full access to duPont's technique. However, duPont has no power to prevent competition from other wrapping materials. The trial court consequently had to determine whether competition from the other wrappings prevented duPont from possessing monopoly power in violation of Section 2. Price and competition are so intimately entwined that any discussion of theory must treat them as one. It is inconceivable that price could be controlled without power over competition or vice versa. This approach to the determination of monopoly power is strengthened by this Court's conclusion in prior cases that, when an alleged monopolist has power over price and competition, an intention to monopolize in a proper case may be assumed.[2]

If a large number of buyers and sellers deal freely in a standardized product, such as salt or wheat, we have complete or pure competition. Patents, on the other hand, furnish the most familiar type of classic monopoly. As the producers of a standardized product bring about significant differentiations of quality, design, or packaging in the product that permit differences of use, competition becomes to a greater or less degree incomplete and the producer's power over price and competition greater over his article and its use, according to the differentiation he is able to create and maintain. A retail seller may have in one sense a monopoly on certain trade because of location, as an isolated country store or filling station, or because no one else makes a product of just the quality or attractiveness of his product, as for example in cigarettes. Thus one can theorize that we have monopolistic competition in every nonstandardized commodity with each manufacturer having power over the price and production of his own product.[3] However, this power that, let us say, automobile or soft-drink manufacturers have over their trademarked products is not the power that makes an illegal monopoly. Illegal power must be appraised in terms of the competitive market for the product.

Determination of the competitive market for commodities depends on how different from one another are the offered commodities in character or use, how far buyers will go to substitute one commodity for another. For example, one can think of building materials as in commodity competition but one could hardly say that brick competed with steel or wood or cement or stone in the meaning of Sherman Act litigation; the products are too different. This is the interindustry competition emphasized by some economists. . . . On the other hand, there are certain differences

---

[2] Here the Court cited *United States* v. *Columbia Steel Co.*, 334 U.S. 495, 525; *United States* v. *Paramount Pictures*, 334 U.S. 131, 173; and *Apex Hosiery Co.* v. *Leader*, 310 U.S. 469, 501. IMS.

[3] Here the Court cited Chamberlin, *Theory of Monopolistic Competition*, c. IV. IMS.

in the formulae for soft drinks but one can hardly say that each one is an illegal monopoly. Whatever the market may be, we hold that control of price or competition establishes the existence of monopoly power under Section 2. Section 2 requires the application of a reasonable approach in determining the existence of monopoly power just as surely as did Section 1. This of course does not mean that there can be a reasonable monopoly. . . . Our next step is to determine whether duPont has monopoly power over cellophane: that is, power over its price in relation to or competition with other commodities. The charge was monopolization of cellophane. The defense, that cellophane was merely a part of the relevant market for flexible packaging materials.

IV. THE RELEVANT MARKET

When a product is controlled by one interest, without substitutes available in the market, there is monopoly power. Because most products have possible substitutes, we cannot, as we said in *Times-Picayune Co.* v. *United States*, 345 U.S. 594, 612, give "that infinite range" to the definition of substitutes. Nor is it a proper interpretation of the Sherman Act to require that products be fungible to be considered in the relevant market.

The Government argues:

> We do not here urge that in *no* circumstances may competition of substitutes negative possession of monopolistic power over trade in a product. The decisions make it clear at the least that the courts will not consider substitutes other than those which are substantially fungible with the monopolized product and sell at substantially the same price.

But where there are market alternatives that buyers may readily use for their purposes, illegal monopoly does not exist merely because the product said to be monopolized differs from others. If it were not so, only physically identical products would be a part of the market. To accept the Government's argument, we would have to conclude that the manufacturers of plain as well as moistureproof cellophane were monopolists, and so with films such as Pliofilm, foil, glassine, polyethylene, and Saran, for each of these wrapping materials is distinguishable. These were all exhibits in the case. New wrappings appear, generally similar to cellophane: is each a monopoly? What is called for is an appraisal of the "cross-elasticity" of demand in the trade. . . . The varying circumstances of each case determine the result. In considering what is the relevant market for determining the control of price and competition, no more definite rule can be declared than that commodities reasonably interchangeable by consumers for the same purposes make up that "part of the trade or commerce," monopolization of which may be illegal. As respects flexible packaging materials, the market . . . is nationwide.

Industrial activities cannot be confined to trim categories. Illegal monopolies under Section 2 may well exist over limited products in narrow fields where competition is eliminated. That does not settle the issue here. In determining the market under the Sherman Act, it is the use or uses to which the commodity is put that control. The selling price between commodities with similar uses and different characteristics may vary, so that the cheaper product can drive out the more expensive. Or, the superior quality of higher priced articles may make dominant the more desirable. Cellophane costs more than many competing products and less than a few. But whatever the price, there are various flexible wrapping materials that are bought by manufacturers for packaging their goods in their own plants or are sold to converters who shape and print them for use in the packaging of the commodities to be wrapped.

Cellophane differs from other flexible packaging materials. From some it differs more than from others. . . . It will adequately illustrate the similarity in characteristics of the various products by noting . . . [that the use of glassine] is almost as extensive as cellophane, . . . and many of its characteristics [are] equally or more satisfactory to users.

It may be admitted that cellophane combines the desirable elements of transparency, strength and cheapness more definitely than any of the others. . . .

But, despite cellophane's advantages, it has to meet competition from other materials in every one of its uses. . . . Food products are the chief outlet, with cigarettes next. The Government makes no challenge to Finding 283 that cellophane furnishes less than 7% of wrappings for bakery products, 25% for candy, 32% for snacks, 35% for meats and poultry, 27% for crackers and biscuits, 47% for fresh produce, and 34% for frozen foods. Seventy-five to 80% of cigarettes are wrapped in cellophane. . . . Thus, cellophane shares the packaging market with others. The over-all result is that cellophane accounts for 17.9% of flexible wrapping materials, measured by the wrapping surface. . . .

Moreover a very considerable degree of functional interchangeability exists between these products. . . . It will be noted . . . that except as to permeability to gases, cellophane has no qualities that are not possessed by a number of other materials. . . . Pliofilm is more expensive . . . but its superior physical characteristics apparently offset cellophane's price advantage. While retailers shift continually between the two, the trial court found that Pliofilm is increasing its share of the business. . . .

An element for consideration as to cross-elasticity of demand between products is the responsiveness of the sales of one product to price changes of the other. If a slight decrease in the price of cellophane causes a considerable number of customers of other flexible wrappings to switch to cellophane, it would be an indication that a high cross-elasticity of demand exists between them; that the products compete in the same market. The court below held that the "[g]reat sensitivity of customers in the flexible packaging markets to price or quality changes" prevented duPont from possessing monopoly control over price. . . . The record sustains these findings. . . .

We conclude that cellophane's interchangeability with the other materials mentioned suffices to make it a part of this flexible packaging material market.

The Government stresses the fact that the variation in price between cellophane and other materials demonstrates they are noncompetitive. As these products are all flexible wrapping materials, it seems reasonable to consider, as was done at the trial, their comparative cost to the consumer in terms of square area. . . . Cellophane costs two or three times as much, surface measure, as its chief competitors for the flexible wrapping market, glassine and greaseproof papers. Other forms of cellulose wrappings and those from other chemical or mineral substances, with the exception of aluminum foil, are more expensive. The uses of these materials . . . are largely to wrap small packages for retail distribution. The wrapping is a relatively small proportion of the entire cost of the article. Different producers need different qualities in wrappings and their need may vary from time to time as their products undergo change. But the necessity for flexible wrappings is the central and unchanging demand. We cannot say that these differences in cost gave duPont monopoly power over prices in view of the findings of fact on that subject.

It is the variable characteristics of the different flexible wrappings and the energy and ability with which the manufacturers push their wares that determine choice. A glance at "Modern Packaging," a trade journal, will give, by its various advertisements, examples of the competition among manufacturers for the flexible packaging market. The trial judge visited the 1952 Annual Packaging Show at Atlantic City, with the consent of counsel. He observed exhibits offered by "machinery manufacturers, converters and manufacturers of flexible packaging materials." He states that these personal observations confirmed his estimate of the competition between cellophane and other packaging materials. . . .

> The record establishes plain cellophane and moistureproof cellophane are each flexible packaging materials which are functionally interchangeable with other flexible packaging materials and sold at same time to same customers for same purpose at competitive prices; there is no cellophane market distinct and separate from the market for flexible packaging materials; the market for flexible packaging materials is the relevant market for determining nature and extent of duPont's market control; and duPont has at all times competed with other cellophane producers and manufacturers of other flexible packaging materials in all aspects of its cellophane business.

The facts above considered dispose also of any contention that competitors have been excluded by duPont from the packaging material market. That market has many producers and there is no proof duPont ever has possessed power to exclude any of them from the rapidly expanding flexible packaging market. The Government apparently concedes as much, for it states that "lack of power to inhibit entry into this so-called market [i.e., flexible packaging materials], comprising widely disparate products, is no indicium of absence of power to exclude competition in the manufacture and sale of cellophane." The record shows the multiplicity of competitors and the financial strength of some with individual assets running to the hundreds of millions. . . . Indeed, the trial court found that duPont could not exclude competitors even from the manufacture of cellophane, . . . an immaterial matter if the market is flexible packaging material. Nor can we say that duPont's profits, while liberal (according to the Government's 15.9% net after taxes on the 1937–1947 average), demonstrate the existence of a monopoly without proof of lack of comparable profits during those years in other prosperous industries. . . . There is no showing that duPont's rate of return was greater or less than that of other producers of flexible packaging materials. . . .

The "market" which one must study to determine when a producer has monopoly power will vary with the part of commerce under consideration. The tests are constant. The market is composed of products that have reasonable interchangeability for the purposes for which they are produced—price, use and qualities considered. While the application of the tests remains uncertain, it seems to us that duPont should not be found to monopolize cellophane when that product has the competition and interchangeability with other wrappings that this record shows.

On the findings of the District Court, its judgment is *Affirmed*.

MR. JUSTICE CLARK and MR. JUSTICE HARLAN took no part in the consideration or decision of this case.

. . . . .

MR. JUSTICE FRANKFURTER, concurring.

. . . . .

MR. CHIEF JUSTICE WARREN, with whom MR. JUSTICE BLACK and MR. JUSTICE DOUGLAS join, dissenting.

This case, like many under the Sherman Act, turns upon the proper definition of the market. In defining the market in which duPont's economic power is to be measured, the majority virtually emasculate Section 2 of the Sherman Act. They admit that "cellophane combines the desirable elements of transparency, strength and cheapness more definitely than any of" a host of other packaging materials. Yet they hold that all of those materials are so indistinguishable from cellophane as to warrant their inclusion in the market. We cannot agree that cellophane, in the language of *Times-Picayune Publishing Co.* v. *United States* . . . is "the selfsame product" as glassine, greaseproof and vegetable parchment papers, waxed papers, sulphite papers, aluminum foil, cellulose acetate, and Pliofilm and other films.

The majority opinion states that "[I]t will adequately illustrate the similarity in characteristics of the various products by noting here Finding 62 as to glassine." But Finding 62 merely states the respects in which the selected flexible packaging materials are as satisfactory as cellophane; it does not compare all the physical properties of cellophane and other materials. The Table incorporated in Finding 59 does make such a comparison, and enables us to note cellophane's unique combination of qualities lacking among less expensive materials in varying degrees.[4] . . . . Indeed, the majority go further than placing cellophane in the same market with such products. They also include the transparent films, which are more expensive than cellophane. These bear even less resemblance to the lower priced packaging materials than does cellophane. . . .

If the conduct of buyers indicated that glassine, waxed and sulphite papers and aluminum foil were actually "the selfsame products" as cellophane, the qualitative differences demonstrated by the comparison of physical properties in Finding 59 would not be conclusive. But the record provides convincing proof that businessmen did not so regard these products. During the period covered by the complaint (1923–1947) cellophane enjoyed phenomenal growth. DuPont's 1924 production was 361,249 pounds, which sold for $1,306,662. Its 1947 production was 133,502,858 pounds, which sold for $55,339,626. Findings 297 and 337. Yet throughout this period the price of cellophane was far greater than that of glassine, waxed paper or sulphite paper. Finding 136 states that in 1929 cellophane's price was even seven times that of glassine; in 1934, four times, and in 1949 still more than twice glassine's price. Reference to DX-994, the graph upon which Finding 136 is based, shows that cellophane had a similar price relation to waxed paper and that sulphite paper sold at even less than glassine and waxed paper. We cannot believe that buyers, practical businessmen, would have bought cellophane in increasing amounts over a quarter of a century if close substitutes were available at from one-seventh to one-half cellophane's price. That they did so is testimony to cellophane's distinctiveness.

The inference yielded by the conduct of cellophane buyers is reinforced by the conduct of sellers other than duPont. Finding 587 states that Sylvania, the only other cellophane producer, absolutely and immediately followed every duPont price change, even dating back its price list to the effective date of duPont's change. Producers of glassine and waxed paper, on the other hand, displayed apparent indifference to duPont's repeated

---

[4] . . . The majority opinion quotes at length from Stocking and Mueller, "The Cellophane Case," XLV *Amer. Economic Rev.* 29, 48–49, in noting the comparative characteristics of cellophane and other products. Unfortunately, the opinion fails to quote the conclusion reached by these economists. They state: "The [trial] court to the contrary notwithstanding, the market in which cellophane meets the 'competition' of other wrappers is narrower than the market for all flexible packaging materials." Id., at 52. And they conclude that ". . . cellophane is so differentiated from other flexible wrapping materials that its cross elasticity of demand gives duPont significant and continuing monopoly power." Id., at 63.

and substantial price cuts. DX-994 shows that from 1924 to 1932 duPont dropped the price of plain cellophane 84%, while the price of glassine remained constant. And during the period 1933–1946 the prices for glassine and waxed paper actually increased in the face of a further 21% decline in the price of cellophane. If "shifts of business" due to "price sensitivity" had been substantial, glassine and waxed paper producers who wanted to stay in business would have been compelled by market forces to meet duPont's price challenge just as Sylvania was. . . . Surely there was more than "a slight decrease in the price of cellophane" during the period covered by the complaint. That producers of glassine and waxed paper remained dominant in the flexible packaging materials market without meeting cellophane's tremendous price cuts convinces us that cellophane was not in effective competition with their products.[5]

Certainly duPont itself shared our view. From the first, duPont recognized that it need not concern itself with competition from other packaging materials. For example, when duPont was contemplating entry into cellophane production, its Development Department reported that glassine "is so inferior that it belongs in an entirely different class and has hardly to be considered as a competitor of cellophane." This was still duPont's view in 1950 when its survey of competitive prospects wholly omitted reference to glassine, waxed paper or sulphite paper and stated that "competition for duPont cellophane will come from competitive cellophane and from non-cellophane films made by us or by others."[6]

DuPont's every action was directed toward maintaining dominance over cellophane. Its 1923 agreements with La Cellophane, the French concern which first produced commercial cellophane, gave duPont exclusive North and Central American rights to cellophane's technology, manufacture and sale, and provided, without any limitation in time, that all existing and future information pertaining to the cellophane process be considered "secret and confidential," and be held in an exclusive common pool. In its subsequent agreements with foreign licensees, duPont was careful to preserve its continental market inviolate. In 1929, while it was still the sole domestic producer of cellophane, duPont won its long struggle to raise the tariff from 25% to 60%, ad valorem, on cellophane imports, substantially foreclosing foreign competition. When Sylvania became the second American cellophane producer the following year and duPont filed suit claiming infringement of its moistureproof patents, they settled the suit by entering into a cross-licensing agreement. . . . If close substitutes for cellophane had been commercially available, duPont, an enlightened enterprise, would not have gone to such lengths to control cellophane.

---

[5] See Stocking and Mueller, "The Cellophane Case," XLV *Amer. Economic Rev.* 29, 56.

[6] R. 4070. It is interesting to note that duPont had almost 70% of the market which this report considered relevant.

As predicted by its 1923 market analysis, duPont's dominance in cellophane proved enormously profitable from the outset. After only five years of production, when duPont bought out the minority stock interests in its cellophane subsidiary, it had to pay more than fifteen times the original price of the stock. But such success was not limited to the period of innovation, limited sales and complete domestic monopoly. A confidential duPont report shows that during the period 1937–1947, despite great expansion of sales, duPont's "operative return" (before taxes) averaged 31%, while its average "net return" (after deduction of taxes, bonuses, and fundamental research expenditures) was 15.9%. Such profits provide a powerful incentive for the entry of competitors.[7] Yet from 1924 to 1951 only one new firm, Sylvania, was able to begin cellophane production. And Sylvania could not have entered if La Cellophane's secret process had not been stolen.[8] It is significant that for 15 years Olin Industries, a substantial firm, was unsuccessful in its attempt to produce cellophane, finally abandoning the project in 1944 after having spent about $1,000,000. . . .

The trial court found that

> DuPont has no power to set cellophane prices arbitrarily. If prices for cellophane increase in relation to prices of other flexible packaging materials it will lose business to manufacturers of such materials in varying amounts for each of duPont's cellophane's major end uses.   Finding 712.

This further reveals its misconception of the antitrust laws. A monopolist seeking to maximize profits cannot raise prices "arbitrarily." Higher prices of course mean smaller sales, but they also mean higher per-unit profit. Lower prices will increase sales but reduce per-unit profit. Within these limits a monopolist has a considerable degree of latitude in determining which course to pursue in attempting to maximize profits. The trial judge thought that, if duPont raised its price, the market would "penalize" it with smaller profits as well as lower sales. DuPont proved him wrong. When 1947 operating earnings dropped below 26% for the first time in 10 years, it increased cellophane's price 7% and boosted its earnings in 1948. DuPont's division manager then reported that "if an opera-

---

[7] See Stocking and Mueller, "The Cellophane Case," XLV *Amer. Economic Rev.* 29, 60–63, where the authors compare the domestic economic history of rayon with that of cellophane. The first American rayon producer earned 64.2% on its investment in 1920, thereby attracting duPont. After a loss in 1921, duPont's average return for the next four years was roughly 32%. As more firms began rayon production, duPont's and the industry's return on investment began to drop. When 6 new firms entered the industry in 1930, bringing the number of producers to 20, average industry earnings for that year declined to 5% and duPont suffered a net loss. "From the beginning of the depression in 1929 through the succeeding recovery and the 1938 recession duPont averaged 29.6 percent before taxes on its cellophane investment. On its rayon investment it averaged only 6.3 percent." Id., at 62–63.

[8] In 1924 two of La Cellophane's principal officials absconded with complete information on the cellophane process. A Belgian concern was then set up to use this process in making cellophane, and it later organized Sylvania as an American affiliate. Findings 615–618.

tive return of 31% is considered inadequate then an upward revision in prices will be necessary to improve the return." It is this latitude with respect to price, this broad power of choice, that the antitrust laws forbid. DuPont's independent pricing policy and the great profits consistently yielded by that policy leave no room for doubt that it had power to control the price of cellophane. The findings of fact cited by the majority cannot affect this conclusion. For they merely demonstrate that, during the period covered by the complaint, duPont was a "good monopolist," *i.e.*, that it did not engage in predatory practices and that it chose to maximize profits by lowering price and expanding sales. Proof of enlightened exercise of monopoly power certainly does not refute the existence of that power.

The majority opinion purports to reject the theory of "interindustry competition." Brick, steel, wood, cement and stone, it says, are "too different" to be placed in the same market. But cellophane, glassine, wax papers, sulphite papers, greaseproof and vegetable parchment papers, aluminum foil, cellulose acetate, Pliofilm and other films are not "too different," the opinion concludes. The majority approach would apparently enable a monopolist of motion picture exhibition to avoid Sherman Act consequences by showing that motion pictures compete in substantial measure with legitimate theatre, television, radio, sporting events and other forms of entertainment. Here, too, "shifts of business" undoubtedly accompany fluctuations in price and "there are market alternatives that buyers may readily use for their purposes." . . . [T]he formula of "reasonable interchangeability," as applied by the majority, appears indistinguishable from the theory of "interindustry competition." The danger in it is that, as demonstrated in this case, it is "perfectly compatible with a fully monopolized economy."[9]

The majority hold in effect that, because cellophane meets competition for many end uses, those buyers for other uses who need or want only cellophane are not entitled to the benefits of competition within the cellophane industry. . . . Furthermore, those buyers who have "reasonable alternatives" between cellophane and other products are also entitled to competition within the cellophane industry, for such competition may lead to lower prices and improved quality.

The foregoing analysis of the record shows conclusively that cellophane is the relevant market. Since duPont has the lion's share of that market, it must have monopoly power, as the majority concede. This being so, we think it clear that, in the circumstances of this case, duPont is guilty of "monopolization." The briefest sketch of duPont's business history precludes it from falling within the "exception to the Sherman Act prohibitions of monopoly power" (majority opinion, pp. 390–391) by suc-

---

[9] Adams, "The 'Rule of Reason': Workable Competition or Workable Monopoly?" 63 *Yale L. F.* 348, 364.

cessfully asserting that monopoly was "thrust upon" it. DuPont was not "the passive beneficiary of a monopoly" within the meaning of *United States* v. *Aluminum Co. of America, supra,* at 429–430. It sought and maintained dominance through illegal agreements dividing the world market, concealing and suppressing technological information, and restricting its licensee's production by prohibitive royalties, and through numerous maneuvers which might have been "honestly industrial" but whose necessary effect was nevertheless exclusionary. DuPont cannot bear "the burden of proving that it owes its monopoly *solely* to superior skill. . . ." (Emphasis supplied.) *United States* v. *United Shoe Machinery Corp. . . .*

Nor can duPont rely upon its moistureproof patents as a defense to the charge of monopolization. Once duPont acquired the basic cellophane process as a result of its illegal 1923 agreements with La Cellophane, development of moistureproofing was relatively easy. DuPont's moistureproof patents were fully subject to the exclusive pooling arrangements and territorial restrictions established by those agreements. And they were the subject of the illicit and exclusionary duPont-Sylvania agreement. Hence, these patents became tainted as part and parcel of duPont's illegal monopoly. Cf., *Mercoid Corp.* v. *Mid-Continent Co.,* 320 U.S. 661, 670. Any other result would permit one who monopolizes a market to escape the statutory liability by patenting a simple improvement on his product.

If competition is at the core of the Sherman Act, we cannot agree that it was consistent with that Act for the enormously lucrative cellophane industry to have no more than two sellers from 1924 to 1951. The conduct of duPont and Sylvania illustrates that a few sellers tend to act like one and that an industry which does not have a competitive structure will not have competitive behavior. The public should not be left to rely upon the dispensations of management in order to obtain the benefits which normally accompany competition. Such beneficence is of uncertain tenure. Only actual competition can assure long-run enjoyment of the goals of a free economy.

We would reverse the decision below and remand the cause to the District Court with directions to determine the relief which should be granted against duPont.

United States v. Grinnell Corporation

384 U.S. 563 (1966)

MR. JUSTICE DOUGLAS delivered the opinion of the Court.

This case presents an important question under §2 of the Sherman Act. . . . The District Court held for the Government and entered a decree. All parties appeal, the United States because it deems the relief inadequate and the defendants both on the merits and on the relief and on the ground that the District Court denied them a fair trial. . . .

Grinnell manufactures plumbing supplies and fire sprinkler systems. It also owns 76% of the stock of ADT, 89% of the stock of AFA, and 100% of the stock of Holmes.[1] ADT provides both burglary and fire protection services; Holmes provides burglary services alone; AFA supplies only fire protection service. Each offers a central station service under which hazard-detecting devices installed on the protected premises automatically transmit an electric signal to a central station. The central station is manned 24 hours a day. Upon receipt of a signal, the central station, where appropriate, dispatches guards to the protected premises and notifies the police or fire department direct. There are other forms of protective services. But the record shows that subscribers to accredited central station service (*i.e.,* that approved by the insurance underwriters) receive reductions in their insurance premiums that are substantially greater than the reduction received by the users of other kinds of protection service. In 1961 accredited companies in the central station service business grossed $65,000,000. ADT, Holmes, and AFA are the three largest companies in the business in terms of revenue: ADT (with 121 central stations in 115 cities) has 73% of the business; Holmes (with 12 central stations in three large cities) has 12.5%; AFA (with three central stations in three large cities) has 2%. Thus the three companies that Grinnell controls have over 87% of the business. . . .

[The Court here detailed the numerous acquisitions—37 by ADT and 3 by Holmes—and the various geographic and product-line market-sharing agreements entered into over the years by ADT, Holmes and others.]

ADT over the year reduced its minimum basic rates to meet competition and renewed contracts at substantially increased rates in cities where it had a monopoly of accredited central station service. ADT threatened retaliation against firms that contemplated inaugurating central station service. And the record indicates that, in contemplating opening a new central station, ADT officials frequently stressed that such action would deter their competitors from opening a new station in that area.

The District Court found that the defendant companies had committed *per se* violations of §1 of the Sherman Act as well as §2 and entered a decree. . . .

I

The offense of monopoly under §2 of the Sherman Act has two elements: (1) the possession of monopoly power in the relevant market and (2) the willful acquisition or maintenance of that power as distinguished

---

[1] These are the record figures. Since the time of the trial, Grinnell's holdings have increased. Counsel for Grinnell has advised this Court that Grinnell now holds 80% of ADT's stock and 90% of the stock of AFA.

from growth or development as a consequence of a superior product, business acumen, or historic accident. We shall see that this second ingredient presents no major problem here, as what was done in building the empire was done plainly and explicitly for a single purpose. In *United States* v. *duPont & Co.,* 351 U.S. 377, 391, we defined monopoly power as "the power to control prices or exclude competition." The existence of such power ordinarily may be inferred from the predominant share of the market. . . . In the present case, 87% of the accredited central station service business leaves no doubt that the congeries of these defendants have monopoly power—power which, as our discussion of the record indicates, they did not hesitate to wield—if that business is the relevant market. The only remaining question therefore is, what is the relevant market?

In case of a product it may be of such a character that substitute products must also be considered, as customers may turn to them if there is a slight increase in the price of the main product. That is the teaching of the *duPont* case . . . , *viz.,* that commodities reasonably interchangeable make up that "part" of trade or commerce which §2 protects against monopoly power.

The District Court treated the entire accredited central station service business as a single market and we think it was justified in so doing. Defendants argue that the different central station services offered are so diverse that they cannot under *duPont* be lumped together to make up the relevant market. For example, burglar alarm services are not interchangeable with fire alarm services. They further urge that *duPont* requires that protective services other than those of the central station variety be included in the market definition.

But there is here a single use, *i.e.,* the protection of property, through a central station that receives signals. It is that service, accredited, that is unique and that competes with all the other forms of property protection. We see no barrier to combining in a single market a number of different products or services where that combination reflects commercial realities. To repeat, there is here a single basic service—the protection of property through use of a central service station—that must be compared with all other forms of property protection.

In §2 cases under the Sherman Act, as in §7 cases under the Clayton Act *(Brown Shoe Co.* v. *United States,* 370 U.S. 294, 325) there may be submarkets that are separate economic entities. We do not pursue that question here. First, we deal with services, not with products; and second, we conclude that the accredited central station is a type of service that makes up a relevant market and that domination or control of it makes out a monopoly of a "part" of trade or commerce within the meaning of §2 of the Sherman Act. The defendants have not made out a case for fragmentizing the types of services into lesser units.

Burglar alarm service is in a sense different from fire alarm service;

from waterflow alarms; and so on. But it would be unrealistic on this record to break down the market into the various kinds of central station protective services that are available. Central station companies recognize that to compete effectively, they must offer all or nearly all types of service.[2] The different forms of accredited central station service are provided from a single office and customers utilize different services in combination. We held in *United States* v. *Philadelphia Nat. Bank,* 374 U.S. 321, 356, that "the cluster" of service denoted by the term "commercial banking" is "a distinct line of commerce." There is, in our view, a comparable cluster of services here. That bank case arose under §7 of the Clayton Act where the question was whether the effect of a merger "in any line of commerce" may be "substantially to lessen competition." We see no reason to differentiate between "line" of commerce in the context of the Clayton Act and "part" of commerce for purposes of the Sherman Act. See *United States* v. *First Nat. Bank & Trust Co.,* 376 U.S. 665, 667–668. In the §7 national bank case just mentioned, *services,* not *products* in the mercantile sense, were involved. In our view the lumping together of various kinds of *services* makes for the appropriate market here as it did in the §7 case.

There are, to be sure, substitutes for the accredited central station service. But none of them appears to operate on the same level as the central station service so as to meet the interchangeability test of the *duPont* case. Nonautomatic and automatic local alarm systems appear on this record to have marked differences, not the low degree of differentiation required of substitute services as well as substitute articles.

Watchman service is far more costly and less reliable. Systems that set off an audible alarm at the site of a fire or burglary are cheaper but often less reliable. They may be inoperable without anyone's knowing it. Moreover, there is a risk that the local ringing of an alarm will not attract the needed attention and help. Proprietary systems that a customer purchases and operates are available; but they can be used only by a very large business or by government and are not realistic alternatives for most concerns. There are also protective services connected directly to municipal police or fire departments. But most cities with an accredited central station do not permit direct, connected service for private businesses. These alternate services and devices differ, we are told, in utility, efficiency, reliability, responsiveness, and continuity, and the rec-

---

[2] Thus, of the 38 nondefendant firms operating a central service station protective service in the United States in 1961, 24 offered all of the following services: automatic fire alarm; waterflow alarm and sprinkler supervision; watchman's reporting and manual fire alarm; and burglar alarm. Of the other firms, 11 provided no watchman's reporting and manual fire alarm service; six provided no automatic fire alarm service; and two offered no sprinkler supervisory and waterflow alarm service. Moreover, of the 14 firms not providing the full panoply of services, 10 lacked only *one* of the above-described services. Appellant ADT's assertion that "very few accredited central stations furnish the full variety of services" is flatly contradicted by the record.

ord sustains that position. And, as noted, insurance companies generally allow a greater reduction in premiums for accredited central station service than for other types of protection.

Defendants earnestly urge that despite these differences, they face competition from these other modes of protection. They seem to us seriously to overstate the degree of competition, but we recognize that (as the District Court found) they "do not have unfettered power to control the price of their services . . . due to the fringe competition of other alarm or watchmen services." 236 F. Supp., at 254. What defendants overlook is that the high degree of differentiation between central station protection and the other forms means that for many customers, only central station protection will do. Though some customers may be willing to accept higher insurance rates in favor of cheaper forms of protection, others will not be willing or able to risk serious interruption to their businesses, even though covered by insurance, and will thus be unwilling to consider anything but central station protection.

The accredited, as distinguished from nonaccredited service, is a relevant part of commerce. Virtually the only central station companies in the status of the nonaccredited are those that have not yet been able to meet the standards of the rating bureau. The accredited ones are indeed those that have achieved, in the eyes of underwriters, superiorities that other central stations do not have. The accredited central station is located in a building of approved design, provided with an emergency lighting system and two alternate main power sources, manned constantly by at least a required minimum of operators, provided with a direct line to fire headquarters and, where possible, a direct line to a police station; and equipped with all the devices, circuits, and equipment meeting the requirements of the underwriters. These standards are important as insurance carriers often require accredited central station service as a condition to writing insurance. There is indeed evidence that customers consider the unaccredited service is inferior. . . .

We have said enough about the great hold that the defendants have on this market. The percentage is so high as to justify the finding of monopoly. And, as the facts already related indicate, this monopoly was achieved in large part by unlawful and exclusionary practices. The restrictive agreements that preempted for each company a segment of the market where it was free of competition of the others were one device. Pricing practices that contained competitors were another. The acquisitions by Grinnell of ADT, AFA, and Holmes were still another. . . . By those acquisitions it perfected the monopoly power to exclude competitors and fix prices.[3]

---

[3] Since the record clearly shows that this monopoly power was consciously acquired, we have no reason to reach the further position of the District Court that once monopoly power is shown to exist, the burden is on the defendants to show that their dominance is due to skill, acumen, and the like.

II

[In this section, the Court considered the scope of the decree imposed by the District Court. It found the decree to be inadequate in terms of the nature of the divestiture conditions imposed upon Grinnell.]

. . . . .

The judgment below is affirmed except as to the decree. We remand for further hearings on the nature of the relief consistent with the views expressed herein.

It is so ordered.

MR. JUSTICE HARLAN, dissenting.

. . . . .

MR. JUSTICE FORTAS, with whom MR. JUSTICE STEWART joins, dissenting.

I agree that the judgment below should be remanded, but I do not agree that the remand should be limited to reshaping the decree. Because I believe that the definition of the relevant market here cannot be sustained, I would reverse and remand for a new determination of this basic issue, subject to proper standards.

We have here a case under both §1 and §2 of the Sherman Act. . . . The judicial task is not difficult to state: Does the record show a combination in restraint of trade or a monopoly or attempt to monopolize? If so, what are its characteristics, scope, and effect? And, finally, what is the appropriate remedy for a court of equity to decree?

Each of these inquiries depends upon two basic referents: definition of the geographical area of trade or commerce restrained or monopolized, and of the products or services involved. In §1 cases this problem ordinarily presents little difficulty because the combination in restraint of trade itself delineates the "market" with sufficient clarity to support the usual injunctive form of relief in those cases. See, e.g., *United States* v. *Griffith,* 334 U.S. 100. In the present case, however, the essence of the offense is monopolization, achieved or attempted, and the major relief is divestiture. For these purposes, "market" definition is of the essence, just as in §7 cases the kindred definition of the "line of commerce" is fundamental. . . .

In §2 cases, the search for "the relevant market" must be undertaken and pursued with relentless clarity. It is, in essence, an economic task put to the uses of the law. Unless this task is well done, the results will be distorted in terms of the conclusion as to whether the law has been violated and what the decree should contain.

In this case, the relevant geographical and product markets have not been defined on the basis of the economic facts of the industry concerned. They have been tailored precisely to fit defendants' business. The Government proposed and the trial court concluded that the relevant market is not the business of fire protection, or burglary protection, or protection against waterflow, etc., or all of these together. It is not even the business of furnishing these from a central location. It is the business, viewed nationally, of supplying "insurance accredited central station protection services" (CSPS)—that is, fire, burglary and other kinds of protection furnished from a central station which is accredited by insurance companies. The business of defendants fits neatly into the product and geographic market so defined. In fact, it comes close to filling the market so defined. This Court has now approved this Procrustean definition.

The geographical market is defined as nationwide. But the need and the service are intensely local—more local by far, for example, than the market which this Court found to be local in *United States* v. *Philadelphia Nat. Bank,* 374 U.S. 321, 357–362. . . . Protection must be provided on the spot. It must be furnished by local personnel able to bring help to the scene within minutes. Even the central stations can provide service only within a 25-mile radius. Where the tenants of the premises turn to central stations for this service, they must make their contracts locally with the central station and purchase their services from it on the basis of local conditions.

But because these defendants, the trial court found, are connected by stock ownership, interlocking management and some degree of national corporate direction, and because there is some national participation in selling as well as national financing, advertising, purchasing of equipment, and the like,[4] the court concluded that the competitive area to be considered is national. This Court now affirms that conclusion.

This is a non sequitur. It is not permissible to seize upon the nationwide scope of defendants' operation and to bootstrap a geographical definition of the market from this. The purpose of the search for the relevant geographical market is to find the area or areas to which a potential buyer may rationally look for the goods or services that he seeks. The test, as this Court said in *United States* v. *Philadelphia Nat. Bank,* is "the geographic structure of supplier-customer relations," 374 U.S. 321, 357, quoting Kaysen & Turner, Antitrust Policy 102 (1959). And, as MR. JUSTICE CLARK put it in *Tampa Electric Co.* v. *Nashville Coal Co.,* 365 U.S. 320, 327, the definition of the relevant market requires "careful selection of the market area in which the seller operates, and to which the purchaser can practicably turn for supplies."[5] The central issue is where does a potential buyer look for potential suppliers of the service—what is

---

[4] . . . There is neither finding nor record to support the implication that rates are to any substantial extent fixed on a nationwide basis, or that there are nationwide contracts with multistate businesses in any significant degree, or that insurers inspect or certify central stations on a nationwide basis.

[5] See also *Brown Shoe Co.* v. *United States,* 370 U.S. 294, 336–37.

the geographical area in which the buyer has, or, in the absence of monopoly, would have, a real choice as to price and alternative facilities? This depends upon the facts of the market place, taking into account such economic factors as the distance over which supplies and services may be feasibly furnished, consistently with cost and functional efficiency. . . .

Here, there can be no doubt that the correct geographic market is local. The services at issue are intensely local: they can be furnished only locally. The business as it is done is local—not nationwide. If, as might well be the case on this record, defendants were found to have violated the Sherman Act in a number of these local areas, a proper decree, directed to those markets, as well as to general corporate features relevant to the condemned practices, could be fashioned. . . . This Court now directs the trial court to require "some [unspecified] divestiture" locally by the alarm companies. This is a recognition of the economic reality that the relevant competitive areas are local. . . .

The trial court's definition of the "product" market even more dramatically demonstrates that its action has been Procrustean—that it has tailored the market to the dimensions of the defendants. It recognizes that a person seeking protective services has many alternative sources. . . . The court relies solely upon its finding that the services offered by accredited central stations are of better quality, and upon its conclusion that the insurance companies tend to give "noticeably larger" discounts to policyholders who use accredited central station protective services. The Court now approves this strange red-haired, bearded, one-eyed man-with-a-limp classification. . . .

Moreover, we are told that the "relevant market" must assume this strange and curious configuration despite evidence in the record and a finding of the trial court that "fringe competition" from such locally available alternatives as watchmen, local alarm systems, proprietary systems, and unaccredited central stations has, in at least 20 cities, forced the defendants to operate at a "loss" even though defendants have a total monopoly in these cities of the "market"—namely, the "accredited central station protective services." And we are led to this odd result even though there is in the record abundant evidence that customers switch from one form of property protection to another, and not always in the direction of accredited central station service.

I believe this approach has no justification in economics, reason or law. . . . As this Court held in *Brown Shoe* . . . , the "reasonable interchangeability of use or the cross-elasticity of demand," determines the boundaries of a product market. 370 U.S., at 325. See also the *Cellophane* case, 351 U.S., at 380. In plain language, this means that the court should have defined the relevant market here to include all services which, in light of geographical availability, price and use characteristics, are in realistic rivalry for all or some part of the business of furnishing protective services to premises. . . .

I do not suggest that wide disparities in quality, price and customer appeal could never affect the definition of the market. But this follows only where the disparities are so great that they create separate and distinct categories of buyers and sellers. The record here and the findings do not approach this standard. They fall far short of justifying the narrowing of the market as practiced here. I need refer only to the exclusion of nonaccredited central stations, which the court seeks to justify by reference to differentials in insurance discounts. These differentials may indeed affect the relative cost to the consumer of the competing modes of protection. But, in the absence of proof that they result in eliminating the competing services from the category of those to which the purchaser "can practicably turn" for supplies,[6] they do not justify such total exclusion. This sort of exclusion of the supposedly not-quite-so-attractive service from the basic definition of the kinds of business and service against which defendants' activity will be measured, is entirely unjustified on this record.[7] . . .

. . . Now, because of this Court's mandate, the market-by-market inquiry must begin for purposes of the decree. But this should have been the foundation of judgment, not its superimposed conclusion. This inquiry should—in my opinion, it must—take into account the *total* economic situation—all of the options available to one seeking protection services. It should not be limited to central stations, and certainly not to "insurance accredited central station protective services" which this Court sanctions as the relevant market. . . .

California Computer Products, Inc., et al. v. *International Business Machines Corp.*

__F.2d__(9th Cir. 1979)

OPINION

CHOY, Circuit Judge. California Computer Products, Inc. (CalComp) appeals from the judgment entered on a directed verdict in favor of appellee International Business Machines Corp. (IBM) as to all counts of its complaint charging IBM with violations of §2 of the Sherman Act. . . . We affirm.

---

[6] *Tampa Electric Co.* v. *Nashville Coal Co.*, 365 U.S., at 327.

[7] The example used by the court in its findings is illuminating and disturbing. In explanation of its narrow market definition, the court says that the difference between the accredited central station protective services and all others "could be compared" to the difference between a compact six-cylinder car and a chauffeur-driven sedan. It is probably true that the degree of direct competition between luxury automobiles and compacts is slight. But it is by no means as clear-cut as the trial court seems to suggest. The question would require careful analysis in light of the total facts and issues. For example, if the antitrust problem at hand involved an acquisition of the business of a manufacturer of compacts by a maker of luxury cars, it is by no means inconceivable that sufficient competitive overlap would be found to place both products in the "relevant market."

I. BACKGROUND AND PROCEEDINGS BELOW

IBM is one of the largest industrial corporations in the world. It achieved technical leadership in the computer industry over other early entrants, such as Sperry Rand, in the mid-1950s and thereafter pioneered the development of many electronic data processing products, including the disk products involved in this litigation.

Disk products are part of a broader category of what is known as peripheral equipment, such as disks, tapes, printers, and terminals, which is connected to the central processing unit (CPU) to enable the data processing system to perform particular functions. . . . Occasionally these devices are built into the CPU; alternatively, they exist as external components that may be "plugged into" the CPU. As a general purpose computer systems manufacturer, IBM sells both CPUs and peripherals, including disk products.

CalComp began manufacturing computer products in 1960. . . . With the acquisition of Century Data Systems in 1969, CalComp entered the disk products market, manufacturing disk drives and controllers that were "plug compatible" with IBM's and other suppliers' CPUs. CalComp's business strategy with respect to IBM-compatible disk products was straightforward: copy and, where possible, improve upon an IBM design, and undersell IBM to its own customers. By the "reverse engineering" of simply buying a device from IBM, taking it apart, and building a similar one, CalComp was able to avoid IBM's expenditures for research and development and pass the savings on through lower prices.

CalComp commenced this lawsuit on October 3, 1973. The complaint alleged that IBM's introduction of new CPUs and disk products, its price cuts on existing disk products, its leasing policies, and other marketing practices prevented CalComp from effectively competing with IBM for disk product sales. . . . CalComp alleged and attempted to prove that these acts by IBM took place within a ten-year span, from late 1963 to 1972, resulting in treble damages of $306 million. . . . At the conclusion of 54 days of trial covering three months, the district court granted IBM's motion for directed verdict on February 11, 1977. . . .

II. ANTITRUST STANDING

CalComp has asserted that IBM's actions created anticompetitive effects on three classes of IBM competitors: (1) general purpose computer systems manufacturers, (2) leasing companies, and (3) IBM-compatible peripheral equipment manufacturers. We believe that CalComp, an IBM-compatible peripheral equipment manufacturer, lacks antitrust standing as to the first two categories of claims. . . .

Section 4 of the Clayton Act . . . §15, authorizing private antitrust suits for damages, . . . confers standing to sue only upon those persons causally injured by antitrust violations. . . . Moreover, in order to prevail the plaintiff must prove not only injury causally linked to the asserted violation, but also that the injury is of the type the antitrust laws were intended to prevent. . . . The plaintiff's burden of proving the former is satisfied by proof of *some* damage flowing from the antitrust violation. . . . Satisfying the latter burden is dependent on a showing that the injury was caused by a reduction, rather than an increase, in competition flowing from the defendant's acts, since "[t]he antitrust laws . . . were enacted 'for the protection of *competition,* not *competitors,*'" *Brunswick Corp.* v. *Pueblo Bowl-O-Mat, Inc.,* 429 U.S. at 488, quoting *Brown Shoe Co.* v. *United States,* 370 U.S. 294, 320 (1962). . . . Accordingly, the plaintiff must demonstrate that the defendant's conduct was intended to or did have some anticompetitive effect beyond his own loss of business or the market's loss of a competitor. . . . Moreover, it is not sufficient for an antitrust plaintiff to allege an indirect ripple effect. . . .

In the present case CalComp has alleged that IBM's actions injured general purpose computer systems manufacturers and leasing companies. But CalComp does not include itself among these two classes of IBM competitors. Nor does CalComp's evidence demonstrate a direct causal injury which would afford it standing. Rather, at best CalComp argues that injury to these two groups has had an indirect ripple effect upon it. As *John Lenore & Co.* [v. *Olympia Brewing Co.,* 550 F.2d 495 (9th Cir. 1977)] indicates, such an indirect ripple effect is not sufficient to allow CalComp to sue for treble damages on its first two categories of claims.

III.   CALCOMP'S CLAIMS AS TO IBM-COMPATIBLE PERIPHERAL EQUIPMENT MANUFACTURERS

A.   Standard of Review on Appeal from Directed Verdict

As a general rule, the district court has the power to direct a verdict if "the evidence permits only one reasonable conclusion as to the verdict." *Fountila* v. *Carter,* 571 F.2d 487, 489–90 (9th Cir. 1978), quoting *Kay* v. *Cessna Aircraft Co.,* 548 F.2d 1370, 1372 (9th Cir. 1977). . . . The district court must consider all the evidence—both favorable and unfavorable. But in order to avoid passing on the credibility of witnesses and weighing contradictory evidence, the court must resolve all inferences in favor of the party with the burden of persuasion, because

[i]t is the jury, not the judge, which "weighs the contradictory evidence and inferences, judges the credibility of witnesses, . . . and draws the ultimate conclusion as to the facts. . . ."

Fount-Wip, Inc. v. *Reddi-Wip, Inc.,* 568 F.2d 1296, 1301 9th Cir. 1978), quoting *Cockrum* v. *Whitney,* 479 F.2d 84, 86 (8th Cir. 1973) and *Tennant* v. *Peoria & Pekin Union Ry.,* 321 U.S. 29, 35 (1944). . . .

B. General §2 Doctrine

CalComp contends that the evidence was sufficient to show that particular conduct on the part of IBM, detailed below, violated either or both the monopolization and attempt to monopolize clauses of §2 of the Sherman Act. . . . In order to reverse the district court's judgment as to either of these claims, it must be that after viewing the evidence in the light most favorable to CalComp, there is substantial evidence of every essential element of that claim.

1. Monopolization. There are three essential elements to a successful claim of §2 monopolization:

a. the possession of monopoly power in the relevant market;
b. the willful acquisition or maintenance of that power; and
c. causal "antitrust" injury.

The first two elements are derived from §2 itself and were explicated in *United States* v. *Grinnell Corp.,* 384 U.S. 563, 570-71 (1966). See *Greyhound Computer Corp.* v. *IBM,* 559 F.2d 488, 492 (9th Cir. 1977). . . .

As reiterated in *Greyhound,* monopoly power—the first element—"is the power to control prices or exclude competition." 559 F.2d at 496, quoting *United States* v. *E. I. duPont de Nemours & Co.,* 351 U.S. 377, 391 (1956). The *duPont* definition of monopoly power has been applied principally with reference to the defendant's share of the relevant product and geographic markets. . . .

The second element of a successful monopolization claim requires that the conceded monopolist have engaged in "willful" acts directed at establishing or retaining its monopoly, "as distinguished from growth or development as a consequence of a superior product, business acumen, or historic accident." *United States* v. *Grinnell Corp.,* 384 U.S. at 571.[1] That case found the defendant's acts sufficient to meet the §2 conduct requirement because they constituted "unlawful and exclusionary practices." Id. at 576.

The plaintiff need not show that the conceded monopolist's acts were of a kind that would be unlawful for an ordinary enterprise. . . . 559 F.2d at 498. Rather, the plaintiff must show that the defendant's acts "unnecessarily excluded competition" from the relevant market. . . . Nor is it necessary to show a specific intent to eliminate a competitor. . . . The defendant's acts are properly analyzed analo-

---

[1] "The Act was deemed by its sponsors not to be applicable to one 'who merely by superior skill and intelligence . . . got the whole business because nobody could do it as well.' [T]he exception was an indication that power obtained or maintained by the kind of behavior that competition is thought to foster, if not compel, was immune even though businesses and business opportunities were destroyed in the process. In short, . . . protection of incentives to competitive behavior would prevail over dispersion of market power." C. Kaysen & D. Turner, *Antitrust Policy 20* (1959), quoting *21 Cong. Rec.* 3151-52 (1890) (remarks of Sen. Hoar).

gously to contracts, combinations and conspiracies under §1 of the Sherman Act: the test is whether the defendant's acts, otherwise lawful, were *unreasonably* restrictive of competition.[2] . . . While this "in large measure" has the effect of making acts of monopolization "merely the end products of conduct which violates §1," "that is not always true." *United States* v. *Griffith*, 334 U.S. 100, 106 (1948). Section 1 is limited to concerted activity and contractual restraints, while under §2, individual activity may also give rise to liability. . . .[3]

The third element—plaintiff's resultant "antitrust" injury—has already been discussed, Part II *supra*.

2. *Attempt to Monopolize*.   There are four elements to a successful claim of §2 attempt to monopolize:

a.   specific intent to control prices or destroy competition with respect to a part of commerce;
b.   predatory or anticompetitive conduct directed to accomplishing the unlawful purpose;
c.   a dangerous probability of success; and
d.   causal antitrust injury.

The first element was explained in *Times-Picayune Publishing Co.* v. *United States*, 345 U.S. 594, 626 (1953), wherein the Supreme Court differentiated the requisite levels of intent under the monopolization and attempt to monopolize clauses of the Sherman Act:

> While the completed offense of monopolization under §2 demands only a general intent to do the act . . . a specific intent to destroy competition or build monopoly is essential to guilt for the mere attempt. . . .

The intent to "build monopoly," given the *duPont* definition of monopoly power, is logically synonymous with the intent to control prices in the relevant market. . . . "Direct evidence" of specific intent to control prices or destroy competition, however, is not always necessary when the attempt claim is "founded upon a substantial claim of restraint of trade"—that is, a §1 violation. In these circumstances the requisite specific intent may be inferred. . . . Market power is relevant to determining whether such an inference is proper; but where a §1 violation "clearly" exists, proof of market power is unnecessary to support an inference of specific intent.[4] . . .

Conversely, "even though the restraint effected may be reasonable

---

[2] Thus, appellant's contention that "*any* act taken by the monopolist satisfies the literal 'monopolizes' language of the statute" is overly broad. . . .

[3] Conversely, not all violations of §1 constitute acts of monopolization under §2. The monopoly must be "acquired or maintained . . . *by means of*" the §1 violation, *United States* v. *Griffith*, 334 U.S. 100, 106 (1948) (emphasis added), "and not all violations of §1 have the requisite causal effect." 3 P. Areeda & D. Turner, *Antitrust Law* ¶626, at 81 (1978).

[4] Since "under the rule of reason market definition is required to establish a §1 violation," such evidence is necessary where specific intent is sought to be shown by inference unless a per se violation of §1 is made out. . . .

under §1, it may constitute an attempt to monopolize forbidden by §2 if a specific intent to monopolize may be shown." *United States* v. *Columbia Steel Co.,* 334 U.S. 495, 531–32 (1948). However, "[o]rdinarily specific intent is difficult to prove," *Hallmark Industry* v. *Reynolds Metals Co.,* 489 F.2d at 12, . . . and thus more commonly it is shown indirectly by proof of illegal conduct and, where necessary, market power.

The "predatory or anticompetitive conduct" element of §2 attempt, like the conduct element of monopolization, encompasses more than violations of §1. . . . The reason for this was stated in *Moore* v. *Jas. H. Matthews & Co.,* 473 F.2d at 322:

> [S]ection 2 is not limited to concerted activity. A jury, therefore, could find that individual actions . . . constituted monopolization or attempted monopolization violating section 2, even if it found no concerted activity.

Additionally, "[s]ection 1 also prohibits 'contracts' that restrain trade," *id.* at 333; and since individual actions may violate §2, no contractual agreement is required. Nonetheless, under §2 attempt—as with §1 monopolization—individual conduct is measured against the same "reasonableness" standard governing concerted and contractual activity under §1. . . .[5]

The third element of §2 attempt, the requirement that a defendant's demonstrated specific intent to control prices or destroy competition have a "dangerous probability of success," may be satisfied either by direct proof of market power . . . or by inference from the proven specific intent itself. . . . Because this element may be inferred from the existence of a specific intent in proper cases, it is not an "essential" element of an attempt claim. . . . For the same reason, neither is proof of any particular degree of market power necessarily an "independent" element of such a claim. . . .[6]

In addition to the first three elements necessary to establish a prima facie case of attempt, the fourth element—causal antitrust injury—is as necessary to confer standing to sue and to support a claim for damages under §2 attempt as it is under §2 monopolization. . . .

C. CalComp's Evidence

The foregoing analysis of the elements of §2 monopolization and attempt to monopolize demonstrates that if CalComp presented sufficient evidence to go to the jury on the issue of IBM's monopoly power in a

---

[5] . . . Because monopoly power is a necessary element of the completed offense of §2 monopolization but is not necessary for attempt, it follows that the same conduct may provide a basis for the monopolization offense and yet be excluded as a basis for the attempt offense. This is so since a defendant's monopoly power—or lack thereof—is part of the "reasonableness" calculus; conduct reasonable for other firms is not necessarily reasonable for the monopolist.

[6] Of course, proof of market power may be necessary to establish specific intent. . . .

relevant market, both of its §2 claims may be analyzed together. The only remaining elements necessary to establish the monopolization offense in this case would be monopolizing conduct and causal "antitrust" injury. If CalComp failed to show either of these, its attempt claim must necessarily also fail: first, because as discussed *supra,*[7] "conduct lawful for a monopolist must, a fortiori, be excluded as a basis for the attempt offense,"[8] and second, because the requirement of causal "antitrust" injury is common to both.

1. Market Evidence. Earlier it was noted that CalComp sought to define three relevant product markets: (a) a general purpose computer systems market; (b) an all disk drive and associated controller market; and (c) a plug-compatible disk drive and associated controller market (which excluded disk products for use with the CPU's of other manufacturers).[9] . . . Not only did the evidence concerning the various market definitions often conflict, but also the testimony and documents purportedly supporting a single market were sometimes internally inconsistent. Still, we assume *arguendo* that the third category is an appropriately defined product market. As noted earlier, it is the only market about which CalComp has standing to sue. See Part II *supra.*

The evidence of IBM's share of the product markets was similarly irresolute. For example, CalComp introduced the testimony of employees of IBM and other industry members concerning IBM's share of the loosely defined general purpose computer systems market; their estimates ranged from as low as 60 percent to as high as 80 percent, while IBM's proof was designed to show that none of these figures was even based on the particular market alleged. CalComp offered expert testimony that in 1970, 1971 and 1972, IBM's share of the all disk drive and associated controller market was 79.4 percent, 70.1 percent and 67.6 percent respectively, while IBM's evidence was that its share was under 30 percent during these years: CalComp's figures reflected cumulative shipments of disk products, while IBM's data was based on annual shipments. IBM contended that because its share of market was rapidly declining (from 100 percent when it invented disk products in 1960 to 25 percent in 1975), cumulative measures were misleading. In the plug-compatible market, IBM—again, because it invented these products—began with a 100-percent share; here too, CalComp's own evidence showed that IBM's share of market declined steadily.

. . . Because we conclude that there was no substantial evidence that any of IBM's alleged acts both constituted unreasonable conduct for a

---

[7] See note 5 *supra.*

[8] 3 P. Areeda & D. Turner, *Antitrust Law* ¶828, at 321 (1978). As stated there, "(i)t would be perversely illogical to hold a defendant without (monopoly) power liable for conduct practiced with legal immunity by a monopolist."

[9] The data presented by both parties assume that the relevant geographic market is the United States.

monopolist and produced causal "antitrust" injury to CalComp, we need not become enmeshed in the hundreds of pages of conflicting and complex evidence on this element of CalComp's claim. For purposes of this decision, we assume that IBM possessed monopoly power in the third purported market during the period 1963 to 1972.

We may therefore accept, with one important addition, CalComp's statement in its brief that the main issue of this appeal is "whether the *acts* and *practices* of IBM . . . constitute a violation of either the monopolization or attempt to monopolize clauses of Section 2 of the Sherman Act, or both." Should we decide this question in the affirmative, the additional question we must answer would be whether any loss Cal-Comp suffered actually resulted from the asserted §2 violation (as opposed to lawful competitive practices).

2. Evidence of §2 Violations. CalComp argues that IBM directly injured it in three ways. Principally, CalComp contends that IBM engaged in "predatory" pricing by cutting its peripheral equipment prices in response to competition from CalComp and other manufacturers. CalComp also attempts to show that IBM made design changes on certain of its CPUs, disk drives and controllers of no technological advantage and solely for the purpose of frustrating competition from plug-compatible manufacturers. Finally, it urges that IBM raised CPU prices in an effort to offset revenue losses caused by its price reductions on peripheral equipment, and that these price increases constituted impermissible conduct for a monopolist.[10]

a. Price cuts on peripherals. When IBM introduced its new System 370 Model 145 in September, 1970, it designated as the standard disk drive for use with this CPU a reworked version of earlier disk drives that had been replaced by competitive equipment and returned to IBM. The monthly rental for this three-drive disk product, the 2319A, was 30 percent below that for IBM's other four- , two- , and single-drive disk products on a per-drive basis—in part because the reuse of earlier disk drives permitted reduced development and manufacturing costs. The integrated control function in the Model 145-2319A system was also priced 60 percent lower than earlier stand-alone controllers, also due at least in part to cost-saving design changes. . . . Viewing all of the relevant evidence in the light most favorable to CalComp, IBM's purpose in offering the lower-priced 2319A disk drive in conjunction with its Model 145 was twofold: primarily, to regain market share from peripheral equipment

---

[10] CalComp also claims that prior to IBM's price cuts on disk products, it offset losses on CPUs with "monopolistic profits" from its then high-priced disk equipment. Even if we were to accept that CalComp's evidence was sufficient to go to a jury on the issue of whether such an antitrust violation occurred, a directed verdict would still be required because of the lack of any showing of causal injury. CalComp did not introduce substantial evidence (and indeed, would have had difficulty if he had attempted to do so) that it was "injured in [its] business or property by reason of" IBM's *high* prices on disk products. . . .

manufacturers who were flourishing under IBM's high price umbrella;[11] . . . and secondarily, to reduce the overall price of the 145 system, thereby providing the lower-priced alternative to the higher-performance, higher-priced models using the 3300 disk product that was to be the 145's market niche.[12] CalComp introduced no evidence that the lower-priced 2319A was not "substantially profitable," as IBM asserted.[13]

Three months after the announcement of the 2319A, IBM introduced the 2319B disk drive for use with all System 360 models. Like the 2319A, this was also a "retread" manufactured from older IBM disk drive that had been replaced with other equipment and returned by customers. IBM similarly priced the three-drive 2319B more than 30 percent below its other disk drives on a per-drive basis. Also, it made no "additional use" charges (for use above a fixed number of hours per month) for the 2319B as it did with its other disk drives, in effect a further reduction in price *vis-a-vis* these other products. . . . The 2319B, viewing all of the evidence in the light most favorable to CalComp, was introduced for the express purpose of abating competitive inroads by other peripheral manufacturers. . . . CalComp introduced no evidence that the 2319B, like the 2319A, was not "substantially profitable".[14]

Following IBM's 2319B announcement, virtually all of the plug-

---

[11] . . . CalComp's Chairman stated that IBM's loss of disk products business "was heading straight toward 100 percent like in two or three years," and that IBM "had to react because they were losing so much business that no other choice was open to them. I wouldn't call that a punitive reaction. I'd call it a defense of market position." . . .

[12] Other evidence indicated that by reducing the price of the system, the 2319A also helped IBM in competing with systems manufacturers such as RCA.

[13] IBM's evidence was that the profit on each of its disk products was greater than 20 percent of revenue before taxes, and that the 2319A in particular was expected to yield a profit of 33 percent.

In its *amicus* brief, Memorex Corp., another peripheral products manufacturer, contended that IBM's cost accounting system is too "inexact" to rely on for such determinations of profitability. Its argument is that by allocating the fixed cost burden for a particular product in part according to the product's revenues, "costs" are artificially reduced when a product's price is cut, and hence profitability is artificially increased. The evidence at trial, however, supports the single conclusion that IBM indeed fairly expected significant profits from its disk products even after price reductions. In response to IBM's price cuts, CalComp and other manufacturers reduced their prices again below IBM's, with the effect that, according to CalComp, they "received much small profit margins" as opposed to incurring losses. CalComp's own evidence established that prior to its price cuts, IBM's projected profits on its disk products ranged from 47 to 58 percent. In addition, IBM's evidence on profitability that Memorex challenges consisted of its internal calculations relied on at the time the decision to go forward with each product was made. As one of CalComp's experts testified, profit expectations at announcement or introduction of a product at a particular price are the primary consideration in analyzing a firm's pricing behavior. Finally, there is *absolutely* no evidence that IBM priced its disk products below marginal cost, which ordinarily is required to show predatory pricing as a means of obtaining or maintaining a monopoly in violation of §2. . . .

[14] . . . IBM's evidence was that the 2319B was expected to return a profit before taxes equal to 32 percent of revenues.

compatible manufacturers reduced their own prices below the 2319B.[15] As a further response to this competition,[16] IBM reduced its prices on peripheral products in still another way with the introduction of its Fixed Term Plan (FTP) on May 27, 1971, described by CalComp as "the single most important act in the CalComp litigation and the principal basis for its damage claim." Prior to the introduction of FTP, IBM offered its products only for sale or 30-day lease, although virtually all of its competitors offered reduced prices for longer leases ranging from one to eight years. Under FTP, IBM customers were given the additional option of an 8 percent discount for signing a one-year lease and a 16 percent discount for a two-year lease on certain peripheral equipment, principally disk drives, tapes and printers. "Additional use" charges were also eliminated on FTP leases, consistent with the practice of most of IBM's competitors. Customers—but not IBM—could cancel the leases in return for a termination charge. Purchase prices on FTP products were also reduced by 15 percent. The evidence at trial was uncontroverted that FTP price reductions were expected to return a profit of 30 percent of revenue before taxes. Lease revenues would be reduced through 1972, but through 1975, FTP was expected to generate $165 million more profit than would have been the case without FTP lease options. This increased profitability due to FTP stemmed not only from an expected increase in market share, but also from longer average lease lives and reduced sales, reconditioning and reinstallation costs.

Finally, following its adoption of FTP, IBM introduced two other new products: the Integrated Storage Controller (ISC) and the Integrated File Adaptor (IFA). ISC and IFA were options available for use with certain System 370 models, allowing direct attachment of disk products to the CPU. Customers choosing one of these "inboard" storage control units could save money by avoiding purchase or lease of a separate controller for some of their disk products, because the price of the ISC and IFA

---

[15] According to CalComp's Chairman, CalComp, like other plug-compatible manufacturers, generally had to offer discounts from the systems manufacturers' prices in order to convince users to take their copy instead of the original.

[16] CalComp introduced evidence of IBM studies reviewed by IBM management shortly before the announcement of FTP that included an analysis of the extent to which two of IBM's competitors, Telex and Memorex, could afford to increase manufacturing and sales volume and reduce prices on disk products. In particular, the studies concluded that Memorex would remain viable despite IBM's introduction of its 2319 disk drives, and that by 1976 IBM would lose 28.8 percent of the plug-compatible disk market. IBM's financial group also reported, however, that if Memorex achieved 60 percent of the plug-compatible disk market, such rapid growth in marketing overhead and working capital requirements would require substantial additional financing—particularly if Memorex met IBM price cuts in the area of 17 to 22 percent.

The obvious concern in these reports to management was the increasing gains by peripheral manufacturers and the lengths to which price competition by Memorex in particular might be carried. Accepting CalComp's inferences from this evidence, FTP was a direct response to these competitor gains, and the level of FTP price cuts was determined by IBM's estimation of the extent of its competitors' willingness to lower prices still further.

options were lower. Thus, ISC and IFA represented price cuts *vis-a-vis* IBM's "outboard" controllers. . . . However, there is little evidence in the record that the ISC and IFA inboard storage control units were priced in response to competition. Rather, the evidence indicates that these products were less expensive to produce. . . . For purposes of analysis, however, we will assume that the IFA and ISC options, like the 2319A, 2319B and FTP products, were priced primarily in response to competition from the plug compatible manufacturers.

The test of the reasonableness of the foregoing pricing actions, and the principal question facing us in this case, is whether IBM—which was the inventor and dominant supplier of the disk products in question—had the right to respond to the lower prices of its competitors with reduced, but still substantially profitable, prices on its own products. We conclude that it did.

CalComp's principal claim is for lost revenues as a result of price reductions it made following IBM's 2319B and FTP announcements. . . . But since these price reductions admittedly resulted from competition by IBM—and since, as both CalComp's and IBM's evidence clearly demonstrates, IBM's stimulus to price competition was in turn competition from peripheral equipment manufacturers such as Cal-Comp—it is impossible to say that CalComp's losses represent compensable "injury" from acts of IBM unnecessarily *excluding* or *restricting* competition. . . . Rather, IBM's price cuts were a part of the very competitive process the Sherman Act was designated to promote. To accept CalComp's position would be to hold that IBM could not compete if competition would result in injury to its competitors, an ill-advised reversal of the Supreme Court's pronouncement that the Sherman Act is meant to protect the competition process, not competitors. . . .

In *Grinnel,* as noted *supra,* the Supreme Court excepted from monopolizing conduct those actions directed toward establishing growth by means of "a superior product, business acumen, or historic accident" (384 U.S. at 571). IBM's dominance in disk products, of course, was not due to historic accident. CalComp witnesses repeatedly testified that IBM's position and success were due to its capable management, technological leadership, market orientation and superior products. Particularly relevant is the fact that IBM invented the disk products that Cal-Comp and other manufacturers copied. . . . [A]ccording to CalComp's Chairman:

> [I]f they [IBM] weren't there and hadn't created the market and hadn't made installations, we wouldn't have any market at all. So it's hard to call the guy who's created your opportunity a competitor—although certainly IBM doesn't give up easily on any particular order.

Granted that IBM's technological innovations resulted in "growth as a consequence of a superior product," it was entitled to maintain its consequent dominate position in the market it created through "business acumen," which we take to include shrewdness in profitable price competition. The Sherman Act does not draw a distinction between competition on the basis of price and of performance: the two are inseparable parts of any competitive offering. Where the opportunity exists to increase or protect market share profitability by offering equivalent or superior performance at a lower price, even a virtual monopolist may do so. . . . As Judge Aldrich observed in *Dehydrating Process Co.* v. *A. O. Smith Corp.*, 292 F.2d 653, 657 (1st Cir. 1961), "the antitrust laws do not require a business to cut its own throat."

The boundaries of reasonable price competition have recently been defined in this circuit. In *Hanson* v. *Shell Oil Co.*, 541 F.2d 1352, 1359 (9th Cir. 1976), cert. denied, 429 U.S. 1074 (1977), we affirmed a directed verdict for a defendant charged with attempted monopolization, holding that the plantiff's failure to show that the defendant's prices were below its marginal or average variable costs[17] "was a failure as a matter of law to present a prima facie case under §2." More recently in *Janich Brothers* [v. *American Distilling Co.*, 570 F.2d 848 (9th Cir. 1978) cert. denied 439 U.S. 829 (1978)], also an attempt case, we stated that "'pricing at marginal cost is the competitive and socially optimal result'" of §2 enforcement. 570 F.2d at 857, quoting Areeda & Turner, "Predatory Pricing and Related Practices Under Section 2 of the Sherman Act," *88 Harv. L. Rev.* 697, 711 (1975). The analysis in *Hanson* and *Janich Brothers* is precisely opposite in the monopolization context. Indeed, the preceding passage quoted in *Janich Brothers* dealt specifically with pricing by a monopolist. The thrust of this analysis is that price reductions up to the point of marginal cost are consistent with competition on the merits, since in this case only less efficient firms will be disadvantaged, while a firm pricing below marginal cost by definition incurs losses, so that competition on the basis of efficiency in this situation is frustrated.

We recognize that refinement of the marginal or average variable cost test will be necessary as future cases arise. For instance, limit pricing by a monopolist might, on a record which presented the issue, be held at impermissible predatory practice. . . . And we do not foreclose the possibility that a monopolist who reduces prices to some point above marginal or average variable costs might still be held to have engaged in a predatory

---

[17] "Marginal cost" refers to the variable cost of the last unit of output, while "average variable cost," appropriately, refers to the average variable cost of all units. See *Janich Brothers*, 570 F.2d at 857, n. 8, 858 n. 11. *Hanson* determined that "because marginal cost is often a sufficient judicial surrogate, 541 F.2d at 1358; *Janich Brothers* concurred that "[a]verage variable cost is likely to approximate marginal cost." 570 F.2d at 858. Given the variation in cost accounting systems among business firms and the likelihood of significant differences in capacity utilization from case to case, we expect that acceptance of this rule of thumb would first require careful scrutiny of the particular facts in a case where the defendant's prices are very near average variable cost. That is not the case here.

act because of other aspects of its conduct. On this record, however, IBM's pricing policies were not predatory.

The case before us presents an *a fortiori* situation as compared to *Hanson* and *Janich Brothers*. CalComp has not only failed to produce evidence of pricing below marginal or average variable cost, but it has also failed as well to introduce any evidence to controvert IBM's substantial proof that its price cuts were highly profitable. Moreover, the evidence of both parties established that IBM's disk price reductions were a response to lower-priced competition to which IBM was rapidly losing its disk business. Were §2 interpreted not to exempt price cuts from attack under these circumstances, there could be no adequate guidelines for a jury to decide the issue of whether the prices at issue were "reasonable." The directed verdict as to CalComp's claims based on IBM's price competition was therefore proper.

b. Design Changes. As noted above, when IBM introduced its System 370 Model 145 in September 1970, it announced the 2319A as the standard disk product for use with the 145. The control function for the 2319A disk drive was integrated into the Model 145 CPU, and thus the interface between the disk drive and its control function was different from earlier models. . . . CalComp claimed that it was competitively disadvantaged as a result of these design changes, because it could not legally begin to copy the 2319A until IBM shipped the first of these disk drives, thereby disclosing the design requirements.

In February 1971, IBM introduced its optional Integrated Storage Controller for use with its System 370 Models 158 and 168 which integrated the disk control function into the CPU. CalComp claimed it was injured by the introduction of ISC and the similar IFA, described above, because it was thereby precluded from replacing the control functions on CPUs with these options. . . .

CalComp characterized these design changes as "technological manipulation" which did not improve performance. It also complained of the fact that the newly integrated functions were priced below their non-integrated counterparts. But as we have stated, price and performance are inseparable parts of any competitive offerings; and equivalent function at lower cost certainly represents a superior product from the buyer's point of view. The evidence at trial was uncontroverted that integration was a cost-saving step, consistent with industry trends, which enabled IBM effectively to reduce prices for equivalent functions. Moreover, there was substantial evidence as well that in the case of Models 145, 158 and 168 the integration of control and memory functions also represented a performance improvement. . . .

IBM, assuming it was a monopolist, had the right to redesign its products to make them more attractive to buyers—whether by reason of lower manufacturing cost and price or improved performance. It was under no duty to help CalComp or other peripheral equipment manufacturers survive or expand. IBM need not have provided its rivals with disk products to examine and copy, . . . nor have constricted its product development so as to facilitate sales of rival products. The reasonableness of IBM's conduct in this regard did not present a jury issue.

  c. *Increases in CPU prices.* In July, 1971, IBM announced price increases on certain of its CPUs of up to 8 percent. The weighted average price increase of all CPUs was 1.5 percent. CalComp argued that these price increases, instituted two months after FTP was announced, were designed to offset the short-term revenue losses expected from FTP price cuts. After FTP users were "locked into" IBM peripherals for one- or two-year lease terms, according to CalComp, they would be unable to change CPUs, thus enabling IBM to raise CPU prices without appreciably affecting demand or profitability.

  However, CalComp's own evidence indicated that the net effect of FTP and the CPU price increases was not expected to be a "wash" with respect to either CPU demand or overall profitability. . . .

  Moreover, there was no evidence the CPU price increases actually offset the FTP price cuts. According to CalComp's amended complaint, "[p]eripheral devices . . . account for between 50 percent and 75 percent of the total value of a system configuration." . . . Since, as discussed *supra,* the FTP price cuts amounted to 8 percent and 16 percent, a jury would be hard pressed to conclude from CalComp's evidence that the CPU price increases in fact offset FTP losses—i.e., that a weighted average price increase of 1.5 percent on CPUs made up for price cuts of 8 percent and 16 percent on peripheral products of equal or greater value.

  Other evidence portrayed IBM's decision to raise CPU prices as motivated by inflation and cost concerns. IBM had not raised its mainframe prices in over four years; its 1971 increases were approved as cost-justified by the newly formed Price Commission under the Economic Stabilization Program then in effect.

  Viewed in the light most favorable to CalComp, this evidence does not provide support for its "offset" theory. Especially since we have already determined that the FTP price cuts allegedly facilitated by the CPU price increases were themselves profitable and reasonable even for a monopolist in any event,[18] it was proper to take the case from the jury on this issue.

---

  [18] In . . . [*Telex Corp.* v. *IBM Corp.* 510 F.2d 894 (10th Cir. 1975)], the Tenth Circuit held that IBM's conduct in this regard was not violative of §2, focusing on the profitability of both the CPU and FTP prices rather than on IBM's possible motivation. Regardless of intent, the court implied, §2 condemns only the monopolist's "use of monopoly power," and the facts in *Telex* showed that IBM's lowering peripheral prices and raising CPU prices was not a case of "an economic giant [dropping] prices to a level where it is not receiving an adequate return and . . . instead [relying] on its reserves or other activities to continue producing and marketing the particular product." See 510 F.2d at 925–26.

IV. CONCLUSION

. . . Having closely analyzed each of CalComp's arguments and the evidence on both sides in support thereof, drawing all reasonable inferences in CalComp's favor, we conclude that the district judge was correct in taking the case from the jury.

Nor does viewing the various acts of IBM collectively change our conclusion. The number of legal and evidentiary issues has required us to consider each instance of IBM's allegedly monopolizing conduct separately for purposes of analytical clarity. However, we are mindful of the fact that "plaintiffs should be given the full benefit of their proof without tightly compartmentalizing the various factual components and wiping the slate clean after scrutiny of each." *Continental Ore Co.* v. *Union Carbide & Carbon Corp.*, 370 U.S. 690, 699 (1962). . . . But there can be no synergistic result such as CalComp claims from a number of acts none of which show causal antitrust injury to CalComp. . . .

Accordingly, the judgment of the district court entered on its directed verdict is affirmed.

Affirmed.

Berkey Photo, Inc. v. Eastman Kodak Company

603 F.2d 263 (2d Cir. 1979)
Cert. denied, _____ U.S. _____ (1980)

KAUFMAN, Chief Judge.

INTRODUCTION

To millions of Americans, the name Kodak is virtually synonymous with photography. Founded over a century ago by George Eastman, the Eastman Kodak Company has long been the preeminent firm in the amateur photographic industry. It provides products and services covering every step in the creation of an enduring photographic record from an evanescent image. Snapshots may be taken with a Kodak camera on Kodak film, developed by Kodak's Color Print and Processing Laboratories, and printed on Kodak photographic paper. The firm has rivals at each stage of this process, but in many of them it stands, and has long stood, dominant. It is one of the giants of American enterprise, with international sales of nearly $6 billion in 1977 and pretax profits in excess of $1.2 billion.

This action, one of the largest and most significant private antitrust suits in history, was brought by Berkey Photo, Inc., a far smaller but still prominent participant in the industry. Berkey competes with Kodak in providing photofinishing services—the conversion of exposed film into finished prints, slides, or movies. Until 1978, Berkey sold cameras as well. It does not manufacture film, but it does purchase Kodak film for resale to its customers, and it also buys photofinishing equipment and supplies, including color print paper, from Kodak.

The two firms thus stand in a complex, multifaceted relationship, for Kodak has been Berkey's competitor in some markets and its supplier in others. In this action, Berkey claims that every aspect of the association has been infected by Kodak's monopoly power in the film, color print paper, and camera markets, willfully acquired, maintained, and exercised in violation of §2 of the Sherman Act. . . . It also charges that Kodak conspired with flashlamp manufacturers in violation of §1 of the Act. . . . A number of the charges arise from Kodak's 1972 introduction of the 110 photographic system, featuring a Pocket Instamatic camera and a new color print film, Kodacolor II, but the case is not limited to that episode. It embraces many of Kodak's activities for the last decade and, indeed, from preceding years as well. . . .

1. THE AMATEUR PHOTOGRAPHIC INDUSTRY

. . . It is, of course, a basic principle in the law of monopolization that the first step in a court's analysis must be a definition of the relevant markets. . . .

The principal markets relevant here, each nationwide in scope, are amateur conventional still cameras, conventional photographic film, photofinishing services, photofinishing equipment, and color print paper. The numerous technological interactions among the products and services constituting these markets are manifest. To take an obvious example, not only are both camera and film required to produce a snapshot, but the two must be in compatible formats. This means that the film must be cut to the right size and spooled in a roll or cartridge that will fit the camera mechanism. Berkey charges that Kodak refused to supply on economical terms film usable with camera formats designed by other manufactures, thereby exploiting its film monopoly to obstruct its rivals in the camera market. Similarly, Berkey contends, since the emulsions and other constituents of a film determine the chemicals and processes required to develop it, Kodak was able to project its power over film into the photofinishing market as well. . . .

A. The Camera Market

The amateur conventional still camera market now consists almost entirely of the so-called 110 and 126 instant-loading cameras. These are the direct descendants of the popular box cameras, the best-known of which was Kodak's so-called Brownie. Small, simple, and relatively inexpensive, cameras of this type are designed for the mass market rather than for the serious photographer.[1]

Kodak has long been the dominant firm in the market thus defined. Between 1954 and 1973 it never enjoyed less than 61 percent of the annual unit sales, nor less than 64 percent of the dollar volume, and in the peak year of 1964, Kodak cameras accounted for 90 percent of market revenues. Much of this success is no doubt due to the firm's history of innovation. In 1963 Kodak first marketed the 126 Instamatic instant-loading camera, . . . and in 1972 it came out with the much smaller 110 Pocket Instamatic. Not only are these cameras small and light, but they employ film packaged in cartridges that can simply be dropped in the back of the camera, thus obviating the need to load and position a roll manually. Their introduction triggered successive revolutions in the industry. Annual amateur still camera sales in the United States averaged 3.9 million units between 1954 and 1963, with little annual variation. In the first full year after Kodak's introduction of the 126, industry sales leaped 22 percent, and they took an even larger quantum jump when the 110 came to market. Other camera manufacturers, including Berkey, copied both these inventions, but for several months after each introduction anyone desiring to purchase a camera in the new format was perforce remitted to Kodak.

Berkey has been a camera manufacturer since its 1966 acquisition of the Keystone Camera Company, a producer of movie cameras and equipment. . . . In 1968 Berkey began to sell amateur still cameras made by other firms, and the following year the Keystone Division commenced manufacturing such cameras itself. From 1970 to 1977, Berkey accounted for 8.2 percent of the sales in the camera market in the United States, . . . reaching a peak of 10.2 percent in 1976. In 1978, Berkey sold its camera division and thus abandoned this market.

B. The Film Market

The relevant market for photographic film comprises color print, color slide, color movie, and black-and-white film.[2] Kodak's grip on this market is even stronger than its hold on cameras. Since 1952, its annual sales have always exceeded 82 percent of the nationwide volume on a unit basis, and 88 percent in revenues. Foreign competition has recently made some inroads into Kodak's monopoly, but the Rochester firm concedes

---

[1] More complicated cameras, such as those in the 135 format (35-millimeter) commonly used by professionals and photographic hobbyists, were found not to be part of this market. The jury also rejected Kodak's request to include in the definition instant cameras, pioneered by the Polaroid Corporation, which produce a finished print within minutes, or even seconds, after the shutter is snapped.

[2] The jury included movie film and 35-millimeter film in this market, presumably because they are substantially identical to the film used in amateur still cameras. Instant film, however, a product chemically distinct from laboratory-processed film, was excluded.

that it dominated film sales throughout the period relevant to this case. Indeed, in his summation, Kodak's trial counsel told the jury that "the film market . . . has been a market where there has not been price competition and where Kodak has been able to price its products pretty much without regard to the products of competitors."

Kodak's monopoly in the film market is particularly important to this case, because the jury accepted Berkey's contention, noted above, that it had been used to disadvantage rivals in cameras, photofinishing, photofinishing equipment, and other markets. Of special relevance to this finding is the color print film segment of the industry, which Kodak has dominated since it introduced Kodacolor, the first amateur color print film, in 1942. . . . In 1963, when Kodak announced the 126 Instamatic camera, it also brought out a new, faster color print film—Kodacolor X—which was initially available to amateur photographers only in the 126 format.[3] Nine years later, Kodak repeated this pattern with the simultaneous introduction of the 110 Pocket Instamatic and Kodacolor II film. For more than a year, Kodacolor II was made only for 110 cameras, and Kodak has never made any other color print film in the 110 size.

C. Photofinishing Services and Photofinishing Equipment

Before 1954, Kodak's Color Print and Processing Laboratories (CP&P) had a nearly absolute monopoly of color photofinishing maintained by a variety of practices. Accounting for over 95 percent of color film sales, Kodak sold every roll with an advance charge for processing included. Consumers had little choice but to purchase Kodak film, and in so doing they acquired the right to have that film developed and printed by CP&P at no further charge. Since few customers would duplicate their costs to procure the services of a non-Kodak photofinisher, Kodak was able to parlay its film monopoly to achieve equivalent market power in photofinishing.[4]

This film/processing tie-in attracted the attention of the Justice Department, and in 1954 a consent decree changed the structure of the color photofinishing market drastically. Kodak was forbidden to link photofinishing to film sales, and it agreed to make its processing technology, chemicals, and paper available to rivals at reasonable rates. As a result, CP&P's share of the market plummeted from 96 percent in 1954 to 69 percent two years later, and it has declined sharply ever since. In 1970, CP&P accounted for but 17 percent of the market, and by 1976 its share

---

[3] . . . "Film speed" refers to an emulsion's sensitivity to light. Thus Kodacolor X—as compared to its predecessor—could produce acceptable images under markedly inferior lighting conditions.

[4] To be sure, Kodak could not in this fashion control the market for color reprints—production of additional prints from slides or negatives. Here it resorted to other tactics. By refusing to sell the special paper or chemicals necessary to produce such reprints to rival photofinishers, it ensured—since there was no other adequate source for these supplies—that even this segment of the market did not escape its grip.

reached a low of 10 percent. There are now approximately 600 independent photofinishers in the United States.

Berkey is one of the largest of these processors. It has been a photofinisher since 1933, but until 1954 its principal business was developing and printing black-and-white film. . . . In addition, Berkey purchased Kodak black-and-white film, which was sold without a processing tie-in, for resale to its photofinishing customers. After the 1954 decree, Berkey applied to Kodak for the appropriate licenses and in 1956 began to process significant amounts of color film. It now finishes more 126 and 110 color print film than does Kodak. . . .

D.   The Color Paper Market

The market for color paper—that is, paper specially treated so that images from color film may be printed on it—effectively came into being after entry of the 1954 consent decree. Before then, Kodak was for all practical purposes the only color photofinisher, and its requirements for color paper were met entirely by the paper division of Kodak Park Works in Rochester. The remaining processors, who dealt with non-Kodak color film and used non-Kodak paper, occupied only 4 percent of the color photofinishing market. Consequently, the vertical foreclosure created by CP&P's lock on photofinishing and its exclusive use of Kodak color paper was virtually complete.

Although the 1954 decree steadily loosened Kodak's grip in photofinishing, it did not immediately affect the firm's control of color paper. For more than a decade, the independent photofinishers that sprang up after the decree was entered looked only to Kodak for their paper supplies. Indeed, although entry by both foreign and domestic paper manufacturers has reduced Kodak's share substantially, to a low of 60 percent in 1976, the firm's color paper operations have remained remarkably profitable. Between 1968 and 1975, while its market share was falling from 94 percent to 67 percent, Kodak's earnings from operations as a percentage of sales remained virtually constant, averaging 60 percent for the period. Moreover, the most recent telling event in the market has not been entry but exit: GAF Corporation announced in 1977 that it was abandoning its effort to sell color paper, leaving Kodak with only one domestic and two foreign competitors.

Kodak, then, is indeed a titan in its field, and accordingly has almost inevitably invited attack under §2 of the Sherman Act. Few, if any, cases have presented so many diverse and difficult problems of §2 analysis. . . .

II.   §2 OF THE SHERMAN ACT

. . . In passing the Sherman Act, Congress recognized that it could not enumerate all the activities that would constitute monopolization. . . . In performing that task, the courts have enunciated certain principles that by now seem almost elementary to any student of antitrust law. But, because §2 must reconcile divergent and sometimes conflicting policies it has been difficult to synthesize the parts into a coherent and consistent whole. To provide a framework for deciding the issues presented by this case, therefore, we begin by stating what we conceive to be the fundamental doctrines of §2.

A. Monopoly Power as the Essence of the §2 Violation

The gravamen of a charge under §1 of the Sherman Act is conduct in restraint of trade; no fundamental alteration of market structure is necessary. Thus, certain restrictive practices among competitors, such as price fixing, are illegal per se. That the conspirators lack the market power to affect prices is immaterial. . . . Section 2, by contrast, is aimed primarily not at improper conduct but at a pernicious market structure in which the concentration of power saps the salubrious influence of competition. . . .

This tenet is well grounded in economic analysis. There is little disagreement that a profit-maximizing monopolist will maintain his prices higher and his output lower than the socially optimal levels that would prevail in a purely competitive market. . . . The price excess represents not a reasonable return on investment but the spoils of the monoplist's power. . . .

It is not a defense to liability under §2 that monopoly power has not been used to charge more than a competitive price or extract greater than a reasonable profit. LEARNED HAND stated the rationale in the *Alcoa* case, *United States* v. *Aluminum Co. of America,* 148 F.2d 416, 427 (2d Cir. 1945). . . . JUDGE HAND explained, in addition, that Congress was not "actuated by economic motives alone" in enacting §2. Id. Considerations of political and social policy form a major part of our aversion to monopolies, for concentration of power in the hands of a few obstructs opportunities for the rest.

Because, like all power, it is laden with the possibility of abuse; because it encourages sloth rather than the active quest for excellence; and because it tends to damage the very fabric of our economy and our society, monopoly power is "inherently evil." *United States* v. *United Shoe Machinery Corp.,* 110 F. Supp. 295, 345 (D. Mass. 1953), *aff'd per curiam,* 347 U.S. 521 (1954). . . . If a finding of monopoly power were all that were necessary to complete a violation of §2, our task in this case would be considerably lightened. Kodak's control of the film and color paper markets clearly reached the level of a monopoly. And, while the issue is a much closer one, it appears that the evidence was sufficient for the jury to find that Kodak possessed such power in the camera market as well.[5] But our inquiry into Kodak's liability cannot end there.

---

[5] . . . Kodak sold approximately two thirds of all amateur conventional still cameras throughout most of the relevant period. The frequency with which flashlamp manufacturers

B.   The Requirement of Anticompetitive Conduct

Despite the generally recognized evils of monopoly power, it is "well settled" . . . that §2 does not prohibit monopoly *simpliciter*—or, as the Supreme Court phased it in the early landmark case of *Standard Oil Co. of New Jersey, supra,* 221 U.S. at 62, "monopoly in the concrete."

Thus, while proclaiming vigorously that monopoly power is the evil at which §2 is aimed, courts have declined to take what would have appeared to be the next logical step—declaring monopolies unlawful per se unless specifically authorized by law. To understand the reason for this, one must comprehend the fundamental tension—one might almost say the paradox—that is near the heart of §2. This tension creates much of the confusion surrounding §2. It makes the cryptic *Alcoa* opinion a litigant's wishing well, into which, it sometimes seems, one may peer and find nearly anthing he wishes.

The conundrum was indicated in characteristically striking prose by Judge Hand, who was not able to resolve it. Having stated that Congress "did not condone 'good trusts' and condemn 'bad' ones; it forbad all," *Alcoa, supra,* 148 F.2d at 427, he declared with equal force, "The successful competitor, having been urged to compete, must not be turned upon when he wins," id. at 430. Hand, therefore, told us that it would be inherently unfair to condemn success when the Sherman Act itself mandates competition. Such a wooden rule, it was feared, might also deprive the leading firm in an industry of the incentive to exert its best efforts. Further success would yield not rewards but legal castigation. The antitrust laws would thus compel the very sloth they were intended to prevent. We must always be mindful lest the Sherman Act be invoked perversely in favor of those who seek protection against the rigors of competition. . . .

In *Alcoa* the crosscurrents and pulls and tugs of §2 law were reconciled by noting that, although the firm controlled the aluminum ingot market, "it may not have achieved monopoly; monopoly may have been thrust upon it." 148 F.2d at 429. In examining this language, which would condemn a monopolist unless it is "the passive beneficiary of a monopoly," id. at 430, we perceive Hand the philosopher. As an operative rule of law, however, the "thrust upon" phrase does not suffice. It has been criticized by scholars, . . . and the Supreme Court appears to have abandoned it. See *United States* v. *Grinnell Corp.,* 384 U.S. 563, 570–71 (1966). . . . *Grinnell* instructs that after possession of monopoly power is found, the second element of the §2 offense is "the willful acquisition or maintenance of that power as distinguished from growth or development as a consequence of a superior product, business acumen, or historic accident." 384 U.S. at 570–71. . . .

---

approached Kodak with suggestions for joint development of products and their willingness to acquiesce in arguably one-sided agreements is further evidence of Kodak's power in the camera market. . . . The precipitous decline, beginning in 1976, of Kodak's share of the camera market was evidence that the jury could consider, although it was not dispositive.

But the law's hostility to monopoly power extends beyond the means of its acquisition. Even if that power has been legitimately acquired, the monopolist may not wield it to prevent or impede competition. Once a firm gains a measure of monopoly power, whether by its own superior competitive skill or because of such actions as restrictive combinations with others, it may discover that the power is capable of being maintained and augmented merely by using it. . . . That is, a firm that has achieved dominance of a market must find its control sufficient to preserve and even extend its market share by excluding or preventing competition. A variety of techniques may be employed to achieve this end—predatory pricing, lease-only policies, and exclusive buying arrangements, to list a few.

Even if the origin of the monopoly power was innocent, therefore, the *Grinnell* rule recognizes that maintaining or extending market control by the exercise of that power is sufficient to complete a violation of §2. As we have explained, only considerations of fairness and the need to preserve proper economic incentives prevent the condemnation of §2 from extending even to one who has gained his power by purely competitive means. The district court judge correctly indicated that such a monopolist is tolerated but not cherished. . . .

The key to analysis, it must be stressed, is the concept of market power. Although power may be derived from size, . . . the two are not identical. . . . A firm that has lawfully acquired a monopoly position is not barred from taking advantage of scale economies by constructing, for example, a large and efficient factory. These benefits are a consequence of size and not an exercise of power over the market.[6] Nevertheless, many anticompetitive actions are possible or effective only if taken by a firm that dominates its smaller rivals. . . . Such conduct is illegal when taken by a monopolist because it tends to destroy competition, although in the hands of a smaller market participant it might be considered harmless, or even "honestly industrial." *Alcoa, supra,* 148 F.2d at 431.

In sum, although the principles announced by the §2 cases often appear to conflict, this much is clear. The mere possession of monopoly power does not ipso facto condemn a market participant. But, to avoid the proscriptions of §2, the firm must refrain at all times from conduct directed at smothering competition. This doctrine has two branches. Unlawfully acquired power remains anathema even when kept dormant. And it is no less true that a firm with a legitimately achieved monopoly may not wield the resulting power to tighten its hold on the market.

---

[6] Nor is a lawful monopolist ordinarily precluded from charging as high a price for its product as the market will accept. True, this is a use of economic power; indeed, the differential between price and marginal cost is used as an indication of the degree of monopoly power. . . . But high prices, far from damaging competition, invite new competitors into the monopolized market. . . . Excessive prices may, however, create an illegal price squeeze in another market. . . .

C.   Monopoly Power as a Lever in Other Markets

It is clear that a firm may not employ its market position as a lever to create—or attempt to create—a monopoly in another market. . . . Kodak, in the period relevant to this suit, was never close to gaining control of the markets for photofinishing equipment or services and could not be held to have attempted to monopolize them. . . . Berkey nevertheless contends that Kodak illicitly gained an advantage in these areas by leveraging its power over film and cameras. Accordingly, we must determine whether a firm violates §2 by using its monopoly power in one market to gain a competitive advantage in another, albeit without an attempt to monopolize the second market. We hold, as did the lower court, that it does.

This conclusion appears to be an inexorable interpretation of the antitrust laws. We tolerate the existence of monopoly power, we repeat, only insofar as necessary to preserve competitive incentives and to be fair to the firm that has attained its position innocently. There is not reason to allow the exercise of such power to the detriment of competition in either the controlled market or any other. That the competition in the leveraged market may not be destroyed but merely distorted does not make it more palatable. Social and economic effects of an extension of monopoly power militate against such conduct. . . .

This rule is linked to the prohibition against tying arrangements in the sale of goods and services. . . . And to condemn a tie, the market for the tied product need not be monopolized. It suffices that a "substantial" amount of competition is foreclosed. . . .

Accordingly, the use of monopoly power attained in one market to gain a competitive advantage in another is a violation of §2, even if there has not been an attempt to monopolize the second market. It is the use of economic power that creates the liability. But, as we have indicated, a large firm does not violate §2 simply by reaping the competitive rewards attributable to its efficient size, nor does an integrated business offend the Sherman Act whenever one of its departments benefits from association with a division possessing a monopoly in its own market. So long as we allow a firm to compete in several fields, we must expect it to seek the competitive advantages of its broad-based activity—more efficient production, greater ability to develop complementary products, reduced transaction costs, and so forth. These are gains that accrue to any integrated firm, regardless of its market share, and they cannot by themselves be considered uses of monopoly power.

We shall now apply to the case at bar the principles we have set forth above.

III.   THE 110 SYSTEM

We commented earlier on the camera revolution sparked by Kodak's introduction of the 126 Instamatic in 1963. Ben Berkey, chairman of Berkey Photo, described the camera's cartridge-loading feature as "fool-proof" and remarked that the new simple system gave the industry "a great boost." Even before the 126 was introduced, however, Kodak had set its sights on a new, smaller line of Instamatic cameras. The aim of Kodak's Project 30, or P-30, as it was often called, was a camera barely one inch thick but capable of producing photographs as clear and large as its bulkier cousins. . . .

The early view at P-30 had been that . . . Kodacolor X [Kodak's color print film then in use] would prove "quite adequate" for the new format. By 1966, however, the Kodacolor Future System Committee, considering Kodak's film sales in the 126 size as well as in the format being created by Project 30, began actively to consider the possibility of developing a new type of Kodacolor film. . . . [T]he committee realized that basic changes in the film would require a new photofinishing process, conducted at temperatures higher than those used in the so-called C-22 method by which prints were made from Kodacolor X. Some committee members, therefore, expressed concern about the effect that a new process might have on independent photofinishers, who developed Kodak film and were purchasers of Kodak equipment and supplies. These concerns were shared by a number of Kodak scientists, such as D. M. Zwick, who feared an "unethical" attempt to create a "deliberate . . . incompatibility with systems other than Kodacolor." . . .

Nevertheless, on May 10, 1967, the committee recommended that Kodak proceed with the development of the new film and finishing process, tentatively labelled P-118. . . . [B]y 1969 Kodak decided that P-118 should be used to help launch the P-30 camera system in March 1972. This decision appears to have been influenced by the views of those Kodak officers who believed that

> [w]ithout a new film, the [camera] program is not a new advertisable system. Without the film, our splicer and processors [for the new high-temperature photo-finishing process] are not required.

. . . Shortly after initial production runs began in October 1971, Kodak recognized that "several product deficiencies" would exist in the film, now called Kodacolor II, at the time of introduction. . . . Not only did Kodacolor II have a significantly shorter shelf life than had been anticipated, but it also proved grainier than Kodak had originally hoped. This problem was highly significant . . . because low graininess was supposedly the quality that made Kodacolor II especially suitable for the Pocket Instamatic cameras.[7]

Despite these deficiencies, Kodak proceeded with its plans for introduction of the 110 system, of which Kodacolor II had become an integral

---

[7] Kodacolor II's grain, though disappointing, was clearly superior to that of Kodacolor X. Berkey does not appear to dispute the point. . . .

part. On March 16, 1972, amid great fanfare, the system was announced. Finally, said Kodak, there was a "little camera that takes big pictures." Kodacolor II was "a remarkable new film"—indeed, the best color negative film Kodak had ever manufactured. . . . In accord with Kodak's 1967 plan, Kodacolor II was sold only in the 110 format for 18 months after introduction. It remains the only 110-size color print film Kodak has ever sold. . . .

As Kodak has hoped, the 110 system proved to be a dramatic success. In 1972—the system's first year—the company sold 2,984,000 Pocket Instamatics, more than 50 percent of its sales in the amateur conventional still camera market. The new camera thus accounted in large part for a sharp increase in total market sales, from 6.2 million units in 1971 to 8.2 million in 1972. Rival manufacturers hastened to market their own 110 cameras, but Kodak stood alone until Argus made its first shipment of the Carefree 110 around Christmas 1972. The next year, although Kodak's competitors sold over 800,000 110 cameras, Kodak retained a firm lead with 5.1 million. Its share of 110 sales did not fall below 50 percent until 1976. Meanwhile, by 1973 the 110 had taken over most of the amateur market from the 126, and three years later it accounted for nearly four fifths of all sales. . . . Berkey contends that the introduction of the 110 system was both an attempt to monopolize and actual monopolization of the camera market. It also alleges that the marketing of the new camera constituted an impermissible leveraging of Kodak's film monopoly into the two photofinishing markets, services and equipment. . . .

A. Attempt to Monopolize and Monopolization of the Camera Market

There is little doubt that the evidence supports the jury's implicit finding that Kodak had monopoly power in cameras. . . . The principal issues presented to us regarding the effect of the 110 introduction in the camera market are whether Kodak engaged in anticompetitive conduct and, if so, whether that conduct caused injury to Berkey.

It will be useful at the outset to present the arguments on which Berkey asks us to uphold its verdict:

1. Kodak, a film and camera monopolist, was in a position to set industry standards. Rivals could not compete effectively without offering products similar to Kodak's. Moreover, Kodak persistently refused to make film available for most formats other than those in which it made cameras. Since cameras are worthless without film, this policy effectively prevented other manufacturers from introducing cameras in new formats. Because of its dominant position astride two markets, and by use of its film monopoly to distort the camera market, Kodak forfeited its own right to reap profits from such innovations without providing its rivals with sufficient advance information to enable them to enter the market with copies of the new product on the day of Kodak's introduction. This is one

of several predisclosure arguments Berkey has advanced in the course of this litigation.

2. The simultaneous introduction of the 110 camera and Kodacolor II film, together with a campaign advertising the two jointly, enabled Kodak to garner more camera sales than if it had merely scaled down Kodacolor X to fit the new camera. The jury could conclude that Kodacolor II was an inferior product and not technologically necessary for the success of the 110. In any event, Kodak's film monopoly prevented any other camera manufacturer from marketing such a film-camera system and the joint introduction was therefore anticompetitive.

3. For 18 months after its introduction, Kodacolor II was available only in the 110 format. Thus it followed that any consumer wishing to use Kodak's "remarkable new film" had to buy a 110 camera. Since Kodak was the leading—and at first the only—manufacturer of such devices, its camera sales were boosted at the expense of its competitors.

For the reasons explained below, we do not believe any of these contentions is sufficient on the facts of this case to justify an award of damages to Berkey. We therefore reverse this portion of the judgment.

1. Predisclosures. Through the 1960s, Kodak followed a checkered pattern of predisclosing innovations to various segments of the industry. Its purpose on these occasions evidently was to ensure that the industry would be able to meet consumers' demand for the complementary goods and services they would need to enjoy the new Kodak products. But predisclosure would quite obviously also diminish Kodak's share of the auxiliary markets. It was therefore, in the words of Walter Fallon, Kodak's chief executive officer, "a matter of judgment on each and every occasion" whether predisclosure would be for or against Kodak's self-interest. Thus, well before the 1965 introduction of Super-8 movie films, Kodak, which had a relatively small share of the movie camera market, provided sufficient information to companies such as Keystone and Bell & Howell to enable them to make cameras to use the new film. It also released processing information so that photofinishers could develop the film. But in 1963, when Kodak came out with Kodacolor X and the 126 Instamatic, it kept its own counsel until the date of introduction.

As early as 1968, some Kodak employees urged that advance warning of the P-30 system would be needed, at least to film processors and manufacturers of photofinishing equipment, to give them time to prepare for Kodacolor II and the new high-temperature finishing process, which was eventually labeled C-41. . . . Nevertheless, Kodak decided not to release advance information about the new film and format. The decision was evidently based on the perception of Dr. Louis K. Eilers, Kodak's chief executive officer at that time, that Kodak would gain more from being first on the market for the sale of all goods and services related to the 110 system than it would lose from the inability of other photofinishers to process Kodacolor II. . . .

. . . We hold that . . . as a matter of law, Kodak did not have a duty to predisclose information about the 110 system to competing camera manufacturers.

As JUDGE FRANKEL indicated, and as Berkey concedes, a firm may normally keep its innovations secret from its rivals as long as it wishes, forcing them to catch up on the strength of their own efforts after the new product is introduced. . . . It is the possibility of success in the marketplace, attributable to superior performance, that provides the incentives on which the proper functioning of our competitive economy rests. If a firm that has engaged in the risks and expenses of research and development were required in all circumstances to share with its rivals the benefits of those endeavors, this incentive would very likely be vitiated.

Withholding from others advance knowledge of one's new products, therefore, ordinarily constitutes valid competitive conduct. Because, as we have already indicated, a monopolist is permitted, and indeed encouraged, by §2 to compete aggressively on the merits, any success that it may achieve through "the process of invention and innovation" is clearly tolerated by the antitrust laws. . . .

. . . [E]nforced predisclosure would cause undesirable consequences beyond merely encouraging the sluggishness the Sherman Act was designed to prevent. A significant vice of the theory propounded by Berkey lies in the uncertainty of its application. Berkey does not contend, in the colorful phrase of JUDGE FRANKEL, that "Kodak has to live in a goldfish bowl," disclosing every innovation to the world at large. . . . However predictable in its application, such an extreme rule would be insupportable. Rather, Berkey postulates that Kodak had a duty to disclose limited types of information to certain competitors under specific circumstances. But it is difficult to comprehend how a major corporation, accustomed though it is to making business decisions with antitrust considerations in mind, could possess the omniscience to anticipate all the instances in which a jury might one day in the future retrospectively conclude that predisclosure was warranted.[8] And it is equally difficult to discern workable guidelines that a court might set forth to aid the firm's decision. For example, how detailed must the information conveyed be? And how far must research have progressed before it is "ripe" for disclosure? These inherent uncertainties would have an inevitable chilling effect on innovation. They go far, we believe, towards explaining why no court has ever imposed the duty Berkey seeks to create here.

An antitrust plaintiff urging a predisclosure rule, therefore, bears a heavy burden in justifying his request. Berkey recognizes the weight of this burden. It contends that it has been met. Kodak is not a monolithic

---

[8] Berkey's argument that Kodak considered predisclosing the 110 system, and so could not be surprised when found liable for failing to do so, is thus a two-edged sword. It illustrates the difficulties in prediction even when the problem has been squarely faced.

monopolist, acting in a single market. Rather, its camera monopoly was supported by its activity as a film manufacturer. Berkey therefore argues that by not disclosing the new format in which it was manufacturing film, Kodak unlawfully enhanced its power in the camera market. Indeed, Kodak not only participates in but monopolizes the film industry. The jury could easily have found that, when Kodak introduced a new film format, rival camera makers would be foreclosed from a substantial segment of the market until they were able to manufacture cameras in the new format. Accordingly, Berkey contended that Kodak illegitimately used its monopoly power in film to gain a competitive advantage in cameras. Thus Berkey insists that the jury was properly permitted to consider whether, on balance, the failure to predisclose the new format was exclusionary. We disagree.

We note that this aspect of Berkey's claim is in large measure independent of the fact that a new film, Kodacolor II, was introduced simultaneously with the new format. It is primarily introduction of the format itself—the size of the film and the cartridge in which it is packaged—of which Berkey complains. . . .

We do not perceive, however, how Kodak's introduction of a new format was rendered an unlawful act of monopolization in the camera market because the firm also manufactured film to fit the cameras. The 110 system was in substantial part a camera development. After all, P-30 existed long before the P-118 film project began, and much of the creative energy behind it was consumed by efforts to produce the camera itself. . . .

Clearly, then, the policy considerations militating against predisclosure requirements for monolithic monopolists are equally applicable here. The first firm, even a monopolist, to design a new camera format has a right to the lead time that follows from its success. The mere fact that Kodak manufactured film in the new format as well, so that its customers would not be offered worthless cameras, could not deprive it of that reward. Nor is this conclusion altered because Kodak not only participated in but dominated the film market. Kodak's ability to pioneer formats does not depend on its possessing a film monopoly. Had the firm possessed a much smaller share of the film market, it would nevertheless have been able to manufacture sufficient quantities of 110-size film—either Kodacolor X or Kodacolor II—to bring the new camera to market. It is apparent, therefore, that the ability to introduce the new format without predisclosure was solely a benefit of integration and not, without more, a use of Kodak's power in the film market to gain a competitive advantage in cameras. . . .

2. Systems Selling. Berkey's claims regarding the introduction of the 110 camera are not limited to its asserted right to predisclosure. The Pocket Instamatic not only initiated a new camera format, it was also promoted together with a new film. As we noted earlier, the view was expressed at Kodak that "[w]ithout a new film, the [camera] program is not a new advertisable system." Responding in large measure to this perception, Kodak hastened research and development of Kodacolor II so that it could be brought to market at the same time as the 110 system. Based on such evidence, and the earlier joint introduction of Kodacolor X and the 126 camera, the jury could readily have found that the simultaneous release of Kodacolor II and the Pocket Instamatic was part of a plan by which Kodak sought to use its combined film and camera capabilities to bolster faltering camera sales. Berkey contends that this program of selling was anticompetitive and therefore violated §2. We disagree.

It is important to identify the precise harm Berkey claims to have suffered from this conduct. It cannot complain of a product introduction *simpliciter* for the same reason it could not demand predisclosure of the new format: any firm, even a monopolist, may generally bring its products to market whenever and however it chooses.[9] Rather, Berkey's argument is more subtle. It claims that by marketing the Pocket Instamatics in a system with a widely advertised new film, Kodak gained camera sales at Berkey's expense. And, because Kodacolor II was not necessary to produce satisfactory 110 photographs and in fact suffered from several deficiencies, these gains were unlawful. . . .

It may be conceded that, by advertising Kodacolor II as a "remarkable new film" capable of yielding "big, sharp pictures from a very small negative," Kodak sold more 110 cameras than it would have done had it merely marketed Kodacolor X in 110-size cartridges. The quality of the end product—a developed snapshot—is at least as dependent upon the characteristics of the film as upon those of the camera. It is perfectly plausible that some customers bought the Kodak 110 camera who would have purchased a competitor's camera in another format had Kodacolor II not been available and widely advertised as capable of producing "big, sharp pictures" from the tiny Pocket Instamatic. Moreover, there was also sufficient evidence for the jury to conclude that a new film was not necessary to bring the new cameras to market. . . .

But necessity is a slippery concept. Indeed, the two [Kodak] scientists, Zwick and Groet, conceded that improvements in the quality of Kodacolor X would be "most welcome." Even if the 110 camera would produce adequate snapshots with Kodacolor X, it would be difficult to fault Kodak for attempting to design a film that could provide better results. The attempt to develop superior products is, as we have explained, an essential element of lawful competition. Kodak could not have violated §2 merely by introducing the 110 camera with an improved film.

---

[9] This is not to say, of course, that new product introductions are ipso facto immune from antitrust scrutiny, and we do not agree with Kodak's argument that they are . . . ; in all such cases, however, it is not the product introduction itself, but some associated conduct, that supplies the violation.

Accordingly, much of the evidence at trial concerned the dispute over the relative merits of Kodacolor II and Kodacolor X. . . . It is undisputed, however, that the grain of Kodacolor II, thought not as fine as Kodak had hoped, was better than that of the older film. . . .

In this context, therefore, the question of product quality has little meaning. A product that commends itself to many users because superior in certain respects may be rendered unsatisfactory to others by flaws they considered fatal. Millions of consumers, for example, evidently found the 110 camera highly attractive because of its "pocket-ability." Others, perhaps more concerned over the quality of their flash pictures, found the original models unsatisfactory because of the high incidence of red-eye.[10] . . .

It is evident, then, that in such circumstances no one can determine with any reasonable assurance whether one product is superior to another. Preference is a matter of individual taste. The only question that can be answered is whether there is sufficient demand for a particular product to make its production worthwhile, and the response, so long as the free choice of consumers is preserved, can only be inferred from the reaction of the market.

When a market is dominated by a monopolist, of course, the ordinary competitive forces of supply may not be fully effective. Even a monopolist, however, must generally be responsive to the demands of customers, for if it persistently markets unappealing goods it will invite a loss of sales and an increase of competition. . . . If a monopolist's products gain acceptance in the market, therefore, it is of no importance that a judge or jury may later regard them as inferior, so long as that success was not based on any form of coercion. Certainly the mere introduction of Kodacolor II along with the Pocket Instamatics did not coerce camera purchasers. . . . Unless consumers desired to use the 110 camera for its own attractive qualities, they were not compelled to purchase Kodacolor II—especially since Kodak did not remove any other films from the market when it introduced the new one. If the availability of Kodacolor II spurred sales of the 110 camera, it did so because some consumers regarded it as superior, at least for the smaller format.[11]

Of course, Kodak's advertising encouraged the public to take a favor-

---

[10] Red-eye is the appearance of a red glint in the eye of the snapshot's subject on a picture taken with a flashlamp. It is a result in large part of the small distance between the flash device and the camera lens. Hence, it was a greater problem for the original 110 cameras than for their larger predecessors in the 126 format.

[11] Thus, the situation might be completely different if, upon the introduction of the 110 system, Kodak had ceased producing film in the 126 size, thereby compelling camera purchasers to buy a Kodak 110 camera. Or had Kodak shifted production in all formats from Kodacolor X to Kodacolor II before other photofinishers could process the new film, it would force photographers to procure their photofinishing services from CP&P. In such a case the technological desirability of the product change might bear on the question of monopolistic intent. . . .

able view of both Kodacolor II and the 110 camera, but that was not improper. A monopolist is not forbidden to publicize its product unless the extent of this activity is so unwarranted by competitive exigencies as to constitute an entry barrier. . . . And in its advertising, a producer is ordinarily permitted, much like an advocate at law, to bathe his cause in the best light possible.[12] Advertising that emphasizes a product's strengths and minimizes its weaknesses does not, at least unless it amounts to deception, constitute anticompetitive conduct violative of §2. . . .

3. *Restriction of Kodacolor II to the 110 Format.*   [In this section, the Court held that although the restriction of Kodacolor II to the 110 format may have been unjustified, there was no evidence that Berkey was injured by this course of action.]

B. Photofinishing and Photofinishing Equipment Markets

1. *Damages.*   Berkey's damages claims here are based on the fact that Kodacolor II, introduced along with the 110 camera, required the new, high-temperature C-41 finishing process instead of the C-22 process used for Kodacolor X and similar films. Thus independent photofinishers could not offer processing service for Kodacolor II—the only color print film Kodak ever offered in the 110 size—until they bought new equipment and received instruction in and supplies for C-41 processing. Moreover, Kodak did not give advance warning to the independents that the new film would be introduced, nor did it predisclose the C-41 process to other makers of photofinishing equipment. Accordingly, CP&P was able to begin processing Kodacolor II several weeks before its competitors. . . .

Because of its early jump and greater efficiency in the C-41 process, CP&P gained a disproportionately high share of 110 finishing, an effect Berkey contends lasted through the end of 1973. There was clear evidence that Kodak was aware of the impact its conduct would have on the business of its photofinishing rivals. . . .

Kodak's conduct with respect to the independent photofinishers perhaps may be criticized as shoddy treatment of firms providing an essential service for Kodak products. Indeed, largely for that reason a number of Kodak employees urged that photofinishers and equipment manufacturers be given advance warning of the C-41 process. The purpose of the Sherman Act, however, is not to maintain friendly business relations among firms in the same industry nor was it designed to keep these firms happy and gleeful. . . . Moreover, it is clear that Kodak did not monopolize or attempt to monopolize the photofinishing or equipment

---

[12] Indeed, Kodak apparently did precisely that in introducing the 110 camera. Aware of the camera's substantial red-eye problem, the firm evidently decided "to provide enough ambient light for exposure without flash" at the press conference announcing the new system. This rather obvious ploy certainly did not amount to the type of deception that might. . . . support an action under §2.

markets.[13] Thus, it is not liable under §2 for the actions described above unless it gained a competitive advantage in these markets by use of the monopoly power it possessed in other segments of the industry.

It bears emphasis that only the wielding of power will support recovery in this context; advantages inuring to Kodak's photofinishing and equipment arms by virtue of membership in an integrated firm will not. As we suggested earlier, a use of monopoly power is an action that a firm would have found substantially less effective, or even counterproductive, if it lacked market control. Thus, the classic example of such a use is a refusal to deal in goods or services needed by a competitor in a second market. . . . But, a firm without control of the market that attempts this will simply drive the purchaser to take its patronage elsewhere. . . .

It is not clear, however, whether in bringing forth the 110 system Kodak did anything that a smaller firm with integrated capabilities but no market control might not have done.[14] Kodak did not use its power to shift the entire photofinishing market from C-22 to the C-41 process, for Kodacolor II was introduced only in the 110 size and at first represented a miniscule percentage of all color print photofinishing. Indeed, the film, was not marketed in other formats until 18 months later, long after the original surprise had worn off.[15] In sum, Kodak's ability to gain a rapidly diminishing competitive advantage with the introduction of the 110 system may have been attributable to its innovation of a new system of photography, and not to its monopoly power. On the other hand, we cannot dismiss the possibility that Kodak's monopoly power in other markets was at least a partial root of its ability to gain an advantage over its photofinishing competitors and to sell them overpriced equipment. For example, it may be that, had Kodak possessed only a small portion of the film market, other manufacturers would have found it more feasible to

---

[13] . . . Although Kodak was for a time the only firm able to finish Kodacolor II, and for a longer period the only company able to provide equipment for the C-41 process, the new process and the machinery used in it did not define separate markets; rather, they were, like Kodacolor II and the 110 camera itself, new entries in markets of wider scope. Kodak held a temporary monopoly in C-41 processing and equipment only in the sense that every firm initially possesses a 100 percent market share in its own innovations and the peripheral products and services associated with it. . . .

[14] We do not, of course, intend to cast any doubt on the well-established doctrine, which we have reaffirmed, see Part II.B *supra,* that certain actions may violate §2 when taken by a monopolist even though they would be perfectly legitimate in the hands of a firm lacking market control. Rather, our consideration rests on a simple proposition: if an action that gains a firm a competitive advantage is effective because of the company's efficiency, prestige, and innovativeness, and not because of its control over the market, the action is not a use of power.

[15] In 1972, fewer than one tenth as many rolls of Kodacolor film were processed in the 110 format as were finished in the 126 size, and CP&P processed only about 15 percent of the 110 rolls. Even in 1973, photofinishers processed more than three times as many 126 Kodacolor rolls—nearly all of it Kodacolor X—as Kodacolor rolls in the 110 format, and CP&P's share in the 110 size fell to approximately 6 percent.

bring out their C-22 films in the 110 size. CP&P would then have had no competitive advantage for a large percentage of 110 photofinishing. Moreover, absent a Kodak film monopoly, the independent photofinishers might not have felt an urgent need to buy expensive equipment for the C-41 process.[16]

We cannot resolve this ambiguity. . . . If the parties wish to pursue these claims to a final determination, therefore, a new trial will be necessary.

2. *Equitable Relief.* [Here the Court reversed Judge Frankel's rulings that Kodak be required (a) to "treat all photofinishers, including CP&P, alike in relevant respects" and (b) to sell color print paper without its Kodak brand name on the reverse side (known as a back print).]

IV. FILM AND COLOR PAPER CLAIMS

. . . In each of these claims Berkey's contention is that it paid an excessive price for Kodak products. They therefore raise similar issues and we shall discuss them together. We remand both claims for retrial.

It is clear that Kodak possessed a monopoly in the film and color paper markets during the period relevant to this suit. Berkey contends that this power, which enabled Kodak to overcharge its customers, was acquired and maintained, at least in part, by anticompetitive conduct. . . .

Excessive prices, maintained through exercise of a monopolist's control of the market, constituted one of the primary evils that the Sherman Act was intended to correct. . . . Where a monopolist has acquired or maintained its power by anticompetitive conduct, therefore, a direct purchaser may recover the overcharge caused by the violation of §2. . . .

But unless the monopoly has bolstered its power by wrongful actions, it will not be required to pay damages merely because its prices may later be found excessive. Setting a high price may be a use of monopoly power, but it is not in itself anticompetitive. Indeed, although a monopolist may be expected to charge a somewhat higher price than would prevail in a competitive market, there is probably no better way for it to guarantee that its dominance will be challenged than by greedily extracting the highest price it can. . . . If a firm has taken no action to destroy competition, it may be unfair to deprive it of the ordinary opportunity to set prices at a profit-maximizing level. Thus, no court has required a lawful monopolist to forfeit to a purchaser three times the increment of its price over that which would prevail in a competitive market. . . . Indeed, as one commentator who might favor such a rule concedes, such judicial oversight of

---

[16] We do not hold that Kodak, which did not have a monopoly in photofinishing equipment, was required to provide such machinery for other photofinishers. But a violation might be found if Kodak's ability to market equipment at an excessive price was attributable to its monopoly power in other areas.

pricing policies would place the courts in a role akin to that of a public regulatory commission. . . . We would be wise to decline that function unless Congress clearly bestows it upon us. . . .

V. THE SECTION 1 CLAIMS

[In this section, the Court affirmed the lower court's ruling that the contracts entered into by Kodak with the General Electric Co. and Sylvania Electronic Products, Inc. constituted illegal conspiracies to restrain trade in the use of new flash devices with amateur cameras.]

2

Direct Price-Fixing Agreements

Cases instituted under Section 1 of the Sherman Act do, in a sense, fall into a simpler and far more consistent pattern than those brought under Section 2. With the exception of the *Appalachian Coals* decision, the Court has steadily refused to consider the reasonableness of direct price-fixing agreements, holding instead that these agreements among individual competitors were per se violations of the law. This, combined with the adoption of a Section 2 rule of reason in the *Standard Oil of New Jersey* decision presented above, introduced into the law what has come to be called the *double standard*. In other words, while agreements among individual competitors concerning matters such as price policy have been held to be illegal in and of themselves, consolidations which yield equal or greater market power have been tested for their reasonableness. Feeling among economists on the double standard is divided. Two otherwise widely divergent groups agree that it is inconsistent to permit a firm to accomplish by consolidation what it is not permitted to do by contract. They part company, however, on the method of eliminating this inconsistency. Some feel that the double standard can best be eliminated by abolishing the rule of reason used in Section 2 cases and thereby expanding the area of per se violation. Others propose to subject Section 1 as well as Section 2 cases to a test of reasonableness, a proposal which would—if adopted—allow defendants to justify conspiratorial activities by showing that favorable economic results were produced. A third group of economists and lawyers, who might be called *traditionalists,* contend that the double standard is necessary if we are to maintain a dynamic, progressive, and noncartelized economy. To accomplish this they feel nothing must be done to penalize business size which may result from successful and fair competition only, while at the same time we must continue to hold any and all attempts to mitigate the force of competition through collusion and conspiracy to be violations of the law.

The cases presented below are intended to show court attitudes toward price-fixing agreements. Although—with the exception *Appalachian*

Coals—price-fixing conspiracies were uniformly condemned, the bases of the opinions vary. Thus, where the *Trenton Potteries* condemnation hinged at least in part on the market power of the conspirators, the later and controlling *Socony-Vacuum* decision held any attempt to influence prices, regardless of the market power of the group, to be illegal. Only in the *Appalachian Coals* case did the Court explicitly attempt to consider the reasonableness of price-fixing agreements, and even here one might contend that it was the lack of market power, not the reasonableness of the agreement, which prevented condemnation.

In any event, since *Socony-Vacuum,* the courts have consistently refused to move from the clear position established therein. In the *Container Corporation* case, one of the latest to be decided under that doctrine, JUSTICE DOUGLAS summarily disposed of any consideration of the reasonableness of price-fixing arrangements. And enforcement authorities have moved with increasing vigor against such conspiracies.

In *U.S. Gypsum,* the first price-fixing case to reach the Supreme Court after criminal antitrust violations were raised to felony status (see Appendix), the Court reaffirmed its antipathy toward price fixing and rejected defendants' argument that interfirm price communication was necessary to satisfy the "meeting-competition" proviso of the Robinson-Patman Act. However, in *ASCAP* the Court has apparently evidenced a willingness, under at least certain circumstances, to consider reasonableness arguments as a defense. Whether this presages anything like a return to *Appalachian Coals* is, of course, too early to tell. And how far businessmen, faced with the increasing possibility of jail sentences, will be willing to test the limits of *ASCAP* remains to be seen.

Addyston Pipe and Steel Company v. United States
175 U.S. 211 (1899)

Note: This case involved an agreement among the six leading manufacturers of iron pipe to divide the market into several regional monopolies, and to fix prices.

MR. JUSTICE PECKHAM . . . delivered the opinion of the court. . . .

We are thus brought to the question whether the contract or combination proved in this case is one which is either a direct restraint or a regulation of commerce among the several States or with foreign nations contrary to the act of Congress [the Sherman Act]. It is objected on the part of the appellants that even if it affected interstate commerce the contract or combination was only a reasonable restraint upon a ruinous competition among themselves, and was formed only for the purpose of protecting the parties thereto in securing prices for their product that were fair and reasonable to themselves and the public. . . .

. . . [W]e are of opinion that the agreement or combination was not one which simply secured for its members fair and reasonable prices for the article dealt in by them. Even if the objection thus set up would, if well founded in fact, constitute a defense, we agree with the Circuit Court of Appeals in its statement of the special facts upon this branch of the case and with its opinion thereon as set forth by Circuit Judge Taft, as follows:

> The defendants being manufacturers and vendors of cast-iron pipe entered into a combination to raise the prices for pipe . . . [in] considerably more than three-quarters of the territory of the United States, . . . significantly called by the associates "pay" territory. . . . Within the margin of the freight per ton which Eastern manufacturers would have to pay to deliver pipe in "pay" territory, the defendants, by controlling two-thirds of the output in "pay" territory, were practically able to fix prices. . . . The most cogent evidence that they had this power is the fact everywhere apparent in the record that they exercised it. . . .
>
> The defendants were by their combination therefore able to deprive the public in a large territory of the advantages otherwise accruing to them from the proximity of defendants' pipe factories and, by keeping prices just low enough to prevent competition by Eastern manufacturers, to compel the public to pay an increase over what the price would have been if fixed by competition between defendants, nearly equal to the advantage in freight rates enjoyed by defendants over Eastern competitors. The defendants acquired this power by voluntarily agreeing to sell only at prices fixed by their committee and by allowing the highest bidder at the secret "auction pool" to become the lowest bidder of them at the public letting. Now, the restraint thus imposed on themselves was only partial. It did not cover the United States. There was not a complete monopoly. It was tempered by the fear of competition and it affected only a part of the price. But this certainly does not take the contract of association out of the annulling effect of the rule against monopolies. . . .
>
> It has been earnestly pressed upon us that the prices at which the cast-iron pipe was sold in "pay" territory were reasonable. . . . We do not think the issue an important one, because . . . we do not think that at common law there is any question of reasonableness open to the courts with reference to such a contract. Its tendency was certainly to give defendants the power to charge unreasonable prices, had they chosen to do so. But if it were important we should unhesitatingly find that the prices charged in the instances which were in evidence were unreasonable. . . .

The facts thus set forth show conclusively that the effect of the combination was to enhance prices beyond a sum which was reasonable. . . .

The views above expressed lead generally to an affirmance of the judgment of the Court of Appeals. . . . [But to] the extent that the present decree includes in its scope the enjoining of defendants thus situated from combining in regard to contracts for selling pipe in their own State, it is modified, and limited to that portion of the combination or agreement which is interstate in its character. As thus modified, the decree is *Affirmed.*

United States v. *Trenton Potteries Co.*

273 U.S. 392 (1927)

MR. JUSTICE STONE delivered the opinion of the Court.

Respondents, twenty individuals and twenty-three corporations, were convicted in the district court . . . of violating the Sherman Anti-Trust Law. . . . The indictment was in two counts. The first charged a combination to fix and maintain uniform prices for the sale of sanitary pottery, in restraint of interstate commerce; the second, a combination to restrain interstate commerce by limiting sales of pottery to a special group known to respondents as "legitimate jobbers." On appeal, the court of appeals . . . reversed the judgment of conviction on both counts on the ground that there were errors in the conduct of the trial. . . . This Court granted certiorari. . . .

Respondents, engaged in the manufacture or distribution of 82 percent of the vitreous pottery fixtures produced in the United States for use in bathrooms and lavatories, were members of a trade organization known as the Sanitary Potters' Association. . . .

There is no contention here that the verdict was not supported by sufficient evidence that respondents, controlling some 82 percent of the business of manufacturing and distributing in the United States vitreous pottery . . . combined to fix prices and to limit sales in interstate commerce to jobbers.

The issues raised here by the government's specification of errors relate only to the decision of the court of appeals upon its review of certain rulings of the district court made in the course of its trial. It is urged that the court below erred in holding in effect . . . that the trial court should have submitted to the jury the question whether the price agreement complained of constituted an unreasonable restraint of trade. . . .

The trial court charged, in submitting the case to the jury that, if it found the agreements or combination complained of, it might return a verdict of guilty without regard to the reasonableness of the prices fixed, or the good intentions of the combining units, whether prices were actually lowered or raised or whether sales were restricted to the special jobbers, since both agreements of themselves were unreasonable restraints.

. . . The court below held specifically that the trial court erred in refusing to charge as requested and held in effect that the charge as given on this branch of the case was erroneous. . . .

. . . The question therefore to be considered here is whether the trial judge correctly withdrew from the jury the consideration of the reasonableness of the particular restraints charged.

That only those restraints upon interstate commerce which are unreasonable are prohibited by the Sherman Law was the rule laid down by the opinions of this Court in the *Standard Oil* and *Tobacco* cases. But it does not follow that agreements to fix or maintain prices are reasonable restraints and therefore permitted by the statute, merely because the prices themselves are reasonable. Reasonableness is not a concept of definite and unchanging content. Its meaning necessarily varies in the different fields of the law, because it is used as a convenient summary of the dominant considerations which control in the application of legal doctrines. Our view of what is a reasonable restraint of commerce is controlled by the recognized purpose of the Sherman Law itself. Whether this type of restraint is reasonable or not must be judged in part at least in the light of its effect on competition, for whatever difference of opinion there may be among economists as to the social and economic desirability of an unrestrained competitive system, it cannot be doubted that the Sherman Law and the judicial decisions interpreting it are based upon the assumption that the public interest is best protected from the evils of monopoly and price control by the maintenance of competition. . . .

The aim and result of every price-fixing agreement, if effective, is the elimination of one form of competition. The power to fix prices, whether reasonably exercised or not, involves power to control the market and to fix arbitrary and unreasonable prices. The reasonable price fixed today may through economic and business changes become the unreasonable price of tomorrow. Once established, it may be maintained unchanged because of the absence of competition secured by the agreement for a price reasonable when fixed. Agreements which create such potential power may well be held to be in themselves unreasonable or unlawful restraints, without the necessity of minute inquiry whether a particular price is reasonable or unreasonable as fixed and without placing on the government in enforcing the Sherman Law the burden of ascertaining from day to day whether it has become unreasonable through the mere variation of economic conditions. Moreover, in the absence of express legislation requiring it, we should hesitate to adopt a construction making the difference between legal and illegal conduct in the field of business relations depend upon so uncertain a test as whether prices are reasonable—a determination which can be satisfactorily made only after a complete survey of our economic organization and a choice between rival philosophies. . . .

The charge of the trial court, viewed as a whole, fairly submitted to the jury the question whether a price-fixing agreement as described in the first count was entered into by the respondents. Whether the prices actually agreed upon were reasonable or unreasonable was immaterial in the circumstances charged in the indictment and necessarily found by the verdict. The requested charge . . . [was] inapplicable to the case in hand and rightly refused. . . .[1]

---

[1] Defendants had requested that the Court charge the following: "The essence of the law is injury to the public. It is not every restraint of competition and not every restraint of trade that works an injury to the public; it is only an undue and unreasonable restraint of trade that has such an effect and is deemed to be unlawful." IMS.

MR. JUSTICE VAN DEVANTER, MR. JUSTICE SUTHERLAND and MR. JUSTICE BUTLER dissent.

MR. JUSTICE BRANDEIS took no part in the consideration or decision of this case.

Appalachian Coals, Inc. v. United States
288 U.S. 344 (1933)

MR. CHIEF JUSTICE HUGHES delivered the opinion of the Court.

This suit was brought to enjoin a combination alleged to be in restraint of interstate commerce in bituminous coal and in attempted monopolization of part of that commerce, in violation of Sections 1 and 2 of the Sherman Anti-Trust Act. . . . The District Court, composed of three Circuit Judges, made detailed findings of fact and entered final decree granting the injunction. . . .

Defendants, other than Appalachian Coals, Inc., are 137 producers of bituminous coal in eight districts (called for convenience Appalachian territory). . . . In 1929 (the last year for which complete statistics were available) the total production of bituminous coal east of the Mississippi river was 484,786,000 tons, of which defendants mined 58,011,367 tons, or 11.96 percent. In the so-called Appalachian territory and the immediately surrounding area, the total production was 107,008,209 tons, of which defendants' production was 54.21 percent, or 64 percent if the output of "captive" mines (16,455,001 tons) be deducted. With a further deduction of 12,000,000 tons of coal produced in the immediately surrounding territory, which however, is not essentially different from the particular area described in these proceedings as Appalachian territory, defendants' production in the latter region was found to amount to 74.4 percent.

The challenged combination lies in the creation by the defendant producers of an exclusive selling agency. This agency is the defendant Appalachian Coals, Inc., which may be designated as the Company. Defendant producers own all its capital stock, their holdings being in proportion to their production. The majority of the common stock, which has exclusive voting right, is held by seventeen defendants. By uniform contracts, separately made, each defendant producer constitutes the Company an exclusive agent for the sale of all coal (with certain exceptions) which the producer mines in Appalachian territory. The Company agrees to establish standard classifications, to sell all the coal of all its principals at the best prices obtainable and, if all cannot be sold, to apportion orders upon a stated basis. . . .

The Government's contention, which the District Court sustained, is that the plan violates the Sherman Anti-Trust Act,—in view that it eliminates competition among the defendants themselves and also gives the selling agency power substantially to affect and control the price of bituminous coal in many interstate markets. . . .

Defendants insist that the primary purpose of the formation of the selling agency was to increase the sale, and thus the production, of Appalachian coal through better methods of distribution, intensive advertising and research, to achieve economies in marketing, and to eliminate abnormal, deceptive and destructive trade practices. . . . Defendants contend that the evidence establishes that the selling agency will not have the power to dominate or fix the price of coal in any consuming market; that the price of coal will continue to be set in an open competitive market; and that their plan by increasing the sale of bituminous coal from Appalachian territory will promote, rather than restrain, interstate commerce.

First.   There is no question as to the test to be applied in determining the legality of the defendants' conduct. The purpose of the Sherman Anti-Trust Act is to prevent undue restraints of interstate commerce, to maintain its appropriate freedom in the public interest, to afford protection from the subversive or coercive influences of monopolistic endeavor. . . . Its general phrases, interpreted to attain its fundamental objects, set up the essential standard of reasonableness. They call for vigilance in the detection and frustration of all efforts unduly to restrain the free course of interstate commerce, but they do not seek to establish a mere delusive liberty either by making impossible the normal and fair expansion of that commerce or the adoption of reasonable measures to protect it from injurious and destructive practices and to promote competition upon a sound basis. . . .

In applying this test, a close and objective scrutiny of particular conditions and purposes is necessary in each case. Realities must dominate the judgment. The mere fact that the parties to an agreement eliminate competition between themselves is not enough to condemn it. . . . The question of the application of the statute is one of intent and effect, and is not to be determined by arbitrary assumptions. It is therefore necessary in this instance to consider the economic conditions peculiar to the coal industry, the practices which have obtained, the nature of defendants' plan of making sales, the reasons which led to its adoption, and the probable consequences of the carrying out of that plan in relation to market prices and other matters affecting the public interest in interstate commerce in bituminous coal.

Second.   The findings of the District Court, upon abundant evidence, leave no room for doubt as to the economic condition of the coal industry. That condition, as the District Court states, "for many years has been indeed deplorable." . . . And in a graphic summary of the economic situation, the court found that "numerous producing companies have gone into bankruptcy or into the hands of receivers, many mines have been shut down, the number of days of operation per week have been greatly curtailed, wages to labor have been substantially lessened, and the States in which coal producing companies are located have found it increasingly difficult to collect taxes.''

Third. The findings also fully disclose the proceedings of the defendants in formulating their plan and the reasons for its adoption. . . . The District Court found that ''the evidence tended to show that other selling agencies with a control of at least 70 percent of the production in their respective districts will be organized if the petition in this case is dismissed''; that in that event ''there will result an organization in most of the districts whose coal is or may be competitive with Appalachian coal; but the testimony tends to show that there will still be substantial, active competition in the sale of coal in all markets in which Appalachian coal is sold.''

Defendants refer to the statement of purposes in their published plan of organization,—that it was intended to bring about ''a better and more orderly marketing of the coals from the region to be served by this company. . . .''

. . . . .

No attempt was made to limit production. The producers decided that it could not legally be limited and, in any event, it could not be limited practically. . . .

Fourth. Voluminous evidence was received with respect to the effect of defendants' plan upon market prices. As the plan has not gone into operation, there are no actual results upon which to base conclusions. The question is necessarily one of prediction. The court below found that, as between defendants themselves, competition would be eliminated. . . .

The more serious question relates to the effect of the plan upon competition between defendants and other producers. As already noted, the District Court found that ''the great bulk'' of the coal produced in Appalachian territory is sold ''in the highly competitive region east of the Mississippi river and north of the Ohio river under an adverse freight rate.'' Elaborate statistics were introduced. . . . It would be impossible to make even a condensed statement of this evidence, . . . but an examination of it fails to disclose an adequate basis for the conclusion that the operation of the defendants' plan would produce an injurious effect upon competitive conditions, in view of the vast volume of coal available, the conditions of production, and the network of transportation facilities at immediate command. . . .

Fifth. We think that the evidence requires the following conclusions:

(1) With respect to defendant's purposes, we find no warrant for determining that they were other than those they declared. Good intentions will not save a plan otherwise objectionable, but knowledge of actual intent is an aid in the interpretation of facts and prediction of conse-

quences. . . . The unfortunate state of the industry would not justify any attempt unduly to restrain competition or to monopolize, but the existing situation prompted defendants to make, and the statute did not preclude them from making, an honest effort to remove abuses, to make competition fairer, and thus to promote the essential interests of commerce. The interests of producers and consumers are interlinked. When industry is grievously hurt, when producing concerns fail, when unemployment mounts and communities dependent upon profitable production are prostrated, the wells of commerce go dry. So far as actual purposes are concerned, the conclusion of the court below was amply supported that defendants were engaged in a fair and open endeavor to aid the industry in a measurable recovery from its plight. The inquiry then, must be whether despite this objective the inherent nature of their plan was such as to create an undue restraint upon interstate commerce.

(2) The question thus presented chiefly concerns the effect upon prices. The evidence as to the conditions of the production and distribution of bituminous coal, the available facilities for its transportation, the extent of developed mining capacity, and the vast potential undeveloped capacity, makes it impossible to conclude that defendants through the operation of their plan will be able to fix the price of coal in the consuming markets. . . . Defendants' coal will continue to be subject to active competition. In addition to the coal actually produced and seeking markets in competition with defendants' coal, enormous additional quantities will be within reach and can readily be turned into the channels of trade if an advance of price invites that course. . . .

The contention is, and the court below found, that while defendants could not fix market prices, the concerted action would "affect" them, that is, that it would have a tendency to stabilize market prices and to raise them to a higher level than would otherwise obtain. But the facts found do not establish, and the evidence fails to show, that any effect will be produced which in the circumstances of this industry will be detrimental to fair competition. . . . The fact that the correction of abuses may tend to stabilize a business, or to produce fairer price levels, does not mean that the abuses should go uncorrected or that cooperative endeavor to correct them necessarily constitutes an unreasonable restraint of trade. The intelligent conduct of commerce through the acquisition of full information of all relevant facts may properly be sought by the cooperation of those engaged in trade, although stabilization of trade and more reasonable prices may be the result. . . .

Decisions cited in support of a contrary view were addressed to very different circumstances from those presented here. They dealt with combinations which on the particular facts were found to impose unreasonable restraints through the suppression of competition, and in actual operation had that effect. . . .

(3)   The question remains whether, despite the foregoing conclusions, the fact that the defendants' plan eliminates competition between themselves is alone sufficient to condemn it. Emphasis is placed upon defendants' control of about 73 percent of the commercial production in Appalachian territory. But only a small percentage of that production is sold in that territory. . . . Defendants insist that . . . no valid objection could have been interposed under the Sherman Act if the defendants had eliminated competition between themselves by a complete integration of their mining properties in a single ownership. . . . We agree that there is no ground for holding defendants' plan illegal merely because they have not integrated their properties and have chosen to maintain their independent plants, seeking not to limit but rather to facilitate production. We know of no public policy, and none is suggested by the terms of the Sherman Act, that, in order to comply with the law, those engaged in industry should be driven to unify their properties and businesses, in order to correct abuses which may be corrected by less drastic measures. Public policy might indeed be deemed to point in a different direction. . . . The argument that integration may be considered a normal expansion of business, while a combination of independent producers in a common selling agency should be treated as abnormal—that one is a legitimate enterprise and the other is not—makes but an artificial distinction. The Anti-Trust Act aims at substance. Nothing in theory or experience indicates that the selection of a common selling agency to represent a number of producers should be deemed to be more abnormal than the formation of a huge corporation bringing various independent units into one ownership. Either may be prompted by business exigencies, and the statute gives to neither a special privilege. The question in either case is whether there is an unreasonable restraint of trade or an attempt to monopolize. If there is, the combination cannot escape because it has chosen corporate form; and, if there is not, it is not to be condemned because of the absence of corporate integration. . . .

. . . We recognize . . . that the case has been tried in advance of the operation of defendants' plan. . . . If in actual operation it should prove to be an undue restraint upon interstate commerce, . . . the decision upon the present record should not preclude the Government from seeking the remedy which would be suited to such a state of facts. . . .

The decree will be reversed and . . . the court shall retain jurisdiction of the cause. . . .

Reversed and remanded.

MR. JUSTICE McREYNOLDS thinks that the court below reached the proper conclusion and that its decree should be affirmed.

United States v. Socony-Vacuum Oil Co., Inc.

310 U.S. 150 (1940)

MR. JUSTICE DOUGLAS delivered the opinion of the Court.

Respondents were convicted by a jury . . . under an indictment charging violations of Section 1 of the Sherman Anti-Trust Act. . . . The Circuit Court of Appeals reversed and remanded for a new trial. . . . The case is here on a petition and cross-petition for certiorari, both of which we granted because of the public importance of the issues raised. . . .

The indictment was returned in December 1936 in the United States District Court for the Western District of Wisconsin. It charges that certain major oil companies, selling gasoline in the Mid-Western area . . . , (1) "combined and conspired together for the purpose of artificially raising and fixing the tank car prices of gasoline" in the "spot markets" in the East Texas and Mid-Continent fields; (2) "have artificially raised and fixed said spot market tank car prices of gasoline and have maintained said prices at artificially high and non-competitive levels, and at levels agreed upon among them and have thereby intentionally increased and fixed the tank car prices of gasoline contracted to be sold and sold in interstate commerce as aforesaid in the Mid-Western area"; (3) "have arbitrarily," by reason of the provisions of the prevailing form of jobber contracts which made the price to the jobber dependent on the average spot market price, "exacted large sums of money from thousands of jobbers with whom they have had such contracts in said Mid-Western area"; and (4) "in turn have intentionally raised the general level of retail prices prevailing in said Mid-Western area."

The *manner* and *means* of effectuating such conspiracy are alleged in substance as follows: Defendants, from February 1935 to December 1936 "have knowingly and unlawfully engaged and participated in two concerted gasoline buying programs" for the purchase "from independent refiners in spot transactions of large quantities of gasoline in the East Texas and Mid-Continent fields at uniform, high, and at times progressively increased prices." The East Texas buying program is alleged to have embraced purchases of gasoline in spot transactions from most of the independent refiners in the East Texas field, who were members of the East Texas Refiners' Marketing Association, formed in February 1935 with the knowledge and approval of some of the defendants "for the purpose of selling and facilitating the sale of gasoline to defendant major oil companies." It is alleged that arrangements were made and carried out for allotting orders for gasoline received from defendants among the members of that association; and that such purchases amounted to more than 50% of all gasoline produced by those independent refiners. The Mid-Continent buying program is alleged to have included "large and increased purchases of gasoline" by defendants from independent refiners located in the Mid-Continent fields pursuant to allotments among themselves. Those purchases, it is charged, were made from independent refiners who were assigned to certain of the defendants at monthly meetings of a group representing defendants. It is alleged that the purchases in this buying program amounted to nearly 50% of all gasoline sold by those independents. As respects both the East Texas and the Mid-Continent buying programs, it is alleged that the purchases of gasoline were in excess of the amounts which defendants would have purchased but for those programs; that at the instance of certain defendants these independent refiners curtailed their production of gasoline. . . .

The *methods of marketing and selling gasoline* in the Mid-Western area are set forth in the indictment in some detail. Since we hereafter develop the facts concerning them, it will suffice at this point to summarize them briefly. Each defendant major oil company owns, operates or leases retail service stations in this area. It supplies those stations, as well as independent retail stations, with gasoline from its bulk storage plants. All but one sell large quantities of gasoline to jobbers in tank car lots under term contracts. In this area these jobbers exceed 4,000 in number and distribute about 50% of all gasoline distributed to retail service stations therein, the bulk of the jobbers' purchases being made from the defendant companies. The price to the jobbers under those contracts with defendant companies is made dependent on the spot market price, pursuant to a formula hereinafter discussed. And the spot market tank car prices of gasoline directly and substantially influence the retail prices in the area. In sum, it is alleged that defendants by raising and fixing the tank car prices of gasoline in these spot markets could and did increase the tank car prices and the retail prices of gasoline sold in the Mid-Western area. The vulnerability of these spot markets to that type of manipulation or stabilization is emphasized by the allegation that spot market prices published in the journals were the result of spot sales made chiefly by independent refiners of a relatively small amount of the gasoline sold in that area—virtually all gasoline sold in tank car quantities in spot market transactions in the Mid-Western area being sold by independent refiners, such sales amounting to less than 5% of all gasoline marketed therein.

So much for the indictment. . . .

The first meeting of the Tank Car Committee[1] was held February 5, 1935, and the second on February 11, 1935. At these meetings the alleged conspiracy was formed, the substance of which, so far as it pertained to the Mid-Continent phase, was as follows:

It was estimated that there would be between 600 and 700 tank cars of distress gasoline produced in the Mid-Continent oil field every month by

---

[1] A division of the NRA-sanctioned Petroleum Administrative Board. IMS.

about 17 independent refiners. These refiners, not having regular outlets for the gasoline, would be unable to dispose of it except at distress prices. Accordingly, it was proposed and decided that certain major companies (including the corporate respondents) would purchase gasoline from these refiners. The Committee would assemble each month information as to the quantity and location of this distress gasoline. Each of the major companies was to select one (or more) of the independent refiners having distress gasoline as its "dancing partner," and would assume responsibility for purchasing its distress supply. In this manner buying power would be coordinated, purchases would be effectively placed, and the results would be much superior to the previous haphazard purchasing. There were to be no formal contractual commitments to purchase this gasoline, either between the major companies or between the majors and the independents. Rather it was an informal gentlemen's agreement or understanding whereby each undertook to perform his share of the joint undertaking. Purchases were to be made at the "fair going market price." . . .

. . . Before . . . [the end of March] all companies alleged to have participated in the program (except one or two) made purchases; 757 tank cars were bought from all but three of the independent refiners who were named in the indictment as sellers. . . .

. . . On May 27, 1935, this Court held . . . that the code-making authority conferred by the National Industrial Recovery Act was an unconstitutional delegation of legislative power. Shortly thereafter the Tank Car Stabilization Committee held a meeting to discuss their future course of action. It was decided that the buying program should continue. . . .

In the meetings when the Mid-Continent buying program was being formulated it was recognized that it would be necessary or desirable to take the East Texas surplus gasoline off the market so that it would not be a "disturbing influence in the Standard of Indiana territory." The reason was that weakness in East Texas spot market prices might make East Texas gasoline competitive with Mid-Continent gasoline in the Mid-Western area and thus affect Mid-Continent spot market prices. . . .

Early in 1935 the East Texas Refiners' Marketing Association was formed to dispose of the surplus gasoline manufactured by the East Texas refiners. . . .

. . . And it is clear that this East Texas buying program was, as we have said, supplementary or auxiliary to the Mid-Continent program. . . .

As a result of these buying programs it was hoped and intended that both the tank car and the retail markets would improve. The conclusion is irresistible that defendants' purpose was not merely to raise the spot market prices but, as the real and ultimate end, to raise the price of gasoline in their sales to jobbers and consumers in the Mid-Western area. Their agreement or plan embraced not only buying on the spot markets but also, at least by clear implication, an understanding to maintain such improvements in Mid-Western prices as would result from those purchases of distress gasoline. The latter obviously would be achieved by selling at the increased prices, not by price cutting. Any other understanding would have been wholly inconsistent with and contrary to the philosophy of the broad stabilization efforts which were under way. In essence the raising and maintenance of the spot market prices were but the means adopted for raising and maintaining prices to jobbers and consumers. . . . Certainly there was enough evidence to support a finding by the jury that such were the scope and purpose of the plan. . . .

Respondents do not contend that the buying programs were not a factor in the price rise and in the stabilization of the spot markets during 1935 and 1936. But they do contend that they were relatively minor ones, because of the presence of other economic forces. . . .

In *United States* v. *Trenton Potteries Co.* . . . , This Court sustained a conviction under the Sherman Act where the jury was charged that an agreement on the part of the members of a combination, controlling a substantial part of an industry, upon the prices which the members are to charge for their commodity is in itself an unreasonable restraint of trade without regard to the reasonableness of the prices or the good intentions of the combining units. . . . This Court pointed out that the so-called "rule of reason" announced in *Standard Oil Co.* v. *United States,* 221 U.S. 1, and in *United States* v. *American Tobacco Co.,* 221 U.S. 106, had not affected this view of the illegality of price-fixing agreements. . . .

But respondents claim that other decisions of this Court afford them adequate defenses to the indictment. Among those on which they place reliance are *Appalachian Coals, Inc.* v. *United States,* 288 U.S. 344. . . .

. . . [I]n reality the only essential thing in common between the instant case and the *Appalachian Coals* case is the presence in each of so-called demoralizing or injurious practices. The methods of dealing with them were quite divergent. In the instant case there were buying programs of distress gasoline which had as their direct purpose and aim the raising and maintenance of spot market prices and of prices to jobbers and consumers in the Mid-Western area, by the elimination of distress gasoline as a market factor. The increase in the spot market prices was to be accomplished by a well organized buying program on that market: regular ascertainment of the amounts of surplus gasoline; assignment of sellers among the buyers; regular purchases at prices which would place and keep a floor under the market. Unlike the plan in the instant case, the plan in the *Appalachian Coals* case was not designed to operate *vis-à-vis* the general consuming market and to fix the prices on that market. Furthermore, the effect, if any, of that plan on prices was not only wholly incidental but also highly conjectural. For the plan had not then been put into operation. Hence this Court expressly reserved jurisdiction in the District Court to take further proceedings if, *inter alia,* in "actual operation" the plan proved to be "an undue restraint upon interstate commerce." And as we have seen it would *per se* constitute such a restraint if price-fixing were involved. . . .

Thus for over forty years this Court has consistently and without deviation adhered to the principle that price-fixing agreements are unlawful *per se* under the Sherman Act and that no showing of so-called competitive abuses or evils which those agreements were designed to eliminate or alleviate may be interposed as a defense. . . .

Therefore the sole remaining question on this phase of the case is the applicability of the rule of the *Trenton Potteries* case to these facts.

Respondents seek to distinguish the *Trenton Potteries* case from the instant one. . . .

But we do not deem those distinctions material.

In the first place, there was abundant evidence that the combination had the purpose to raise prices. And likewise, there was ample evidence that the buying programs at least contributed to the price rise and the stability of the spot markets, and to increases in the price of gasoline sold in the Mid-Western area during the indictment period. That other factors also may have contributed to that rise and stability of the markets is immaterial. . . . Proof that there was a conspiracy, that its purpose was to raise prices, and that it caused or contributed to a price rise is proof of the actual consummation or execution of a conspiracy under Section 1 of the Sherman Act.

Secondly, the fact that sales on the spot markets were still governed by some competition is of no consequence. For it is indisputable that that competition was restricted through the removal by respondents of a part of the supply which but for the buying programs would have been a factor in determining the going prices on those markets. . . . Competition was not eliminated from the markets; but it was clearly curtailed, since restriction of the supply of gasoline, the timing and placement of the purchases under the buying programs and the placing of a floor under the spot markets obviously reduced the play of the forces of supply and demand.

The elimination of so-called competitive evils is no legal justification for such buying programs. . . . If the so-called competitive abuses were to be appraised here, the reasonableness of prices would necessarily become an issue in every price-fixing case. In that event the Sherman Act would soon be emasculated; its philosophy would be supplanted by one which is wholly alien to a system of free competition; it would not be the charter of freedom which its framers intended.

. . . Those who controlled the prices. . . . would have it in their power to destroy or drastically impair the competitive system. But the thrust of the rule is deeper and reaches more than monopoly power. Any combination which tampers with price structures is engaged in an unlawful activity. Even though the members of the price-fixing group were in no position to control the market, to the extent that they raised, lowered, or stabilized prices they would be directly interfering with the free play of market forces. The Act places all such schemes beyond the pale and protects that vital part of our economy against any degree of interference. Congress . . . has not permitted the age-old cry of ruinous competition and competitive evils to be a defense to price-fixing conspiracies. It has no more allowed genuine or fancied competitive abuses as a legal justification for such schemes than it has the good intentions of the members of the combination. If such a shift is to be made, it must be done by the Congress. Certainly Congress has not left us with any such choice. . . .

Nor is it important that the prices paid by the combination were not fixed in the sense that they were uniform and inflexible. Price-fixing as used in the *Trenton Potteries* case has no such limited meaning. . . . Hence, prices are fixed within the meaning of the *Trenton Potteries* case. . . . because they are agreed upon. And the fact that, as here, they are fixed at the fair going market price is immaterial. . . .

Under the Sherman Act a combination formed for the purpose and with the effect of raising, depressing, fixing, pegging, or stabilizing the price of a commodity in interstate or foreign commerce is illegal *per se*. . . . Price-fixing agreements may have utility to members of the group though the power possessed or exerted falls far short of domination and control. Monopoly power . . . is not the only power which the Act strikes down, as we have said. Proof that a combination was formed for the purpose of fixing prices and that it caused them to be fixed or contributed to that result is proof of the completion of a price-fixing conspiracy under Section 1 of the Act. The indictment in this case charged that this combination had that purpose and effect. And there was abundant evidence to support it. Hence the existence of power on the part of members of the combination to fix prices was but a conclusion from the finding that the buying programs caused or contributed to the rise and stability of prices. . . .

The judgment of the Circuit Court of Appeals is reversed and that of the District Court affirmed. . . .

[The CHIEF JUSTICE and MR. JUSTICE MURPHY did not participate in the consideration or decision of this case. MR. JUSTICE ROBERTS, with whom MR. JUSTICE McREYNOLDS concurred, dissented.]

United States v. *Container Corp. of America, et al.*

393 U.S. 333 (1969)

MR. JUSTICE DOUGLAS delivered the opinion of the Court.

This is a civil antitrust action charging a price-fixing agreement in violation of §1 of the Sherman Act. . . .

The case as proved is unlike any of other price decisions we have rendered. There was here an exchange of price information but no agreement to adhere to a price schedule as in *Sugar Institute* v. *United States,* 297 U.S. 553, or *United States* v. *Socony-Vacuum Oil Co.,* 310 U.S. 150. There was here an exchange of information concerning specific sales to identified customers, not a statistical report on the average cost to all members, without identifying the parties to specific transactions, as in *Maple Flooring Mfrs. Assn.* v. *United States,* 268 U.S. 563. While there was present here, as in *Cement Mfrs. Protective Assn.* v. *United States,* 268 U.S. 588, an exchange of prices to specific customers, there was absent the controlling circumstance, *viz.,* that cement manufacturers, to protect themselves from delivering to contractors more cement than was needed for a specific job and thus receiving a lower price, exchanged price information as a means of protecting their legal rights from fraudulent inducements to deliver more cement than needed for a specific job.

Here all that was present was a request by each defendant of its competitor for information as to the most recent price charged or quoted, whenever it needed such information and whenever it was not available from another source. Each defendant on receiving that request usually furnished the data with the expectation that it would be furnished reciprocal information when it wanted it. That concerted action is of course sufficient to establish the combination or conspiracy, the initial ingredient of a violation of §1 of the Sherman Act.

There was of course freedom to withdraw from the agreement. But the fact remains that when a defendant requested and received price information, it was affirming its willingness to furnish such information in return.

There was to be sure an infrequency and irregularity of price exchanges between the defendants; and often the data were available from the records of the defendants or from the customers themselves. Yet the essence of the agreement was to furnish price information whenever requested.

Moreover, although the most recent price charged or quoted was sometimes fragmentary, each defendant had the manuals with which it could compute the price charged by a competitor on a specific order to a specific customer.

Further, the price quoted was the current price which a customer would need to pay in order to obtain products from the defendant furnishing the data.

The defendants account for about 90% of the shipment of corrugated containers from plants in the Southeastern United States. While containers vary as to dimensions, weight, color, and so on, they are substantially identical, no matter who produces them, when made to particular specifications. The prices paid depend on price alternatives. Suppliers when seeking new or additional business or keeping old customers, do not exceed a competitor's price. It is common for purchasers to buy from two or more suppliers concurrently. A defendant supplying a customer with containers would usually quote the same price on additional orders, unless costs had changed. Yet where a competitor was charging a particular price, a defendant would normally quote the same price or even a lower price.

The exchange of price information seemed to have the effect of keeping prices within a fairly narrow ambit. Capacity has exceeded the demand from 1955 to 1963, the period covered by the complaint, and the trend of corrugated container prices has been downward. Yet despite this excess capacity and the downward trend of prices, the industry has expanded in the Southeast from 30 manufacturers with 49 plants to 51 manufacturers with 98 plants. An abundance of raw materials and machinery makes entry into the industry easy with an investment of $50,000 to $75,000.

The result of this reciprocal exchange of prices was to stabilize prices though at a downward level. Knowledge of a competitor's price usually meant matching that price. The continuation of some price competition is not fatal to the Government's case. The limitation or reduction of price competition brings the case within the ban, for as we held in *United States* v. *Socony-Vacuum Oil Co., supra,* at 224, n. 59, interference with the setting of price by free market forces is unlawful *per se.* Price information exchanged in some markets may have no effect on a truly competitive price. But the corrugated container industry is dominated by relatively few sellers. The product is fungible and the competition for sales is price. The demand is inelastic, as buyers place orders only for immediate, short-run needs. The exchange of price data tends toward price uniformity. For a lower price does not mean a larger share of the available business but a sharing of the existing business at a lower return. Stabilizing prices as well as raising them is within the ban of §1 of the Sherman Act. . . . The inferences are irresistible that the exchange of price information has had an anticompetitive effect in the industry, chilling the vigor of price competition. . . .

Price is too critical, too sensitive a control to allow it to be used even in an informal manner to restrain competition.[1]

Reversed.

MR. JUSTICE FORTAS, concurring.

I join in the judgment and opinion of the Court. I do not understand the Court's opinion to hold that the exchange of specific information among sellers as to prices charged to individual customers, pursuant to mutual arrangement, is a *per se* violation of the Sherman Act.

---

[1] Thorstein Veblen in *The Theory of Business Enterprise* (1904) makes clear how the overabundance of a commodity creates a business appetitie to regulate or control prices or output or both. Measures short of monopoly may have "a salutary effect," as for example a degree of control or supervision over prices not obtainable while the parties "stood on their old footing of severalty." But that relief is apt to be "only transient," for as the costs of production decline and growth of the industry "catches up with the gain in economy," the need for further controls or restraints increases. And so the restless, never-ending search for price control and other types of restraint. . . .

Absent *per se* violation, proof is essential that the practice resulted in an unreasonable restraint of trade. There is no single test to determine when the record adequately shows an "unreasonable restraint of trade"; but a practice such as that here involved, which is adopted for the purpose of arriving at a determination of prices to be quoted to individual customers, inevitably suggests the probability that it so materially interfered with the operation of the price mechanism of the marketplace as to bring it within the condemnation of this Court's decisions. . . .

MR. JUSTICE MARSHALL, with whom MR. JUSTICE HARLAN and MR. JUSTICE STEWART join, dissenting.

I agree with the Court's holding that there existed an agreement among the defendants to exchange price information whenever requested. However, I cannot agree that the agreement should be condemned, either as illegal *per se* or as having had the purpose or effect of restricting price competition in the corrugated container industry in the Southeastern-United States. . . .

Per se rules always contain a degree of arbitrariness. They are justified on the assumption that the gains from imposition of the rule will far outweigh the losses and that significant administrative advantages will result. In other words, the potential competitive harm plus the administrative costs of determining in what particular situations the practice may be harmful must far outweigh the benefits that may result. If the potential benefits in the aggregate are outweighed to this degree, then they are simply not worth identifying in individual cases.

I do not believe that the agreement in the present case is so devoid of potential benefit or so inherently harmful that we are justified in condemning it without proof that it was entered into for the purpose of restraining price competition or that it actually had that effect. The agreement in this case was to supply, when requested, price data for identified customers. Each defendant supplied the necessary information on the expectation that the favor would be returned. The nature of the exchanged information varied from case to case. In most cases, the price obtained was the price of the last sale to the particular customer; in some cases, the price was a current quotation to the customer. In all cases, the information obtained was sufficient to inform the defendants of the price they would have to beat in order to obtain a particular sale.

Complete market knowledge is certainly not an evil in perfectly competitive markets. This is not, however, such a market, and there is admittedly some danger that price information will be used for anticompetitive purposes, particularly the maintenance of prices at a high level. If the danger that price information will be so used is particularly high in a given situation, then perhaps exchange of information should be condemned.

I do not think the danger is sufficiently high in the present case. Defendants are only 18 of the 51 producers of corrugated containers in the

Southeastern United States. Together, they do make up 90% of the market and the six largest defendants do control 60% of the market. But entry is easy; an investment of $50,000 to $75,000 is ordinarily all that is necessary. In fact, the number of sellers has increased from 30 to the present 51 in the eight-year period covered by the complaint. The size of the market has almost doubled because of increased demand for corrugated containers. Nevertheless, some excess capacity is present. The products produced by defendants are undifferentiated. Industry demand is inelastic, so that price changes will not, up to a certain point, affect the total amount purchased. The only effect of price changes will be to reallocate market shares among sellers.

In a competitive situation, each seller will cut his price in order to increase his share of the market, and prices will ultimately stabilize at a competitive level—*i.e.,* price will equal cost, including a reasonable return on capital. Obviously, it would be to a seller's benefit to avoid such price competition and maintain prices at a higher level, with a corresponding increase in profit. In a market with very few sellers, and detailed knowledge of each other's price, such action is possible. However, I do not think it can be concluded that this particular market is sufficiently oligopolistic, especially in light of the ease of entry, to justify the inference that price information will necessarily be used to stabilize prices. Nor do I think that the danger of such a result is sufficiently high to justify imposing a *per se* rule without actual proof.

In this market, we have a few sellers presently controlling a substantial share of the market. We have a large number competing for the remainder of the market, also quite substantial. And total demand is increasing. In such a case, I think it just as logical to assume that the sellers, especially the smaller and newer ones, will desire to capture a larger market share by cutting prices as it is that they will acquiesce in oligopolistic behavior. The likelihood that prices will be cut and that those lower prices will have to be met acts as a deterrent to setting prices at an artificially high level in the first place. Given the uncertainty about the probable effect of an exchange of price information in this context, I would require that the Government prove that the exchange was entered into for the purpose of, or that it had the effect of, restraining price competition. . . .

The Court does not hold that the agreement in the present case was a deliberate attempt to stabilize prices. . . . The weight of the evidence in the present case indicates that the price information was employed by each defendant on an individual basis, and was used by that defendant to set its prices for a specific customer; ultimately each seller wanted to obtain all or part of that customer's business at the expense of a competitor. The District Court found that there was no explicit agreement among defendants to stabilize prices and I do not believe that the desire of a few industry witnesses to use the information to minimize price cuts supports the conclusion that such an agreement was implicit. On the contrary, the evidence establishes that the information was used by defendants as each pleased and was actually employed for the purpose of engaging in active price competition. . . .

The record indicates that defendants have offered voluminous evidence concerning price trend and competitive behavior in the corrugated container market. Their exhibits indicate a downward trend in prices, with substantial price variations among defendants and among their different plants. There was also a great deal of shifting of accounts. The District Court specifically found that the corrugated container market was highly competitive and that each defendant engaged in active price competition. The Government would have us ignore this evidence and these findings, and assume that because we are dealing with an industry with overcapacity and yet continued entry, the new entrants must have been attracted by high profits. The Government then argues that high profits can only result from stabilization of prices at an unduly high level. Yet, the Government did not introduce any evidence about the level of profits in this industry, and no evidence about price levels. . . . The Government admits that the price trend was down, but asks the Court to assume that the trend would have been accelerated with less informed, and hence more vigorous, price competition.[2] In the absence of any proof whatsoever, I cannot make such an assumption. It is just as likely that price competition was furthered by the exchange as it is that it was depressed.

Finally, the Government focuses on the finding of the District Court that in a majority of instances a defendant, when it received what it considered reliable price information, would quote or charge substantially the same price.[3] The Court and my Brother FORTAS also focus on this finding. Such an approach ignores, however, the remainder of the District Court's findings. The trial judge found that price decisions were individual decisions, and that defendants frequently did cut prices in order to obtain a particular order. And, the absence of any price parallelism or price uniformity and the downward trend in the industry undercut the conclusion that price information was used to stabilize prices.[4]

The Government is ultimately forced to fall back on the theoretical argument that prices would have been more unstable and would have fallen faster without price information. As I said earlier, I cannot make this as-

---

[2] There was no effort to demonstrate that the price behavior of those manufacturers who did not exchange price information, if any, varied significantly from the price behavior of those who did. In fact, several of the District Court's findings indicate that when certain defendants stopped exchanging price information, their price behavior remained essentially the same, and, in some cases, prices actually increased.

[3] It should be noted that, in most cases, this information was obtained from a customer rather than a competitor, a practice the Government does not condemn.

[4] As mentioned above, no evidence was introduced that would indicate that more than minimal price cuts were economically feasible.

sumption on the basis of the evidence in this record. The findings of the court below simply do not indicate that the exchange of information had a significant anticompetitive effect; if we rely on these findings, at worst all we can assume is that the exchange was a neutral factor in the market. . . . [T]he record indicates that, while each defendant occasionally received price information from a competitor, that information was used in the same manner as other reliable market information—*i.e.*, to reach an individual price decision based upon all available information. The District Court's findings that this was a competitive industry, lacking any price parallelism or uniformity, effectively refute the Government's assertion that the result of those decisions was to maintain or tend to maintain prices at other than a competitive level. Accordingly, I would affirm the decision of the court below.

United States v. *United States Gypsum Co. et al.*
438 U.S. 422 (1978)

MR. CHIEF JUSTICE BURGER delivered the opinion of the Court.

I

Gypsum board, a laminated type of wall board composed of paper, vinyl or other specially treated coverings over a gypsum core, has in the last 30 years substantially replaced wet plaster as the primary component of interior walls and ceilings in residential and commercial construction. The product is essentially fungible; differences in price, credit terms and delivery services largely dictate the purchasers' choice between competing suppliers. Overall demand, however, is governed by the level of construction activity and is only marginally affected by price fluctuations.

The gypsum board industry is highly concentrated with the number of producers ranging from nine to 15 in the period 1960 to 1973. The eight largest companies accounted for some 94 percent of the national sales with the seven single-plant producers[1] accounting for the remaining 6 percent. Most of the major producers and a large number of the single-plant producers are members of the Gypsum Association which since 1930 has served as a trade association of gypsum board manufacturers.

A

Beginning in 1966, the Justice Department, as well as the Federal Trade Commission, became involved in investigations into possible antitrust violations in the gypsum board industry. In 1971, a grand jury was em-

---

[1] The major producers operate numerous plants to serve a wide range of geographical markets. The single-plant producers are limited in terms of the markets they can serve because of the difficulties and expense involved in long-distance transportation of gypsum board.

paneled and the investigation continued for an additional 28 months. In late 1973, an indictment was filed in the United States District Court for the Western District of Pennsylvania charging six major manufacturers and various of their corporate officials with violations of §1 of the Sherman Act. . . .

The indictment charged that the defendants had engaged in a combination and conspiracy "[b]eginning sometime prior to 1960 and continuing thereafter at least until sometime in 1973," . . . in restraint of interstate trade and commerce in the manufacture and sale of gypsum board. . . . The indictment proceeded to specify some 13 types of actions taken by conspirators "in formulating and effectuating" the combination and conspiracy, the most relevant of which, for our purposes, is specification (h) which alleged that the conspirators:

> telephoned or otherwise contacted one another to exchange and discuss current and future published or market prices and published or standard terms and conditions of sale and to ascertain alleged deviations therefrom.

B

. . . The focus of the Government's price fixing case at trial was interseller price verification—that is, the practice allegedly followed by the gypsum board manufacturers of telephoning a competing producer to determine the price currently being offered on gypsum board to a specific customer. The Government contended that these price exchanges were part of an agreement among the defendants, had the effect of stabilizing prices and policing agreed upon price increases, and were undertaken on a frequent basis until sometime in 1973. Defendants disputed both the scope and duration of the verification activities, and further maintained that those exchanges of price information which did occur were for the purposes of complying with the Robinson-Patman Act[2] and preventing customer fraud. . . .

The instructions on the verification issue given by the trial judge provided that if the exchanges of price information were deemed by the jury to have been undertaken "in a good faith effort to comply with the Robinson-Patman Act," verification standing alone would not be sufficient to establish an illegal price-fixing agreement. The paragraphs immediately following, however, provided that the purpose was essentially irrelevant if the jury found that the effect of verification was to raise, fix, maintain or stabilize prices. The instructions on verification closed with the observation that

"[t]he law presumes that a person intends the necessary and natural consequences of his acts. Therefore, if the effect of the exchanges of

---

[2] Defendants contended that the exchange of price information or verification was necessary to enable them to take advantage of the meeting competition defense contained in §2(b) of the Robinson-Patman Act. . . . See Part III, *infra*.

pricing information was to raise, fix, maintain and stabilize prices, then the parties to them are presumed, as a matter of law, to have intended that result.". . .

C

[Section C discusses the sequence of events leading to the jury's decision in favor of the Government, which included conversations and communications between the judge and the jury foreman.]

D

The Court of Appeals for the Third Circuit reversed the convictions. . . .

Two judges agreed that the trial judge erred in instructing the jury that an effect on prices resulting from an agreement to exchange price information made out a Sherman Act violation regardless of whether respondents' sole purpose in engaging in such exchanges was to establish a defense to price discrimination charges. Instead, they regarded such a purpose if certain conditions were met,[3] as constituting a "controlling circumstance" which under *United States* v. *Container Corp. of America,* 393 U.S. 333 . . . (1969) would excuse what might otherwise constitute an antitrust violation. . . .

One judge, in dissent, would have sustained the convictions. He regarded the charge on verification to be consistent with *Container Corp.,* and rejected the notion that the Robinson-Patman Act required the exchange of price information even in the limited circumstances identified by the majority. . . .

We granted certiorari, . . . and we affirm.

II

We turn first to consider the jury instructions regarding the elements of the price-fixing offense charged in the indictment. Although the trial judge's instructions on the price-fixing issue are not without ambiguity, it seems reasonably clear that he regarded an effect on prices as the crucial element of the charged offense. The jury was instructed that if it found interseller verification had the effect of raising, fixing, maintaining or stabilizing the price of gypsum board, then such verification could be considered as evidence of an agreement to so affect prices. They were further charged, and it is this point which gives rise to our present concern, that "if the effect of the exchanges of pricing information was to raise, fix,

---

[3] "Therefore, appellants were entitled to an instruction that their verification practice would not violate the Sherman Act if the jury found: (1) the appellants engaged in the practice solely to comply with the strictures of Robinson-Patman; (2) they had first resorted to all other reasonable means of corroboration, without success; (3) they had good, independent reason to doubt the buyers' truthfulness; and (4) their communication with competitors was strictly limited to the one price and one buyer at issue." 550 F.2d 115, 126.

maintain and stabilize prices, then the parties to them are presumed, *as a matter of law,* to have intended that result.". . . (Emphasis added.)

The Government characterizes this charge as entirely consistent with "this Court's long-standing rule that an agreement among sellers to exchange information on current offering prices violates Section 1 of the Sherman Act if it has either the purpose or the effect of stabilizing prices,". . . and relies primarily on our decision in *United States* v. *Container Corp. of America,* 393 U.S. 333, . . . a civil case, to support its position. . . . The Court of Appeals rejected the Government's "effects alone" test, holding instead that in certain limited circumstances, a purpose of complying with the Robinson-Patman Act would constitute a controlling circumstance excusing Sherman Act liability, and hence an instruction allowing the jury to ignore purpose could not be sustained.

We agree with the Court of Appeals that an effect on prices, without more, will not support a criminal conviction under the Sherman Act, but we do not base that conclusion on the existence of any conflict between the requirements of the Robinson-Patman and the Sherman Acts.[4] Rather, we hold that a defendant's state of mind or intent is an element of a criminal antitrust offense which must be established by evidence and inferences drawn therefrom and cannot be taken from the trier of fact through reliance on a legal presumption of wrongful intent from proof of an effect on prices. . . . Since the challenged instruction, as we read it, had this prohibited effect, it is disapproved. We are unwilling to construe the Sherman Act as mandating a regime of strict liability criminal offenses.[5]

A

[This section discusses the general legal concept of the strict liability offense and the limited circumstances in which Congress has created, and the Supreme Court has recognized, such offenses.]

B

The Sherman Act, unlike most traditional criminal statutes, does not, in clear and categorical terms, precisely identify the conduct which it proscribes.[6] Both civil remedies and criminal sanctions are authorized

---

[4] See Part III, *infra.*

[5] Our analysis focuses solely on the elements of a criminal offense under the antitrust laws, and leaves unchanged the general rule that a civil violation can be established by proof of either an unlawful purpose or an anticompetitive effect. See *United States* v. *Container Corp.,* 393 U.S., at 337; id., at 341 . . . (MARSHALL, J., dissenting). Of course, consideration of intent may play an important role in divining the actual nature and effect of the alleged anticompetitive conduct. See *Chicago Bd. of Trade* v. *United States,* 246, U.S. 231, 238 . . . (1918).

[6] Senator Sherman adverted to the open-texture of the statutory language in 1890 and accurately forecast its consequence—a central role for the courts in giving shape and content to the Act's proscriptions.

"I admit that it is difficult to define in legal language the precise line between lawful and unlawful combinations. This must be left for courts to determine in each particular case. All

with regard to the same generalized definitions of the conduct proscribed—restraints of trade or commerce and illegal monopolization—without reference to or mention of intent or state of mind. Nor has judicial elaboration of the Act always yielded the clear and definitive rules of conduct which the statute omits; instead open-ended and fact-specific standards like the rule of reason have been applied to broad classes of conduct falling within the purview of the Act's general provisions. . . . Simply put, the Act has not been interpreted as if it were primarily a criminal statute; it has been construed to have a "generality and adaptability comparable to that found desirable in constitutional provisions.". . .

Close attention to the type of conduct regulated by the Sherman Act butresses this conclusion. With certain exceptions for conduct regarded as per se illegal because of its unquestionably anticompetitive effects, see, e.g., *United States* v. *Socony-Vacuum Oil Co.,* 310 U.S. 150, the behavior proscribed by the Act is often difficult to distinguish from the gray zone of socially acceptable and economically justifiable business conduct. Indeed, the type of conduct charged in the indictment in this case—the exchange of price information among competitors—is illustrative in this regard.[7] The imposition of criminal liability on a corporate official, or for that matter on a corporation directly, for engaging in such conduct which only after the fact is determined to violate the statute because of anticompetitive effects, without inquiring into the intent with which it was undertaken, holds out the distinct possibility of overdeterrence; salutary and procompetitive conduct lying close to the borderline of impermissible conduct might be shunned by businessmen who chose to be excessively cautious in the face of uncertainty regarding possible exposure to criminal punishment for even a good-faith error of judgment.[8]. . .

. . . [W]e conclude that the criminal offenses defined by the Sherman Act should be construed as including intent as an element.

---

that we, as lawmakers, can do is to declare general principles, and we can be assured that courts will apply them so as to carry out the meaning of the law. . . ." *21 Cong. Rec.* 2460 (1890).

[7] The exchange of price data and other information among competitors does not invariably have anticompetitive effects; indeed such practices can in certain circumstances increase economic efficiency and render markets more rather than less competitive. For this reason, we have held that such exchanges of information do not constitute a per se violation of the Sherman Act. . . . A number of factors including most prominently the structure of the industry involved and the nature of the information exchanged are generally considered in divining the pro or anticompetitive effects of this type of interseller communication. . . . Exchanges of current price information, of course, have the greatest potential for generating anticompetitive effects and although not per se unlawful have consistently been held to violate the Sherman Act. . . .

[8] Congress has recently increased the criminal penalties for violation of the Sherman Act. Individual violations are now treated as felonies punishable by a fine not to exceed $100,000, or by imprisonment for up to three years, or both. Corporate violators are subject to a $1 million fine. . . . The severity of these sanctions provides further support for our conclusion that the Sherman Act should not be construed as creating strict liability crimes. . . . Respondents here were not prosecuted under the new penalty provisions since they were indicted prior to the December 21, 1974 effective date for the increased sanctions.

C

Having concluded that intent is a necessary element of a criminal antitrust violation, the task remaining is to treat the practical aspects of this requirement. . . . As we have noted, the language of the Act provides minimal assistance in determining what standard of intent is appropriate and the sparse legislative history of the criminal provisions is similarly unhelpful. We must therefore turn to more general sources and traditional understandings of the nature of the element of intent in the criminal law. . . .

. . . Our question . . . is whether a criminal violation of the antitrust laws requires, in addition to proof of anticompetitive effects, a demonstration that the disputed conduct was undertaken with the conscious object of producing such effects or whether it is sufficient that the conduct is shown to have been undertaken with knowledge that the proscribed effects would most likely follow. While the difference between these formulations is a narrow one, . . . we conclude that action taken with knowledge of its probable consequences and having the requisite anticompetitive effects can be a sufficient predicate for a finding of criminal liability under the antitrust laws.[9]

Nothing in our analysis of the Sherman Act persuades us that this general understanding of intent should not be applied to criminal antitrust violations such as charged here. The business behavior which is likely to give rise to criminal antitrust charges is conscious behavior normally undertaken only after a full consideration of the desired results and a weighing of the costs, benefits and risks. A requirement of proof not only of this knowledge of likely effects, but also of a conscious desire to bring them to fruition or to violate the law would seem, particularly in such a context, both unnecessarily cumulative and unduly burdensome. . . .

D

When viewed in terms of this standard, the jury instructions on the price-fixing charge cannot be sustained. . . . [T]he jury was told that the requisite intent followed, *as a matter of law,* from a finding that the exchange of price information had an impact on prices. Although an effect on prices may well support an inference that the defendant had knowledge of the probability of such a consequence at the time he acted, the jury must remain free to consider additional evidence before accepting or rejecting the inference. Therefore, although it would be correct to instruct the jury that it may infer intent from an effect on prices, ultimately the de-

---

[9] In so holding, we do not mean to suggest that conduct undertaken with the purpose of producing anticompetitive effects would not also support criminal liability, even if such effects did not come to pass. . . . We hold only that this elevated standard of intent need not be established in cases where anticompetitive effects have been demonstrated; instead, proof that the defendant's conduct was undertaken with knowledge of its probable consequences will satisfy the Government's burden.

cision on the issue of intent must be left to the trier of fact alone. The instruction given invaded this fact-finding function. . . .

III

Our construction of the Sherman Act to require proof of intent as an element of a criminal antitrust violation leaves unresolved the question upon which the Court of Appeals focused, whether verification of price concessions with competitors for the sole purpose of taking advantage of the §2(b) meeting competition defense of the Robinson-Patman Act should be treated as a controlling circumstance precluding liability under §1 of the Sherman Act. We now turn to that question.[10]

A

In *Cement Mfgrs. Protective Assn.* v. *United States,* 268 U.S. 588, . . . the Court held exampt from Sherman §1 liability an exchange of price information among competitors because the exchange of information was necessary to protect the cement manufacturers from fraudulent behavior by contractors. . . . Over 40 years later, in *United States* v. *Container Corp.,* 393 U.S. 333, . . . MR. JUSTICE DOUGLAS characterized the *Cement* holding in the following terms:

> While there was present here, as in *Cement Mfgrs. Protective Association* v. *United States,* 268 U.S. 588, an exchange of prices to specific customers, there was absent the controlling circumstance, viz., that cement manufacturers, to protect themselves from delivering to contractors more cement than was needed for a specific job and thus receiving a lower price, exchanged price information as a means of protecting their legal rights from fraudulent inducements to deliver more cement than needed for a specific job.

The use of the phrase *controlling circumstance* in *Container* implied that the exception from Sherman Act liability recognized in *Cement Mfgrs.* was not necessarily limited to special circumstances of that case, although the exact scope of the exception remained largely undefined.

Since *Container,* several courts have read the controlling circumstance exception as encompassing exchanges of price information when undertaken for the purpose of compliance with §2(b) of the Robinson-Patman Act. . . . The Court of Appeals in the instant case essentially adopted the same tack—albeit with some additional limitations . . . — finding

---

[10] This question was not resolved by the prior discussion because a purpose of complying with the Robinson-Patman Act by exchanging price information is not inconsistent with knowledge that such exchanges of information will have the probable effect of fixing or stabilizing prices. Since we hold knowledge of the probable consequences of conduct to be the requisite mental state in a criminal prosecution like the instant one where an effect on prices is also alleged, a defendant's purpose in engaging in proscribed conduct will not insulate him from liability unless it is deemed sufficient merit to justify a general exception to the Sherman Act's proscriptions. . . .

such a step necessary to eliminate a perceived conflict between the Sherman Act's proscriptions regarding the exchange of price information among competitors and the claimed necessity of such exchanges to perfect the §2(b) defense of the Robinson-Patman Act. The Government challenges that resolution on two grounds: first, that there is no general controlling circumstance exception to the Sherman Act and, second, that in any event, there is no conflict between the two antitrust statutes which would require the prohibitions of the Sherman Act to be tempered even to the degree mandated by the Court of Appeals' carefully circumscribed holding in this case. We agree generally with the Government as to the proper accommodation of the Sherman and Robinson-Patman Acts, and therefore find it unnecessary to address the more general question going to the existence and proper scope of the so-called controlling circumstance exception.

B

Section 2(a) of the Robinson-Patman Act, 15 U.S.C. §13(a), embodies a general prohibition of price discrimination between buyers when an injury to competition is the consequence. The primary exception to the §2(a) bar is the meeting competition defense which is incorporated as a proviso to the burden of proof requirements set out in §2(b) of the Act. . . . The role of the §2(b) proviso in tempering the §2(a) prohibition of price discrimination was highlighted in *Standard Oil Co.* v. *Trade Commission,* 340 U.S.231. . . . There we recognized the potential tension between the rationales underlying the Sherman and Robinson-Patman Acts and sought to effect a partial accommodation by construing §2(b) to provide an absolute defense to liability for price discrimination.

. . . The Court of Appeals . . . concluded that only a very narrow exception to Sherman Act liability should be recognized; that exception would cover the relatively few situations where the veracity of the buyer seeking the matching discount was legitimately in doubt, other reasonable means of corroboration were unavailable to the seller, and the interseller communication was for the sole purpose of complying with the Robinson-Patman Act. Despite the court's efforts to circumscribe the scope of the exception it was constrained to recognize, we find its analysis unacceptable.

C

A good-faith belief, rather than absolute certainty, that a price concession is being offered to meet an equally low price offered by a competitor is sufficient to satisfy the Robinson-Patman's §2(b) defense. While casual reliance on uncorroborated reports of buyers or sales representatives without further investigation may not . . . be sufficient to make the requisite showing of good faith, nothing in the language of §2(b) . . . indicates that direct discussions of price between competitors are required.

Nor has any court, so far as we are aware, ever imposed such a requirement. . . . On the contrary, the §2(b) defense has been successfully invoked in the absence of interseller verification on numerous occasions. . . . And in *Kroger Co.* v. *FTC*, 438 F.2d 1372, 1376–1377 (CA6 1971), aff'g *Beatrice Foods Co.*, 76 F.T.C. 719, the defense was recognized despite the fact that the price concession was ultimately found to have undercut that of the competition and thus technically to have fallen outside the "meet not beat" structures of the defense. As these cases indicate, and as the Federal Trade Commission observed, it is the concept of good faith which lies at the core of the meeting-competition defense. . . .

The so-called problem of the untruthful buyer which concerned the Court of Appeals does not in our view call for a different approach to the §2(b) defense. The good-faith standard remains the benchmark against which the seller's conduct is to be evaluated, and we agree with the government and the FTC that this standard can be satisfied by efforts falling short of interseller verification in most circumstances where the seller has only vague, generalized doubts about the realiability of its commercial adversary—the buyer. . . . Given the fact specific nature of the inquiry, it is difficult to predict all the factors the FTC or a court would consider in appraising a seller's good faith in matching a competing offer in these circumstances. Certainly, evidence that a seller had received reports of similar discounts from other customers . . . or was threatened with a termination of purchases if the discount were not met . . . would be relevant in this regard. Efforts to corroborate the reported discount by seeking documentary evidence or by appraising its reasonableness in terms of available market data would also be probative as would the seller's past experience with the particular buyer in question.[11]

There remains the possibility that in a limited number of situations a seller may have substantial reasons to doubt the accuracy of reports of a competing offer and may be unable to corroborate such reports in any of the generally accepted ways. Thus the defense may be rendered unavailable since unanswered questions about the reliability of a buyer's representations may well be inconsistent with a good-faith belief that a com-

---

[11] It may also turn out that sustained enforcement of §2(f) of the Robinson-Patman Act, which imposes liability on buyers for inducing illegal price discounts, will serve to bolster the credibility of buyer's representations and render reliance thereon by sellers a more reasonable and secure predicate for a finding of good faith under §2(b). See generally Note, "Meeting Competition Under the Robinson-Patman Act," *90 Harv.L.Rev.* 1476, 1495–1496 (1977). In both *Great Atlantic and Pacific Tea Co.* v. *FTC*, 557 F.2d 971 (CA2 1977) and *Kroger* v. *FTC*, *supra*, buyers have been held liable under §2(f) despite the fact that the sellers were either found not to have violated the Robinson-Patman Act (Kroger) or were not charged with such a violation (A&P). Certiorari has been granted in *Great Atlantic and Pacific Tea Co.* to consider the permissibility of enforcing the Robinson-Patman Act in this manner. . . . [Subsequent to this opinion, the Supreme Court ruled in favor of A&P, on the grounds that, since its suppliers acted in good faith to meet competition within the meaning of §2(b), it could not be liable under §2(f). (See Chapter 9 below.)]

peting offer had in fact been made.[12] As an abstract proposition, resort to interseller verification as a means of checking the buyer's reliability seems a possible solution to the seller's plight, but careful examination reveals serious problems with the practice.

Both economic theory and common human experience suggest that interseller verification—if undertaken on an isolated and infrequent basis with no provision for reciprocity or cooperation—will not serve its putative function of corroborating the representations of unreliable buyers regarding the existence of competing offers. Price concessions by oligopolists generally yield competitive advantages only if secrecy can be maintained; when the terms of the concession are made publicly known, other competitors are likely to follow and any advantage to the initiator is lost in the process. . . . Thus, if one seller offers a price concession or the purpose of winning over one of his competitor's customers, it is unlikely that the same seller will freely inform its competitor of the details of the concession so that it can be promptly matched and diffused. Instead, such a seller would appear to have at least as great an incentive to misrepresent the existence or size of the discount as would the buyer who received it. Thus verification, if undertaken on a one-shot basis for the sole purpose of complying with the §2(b) defense, does not hold out much promise as a means of shoring up buyers' representations.

The other variety of interseller verification is, like the conduct charged in the instant case, undertaken pursuant to an agreement, either tacit or express, providing for the reciprocity among competitors in the exchange of price information. Such an agreement would make little economic sense, in our view, if its sole purpose were to guarantee all participants the opportunity to match the secret price concessions of other participants under §2(b) of the Robinson-Patman Act. For in such circumstances, each seller would know that his price concession could not be kept from his competitors and no seller participating in the information exchange arrangement would, therefore, have any incentive for deviating from the prevailing price level in the industry. . . . Regardless of its putative purpose, the most likely consequence of any such agreement to exchange price information would be the stabilization of industry prices. . . . Instead of facilitating use of the §2(b) defense, such an agreement would have the effect of eliminating the very price concessions which provide the main element of competition in oligopolistic industries and the primary occasion for resort to the meeting competition defense.

Especially in oligopolistic industries such as the gypsum board industry, the exchange of price information among competitors carries with it

---

[12] We need not and do not decide that in all such circumstances the defense would be unavailable. The case by case interpretation and elaboration [of] the §2(b) defense is properly left to the other federal courts and the FTC in the context of concrete fact situations. We note also that our conclusions regarding the proper interpretation of §2(f) of the Robinson-Patman Act, see n. 30 *supra,* may well affect subsequent application of the §2(b) defense.

the added potential for the development of concerted price-fixing arrangements which lie at the core of the Sherman Act's prohibitions. . . .

We are left, therefore, on the one hand, with doubts about both the need for and the efficacy of interseller verification as a means of facilitating compliance with §2(b) of the Robinson-Patman Act, and, on the other, with recognition of the tendency for price discussions between competitors to contribute to the stability of oligopolistic prices and open the way for the growth of prohibited anticompetitive activity. To recognize even a limited controlling circumstance exception for interseller verification in such circumstances would be to remove from scrutiny under the Sherman Act conduct falling near its core with no assurance, and indeed with serious doubts, that competing antitrust policies would be served thereby. In *Automatic Canteen* v. *FTC,* 346 U.S. 61 . . . (1953), the Court suggested that as a general rule the Robinson-Patman Act should be construed so as to insure its coherence with "the broader antitrust policies that have been laid down by Congress;" that observation buttresses our conclusion that exchanges of price information—even when putatively for purposes of Robinson-Patman Act compliance—must remain subject to close scrutiny under the Sherman Act. . . .

IV

[In Section IV, the Court noted its agreement with the Court of Appeals as to the impropriety of the contacts between the judge and the jury foreman.]

V

[In Section V, the Court affirmed the Court of Appeals' ruling that certain written instructions to the jury were improperly framed.]

Accordingly, the judgment of the Court of Appeals is

Affirmed.

MR. JUSTICE STEWART joins all but Part IV of this opinion.

MR. JUSTICE BLACKMUN took no part in the consideration or decision of this case.

. . . . .

MR. JUSTICE POWELL, concurring in part.

I join the judgment and Parts I, II, and V of the Court's opinion. I also join so much of Part III as holds that a seller's intention to establish a meeting competition defense under §2(b) of the Robinson-Patman Act to a charge of price discrimination under §2(a) of that Act is not in itself a "controlling circumstance" excusing liability under §1 of the Sherman Act for otherwise unlawful direct price verification practices.

I do not join those portions of Part III, however, that might be read as suggesting that there are cases where the §2(b) defense is unavailable even though a seller made every reasonable, lawful effort to corroborate his buyer's report that a competitor had offered a lower price before reducing his own price to that buyer. . . . In my view, a proper accommodation between the policies of the Robinson-Patman Act and the Sherman Act would result in recognition of the §2(b) defense in such cases. Otherwise, sellers sometimes would face the unenviable choice of reducing prices to one buyer and risking Robinson-Patman Act liability, refusing to do so and losing the sale, or reducing prices to all buyers.

A prudent businessman faced with this choice often would forego the price reduction altogether. This reaction would disserve the procompetitive policy of the Sherman Act without advancing materially the antidiscrimination policy of the Robinson-Patman Act. The Court already has made clear that the Robinson-Patman Act "does not require the seller to justify price discriminations by showing that in fact they met a competitor's price." *FTC* v. *A. E. Staley Manufacturing Co.*, 324 U.S. 746 . . . (1945). Today the Court confirms that "it is the concept of good faith which lies at the core of the meeting-competition defense and good faith 'is a flexible and pragmatic, not technical or doctrinaire, concept.'". . . A seller who has attempted to verify his buyer's report by every reasonable, lawful means before reducing his price to meet a competitor's price, in my view, has met the test of "good faith." In such a case, if the buyer's report proves to have been untruthful, it is the buyer alone, not the seller, who has acted in bad faith.

[MR. JUSTICE REHNQUIST concurred in part and dissented in part.]

MR. JUSTICE STEVENS, concurring in part and dissenting in part.

There are three reasons why I am unable to subscribe to the bifurcated construction of §1 of the Sherman Act which the Court adopts in Part II of its opinion.

In 1955 I subscribed to the view that criminal enforcement of the Sherman Act is inappropriate unless the defendants have deliberately violated the law. . . . I adhere to that view today. But since 1890 when the Sherman Act was enacted, the statute has had the same substantive reach in criminal and civil cases. No matter how wise the new rule that the Court adopts today may be, I believe it is an amendment only Congress may enact.

If I were fashioning a new test of criminal liability, I would require proof of a specific purpose to violate the law rather than mere knowledge that the defendants' agreement has had an adverse effect on the market. . . . There is, of course, a theoretical possibility that defendants could engage in a practice of exchanging current price information that was sufficiently prevalent to have had a market-wide impact that they did not know about, but as a practical matter that possibility is surely remote.

Finally, I am afraid that the new civil-criminal dichotomy may work mischief in the civil enforcement of the prohibition against tampering with prices in a free market. Conclusive presumptions play a central role in the enforcement, both civil and criminal, of the Sherman Act. Thus, an agreement to charge the same price,[13] or to adopt a common purchasing policy that determines the market price[14] is unreasonable, and therefore unlawful, without any proof of the purpose of the actual effect of the agreement. The law presumes that those who entered the price-fixing agreement knew that forbidden effects would follow, and it also presumes, conclusively, that those effects will follow. In a criminal prosecution for price-fixing in violation of the Sherman Act it is, therefore, irrelevant whether the prices fixed were reasonable or whether the defendant's intentions were good.[15] See *United States* v. *Trenton Potteries,* 273 U.S. 392. . . .

To be sure, cases such as *Trenton Potteries* involved conduct that was determined to be illegal on its face, while in this case the trial court appraised respondents' agreement under rule of reason analysis.[16] But properly understood, rule of reason analysis is not distinct from per se analysis. On the contrary, agreements that are illegal per se are merely a species within the broad category of agreements that unreasonably restrain trade; less proof is required to establish their illegality, but they nonetheless violate the basic rule of reason. . . .

As applied to an agreement among major producers to exchange current price information, the rule of reason requires an element in addition to proof of the agreement itself—either an actual market effect or an express purpose to affect market price—but once that element is shown any additional showing of intent is unnecessary. . . . The rule is premised on the assumption that if the practice of exchanging current price information is sufficiently prevalent to affect the market price then there is an extremely high probability that the sales representatives of these companies

---

[13] *United States* v. *Trenton Potteries Co.,* 273 U.S. 392, 47 S.Ct. 377, 71 L.Ed. 700.

[14] *United States* v. *Socony-Vacuum Oil Co.,* 310 U.S. 150, 60 S.Ct. 811, 84 L.Ed. 1129.

[15] In fact, early in the development of criminal enforcement of the Sherman Act, this Court stated: "[T]he conspirators must be held to have intended the necessary and direct consequences of their acts and cannot be heard to say the contrary. In other words, by purposely engaging in a conspiracy which necessarily and directly produces the result which the statute is designed to prevent, they are, in legal contemplation, chargeable with intending that result." *United States* v. *Patten,* 226 U.S. 525, 543, 33 S.Ct. 141, 145, 57 L.Ed. 333.

[16] An argument can be made that an agreement among the major producers in the market to exchange current price information should be considered illegal on its face. . . .

had actual knowledge of that fact. Given the language of §1, that premise is as valid in the context of a criminal prosecution as it is in the context of a treble-damage civil action.

Accordingly, although I agree with much of the abstract discussion in Part II of the Court's opinion, I concur only in Parts I, III, IV, and V, and in the judgment.

Note: On remand, the defendants again were found guilty of price fixing [1972-2 Trade Cases ¶62,360 (W.D. Penn. 1978)]. This was sustained by the Court of Appeals [600 F.2d 414 (3rd Cir. 1979)]; a petition for certiorari was denied by the Supreme Court [___ U.S. ___ (1979)].

American Society of Composers, Authors and Publishers, et. al. v. *Columbia Broadcasting System, et al.*
441 U.S. 1 (1979)

MR. JUSTICE WHITE delivered the opinion of the Court:

This case involves an action under the antitrust and copyright laws brought by respondent Columbia Broadcasting System, Inc. (CBS), against petitioners, American Society of Composers, Authors and Publishers (ASCAP) and Broadcast Music, Inc. (BMI), and their members and affiliates. . . . The basic question presented is whether the issuance by ASCAP and BMI to CBS of blanket licenses to copyrighted musical compositions at fees negotiated by them is price fixing per se unlawful under the antitrust laws.

I

CBS operates one of three national commercial television networks, supplying programs to approximately 200 affiliated stations and telecasting approximately 7,500 network programs per year. Many, but not all, of these programs make use of copyrighted music recorded on the soundtrack. CBS also owns television and radio stations in various cities. It is "the giant of the world in the use of music rights," the "No. 1 outlet in the history of entertainment.". . .

Since 1897 the copyright laws have vested in the owner of a copyrighted musical composition the exclusive right to perform the work publicly for profit, . . . but the legal right is not self-enforcing. In 1914 Victor Herbert and a handful of other composers organized ASCAP because those who performed copyrighted music for profit were so numerous and widespread, and most performances so fleeting, that as a practical matter is was impossible for the many individual copyright owners to negotiate with and license the users and to detect unauthorized users. . . . As ASCAP operates today, its 22,000 members grant it nonexclusive rights to license nondramatic performances of their works, and ASCAP issues licenses and distributes royalties to copyright owners in accordance with a schedule reflecting the nature and amount of the use of their music and other factors.

BMI, a nonprofit corporation owned by members of the broadcasting industry, . . . was organized in 1939, is affiliated with or represents some 10,000 publishing companies and 20,000 authors and composers, and operates in much the same manner as ASCAP. Almost every domestic copyrighted composition is in the repertory either of ASCAP, with a total of 3 million compositions, or of BMI, with 1 million.

Both organizations operate primarily through blanket licenses, which give the licensees the right to perform any and all of the compositions owned by the members or affiliates as often as the licensees desire for a stated term. Fees for blanket licenses are ordinarily a percentage of total revenues or a flat dollar amount, and do not directly depend on the amount or type of music used. Radio and television broadcasters are the largest users of music, and almost all of them hold blanket licenses from both ASCAP and BMI. Until this litigation, CBS held blanket licenses from both organizations for its television network on a continuous basis since the late 1940s and had never attempted to secure any other form of license from either ASCAP[1] or any of its members. . . .

The complaint filed by CBS charged various violations of the Sherman Act . . . and the copyright laws. . . . CBS argued that ASCAP and BMI are unlawful monopolies and that the blanket license is illegal price fixing, an unlawful tying arrangement, a concerted refusal to deal, and a misuse of copyrights. The District Court, though denying summary judgment to certain defendants, ruled that the practice did not fall within the per se rule. . . . After an eight-week trial, limited to the issue of liability, the court dismissed the complaint, rejecting again the claim that the blanket license was price fixing and a per se violation of §1 of the Sherman Act, and holding that since direct negotiation with individual copyright owners is available and feasible there is no undue restraint of trade, illegal tying, misuse of copyrights or monopolization. . . .

Though agreeing with the District Court's fact-finding and not disturbing its legal conclusions on the other antitrust theories of liability, . . . the Court of Appeals held that the blanket license issued to television networks was a form of price fixing illegal per se under the Sherman Act. . . .

. . . Because we disagree with the Court of Appeals' conclusions with respect to the per se illegality of the blanket license, we reverse its judgment and remand the cause for further appropriate proceedings.

---

[1] Unless the context indicates otherwise, references to ASCAP alone in this opinion usually apply to BMI as well. . . .

II

In construing and applying the Sherman Act's ban against contracts, conspiracies, and combinations in restraint of trade, the Court has held that certain agreements or practices are so "plainly anticompetitive," *National Society of Professional Engineers* v. *United States,* 435 U.S. 679, 692 (1978), . . . and so often "lack . . . any redeeming virtue," *Northern Pac. R. Co.* v. *United States,* 356 U.S. 1, 5 (1958), that they are conclusively presumed illegal without further examination under the rule of reason generally applied in Sherman Act cases. This per se rule is a valid and useful tool of antitrust policy and enforcement.[2] And agreements among competitors to fix prices on their individual goods or services are among those concerted activities that the Court has held to be within the per se category. . . . But easy labels do not always supply ready answers.

A

To the Court of Appeals and CBS, the blanket license involves price fixing in the literal sense: the composers and publishing houses have joined together into an organization that sets its price for the blanket license it sells.[3] But this is not a question simply of determining whether two or more potential competitors have literally "fixed" a "price." As generally used in the antitrust field, price fixing is a shorthand way of describing certain categories of business behavior to which the per se rule has been held applicable. The Court of Appeals' literal approach does not alone establish that this particular practice is one of those types or that it is "plainly anticompetitive" and very likely without "redeeming virtue." Literalness is overly simplistic and often overbroad. When two partners set the price of their goods or services they are literally price fixing, but they are not per se in violation of the Sherman Act. . . . Thus, it is necessary to characterize the challenged conduct as falling within or without that category of behavior to which we apply the label "per se

---

[2] "This principle of per se unreasonableness not only makes the type of restraints which are proscribed by the Sherman Act more certain to the benefit of everyone concerned, but it also avoids the necessity for an incredibly complicated and prolonged economic investigation into the entire history of the industry involved, as well as related industries, in an effort to determine at large whether a particular restraint has been unreasonable—an inquiry so often wholly fruitless when undertaken." *Northern Pac. R. C.* v. *United States,* 356, U.S. 1, 5 (1958). . . .

[3] CBS also complains that it pays a flat fee regardless of the amount of use it makes of ASCAP compositions and even though many of its programs contain little or no music. We are unable to see how that alone could make out an antitrust violation or misuse of copyrights:

"Sound business judgment could indicate that such payment represents the most convenient method of fixing the business value of the privileges granted by the licensing agreement. . . ." *Automatic Radio Manufacturing Co.* v. *Hazeltine Research, Inc.,* 339 U.S. 827, 834 (1950).

See also *Zenith Radio Corp.* v. *Hazeltine Research, Inc.,* 395 U.S. 100 (1969).

price fixing." That will often, but not always, be a simple matter. . . .

. . . We have never examined a practice like this one before; indeed, the Court of Appeals recognized that "[i]n dealing with performing rights in the music industry we confront conditions both in copyright law and in antitrust law which are *sui generis*." . . . And though there has been rather intensive antitrust scrutiny of ASCAP and its blanket licenses, that experience hardly counsels that we should outlaw the blanket license as a per se restraint of trade.

B

This and other cases involving ASCAP and its licensing practices have arisen out of the efforts of the creators of copyrighted musical compositions to collect for the public performance of their works, as they are entitled to do under the Copyright Act. As already indicated, ASCAP and BMI originated to make possible and to facilitate dealings between copyright owners and those who desire to use their music. Both organizations plainly involve concerted action in a large and active line of commerce, and it is not surprising that, as the District Court found, [n]either ASCAP nor BMI is a stranger to antitrust litigation.". . .

The Department of Justice first investigated allegations of anticompetitive conduct by ASCAP over 50 years ago. . . .

Under . . . [a 1941 consent decree, amended in 1950] which still substantially controls the activities of ASCAP, members may grant ASCAP only nonexclusive rights to license their works for public performance. Members, therefore, retain the rights individually to license public performances, along with the rights to license the use of their compositions for other purposes. ASCAP itself is forbidden to grant any license to perform one or more specified compositions in the ASCAP repertory unless both the user and the owner have requested it in writing to do so. ASCAP is required to grant to any user making written application a nonexclusive license to perform all ASCAP compositions, either for a period of time or on a per-program basis. ASCAP may not insist on the blanket license, and the fee for the per-program license, which is to be based on the revenues for the program on which ASCAP music is played, must offer the applicant a genuine economic choice between the per-program license and the more common blanket license. If ASCAP and a putative licensee are unable to agree on a fee within 60 days, the applicant may apply to the District Court for a determination of a reasonable fee, with ASCAP having the burden of proving reasonableness. . . .

Of course, a consent judgment, even one entered at the behest of the Antitrust Division, does not immunize the defendant from liability for actions, including those contemplated by the decree, that violate the rights of nonparties. . . . But it cannot be ignored that the Federal Executive and Judiciary have carefully scrutinized ASCAP and the challenged conduct, have imposed restrictions on various of ASCAP's practices, and, by the terms of the decree, stand ready to provide further consideration, supervision, and perhaps invalidation of asserted anticompetitive practices. . . . In these circumstances, we have a unique indicator that the challenged practice may have redeeming competitive virtues and that the search for those values is not almost sure to be in vain.[4] Thus, although CBS is not bound by the Antitrust Division's actions, the decree is a fact of economic and legal life in this industry, and the Court of Appeals should not have ignored it completely in analyzing the practice. . . .

After the consent decrees, the legality of the blanket license was challenged in suits brought by certain ASCAP members against individual radio stations for copyright infringement. The stations raised as a defense that the blanket license was a form of price fixing illegal under the Sherman Act. The parties stipulated that it would be nearly impossible for each radio station to negotiate with each copyright holder separate licenses for the performance of his works on radio. Against this background, and relying heavily on the 1950 consent judgments, the Court of Appeals for the Ninth Circuit rejected claims that ASCAP was a combination in restraint of trade and that the blanket license constituted illegal price fixing. *K-91, Inc.* v. *Gershwin Publishing Corp.*, 372 F.2d 1 (CA9 1967), cert. denied, 389 U.S. 1045 (1968).

The Department of Justice, with the principal responsibility for enforcing the Sherman Act and administering the consent decrees relevant to this case, agreed with the result reached by the Ninth Circuit. In a submission *amicus curiae* opposing one station's petition for certiorari in this Court, the Department stated that there must be "some kind of central licensing agency by which copyright holders may offer their works in a common pool to all who wish to use them." . . . The Department concluded that, in the circumstances of that case, the blanket licenses issued by ASCAP to individual radio stations were neither a per se violation of the Sherman Act nor an unreasonable restraint of trade.

As evidenced by its *amicus* brief in the present case, the Department remains of that view. Furthermore, the United States disagrees with the Court of Appeals in this case and urges that the blanket licenses, which the consent decree authorizes ASCAP to issue to television networks, are not per se violations of the Sherman Act. It takes no position, however, on whether the practice is an unreasonable restraint of trade in the context of the network television industry.

Finally, we note that Congress, in the new Copyright Act, has itself chosen to employ the blanket license and similar practices. . . . Though these provisions are not directly controlling, they do reflect an opinion that the blanket license, and ASCAP, are economically beneficial in at least some circumstances. . . .

---

[4] . . . Moreover, unthinking application of the per se rule might upset the balancing of economic power and of pro- and anticompetitive effects presumably worked out in the decree.

III

Of course, we are no more bound than in CBS by the views of the Department of Justice, the results in the prior lower court cases, or the opinions of various experts about the merits of the blanket license. But while we must independently examine this practice, all those should caution us against too easily finding blanket licensing subject to per se invalidation.

A

As a preliminary matter, we are mindful that the Court of Appeals' holding would appear to be quite difficult to contain. If, as the court held, there is a per se antitrust violation whenever ASCAP issues a blanket license to a television network for a single fee, why would it not also be automatically illegal for ASCAP to negotiate and issue blanket licenses to individual radio or television stations or to other users who perform copyrighted music for profit? . . . Likewise, if the present network licenses issued through ASCAP on behalf of its members are per se violations, why would it not be equally illegal for the members to authorize ASCAP to issue licenses establishing various categories of uses that a network might have for copyrighted music and setting a standard fee for each described use?

Although the Court of Appeals apparently thought the blanket license could be saved in some or even many applications, it seems to us that the per se rule does not accommodate itself to such flexibility and that the observations of the Court of Appeals with respect to remedy tend to impeach the per se basis for the holding of liability.[5]

CBS would prefer that ASCAP be authorized, indeed directed, to make all its compositions available at standard per-use rates within negotiated categories of use. . . .[6] But if this in itself or in conjunction with blanket licensing constitutes illegal price fixing by copyright owners, CBS urges

---

[5] . . . The Court of Appeals would apparently not outlaw the blanket license across the board but would permit it in various circumstances where it is deemed necessary of sufficiently desirable. It did not even enjoin blanket licensing with the television networks, the relief it realized would normally follow a finding of per se illegality of the license in that context. Instead, as requested by CBS, it remanded to the District Court to require ASCAP to offer in addition to blanket licensing some competitive form of per-use licensing. But per-use licensing by ASCAP, as recognized in the consent decrees, might be even more susceptible to the per se rule than blanket licensing.

The rationale for this unusual relief in a per se case was that "[t]he blanket license is not simply a 'naked restraint' ineluctably doomed for extinction.". . . To the contrary, the Court of Appeals found that the blanket license might well "serve a market need" for some. . . . This, it seems to us, is not the per se approach, which does not yield so readily to circumstances, but in effect is a rather bobtailed application of the rule of reason, bobtailed in the sense that it is unaccompanied by the necessary analysis demonstrating why the particular licensing system is an undue competitive restraint.

[6] Surely, if ASCAP abandoned the issuance of all licenses and confined its activities to policing the market and suing infringers, it could hardly be said that member copyright owners would be in violation of the antitrust laws by not having a common agent issue per-use

that an injunction issue forbidding ASCAP to issue any blanket license or to negotiate any fee except on behalf of an individual member for the use of his own copyrighted work or works.[7] Thus, we are called upon to determine that blanket licensing is unlawful across the board. We are quite sure, however, that the per se rule does not require any such holding.

B

In the first place, the line of commerce allegedly being restrained, the performing rights to copyrighted music, exists at all only because of the copyright laws. Those who would use copyrighted music in public performances must secure consent from the copyright owner or be liable at least for the statutory damages for each infringement and, if the conduct is willful and for the purpose of financial gain, to criminal penalties. . . . Although the copyright law confers no rights on copyright owners to fix prices among themselves or otherwise to violate the antitrust laws, we would not expect that any market arrangements reasonably necessary to effectuate the rights that are granted would be deemed a per se violation of the Sherman Act. Otherwise, the commerce anticipated by the Copyright Act and protected against restraint by the Sherman Act would not exist at all or would exist only as a pale reminder of what Congress envisioned.[8]

C

More generally, in characterizing this conduct under the per se rule, . . . our inquiry must focus on whether the effect and, here because it tends to show effect, . . . the purpose of the practice is to threaten the proper operation of our predominantly free market economy—that is, whether the practice facially appears to be one that would always or almost always tend to restrict competition and decrease output, and in what portion of the market, or instead one designed to "increase economic efficiency and render markets more rather than less competitive.". . .

The blanket license, as we see it, is not a "naked restraint of trade with no purpose except stifling of competition," *White Motor Co.* v. *United*

---

licenses. Under the copyright laws, those who publicly perform copyrighted music have the burden of obtaining prior consent. . . .

[7] In its complaint, CBS alleged that it would be "wholly impracticable" for it to obtain individual licenses directly from the composers and publishing houses, but it now says that it would be willing to do exactly that if ASCAP were enjoined from granting blanket licenses to CBS or its competitors in the network television business.

[8] . . . Because a musical composition can be "consumed" by many different people at the same time and without the creator's knowledge, the "owner" has no real way to demand reimbursement for the use of his property except through the copyright laws *and* an effective way to enforce those legal rights. . . . It takes an organization of rather large size to monitor most or all uses and to deal with users on behalf of the composers. Moreover, it is insufficient [sic.] to have too many such organizations duplicating each other's monitoring of use.

States, 372 U.S. 253, 263 (1963), but rather accompanies the integration of sales, monitoring, and enforcement against unauthorized copyright use. . . . As we have already indicated, ASCAP and the blanket license developed together out of the practical situation in the market place: thousands of users, thousands of copyright owners, and millions of compositions. Most users want unplanned, rapid and indemnified access to any and all of the repertory of compositions, and the owners want a reliable method of collecting for the use of their copyrights. Individual sales transactions in this industry are quite expensive, as would be individual monitoring and enforcement, especially in light of the resources of single composers. . . .

A middleman with a blanket license was an obvious necessity if the thousands of individual negotiations, a virtual impossibility, were to be avoided. Also, individual fees for the use of individual compositions would presuppose an intricate schedule of fees and uses, as well as a difficult and expensive reporting problem for the user and policing task for the copyright owner. Historically, the market for public performance rights organized itself largely around the single-fee blanket license, which gave unlimited access to the repertory and reliable protection against infringement. When ACASP's major and user-created competitor, BMI, came on the scene, it also turned to the blanket license.

With the advent of radio and television networks, market conditions changed, and the necessity for and advantages of a blanket license for those users may be far less obvious than is the case when the potential users are individual television or radio stations or the thousands of other individuals and organizations performing copyrighted compositions in public.[9] But even for television network licenses, ASCAP reduces costs absolutely by creating a blanket license that is sold only a few, instead of thousands,[10] of times, and that obviates the need for closely monitoring the networks to see that they do not use more than they pay for. . . . ASCAP also provides the necessary resources for blanket sales and enforcement, resources unavailable to the vast majority of composers and publishing houses. Moreover, a bulk license of some type is a necessary consequence of the integration necessary to achieve these efficiencies, and a necessary consequence of an aggregate license is that its price must be established.

D

This substantial lowering of costs, which is of course potentially bene-

---

[9] And of course changes brought about by new technology or new marketing techniques might also undercut the justification for the practice.

[10] The District Court found that CBS would require between 4,000 and 8,000 individual license transactions per year. . . .

ficial to both sellers and buyers, differentiates the blanket license from individual use licenses. The blanket license is composed of the individual compositions plus the aggregating service. Here, the whole is truly greater than the sum of its parts; it is, to some extent, a different product. The blanket license has certain unique characteristics: It allows the licensee immediate use of covered compositions, without the delay of prior individual negotiations,[11] and great flexibility in the choice of musical material. Many consumers clearly prefer the characteristics and cost advantages of this marketable package, . . . and even small performing rights societies that have occasionally arisen to compete with ASCAP and BMI have offered blanket licenses. . . . Thus, to the extent the blanket license is a different product, ASCAP is not really a joint sales agency offering the individual goods of many sellers, but is a separate seller offering its blanket license, of which the individual compositions are raw material.[12] ASCAP, in short, made a market in which individual composers are inherently unable to fully effectively compete. . . .

E

Finally, we have some doubt—enough to counsel against application of the per se rule—about the extent to which this practice threatens the "central nervous system of the economy," *United States* v. *Socony Vacuum,* 310 U.S. 150, 226 n. 59 (1940), that is, competitive pricing as the free market's means of allocating resources. Not all arrangements among actual or potential competitors that have an impact on price are per se violations of the Sherman Act or even unreasonable restraints. Mergers among competitors eliminate competition, including price competition, but they are not per se illegal and many of them withstand attack under any existing antitrust standard. Joint ventures and other cooperative arrangements are also not usually unlawful, at least not as price-fixing schemes, where the agreement on price is necessary to market the product at all.

Here, the blanket license fee is not set by competition among individual copyright owners, and it is a fee for the use of any of the compositions covered by the license. But the blanket license cannot be wholly equated with a simple horizontal arrangement among competitors. ASCAP does set the price for its blanket license, but that license is quite different from

---

[11] . . . Significantly, ASCAP deals only with nondramatic performance rights. Because of their nature, dramatic rights, such as for musicals, can be negotiated individually and well in advance of the time of performance. The same is true of various other rights, such as sheet music, recording, and synchronization, which are licensed on an individual basis.

[12] Moreover, because of the nature of the product—a composition can be simultaneously "consumed" by many users—composers have numerous markets and numerous incentives to produce, so the blanket license is unlikely to cause decreased output, one of the normal undesirable effects of a cartel. And since popular songs get an increased share of ASCAP's revenue distributions, composers compete even within the blanket license in terms of productivity and consumer satisfaction.

anything any individual owner could issue. The individual composers and authors have neither agreed not to sell individually in any other market nor use the blanket license to mask price fixing in such other markets. . . . Moreover, the substantial restraints placed on ASCAP and its members by the consent decree must not be ignored. The District Court found that there was no legal, practical, or conspiratorial impediment to CBS obtaining individual licenses; CBS, in short, had a real choice.

With this background in mind, which plainly enough indicates that over the years, and in the face of available alternatives, the blanket license has provided an acceptable mechanism for at least a large part of the market for the performing rights to copyrighted musical compositions, we cannot agree that it should automatically be declared illegal in all of its many manifestations. Rather, when attacked, it should be subjected to a more discriminating examination under the rule of reason. It may not ultimately survive that attack, but that is not the issue before us today.

IV

. . . . .

The judgment of the Court of Appeals is reversed and the case is remanded to that court for further proceedings consistent with this opinion.

It is so ordered.

MR. JUSTICE STEVENS, dissenting.

The Court holds that ASCAP's blanket license is not a species of price fixing categorically forbidden by the Sherman Act. I agree with that holding. The Court remands the case to the Court of Appeals, leaving open the question whether the blanket license as employed by ASCAP and BMI is unlawful under a rule of reason inquiry. I think that question is properly before us now and should be answered affirmatively.
. . . The record before this Court is a full one, reflecting extensive discovery and eight weeks of trial. The District Court's findings of fact are thorough and well supported. They clearly reveal that the challenged policy does have a significant adverse impact on competition. I would therefore affirm the judgment of the Court of Appeals.

I

. . . Neither ASCAP or BMI has ever offered to license anything less than its entire portfolio, even on an experimental basis. . . . It is the refusal to license anything less than the entire repertoire—rather than the decision to offer blanket licenses themselves—that raises the serious antitrust questions in this case.

II

Under our prior cases, there would be no question about the illegality of the blanket-only licensing policy if ASCAP and BMI were the exclusive sources of all licenses. A copyright, like a patent, is a statutory grant of monopoly privileges. The rules which prohibit a patentee from enlarging his statutory monopoly by conditioning a license on the purchase of unpatented goods, . . . or by refusing to grant a license under one patent unless the licensee also takes a license under another, are equally applicable to copyrights.[13]

It is clear, however, that the mere fact that the holder of several patents has granted a single package license covering them all does not establish any illegality. This point was settled by *Automatic Radio Manufacturing Co.* v. *Hazeltine Research, Inc.,* 339 U.S. 827, 834 and reconfirmed in *Zenith Radio Corp.* v. *Hazeltine Research, Inc.,* 395 U.S. 100, 137–138. The Court is therefore unquestionably correct in its conclusion that ASCAP's issuance of blanket licenses covering its entire inventory is not, standing alone, automatically unlawful. But both of those cases identify an important limitation on this rule. In the former, the Court was careful to point out that the record did not present the question whether the package license would have been unlawful if *Hazeltine* had refused to license on any other basis. . . . And in the latter case, the Court held that the package license was illegal because of such a refusal. . . .

Since ASCAP offers only blanket licenses, its licensing practices fall on the illegal side of the line drawn by the two *Hazeltine* cases. But there is a significant distinction: unlike *Hazeltine,* ASCAP does not have exclusive control of the copyrights in its portfolio, and it is perfectly possible—at least as a legal matter—for a user of music to negotiate directly with composers and publishers for whatever rights he may desire. The availability of a practical alternative alters what would otherwise be the competitive effect of a blockbooking or blanket licensing policy. ASCAP is therefore quite correct in its insistence that its blanket license cannot be categorically condemned on the authority of the blockbooking and package licensing cases. While these cases are instructive, they do not directly answer the question whether the ASCAP practice is unlawful.

The answer to that question depends on an evaluation of the effect of the practice on competition in the relevant market. And, of course, it is well settled that a sales practice that is permissible for a small vendor, at least when no coercion is present, may be unreasonable when employed by a company that dominates the market. . . . We therefore must consider what the record tells us about the competitive character of this market.

---

[13] Indeed, the leading cases condemning the practice of "blockbooking" involved copyrighted motion pictures, rather than patents. See *United States* v. *Paramount Pictures,* 334 U.S. 131; *United States* v. *Loew's Inc.,* 371 U.S. 38.

III

The market for music at issue here is wholly dominated by ASCAP-issued blanket licenses.[14] Virtually every domestic copyrighted composition is in the repertoire of either ASCAP or BMI. And again, virtually without exception, the only means that has been used to secure authority to perform such compositions is the blanket license.

The blanket all-or-nothing license is patently discriminatory. . . . The user purchases full access to ASCAP's entire repertoire, even though his needs could be satisfied by a far more limited selection. The price he pays for this access is unrelated either to the quantity or the quality of the music he actually uses, or, indeed to what he would probably use in a competitive system. Rather, in this unique all-or-nothing system, the price is based on a percentage of the user's advertising revenues, . . . a measure that reflects the customer's ability to pay . . . but is totally unrelated to factors—such as the cost, quality, or quantity of the product—that normally affect price in a competitive market. The ASCAP system requires users to buy more music than they want at a price which, while not beyond their ability to pay and perhaps not even beyond what is "reasonable" for the access they are getting, . . . may well be far higher than what they would choose to spend for music in a competitive system. It is a classic example of economic discrimination.

The record plainly establishes that there is no price competition between separate musical compositions. . . . Under a blanket license, it is no more expensive for a network to play the most popular current hit in prime time than it is to use an unknown competition as background music in a soap opera. Because the cost to the user is unaffected by the amount used on any program or on all programs, the user has no incentive to economize by, for example, substituting what would otherwise be less expensive songs for established favorites or by reducing the quantity of music used on a program. The blanket license thereby tends to encourage the use of more music, and also of a larger share of what is really more valuable music, than would be expected in a competitive system characterized by separate licenses. And since revenues are passed on to composers on a basis reflecting the character and frequency of the use of their music, . . . the tendency is to increase the rewards of the established composers at the expense of those less well known. Perhaps the prospect is in any event unlikely, but the blanket license does not present a new songwriter with any opportunity to try to break into the market by offering his product for sale at an unusually low price. The absence of that opportunity, however unlikely it may be, is characteristic of a cartelized rather than a competitive market. . . .

The current state of the market cannot be explained on the ground that

---

[14] As in the majority opinion, my references to ASCAP generally encompass BMI as well.

it could not operate competitively, or that issuance of more limited—and thus less restrictive—licenses by ASCAP is not feasible. The District Court's findings disclose no reason why music performing rights could not be negotiated on a per-composition or per-use basis, either with the composer or publisher directly or with an agent such as ASCAP. In fact, ASCAP now compensates composers and publishers on precisely those bases. . . . If distributions of royalties can be calculated on a per-use and per-composition basis, it is difficult to see why royalties could not also be collected in the same way. Moreover, the record also shows that where ASCAP's blanket license scheme does not govern, competitive markets do. A competitive market for synch rights exists,[15] and after the use of blanket licenses in the motion picture industry was discontinued, . . . such a market promptly developed in that industry. . . . In sum, the record demonstrates that the market at issue here is one that could be highly competitive, but is not competitive at all.

IV

Since the record describes a market that could be competitive and is not, and since that market is dominated by two firms engaged in a single, blanket method of dealing, it surely seems logical to conclude that trade has been restrained unreasonably. ASCAP argues, however, that at least as to CBS, there has been no restraint at all since the network is free to deal directly with copyright holders.

The District Court found that CBS had failed to establish that it was compelled to take a blanket license from ASCAP. While CBS introduced evidence suggesting that a significant number of composers and publishers, satisfied as they are with the ASCAP system, would be "disinclined" to deal directly with the network, the court found such evidence unpersuasive in light of CBS' substantial market power in the music industry and the importance to copyright holders of network television exposure. . . .

. . . ASCAP's underlying argument that CBS must be viewed as having acted with complete freedom in choosing the blanket license is not supported by the District Court's findings. The District Court did not find that CBS could cancel its blanket license "tomorrow" and continue to use music in its programming and compete with the other networks. Nor did the District Court find that such a course was without any risk or expense. Rather, the District Court's finding was that within a year, during which it would continue to pay some millions of dollars for its annual blanket license, CBS could be able to develop the needed machinery and enter into the necessary contracts. . . . In other words, although the barriers

---

[15] The synch right is the right to record a copyrighted song in synchronization with the film or videotape, and is obtained separately from the right to perform the music. It is the latter which is controlled by ASCAP and BMI. . . .

to direct dealing by CBS as an alternative to paying for a blanket license are real and significant, they are not insurmountable.

Far from establishing ASCAP's immunity from liability, these District Court findings, in my judgment, confirm the illegality of its conduct. Neither CBS nor any other user has been willing to assume the costs and risks associated with an attempt to purchase music on a competitive basis. The fact that an attempt by CBS to break down the ASCAP monopoly might well succeed does not preclude the conclusion that smaller and less powerful buyers are totally foreclosed from a competitive market.[16] Despite its size, CBS itself may not obtain music on a competitive basis without incurring unprecedented costs and risks. The fear of unpredictable consequences, coupled with the certain and predictable costs and delays associated with a change in its method of purchasing music, unquestionably inhibits any CBS management decision to embark on a competitive crusade. Even if ASCAP offered CBS a special bargain to forestall any such crusade, that special arrangement would not cure the marketwide restraint.

Whatever management decision CBS should or might have made, it is perfectly clear that the question whether competition in the market has been unduly restrained is not one that any single company's management is authorized to answer. It is often the case that an arrangement among competitors will not serve to eliminate competition forever, but only to delay its appearance or to increase the costs of new entry. That may well be the state of this market. Even without judicial intervention, the ASCAP monopoly might eventually be broken by CBS, if the benefits of doing so outweigh the significant costs and risks involved in commencing direct dealing.[17] But that hardly means that the blanket licensing policy at issue here is lawful. An arrangement that produces marketwide price discrimination and significant barriers to entry unreasonably restrains trade even if the discrimination and the barriers have only a limited life expectancy. History suggests, however, that these restraints have an enduring character.

Antitrust policy requires that great aggregations of economic power be closely scrutinized. That duty is especially important when the aggrega-

---

[16] For an individual user, the transaction costs involved in direct dealing with individual copyright holders may well be prohibitively high, at least in the absence of any broker or agency routinely handling such requests. Moreover, the District Court found that writers and publishers support and prefer the ASCAP system to direct dealing. . . . While their apprehension at direct dealing with CBS could be overcome, the District Court found, by CBS' market power and the importance of television exposure, a similar conclusion is far less likely with respect to other users.

[17] The risks involved in such a venture appear to be substantial. One significant risk, which may be traced directly to ASCAP and its members, relates to music "in the can"—music which has been performed on shows and movies already in the network's inventory, but for which the network must still secure performing rights. The networks accumulate substantial inventories of shows "in the can.". . .

tion is composed of statutory monopoly privileges. Our cases have repeatedly stressed the need to limit the privileges conferred by patent and copyright strictly to the scope of the statutory grant. The record in this case plainly discloses that the limits have been exceeded and that ASCAP and BMI exercise monopoly powers that far exceed the sum of the privileges of the individual copyright holders. Indeed, ASCAP itself argues that its blanket license constitutes a product that is significantly different from the sum of its component parts. I agree with that premise, but I conclude that the aggregate is a monopolistic restraint of trade proscribed by the Sherman Act.

PART TWO

Indirect Conspiracies and Oligopoly

3

Trade Association Activities

The problem of distinguishing between those trade association activities which serve to improve businessmen's knowledge of market conditions and thereby make competition more perfect, and those which have as their purpose the elimination of competition, is often a difficult one. The dissemination of trade statistics, for example, may result in greater price uniformity, either by making competition more perfect—theoretically, better knowledge enables entrepreneurs to perform their economic functions more intelligently—or by making overt collusion unnecessary—potential price-cutters might be deterred by the knowledge that such moves would become immediately and widely known.

Although difficult, the problem is not insoluble. The following cases indicate that it is possible to distinguish the legal from the illegal, the economically desirable from the economically undesirable. In *American Column and Lumber Co.* v. *United States*,[1] one of the first such cases to reach the Supreme Court, it was held that minute disclosure of the operations of individual members provided the lumber manufacturers' trade organization with information that was used to convince firms of the necessity of maintaining a spirit of harmony. This substitution of cooperation for competition was found to have gone too far: the Sherman Act had been violated. The *Cement Institute* case set forth the doctrine that collusive adoption of a delivered price system by members of a trade association was an unfair method of competition within the meaning of the Federal Trade Commission Act. In the *Tag Manufacturers* case, the various criteria which have evolved over the years for determining the permissible sphere of trade association activities were applied to exonerate the circulation of some price information by an association whose members accounted for some 95 percent of the industry's capacity. A comparison of the *Tag* case with those preceding it illustrates the development of these criteria and throws light on what may be a broader interpretation of the legality of the exchange of certain types of trade information. Of

---

[1] 257 U.S. 377 (1921).

course, as *Container Corporation* and *U.S. Gypsum* illustrate (see Chapter 2 above), certain activities will continue to be challenged.

Federal Trade Commission v. *Cement Institute*
333 U.S. 683 (1948)
MR. JUSTICE BLACK delivered the opinion of the Court.

We granted certiorari to review the decree of the Circuit Court of Appeals which, with one judge dissenting, vacated and set aside a cease and desist order issued by the Federal Trade Commission against the respondents. . . . Those respondents are: The Cement Institute . . . ; the 74 corporate members of the Institute; and 21 individuals who are associated with the Institute. . . .

The proceedings were begun by a Commission complaint of two counts. The first charged that certain alleged conduct set out at length constituted an unfair method of competition in violation of Section 5 of the Federal Trade Commission Act. . . . The core of the charge was that the respondents had restrained and hindered competition in the sale and distribution of cement by means of a combination among themselves made effective through mutual understanding or agreement to employ a multiple basing point system of pricing. It was alleged that this system resulted in the quotation of identical terms of sale and identical prices for cement by the respondents at any given point in the United States. This system had worked so successfully, it was further charged, that for many years prior to the filing of the complaint, all cement buyers throughout the nation, with rare exceptions, had been unable to purchase cement for delivery in any given locality from any one of the respondents at a lower price or on more favorable terms than from any of the other respondents.

The second count of the complaint, resting chiefly on the same allegations of fact set out in Count I, charged that the multiple basing point system of sales resulted in systematic price discriminations between the customers of each respondent. These discriminations were made, it was alleged, with the purpose of destroying competition in price between the various respondents in violation of Section 2 of the Clayton Act, . . . as amended by the Robinson-Patman Act. . . .

Resting upon its findings, the Commission ordered that respondents cease and desist from "carrying out any planned common course of action, understanding, agreement, combination, or conspiracy" to do a number of things . . . , all of which things, the Commission argues, had to be restrained in order effectively to restore individual freedom of action among the separate units in the cement industry. . . .

Jurisdiction. At the very beginning we are met with a challenge to the Commission's jurisdiction. . . . [Respondents'] argument runs this way: Count I in reality charges a combination to restrain trade. Such a combi-

nation constitutes an offense under Section 1 of the Sherman Act . . . .
Hence, continue respondents, the Commission, whose jurisdiction is limited to "unfair methods of competition," is without power to institute
proceedings. . . . Assuming, without deciding, that the conduct charged
in each count constitutes a violation of the Sherman Act, we hold that the
Commission does have jurisdiction to conclude that such conduct may
also be an unfair method of competition and hence constitute a violation
of Section 5 of the Federal Trade Commission Act. . . .

The Multiple Basing Point Delivered Price System. Since the multiple
basing point delivered price system of fixing prices and terms of cement
sales is the nub of this controversy, it will be helpful at this preliminary
stage to point out in general what it is and how it works. A brief reference
to the distinctive characteristics of "factory" or "mill prices" and
"delivered prices" is of importance to an understanding of the basing
point delivered price system here involved.

Goods may be sold and delivered to customers at the seller's mill or
warehouse door or may be sold free on board (f.o.b.) trucks or railroad
cars immediately adjacent to the seller's mill or warehouse. In either
event the actual cost of the goods to the purchaser is, broadly speaking,
the seller's "mill price" plus the purchaser's cost of transportation. However, if the seller fixes a price at which he undertakes to deliver goods to
the purchaser where they are to be used, the cost to the purchaser is the
"delivered price." A seller who makes the "mill price" identical for all
purchasers of like amount and quality simply delivers his goods at the
same place (his mill) and for the same price (price at the mill). He thus receives for all f.o.b. mill sales an identical net amount of money for like
goods from all customers. But a "delivered price" system creates compli-
cations which may result in a seller's receiving different net returns from
the sale of like goods. The cost of transporting 500 miles is almost always
more than the cost of transporting 100 miles. Consequently if customers
100 and 500 miles away pay the same "delivered price," the seller's net
return is less from the more distant customer. This difference in the producer's net return from sales to customers in different localities under a
"delivered price" system is an important element in the charge under
Count I of the complaint and is the crux of Count II.

The best known early example of a basing point price system was
called "Pittsburgh plus." It related to the price of steel. The Pittsburgh
price was the base price, Pittsburgh being therefore called a price basing
point. In order for the system to work, sales had to be made only at delivered prices. Under this system the delivered price of steel from anywhere in the United States to a point of delivery anywhere in the United
States was in general the Pittsburgh price plus the railroad freight rate
from Pittsburgh to the point of delivery. Take Chicago, Illinois, as an
illustration of the operation and consequences of the system. A Chicago
steel producer was not free to sell his steel at cost plus a reasonable profit.

He must sell it at the Pittsburgh price plus the railroad freight rate from Pittsburgh to the point of delivery. Chicago steel customers were by this pricing plan thus arbitrarily required to pay for Chicago produced steel the Pittsburgh base price plus what it would have cost to ship the steel by rail from Pittsburgh to Chicago had it been shipped. The theoretical cost of this ficitious shipment became known as "phantom freight." But had it been economically possible under this plan for a Chicago producer to ship his steel to Pittsburgh, his "delivered price" would have been merely the Pittsburgh price, although he actually would have been required to pay the freight from Chicago to Pittsburgh. Thus the "delivered price" under these latter circumstances required a Chicago (non-basing point) producer to "absorb" freight costs. That is, such a seller's net returns became smaller and smaller as his deliveries approached closer and closer to the basing point.

Several results obviously flow from use of a single basing point system such as "Pittsburgh plus" originally was. One is that the "delivered prices" of all producers in every locality where the deliveries are made are always the same regardless of the producers' different freight costs. Another is that sales made by a non-base mill for delivery at different localities result in net receipts to the seller which vary in amounts equivalent to the "phantom freight" included in, or the "freight absorption" taken from the "delivered price."

As commonly employed by respondents, the basing point system is not single but multiple. That is, instead of one basing point, like that in "Pittsburgh plus," a number of basing point localities are used. In the multiple basing point system, just as in the single basing point system, freight absorption or phantom freight is an element of the delivered price on all sales not governed by a basing point actually located at the seller's mill. And all sellers quote identical delivered prices in any given locality regardless of their different costs of production and their different freight expenses. Thus the multiple and single systems function in the same general manner and produce the same consequences—identity of prices and diversity of net returns.[1] Such differences as there are in matters here pertinent are therefore differences of degree only. . . .

---

[1] The Commission in its findings explained . . . , "The formula used to make this system operative is that the delivered price at any location shall be the lowest combination of base price plus all-rail freight. Thus, if Mill A has a base price of $1.50 per barrel, its delivered price at each location where it sells cement will be $1.50 per barrel plus the all-rail freight from its mill to the point of delivery, except that when a sale is made for delivery at a location at which the combination of the base price plus all-rail freight from another mill is a lower figure, Mill A uses this lower combination so that its delivered price at such location will be the same as the delivered price of the other mill. At all locations where the base price of Mill A plus freight is the lowest combination, Mill A recovers $1.50 net at the mill, and at locations where the combination of base price plus freight of another mill is lower, Mill A shrinks its mill net sufficiently to equal that price. Under these conditions it is obvious that the highest mill net which can be recovered by Mill A is $1.50 per barrel, and on sales where it has been necessary to shrink its mill net in order to match the delivered price of another mill, its net recovery at the mill is less than $1.50.". . .

Findings and Evidence.   It is strongly urged that the Commission failed to find, as charged in both counts of the complaint, that the respondents had by combination, agreements, or understandings among themselves utilized the multiple basing point delivered price system as a restraint to accomplish uniform prices and terms of sale. A subsidiary contention is that assuming the Commission did so find, there is no substantial evidence to support such a finding. We think that adequate findings of combination were made and that the findings have support in the evidence.

The Commission's findings of fact set out at great length and with painstaking detail numerous concerted activities carried on in order to make the multiple basing point system work in such way that competition in quality, price and terms of sale of cement would be non-existent, and that uniform prices, job contracts, discounts, and terms of sale would be continuously maintained. . . . Among the collective methods used to accomplish these purposes, according to the findings, were boycotts; discharge of uncooperative employees; organized opposition to the erection of new cement plants; selling cement in a recalcitrant price cutter's sales territory at a price so low that the recalcitrant was forced to adhere to the established basing point prices; discouraging the shipment of cement by truck or barge; and preparing and distributing freight rate books which provided respondents with similar figures to use as actual or "phantom" freight factors, thus guaranteeing that their delivered prices (base prices plus freight factors) would be identical on all sales whether made to individual purchasers under open bids or to governmental agencies under sealed bids. These are but a few of the many activities of respondents which the Commission found to have been done in combination to reduce or destroy price competition in cement. . . .

Thus we have a complaint which charged collective action by respondents designed to maintain a sales technique that restrained competition, detailed findings of collective activities by groups of respondents to achieve that end, then a general finding that respondents maintained the combination, and finally an order prohibiting the continuance of the combination. It seems impossible to conceive that anyone reading these findings in their entirety could doubt that the Commission found that respondents collectively maintained a multiple basing point delivered price system for the purpose of suppressing competition in cement sales. The findings are sufficient. The contention that they are not is without substance. . . .

Although there is much more evidence to which reference could be made, we think that the following facts shown by evidence in the record, some of which are in dispute, are sufficient to warrant the Commission's finding of concerted action.

When the Commission rendered its decision there were about 80 cement manufacturing companies in the United States operating about 150 mills. Ten companies controlled more than half of the mills and there were substantial corporate affiliations among many of the others. This concentration of productive capacity made concerted action far less difficult than it would otherwise have been. The belief is prevalent in the industry that because of the standardized nature of cement, among other reasons, price competition is wholly unsuited to it. That belief is historic. It has resulted in concerted activities to devise means and measures to do away with competition in the industry. Out of those activities came the multiple basing point delivered price system. Evidence shows it to be a handy instrument to bring about elimination of any kind of price competition. The use of the multiple basing point delivered price system by the cement producers has been coincident with a situation whereby for many years, with rare exceptions, cement has been offered for sale in every given locality at identical prices and terms by all producers. Thousands of secret sealed bids have been received by public agencies which corresponded in prices of cement down to a fractional part of a penny.[2]

Occasionally foreign cement has been imported, and cement dealers have sold it below the delivered price of the domestic product. Dealers who persisted in selling foreign cement were boycotted by the domestic producers. Officers of the Institute took the lead in securing pledges by producers not to permit sales f.o.b. mill to purchasers who furnished their own trucks, a practice regarded as seriously disruptive of the entire delivered price structure of the industry.

During the depression in the 1930s, slow business prompted some producers to deviate from the prices fixed by the delivered price system. Meetings were held by other producers; an effective plan was devised to punish the recalcitrants and bring them into line. The plan was simple but successful. Other producers made the recalcitrant's plant an involuntary base point. The base price was driven down with relatively insignificant losses to the producers who imposed the punitive basing point, but with heavy losses to the recalcitrant who had to make all its sales on this basis. In one instance, where a producer had made a low public bid, a punitive base point price was put on its plant and cement was reduced 10¢ per barrel; further reductions quickly followed until the base price at which this recalcitrant had to sell its cement dropped to 75¢ per barrel, scarcely one-half of its former base price of $1.45. Within six weeks after the base price hit 75¢ capitulation occurred and the recalcitrant joined a Portland cement association. Cement in that locality then bounced back to $1.15, later to $1.35, and finally to $1.75.

The foregoing are but illustrations of the practices shown to have been utilized to maintain the basing point price system. Respondents offered testimony that cement is a standardized product, that "cement is cement," that no differences existed in quality or usefulness, and that purchasers demanded delivered price quotations because of the high cost of

---

[2] A footnote table pointed out that each of eleven companies, bidding for a 6,000-barrel U.S. government order in 1936, entered sealed bids of $3.286854 per barrel. IMS.

transportation from mill to dealer. There was evidence, however, that the Institute and its members had, in the interest of eliminating competition, suppressed information as to the variations in quality that sometimes exist in different cements. Respondents introduced the testimony of economists to the effect that competition alone could lead to the evolution of a multiple basing point system of uniform delivered prices and terms of sale for an industry with a standardized product and with relatively high freight costs. These economists testified that for the above reasons no inferences of collusion, agreement, or understanding could be drawn from the admitted fact that cement prices of all United States producers had for many years almost invariably been the same in every given locality in the country. There was also considerable testimony by other economic experts that the multiple basing point system of delivered prices as employed by respondents contravened accepted economic principles and could only have been maintained through collusion.

The Commission did not adopt the views of the economists produced by the respondents. It decided that even though competition might tend to drive the price of standardized products to a uniform level, such a tendency alone could not account for the almost perfect identity in prices, discounts, and cement containers which had prevailed for so long a time in the cement industry. The Commission held that the uniformity and absence of competition in the industry were the results of understandings or agreements entered into or carried out by concert of the Institute and the other respondents. It may possibly be true, as respondents' economists testified, that cement producers will, without agreement express or implied and without understanding explicit or tacit, always and at all times (for such has been substantially the case here) charge for their cement precisely, to the fractional part of a penny, the price their competitors charge. Certainly it runs counter to what many people have believed, namely, that without agreement, prices will vary—that the desire to sell will sometimes be so strong that a seller will be willing to lower his prices and take his chances. We therefore hold that the Commission was not compelled to accept the views of respondents' economist-witnesses that active competition was bound to produce uniform cement prices. The Commission was authorized to find understanding, express or implied, from evidence that the industry's Institute actively worked, in cooperation with various of its members, to maintain the multiple basing point delivered price system; that this pricing system is calculated to produce, and has produced, uniform prices and terms of sale throughout the country; and that all of the respondents have sold their cement substantially in accord with the pattern required by the multiple basing point system. . . .

Unfair Methods of Competition.   We sustain the Commission's holding that concerted maintenance of the basing point delivered price system is an unfair method of competition prohibited by the Federal Trade Commission Act. . . .

We cannot say that the Commission is wrong in concluding that the delivered-price system as here used provides an effective instrument which, if left free for use of the respondents, would result in complete destruction of competition and the establishment of monopoly in the cement industry. . . . We uphold the Commission's conclusion that the basing point delivered price system employed by respondents is an unfair trade practice which the Trade Commission may suppress.[3]

The Price Discrimination Charge in Count Two. The Commission found that respondents' combination to use the multiple basing point delivered price system had effected systematic price discrimination in violation of Section 2 of the Clayton Act as amended by the Robinson-Patman Act. . . .

The Commission held that the varying mill nets received by respondents on sales between customers in different localities constituted a "discrimination in price between different purchasers" within the prohibition of Section 2(a), and that the effect of this discrimination was the substantial lessening of competition between respondents. The Circuit Court of Appeals reversed the Commission on this count. It agreed that respondents' prices were unlawful insofar as they involved the collection of phantom freight, but it held that prices involving only freight absorption came within the "good faith" proviso of Section 2(b).

The respondents contend that the differences in their net returns from sales in different localities which result from use of the multiple basing point delivered price system are not price discriminations within the meaning of Section 2(a). If held that these net return differences are price discriminations prohibited by Section 2(a), they contend that the discriminations were justified under Section 2(b) because "made in good faith to meet an equally low price of a competitor." Practically all the arguments presented by respondents in support of their contentions were considered by this Court and rejected in 1945 in *Corn Products Co.* v. *Federal Trade Comm'n* . . . , and in the related case of *Federal Trade Comm'n* v. *Staley Co.* . . . Consequently, we see no reason for again reviewing the questions that were there decided.

In the *Corn Products* case the Court, in holding illegal a single basing point system, specifically reserved decision upon the legality under the Clayton Act of a multiple basing point price system, but only in view of the "good faith" proviso of Section 2(b), and referred at that point to the companion *Staley* opinion. . . . The latter case held that a seller could not justify the adoption of a competitor's basing point price system under Section 2(b) as a good faith attempt to meet the latter's equally low price. Thus the combined effect of the two cases was to forbid the adoption for sales purposes of any basing point pricing system. . . .

---

[3] While we hold that the Commission's findings of combination were supported by evidence, that does not mean that existence of a "combination" is an indispensable ingredient of an "unfair method of competition" under the Trade Commission Act. . . .

Section 2(*b*) permits a single company to sell one customer at a lower price than it sells to another if the price is "made in good faith to meet an equally low price of a competitor." But this does not mean that Section 2(*b*) permits a seller to use a sales system which constantly results in his getting more money for like goods from some customers than he does from others. We held to the contrary in the *Staley* case. . . . Each of the respondents, whether all its mills were basing points or not, sold some cement at prices determined by the basing point formula and governed by other base mills. Thus, all respondents to this extent adopted a discriminatory pricing system condemned by Section 2. As this in itself was evidence of the employment of the multiple basing point system by the respondents as a practice rather than as a good faith effort to meet "individual competitive situations," we think the Federal Trade Commission correctly concluded that the use of this cement basing point system violated the Act. Nor can we discern under these circumstances any distinction between the "good faith" proviso as applied to a situation involving only phantom freight and one involving only freight absorption. Neither comes within its terms. . . .

The Order.   There are several objections to the Commission's cease and desist order. We consider the objections, having in mind that the language of its prohibitions should be clear and precise in order that they may be understood by those against whom they are directed. . . . But we also have in mind that the Commission has a wide discretion generally in the choice of remedies to cope with trade problems entrusted to it by the Commission Act. . . .

There is a special reason, however, why courts should not lightly modify the Commission's orders made in efforts to safeguard a competitive economy. . . .

In the present proceeding the Commission has exhibited the familiarity with the competitive problems before it which Congress originally anticipated the Commission would achieve from its experience. The order it has prepared is we think clear and comprehensive. At the same time the prohibitions in the order forbid no activities except those which if continued would directly aid in perpetuating the same old unlawful practices. Nor do we find merit to the charges of surplusage in the order's terms.

Most of the objections to the order appear to rest on the premise that its terms will bar an individual cement producer from selling cement at delivered prices such that its net return from one customer will be less than from another, even if the particular sale be made in good faith to meet the lower price of a competitor. The Commission disclaims that the order can possibly be so understood. Nor do we so understand it. As we read the order, all of its separate prohibiting paragraphs and subparagraphs, which need not here be set out, are modified and limited by a preamble. This preamble directs that all of the respondents "do forthwith cease and desist from entering into, continuing, cooperating in, or carrying out any planned common course of action, understanding, agreement, combination, or conspiracy between and among any two or more of said respondents, or between any one or more of said respondents and others not parties hereto, to do or perform any of the following things. . . ." Then follow the prohibitory sentences. It is thus apparent that the order by its terms is directed solely at concerted, not individual activity on the part of the respondents. . . .

The Commission's order should not have been set aside by the Circuit Court of Appeals. Its judgment is reversed and the cause is remanded to that court with directions to enforce the order.

It is so ordered.

MR. JUSTICE DOUGLAS and MR. JUSTICE JACKSON took no part in the consideration or decision of these cases.

[MR. JUSTICE BURTON dissented.]

Tag Manufacturers Institute v. Federal Trade Commission
174 F.2d 452 (1st. Cir. 1949)

Before MAGRUDER, Chief Judge, WOODBURY, Circuit Judge, and PETERS, District Judge.

MAGRUDER, Chief Judge.

Petitioners in this case ask us . . . to review and set aside or modify a cease and desist order of the Federal Trade Commission. . . .

On May 2, 1941, the Commission issued its complaint. . . . The complaint alleged that . . . petitioners "have entered into and carried out an understanding, agreement, combination, and conspiracy to restrict, restrain, suppress and eliminate price competition in the sale and distribution of said tag products" in interstate commerce; that pursuant to said agreement, petitioners "have fixed and maintained, and still fix and maintain, uniform prices, terms and conditions of sale for said tag products"; that the acts and practices of petitioners "have a dangerous tendency to and have actually hindered and prevented price competition" in the sale of tags in interstate commerce, have placed in petitioners the power to control and enhance prices on said products, have unreasonably restrained such commerce "and constitute unfair methods of competition in commerce within the intent and meaning of the Federal Trade Commission Act.". . .

The manufacturing petitioners sell and distribute approximately 95 percent of the tag products purchased and used in the United States, with 55 percent of the business of the industry shared by the four largest manufacturers.

Certain standardized tags are made in advance of sale and sold out of stock, such as plain unprinted stock shipping tags. However, over 80 percent of the business is in made-to-order tags, the varieties of which are almost unlimited, representing as they do selective combinations of materials and processes, or component elements, in various sizes and shapes. The much greater part of the products of the industry, particularly of made-to-order tags, is sold direct to consumers, but there is a considerable volume of sales to distributors and others for resale. To some extent, tag manufacturers buy from other manufacturers, for resale, types of tags which they do not themselves manufacture. Orders for tags are generally small in dollar value, averaging between $20 to $40, and a thousand or more orders for tags are placed with manufacturers each business day.

In such an industry, it would evidently not be practicable for a manufacturer to give a price on each order, based upon an individual cost estimate of that order. Hence, early in the history of the industry, manufacturers began to issue price lists to their salesmen, distributors and customers. The simple stock tags were customarily listed at stated prices for the finished product. With respect to the more elaborate, and infinitely various made-to-order tags, the price lists would enumerate the prices of the various basic components, such as tag stock, strings, wires, punches, eyelets, stapling, gumming, printing, etc.—from which the price for any particular tag, made up from the desired combination of components, might be computed.

. . . The price list does serve to indicate to the trade the scale of prices which the seller hopes and expects to maintain in the generality of future transactions until further notice. . . . In other words, from the nature of things it is reasonably to be expected that off-list sales would be the exception rather than the rule, and that the greater portion of sales would be at the prices stated in the seller's current price list. This is particularly true in an industry such as the tag industry, with its wide variety of products and tremendous number of sales transactions each of small dollar volume on the average.

The issuance of price lists by tag manufacturers had become established as a general practice in the industry prior to the formation of the Institute and prior to the execution of the various Tag Industry Agreements, later to be described, which formed the principal basis of the Commission's complaint against petitioners.

The Institute was organized in 1933, and has operated continuously since that time. All the manufacturing petitioners have become members of the Institute. At all times since its organization, the active management of the Institute has been in the hands of petitioner Frank H. Baxter, its secretary-treasurer and executive director. The Institute has concerned itself with typical trade association activities, and among other things has fostered efforts at more refined standardization of tag products and components thereof.

While the National Industrial Recovery Act . . . was in effect, a Code of Fair Competition for the Tag Industry was promulgated. . . . Under the Code, a so-called "open-price plan of selling" was prescribed, under which each member of the industry was required to file a schedule of his prices and terms of sale. . . . Further, it was provided that no member of the industry "shall sell such product for less than such price or upon terms or conditions more favorable" than stated in his filed price schedule. . . .

After the National Industrial Recovery Act was invalidated . . . members of the industry adopted a succession of four Tag Industry Agreements, so-called, in 1935, 1936, 1937 and 1940. The 1940 agreement was in effect when the Commission's complaint was filed, and was still in effect at the time of the final hearing before the Commission. . . .

. . . [T]he agreements were concerned chiefly with the reporting and dissemination of industry statistics. . . .

Article II of the 1940 agreement requires the Subscribers to report to the Associates (Baxter) the prices, terms and conditions of each sale or contract to sell any tag products covered by the agreement. . . .

A further important provision of Article II is as follows:

> . . . Nothing herein shall be construed as a limitation or restriction upon the right of each Subscriber independently to establish such prices, or such terms and conditions of sale, or policies of whatever nature affecting prices or sales, as he may deem expedient. Nothing in any report made to the Associates by any Subscriber hereunder shall be construed as a representation or pledge as to prices, terms, conditions of sale, or policies in current or future transactions.

With reference to the use by Baxter of the foregoing information, it is provided: . . .

> All information relating to prices, terms and conditions of sale disseminated to the Subscribers pursuant hereto shall be freely and fully available to public agencies, distributors and consumers of the products, and to any other properly interested persons; and shall be disseminated in the same manner as to Subscribers, to such of them as may apply therefore and arrange for payment of the reasonable cost of such service.
>
> Each Subscriber agrees that he will notify purchasers from him of the availability of this information.

Article III of the 1940 agreement requires each Subscriber throughout the life of the agreement to mail to Baxter "duplicates of every invoice or other memorandum of shipment or delivery of the products and of all credit memoranda applicable thereto. . . ." . . . It is provided that the Associates (Baxter) "shall compile the information submitted to them pursuant to this Article in such a way as not to disclose the information of any one Subscriber or the names of any purchasers. . . ."

Article IV of the 1940 agreement relates to the enforcement of the aforesaid reporting undertakings. It is recited that a breach of Article II or

Article III by any Subscriber . . . [shall cause to be imposed on him fines ranging from $5-$25 per day; and for] failure to transmit copies of invoices or memoranda as described in Article III "within ten (10) days after the date of mailing of the original of each such invoice or memorandum," the "liquidated damages" [fines] are stated to be an amount equivalent to 10 percent of the aggregate value of all the Subscriber's transactions proved to be affected by such failure, up to a maximum of $100 applicable to a single day's billing by one Subscriber. . . .

The final Article in the 1940 agreement, Article V, provides for termination of the entire agreement "by written agreement of a majority of the parties." . . . It is further provided that any manufacturer of tag products "may become a Subscriber to this Agreement at any time by signing the same and making the payments provided in Article I hereof." . . .

We think the evidence does warrant a finding that during the life of the Tag Industry Agreements there has from time to time been considerable list price uniformity with respect to types of tags constituting a large portion of the industry's business. Such a finding, in conjunction with the unchallenged finding that on the average 75 percent of the industry's business is done at list, would warrant the inference that during the years in which the Tag Industry Agreements have been in effect there has been a considerable uniformity of actual selling prices. The evidence does not, however, warrant the Commission's finding that the effect of the operation of the Tag Industry Agreements "has resulted in a substantial uniformity of prices for tags and tag products among the respondent members." In the first place, this implies that the instances of departure from uniformity are insignificant and unsubstantial—which certainly cannot be said. In the second place, there is no evidence that such uniformity as has existed is a result of the operation of the Tag Industry Agreements, for it does not appear whether there has been an increase or decrease of uniformity either in list prices or in actual selling prices since the agreements have been in operation. . . .

In support of its conclusion, the Commission refers to the provisions in the Tag Industry Agreements designed to insure compliance with the reporting commitments of the Subscribers. . . . The evidence is uncontradicted that Baxter's only concern with off-list transactions was to find out if they had been reported, after the event, as the agreement required. If the investigation indicated a violation of any reporting obligation of a Subscriber, Baxter would institute proceedings for assessment of "liquidated damages" as specified in the agreement. Total assessments for acts of noncompliance amounted to less than $10,000 for the period 1935–1941. The record contains not a single instance of an assessment for failure to adhere to a list price. . . .

Whether they are "liquidated damages," as they purport to be, or "penalties," as the Commission calls them, is hardly decisive. If the reporting commitments they are designed to buttress are otherwise lawful, the agreement does not become a violation of the anti-trust laws or the Federal Trade Commission Act merely because the reporting plan is accompanied by a penalty provision which would not be legally enforceable. . . .

There has been some tendency to look askance at reporting agreements between competitors, where the information exchanged is reserved exclusively to themselves and withheld from buyers or the public generally. Presumably this is because such secrecy more readily suggests the inference that the agreement is inspired by some unlawful purpose and precludes the argument that the information thus secretly exchanged serves a function similar to that of market information made available through the activities of commodity exchanges, trade journals, etc. . . .

. . . It is noteworthy that the Commission has failed to produce a single tag buyer to testify that he was unaware of the existence of this information service, or that he sought information from Baxter and could not get it, or that he sought to subscribe to the service and was refused. . . .

We have come to the conclusion that the reporting agreements herein, and the practices of petitioners thereunder, are lawful under the controlling authorities. . . . Once a price list has been issued to the trade it necessarily becomes pretty much public property. There is certainly nothing secret about it. It would be no great feat for a manufacturer to obtain copies of his competitors' price lists. The Tag Industry Agreement merely facilitates the assembling of such data. As to the obligation of Subscribers to report off-list sales and to furnish copies of all invoices, that is no more than the reporting of past transactions. The Commission has endeavored to show that the agreement was something more than this, that it was a price-fixing agreement having the purpose and actual effect of restraining and preventing price competition. We believe that such findings are unsupported by the evidence or by any reasonable inferences to be drawn therefrom. We say this with full recognition of our limited scope of review of findings of fact by the Commission. . . .

Since in our view of the case, the cease and desist order will have to be set aside, it becomes unnecessary for us to consider certain seriously pressed objections by petitioners to the breadth of the order.

A judgment will be entered setting aside the order of the Commission.

4

Oligopoly

In cases involving overwhelming market dominance, consciously achieved, either by a single firm or by direct conspiracy among competitors, the government had a relatively easy time of it. Once evidence of either had been established, the outcome, for all practical purposes, was no longer in doubt. (Whether *CalComp* and *Berkey* are the harbingers of change, as we have pointed out in Chapter 1, remains to be seen.) There remained, however, the thorny question of what to do about an industry made up of a small number of firms of intermediate size, whose behavior exhibited all the manifestations of a concerted agreement, yet where no such overt agreement could be found to exist. As we saw in Chapter 1, this issue was first explored (tentatively, to be sure) in *U.S.* v. *U.S. Steel*. In that case, U.S. Steel did not have a large enough market share to come under the doctrine of the *Standard Oil* decision, nor was the government able to establish the existence of a concerted agreement.

As a result of the *Steel* case, the government did not pursue cases of that type for many years. Consequently, the issue remained relatively dormant until 1946, when the *American Tobacco* decision was handed down. For the first time, it was established that the existence of an agreement could be inferred from the identical nature of the behavior of the defendants. This finding was hailed by a number of commentators as an implicit recognition by the Supreme Court of the economic theory of oligopoly—that in an industry characterized by a small number of firms, these firms, independently pursuing their self-interest, may refrain from actively competing with one another. Thus it seemed that the bulk of American industry, whose structural characteristics were not unlike those of an oligopoly, was now fair game for the antitrust authorities.

But the courts proceeded to fashion new distinctions. In *Triangle Conduit & Cable* the concept of conscious parallelism was developed, and the *Theatre Enterprises* case provided the Supreme Court with the opportunity to employ this concept as a device for distinguishing lawful from unlawful activity. The Government, therefore, became reluctant to continue its frontal attack on oligopoly, which after the *American Tobacco* decision had seemed so promising. Evidence that this reluctance has been justified can be found in the recent affirmation, by an evenly divided Supreme Court, of the Court of Appeals decision in *U.S.* v. *Chas. Pfizer,* which is apparently consistent with the doctrine enunciated in *Theatre Enterprises.* Thus, at least for the present, it does not appear as though the Supreme Court is prepared to reconsider its earlier position: independent but parallel action by firms in an industry with few sellers, taken in pursuit of each firm's self-interest, is acceptable.

American Tobacco Company v. United States

328 U.S. 781 (1946)

MR. JUSTICE BURTON delivered the opinion of the Court.

The petitioners are The American Tobacco Company, Liggett & Myers Tobacco Company, R. J. Reynolds Tobacco Company, American Suppliers, Inc., a subsidiary of American, and certain officials of the respective companies who were convicted by a jury, in the District Court of the United States for the Eastern District of Kentucky, of violating §§1 and 2 of the Sherman Anti-trust Act. . . .

Each petitioner was convicted on four counts: (1) conspiracy in restraint of trade, (2) monopolization, (3) attempt to monopolize, and (4) conspiracy to monopolize. Each count related to interstate and foreign trade and commerce in tobacco. No sentence was imposed under the third count as the Court held that count was merged in the second. Each petitioner was fined $5,000 on each of the other counts, making $15,000 for each petitioner and a total of $255,000. . . .

The Circuit Court of Appeals for the Sixth Circuit . . . affirmed each conviction. . . . This opinion is limited to the convictions under §2 of the Sherman Act. . . .

The issue . . . emphasized in the order allowing certiorari and primarily argued by the parties has not been previously decided by this Court. It is raised by the following instructions which were especially applicable to the second count but were related also to the other counts under §2 of the Sherman Act:

> Now, the term *monopolize* as used in Section 2 of the Sherman Act, as well as in the last three counts of the Information, means the joint acquisition or maintenance by the members of the conspiracy formed for that purpose, of the *power to control and dominate interstate trade and commerce in a commodity to such an extent that they are able, as a group, to exclude actual or potential competitors from the field, accompanied with the intention and purpose to exercise such power.*
>
> The phrase *attempt to monopolize* means the employment of methods, means and practices which would, if successful, accomplish monopolization, and which, though falling short, nevertheless approach so close as to

create a dangerous probability of it, which methods, means and practices are so employed by the members of and pursuant to a combination or conspiracy formed for the purpose of such accomplishment.

It is in no respect a violation of the law that a number of individuals or corporations, each acting for himself or itself, may own or control a large part, or even all of a particular commodity, or all the business in a particular commodity.

An essential element of the illegal monopoly or monopolization charged *in this case is the existence of a combination or conspiracy to acquire and maintain the power to exclude competitors to a substantial extent.*

Thus you will see that *an indispensable ingredient of each of the offenses charged in the Information is a combination or conspiracy.* (Italics supplied [by the Supreme Court].) . . .

. . . The trial court's instructions did not call for proof of an "actual exclusion" of competitors on the part of the petitioners. For the purposes of this opinion, we shall assume, therefore, that an actual exclusion of competitors by the petitioners was not claimed or established by the prosecution. Simply stated the issue is: Do the facts called for by the trial court's definition of monopolization amount to a violation of §2 of the Sherman Act? . . .

. . . To support the verdicts it was not necessary to show power and intent to exclude *all* competitors, or to show a conspiracy to exclude *all* competitors. The requirement stated to the jury and contained in the statute was only that the offenders shall "monopolize any part of the trade or commerce among the several States, or with foreign nations." This particular conspiracy may well have derived special vitality, in the eyes of the jury, from the fact that its existence was established, not through the presentation of a formal written agreement, but through the evidence of widespread and effective conduct on the part of petitioners in relation to their existing or potential competitors. . . .

First of all, the monopoly found by the jury to exist in the present cases appears to have been completely separable from the old American Tobacco Trust which was dissolved in 1911. The conspiracy to monopolize and the monopolization charged here do not depend upon proof relating to the old tobacco trust but upon a dominance and control by petitioners in recent years over purchases of the raw material and over the sale of the finished product in the form of cigarettes. The fact, however, that the purchases of leaf tobacco and the sales of so many products of the tobacco industry have remained largely within the same general group of business organizations for over a generation, inevitably has contributed to the ease with which control over competition within the industry and the mobilization of power to resist new competition can be exercised. . . . The verdicts indicate that practices of an informal and flexible nature were adopted and that the results were so uniformly beneficial to the petitioners in protecting their common interests as against those of competitors that, entirely from circumstantial evidence, the jury found that a combination or conspiracy existed among the petitioners from 1937 to 1940, with power and intent to exclude competitors to such a substantial extent as to violate the Sherman Act as interpreted by the trial court.

The position of the petitioners in the cigarette industry from 1931 to 1939 is clear. . . . [A]lthough American, Liggett and Reynolds gradually dropped in their percentage of the national domestic cigarette production from 90.7% in 1931 to 73.3%, 71% and 68%, respectively, in 1937, 1938 and 1939, they have accounted at all times for more than 68%, and usually for more than 75%, of the national production. The balance of the cigarette production has come from six other companies. No one of those six ever has produced more than 10.6% once reached by Brown & Williamson in 1939. . . . [W]hile the percentage of cigarettes produced by American, Liggett and Reynolds in the United States dropped gradually from 90.7% to 68%, their combined volume of production actually increased. . . .

The further dominance of American, Liggett and Reynolds within their special field of burley blend cigarettes, as compared with the so-called "10-cent cigarettes," is also apparent. In 1939, the 10-cent cigarettes constituted about 14½% of the total domestic cigarette production. Accordingly, the 68% of the total cigarette production enjoyed by American, Liggett and Reynolds amounted to 80% of that production within their special field of cigarettes. . . . In addition . . . they also produced over 63% of the smoking tobacco and over 44% of the chewing tobacco. They never were important factors in the cigar or snuff fields of the tobacco industry.

The foregoing demonstrates the basis of the claim of American, Liggett and Reynolds to the title of the "Big Three." . . . Without adverse criticism of it, comparative size on this great scale inevitably increased the power of these three to dominate all phases of their industry. . . . An intent to use this power to maintain a monopoly was found by the jury in these cases.

The record further shows that . . . [i]n each of the years 1937, 1938 and 1939, American, Liggett and Reynolds expended a total of over $40,000,000 a year for advertising. Such advertising is not here criticized as a business expense. Such advertising may benefit indirectly the entire industry, including the competitors of the advertisers. Such tremendous advertising, however, is also a widely published warning that these companies possess and know how to use a powerful offensive and defensive weapon against new competition. New competition dare not enter such a field, unless it be well supported by comparable national advertising. Large inventories of leaf tobacco, and large sums required for payment of federal taxes in advance of actual sales, further emphasize the effectiveness of a well financed monopoly in this field against potential competitors if there merely exists an intent to exclude such competitors. Prevention of all potential competition is the natural program for maintaining a monopoly here, rather than any program of actual exclusion. "Prevention" is cheaper and more effective than any amount of "cure." . . .

The verdicts show that the jury found that the petitioners conspired to fix prices and to exclude undesired competition against them in the purchase of the domestic type of flue-cured tobacco and of burley tobacco. These are raw materials essential to the production of cigarettes of the grade sold by the petitioners and also, to some extent, of the 10-cent grade of cigarettes which constitutes the only substantial competition to American, Liggett and Reynolds in the cigarette field of the domestic tobacco industry. . . . The petitioners purchased a combined total of between 50% and 80% of the domestic flue-cured tobacco. . . . [and] from 60% to 80% of the annual crop of burley.[1] . . .

The Government introduced evidence showing . . . that petitioners refused to purchase tobacco on these [auction] markets unless the other petitioners were also represented thereon. There were attempts made by others to open new tobacco markets but none of the petitioners would participate in them unless the other petitioners were present. Consequently, such markets were failures due to the absence of buyers. . . . In this way the new tobacco markets and their locations were determined by the unanimous consent of the petitioners and, in arriving at their determination, the petitioners consulted with each other as to whether or not a community deserved a market.

The Government presented evidence to support its claim that, before the markets opened, the petitioners placed limitations and restrictions on the prices which their buyers were permitted to pay for tobacco. None of the buyers exceeded these price ceilings. Grades of tobacco were formulated in such a way as to result in the absence of competition between the petitioners. There was manipulation of the price of lower grade tobaccos in order to restrict competition from manufacturers of the lower priced cigarettes. Methods used included the practice of the petitioners of calling their respective buyers in, prior to the opening of the annual markets, and giving them instructions as to the prices to be paid for leaf tobacco in each of the markets. These instructions were in terms of top prices or price ranges. The price ceilings thus established for the buyers were the same for each of them. . . .

Where one or two of the petitioners secured their percentage of the crop on a certain market or were not interested in the purchase of certain offerings of tobacco, their buyers, nevertheless, would enter the bidding in order to force the other petitioners to bid up to the maximum price. The petitioners were not so much concerned with the prices they paid for the

---

[1] Flue-cured, or bright tobacco, takes its name from the fact that it is cured in barns heated by a system of flues. Burley tobacco is produced largely in Kentucky and Tennessee, and is cured by exposing the leaves to the air, without heat. IMS.

leaf tobacco as that each should pay the same price for the same grade and that none would secure any advantage in purchasing tobacco. . . .

At a time when the manufacturers of lower priced cigarettes were beginning to manufacture them in quantity, the petitioners commenced to make large purchases of the cheaper tobacco leaves used for the manufacture of such lower priced cigarettes. No explanation was offered as to how or where this tobacco was used by petitioners. The compositions of their respective brands of cigarettes calling for the use of more expensive tobaccos remained unchanged during this period of controversy and up to the end of the trial. The Government claimed that such purchases of cheaper tobacco evidenced a combination and a purpose among the petitioners to deprive the manufacturers of cheaper cigarettes of the tobacco necessary for their manufacture, as well as to raise the price of such tobacco to such a point that cigarettes made therefrom could not be sold at a sufficiently low price to compete with the petitioners' more highly advertised brands.

The verdicts show also that the jury found that the petitioners conspired to fix prices and to exclude undesired competition in the distribution and sale of their principal products. The petitioners sold and distributed their products to jobbers and to selected dealers who bought at list prices less discounts. . . . The list prices charged and the discounts allowed by petitioners have been practically identical since 1923 and absolutely identical since 1928. Since the latter date, only seven changes have been made by the three companies and those have been identical in amount. The increases were first announced by Reynolds. American and Liggett thereupon increased their list prices in identical amounts.

The following record of price changes is circumstantial evidence of the existence of a conspiracy and of a power and intent to exclude competition coming from cheaper grade cigarettes. . . . [1931] was one of the worst years of financial and economic depression in the history of the country. On June 23, 1931, Reynolds, without previous notification or warning to the trade or public, raised the list price of Camel cigarettes, constituting its leading cigarette brand, from $6.40 to $6.85 a thousand. The same day, American increased the list price for Lucky Strike cigarettes, its leading brand, and Liggett the price for Chesterfield cigarettes, its leading brand, to the identical price of $6.85 a thousand. No economic justification for this raise was demonstrated. The president of Reynolds stated that it was "to express our own courage for the future and our own confidence in our industry." The president of American gave as his reason for the increase, "the opportunity of making some money." . . .The officials of Liggett claimed that they thought the increase was a mistake . . . but they contended that unless they also raised their list price for Chesterfields, the other companies would have greater resources to spend in advertising and thus would put Chesterfield cigarettes at a competitive disadvantage. This general price increase soon resulted in higher retail prices and in a loss in volume of sales. Yet in 1932, in the midst of the national depression with the sales of the petitioners' cigarettes falling off greatly in number, the petitioners still were making tremendous profits as a result of the price increase. Their net profits in that year amounted to more than $100,000,000. This was one of the three biggest years in their history.

. . . [A]fter the above described increase in list prices of the petitioners in 1931, the 10-cent brands made serious inroads upon the sales of the petitioners. These cheaper brands of cigarettes were sold at a list price of $4.75 a thousand and from 1931 to 1932 the sales of these cigarettes multiplied 30 times, rising from 0.28% of the total cigarette sales of the country in June, 1931, to 22.78% in November, 1932. In response to this threat of competition . . . the petitioners . . . cut the list price of their three leading brands . . . to $5.50 a thousand. The evidence tends to show that this cut was directed at the competition of the 10-cent cigarettes. . . . Following the . . . price cut by petitioners, the sales of the 10-cent brands fell off considerably. . . . When the sale of the 10-cent brands had dropped from 22.78% of the total cigarette sales in November, 1932, to 6.43% in May, 1933, the petitioners, in January, 1934, raised the list price of their leading brands from $5.50 back up to $6.10 a thousand. During the period that the list price of $5.50 a thousand was in effect, Camels and Lucky Strikes were being sold at a loss by Reynolds and American. Liggett at the same time was forced to curtail all of its normal business activities and cut its advertising to the bone in order to sell at this price. [Subsequent increases brought the price to $6.53 by 1940.] . . .

Certain methods used by the petitioners to secure a reduction in the retail prices of their cigarettes were in evidence. Reynolds and Liggett required their retailers to price the 10-cent brands at a differential of not more than 3 cents below Camel and Chesterfield cigarettes. They insisted upon their dealers correcting a greater differential by increasing the retail price of the 10 cent brands to 11 cents with petitioners' brands at 14 cents a package, or by requiring that petitioners' brands be priced at 13 cents with the lower priced cigarettes at 10 cents a package. . . . After the list price reductions were made and at the height of the price war, the petitioners commenced the distribution of posters advertising their brands at 10 cents a package and made attempts to have dealers meet these prices. . . . In addition to the use of . . . inducements, petitioners also used threats and penalties to enforce compliance with their retail price program. . . . There was evidence that when dealers received an announcement of the price increase from one of the petitioners and attempted to purchase some of the leading brands of cigarettes from the other petitioners at their unchanged prices before announcement of a similar change, the latter refused to fill such orders until their prices were also raised, thus bringing about the same result as if the changes had been precisely simultaneous.

It was on the basis of such evidence that the Circuit Court of Appeals found that the verdicts of the jury were sustained by sufficient evidence on each count. The question squarely presented here by the order of this Court in allowing the writs of certiorari is whether actual exclusion of competitors is necessary to the crime of monopolization in these cases under §2 of the Sherman Act. We agree with the lower courts that such actual exclusion of competitors is not necessary to that crime in these cases and that the instructions given to the jury, and hereinbefore quoted, correctly defined the crime. A correct interpretation of the statute and of the authorities makes it the crime of monopolizing, under §2 of the Sherman Act, for parties, as in these cases, to combine or conspire to acquire or maintain the power to exclude competitors from any part of the trade or commerce among the several states or with foreign nations, provided they also have such a power that they are able, as a group, to exclude actual or potential competition from the field and provided that they have the intent and purpose to exercise that power. See *United States v. Socony-Vacuum Oil Co.* . . .

It is not the form of the combination or the particular means used but the result to be achieved that the statute condemns. It is not of importance whether the means used to accomplish the unlawful objectives are in themselves lawful or unlawful. Acts done to give effect to the conspiracy may be in themselves wholly innocent acts. Yet, if they are part of the sum of the acts which are relied upon to effectuate the conspiracy which the statute forbids, they come within its prohibition. No formal agreement is necessary to constitute an unlawful conspiracy. Often crimes are a matter of inference deduced from the acts of the person accused and done in pursuance of a criminal purpose. Where the conspiracy is proved, as here, from the evidence of the action taken in concert by the parties to it, it is all the more convincing proof of an intent to exercise the power of exclusion acquired through that conspiracy. The essential combination or conspiracy in violation of the Sherman Act may be found in a course of dealing or other circumstances as well as in an exchange of words. . . . Where the circumstances are such as to warrant a jury in finding that the conspirators had a unity of purpose or a common design and understanding, or a meeting of minds in an unlawful arrangement, the conclusion that a conspiracy is established is justified. Neither proof of exertion of the power to exclude nor proof of actual exclusion of existing or potential competitors is essential to sustain a charge of monopolization under the Sherman Act. . . .

[The Court then took this opportunity to endorse the key portions of Judge Learned Hand's decision in *United States* v. *Aluminum Company of America,* 148 F.2d 416.]

In the present cases, the petitioners have been found to have conspired to establish a monopoly and also to have the power and intent to establish and maintain the monopoly. To hold that they do not come within the prohibition of the Sherman Act would destroy the force of that Act. Accordingly, the instructions of the trial court under §2 of the Act are approved and the judgment of the Circuit Court of Appeals is *Affirmed.*

MR. JUSTICE FRANKFURTER entirely agrees with the judgment and opinion in these cases. He, however, would have enlarged the scope of the orders allowing the petitions for certiorari so as to permit consideration of the alleged errors in regard to the selection of the jury.

MR. JUSTICE REED and MR. JUSTICE JACKSON took no part in the consideration or decision of these cases.

[MR. JUSTICE RUTLEDGE concurred.]

Triangle Conduit & Cable Co., Inc. v. *Federal Trade Commission*
168 F.2d 175 (7th Cir. 1948)[1]
Before SPARKS, KERNER, and MINTON, Circuit Judges.
KERNER, Circuit Judge.

Petitioners, fourteen corporate manufacturers of rigid steel conduit,[2] and five representatives of these corporations ask us to review and set aside a cease and desist order of the Federal Trade Commission, upon a complaint in two counts, charging that petitioners collectively have violated Section 5 of the Federal Trade Commission Act . . . , which declares unlawful "unfair methods of competition in commerce." . . .

In substance the first count alleged the existence and continuance of a conspiracy for the purpose and with the effect of substantially restricting and suppressing actual and potential competition in the distribution and sale of rigid steel conduit in commerce, effectuated by the adoption and use of a basing point method of quoting prices for rigid steel conduit. The second count did not rest upon an agreement or combination. It charged

---

[1] On April 25, 1949 the Supreme Court upheld the Federal Trade Commission order—affirmed in this lower court decision—under Count II of the complaint by a four-to-four tie vote. *Clayton Mark et al.* v. *Federal Trade Commission,* 336 U.S. 956 (1949) consists of a 23-word order. Mr. Justice Jackson took no part in the case. IMS.

[2] Rigid steel conduit is a steel pipe, used primarily in the roughing-in stage of building construction where electrical wiring is necessary in order to furnish a container for the wiring. It is a standard commodity made from standard steel pipe. IMS.

that each corporate petitioner and others violated Section 5 of the Federal Trade Commission Act "through their concurrent use of a formula method of making delivered price quotations with the knowledge that each did likewise, with the result that price competition between and among them was unreasonably restrained." It alleged that nearby customers were deprived of price advantages which they would have naturally enjoyed by reason of their proximity to points of production, and that such course of action created in said conduit sellers a monopolistic control over price in the sale and distribution of rigid steel conduit.

Petitioners answered the complaint. They denied any agreement or combination. After extensive hearings before a trial examiner, the Commission made its findings of fact and conclusions of law therefrom. It found the charges to be fully substantiated by the evidence. . . .

The argument [of defendants] is that there is no direct evidence of any conspiracy; that if the Commission made such a finding, it is based upon a series of inferences; and that the general use of the basing point method of pricing and the uniformity of prices does not justify an inference of conspiracy. We think there was direct proof of the conspiracy, but whether there was or not, in determining if such a finding is supported, it is not necessary that there be direct proof of an agreement. Such an agreement may be shown by circumstantial evidence. . . .

In this case there was evidence showing collective action to eliminate the Evanston basing point, and collective activities in promoting the general use of the formula presently to be noted. The record clearly establishes the fact that conduit manufacturers controlling 93% of the industry use a system under which they quote only delivered prices, which are determined in accordance with a formula consisting of a base price at Pittsburgh or Chicago plus rail freight, depending upon which basing point price controls at any particular destination or in any particular section of the United States; that as a result of using that formula the conduit producers were enabled to match their delivered price quotations, and purchasers everywhere were unable to find price advantages anywhere; and that purchaser at or near a place of production could not buy more cheaply from their nearby producer than from producers located at greater distances, and producers located at great distances from any given purchaser quoted as low a delivered price as that quoted by the nearest producer.

. . . Not only did petitioners match their bids when submitted under seal to agencies of public bodies, but each, with the knowledge of the others, did likewise—used the formula for the purpose of presenting to prospective private purchasers conditions of matched price quotations.

. . . Our study of this record and of applicable law has convinced us that the Commission was justified in drawing the inference that the petitioners acted in concert in a price-fixing conspiracy.

We now turn to consider petitioners' contention that the individual use of the basing point method, with knowledge that other sellers use it, does not constitute an unfair method of competition. This contention embodies the theory of the second count of the complaint. . . .

Briefly, the argument is that individual freight absorption is not illegal per se, and that the Commission's order is a denial of the right to meet competition. More specifically, petitioners say that conduit is a homogeneous product; that no buyer will pay more for the product of one seller than he will for that of another; that the buyer is not interested in the seller's cost of transportation or in any other factor of the seller's cost; that effective competition requires that traders have large freedom of action when conducting their own affairs; that in any particular market, the seller must adjust his own price to meet the market price or retire from that market altogether; that it has always been the custom of merchants to send their goods to distant markets to be sold at the prices there prevailing; that there is no lessening of competition, or injury to competitors, when a seller absorbs freight traffic to meet lawful competition; and that it is for the court to decide as a matter of law what constitutes an unfair method of competition under Section 5 of the Act. . . .

On the other hand, the Commission contends that unfair methods of competition include not only methods that involve deception, bad faith, and fraud, but methods that involve oppression or such as are against public policy because of their dangerous tendency unduly to hinder competition or create monopoly.

As already noted, each conduit seller knows that each of the other sellers is using the basing point formula; each knows that by using it he will be able to quote identical delivered prices and thus present a condition of matched prices under which purchasers are isolated and deprived of choice among sellers so far as price advantage is concerned. Each seller must systematically increase or decrease his mill net price for customers at numerous destinations in order to match the delivered prices of his competitors. Each seller consciously intends not to attempt the exclusion of any competition from his natural freight advantage territory by reducing the price, and in effect invites the others to share the available business at matched prices in his natural market in return for a reciprocal invitation.

In this situation, and indeed all parties to these proceedings agree, the legal question presented is identical with the one the Supreme Court considered in the *Federal Trade Commission* v. *Cement Institute* case. . . .

In the light of that opinion, we cannot say that the Commission was wrong in concluding that the individual use of the basing point method as here used does constitute an unfair method of competition. . . .

The Commission's order is affirmed and an enforcement decree will be entered. It is so ordered.

Theatre Enterprises, Inc. v. Paramount Film Distributing Corp.

346 U.S. 537 (1954)

MR. JUSTICE CLARK delivered the opinion of the Court.

Petitioner brought this suit for treble damages and an injunction under §§4 and 16 of the Clayton Act, alleging that respondent motion picture producers and distributors had violated the antitrust laws by conspiring to restrict "first-run"[1] pictures to downtown Baltimore theatres, thus confining its suburban theatre to subsequent runs and unreasonable "clearances."[2] After hearing the evidence a jury returned a general verdict for respondents. The Court of Appeals for the Fourth Circuit affirmed the judgment based on the verdict. . . .

The opinion of the Court of Appeals contains a complete summary of the evidence presented to the jury. We need not recite that evidence again. It is sufficient to note that petitioner owns and operates the Crest Theatre, located in a neighborhood shopping district some six miles from the downtown shopping center in Baltimore, Maryland. The Crest, possessing the most modern improvements and appointments, opened on February 26, 1949. Before and after the opening, petitioner, through its president, repeatedly sought to obtain first-run features for the theatre. Petitioner approached each respondent separately, initially requesting exclusive first-runs, later asking for first-runs on a "day-and-date" basis.[3] But respondents uniformly rebuffed petitioner's efforts and adhered to an established policy of restricting first-runs in Baltimore to the eight downtown theatres. Admittedly there is no direct evidence of illegal agreement between the respondents and no conspiracy is charged as to the independent exhibitors in Baltimore, who account for 63% of first-run exhibitions. The various respondents advanced much the same reasons for denying petitioner's offers. Among other reasons, they asserted that day-and-date first-runs are normally granted only to noncompeting theatres. Since the Crest is in "substantial competition" with the downtown theatres, a day-and-date arrangement would be economically unfeasible. And even if respondents wished to grant petitioner such a

---

[1] "Runs are successive exhibitions of a feature in a given area, first-run being the first exhibition in that area, second-run being the next subsequent, and so on. . . ." *United States* v. *Paramount Pictures, Inc.,* 334 U.S. 131, 144–45, n. 6 (1948).

[2] "A clearance is the period of time, usually stipulated in license contracts, which must elapse between runs of the same feature within a particular area or in specified theatres." *United States* v. *Paramount Pictures, Inc.,* 334 U.S. 131, 144, n. 6 (1948).

[3] A first-run "day-and-date" means that two theatres exhibit a first-run at the same time. Had petitioner's request for a day-and-date first-run been granted, the Crest and a downtown theatre would have exhibited the same features simultaneously.

license, no downtown exhibitor would waive his clearance rights over the Crest and agree to a simultaneous showing. As a result, if petitioner were to receive first-runs, the license would have to be an exclusive one. However, an exclusive license would be economically unsound because the Crest is a suburban theatre, located in a small shopping center, and served by limited public transportation facilities; and, with a drawing area of less than one-tenth that of a downtown theatre, it cannot compare with those easily accessible theatres in the power to draw patrons. Hence the downtown theatres offer far greater opportunities for the widespread advertisement and exploitation of newly released features, which is thought necessary to maximize the over-all return from subsequent runs as well as first-runs. The respondents, in the light of these conditions, attacked the guaranteed offers of petitioner, one of which occurred during the trial, as not being made in good faith. Respondents Loew's and Warner refused petitioner an exclusive license because they owned the three downtown theatres receiving their first-run product.

The crucial question is whether respondents' conduct toward petitioner stemmed from independent decision or from an agreement, tacit or express. To be sure, business behavior is admissible circumstantial evidence from which the fact finder may infer agreement. . . . But this Court has never held that proof of parallel business behavior conclusively establishes agreement or, phrased differently, that such behavior itself constitutes a Sherman Act offense. Circumstantial evidence of consciously parallel behavior may have made heavy inroads into the traditional judicial attitude toward conspiracy; but "conscious parallelism" has not yet read conspiracy out of the Sherman Act entirely. Realizing this, petitioner attempts to bolster its argument . . . by urging that the conscious unanimity of action by respondents should be "measured against the background and findings in the *Paramount* case." In other words, since the same respondents had conspired in the *Paramount* case to impose a uniform system of runs and clearances without adequate explanation to sustain them as reasonable restraints of trade, use of the same device in the present case should be legally equated to conspiracy. But the *Paramount* decrees, even if admissible, were only prima facie evidence of a conspiracy covering the area and existing during the period there involved. Alone or in conjunction with the other proof of the petitioner, they would form no basis for a directed verdict. Here each of the respondents had denied the existence of any collaboration and in addition had introduced evidence of the local conditions surrounding the Crest operation which, they contended, precluded it from being a successful first-run house. They also attacked the good faith of the guaranteed offers of the petitioner for first-run pictures and attributed uniform action to individual business judgment motivated by the desire for maximum revenue. This evidence, together with other testimony of an explanatory nature, raised fact issues requiring the trial judge to submit the issue of conspiracy to the jury. . . .

Affirmed.

United States v. Chas. Pfizer & Co., Inc.
367 F. Supp. 91 (S.D.N.Y. 1973)
. . . . .

CANNELLA, District Judge.

. . . This criminal antitrust prosecution was commenced by the filing of an indictment on August 17, 1961. The indictment charges that the defendants, Chas. Pfizer & Co., Inc. (Pfizer), American Cyanamid Company (Cyanamid) and Bristol-Myers Company (Bristol) and the co-conspirators, Olin Mathieson Chemical Corporation (Squibb) and the Upjohn Company (Upjohn) violated sections one and two of the Sherman Act . . . by virtue of their manufacture, use and sale of the broad spectrum antibiotic drug tetracycline. . . .

THE CHARGES

Each defendant is charged in three counts with having violated the Sherman Act during the years 1953–1961 by: (1) count one—conspiring to exclude competitors and fix and maintain prices in the broad spectrum antibiotic market in violation of section 1 of the Act; (2) count two—conspiring to monopolize; and (3) count three—monopolization of the broad spectrum antibiotic market, both in violation of section 2 of the Act. The terms of the conspiracy charged in counts one and two of the indictment are as follows:

    (a) The manufacture of tetracycline be confined to Pfizer, Cyanamid and Bristol;
    (b) The sale of tetracycline products be confined to Pfizer, Cyanamid, Bristol, Upjohn and Squibb;
    (c) The sale of bulk tetracycline be confined to Bristol and bulk tetracycline be sold by Bristol only to Upjohn and Squibb; and
    (d) The sale of broad spectrum antibiotic products by the defendant companies and the co-conspirator companies be at substantially identical and non-competitive prices.[1]

The indictment sets forth twelve "means and methods" by which the defendants are alleged to have accomplished the illegal acts specified:

    (a) Cyanamid licensed Pfizer and Bristol to use its aureomycin patent in the manufacture of tetracycline and refused to license all other applicants.

---

[1] Indictment, ¶45.

(b)   Pfizer licensed Cyanamid and Bristol under its tetracycline patent and refused to license all other applicants.

(c)   Cyanamid assisted and cooperated with Pfizer in obtaining for Pfizer a patent on tetracycline.

(d)   Pfizer, Cyanamid and Bristol suppressed litigation involving the validity of Pfizer's tetracycline patent.

(e)   Pfizer and Cyanamid and Bristol withheld pertinent and material information from the Patent Office and otherwise misled the Patent Office prior to the issuance of Pfizer's tetracycline patent.

(f)   Cyanamid acquired the competing Heyden patent application of tetracycline and abandoned the product claims therein.

(g)   Bristol sold bulk tetracycline only to Upjohn and Squibb. Each of the defendant companies refused to sell bulk tetracycline to all others except that Cyanamid sold a large amount of bulk tetracycline to Pfizer in early 1954 in assisting Pfizer to make a prompt entry into the tetracycline product market.

(h)   Bristol entered into agreements with Upjohn and Squibb respectively which required Upjohn and Squibb to purchase all their requirement of bulk tetracycline from Bristol.

(i)   Pfizer issued licenses to Upjohn and Squibb, respectively, limited, however, at Bristol's request, to the sale of tetracycline products.

(j)   Pfizer and Cyanamid maintained substantially identical, non-competitive and unreasonably high prices on terramycin products and aureomycin products, respectively.

(k)   Pfizer, Cyanamid, Bristol, Upjohn and Squibb each introduced its tetracycline products on the market at prices which were substantially identical with each other and which conformed to the non-competitive prices of terramycin products and aureomycin products in effect as of November 1953, and all these companies maintained such substantially identical, non-competitive and unreasonably high prices until at least July 1960.

(l)   Pfizer, Cyanamid, Bristol, Upjohn and Squibb each introduced its tetracycline products on the market in dosage forms and customer classifications substantially identical with the terramycin product and aureomycin product dosage forms and customer classifications in effect as of November 1953, and have continued to use such substantially identical dosage forms and classifications to date.[2]

These "means and methods" form the essence of the Government's case and outline its position at trial.

FACTUAL FRAMEWORK AND CONTENTIONS
OF THE PARTIES

•   •   •   •   •

Pre-tetracycline

Three effective, patented broad spectrum antibiotics were produced and marketed prior to the discovery of tetracycline in 1952: aureomycin,

---

[2] Id., ¶46.

terramycin, and chloromycetin. Aureomycin was first made available to the public in September 1948 by Cyanamid, who later obtained a patent for the drug in September 1949. Terramycin, the Pfizer product, was first marketed in March 1950 and was patented in July of that year. Chloromycetin was released in January 1949 and was patented in October 1949 by Parke-Davis, a pharmaceutical manufacturer not charged herein. During the pre-tetracycline period none of these manufacturers granted licenses or cross-licenses for these patented drugs. (No licenses or cross-licenses for these drugs have been subsequently granted, except to the extent indicated herein.)

Each of these antibiotics are prescription drugs, available only on a doctor's prescription and their sales, therefore, are largely dependent upon the physician's opinion of their effectiveness in treating the specific patient involved, despite their interchangeability due to chemical and functional similarities. Each manufacturer, cognizant of this, sought to price his drug, at a level which was competitive with the price fixed by the other two producers, thereby creating a stable and parallel price structure in the broad spectrum antibiotic market during the pre-tetracycline period. Price reductions by one manufacturer were met by all others during these years. Neither this price parallelism nor the companies' refusal to grant licenses for these earlier drugs is relied on by the Government to support the charges of the indictment.

Tetracycline

In June 1952, a Pfizer scientist, Dr. Conover, discovered tetracycline through the application of a deschlorination process to aureomycin. Tetracycline was considered by some to be a product superior to the earlier broad spectrum antibiotics, and Pfizer filed an application for a product and process patent in October 1952. The publicity surrounding the Pfizer discovery led Cyanamid to apply for a similar patent in March 1953. The entry of these competing claims caused the Patent Office to declare an interference (the first interference) on December 23, 1953.

This turn of events placed Pfizer in a difficult position. On the one hand, Pfizer believed that it possessed priority of invention (June 1952, as opposed to March 1953). On the other hand, if it were awarded the tetracycline patent, Pfizer's sole method of tetracycline production would be through the application of a deschlorination process to Cyanamid's patented aureomycin, thereby making it wholly dependent upon Cyanamid for bulk aureomycin, either by purchase or license to manufacture. In an attempt to resolve both the pending interference and the potential patent block, Pfizer's President, McKeen, met with Malcolm, President of Cyanamid's Lederle Laboratories in November 1953. These McKeen-Malcolm meetings, and not any antecedent event, mark the inception of the alleged conspiracy to violate the Sherman Act charged herein, according to the government's theory of the case. . . .

The government relies upon the testimony of the four individuals present at either the first or second meeting to develop what transpired at those times. All four agree that the subject under discussion was the pending Patent Office interference and the hollowness of a Pfizer victory in that proceeding unless such a victory was coupled with access to substantial quantities of aureomycin. Similarly, they agree that Cyanamid was concerned over a potential patent block to its tetracycline production, if Pfizer's Conover application ultimately prevailed. All of the participants testified that the agreement which emerged from these meetings and which settled the pending interference was a product of independent business judgment exercised in pursuit of their respective corporate interests. . . .

The Government does not contend that the . . . agreement is unlawful *per se*. Rather, the Government views the Pfizer-Cyanamid meetings of 1953 and the resulting agreement as initial evidence of the conspiracy charged in the indictment and that this evidence, viewed together with the subsequent factual developments, supports a conviction in this case. The record, which is fully developed by extensive direct and cross-examination, does not reveal that any discussion of prices, price fixing, exclusion of competitors or licensing restrictions occurred at the November meetings, and the individuals present have vigorously denied any illegal motive for their conduct. The testimony given stresses the business reasons for the action taken and the actors exercise of business judgment as free agents, and not as conspirators.

Bristol, the third defendant herein, was not dormant in the tetracycline field during the pendency of the Pfizer and Cyanamid applications. It developed a fermentation process for tetracycline production and applied for a process patent in October 1953. The Patent Office rejected this claim on December 8, 1953, and Bristol subsequently filed a second application asserting the separate patentability of tetracycline hydrochloride. This claim resulted in the declaration of another interference by the Patent Office in March 1954, to which Bristol, Pfizer and Cyanamid were parties (the second interference).

As was stated earlier, Cyanamid conceded priority of invention to Pfizer in February 1954, thereby increasing the likelihood that Pfizer would soon be issued the tetracycline patent. In that same month, a trade paper published a report that upon receipt of the patent, Pfizer would license no one, other than Cyanamid, to manufacture, use or sell the drug. Both of these events caused concern at Bristol, and Bristol, facing total exclusion from the tetracycline market, entered into communications with Pfizer. McKeen confirmed Pfizer's policy to license Cyanamid and no one else and he indicated that, upon receipt of the patent, Pfizer would bring infringement actions to enforce its rights. Despite these foreboding signs, Bristol, in mid-1954, entered into agreements with both Squibb and Upjohn under which Bristol was to sell bulk tetracycline to Squibb and Upjohn for resale under their own brand names and pursuant to which Squibb and Upjohn agreed to indemnify Bristol against any loss occasioned by an infringement action involving tetracycline.

Pfizer was issued the tetracycline patent on January 11, 1955. . . .

On the day the patent was issued, Pfizer commenced patent infringement actions against Bristol, Squibb and Upjohn. In response, Bristol, Squibb and Upjohn commenced independent actions seeking a declaratory judgment invalidating the Pfizer patent. . . .

During the pendency of these lawsuits, Upjohn attempted to negotiate an independent settlement with Pfizer. These efforts were unavailing however. Bristol, faced with the loss of its two largest customers, became most anxious to reach an early accord with Pfizer. These events prompted Bristol to renegotiate its agreement with Squibb and Upjohn in November 1955. . . .

From the outset, Pfizer maintained a policy against licensing others to produce tetracycline. This approach paralleled the nonlicensing policy adhered to by the manufacturers of the three pre-tetracycline broad spectrum antibiotics. The infringement actions against Bristol, Squibb and Upjohn can be said to demonstrate this approach. This policy was first abrogated to resolve the Pfizer-Cyanamid patent block, discussed earlier, but was otherwise enforced throughout this period until the "Broady incident."

John G. Broady, a lawyer-investigator, was tried in the New York state courts in November–December 1955 and convicted of wire-tapping numerous telephones, including those of Bristol and Squibb. The proof adduced at trial indicated that Broady had been retained by Pfizer's general counsel to make certain investigations and that his illegal actions stemmed therefrom. Bristol advantageously seized upon this Broady material by asserting that it would exploit the incident in its defense of the infringement suit. Pfizer, fearful that the adverse publicity created by such disclosure would damage its reputation, quickly arranged a meeting between McKeen and Schwartz, President of Bristol, to discuss the possibilities of a settlement.

The Pfizer-Bristol meetings took place on December 14 and 15, 1955 and were attended by McKeen, Schwartz and their respective patent counsel. The government contends that as a result of these meetings Bristol was brought into the alleged conspiracy for the first time.

The Pfizer-Bristol meetings resulted in a settlement of the pending litigation. A formal agreement embodying the agreed upon terms was executed on March 25, 1956. . . .

The Government contends that Bristol's entry into the alleged conspiracy occurred during the meetings of December 1955 and that the agreement reached was a product of conspiratorial conduct, although the legality of the agreement itself is not challenged. The Government does not question the propriety of Bristol's conduct antecedent to these meetings, despite the close parallels in Bristol's actions both before and after December 1955. The Government places stress on the limited nature of the licenses granted to Squibb and Upjohn, asserting that this evidences the crimes charged and Bristol's participation therein. In derogation of these charges, both McKeen and Schwartz have testified that the agreement was in all respects the product of sound business judgment that in no way involved actions of a conspiratorial nature.

The facts set out above are not, in the main, substantially in dispute. It is not disputed that throughout the period covered by the indictment the defendants and co-conspirators maintained substantially similar and parallel prices on tetracycline in the retail, wholesale and private hospital markets and that the only price deviations between them occurred in instances of competitive bidding.[3] Nor is it disputed that only the five firms named in the indictment manufactured or sold tetracycline on the domestic market, to the exclusion of all others. Rather, the question in this case is whether the Government has shown, by proof adduced at trial, that the defendants and co-conspirators agreed or conspired to fix or maintain prices, to exclude competitors and to monopolize the tetracycline market or achieved monopolization of that market by virtue of their conspiratorial conduct or whether the facts demonstrate nothing more than the natural and normal consequences of the exercise of independent business judgment and the free-flow of marketplace forces.

THE WEIGHT AND SUFFICIENCY OF THE EVIDENCE

. . . The *sine qua non* of the charges against these defendants is proof of an agreement or conspiracy to engage in the illegal acts of which they stand accused. Such agreement need not be in writing or formalized in other fashion. . . . The behavior and conduct of the alleged conspirators may sufficiently evidence the existence of a tacit agreement or conspiracy to commit the illegal acts. . . . The facts and circumstances of the case

---

[3] The prices charged by the defendants and co-conspirators during this period are based on suggested list prices which were discounted in order to arrive at the actual prices charged to the various purchasers. The discount structure was as follows: (1) retailer, 40% off list; (2) private hospital, 40% off list; (3) wholesaler, 40% off list reduced by an additional 16⅔% and then further reduced by 5% (Pfizer's discount was 40% plus 20% off list, Squibb's was 40% plus 16% and Upjohn did not sell to wholesalers). After discounting, the published (actual) prices for each available broad spectrum antibiotic, 250 milligram capsules in bottles of 100, during this period were:

List price	$51.00
Retail	30.60
Private hospital	30.60
Wholesale	24.22*

* Upjohn did not sell to wholesalers. Squibb's price to wholesalers was $25.70 and Pfizer's $24.48.

as a whole may be employed to prove the conduct necessary to sustain a conviction. . . .

The law governing count two, the conspiracy to monopolize, is in substance the same as that set out above, with an additional necessary element—proof of specific intent to monopolize. . . . The monopolization count of the indictment, count three, requires proof of monopoly power in the relevant market plus either proof of a combination or conspiracy to monopolize (proof of count two would suffice) or proof of other purposeful and intentional acts going to the acquisition, maintenance or exercise of the monopoly power. . . .

The Government has sought to prove the various elements of the crimes charged herein by means of circumstantial evidence and attempts to predicate a finding of guilt upon the inferences arising therefrom. The Court of Appeals has recognized circumstantial proof as proper evidence in this case, . . . and the rule is clear that such circumstantial evidence need not preclude every reasonable hypothesis of innocence in order to support a conviction, if the prosecution otherwise meets its burden of proof. . . .

In the face of the Government's circumstantial proof and argument, stand the defendants' vigorous and complete denials of the existence of any agreement or conspiracy to engage in the illegal acts charged in the indictment. The defendants assert that their conduct and the consequences flowing therefrom were the natural results of independently exercised business judgment and not the product of any illegal conspiracy. They urge that the proof demonstrates nothing more than "conscious parallelism" and similarity of business practices, neither of which are illegal standing alone. . . .

The Court, faced with a case that presents neither substantially disputed facts nor turns upon questions addressed to the applicable law but, rather, revolves around the possible interpretations emanating from the proof, finds guidance for the decisional process in Judge Medina's statement in the *Investment Bankers'* case, *United States* v. *Morgan,* 118 F. Supp. 621, 634 (S.D.N.Y. 1953).

> True it is that conspiracies whether by businessmen or others engaged in unlawful schemes are often hard to detect. No direct proof of agreement between the wrongdoers is necessary; circumstantial evidence of the illegal combination is here as elsewhere often most convincing and satisfactory. But, when all is said and done, it is the true and ultimate fact which must prevail. Either there is some agreement, combination or conspiracy or there is not. The answer must not be found in some crystal ball or vaguely sensed by some process of intuition, based upon a chance phrase used here or there, but in *the evidence adduced in the record of the case which must be carefully sifted, weighed and considered in its every aspect.* This is an arduous but necessary task. (emphasis added)

⋅ ⋅ ⋅ ⋅ ⋅

CONCLUSION

. . . After a careful and laborious review of all of the evidence in this case the Court finds that the Government has failed to meet its burden of proof. The Court is not convinced beyond a reasonable doubt that the defendants are guilty of the crimes of which they stand accused. The Court is not persuaded beyond the "hesitation point" that the defendants Pfizer and Cyanamid engaged in anything other than the exercise of independent business judgment when they entered into the January 11, 1954 agreement that settled the patent block situation. The Court is of a similar opinion with regard to the Bristol-Pfizer agreement that terminated the infringement suits in March 1956. The leverage Bristol gained from the "Broady" incident and not any secretive transaction best explains the impetus for this settlement. The parallel pricing among the tetracycline producers, standing alone, does not indicate price fixing,[4] and the court finds the parallel and substantially similar price structure maintained by Parke-Davis[5] and the absence of any provable agreement between the defendants are together sufficient to cast doubt upon an inference of illegality. The Court is not convinced that the illegal conduct alleged here is demonstrated by the "Patent Office"[6] or "excess profits" evidence[7] offered by the Government. In short, the Court finds that the Government has not proved the requisite elements of the crimes charged beyond a reasonable doubt. . . .

The motions for acquittal made by all defendants as to all counts of the indictment are granted. The Clerk of this Court is directed to enter judgment dismissing the indictment.

So ordered.

---

[4] The fact that tetracycline is a prescription drug and therefore, is largely dependent upon physicians' recommendations for its sales volume is significant to the pricing policies that emerged during the period in question. The defendants assert that the market structure for tetracycline and tetracycline products during these years followed that of the pre-tetracycline broad spectrum antibiotics (the legality of which has not been questioned), . . . and the Court agrees with this construction.

[5] The pricing policies of Parke-Davis, a competitor of the defendants not charged in the indictment, was largely excluded at the first trial. The Court of Appeals found this evidence most significant on the question of whether or not a conspiracy did in fact exist and premised its reversal, in large part, upon the restriction placed upon the use of this proof by the first trial judge. This Court has followed the mandate of the Court of Appeals and has carefully considered the Parke-Davis evidence. The Court concludes that this evidence is entitled to substantial weight and bears heavily against a verdict of guilty in this case. . . .

[6] This refers to the meetings attended by representatives of Pfizer, Bristol and Cyanamid at the time of the issuance of the tetracycline patent. These meetings were cited by the government as evidence of the conspiracy between Pfizer and Cyanamid. IMS.

[7] This Court is not convinced that excess profits demonstrate guilt any more than nominal profits would prove innocence of a price-fixing charge.

PART THREE

Mergers and the Problems They Pose

5

Mergers and Market Power

Traditionally, corporate mergers have been grouped into three categories: horizontal, vertical, and conglomerate. The cases presented in this chapter provide a history of the legislative and judicial attitudes toward mergers of the first two types, that is, those involving two or more firms in the same market and those in which the acquired firm is either a customer or a supplier of the acquiring firm. In the *Thatcher* case (which marked what most observers considered the judicial attenuation of the original Section 7 of the Clayton Act), the Court decided that the Federal Trade Commission's power to prevent mergers which might substantially lessen competition extended only to acquisitions of stock. This opened the way to merger via *asset* acquisition and, for all practical purposes, eliminated the Clayton Act as an effective antimerger weapon until 1950. Congress then enacted the Celler-Kefauver Amendment, which brought asset acquisitions under the purview of Section 7. It also eliminated the requirement that competition be shown to have been lessened "between the corporation . . . so acquired and the corporation making the acquisition," thereby extending the reach of Section 7, at least potentially, to horizontal and conglomerate mergers.

Brown Shoe represents the first comprehensive Supreme Court interpretation of the legal-economic goals of the amended Clayton Act. It provides useful insight into judicial treatment of such economic concepts as the geographic and product scope of a market. In the *Von's* decision, the Court extended the doctrine of reasonable probability of competitive injury to proscribe a horizontal merger where the effect on market concentration did not appear to be significant; in *General Dynamics,* however, the Court has seemingly retreated from this position (perhaps in deference to Justice Stewart's dissenting opinion in *Von's*).

181

Thatcher Manufacturing Company v. *Federal Trade Commission*
272 U.S. 554 (1926)
MR. JUSTICE McREYNOLDS delivered the opinion of the Court.

. . . . .

The Commission entered complaint against the petitioner, March 1, 1921, and charged that the latter contrary to Section 7 of the Clayton Act, first acquired the stock of four competing corporations—Lockport Glass Company, Essex Glass Company, Travis Glass Company and Woodbury Glass Company—and thereafter took transfers of all the business and assets of the first three and caused their dissolution. . . . [T]he Commission ruled that the acquisitions of all these stocks were unlawful and ordered the petitioner to cease and desist from ownership, operation, management and control of the assets, properties, rights, etc., of the Lockport, Essex and Travis Glass Companies secured through such stock ownership, and to divest itself of the assets, properties, rights, etc., formerly held by them. Also, that it should divest itself of the stock of the Woodbury Glass Company.

The court below held that the last-named company was not in competition with petitioner within the meaning of the statute and modified the order accordingly. Therein we agree and to that extent affirm its decree.

The court further ruled, in effect, that as the stocks of the remaining three companies were unlawfully obtained and ownership of the assets came through them, the Commission properly ordered the holder so to dispossess itself of the properties as to restore prior lawful conditions. With this we cannot agree. When the Commission institutes a proceeding based upon the holding of stock contrary to Section 7 of the Clayton Act, its power is limited by Section 11 to an order requiring the guilty person to cease and desist from such violation, effectually to divest itself of the stock, and to make no further use of it. The Act has no application to ownership of a competitor's property and business obtained prior to any action by the Commission, even though this was brought about through stock unlawfully held. The purpose of the Act was to prevent continued holding of stock and the peculiar evils incident thereto. If purchase of property has produced an unlawful status a remedy is provided through the courts. . . . The Commission is without authority under such circumstances.

Affirmed in part; reversed in part.

[MR. JUSTICE BRANDEIS, with whom the Chief Justice, MR. JUSTICE HOLMES and MR. JUSTICE STONE joined, dissented in part.]

Brown Shoe Co., Inc. v. United States

370 U.S. 294 (1962)

MR. CHIEF JUSTICE WARREN delivered the opinion of the Court.

I

This suit was initiated in November 1955 when the Government filed a civil action in the United States District Court for the Eastern District of Missouri alleging that a contemplated merger between the G. R. Kinney Company, Inc. (Kinney), and the Brown Shoe Company, Inc. (Brown), through an exchange of Kinney for Brown stock, would violate Section 7 of the Clayton Act. . . .

The Industry

The District Court found that although domestic shoe production was scattered among a large number of manufacturers, a small number of large companies occupied a commanding position. Thus, while the 24 largest manufacturers produced about 35% of the Nation's shoes, the top 4— International, Endicott-Johnson, Brown (including Kinney) and General Shoe—alone produced approximately 23% of the Nation's shoes or 65% of the production of the top 24.

In 1955, domestic production of nonrubber shoes was 509.2 million pairs, of which about 103.6 million pairs were men's shoes, about 271 million pairs were women's shoes, and about 134.6 million pairs were children's shoes. The District Court found that men's, women's, and children's shoes are normally produced in separate factories.

The public buys these shoes through about 70,000 retail outlets, only 22,000 of which, however, derive 50% or more of their gross receipts from the sale of shoes and are classified as "shoe stores" by the Census Bureau. These 22,000 shoe stores were found generally to sell (1) men's shoes only, (2) women's shoes only, (3) women's and children's shoes, or (4) men's, women's, and children's shoes.

The District Court found a "definite trend" among shoe manufacturers to acquire retail outlets. . . . Brown, itself, with no retail outlets of its own prior to 1951, had acquired 845 such outlets by 1956. Moreover, between 1950 and 1956 nine independent shoe store chains, operating 1,114 retail shoe stores, were found to have become subsidiaries of these large firms and to have ceased their independent operations.

And once the manufacturers acquired retail outlets, the District Court found there was a "definite trend" for the parent-manufacturers to supply an ever increasing percentage of the retail outlets' needs, thereby foreclosing other manufacturers from effectively competing for the retail accounts. Manufacturer-dominated stores were found to be "drying up" the available outlets for independent producers.

Another "definite trend" found to exist in the shoe industry was a decrease in the number of plants manufacturing shoes. And there appears to have been a concomitant decrease in the number of firms manufacturing shoes. In 1947, there were 1,077 independent manufacturers of shoes, but by 1954 their number had decreased about 10% to 970.[1]

Brown Shoe

Brown Shoe was found not only to have been a participant, but also a moving factor, in these industry trends. Although Brown had experimented several times with operating its own retail outlets, by 1945 it had disposed of them all. However, in 1951, Brown again began to seek retail outlets by acquiring the Nation's largest operator of leased shoe departments, Wohl Shoe Company (Wohl), which operated 250 shoe departments in department stores throughout the United States. Between 1952 and 1955 Brown made a number of smaller acquisitions. . . . In 1954, Brown made another major acquisition: Regal Shoe Corporation which, at the time, operated one manufacturing plant producing men's shoes and 110 retail outlets.

The acquisition of these corporations was found to lead to increased sales by Brown to the acquired companies. . . .

During the same period of time, Brown also acquired the stock or assets of seven companies engaged solely in shoe manufacturing. As a result, in 1955, Brown was the fourth largest shoe manufacturer in the country, producing about 25.6 million pairs of shoes or about 4% of the Nation's total footwear prouction.

Kinney

Kinney is principally engaged in operating the largest family-style shoe store chain in the United States. At the time of trial, Kinney was found to be operating over 400 such stores in more than 270 cities. These stores were found to make about 1.2% of all national retail shoe sales by dollar volume. Moreover, in 1955 the Kinney stores sold approximately 8 million pairs of nonrubber shoes or about 1.6% of the national pairage sales of such shoes. . . .

In addition to this extensive retail activity, Kinney owned and operated four plants which manufactured men's, women's, and children's shoes and whose combined output was 0.5% of the national shoe production in 1955, making Kinney the twelfth largest shoe manufacturer in the United States.

Kinney stores were found to obtain about 20% of their shoes from Kinney's own manufacturing plants. At the time of the merger, Kinney bought no shoes from Brown; however, in line with Brown's conceded

---

[1] U.S. Bureau of the Census, 1958 Census of Manufacturers, MC 58(2)-31A-6. By 1958, the number of independent manufacturers had decreased by another 10% to 872. *Ibid.*

reasons[2] for acquiring Kinney, Brown had, by 1957, become the largest outside supplier of Kinney's shoes, supplying 7.9% of all Kinney's needs.

. . . . .

III. LEGISLATIVE HISTORY

This case is one of the first to come before us in which the Government's complaint is based upon allegations that the appellant has violated Section 7 of the Clayton Act, as that section was amended in 1950. The amendments adopted in 1950 culminated extensive efforts over a number of years, on the parts of both the Federal Trade Commission and some members of Congress, to secure revision of a section of the antitrust laws considered by many observers to be ineffective in its then existing form. . . . In the light of this extensive legislative attention to the measure, and the broad, general language finally selected by Congress for the expression of its will, we think it appropriate to review the history of the amended Act in determining whether the judgment of the court below was consistent with the intent of the legislature. . . .

The dominant theme pervading congressional consideration of the 1950 amendments was a fear of what was considered to be a rising tide of economic concentration in the American economy. Apprehension in this regard was bolstered by the publication in 1948 of the Federal Trade Commission's study on corporate mergers. Statistics from this and other current studies were cited as evidence of the danger to the American economy in unchecked corporate expansions through merger. Other considerations cited in support of the bill were the desirability of retaining "local control" over industry and the protection of small businesses.[3] Throughout the recorded discussion may be found examples of Congress' fear not only of accelerated concentration of economic power on economic grounds, but also of the threat to other values a trend toward concentration was thought to pose.

What were some of the factors, relevant to a judgment as to the validity of a given merger, specifically discussed by Congress in redrafting Section 7?

---

[2] As stated in the testimony of Clark R. Gamble, President of Brown Shoe Company:
"It was our feeling, in addition to getting a distribution into the field of prices which we were not covering, it was also the feeling that as Kinney moved into the shopping centers in these free standing stores, they were going into a higher income neighborhood and they would probably find the necessity of up-grading and adding additional lines to their very successful operation that they had been doing and it would give us an opportunity we hoped to be able to sell them in that category. Besides that, it was a very successful operation and would give us a good diversified investment to stabilize our earnings." . . .

[3] . . . Cf. *United States* v. *Aluminum Co. of America,* 148 F.2d 416, 429 (C.A.2d Cir., per Learned Hand, J.): "Throughout the history of these [antitrust] statutes it has been constantly assumed that one of their purposes was to perpetuate and preserve, for its own sake and in spite of possible cost, an organization of industry in small units which can effectively compete with each other."

First, there is no doubt that Congress did wish to "plug the loophole" and to include within the coverage of the Act the acquisition of assets no less than the acquisition of stock.

Second, by the deletion of the "acquiring-acquired" language in the original text, it hoped to make plain that Section 7 applied not only to mergers between actual competitors, but also to vertical and conglomerate mergers whose effect may tend to lessen competition in any line of commerce in any section of the country.[4]

Third, it is apparent that a keystone in the erection of a barrier to what Congress saw was the rising tide of economic concentration, was its provision of authority for arresting mergers at a time when the trend to a lessening of competition in a line of commerce was still in its incipiency. Congress saw the process of concentration in American business as a dynamic force; it sought to assure the Federal Trade Commission and the courts the power to brake this force at its outset and before it gathered momentum.

Fourth, and closely related to the third, Congress rejected, as inappropriate to the problem it sought to remedy, the application to Section 7 cases of the standards for judging the legality of business combinations adopted by the courts in dealing with cases arising under the Sherman Act, and which may have been applied to some early cases arising under original Section 7.

Fifth, at the same time that it sought to create an effective tool for preventing all mergers having demonstrable anticompetitive effects, Congress recognized the stimulation to competition that might flow from particular mergers. When concern as to the Act's breadth was expressed, supporters of the amendments indicated that it would not impede, for example, a merger between two small companies to enable the combination to compete more effectively with larger corporations dominating the relevant market, nor a merger between a corporation which is financially healthy and a failing one which no longer can be a vital competitive factor in the market. The deletion of the word "community" in the original Act's description of the relevant geographic market is another illustration of Congress' desire to indicate that its concern was with the adverse effects of a given merger on competition only in an economically significant "section" of the country. Taken as a whole, the legislative history illuminates congressional concern with the protection of *competition,* not *competitors,* and its desire to restrain mergers only to the extent that such combinations may tend to lessen competition.

---

[4] That Section 7 was intended to apply to all mergers—horizontal, vertical or conglomerate—was specifically reiterated by the House Report on the final bill. H. R. Rep. No. 1191, 81st Cong., 1st Sess. 11. . . .

Sixth, Congress neither adopted nor rejected specifically any particular tests for measuring the relevant markets, either as defined in terms of product or in terms of geographic locus of competition, within which the anticompetitive effects of a merger were to be judged. Nor did it adopt a definition of the word "substantially," whether in quantitative terms of sales or assets or market shares or in designated qualitative terms, by which a merger's effects on competition were to be measured.

Seventh, while providing no definite quantitative or qualitative tests by which enforcement agencies could gauge the effects of a given merger to determine whether it may "substantially" lessen competition or tend toward monopoly, Congress indicated plainly that a merger had to be functionally viewed, in the context of its particular industry. That is, whether the consolidation was to take place in an industry that was fragmented rather than concentrated, that had seen a recent trend toward domination by a few leaders or had remained fairly consistent in its distribution of market shares among the participating companies, that had experienced easy access to markets by suppliers and easy access to suppliers by buyers or had witnessed foreclosure of business, that had witnessed the ready entry of new competition or the erection of barriers to prospective entrants, all were aspects, varying in importance with the merger under consideration, which would properly be taken into account.[5]

Eighth, Congress used the words "*may be* substantially to lessen competition" (emphasis supplied), to indicate that its concern was with probabilities, not certainties. Statutes existed for dealing with clear-cut menaces to competition; no statute was sought for dealing with ephemeral possibilities. Mergers with a probable anticompetitive effect were to be proscribed by this Act.

It is against this background that we must return to the case before us.

IV. THE VERTICAL ASPECTS OF THE MERGER

Economic arrangements between companies standing in a supplier-customer relationship are characterized as "vertical." The primary vice of a vertical merger or other arrangement tying a customer to a supplier is that, by foreclosing the competitors of either party from a segment of the market otherwise open to them, the arrangement may act as a "clog on competition," *Standard Oil Co. of California* v. *United States,* 337 U.S.

---

[5] Subsequent to the adoption of the 1950 amendments, both the Federal Trade Commission and the courts have, in the light of Congress' expressed intent, recognized the relevance and importance of economic data that places any given merger under consideration within an industry framework almost inevitably unique in every case. Statistics reflecting the shares of the market controlled by the industry leaders and the parties to the merger are, of course, the primary index of market power; but only a further examination of the particular market—its structure, history and probably future—can provide the appropriate setting for judging the probable anticompetitive effect of the merger. . . .

293, 314, which "deprive[s] . . . rivals of a fair opportunity to compete."[6] . . . Every extended vertical arrangement by its very nature, for at least a time, denies to competitors of the supplier the opportunity to compete for part or all of the trade of the customer-party to the vertical arrangement. However, the Clayton Act does not render unlawful all such vertical arrangements, but forbids only those whose effect "may be substantially to lessen competition, or to tend to create a monopoly" "in any line of commerce in any section of the country." . . . The "area of effective competition" must be determined by reference to a product market (the "line of commerce") and a geographic market (the "section of the country").

The Product Market

The outer boundaries of a product market are determined by the reasonable interchangeability of use or the cross-elasticity of demand between the product itself and substitutes for it.[7] However, within this broad market, well-defined submarkets may exist, which, in themselves, constitute product markets for antitrust purposes. *United States* v. *E. I. duPont de Nemours & Co.*, 353 U.S. 586, 593-595. The boundaries of such a submarket may be determined by examining such practical indicia as industry or public recognition of the submarket as a separate economic entity, the product's peculiar characteristics and uses, unique production facilities, distinct customers, distinct prices, sensitivity to price changes, and specialize vendors. Because Section 7 of the Clayton Act prohibits any merger which may substantially lessen competition "in *any* line of commerce" (emphasis supplied), it is necessary to examine the effects of a merger in each such economically significant submarket to determine if there is a reasonable probability that the merger will substantially lessen competition. If such a probability is found to exist, the merger is proscribed.

Applying these considerations to the present case, we conclude that the record supports the District Court's finding that the relevant lines of commerce are men's, women's, and children's shoes. These product lines are recognized by the public; each line is manufactured in separate plants; each has characteristics peculiar to itself rendering it generally noncompetitive with the others; and each is, of course, directed toward a distinct class of customers.

Appellant, however, contends that the District Court's definitions fail to recognize sufficiently "price/quality" and "age/sex" distinctions in

---

[6] In addition, a vertical merger may disrupt and injure competition when those independent customers of the supplier who are in competition with the merging customer, are forced either to stop handling the supplier's lines, thereby jeopardizing the goodwill they have developed, or to retain the supplier's lines, thereby forcing them into competition with their own supplier. . . .

[7] The cross-elasticity of production facilities may also be an important factor in defining a product market within which a vertical merger is to be viewed. . . .

shoes. Brown argues that the predominantly medium-priced shoes which it manufactures occupy a product market different from the predominantly low-priced shoes which Kinney sells. But agreement with that argument would be equivalent to holding that medium-priced shoes do not compete with low-priced shoes. We think the District Court properly found the facts to be otherwise. It would be unrealistic to accept Brown's contention that, for example, men's shoes selling below $8.99 are in a different product market from those selling above $9.00.

This is not to say, however, that "price/quality" differences, where they exist, are unimportant in analyzing a merger; they may be of importance in determining the likely effect of a merger. But the boundaries of the relevant market must be drawn with sufficient breadth to include the competing products of each of the merging companies and to recognize competition where, in fact, competition exists. Thus we agree with the District Court that in this case a further division of product lines based on "price/quality" differences would be "unrealistic."

Brown's contention that the District Court's product market definitions should have recognized further "age/sex" distinctions raises a different problem. Brown's sharpest criticism is directed at the District Court's finding that children's shoes constituted a single line of commerce. Brown argues, for example, that "a little boy does not wear a little girl's black patent leather pump" and that "[a] male baby cannot wear a growing boy's shoes." Thus Brown argues that "infants' and babies'" shoes, "misses' and children's" shoes and "youths' and boys'" shoes should each have been considered a separate line of commerce. Assuming, *arguendo,* that little boys' shoes, for example, do have sufficient peculiar characteristics to constitute one of the markets to be used in analyzing the effects of this merger, we do not think that in this case the District Court was required to employ finer "age/sex" distinctions than those recognized by its classifications of "men's," "women's," and "children's" shoes. Further division does not aid us in analyzing the effects of this merger. . . .

The Geographic Market

We agree with the parties and the District Court that insofar as the vertical aspect of this merger is concerned, the relevant geographic market is the entire Nation. The relationships of product value, bulk, weight and consumer demand enable manufacturers to distribute their shoes on a nationwide basis, as Brown and Kinney, in fact, do. The anticompetitive effects of the merger are to be measured within this range of distribution.

The Probable Effect of the Merger

Once the area of effective competition affected by a vertical arrangement has been defined, an analysis must be made to determine if the effect of the arrangement "may be substantially to lessen competition, or to tend to create a monopoly" in this market.

Since the diminution of the vigor of competition which may stem from a vertical arrangement results primarily from a foreclosure of a share of the market otherwise open to competitors, an important consideration in determining whether the effect of a vertical arrangement "may be substantially to lessen competition, or to tend to create a monopoly" is the size of the share of the market foreclosed. However, this factor will seldom be determinative. If the share of the market foreclosed is so large that it approaches monopoly proportions, the Clayton Act will, of course, have been violated; but the arrangement will also have run afoul of the Sherman Act. And the legislative history of Section 7 indicates clearly that the tests for measuring the legality of any particular economic arrangement under the Clayton Act are to be less stringent than those used in applying the Sherman Act. On the other hand, foreclosure of a *de minimis* share of the market will not tend "substantially to lessen competition."

Between these extremes, in cases such as the one before us, in which the foreclosure is neither of monopoly nor *de minimis* proportions, the percentage of the market foreclosed by the vertical arrangement cannot itself be decisive. In such cases, it becomes necessary to undertake an examination of various economic and historical factors in order to determine whether the arrangement under review is of the type Congress sought to proscribe.

A most important such factor to examine is the very nature and purpose of the arrangement.[8] Congress not only indicated that "the tests of illegality [under Section 7] are intended to be similar to those which the courts have applied in interpreting the same language as used in other sections of the Clayton Act," but also chose for Section 7 language virtually identical to that of Section 3 of the Clayton Act, 15 U.S.C. Section 14, which had been interpreted by this Court to require an examination of the interdependence of the market share foreclosed by, and the economic purpose of, the vertical arrangement. Thus, for example, if a particular vertical arrangement, considered under Section 3, appears to be a limited term exclusive-dealing contract, the market foreclosure must generally be significantly greater than if the arrangement is a tying contract before the arrangement will be held to have violated the Act. . . . The reason for this is readily discernible. The usual tying contract forces the customer to take a product or brand he does not necessarily want in order to secure one which he does desire. Because such an arrangement is inherently anticompetitive, we have held that its use by an established company is likely "substantially to lessen competition" although only a relatively

---

[8] Although it is "unnecessary for the Government to speculate as to what is in the 'back of the minds' of those who promote a merger," H.R. Rep. No. 1191, 81st Cong., 1st Sess. 8, evidence indicating the purpose of the merging parties, where available, is an aid in predicting the probable future conduct of the parties and thus the probable effects of the merger. *Swift & Co.* v. *United States,* 196 U.S. 375, 396; *United States* v. *Maryland & Virginia Milk Producers Assn.,* 167 F. Supp. 799, 804 (D.C.D.C.), aff'd, 362 U.S. 458.

small amount of commerce is affected. *International Salt Co.* v. *United States.* . . . Thus, unless the tying device is employed by a small company in an attempt to break into a market . . . the use of a tying device can rarely be harmonized with the strictures of the antitrust laws, which are intended primarily to preserve and stimulate competition. . . . On the other hand, requirement contracts are frequently negotiated at the behest of the customer who has chosen the particular supplier and his product upon the basis of competitive merit. . . . Of course, the fact that requirement contracts are not inherently anticompetitive will not save a particular agreement if, in fact, it is likely "substantially to lessen competition, or tend to create a monopoly." . . . Yet requirement contract may escape censure if only a small share of the market is involved, if the purpose of the agreement is to insure to the customer a sufficient supply of a commodity vital to the customer's trade or to insure to the supplier a market for his output and if there is no trend toward concentration in the industry. . . . Similar considerations are pertinent to a judgment under Section 7 of the Act.

The importance which Congress attached to economic purpose is further demonstrated by the Senate and House Reports on H. R. 2734, which evince an intention to preserve the "failing company" doctrine. . . . Similarly, Congress foresaw that the merger of two large companies or a large and a small company might violate the Clayton Act while the merger of two small companies might not, although the share of the market foreclosed be identical, if the purpose of the small companies is to enable them in combination to compete with larger corporations dominating the market.

The present merger involved neither small companies nor failing companies. In 1955, the date of this merger, Brown was the fourth largest manufacturer in the shoe industry with sales of approximately 25 million pairs of shoes and assets of over $72,000,000 while Kinney had sales of about 8 million pairs of shoes and assets of about $18,000,000. Not only was Brown one of the leading manufacturers of men's, women's, and children's shoes but Kinney, with over 350 retail outlets, owned and operated the largest independent chain of family shoe stores in the Nation. Thus, in this industry, no merger between a manufacturer and an independent retailer could involve a larger potential market foreclosure. Moreover, it is apparent both from past behavior of Brown and from the testimony of Brown's President, that Brown would use its ownership of Kinney to force Brown shoes into Kinney stores. Thus, in operation this vertical arrangement would be quite analogous to one involving a tying clause.[9]

Another important factor to consider is the trend toward concentration

---

[9] Moreover, ownership integration is a more permanent and irreversible tie than is contract integration. See Kessler and Stern, "Competition, Contract, and Vertical Integration," 69 *Yale L. J.* 1, 78 (1959).

in the industry. It is true, of course, that the statute prohibits a given merger only if the effect of *that* merger may be substantially to lessen competition. But the very wording of Section 7 requires a prognosis of the probable *future* effect of the merger.

The existence of a trend toward vertical integration, which the District Court found, is well substantiated by the record. Moreover, the court found a tendency of the acquiring manufacturers to become increasingly important sources of supply for their acquired outlets. The necessary corollary of these trends is the foreclosure of independent manufacturers from markets otherwise open to them. And because these trends are not the product of accident but are rather the result of deliberate policies of Brown and other leading shoe manufacturers, account must be taken of these facts in order to predict the probable future consequences of this merger. It is against this background of continuing concentration that the present merger must be viewed.

Brown argues, however, that the shoe industry is at present composed of large number of manufacturers and retailers, and that the industry is dynamically competitive. But remaining vigor cannot immunize a merger if the trend in that industry is toward oligopoly. . . . It is the probable effect of the merger upon the future as well as the present which the Clayton Act commands the courts and the Commission to examine.

Moreover, as we have remarked above, not only must we consider the probable effects of the merger upon the economics of the particular markets affected but also we must consider its probable effects upon the economic way of life sought to be preserved by Congress. Congress was desirous of preventing the formation of further oligopolies with their attendant adverse effects upon local control of industry and upon small business. Where an industry was composed of numerous independent units, Congress appeared anxious to preserve this structure. . . .

The District Court's findings, and the record facts, many of them set forth in Part I of this opinion, convince us that the shoe industry is being subjected to just such a cumulative series of vertical mergers which, if left unchecked, will be likely "substantially to lessen competition."

We reach this conclusion because the trend toward vertical integration in the shoe industry, when combined with Brown's avowed policy of forcing its own shoes upon its retail subsidiaries, may foreclose competition from a substantial share of the markets for men's, women's, and children's shoes, without producing any countervailing competitive, economic, or social advantages.

V. THE HORIZONTAL ASPECTS OF THE MERGER

An economic arrangement between companies performing similar functions in the production or sale of comparable goods or services is characterized as "horizontal." The effect on competition of such an arrangement depends, of course, upon its character and scope. Thus, its validity in the face of the antitrust laws will depend upon such factors as: the relative size and number of the parties to the arrangement; whether it allocates shares of the market among the parties; whether it fixes prices at which the parties will sell their product; or whether it absorbs or insulates competitors. Where the arrangement effects a horizontal merger between companies occupying the same product and geographic market, whatever competition previously may have existed in that market between the parties to the merger is eliminated. Section 7 of the Clayton Act, prior to its amendment, focused upon this aspect of horizontal combinations by proscribing acquisitions which might result in a lessening of competition between the acquiring and the acquired companies. The 1950 amendments made plain Congress' intent that the validity of such combinations was to be gauged on a broader scale: their effect on competition generally in an economically significant market.

Thus, again, the proper definition of the market is a "necessary predicate" to an examination of the competition that may be affected by the horizontal aspects of the merger. The acquisition of Kinney by Brown resulted in a horizontal combination at both the manufacturing and retailing levels of their businesses. Although the District Court found that the merger of Brown's and Kinney's *manufacturing* facilities was economically too insignificant to come within the prohibitions of the Clayton Act, the Government has not appealed from this portion of the lower court's decision. Therefore, we have no occasion to express our views with respect to that finding. On the other hand, appellant does contest the District Court's finding that the merger of the companies' *retail* outlets may tend substantially to lessen competition.

The Product Market

Shoes are sold in the United States in retail shoe stores and in shoe departments of general stores. These outlets sell: (1) men's shoes, (2) women's shoes, (3) women's or children's shoes, or (4) men's, women's or children's shoes. Prior to the merger, both Brown and Kinney sold their shoes in competition with one another through the enumerated kinds of outlets characteristic of the industry. . . .

The Geographic Market

The criteria to be used in determining the appropriate geographic market are essentially similar to those used to determine the relevant product market. . . . Moreover, just as a product submarket may have Section 7 significance as the proper "line of commerce," so may a geographic submarket be considered the appropriate "section of the country." . . . Congress prescribed a pragmatic, factual approach to the definition of the relevant market and not a formal, legalistic one. The geographic market selected must, therefore, both "correspond to the commercial realities" of the industry and be economically significant. Thus, although the geographic market in some instances may encompass the entire Nation, under other circumstances it may be as small as a single metropolitan area. . . . The fact that two merging firms have competed directly on the horizontal level in but a fraction of the geographic markets in which either has operated, does not, in itself, place their merger outside the scope of Section 7. That section speaks of "any . . . section of the country," and if anticompetitive effects of a merger are probable in "any" significant market, the merger—at least to that extent—is proscribed.

The parties do not dispute the findings of the District Court that the Nation as a whole is the relevant geographic market for measuring the anticompetitive effects of the merger viewed vertically or of the horizontal merger of Brown's and Kinney's manufacturing facilities. As to the retail level, however, they disagree. . . .

We believe, however, that the record fully supports the District Court's findings that shoe stores in the outskirts of cities compete effectively with stores in central downtown areas, and that while there is undoubtedly some commercial intercourse between smaller communities within a single "standard metropolitan area," the most intense and important competition in retail sales will be confined to stores within the particular communities in such an area and their immediate environs.

We therefore agree that the District Court properly defined the relevant geographic markets in which to analyze this merger as those cities with a population exceeding 10,000 and their environs in which both Brown and Kinney retailed shoes through their own outlets. Such markets are large enough to include the downtown shops and suburban shopping centers in areas contiguous to the city, which are the important competitive factors, and yet are small enough to exclude stores beyond the immediate environs of the city, which are of little competitive significance.

The Probable Effect of the Merger

Having delineated the product and geographic markets within which the effects of this merger are to be measured, we turn to an examination of the District Court's finding that as a result of the merger competition in the retailing of men's, women's and children's shoes may be lessened substantially in those cities in which both Brown and Kinney stores are located. . . .

. . . [W]e believe the record is adequate to support the findings of the District Court. While it is true that the court concentrated its attention on the structure of competition in the city in which it sat and as to which detailed evidence was most readily available, it also heard witnesses from no less than 40 other cities in which the parties to the merger operated. The court was careful to point out that it was on the basis of all the evidence that it reached its conclusions concerning the boundaries of the relevant markets and the merger's effects on competition within them. We recognize that variations of size, climate and wealth as enumerated by Brown exist in the relevant markets. However, we agree with the court below that the markets with respect to which evidence was received provide a fair sampling of all the areas in which the impact of this merger is to be measured. The appellant has not shown how the variables it has mentioned could affect the structure of competition within any particular market so as to require a change in the conclusions drawn by the District Court. Each competitor within a given market is equally affected by these factors, even though the city in which he does business may differ from St. Louis in size, climate or wealth. Thus, we believe the District Court properly reached its conclusions on the basis of the evidence available to it. There is no reason to protract already complex antitrust litigation by detailed analyses of peripheral economic facts, if the basic issues of the case may be determined through study of a fair sample.[10]

In the case before us, not only was a fair sample used to demonstrate the soundness of the District Court's conclusions, but evidence of record fully substantiates those findings as to each relevant market. An analysis of undisputed statistics of sales of shoes in the cities in which both Brown and Kinney sell shoes at retail, separated into the appropriate lines of commerce, provides a persuasive factual foundation upon which the required prognosis of the merger's effects may be built. Although Brown objects to some details in the Government's computations used in drafting these exhibits, appellant cannot deny the correctness of the more general picture they reveal. . . . They show, for example, that during 1955 in 32 separate cities, ranging in size and location from Topeka, Kansas, to Batavia, New York, and Hobbs, New Mexico, the combined share of Brown and Kinney sales of women's shoes (by unit volume) exceeded 20%.[11] In 31 cities—some the same as those used in measuring the effect of the merger in the women's line—the combined share of children's shoes sales exceeded 20%; in 6 cities their share exceeded 40%. In Dodge City, Kansas, their combined share of the market for woman's shoes was over 57%; their share of the children's shoe market in that city was 49%. In the 7 cities in which Brown's and Kinney's combined shares of the market for women's shoes were greatest (ranging from 33% to 57%) each of the parties alone, prior to the merger, had captured substantial portions of those markets (ranging from 13% to 34%); the merger intensified this

---

[10] See . . . U.S. Atty. Gen. Nat. Comm. to Study the Antitrust Laws, Report 126 (1955): "While sufficient data to support a conclusion is required, sufficient data to give the enforcement agencies, the courts and business certainty as to competitive consequences would nullify the words 'Where the effect may be' in the Clayton Act and convert them into 'Where the effect is.'" And the Committee of the Judicial Conference of the United States on Procedure in Antitrust and Other Protracted Cases has also emphasized the need for limiting the mass of possibly relevant evidence in cases of this type in order to avoid confusion and its concomitant increased possibility of error. 13 F.R.D. 62, 64.

[11] Although the sum of the parties' pre-existing shares of the market will normally equal their combined share of the immediate post-merger market, we recognize that this share need not remain stable in the future. Nevertheless, such statistics provide a graphic picture of the immediate impact of a merger, and, as such, also provide a meaningful base upon which to build conclusions of the probable future effects of the merger.

existing concentration. In 118 separate cities the combined shares of the market of Brown and Kinney in the sale of one of the relevant lines of commerce exceeded 5%. In 47 cities, their share exceeded 5% in all three lines.

The market share which companies may control by merging is one of the most important factors to be considered when determining the probable effects of the combination on effective competition in the relevant market. In an industry as fragmented as shoe retailing, the control of substantial shares of the trade in a city may have important effects on competition. If a merger achieving 5% control were now approved, we might be required to approve future merger efforts by Brown's competitors seeking similar market shares. The oligopoly Congress sought to avoid would then be furthered and it would be difficult to dissolve the combinations previously approved. Furthermore, in this fragmented industry, even if the combination controls but a small share of a particular market, the fact that this share is held by a large national chain can adversely affect competition. Testimony in the record from numerous independent retailers, based on their actual experience in the market, demonstrates that a strong, national chain of stores can insulate selected outlets from the vagaries of competition in particular locations and that the large chains can set and alter styles in footwear to an extent that renders the independents unable to maintain competitive inventories. A third significant aspect of this merger is that it creates a large national chain which is integrated with a manufacturing operation. The retail outlets of integrated companies, by eliminating wholesalers and by increasing the volume of purchases from the manufacturing division of the enterprise, can market their own brands at prices below those of competing independent retailers. Of course, some of the results of large integrated or chain operations are beneficial to consumers. Their expansion is not rendered unlawful by the mere fact that small independent stores may be adversely affected. It is competition, not competitors, which the Act protects. But we cannot fail to recognize Congress' desire to promote competition through the protection of viable, small, locally owned businesses. Congress appreciated that occasional higher costs and prices might result from the maintenance of fragmented industries and markets. It resolved these competing considerations in favor of decentralization. We must give effect to that decision.

Other factors to be considered in evaluating the probable effects of a merger in the relevant market lend additional support to the District Court's conclusion that this merger may substantially lessen competition. One such factor is the history of tendency toward concentration in the industry.[12] As we have previously pointed out, the shoe industry has, in re-

---

[12] . . . A Company's history of expansion through mergers presents a different economic picture than a history of expansion through unilateral growth. Internal expansion is more likely to be the result of increased demand for the company's products and is more likely to provide increased investment in plants, more jobs and greater output. Conversely,

cent years, been a prime example of such a trend. Most combinations have been between manufacturers and retailers, as each of the larger producers has sought to capture an increasing number of assured outlets for its wares. Although these mergers have been primarily vertical in their aim and effect, to the extent that they have brought ever greater numbers of retail outlets within fewer and fewer hands, they have had an additional important impact on the horizontal plane. By the merger in this case, the largest single group of retail stores still independent of one of the large manufacturers was absorbed into an already substantial aggregation of more or less controlled retail outlets. As a result of this merger, Brown moved into second place nationally in terms of retail stores directly owned. Including the stores on its franchise plan, the merger placed under Brown's control almost 1,600 shoe outlets, or about 7.2% of the Nation's retail "shoe stores" as defined by the Census Bureau and 2.3% of the Nation's total retail shoe outlets.[13] We cannot avoid the mandate of Congress that tendencies toward concentration in industry are to be curbed in their incipiency, particularly when those tendencies are being accelerated through giant steps striding across a hundred cities at a time. In the light of the trends in this industry we agree with the Government and the court below that this is an appropriate place at which to call a halt.

At the same time appellant has presented no mitigating factors, such as the business failure or the inadequate resources of one of the parties that may have prevented it from maintaining its competitive position, nor a demonstrated need for combination to enable small companies to enter into a more meaningful competition with those dominating the relevant markets. On the basis of the record before us, we believe the Government sustained its burden of proof. We hold that the District Court was correct in concluding that this merger may tend to lessen competition substantially in the retail sale of men's, women's, and children's shoes in the overwhelming majority of those cities and their environs in which both Brown and Kinney sell through owned or controlled outlets.

The judgment is *Affirmed.*

Note: In a subsequent decision, *U.S.* v. *Continental Can Co.,* 378 U.S. 441 (1964), the Supreme Court sharpened the economic tools developed in *Brown Shoe,* particularly in connection with their use to define relevant product markets. (See especially pp. 447–58 of that decision.)

---

expansion through merger is more likely to reduce available consumer choice while providing no increase in industry capacity, jobs or output. It was for these reasons, among others, Congress expressed its disapproval of successive acquisitions. Section 7 was enacted to prevent even small mergers that added to concentration in an industry. . . .

[13] Although statistics concerning the degree of concentration and the rank of Brown-Kinney in terms of controlled retail stores in each of the relevant product and geographic markets would have been more helpful in analyzing the results of this merger, neither side has presented such statistics. The figures in the record, based on national rank, are, nevertheless, useful in depicting the trends in the industry.

United States v. Von's Grocery Company

384 U.S. 270 (1966)

MR. JUSTICE BLACK delivered the opinion of the Court.

On March 25, 1960, the United States brought this action charging that the acquisition by Von's Grocery Company of its direct competitor Shopping Bag Food Stores, both large retail grocery companies in Los Angeles, California, violated §7 of the Clayton Act . . . as amended in 1950 by the Celler-Kefauver Anti-Merger Act. . . . On March 28, 1960, three days later, the District Court refused to grant the Government's motion for a temporary restraining order and immediately Von's took over all of Shopping Bag's capital stock and assets including 36 grocery stores in the Los Angeles area. After hearing evidence on both sides, the District Court made findings of fact and concluded as a matter of law that there was "not a reasonable probability" that the merger would tend "substantially to lessen competition" or "create a monopoly" in violation of §7. For this reason the District Court entered judgment for the defendants. . . . The Government appealed directly to this Court. . . . The sole question here is whether the District Court properly concluded on the facts before it that the Government had failed to prove a violation of §7.

The record shows the following facts relevant to our decision. The market involved here is the retail grocery market in the Los Angeles area. In 1958 Von's retail sales ranked third in the area and Shopping Bag's ranked sixth. In 1960 their sales together were 7.5% of the total two and one-half billion dollars of retail groceries sold in the Los Angeles market each year. For many years before the merger both companies had enjoyed great success as rapidly growing companies. From 1948 to 1958 the number of Von's stores in the Los Angeles area practically doubled from 14 to 27, while at the same time the number of Shopping Bag's stores jumped from 15 to 34. During that same decade, Von's sales increased fourfold and its share of the market almost doubled while Shopping Bag's sales multiplied seven times and its share of the market tripled. The merger of these two highly successful, expanding and aggressive competitors created the second largest grocery chain in Los Angeles with sales of almost $172,488,000 annually. In addition the findings of the District Court show that the number of owners operating single stores in the Los Angeles retail grocery market decreased from 5,365 in 1950 to 3,818 in 1961. By 1963, three years after the merger, the number of single-store owners had dropped still further to 3,590.[1] During roughly the same period from 1953 to 1962, the number of chains with two or more grocery

---

[1] Despite this steadfast concentration of the Los Angeles grocery business into fewer and fewer hands, the District Court, in Finding of Fact No. 80, concluded as follows:

"There has been no increase in concentration in the retail grocery business in the Los

stores increased from 96 to 150. While the grocery business was being concentrated into the hands of fewer and fewer owners, the small companies were continually being absorbed by the larger firms through mergers. According to an exhibit prepared by one of the Government's expert witnesses, in the period from 1949 to 1958 nine of the top 20 chains acquired 126 stores from their smaller competitors. . . . Moreover, . . . acquisitions and mergers in the Los Angeles retail grocery market have continued at a rapid rate since the merger. These facts alone are enough to cause us to conclude contrary to the District Court that the Von's-Shopping Bag merger did violate §7. Accordingly, we reverse. . . .

Like the Sherman Act in 1890 and the Clayton Act in 1914, the basic purpose of the 1950 Celler-Kefauver Act was to prevent economic concentration in the American economy by keeping a large number of small competitors in business. . . . As we said in *Brown Shoe Co.* v. *United States,* 370 U.S. 294, 315, "The dominant theme pervading congressional consideration of the 1950 amendments was a fear of what was considered to be a rising tide of economic concentration in the American economy." To arrest this "rising tide" toward concentration into too few hands and to halt the gradual demise of the small businessman, Congress decided to clamp down with vigor on mergers. . . .

The facts of this case present exactly the threatening trend toward concentration which Congress wanted to halt. The number of small grocery companies in the Los Angeles retail grocery market had been declining rapidly before the merger and continued to decline rapidly afterwards. This rapid decline in the number of grocery store owners moved hand in hand with a large number of significant absorptions of the small companies by the larger ones. In the midst of this steadfast trend toward concentration, Von's and Shopping Bag, two of the most successful and largest companies in the area, jointly owning 66 grocery stores merged to become the second largest chain in Los Angeles. This merger cannot be defended on the ground that one of the companies was about to fail or that the two had to merge to save themselves from destruction by some larger and more powerful competitor. What we have on the contrary is simply the case of two already powerful companies merging in a way which makes them even more powerful than they were before. If ever such a merger would not violate §7, certainly it does when it takes place in a market characterized by a long and continuous trend toward fewer and

---

Angeles Metropolitan Area either in the last decade or since the merger. On the contrary, economic concentration has decreased. . . ."

This conclusion is completely contradicted by Finding No. 23 which makes plain the steady decline in the number of individual grocery store owners referred to above. It is thus apparent that the District Court, in Finding No. 80, used the term "concentration" in some sense other than a total decrease in the number of separate competitors which is the crucial point here.

fewer owner-competitors which is exactly the sort of trend which Congress, with power to do so, declared must be arrested.

Appellees' primary argument is that the merger between Von's and Shopping Bag is not prohibited by §7 because the Los Angeles grocery market was competitive before the merger, has been since, and may continue to be in the future. Even so, §7 "requires not merely an appraisal of the immediate impact of the merger upon competition, but a prediction of its impact upon competitive conditions in the future; this is what is meant when it is said that the amended §7 was intended to arrest anticompetitive tendencies in their 'incipiency.'" *U.S.* v. *Philadelphia Nat. Bank,* 374 U.S. 321, 362. It is enough for us that Congress feared that a market marked at the same time by both a continuous decline in the number of small businesses and a large number of mergers would slowly but inevitably gravitate from a market of many small competitors to one dominated by one or a few giants, and competition would thereby be destroyed. Congress passed the Celler-Kefauver Act to prevent such a destruction of competition. Our cases since the passage of that Act have faithfully endeavored to enforce this congressional command. We adhere to them now.

Here again as in *United States* v. *El Paso Gas Co.,* 376 U.S. 651, 662, since appellees "have been on notice of the antitrust charge from almost the beginning . . . we not only reverse the judgment below but direct the District Court to order divestiture without delay." . . .

Reversed and remanded.

[MR. JUSTICE FORTAS took no part in the consideration or decision of this case. MR. JUSTICE WHITE concurred.]

MR. JUSTICE STEWART, with whom MR. JUSTICE HARLAN joins, dissenting.

We first gave consideration to the 1950 amendment of §7 of the Clayton Act in *Brown Shoe Co.* v. *United States.* . . . The thorough opinion THE CHIEF JUSTICE wrote for the Court in that case made two things plain: First, the standards of §7 require that every corporate acquisition be judged in the light of the contemporary economic context of its industry. Second, the purpose of §7 is to protect competition, not to protect competitors, and every §7 case must be decided in the light of that clear statutory purpose. Today the Court turns its back on these two basic principles and on all the decisions that have followed them.

The Court makes no effort to appraise the competitive effects of this acquisition in terms of the contemporary economy of the retail food industry in the Los Angeles area.[2] Instead, through a simple exercise in sums, it finds that the number of individual competitors in the market has decreased over the years, and, apparently on the theory that the degree of competition is invariably proportional to the number of competitors, it holds that this historic reduction in the number of competing units is enough under §7 to invalidate a merger within the market, with no need to examine the economic concentration of the market, the level of competition in the market, or the potential adverse effect of the merger on that competition. This startling *per se* rule is contrary not only to our previous decisions, but contrary to the language of §7, contrary to the legislative history of the 1950 amendment, and contrary to economic reality.

Under §7, as amended, a merger can be invalidated if, and only if, "the effect of such acquisition may be substantially to lessen competition, or to tend to create a monopoly." No question is raised here as to the tendency of the present merger to create a monopoly. Our sole concern is with the question whether the effect of the merger may be substantially to lessen competition.

The principal danger against which the 1950 amendment was addressed was the erosion of competition through the cumulative centripetal effect of acquisitions by large corporations, none of which by itself might be sufficient to constitute a violation of the Sherman Act. Congress' immediate fear was that of large corporations buying out small companies. A major aspect of that fear was the perceived trend toward absentee ownership of local business. Another, more generalized, congressional purpose revealed by the legislative history was to protect small businessmen and to stem the rising tide of concentration in the economy.[3] These goals, Congress thought, could be achieved by "arresting mergers at a time when the trend to a lessening of competition in a line of commerce was still in its incipiency." *Brown Shoe Co.* v. *United States, supra,* at 317.

---

[2] This is the first case to reach the Court under the 1950 amendment to §7 that involves a merger between firms engaged solely in retail food distribution. Kaysen & Turner, *Antitrust Policy* 40 (1959), have discussed this industry in the following terms: "As a guess, we can say that the most important distributive trades, especially the food trades, are structurally unconcentrated in the metropolitan areas. . . . [T]he significance of structural oligopoly in terms of policy is far different in [these trades] than in manufacturing and mining. . . . [T]he traditional view that the local-market industries are essentially competitive in character is probably correct. . . ."

[3] Much of the fuel for the congressional debates on concentration in the American economy was derived from a contemporary study by the Federal Trade Commission on corporate acquisitions between 1940 and 1947. See Report of the Federal Trade Commission on the Merger Movement: A Summary Report (1948). A critical study of the FTC report, published while the 1950 amendment was pending in Congress, concluded that the effect of the recent merger movement on concentration had been slight. Lintner & Butters, "Effect of Mergers on Industrial Concentration, 1940–1947," 32 *Rev. of Econ. & Statistics* 30 (1950). Two economists for the Federal Trade Commission later acquiesced in that conclusion. Blair & Houghton, "The Lintner-Butters Analysis of the Effect of Mergers on Industrial Concentration, 1940–1947," 33 *Rev. of Econ. & Statistics* 63, 67, n. 12 (1951).

. . . The legislative history leaves no doubt that the applicable standard for measuring the substantiality of the effect of a merger on competition was that of a "reasonable probability" of lessening competition. The standard was thus more stringent than that of a "mere possibility" on the one hand and more lenient than that of a "certainty" on the other.[4] I cannot agree that the retail grocery business in Los Angeles is in an incipient or any other stage of a trend toward a lessening of competition, or that the effective level of concentration in the industry has increased. Moreover, there is no indication that the present merger, or the trend in this industry as a whole, augurs any danger whatsoever for the small businessman. The Court has substituted bare conjecture for the statutory standard of a reasonable probability that competition may be lessened.

The Court rests its conclusion on the "crucial point" that, in the 11-year period between 1950 and 1961, the number of single-store grocery firms in Los Angeles decreased 29% from 5,365 to 3,818.[5] Such a decline should, of course, be no more than a fact calling for further investigation of the competitive trend in the industry. For the Court, however, that decline is made the end, not the beginning, of the analysis. . . .

I believe that even the most superficial analysis of the record makes plain the fallacy of the Court's syllogism that competition is necessarily reduced when the bare number of competitors has declined. In any meaningful sense, the structure of the Los Angeles grocery market remains unthreatened by concentration. Local competition is vigorous to a

---

[4] Although Congress eschewed exclusively mathematical tests for assessing the impact of a merger, it offered several generalizations indicative of the sort of merger that might be proscribed, e.g.: Whether the merger eliminated an enterprise that had been a substantial factor in competition; whether the increased size of the acquiring corporation threatened to give it a decisive advantage over competitors; whether an undue number of competing enterprises had been eliminated. H. R. Rep. No. 1191, 81st Cong., 1st Sess., p. 8. See *Brown Shoe Co.* v. *United States,* 370 U.S. 294, 321, n. 36. Only the first of these generalizations is arguably applicable to the present merger; the market-extension aspects of the merger, as well as the evidence of Shopping Bag's declining profit margin and weak price competition, suggest that any conclusion under this test would be equivocal. See infra, pp. 295–296; 298, n. 30. Senator Kefauver stated explicitly on the Senate floor that the mere elimination of competition between the merged firms would not make the acquisition illegal; rather, "the merger would have to have the effect of lessening competition generally." 96 Cong. Rec. 16456.

[5] The decline continued at approximately the same rate to 1963, the last year for which data are available, when there were 3,590 single-store grocery firms in the area. The record contains no breakdown of the figures on single-store concerns. In an extensive study of the retail grocery industry on a national scale, the Federal Trade Commission found that between 1939 and 1954 the total number of grocery stores in the United States declined by 109,000, or 28%. The entire decrease was suffered by stores with annual *gross* sales of less than $50,000. During the same period, the number of stores in all higher sales brackets increased. The Commission noted that the census figures, from which its data were taken, included an undetermined number of grocery firms liquidating after 1948 that merely closed their grocery operations and continued their remaining lines of business, such as nongrocery retailing, food wholesaling, food manufacturing, etc. Staff Report to the Federal Trade Commission, Economic Inquiry Into Food Marketing, Part I, Concentration and Integration in Retailing 48, 54 (1960).

fault, not only among chain stores themselves but also between chain stores and single-store operators. The continuing population explosion of the Los Angeles area, which has outrun the expansion plans of even the largest chains, offers a surfeit of business opportunity for stores of all sizes. Affiliated with cooperatives that give the smallest store the buying strength of its largest competitors, new stores have taken full advantage of the remarkable ease of entry into the market. And, most important of all, the record simply cries out that the numerical decline in the number of single-store owners is the result of transcending social and technological changes that positively preclude the inference that competition has suffered because of the attrition of competitors.

Section 7 was never intended by Congress for use by the Court as a charter to roll back the supermarket revolution. Yet the Court's opinion is hardly more than a requiem for the so-called "Mom and Pop" grocery stores—the bakery and butcher shops, and vegetable and fish markets—that are now economically and technologically obsolete in many parts of the country. No action by this Court can resurrect the old single-line Los Angeles food stores that have been run over by the automobile or obliterated by the freeway. . . . Today's dominant enterprise in food retailing is the supermarket. Accessible to the housewife's automobile from a wide radius, it houses under a single roof the entire food requirements of the family. Only through . . . [a] reactionary philosophy . . . can the Court read into the legislative history of §7 its attempt to make the automobile stand still, to mold the food economy of today into the market pattern of another era.

. . . [T]he record offers abundant evidence of the dramatic history of growth and prosperity of the retail food business in Los Angeles.

. . . Between 1948 and 1958, the market share of Safeway, the leading grocery chain in Los Angeles, declined from 14% to 8%. The combined market shares of the top two chains declined from 21% to 14% over the same period; for the period 1952–1958, the combined shares of the three, four, and five largest firms also declined. It is true that between 1948 and 1958, the combined shares of the top 20 firms in the market increased from 44% to 57%. The crucial fact here, however, is that seven of these top 20 firms in 1958 were not even in existence as chains in 1948. Because of the substantial turnover in the membership of the top 20 firms, the increase in market share of the top 20 as a group is hardly a reliable indicator of any tendency toward market concentration.[6]

In addition, statistics in the record for the period 1953–1962 strongly suggest that the retail grocery industry in Los Angeles is less concentrated today than it was a decade ago. During this period, the number of chain

---

[6] See Joskow, "Structural Indicia: Rank-Shift Analysis as a Supplement to Concentration Ratios," VI *Antitrust Bulletin* 9 (1961). In addition, the overall market share of the top 20 firms in fact showed a slight decline between 1958 and 1960. . . .

store firms in the area rose from 96 to 150, or 56%. That increase occurred overwhelmingly among chains of the very smallest size, those composed of two or three grocery stores. Between 1953 and 1962, the number of such "chains" increased from 56 to 104, or 86%. Although chains of 10 or more stores increased from 10 to 24 during the period, seven of these 24 chains were not even in existence as chains in Los Angeles in 1953.

Yet even these dramatic statistics do not fully reveal the dynamism and vitality of competition in the retail grocery business in Los Angeles during the period. The record shows that . . . during the period 1953–1962 . . . 173 new chains made their appearance in the market area, and 119 chains went out of existence as chain stores. The vast majority of this market turbulence represented turnover in chains of two or three stores. . . . [A]lmost without exception, these new chains were the outgrowth of successful one-store operations.[7] There is no indication that comparable turmoil did not equally permeate single-store operations in the area.[8] In fashioning its *per se* rule, based on the net arithmetical decline in the number of single-store operators, the Court completely disregards the obvious procreative vigor of competition in the market as reflected in the turbulent history of entry and exit of competing small chains.

To support its conclusion the Court invokes three sets of data regarding absorption of smaller firms by merger with larger firms. In each of the acquisitions detailed in . . . the Court's opinion, the acquired units were grocery *chains*. Not one of these acquisitions was of a firm operating only a single store.[9] The Court cannot have it both ways. It is only among single-store operators that the decline in the unit number of competitors, so heavily relied upon by the Court, has taken place. Yet the . . . [data] show not a trace of merger activity involving the acquisition of single-store operators. And the number of *chains* in the area has in fact shown a

---

[7] On the basis of these facts, one witness concluded: ". . . It must be remembered that in 1953, only 10 chains with as many as 10 stores each were operating in the area. These chains are recognized as being among the best managed, most successful and most aggressive supermarket operators in the country. They themselves have engaged in expansion programs of significant proportions since 1953. Yet, 10 years later, instead of having swept aside all competition and being left alone to compete among themselves, these same 10 chains are now faced with the necessity of competing against no less than 14 new chains of 10 or more stores each, a significantly greater number of smaller chains and a host of successful single-store operators, of whom many are affiliated with powerful voluntary chains or other cooperative groups. . . .'"

[8] Data for 1960, the only year for which such figures are available in the record, reveal a comparable agitation of entry and exit among operators of single stores. Although there was a net loss of 132 single-outlet stores in 1960, 128 new single-outlet stores opened during the year.

[9] As to Table 1 in the Appendix of the Court's opinion, this fact is obvious on the face of the table. As to Table 2 in the Appendix, examination of the record discloses that each of the nine acquisitions listed as involving a single store represented purchases of single stores from chains ranging in size from two to 49 stores.

substantial net increase during the period, in spite of the fact that some of the chains have been absorbed by larger firms. How then can the Court rely on these acquisitions as evidence of a tendency toward market concentration in the area? . . .

The Court's reliance on the fact that nine of the top 20 chains acquired 120 stores in the Los Angeles area between 1949 and 1958 does not withstand analysis in light of the complete record. Forty percent of these acquisitions . . . were made by [chains] . . . which ranked 9th, 11th, and 20th, . . . according to 1958 sales in the market. Each of these firms subsequently went into bankruptcy as a result of overexpansion, undercapitalization, or inadequate managerial experience. This substantial post-acquisition demise of relatively large chains hardly comports with the Court's tacit portrayal of the inexorable march of the market toward oligopoly.

Further, the table relied on by the Court to sustain its view that acquisitions have continued in the Los Angeles area at a rapid rate in the three-year period following this merger indiscriminately lumps together horizontal and market-extension mergers. . . . [A]t a time when the number of single-store concerns was well over 3,500, horizontal mergers over a three-year period between going concerns achieved at most only the *de minimis* level of 10 acquisitions involving 20 stores. It cannot seriously be maintained that the effect of the negligible market share foreclosed by these horizontal mergers may be substantially to lessen competition within the meaning of §7. . . .

Moreover, contrary to the assumption on which the Court proceeds, the record establishes that the present merger itself has substantial, even predominant, market-extension overtones. The District Court found that the Von's stores were located in the southern and western portions of the Los Angeles metropolitan area, and that the Shopping Bag stores were located in the northern and eastern portions. In each of the areas in which Von's and Shopping Bag stores competed directly, there were also at least six other chain stores and several smaller stores competing for the patronage of customers. . . . Even among these stores which competed at least partially with one another, the overlap in sales represented only approximately 25% of the combined sales of the two chains in the overall Los Angeles area. The present merger was thus three parts market-extension and only one part horizontal, but the Court nowhere recognizes this market-extension aspect that exists within the local market itself. The actual market share foreclosed by the elimination of Shopping Bag as an independent competitor was thus slightly less than 1% of the total grocery store sales in the area. The share of the market preempted by the present merger was therefore practically identical with the 0.77% market foreclosure accepted as "quite insubstantial" by the Court in *Tampa Electric Co.* v. *Nashville Coal Co.,* 365 U.S. 320, 331–333.

The irony of this case is that the Court invokes its sweeping new construction of §7 to the detriment of a merger between two relatively successful, local, largely family-owned concerns, each of which had less than 5% of the local market and neither of which had any prior history of growth by acquisition.[10] In a sense, the defendants are being punished for the sin of aggressive competition. The Court is inaccurate in its suggestions, *ante,* pp. 277–278, that the merger makes these firms more "powerful" than they were before, and that Shopping Bag was itself a "powerful" competitor at the time of the merger. There is simply no evidence in the record, and the Court makes no attempt to demonstrate, that the increment in market *share* obtained by the combined stores can be equated with an increase in the market *power* of the combined firm. . . .

With regard to the "plight" of the small businessman, the record is unequivocal that his competitive position is strong and secure in the Los Angeles retail grocery industry. The most aggressive competitors against the larger retail chains are frequently the operators of single stores.[11] The vitality of these independents is directly attributable to the recent and spectacular growth in California of three large cooperative buying organizations. . . . The rise of these cooperative organizations has introduced a significant new source of countervailing power against the market power of the chain stores, without in any way sacrificing the advantages of independent operation. In the face of the substantial assistance available to independents through membership in such cooperatives, the Court's implicit equation between the market power and the market share resulting from the present merger seems completely invalid.

Moreover, it is clear that there are no substantial barriers to market entry. The record contains references to numerous highly successful instances of entry with modest initial investments. . . . Enhancing free access to the market is the absence of any such restrictive factors as patented technology, trade secrets, or substantial product differentiation.

---

[10]   . . . So far as the record reveals, the competitive behavior of these firms was impeccable throughout their expansion, which took place solely by internal growth. In discussing the success of comparable firms *vis-à-vis* the Sherman Act, Judge Learned Hand stated: ". . . The successful competitor, having been urged to compete, must not be turned upon when he wins." *United States* v. *Aluminum Co. of America,* 148 F.2d 416, 430.

[11] One single-store operator, located adjacent to one supermarket and within a mile of two others, testified, "I have often been asked if I could compete successfully against this sort of competition. My answer is and always has been that the question is not whether I can compete against them, but whether they can compete against me."

Another single-store operator testified, "Competition in the grocery business is on a store-by-store basis and any aggressive and able operator like myself can out-compete the store of any of the chains because of personalized service, better labor relations, and being in personal charge of the store and seeing that it is run properly."

A third single-store operator testified, "The chains in this area are good operators, but when they grow too large, they are actually easier to compete with from an independent's viewpoint. If I had a choice, I would rather operate a store near a chain unit than near another independent."

Numerous other factors attest to the pugnacious level of grocery competition in Los Angeles, all of them silently ignored by the Court in its emphasis solely on the declining number of single-store competitors in the market. Three thousand five hundred and ninety single-store firms is a lot of grocery stores. The large number of separate competitors and the frequent price battles between them belie any suggestion that price competition in the area is even remotely threatened by a descent to the sort of consciously interdependent pricing that is characteristic of a market turning the corner toward oligopoly. The birth of dynamic new competitive forces—discount food houses and food departments in department stores, bantams and superettes, deli-liquor stores and drive-in dairies—promises unremitting competition in the future. In the more than four years following the merger, the District Court found not a shred of evidence that competition had been in any way impaired by the merger. . . .

The harsh standard now applied by the Court to horizontal mergers may prejudice irrevocably the already difficult choice by numerous successful small and medium-sized businessmen in the myriad smaller markets where the effect of today's decision will be felt, whether to expand by buying or by building additional facilities. And by foreclosing future sale as one attractive avenue of eventual market exit, the Court's decision may over the long run deter new market entry and tend to stifle the very competition it seeks to foster.

In a single sentence and an omnibus footnote at the close of its opinion, the Court pronounces its work consistent with the line of our decisions under §7 since the passage of the 1950 amendment. The sole consistency that I can find is that in litigation under §7, the Government always wins. The only precedent that is even within sight of today's holding is *U.S.* v. *Philadelphia Nat. Bank,* 374 U.S. 321. In that case, in the interest of practical judicial administration, the Court proposed a simplified test of merger illegality: "[W]e think that a merger which produces a firm controlling an undue percentage share of the relevant market, and results in a significant increase in the concentration of firms in that market, is so inherently likely to lessen competition substantially that it must be enjoined in the absence of evidence clearly showing that the merger is not likely to have such anticompetitive effects." *U.S.* v. *Philadelphia Nat. Bank, supra,* at 363. The merger between Von's and Shopping Bag produced a firm with 1.4% of the grocery stores and 7.5% of grocery sales in Los Angeles, and resulted in an increase of 1.1% in the market share enjoyed by the two largest firms in the market and 3.3% in the market share of the six largest firms. The former two figures are hardly the "undue percentage" of the market, nor are the latter two figures the "significant increase" in concentration, that would make this merger inherently suspect under the standard of *Philadelphia Nat. Bank.* Instead, the circumstances of the present merger fall far outside the simplified test established by that case for precisely the sort of merger here involved.[12] . . .

The emotional impact of a merger between the third and sixth largest competitors in a given market, however fragmented, is understandable, but that impact cannot substitute for the analysis of the effect of the merger on competition that Congress required by the 1950 amendment. Nothing in the present record indicates that there is more than an ephemeral possibility that the effect of this merger may be substantially to lessen competition. Section 7 clearly takes "reasonable probability" as its standard. That standard has not been met here, and I would therefore affirm the judgment of the District Court.

United States v. General Dynamics Corp.

415 U.S. 486 (1974)

* * * * *

MR. JUSTICE STEWART delivered the opinion of the Court. . . .

I

At the time of the acquisition involved here, Material Service Corp. was a large midwest producer and supplier of building materials, concrete, limestone, and coal. All of its coal production was from deep-shaft mines operated by it or its affiliate, appellee Freeman Coal Mining Corp., and production from these operations amounted to 6.9 million tons of coal in 1959 and 8.4 million tons in 1967. In 1954, Material Service began to

---

[12] . . .The Court's opinion is remarkable for its failure to support its conclusion by reference to even a single piece of economic theory. I shall not dwell here on the barometers of competition that have been suggested by the commentators. But it seems important to note that the present merger falls either outside, or at the very fringe, of the various mechanical tests that had been proposed. See, *e.g.*, Kaysen & Turner, *Antitrust Policy* 133–136 (1959) (horizontal merger with direct competitor is prima facie unlawful where acquiring company accounts for 20% or more of the market, or where merging companies together constitute 20% or more of the market; acquisitions producing less than 20% market control unlawful only where special circumstances are present, such as serious barriers to entry or substantial influence on prices by the acquired company); Stigler, "Mergers and Preventive Antitrust Policy," 104 *U. Pa. L. Rev.* 176, 179–182 (1955) (acquisition unlawful if it produces a combined market share of 20% or more; acquisition permitted if the combined share is less than 5–10%); Bok, Section 7 of The Clayton Act and the Merging of Law and Economics, 74 *Harv. L. Rev.* 226, 308–329 (1960) (no merger by the dominant firm in an industry if its market share is increased by more than 2–3%; no merger by other large firms in the industry where the combined market shares of the two-to-eight largest firms after the merger are increased by 7–8% or more over the shares that existed at any time during the preceding 5–10 years; no merger where acquired firm has 5% market share or more). See also Markham, "Merger Policy Under the New Section 7: A Six-Year Appraisal," 43 *Va. L. Rev.* 489, 521–522 (1957). The 40% rule promoted by the concurring opinion in the present case seems no more than an ad hoc endeavor to rationalize the holding of the Court.

acquire the stock of United Electric Coal Companies. United Electric at all relevant times operated only strip or open-pit mines in Illinois and Kentucky; at the time of trial in 1970 a number of its mines had closed and its operations had been reduced to four mines in Illinois and none in Kentucky. . . . Material Service's purchase of United Electric stock continued until 1959. At this point Material's holdings amounted to more than 34% of United Electric's outstanding shares and—all parties are now agreed on this point—Material had effective control of United Electric. . . .

Some months after this takeover, Material Service was itself acquired by the appellee General Dynamics Corp. General Dynamics is a large diversified corporation, much of its revenues coming from sales of aircraft, communications, and marine products to Government agencies. . . . As a result of the purchase of Material Service, and through it, of Freeman and United Electric, General Dynamics became the Nation's fifth largest commercial coal producer. During the early 1960s General Dynamics increased its equity in United Electric by direct purchases of United Electric stock, and by 1966 it held or controlled 66.15% of United Electric's outstanding shares. In September 1966 the board of directors of General Dynamics authorized a tender offer to holders of the remaining United Electric stock. This offer was successful, and United Electric shortly thereafter became a wholly owned subsidiary of General Dynamics.

The thrust of the Government's complaint was that the acquisition of United Electric by Material Service in 1959 violated §7 of the Clayton Act . . . because the takeover substantially lessened competition in the production and sale of coal in either or both of two geographic markets. It contended that a relevant "section of the country" within the meaning of §7 was, alternatively, the State of Illinois or the Eastern Interior Coal Province Sales Area, the latter being one of four major coal distribution areas recognized by the coal industry and comprising Illinois and Indiana, and parts of Kentucky, Tennessee, Iowa, Minnesota, Wisconsin, and Missouri.[1]

At trial controversy focused on three basic issues: the propriety of coal as a "line of commerce," the definition of Illinois or the Eastern Interior Coal Province Sales Area as a relevant "section of the country," and the

---

[1] Testimony at trial indicated that the Eastern Interior Coal Province—the area of coal production upon which the Eastern Coal Province Sales Area was based—was originally named by United States Geological Survey maps of the coalfields in the United States and described one portion of a sequence of coal-bearing rock formations known geologically as the Pennsylvania System. The Sales Area of the Eastern Interior Coal Province was derived from the assumption, acknowledged in the trial court's opinion, that the high costs of transporting coal—which may amount to 40% of the price of delivered coal—will inevitably give producers of coal a clear competitive advantage in sales in the immediate areas of the mines.

probability of a lessening of competition within these or any other product and geographic markets resulting from the acquisition. The District Court decided against the Government on each of these issues. . . .

II

The Government sought to prove a violation of §7 of the Clayton Act principally through statistics showing that within certain geographic markets the coal industry was concentrated among a small number of large producers; that this concentration was increasing; and that the acquisition of United Electric would materially enlarge the market share of the acquiring company and thereby contribute to the trend toward concentration.

The concentration of the coal market in Illinois and, alternatively, in the Eastern Interior Coal Province was demonstrated by a table of the share of the largest two, four, and ten coal producing firms in each of these areas for both 1957 and 1967 that revealed the following:[2]

	Eastern Interior Coal Province		Illinois	
	1957	1967	1957	1967
Top 2 firms	29.6	48.6	37.8	52.9
Top 4 firms	43.0	62.9	54.5	75.2
Top 10 firms	65.5	91.4	84.0	98.0

These statistics, the Government argued, showed not only that the coal industry was concentrated among a small number of leading producers, but that the trend had been toward increasing concentration.[3] Furthermore, the undisputed fact that the number of coal-producing firms in Illinois decreased almost 73% during the period of 1957 to 1967 from 144 to 39 was claimed to be indicative of the same trend. The acquisition of United Electric by Material Service resulted in increased concentration of coal sales among the leading producers in the areas chosen by the Government, as shown by the following table: [4]

---

[2] The figures for 1967 reflect the impact on market concentration of the acquisition involved here.

[3] The figures demonstrating the degree of concentration in the two coal markets chosen by the Government were roughly comparable to those in *United States* v. *Von's Grocery Co.*, 384 U.S. 270, where the top four firms in the market controlled 24.4% of the sales, the top eight 40.9%, and the top 12 48.8%. See, *id.*, at 281 (WHITE J., concurring). See also *United States* v. *Pabst Brewing Co.*, 384 U.S. 546, 551, where the top four producers of beer in Wisconsin were found to control 47.74% of the market, and the top 10 in the Nation and the local three-state area to control 45.06% and 58.93%, respectively. . . .

[4] The percentage increase in concentration asserted here was thus analogous to that found in *Von's Grocery, supra,* where the concentration among the top four, eight, and 12

	1959			1967		
	Share of Top 2 but for Merger	Share of Top 2 Given Merger	Percent Increase	Share of Top 2 but for Merger	Share of Top 2 Given Merger	Percent Increase
Province	33.1	37.9	14.5	45.0	48.6	8.0
Illinois	36.6	44.3	22.4	44.0	52.9	20.2

Finally, the Government's statistics indicated that the acquisition increased the share of the merged company in the Illinois and Eastern Interior Coal Province coal markets by significant degrees:[5]

	Province		Illinois	
	Rank	Share (percent)	Rank	Share (percent)
1959				
Freeman	2	7.6	2	15.1
United Electric	6	4.8	5	8.1
Combined	2	12.4	1	23.2
1967				
Freeman	5	6.5	2	12.9
United Electric	9	4.4	6	8.9
Combined	2	10.9	2	21.8

The effect of adopting this approach to a determination of a "substantial" lessening of competition is to allow the Government to rest its case on a showing of even small increases of market share or market concentration in those industries or markets where concentration is already great or has been recently increasing, since "if concentration is already great, the importance of preventing even slight increases in concentration and so preserving the possibility of eventual deconcentration is correspondingly great." *United States* v. *Aluminum Co. of America,* 377 U.S. 271, 279, citing *United States* v. *Philadelphia National Bank,* 374 U.S., at 365 n. 42.

While the statistical showing proffered by the Government in this case,

---

firms was increased, respectively, by 18.0%, 7.6%, and 2.5% as a result of the merger invalidated there.

[5] The 1959 Illinois figure of 23.2% was asserted by the Government to be comparable to the 23.94% share of the Wisconsin beer market found to be significant in *Pabst, supra,* and the 25% share controlled by the merged company in *United States* v. *Continental Can Co.,* 378 U.S. 441, 461. The Province figure of 12.4% was compared with the shares held by the merged companies in *Von's Grocery* (7.5%), and in the *Pabst* national (4.49%) and three-state (11.32%) markets.

the accuracy of which was not discredited by the District Court or contested by the appellees, would under this approach have sufficed to support a finding of "undue concentration" in the absence of other considerations, the question before us is whether the District Court was justified in finding that other pertinent factors affecting the coal industry and the business of the appellees mandated a conclusion that no substantial lessening of competition occurred or was threatened by the acquisition of United Electric. We are satisfied that the court's ultimate finding was not in error.

In *Brown Shoe* v. *United States* . . . [370 U.S. 294 (1962)], we cautioned that statistics concerning market share and concentration, while of great significance, were not conclusive indicators of anticompetitive effects:

> Congress indicated plainly that a merger had to be functionally viewed, in the context of its particular industry. 370 U.S., at 321–322.

> Statistics reflecting the shares of the market controlled by the industry leaders and the parties to the merger are, of course, the primary index of market power; but only a further examination of the particular market—its structure, history and probable future—can provide the appropriate setting for judging the probable anticompetitive effect of the merger. *Id.*, at 322 n. 38.

. . . In this case, the District Court assessed the evidence of the "structure, history and probable future" of the coal industry, and on the basis of this assessment found no substantial probability of anticompetitive effects from the merger.

Much of the District Court's opinion was devoted to a description of the changes that have affected the coal industry since World War II. . . . First, it found that coal had become increasingly less able to compete with other sources of energy in many segments of the energy market. . . . Because of these changes in consumption patterns, coal's share of the energy resources consumed in this country fell from 78.4% in 1920 to 21.4% in 1968. The court reviewed evidence attributing this decline not only to the changing relative economies of alternative fuels and to new distribution and consumption patterns, but also to more recent concern with the effect of coal use on the environment and consequent regulation of the extent and means of such coal consumption.

Second, the court found that to a growing extent since 1954, the electric utility industry has become the mainstay of coal consumption. While electric utilities consumed only 15.76% of the coal produced nationally in 1947, their share of total consumption increased every year thereafter, and in 1968 amounted to more than 59% of all the coal consumed throughout the Nation. . . .

Third, and most significantly, the court found that to an increasing degree, nearly all coal sold to utilities is transferred under long-term requirements contracts, under which coal producers promise to meet utilities' coal consumption requirements for a fixed period of time, and at predetermined prices. . . . These developments in the patterns of coal distribution and consumption, the District Court found, have limited the amounts of coal immediately available for "spot" purchases on the open market, since "[t]he growing practice by coal producers of expanding mine capacity only to meet long-term contractual commitments and the gradual disappearance of the small truck mines has tended to limit the production capacity available for spot sales." [341 F. Supp., at 543.]

Because of these fundamental changes in the structure of the market for coal, the District Court was justified in viewing the statistics relied on by the Government as insufficient to sustain its case. Evidence of past production does not, as a matter of logic, necessarily give a proper picture of a company's future ability to compete. In most situations, of course, the unstated assumption is that a company that has maintained a certain share of a market in the recent past will be in a position to do so in the immediate future. Thus, companies that have controlled sufficiently large shares of a concentrated market are barred from merger by §7, not because of their past acts, but because their past performances imply an ability to continue to dominate with at least equal vigor. . . . Evidence of the amount of annual sales is relevant as a prediction of future competitive strength, since in most markets distribution systems and brand recognition are such significant factors that one may reasonably suppose that a company which has attracted a given number of sales will retain that competitive strength.

In the coal market, as analyzed by the District Court, however, statistical evidence of coal *production* was of considerably less significance. The bulk of the coal produced is delivered under long-term requirements contracts, and such sales thus do not represent the exercise of competitive power but rather the obligation to fulfill previously negotiated contracts at a previously fixed price. The focus of competition in a given time frame is not on the disposition of coal already produced but on the procurement of new long-term supply contracts. In this situation, a company's past ability to produce is of limited significance, since it is in a position to offer for sale neither its past production nor the bulk of the coal it is presently capable of producing, which is typically already committed under a long-term supply contract. A more significant indicator of a company's power effectively to compete with other companies lies in the state of a company's uncommitted reserves of recoverable coal. A company with relatively large supplies of coal which are not already under contract to a consumer will have a more important influence upon competition in the contemporaneous negotiation of supply contracts than a firm with small reserves, even though the latter may presently produce a greater tonnage of coal. In a market where the availability and price for coal are set by long-term contracts rather than immediate or short-term purchases and sales, reserves rather than past production are the best measure of a company's ability to compete.

The testimony and exhibits in the District Court revealed that United Electric's coal reserve prospects were "unpromising." 341 F. Supp., at 559. United's relative position of strength in reserves was considerably weaker than its past and current ability to produce. While United ranked fifth among Illinois coal producers in terms of annual production, it was 10th in reserve holdings, and controlled less than 1% of the reserves held by coal producers in Illinois, Indiana, and western Kentucky. *Id.,* at 538. . . . Even more significantly, the District Court found that of the 52,033,304 tons of currently mineable reserves in Illinois, Indiana, and Kentucky controlled by United, only four million tons had not already been committed under long-term contracts. United was found to be facing the future with relatively depleted resources at its disposal, and with the vast majority of those resources already committed under contracts allowing no further adjustment in price. In addition, the District Court found that "United Electric has neither the possibility of acquiring more [reserves] nor the ability to develop deep coal reserves," and thus was not in a position to increase its reserves to replace those already depleted or committed. *Id.,* at 560.

Viewed in terms of present and future reserve prospects—and thus in terms of probable future ability to compete—rather than in terms of past production, the District Court held that United Electric was a far less significant factor in the coal market than the Government contended or the production statistics seemed to indicate. While the company had been and remained a "highly profitable" and efficient producer of relatively large amounts of coal, its current and future power to compete for subsequent long-term contracts was severely limited by its scarce uncommitted resources. . . . Irrespective of the company's size when viewed as a producer, its weakness as a competitor was properly analyzed by the District Court and fully substantiated that court's conclusion that its acquisition by Material Service would not "substantially . . . lessen competition. . . ."

III

[In this section, MR. JUSTICE STEWART rejected the Government's allegations (1) that the District Court gave undue consideration to post-acquisition evidence; (2) that the District Court's reliance on depleted and uncommitted reserves is essentially a "failing company" defense which must meet the strict limits places on that defense by the Court in previous decisions; and (3) that the factual underpinning of the District Court's decision lacked adequate evidentiary support.]

. . . One factual claim by the Government . . . goes to the heart of the reasoning of the District Court and thus is worthy of explicit note here. The Government asserts that the paucity of United Electric's coal reserves could not have the significance perceived by the District Court, since all companies engaged in extracting minerals at some point deplete their reserves and then acquire new reserves or the new technology required to extract more minerals from their existing holdings. United Electric, the Government suggests, could at any point either purchase new strip reserves or acquire the expertise to recover currently held deep reserves.

But the District Court specifically found new strip reserves not to be available: "Evidence was presented at trial by experts, by state officials, by industry witnesses and by the Government itself indicating that economically mineable strip reserves that would permit United Electric to continue operations beyond the life of its present mines are not available. The Government failed to come forward with any evidence that such reserves are *presently* available." 341 F. Supp., at 559. In addition, there was considerable testimony at trial, apparently credited by the District Court, indicating that United Electric and others had tried to find additional strip reserves not already held for coal production, and had been largely unable to do so.

Moreover, the hypothetical possibility that United Electric might in the future acquire the expertise to mine deep reserves proves nothing—or too much. As the Government pointed out in its brief and at oral argument, in recent years a number of companies with no prior experience in extracting coal have purchased coal reserves and entered the coal production business in order to diversify and complement their current operations. The mere possibility that United Electric, in common with all other companies with the inclination and the corporate treasury to do so, could some day expand into an essentially new line of business does not depreciate the validity of the conclusion that United Electric at the time of the trial did not have the power to compete on a significant scale for the procurement of future long-term contracts, nor does it vest in the production statistics relied on by the Government more significance than ascribed to them by the District Court.

IV

In addition to contending that the District Court erred in finding that the acquisition of United Electric would not substantially lessen competition, the Government urges us to review the court's determinations of the proper product and geographic markets. The Government suggests that while the "energy market" might have been *an* appropriate "line of commerce," coal also had sufficient "practical indicia" as a separate "line of commerce" to qualify as an independent and consistent submarket. . . . It also suggests that irrespective of the validity of the criteria adopted by the District Court in selecting its 10 geographic markets, competition between United Electric and Material Service within the larger alternative geographic markets claimed by the Government established those areas as a permissible "section of the country" within the meaning of §7.

While under normal circumstances a delineation of proper geographic and product markets is a necessary precondition to assessment of the probabilities of a substantial effect on competition within them, in this case we nevertheless affirm the District Court's judgment without reaching these questions. . . . Irrespective of the markets within which the acquiring and the acquired company might be viewed as competitors for purposes of this §7 suit, the Government's statistical presentation simply did not establish that a substantial lessening of competition was likely to occur in any market. By concluding that "divestiture [would not] benefit competition even were this court to accept the Government's unrealistic product and geographic market definitions," 341 F. Supp., at 560, the District Court rendered superfluous its further determinations that the Government also erred in its choice of relevant markets. Since we agree with the District Court that the Government's reliance on production statistics in the context of this case was insufficient, it follows that the judgment before us may be affirmed without reaching the issues of geographic and product markets.

The judgment of the District Court is *affirmed*.

It is so ordered.

MR. JUSTICE DOUGLAS, with whom MR. JUSTICE BRENNAN, MR. JUSTICE WHITE, and MR. JUSTICE MARSHALL concur, dissenting. . . .

I

[In this section the facts surrounding the acquisition and the nature of the participants were described.]

II

. . . The court below concluded that "the energy market is the appropriate line of commerce for testing the competitive effect of the United Electric-Freeman combination." 341 F. Supp., at 555. The court rejected the Government's hypothesis of coal as a submarket for antitrust purposes as "untenable," finding that *United States* v. *Continental Can Co.*, 378 U.S. 441 (1964), "compel[s] this court to conclude that since coal competes with gas, oil, uranium and other forms of energy, the relevant line of commerce must encompass interfuel competition." 341 F. Supp., at 556.

I read *Continental Can* to import no such compulsion. . . .

The District Court here found an energy market in which the combination did not work the prohibited effect. Whatever the correctness of that finding, *Continental Can* teaches us that it is of no help to appellees if their exist other lines of commerce in which the effect is present. Any combination may involve myriad lines of commerce; the existence of an energy market is not inconsistent with and does not negate the existence of a narrower coal market for "within this broad market, well-defined submarkets may exist which, in themselves, constitute product markets for antitrust purposes." *Brown Shoe Co.* v. *United States,* 370 U.S. 294, 325 (1962).

This principle found recognition in *Continental Can* where we recognized glass and metal containers "to be two separate lines of commerce," despite finding that competition between the lines "necessarily implied one or more *other* lines of commerce embracing both industries." 378 U.S., at 456–457 (emphasis added). . . .

Coal has both price advantages and operational disadvantages which combine to delineate within the energy market "economically significant submarket[s]."[6] The consumers for whom price is determinative mark out a submarket in which coal is the overwhelming choice; the boundaries of this submarket are strengthened by coal's virtual inability to compete in other significant sectors of the energy market. Energy-use technology in highway and air transportation necessitates the use of liquid fuels. The relative operational ease of dieselized power plants has worked to virtually foreclose coal from the rail transportation market. . . . Despite their higher cost, gas and oil enjoy a competitive edge in the space-heating market because of simple consumer preference for these sources of energy over coal. . . .

The market for coal is therefore effectively limited to large industrial energy consumers such as electric utilities and certain manufacturers with the ability and economic incentive to consider coal as an energy source.[7] The court below noted that the "utility market has become the mainstay of coal production," 341 F. Supp., at 539, accounting for 72% of total national coal consumption in 1968. Within this sector coal's economic advantage yields it an overwhelming share of the market. In each year from 1960 to 1967 (the period during which the Freeman-United Electric union solidified) coal accounted for over 90% of the B.t.u.'s consumed by steam electric utility plants in the EICP sales area; it also provided 74% of the B.t.u.'s consumed by cement plants in the same area and 94% of the B.t.u.'s consumed by such plants in Illinois.[8]

The coal market is therefore viewed by energy consumers as a separate

---

[6] See *Brown Shoe Co.* v. *United States,* 370 U.S. 294, 325 (1962).

[7] The only other significant use for coal is metallurgical in nature. Metallurgical coal is used as a product in the manufacture of steel. The use of such coal as a product sets it off in a separate market from nonmetallurgical coal which is used as an energy source.

[8] Although nuclear and geothermal power may draw some utility consumers from the coal market in the future, nuclear fuel is not consumable in existing fossil-fuel plants nor is nuclear fuel presently an alternative for nonutility coal consumers. Thus, whatever the future inroads of alternative fuels, there remains a significant class of energy consumers which looks only to coal.

economic entity confined to those users with the technological capability to allow the use of coal and the incentive for economy to mandate it. Within that market coal experiences little competition from other fuels since coal's delivered price per B.t.u. in the areas served by Freeman and United Electric is significantly lower than that for any other combustible fuel except interruptible natural gas which is available only on a seasonal basis.[9] Central Illinois Light Co., for example, purchases coal at 27 cents per million B.t.u.'s, firm natural gas at 45 cents, and oil (for ignition purposes) at 70 cents. . . . Since coal consumption facilities are unique and not readily adaptable to alternative energy sources, there is little interfuel price sensitivity. As the Court in *Kennecott Copper Corp.* v. *FTC,* 467 F.2d 67, 79 (CA10 1972), stated in finding that "[t]he coal industry is a distinct submarket which has characteristics which are not shared by the other fuel industries," coal prices "are now, and promise to be in the future, subject to the peculiarities of the coal business [since] other fuels appear to have a limited effect." . . .

III

[In this section MR. JUSTICE DOUGLAS discussed the District Court's delineation of the appropriate relevant geographic markets. Since this issue was not addressed by the majority I have omitted it herein.]

IV

While finding no violation of §7 in the Freeman-United Electric combination, the District Court did not make clear the standard used in reaching that ultimate conclusion. The court did not mention what it thought to be the relevant market shares nor did it discuss the effect of the combination on industry concentration. The court merely found that Freeman and United Electric do not compete because they are located in different FRD geographic markets, and because they sell different types of coal. . . .

The . . . [majority] urges that United's weak reserve position, rather than establishing a failing-company defense, "went to the heart of the Government's statistical prima facie case based on production figures." Under this view United's weak reserve position at the time of trial constitutes postacquisition evidence which diminishes the possibility of anticompetitive impact and thus directly affects the strength of time-of-acquisition findings. The problem with this analysis is that this District Court made no time-of-acquisition findings which such postacquisition evidence could affect. The majority concedes the obvious need for a limitation on the weight given postacquisition evidence and notes that we have reversed cases where "too much weight" has been given. Here the

---

[9] Interruptible gas is sold at a lower rate and is available only when it is not required by firm-rate customers which are supplied according to their needs and which always have priority.

postacquisition events were given *all* the weight because *all* the District Court's findings were made as of the time of the trial. While findings made as of the time of the merger could concededly be tempered to a limited degree by postacquisition events, no such findings were ever made.

Many of the commitments here which reduced United's available reserves occurred after the acquisition; 21 million tons for example were committed in 1968. Similarly, though the District Court found further mineable strip reserves unavailable at the time of trial, there is no finding that they were unavailable in 1959 or 1967. To the contrary, the record demonstrates that other coal producers did acquire new strip reserves during the 1960s. . . . United's 1959 viability is further supported by the fact that it possessed 27 million tons of deep reserves. While we do not know if all these reserves were economically mineable at the time of the acquisition, there was no finding that they would not become so in the near future with advances in technology or changes in the price structure of the coal market.[10] Further there was no contention or finding that further deep reserves were not available for acquisition.[11] The District Court merely concluded that United had no "ability to develop deep coal reserves."[12]

While it is true that United is a strip-mining company which has not extracted deep reserves since 1954, this does not mean that United would not develop deep-mining expertise if deep reserves were all it had left or that it could not sell the reserves to some company which poses less of a threat to increased concentration in the coal market than does Freeman. United Electric was not, as the Court suggests, merely one of many companies with the possible "inclination and the corporate treasury" to allow expansion into "an essentially new line of business." United was a coal company with a thriving coal-marketing structure. At the time of the merger it had access to at least 27 million tons of deep reserves and it had operated a deep mine only five years previously. While deep-coal mining may have been an essentially new line of business for many, it was for

---

[10] Research into new methods of extraction or a rise in the price of coal could make reserves which are uneconomical to mine at any given time economically mineable in the future.

[11] To the contrary, United Electric acquired substantial new deep reserves after the time of the acquisition since it now owns about 44 million tons of deep reserves and controls by location another 40 to 50 million tons. Reserves are controlled by location if, in order to be mined at all, they must be mined by those who control, by ownership, lease, or option, the contiguous reserves.

[12] If that conclusion is to lend support to the combination on the ground that United "standing alone, cannot contribute meaningfully to competition," it must be made in light of the stringent standards applicable to the failing-company defense. In *Citizen Publishing Co.* v. *United States*, 394 U.S. 131, 138–139 (1969), we said that the defense is one of "narrow scope" and that the burden of proving the defense is "on those who seek refuge under it." We also stated that the prospects of continued independent existence must be "dim or nonexistent" and that it must be established that the acquiring company is the only available purchaser. See also *United States* v. *Greater Buffalo Press*, 402 U.S. 549, 555–556 (1971), and *United States* v. *Third National Bank of Nashville*, 390 U.S. 171, 189 (1968).

United merely a matter of regaining the expertise it once had to extract reserves it already owned for sale in a market where it already had a good name.

V

Thus, from product and geographic markets to market-share and industry-concentration analysis to the failing-company defense, the findings below are based on legal standards which are either incorrect or not disclosed. While the court did gratuitously state that no §7 violation would be found "even were this court to accept the Government's unrealistic product and market definitions," this conclusory statement is supported by no analysis sufficient to allow review in this Court. The majority notes that production figures are of limited significance because they include deliveries under long-term contracts entered into in prior years. It is true that uncommitted reserves or sales of previously uncommitted coal would be preferable indicia of competitive strength, but the District Court made *no* findings as to United's or Freeman's respective market shares at the time of the acquisition under either of these standards. . . .

6

Mergers and Product/ Market Extension

The third category of mergers—conglomerates—involves those among firms which formerly were neither customers, suppliers, nor direct competitors of one another. This third category can be divided into three types of mergers. First, there are product-extension mergers. These involve industries and products into which either or both of the merger partners might logically be expected to enter *de novo*—without using merger as the entry route. Second, there are market-extension mergers, involving firms which produce substitutable products, but which market them in separate geographic areas. As with product-extension mergers, there is often a possibility that, absent the merger, *de novo* entry might occur.

Third, there are what might be called pure conglomerates—mergers of firms with no discernible relationship to one another. These are generally aimed at achieving greater use of management or other generalized capabilities, attaining financial or strategic advantages, or enhancing an organization's sheer size.

Adjudication of product- and market-extension mergers has frequently involved a determination of the importance of the acquiring firm as a potential competitor—would the firm either have entered by itself, thereby increasing the number of competitors? Or would it at least have remained at the edge of the market, thereby providing a constraint upon the activities of those firms already a part of the market?

Another aspect which has often been crucial to the outcome of these cases has been the Court's estimate of the power brought to the industry by the acquiring firm. More specifically, will the "deep financial pockets" of the acquiring firm give the newly acquired firm an unfair advantage over its rivals, ultimately lessening competition?

These issues were graphically presented in the *Procter & Gamble, Falstaff, Budd* and *Marine Bancorporation* cases. The *Budd* decision is particularly interesting in that it attempts to enunciate a rule for identifying toehold acquisitions, whereby product-extension mergers may be

221

permitted by a powerful outsider with an industry's smaller firms, so as to enable the acquiring firm to gain a toehold in the industry. *Falstaff* and *Marine Bancorporation* are of interest both for their treatment of market-extension and potential competition factors generally and for their analysis of the means by which potential entrants are identified and evaluated.

Finally, related collaterally to market extension is reciprocity: the possibility that a firm engaged in many areas of activity can demand from suppliers of one division reciprocal business for another, thereby foreclosing potentially important markets to competing suppliers. While enforcement activity in this area has not been particularly active, *Consolidated Foods* illustrates the willingness of the Supreme Court to consider evidence of the extent to which an acquiring firm actively sought reciprocity and the effect thereon of the challenged acquisition.

Pure conglomerate mergers remain one of the more difficult areas: antitrust traditionalists contend that, by definition, these lead to no enhancement of power in any relevant market, while enforcers worry about the social and economic consequences of the massive size of some of these combinations. But the courts have not spoken clearly on this subject—yet.

Federal Trade Commission v. *Consolidated Foods Corp.*

380 U.S. 592 (1965)

MR. JUSTICE DOUGLAS delivered the opinion of the Court.

The question presented involves an important construction and application of Section 7 of the Clayton Act . . . amended. . . . Consolidated Foods Corp.—which owns food processing plants and a network of wholesale and retail food stores—acquired Gentry, Inc., in 1951. Gentry manufactures principally dehydrated onion and garlic. The Federal Trade Commission held that the acquisition violated Section 7 because it gave respondent the advantage of a mixed threat and lure of reciprocal buying in its competition for business and "the power to foreclose competition from a substantial share of the markets for dehydrated onion and garlic." It concluded, in other words, that the effect of the acquisition "may be substantially to lessen competition" within the meaning of Section 7, and it ordered divestiture and gave other relief. . . . The Court of Appeals, relying mainly on 10 years of post-acquisition experience, held that the Commission had failed to show a probability that the acquisition would substantially lessen competition. . . . The case is here on certiorari. . . .

We hold at the outset that the "reciprocity" made possible by such an acquisition is one of the congeries of anticompetitive practices at which the antitrust laws are aimed. The practice results in "an irrelevant and alien factor," . . . intruding into the choice among competing products, creating at the least "a priority on the business at equal prices." *International Salt Co.* v. *United States* . . . ; *Northern Pac. R. Co.* v. *United States.* . . . Reciprocal trading may ensue not from bludgeoning or coercion but from more subtle arrangements. A threatened withdrawal of orders if products of an affiliate cease being bought, as well as a conditioning of future purchases on the receipt of orders for products of that affiliate, is an anticompetitive practice. Section 7 of the Clayton Act is concerned "with probabilities, not certainties." *Brown Shoe Co.* v. *United States* . . . ; *United States* v. *Philadelphia Nat. Bank.* . . . Reciprocity in trading as a result of an acquisition violates Section 7, if the probability of a lessening of competition is shown. We turn then to that, the principal, aspect of the present case.

Consolidated is a substantial purchaser of the products of food processors who in turn purchase dehydrated onion and garlic for use in preparing and packaging their food. Gentry, which as noted is principally engaged in the manufacture of dehydrated onion and garlic, had in 1950, immediately prior to its acquisition by Consolidated, about 32% of the total sales of the dehydrated garlic and onion industry and, together with its principal competitor, Basic Vegetable Products, Inc., accounted for almost 90% of the total industry sales. The remaining 10% was divided between two other firms. By 1958 the total industry output of both products had doubled, Gentry's share rising to 35% and the combined share of Gentry and Basic remaining at about 90%.

After the acquisition Consolidated (though later disclaiming adherence to any policy of reciprocity) did undertake to assist Gentry in selling. An official of Consolidated wrote as follows to its distributing divisions:

> Oftentimes, it is a great advantage to know when you are calling on a prospect, whether or not that prospect is a supplier of someone within your own organization. Everyone believes in reciprocity providing all things are equal.
>
> Attached is a list of prospects for our Gentry products. We would like to have you indicate on the list whether or not you are purchasing any of your supplies from them. If so, indicate whether your purchases are relatively large, small or insignificant. . . .

Food processors who sold to Consolidated stated they would give their onion and garlic business to Gentry for reciprocity reasons if it could meet the price and quality of its competitors' products. . . .

Some suppliers responded and gave reciprocal orders. Some who first gave generous orders later reduced them or abandoned the practice. It is impossible to recreate the precise anatomy of the market arrangements following the acquisition, though respondent offers a factual brief seeking to prove that "reciprocity" either failed or was not a major factor in the post-acquisition history.

The Commission found, however, that "merely as a result of its connection with Consolidated, and without any action on the latter's part, Gentry would have an unfair advantage over competitors enabling it to make sales that otherwise might not have been made." . . .

The Court of Appeals, on the other hand, gave post-acquisition evidence almost conclusive weight. It pointed out that, while Gentry's share of the dehydrated onion market increased by some 7%, its share of the dehydrated garlic market decreased 12%. . . . It also relied on apparently unsuccessful attempts at reciprocal buying. . . . The Court of Appeals concluded that "Probability can best be gauged by what the past has taught." . . .

The Court of Appeals was not in error in considering the post-acquisition evidence in this case. . . . But we think it gave too much weight to it. . . . No group acquiring a company with reciprocal buying opportunities is entitled to a "free trial" period. To give it such would be to distort the scheme of Section 7. . . . Probability of the proscribed evil is required, as we have noted. If the post-acquisition evidence were given conclusive weight or allowed to override all probabilities, then acquisitions would go forward willy-nilly, the parties biding their time until reciprocity was allowed fully to bloom. It is, of course, true that post-acquisition conduct may amount to a violation of Section 7 even though there is no evidence to establish probability *in limine*. . . . But the force of Section 7 is still in probabilities, not in what later transpired. That must necessarily be the case, for once the two companies are united no one knows what the fate of the acquired company and its competitors would have been but for the merger.

Moreover, the post-acquisition evidence here tends to confirm, rather than cast doubt upon, the probable anticompetitive effect which the Commission found the merger would have. The Commission found that Basic's product was superior to Gentry's—as Gentry's president freely and repeatedly admitted. Yet Gentry, in a rapidly expanding market, was able to increase its share of onion sales by 7% and to hold its losses in garlic to a 12% decrease. . . .

We do not go so far as to say any acquisition, no matter how small, violates Section 7 if there is a probability of reciprocal buying. Some situations may amount only to *de minimis*. But where, as here, the acquisition is of a company that commands a substantial share of a market, a finding of probability of reciprocal buying by the Commission, whose expertise the Congress trusts, should be honored, if there is substantial evidence to support it.

The evidence is in our view plainly substantial. Reciprocity was tried over and again and it sometimes worked. The industry structure was peculiar, Basic being the leader with Gentry closing the gap. Moreover there is evidence, as the Commission found, "that many buyers have determined that their source of supply may best be protected by a policy of buying from two suppliers." When reciprocal buying—or the inducement of it—is added, the Commission observed:

> Buyers are likely to lean toward Basic on the ground of quality, but, in seeking a second, protective supply channel, to purchase from Gentry in the belief that this will further their sales to Consolidated. Not only does Gentry thus obtain sales that might otherwise go to Basic or Puccinelli, but the two-firm oligopoly structure of the industry is strengthened and solidified and new entry by others is discouraged. . . .

We conclude that there is substantial evidence to sustain that conclusion and that the order of the Commission should not have been denied enforcement. The judgment of the Court of Appeals is accordingly

Reversed.

[MR. JUSTICE HARLAN concurred.]

MR. JUSTICE STEWART, concurring in the judgment.

. . . While I agree with the result that the Court has reached, I am persuaded to file this separate statement of my views regarding the issues involved.

Clearly the opportunity for reciprocity is not alone enough to invalidate a merger under Section 7. The Clayton Act was not passed to outlaw diversification. Yet large scale diversity of industrial interests almost always presents the possibility of some reciprocal relationships. Often the purpose of diversification is to acquire companies whose present management can benefit from the technical skills and sales acumen of the acquiring corporation. Without more, Section 7 of the Clayton Act does not prohibit mergers whose sole effect is to introduce into an arena of "soft" competition the experience and skills of a more aggressive organization.

It obviously requires more than this kind of bare potential for reciprocal buying to bring a merger within the ban of Section 7. Before a merger may be properly outlawed under Section 7 on the basis solely of reciprocal buying potentials, the law requires a more closely textured economic analysis. . . .

. . . Certainly the mere effort at reciprocity cannot be the basis for finding the probability of a significant alteration in the market structure. Section 7 does not punish intent. No matter how bent on reciprocity Consolidated might have been, if its activities would not have the requisite probable impact on competition, it cannot be held to have violated this law. And, I think, it is not enough to say that the merger is illegal merely because the reciprocity attempts "sometimes worked." If the opportunity for reciprocity itself is not a violation of the Act when the merger occurs, then some standard must be established for determining how effective reciprocity must be before the merger is subject to invalidation. Nor do I think that illegality of this merger can be rested upon the fact that "[t]he industry structure was peculiar, Basic being the leader with Gentry closing the gap." There is evidence that in the years following 1951, when the merger took place, increased emphasis was placed on solving technical problems which had prevented some processors from relying on dehydrated, rather than raw, onions. The 1950s were a time of flux for the industry. Basic was sometimes the innovator of technological change leading to increased sales; sometimes Gentry had the upper hand. It is possible that this shift to more intensive competition was connected with the merger. Faced with a new competitive situation, Basic may have determined to solve quality control problems which had long been dormant. Indeed, the evidence seems to show that, after the acquisition, the industry reflected the salutary qualities normally associated with free competition. Overall, both Basic and Gentry were furnishing a better product at the end of this period than at the beginning. It is true that the industry had oligopolistic features, but there is no evidence to indicate that barriers to entry were particularly severe.[1] And Gentry, while it was "closing the gap" with regard to dehydrated onions, was falling even farther behind Basic in the sales of dehydrated garlic. Finally, I can attach no significance to the fact that processors, seeking a second source of supply, normally relied on Gentry rather than Puccinelli. That fact can rest on so many alternative hypotheses that it is persuasive as to none.

The touchstone of Section 7 is the probability that competition will be lessened. But before a court takes the drastic step of ordering divestiture, the evidence must be clear that such a probability exists. . . .

To determine that probability, the courts and the Commission should rely on the best information available, whether it is an examination of the market structure before the merger has taken place, or facts concerning the changes in the market after the merger has been consummated. For that reason, I differ with the Court in its assessment of the weight to be accorded post-acquisition evidence. That evidence is the best evidence available to determine whether the merger will distort market forces in the dehydrated onion and garlic industry. The Court of Appeals, in my view, was not wrong because it "gave too much weight" to the post-acquisition evidence. It erred because of the gloss it placed on the statistics and testimony adduced before the hearing examiner and the Commission. . . .

---

[1] Indeed, by the time of the Commission's decision an additional firm, Gilroy Foods, Inc., had entered this market.

Federal Trade Commission v. Procter & Gamble Co.

386 U.S. 568 (1967)

MR. JUSTICE DOUGLAS delivered the opinion of the Court.

This is a proceeding initiated by the Federal Trade Commission charging that respondent, Procter & Gamble Co., had acquired the assets of Clorox Chemical Co. in violation of §7 of the Clayton Act, . . . as amended by the Celler-Kefauver Act. . . . The charge was that Procter's acquisition of Clorox might substantially lessen competition or tend to create a monopoly in the production and sale of household liquid bleaches. . . .

As indicated by the Commission in its painstaking and illuminating report, it does not particularly aid analysis to talk of this merger in conventional terms, namely, horizontal or vertical or conglomerate. This merger may most appropriately be described as a "product-extension merger," as the Commission stated. . . .

At the time of the merger, in 1957, Clorox was the leading manufacturer in the heavily concentrated household liquid bleach industry. It is agreed that household liquid bleach is the relevant line of commerce. The product is used in the home as a germicide and disinfectant, and, more importantly, as a whitening agent in washing clothes and fabrics. It is a distinctive product with no close substitutes. Liquid bleach is a low-price, high-turnover consumer product sold mainly through grocery stores and supermarkets. The relevant geographical market is the Nation and a series of regional markets. Because of high shipping costs and low sales price, it is not feasible to ship the product more than 300 miles from its point of manufacture. Most manufacturers are limited to competition within a single region since they have but one plant. Clorox is the only firm selling nationally; it has 13 plants distributed throughout the Nation. Purex, Clorox's closest competitor in size, does not distribute its bleach in the northeast or mid-Atlantic States; in 1957, Purex's bleach was available in less than 50% of the national market.

At the time of the acquisition, Clorox was the leading manufacturer of household liquid bleach, with 48.8% of the national sales—annual sales of slightly less than $40,000,000. Its market share had been steadily increasing for the five years prior to the merger. Its nearest rival was Purex, which manufacturers a number of products other than household liquid bleaches, including abrasive cleaners, toilet soap, and detergents. Purex accounted for 15.7% of the household liquid bleach market. The industry is highly concentrated; in 1957, Clorox and Purex accounted for almost 65% of the Nation's household liquid bleach sales, and, together with four other firms, for almost 80%. The remaining 20% was divided among over 200 small producers. Clorox had total assets of $12,000,000; only eight producers had assets in excess of $1,000,000 and very few had assets of more than $75,000.

In light of the territorial limitations on distribution, national figures do not give an accurate picture of Clorox's dominance in the various regions. Thus, Clorox's seven principal competitors did no business in New England, the mid-Atlantic States, or metropolitan New York. Clorox's share of the sales in those areas was 56%, 72%, and 64% respectively. Even in regions where its principal competitors were active, Clorox maintained a dominant position. Except in metropolitan Chicago and the west-central States Clorox accounted for at least 39%, and often a much higher percentage, of liquid bleach sales.

Since all liquid bleach is chemically identical, advertising and sales promotion are vital. In 1957 Clorox spent almost $3,700,000 on advertising, imprinting the value of its bleach in the mind of the consumer. In addition, it spent $1,700,000 for other promotional activities. The Commission found that these heavy expenditures went far to explain why Clorox maintained so high a market share despite the fact that its brand, though chemically indistinguishable from rival brands, retailed for a price equal to or, in many instances, higher than its competitors.

Procter is a large, diversified manufacturer of low-price, high-turnover household products sold through grocery, drug, and department stores. Prior to its acquisition of Clorox, it did not produce household liquid bleach. Its 1957 sales were in excess of $1,100,000,000 from which it realized profits of more than $67,000,000; its assets were over $500,000,000. Procter has been marked by rapid growth and diversification. It has successfully developed and introduced a number of new products. Its primary activity is in the general area of soaps, detergents, and cleansers; in 1957, of total domestic sales, more than one-half (over $500,000,000) were in this field. Procter was the dominant factor in this area. It accounted for 54.4% of all packaged detergent sales. The industry is heavily concentrated—Procter and its nearest competitors, Colgate-Palmolive and Lever Brothers, account for 80% of the market.

In the marketing of soaps, detergents, and cleansers, as in the marketing of household liquid bleach, advertising and sales promotion are vital. In 1957, Procter was the Nation's largest advertiser, spending more than $80,000,000 on advertising and an additional $47,000,000 on sales promotion. Due to its tremendous volume, Procter receives substantial discounts from the media. As a multiproduct producer Procter enjoys substantial advantages in advertising and sales promotion. Thus, it can and does feature several products in its promotions, reducing the printing, mailing, and other costs for each product. It also purchases network programs on behalf of several products, enabling it to give each product network exposure at a fraction of the cost per product that a firm with only one product to advertise would incur.

Prior to the acquisition, Procter was in the course of diversifying into product lines related to its basic detergent-soap-cleanser business. Liquid bleach was a distinct possibility since packaged detergents—Procter's primary product line—and liquid bleach are used complementarily in washing clothes and fabrics, and in general household cleaning. As noted by the Commission:

> . . . From the consumer's viewpoint, packaged detergents and liquid bleach are closely related products. But the area of relatedness between products of Procter and of Clorox is wider. Household cleansing agents in general, like household liquid bleach, are low-cost, high-turnover household consumer goods marketed chiefly through grocery stores and pre-sold to the consumer by the manufacturer through mass advertising and sales promotions. Since products of both parties to the merger are sold to the same customers, at the same stores, and by the same merchandising methods, the possibility arises of significant integration at both the marketing and distribution levels. . . .

The decision to acquire Clorox was the result of a study conducted by Procter's promotion department designed to determine the advisability of entering the liquid bleach industry. The initial report noted the ascendancy of liquid bleach in the large and expanding household bleach market, and recommended that Procter purchase Clorox rather than enter independently. Since a large investment would be needed to obtain a satisfactory market share, acquisition of the industry's leading firm was attractive. . . .

The Commission found that the acquisition might substantially lessen competition. . . .

The Court of Appeals said that the Commission's finding of illegality had been based on "treacherous conjecture," mere possibility and suspicion. . . . [It] also heavily relied on post-acquisition "evidence . . . to the effect that the other producers subsequent to the merger were selling more bleach for more money than ever before" (358 F.2d, at 80), and that "[t]here [had] been no significant change in Clorox's market share in the four years subsequent to the merger" (*ibid.*). . . . The Court of Appeals, in our view, misapprehended the standards for its review and the standards applicable in a §7 proceeding.

Section 7 of the Clayton Act was intended to arrest the anticompetitive effects of market power in their incipiency. The core question is whether a merger may substantially lessen competition, and necessarily requires a prediction of the merger's impact on competition, present and future. . . . The section can deal only with probabilities, not with certainties. . . . And there is certainly no requirement that the anticompetitive power manifest itself in anticompetitive action before §7 can be called into play. If the enforcement of §7 turned on the existence of actual anticompetitive practices, the congressional policy of thwarting such practices in their incipiency would be frustrated.

All mergers are within the reach of §7, and all must be tested by the same standard, whether they are classified as horizontal, vertical, conglomerate[1] or other. As noted by the Commission, this merger is neither horizontal, vertical, nor conglomerate. Since the products of the acquired company are complementary to those of the acquiring company and may be produced with similar facilities, marketed through the same channels and in the same manner, and advertised by the same media, the Commission aptly called this acquisition a "product-extension merger." . . .

The anticompetitive effects with which this product-extension merger is fraught can easily be seen: (1) the substitution of the powerful acquiring firm for the smaller, but already dominant, firm may substantially reduce the competitive structure of the industry by raising entry barriers and by dissuading the smaller firms from aggressively competing; (2) the acquisition eliminates the potential competition of the acquiring firm.

The liquid bleach industry was already oligopolistic before the acquisition, and price competition was certainly not as vigorous as it would have been if the industry were competitive. Clorox enjoyed a dominant position nationally, and its position approached monopoly proportions in certain areas. The existence of some 200 fringe firms certainly does not belie that fact. Nor does the fact, relied upon by the court below, that, after the merger, producers other than Clorox "were selling more bleach for more money than ever before." 358 F.2d, at 80. In the same period, Clorox increased its share from 48.8% to 52%. The interjection of Procter into the market considerably changed the situation. There is every reason to assume that the smaller firms would become more cautious in competing due to their fear of retaliation by Procter. It is probable that Procter would become the price leader and that oligopoly would become more rigid.

The acquisition may also have the tendency of raising the barriers to new entry. The major competitive weapon in the successful marketing of bleach is advertising. Clorox was limited in this area by its relatively small budget and its inability to obtain substantial discounts. By contrast, Procter's budget was much larger; and, although it would not devote its entire budget to advertising Clorox, it could divert a large portion to meet the short-term threat of a new entrant. Procter would be able to use its volume discounts to advantage in advertising Clorox. Thus, a new entrant would be much more reluctant to face the giant Procter than it would have been to face the smaller Clorox.[2]

---

[1] A pure conglomerate merger is one in which there are no economic relationships between the acquiring and the acquired firm.

[2] The barriers to entry have been raised both for entry by new firms and for entry into new geographical markets by established firms. The latter aspect is demonstrated by Purex's lesson in Erie, Pennsylvania. In October 1957, Purex selected Erie, Pennsylvania—where it had not sold previously—as an area in which to test the salability, under competitive conditions, of a new bleach. The leading brands in Erie were Clorox, with 52%, and the "101"

Possible economies cannot be used as a defense to illegality. Congress was aware that some mergers which lessen competition may also result in economies but it struck the balance in favor of protecting competition . . . .

The Commission also found that the acquisition of Clorox by Procter eliminated Procter as a potential competitor. The Court of Appeals declared that this finding was not supported by evidence because there was no evidence that Procter's management had ever intended to enter the industry independently and that Procter had never attempted to enter. The evidence, however, clearly shows that Procter was the most likely entrant. Procter had recently launched a new abrasive cleaner in an industry similar to the liquid bleach industry, and had wrested leadership from a brand that had enjoyed even a larger market share than had Clorox. Procter was engaged in a vigorous program of diversifying into product lines closely related to its basic products. Liquid bleach was a natural avenue of diversification since it is complementary to Procter's products, is sold to the same customers through the same channels, and is advertised and merchandised in the same manner. Procter had substantial advantages in advertising and sales promotion, which, as we have seen, are vital to the success of liquid bleach. No manufacturer had a patent on the product or its manufacture, necessary information relating to manufacturing methods and processes was readily available, there was no shortage of raw material, and the machinery and equipment required for a plant of efficient capacity were available at reasonable costs. Procter's management was experienced in producing and marketing goods similar to liquid bleach. Procter had considered the possibility of independently entering but decided against it because the acquisition of Clorox would enable Procter to capture a more commanding share of the market.

It is clear that the existence of Procter at the edge of the industry exerted considerable influence on the market. First, the market behavior of the liquid bleach industry was influenced by each firm's prediction of the market behavior of its competitors, actual and potential. Second, the barriers to entry by a firm of Procter's size and with its advantages were not significant. There is no indication that the barriers were so high that the price Procter would have to charge would be above the price that would maximize the profits of the existing firms. Third, the number of potential entrants was not so large that the elimination of one would be insignificant. Few firms would have the temerity to challenge a firm as

---

brand, sold by Gardner Manufacturing Company, with 29% of the market. Purex launched an advertising and promotional campaign to obtain a broad distribution in a short time, and in five months captured 33% of the Erie market. Clorox's share dropped to 35% and 101's to 17%. Clorox responded by offering its bleach at reduced prices, and then added an offer of a $1-value ironing board cover for 50¢ with each purchase of Clorox at the reduced price. It also increased its advertising with television spots. The result was to restore Clorox's lost market share and, indeed, to increase it slightly. Purex's share fell to 7%. . . .

solidly entrenched as Clorox. Fourth, Procter was found by the Commission to be the most likely entrant. These findings of the Commission were amply supported by the evidence.

The judgment of the Court of Appeals is reversed and remanded with instructions to affirm and enforce the Commission's order.

It is so ordered.

MR. JUSTICE STEWART and MR. JUSTICE FORTAS took no part in the consideration or decision of this case.

MR. JUSTICE HARLAN, concurring.

I agree that the Commission's order should be sustained, but . . . [i]t is regrettable to see this Court as it enters this comparatively new field of economic adjudication starting off with what has almost become a kind of *res ipsa loquitur* approach to antitrust cases.

The type of merger represented by the transaction before us is becoming increasingly important as large corporations seek to diversify their operations . . . and "[c]ompanies looking for new lines of business tend to buy into those fields with which they have at least some degree of familiarity, and where economies and efficiencies from assimilation are at least possible." Turner, Conglomerate Mergers and Section 7 of the Clayton Act, 78 Harv. L. Rev. 1313, 1315. Application of §7 to such mergers has been troubling to the Commission and the lower courts. . . .

I thus believe that it is incumbent upon us to make a careful study of the facts and opinions below in this case, and at least to embark upon the formulation of standards for the application of §7 to mergers which are neither horizontal nor vertical and which previously have not been considered in depth by this Court. . . . My prime difficulty with the Court's opinion is that it makes no effort in this direction at all, and leaves the commission, lawyers, and businessmen at large as to what is to be expected of them in future cases of this kind.

I

The Court's opinion rests on three separate findings of anticompetitive effect. The Court first declares that the market here was "oligopolistic" and that interjection of Procter would make the oligopoly "more rigid" because "[t]here is every reason to assume that the smaller firms would become more cautious in competing due to their fear of retaliation by Procter." The Court, however, does not indicate exactly what reasons lie behind this assumption or by what standard such an effect is deemed "reasonably probable." It could equally be assumed that smaller firms would become more aggressive in competing due to their fear that otherwise Procter might ultimately absorb their markets and that Procter, as a new entrant in the bleach field, was vulnerable to attack.

But assumption is no substitute for reasonable probability as a measure of illegality under §7 . . . and Congress has not mandated the Commission or the courts "to campaign against 'superconcentration' in the absence of any evidence of harm to competition." Turner *supra*, at 1395. . . .

The Court next stresses the increase in barriers to new entry into the liquid bleach field caused primarily, it is thought, by the substitution of the larger advertising capabilities of Procter for those of Clorox. Economic theory would certainly indicate that a heightening of such barriers has taken place. But the Court does not explain why it considers this change to have significance under §7, nor does it indicate when or how entry barriers affect competition in a relevant market. In this case, for example, the difficulties of introducing a new nationally advertised bleach were already so great that even a great company like Procter, which the Court finds the most likely entrant, believed that entry would not "pay out." Why then does the Court find that a further increase of incalculable proportions in such barriers substantially lessens competition? Such a conclusion at least needs the support of reasoned analysis.[3]

Finally, the Court places much emphasis on the loss to the market of the most likely potential entrant, Procter. Two entirely separate anticompetitive effects might be traced to this loss, and the Court fails to distinguish between them. The first is simply that loss of the most likely entrant increases the operative barriers to entry by decreasing the likelihood that any firm will attempt to surmount them.[4] But this effect merely reinforces the Court's previous entry-barrier argument, which I do not find convincing as presented. The second possible effect is that a reasonably probable entrant has been excluded from the market and a measure of horizontal competition has been lost. Certainly the exclusion of what would promise to be an important independent competitor from the market may be sufficient, in itself, to support a finding of illegality under §7, . . . when the market has few competitors. The Commission, however, expressly refused to find a reasonable probability that Procter would

---

[3] The need for analysis is even clearer in light of the fact that entry into the market by producers of nonadvertised, locally distributed bleaches was found to be easy. There were no technological barriers to entry, and the capital requirements for entry, with the exception of advertising costs, were small. The Court must at least explain why the threat of such entry and the presence of small competitors in existing regional markets cannot be considered the predominant, and unaffected, form of competition. To establish its point, the Court must either minimize the importance of such competition or show why it would be substantially lessened by the merger.

[4] Bain's pioneering study of barriers to entry, *Barriers to New Competition*, recognized that such barriers could be surmounted at different price levels by different potential entrants. Thus even without change in the nature of the barriers themselves, the market could become more insulated through loss of the most likely entrant simply because the prevailing market price would have to rise to a higher level than before to induce entry.

have entered this market on its own, and the Sixth Circuit was in emphatic agreement. . . .

Thus I believe, with all respect, that the Court has failed to make a convincing analysis of the difficult problem presented, and were no more to be said in favor of the Commission's order I would vote to set it aside.

II

The Court, following the Commission, points out that this merger is not a pure "conglomerate" merger but may more aptly be labeled a "product-extension" merger. . . .

At the outset, it seems to me that there is a serious question whether the state of our economic knowledge is sufficiently advanced to enable a surefooted administrative or judicial determination to be made *a priori* of substantial anticompetitive effect in mergers of this kind. It is clear enough that Congress desired that conglomerate and product-extension mergers be brought under §7 scrutiny, but well versed economists have argued that such scrutiny can never lead to a valid finding of illegality. . . .

Lending strength to this position is the fact that such mergers do provide significant economic benefits which argue against excessive controls being imposed on them. The ability to merge brings large firms into the market for capital assets and encourages economic development by holding out the incentive of easy and profitable liquidation to others. Here, for example, the owners of Clorox who had built the business, were able to liquefy their capital on profitable terms without dismantling the enterprise they had created. Also merger allows an active management to move rapidly into new markets bringing with its intervention competitive stimulation and innovation. It permits a large corporation to protect its shareholders from business fluctuation through diversification, and may facilitate the introduction of capital resources, allowing significant economies of scale, into a stagnating market. . . .

At the other end of the spectrum, it has been argued that the entry of a large conglomerate enterprise may have a destructive effect on competition in any market. . . . Thus it is contended that a large conglomerate may underprice in one market, adversely affecting competition, and subsidize the operation by benefits accruing elsewhere.[5] It is also argued that the large company generates psychological pressure which may force smaller ones to follow its pricing policies, and that its very presence in the market may discourage entrants or make lending institutions unwilling to finance them. . . . [T]hese observations do indicate that significant dangers to competition may be presented by some conglomerate and prod-

---

[5] But see Turner, "Conglomerate Mergers and Section 7 of the Clayton Act," 78 *Harv. L. Rev.* 1313, 1340. "[T]he belief that predatory pricing is a likely consequence of conglomerate size, and hence of conglomerate merger, is wholly unverified by any careful studies . . . ."

uct-extension mergers. Further, congressional concern in enacting §7 extended not only to anticompetitive behavior in particular markets, but also to the possible economic dominance of large companies which had grown through merger. Thus, while fully agreeing that mergers of this kind are not to be regarded as something entirely set apart from scrutiny under §7, I am of the view that when this Court does undertake to establish the standards for judging their legality, it should proceed with utmost circumspection. . . .

III

In adjudicating horizontal and vertical combinations under §7 where the effects on competition are reasonably obvious and substantiality is the key issue, the responsible agencies have moved away from an initial emphasis on comprehensive scrutiny and opted for more precise rules of thumb which provide advantages of administrative convenience and predictability for the business world. . . . A conglomerate case, however, is not only too new to our experience to allow the formulation of simple rules but also involves "concepts of economic power and competitive effect that are still largely unformulated." . . .

Procter . . . has insisted throughout this proceeding that anticompetitive effects must be proved *in fact* from post-merger evidence in order for §7 to be applied. The Court gives little attention to this contention, but I think it must be considered seriously, both because it is arguable and because it was, in a sense, the main source of difference between the Commission and the Sixth Circuit. . . .

If §7 is to serve the purposes Congress intended for it, we must, I think, stand with the Commission on this issue. Only by focusing on market structure can we begin to formulate standards which will allow the responsible agencies to give proper consideration to such mergers and allow businessmen to plan their actions with a fair degree of certainty . . . . The value of post-merger evidence seems more than offset by the difficulties encountered in obtaining it. And the post-merger evidence before us in this proceeding is at best inconclusive.

Deciding that §7 inquiry in conglomerate or product-extension merger cases should be directed toward reasonably probable changes in market structure does not, however, determine how that inquiry should be narrowed and focused. The Commission and the Court isolate two separate structural elements, the degree of concentration in the existing market and the "condition of entry." The interplay of these two factors is said to determine the existence and extent of market power, since the "condition of entry" determines the limits potential competition places on the existing market. It must be noted, however, that economic theory teaches that potential competition will have no effect on the market behavior of existing firms unless present market power is sufficient to drive the market price to the point where entry would become a real possibility. So long as existing competition is sufficient to keep the market price below that point, potential competition is of marginal significance as a market regulator. Thus in a conglomerate or product-extension case, where the effects on market structure which are easiest to discover are generally effects on the "condition of entry," an understanding of the workings of the premerger market cannot be ignored, and indeed, is critical to a determination whether the visible effects on "condition of entry" have any competitive significance.

The Commission pinned its analysis of the premerger market exclusively on its concentration, the large market share enjoyed by the leading firms. . . . The Sixth Circuit discounted the Commission's analysis because of the presence of some 200 small competitors in the market. The Court bases its agreement with the Commission and its rejection of the Court of Appeals' position on Clorox's alleged domination of the market. But domination is an elusive term, for dominance in terms of percentage of sales is not the equivalent of dominance in terms of control over price or other aspects of market behavior. Just as the total number of sellers in the market is not determinative of its operation, the percentage of sales made by any group of sellers is similarly not conclusive. The determinative issue is, instead, how the sellers interact and establish the pattern of market behavior. The significance of concentration analysis is that it allows measurement of one easily determined variable to serve as an opening key to the pattern of market behavior.

I think that the Commission, on *this* record, was entitled to regard the market as "oligopolistic" and that it could properly ignore the impact of the smaller firms. I hasten to add, however, that there are significant "economic dissents" from oligopoly analysis in general. . . . In adjudicating §7 questions in a conglomerate or product-extension merger context where the pattern of behavior in the existing market is apt to be crucial, I would, therefore, allow the introduction by a defendant of evidence designed to show that the actual operation of the market did not accord with oligopoly theory, or whatever other theory the Commission desires to apply. In other words, I believe that defendants in §7 proceedings are entitled, in the case of conglomerate or product-extension mergers, to build their own economic cases for the proposition that the mergers will not substantially impair competition. . . . But to challenge effectively the presumption which the Commission is entitled to draw from general economic theory, a defendant must present, in my opinion, not only contradictory facts but a more cogent explanation of the pattern of market behavior.

If the proof as a whole establishes that pricing power may be exercised by a firm or firms in the market—that prices may be raised in the long run over competitive prices—then the Commission may legitimately focus on the role of potential competition and the "condition of entry." . . . In so doing, however, a new difficulty is encountered. The threat of potential competition merely affects the range over which price power extends. Potential competition does not compel more vigorous striving in the market, nor advance any other social goal which Congress might be said to have favored in passing §7. Thus it may legitimately be questioned whether even a substantial increase in entry barriers creates a substantial lessening of competition or tendency to monopoly as required by §7.

Two justifications for the use of entry barriers as a determinant under §7 can be given. The first is that an increased range over which pricing power may be exercised is contrary to the mandate of §7 because Congress' use of the word "competition" was a shorthand for the invocation of the benefits of a competitive market, one of which is a price close to average cost. Such an approach leads also to the conclusion that economic efficiencies produced by the merger must be weighed against anticompetitive consequences in the final determination whether the net effect on competition is substantially adverse. . . . The second justification is found in the tendency-to-monopoly clause of §7. Certainly the clearest evil of monopoly is the excessive power the monopolist has over price. Since "antitrust operates to forestall concentrations of economic power which, if allowed to develop unhindered, would call for much more intrusive government supervision of the economy," Blake & Jones, In Defense of Antitrust, 65 Col. L. Rev. 377, 383, increased power over price should be attackable under §7. . . . For these reasons I conclude that the Commission may properly find a conglomerate or product-extension merger illegal under §7 because it substantially increases pricing power in the relevant market.

Given the development of a case against the merger in this area, however, the problem of efficiencies raised above must still be faced. The Court attempts to brush the question aside by asserting that Congress preferred competition to economies, but neglects to determine whether certain economies are inherent in the idea of competition. If it is conceded, as it must be, that Congress had reasons for favoring competition, then more efficient operation must have been among them. It is of course true that a firm's ability to achieve economies enhances its competitive position, but adverse effects on competitors must be distinguished from adverse effects on competition. . . . Economies achieved by one firm may stimulate matching innovation by others, the very essence of competition. They always allow the total output to be delivered to the consumer with an expenditure of fewer resources. Thus when the case against a conglomerate or product-extension merger rests on a market-structure demonstration that the likelihood of anticompetitive consequences has been substantially increased, the responsible agency should then move on to examine and weigh possible efficiencies arising from the merger in order to determine whether, on balance, competition has been substantially lessened. Where detriments to competition are apt to be "highly speculative" it seems wisest to conclude that "possibilities of adverse effects on competitive behavior are worth worrying about only when the merger does not involve substantial economies. . . ." Turner, *supra,* at 1354. . . .

To summarize then, four important guides to the adjudication of conglomerate or product-extension mergers under §7 seem to come forward. First, the decision can rest on analysis of market structure without resort to evidence of post-merger anticompetitive behavior. Second, the operation of the premerger market must be understood as the foundation of successful analysis. The responsible agency may presume that the market operates in accord with generally accepted principles of economic theory, but the presumption must be open to challenge of alternative operational formulations. Third, if it is reasonably probable that there will be a change in market structure which will allow the exercise of substantially greater market power, then a prima facie case has been made out under §7. Fourth, where the case against the merger rests on the probability of increased market power, the merging companies may attempt to prove that there are countervailing economies reasonably probable which should be weighed against the adverse effects.

IV

The Commission's decision did, I think, conform to this analysis. . . .

To hold the merger unlawful, the Commission relied on five factors which taken together convinced it that "substantial" anticompetitive consequences could be expected. A "substantial" impact was said to be "significant and real, and discernible not merely to theorists or scholars but to practical, hard-headed businessmen." . . . The relevant factors were (1) the excessive concentration in the industry at the time of the merger and the commanding market position of Clorox, (2) the relative disparity in size and strength between Procter and the firms in the liquid bleach industry, (3) the position of Procter in other markets, (4) the elimination of Procter as a potential competitor, and (5) the nature of the "economies" expected from the merger. The net of these factors was to establish a substantial effect on the market structure variable involved, condition of entry. . . .

. . . The Commission—in my opinion quite correctly—seemed to accept the idea that economies could be used to defend a merger, noting that "[a] merger that results in increased efficiency of production, distribution or marketing may, in certain cases, increase the vigor of competition in the relevant market." . . . But advertising economies were placed in a different classification since they were said "only to increase the barriers to new entry" and to be "offensive to at least the spirit, if not the letter, of the antitrust laws." . . . Advertising was thought to benefit only the sellers by entrenching his market position, and to be of no use to the consumer.

I think the Commission's view overstated and oversimplified. Proper advertising serves a legitimate and important purpose in the market by educating the consumer as to available alternatives. This process contributes to consumer demand being developed to the point at which economies of scale can be realized in production. The advertiser's brand name may also be an assurance of quality, and the value of this benefit is demonstrated by the general willingness of consumers to pay a premium for the advertised brands. Undeniably advertising may sometimes be used to create irrational brand preferences and mislead consumers as to the actual differences between products, but it is very difficult to discover at what point advertising ceases to be an aspect of healthy competition. . . . It is not the Commission's function to decide which lawful elements of the "product" offered the consumer should be considered useful and which should be considered the symptoms of industrial "sickness." It is the consumer who must make that election through the exercise of his purchasing power. In my view, true efficiencies in the use of advertising must be considered in assessing economies in the marketing process, which as has been noted are factors in the sort of §7 proceeding involved here.

I do not think, however, that on the record presented Procter has shown any true efficiencies in advertising. Procter has merely shown that it is able to command equivalent resources at a lower dollar cost than other bleach producers. No peculiarly efficient marketing techniques have been demonstrated, nor does the record show that a smaller net advertising expenditure could be expected. Economies cannot be premised solely on dollar figures, lest accounting controversies dominate §7 proceedings. Economies employed in defense of a merger must be shown in what economists label "real" terms, that is in terms of resources applied to the accomplishment of the objective. For this reason, the Commission, I think, was justified in discounting Procter's efficiency defense.

In the Matter of the Budd Company
86 F.T.C. 518 (1975)

OPINION OF THE COMMISSION

By ENGMAN, Commissioner: The Budd Company appeals from the Initial Decision in this matter in which the Administrative Law Judge found that its acquisition of the Gindy Manufacturing Corporation (Gindy) in 1968 violated Section 7 of the Clayton Act.

According to the *Fortune Directory of the 500 Largest United States Industrial Corporations,* in 1967 Budd was the 250th largest industrial corporation in the nation in terms of sales ($469.5 million) and was one of the largest independent automotive suppliers in the nation and the largest independent supplier of body parts to the automotive industry. Budd principally manufactured automotive bodies, wheels, rims, hubs, drums, brakes, jigs and dies used in the manufacture of automotive body parts. In addition it was a leading manufacturer of railroad and mass transit cars.

Prior to its acquisition by Budd on October 22, 1968, Gindy was a Pennsylvania corporation engaged in the manufacture and sale of van trailers, containers and container chassis. For fiscal year 1968, Gindy sales were approximately $32 million and its assets amounted to about $44 million. . . .

The complaint alleges that prior to the acquisition Budd was one of the most likely potential entrants into the manufacture and sale of van trailers, closed-top dry freight van trailers, open-top van trailers, and containers and container chassis, and that by acquiring Gindy, Budd eliminated itself as a substantial potential competitor in these markets. The complaint further alleges that these markets and segments thereof are highly concentrated and characterized by high entry barriers. . . .

I. Relevant Product Markets

The broadest product markets found by the ALJ to be appropriate for this case are (1) van trailers and (2) containers and chassis. Van trailers refers to the large box-type trailers attached permanently to a chassis with wheels that are pulled by a truck tractor. Truck trailers are *not* van trailers. Truck trailers would include tank and bulk commodity trailers (for hauling liquids, gas, cement, and the like); platform trailers and low bed heavy haulers (used, for instance, to transport heavy machinery and girders); pole and logging trailers; and dump trailers. Trucks and truck bodies are not included with the term "van trailers" which is used exclusively to refer to trailers of five-ton capacity or more that are pulled by a truck tractor. A van trailer can be open or closed at the top and is usually made with aluminum or steel or both. Vans represent by far the largest percentage of all types of truck trailers.

Containers and chassis refer to large, closed box-type structures which can be used for intermodal transportation of goods, by rail, motor carrier, or ship. The container is designed to be detachable from the chassis on which it sits when pulled by a truck. Sizes are standardized and containers must be strong enough to be hoisted and stacked on top of one another during shipboard transit. . . .

We are satisfied that the van trailers and containers and chassis each constitute appropriate markets for purposes of the case. It is not disputed that van trailers are produced on fairly unique production lines which cannot be quickly utilized to produce other types of non-van trailers such as tank, platform, logging, or dump trailers. Also, because of their special design, there is little or no substitution in end use between van trailers and these other types of truck trailers. Likewise, containers and chassis serve a distinct function that separates them from van trailers and they are usually constructed on different assembly lines than those used to build van trailers.

In addition to the foregoing product markets, the ALJ found that subcategories of van trailers listed by the Department of Census as closed-top van trailers, constitute relevant submarkets for purposes of this case. Respondent takes sharp issue that these finer divisions constitute markets. . . .

We agree with respondent . . . that closed-top dry freight van trailers and open-top van trailers do not constitute meaningful economic markets. The market for open-top trailers is limited as they are used mainly to carry freight, such as steel lengths, which must be loaded from the top by cranes. . . . Although it is true that a buyer may not find these types substitutable for particular end uses, the record nevertheless establishes that production and distribution facilities for each are identical and are essentially identical among other types of vans. Both closed- and open-top vans are commonly made by all van trailer manufacturers, including Gindy, and do not require separate assembly lines. . . .

No doubt the reason that complaint counsel urge the existence of separate closed-top and open-top van markets is that Gindy's market share is much higher if these product lines are used. . . . The inappropriateness of making a distinction in market definitions based on the presence or absence of a top on the trailer[1] is evidenced by the fact that in the following year, although Gindy's market share and ranking stayed nearly the same in overall van sales, its shipment of open-top trailers declined precipitously from $3,150,000 to $1,268,000 resulting in a drop from 15 percent to 7.8 percent of the industry total in just one year. The difference was made up by the production of other types of van trailers, thus evidencing ease of production flexibility. . . .

The ALJ, in accepting complaint counsel's argument that closed-top and open-top van trailers each constitute a relevant submarket, mechanically relied on the fact that several of the submarket criteria referred to in *Brown Shoe Co.* v. *United States,* 370 U.S. 294, 325 (1962) were applicable, such as peculiar characteristics and uses, distinct prices, and industry recognition of open-top van trailers as a category of truck trailers. But as the Court observed in a later case, "[T]hese [*Brown Shoe*] guidelines offer no precise formula for judgment and they necessitate, rather than avoid, careful consideration based upon the entire record" *United States* v. *Continental Can Co.,* 378 U.S. 441, 449 (1964). Cross-elasticity of supply can also be an important consideration in defining markets. . . . The interchangeability of production and distribution facilities between two

---

[1] There are differences in construction between open-top and closed-top freight trailers in addition to the presence or absence of a roof. Open-top trailers must have stronger top rails among other things and in fact sell for a slightly higher price than equivalent size closed-top vans. Nevertheless, as noted, production procedures and equipment are the same. Both types of trailers are produced on the same assembly line, and no additional expenditures are required to switch production capability from one to the other (Tr. 386–87, 1343).

products is a strong indication that in measuring the relevant market and the degree of market power held by firms, the output of both products should be included since the manufacturer of one can shift readily to the production and sale of the other in response to profit opportunities. . . . Because the record establishes such a high degree of cross-elasticity of production, and identical marketing ease, among van trailers, we conclude that open-top and closed-top van trailers do not constitute separate submarkets.

In adopting van trailers and containers and chassis as lines of commerce, we not deny that there is probably an even broader economic market encompassing these and other trailers. It appears that there is considerable interchangeability in production equipment and skills over the long-run between all types of truck trailers, except for tank and bulk commodity trailers which seem to fall in a specialized production class all of their own. . . . Consequently, in addition to the two product markets adopted in the initial decision, we will also examine the instant acquisition in terms of market share statistics for a broader market consisting of all truck trailers (except tank and bulk commodity trailers).

II. Geographic Market

The record supports the ALJ's findings that the relevant geographic market . . . [is] in the United States as a whole for sales of van trailers and containers and chassis. This is not to say that all trailer manufacturers are able to compete uniformly throughout the nation. High transportation costs, even for such mobile products as trailers, make it difficult to supply trailers to distant locations. Nevertheless neither party suggests that anything less than the nation should be considered the proper geographic market.

Respondent does argue that foreign producers of containers have competed with domestic producers of containers and that purchasers of containers look beyond the boundaries of the United States for supplies of this product. . . . The record indicates that there has been little competition from foreign-made containers insofar as domestic consumption in this country is concerned. Shipping lines are the primary buyers of containers and federal regulations prohibit American shipping line operators from purchasing cargo containers of foreign manufacture with capital reserve funds. . . . Furthermore, since the devaluation of the U.S. dollar, foreign container manufacturers have found it particularly difficult to sell containers in this country.

III. Market Concentration

Universe figures for the various lines of commerce described above were taken from Census Bureau publications. Shipments of individual firms were obtained directly from the manufacturers. . . .

. . . Before the loss of a potential entrant can be viewed as violating Section 7, it must be established that the market is concentrated or threatens to become so, that entry barriers are high, and that the acquired firm is a leading factor in the market. . . . If the market is not concentrated, there is usually little opportunity for the sellers to collectively maintain prices above competitive levels and any diminution of potential competition will not be material. On the other hand, if the market is concentrated but entry barriers are low, potential competition will be important but since there will be a large number of firms able to come into the market under approximately the same conditions, the merger of one of those firms with an existing seller will make no difference because the threat of new entry will remain approximately the same. . . .

As the [available data] . . . show, four-firm concentration ratios are approximately 60 percent or more, with the largest firm, Fruehauf, usually representing about 25 percent of output. The top three firms (Fruehauf, Trailmobile, and Strick) collectively shared more than 50 percent of the output in each of the markets during the three years leading up to the year of acquisition. Although the record indicates that the balance of the markets are shared by nearly a hundred firms, clearly these markets are substantially concentrated. . . .

In addition, the ALJ found that there were substantial barriers to entry insofar as entering on a substantial level of production is concerned. . . . [W]e think the record bears out the ALJ's finding, although the term *barriers to effective competition* might convey a more accurate picture than *barriers to entry.* . . . Small van trailer manufacturers generally do not have the ability to extend or obtain credit to finance a sale of a large number of trailers to large customers or to offer finance terms competitive with terms offered by the large trailer manufacturers. It is not uncommon for the largest companies in the industry to sell trailers to fleet operators with virtually no downpayment on six- to eight-year credit terms. . . . Manufacturers who do not have the capital resources to finance sales on these terms generally cannot arrange such favorable terms through banks. . . .

In addition, the larger van manufacturers have an advantage as they have geographically-dispersed branch outlets that enable them to service and resell large lots of used trailers that have been accepted as trade-ins in sales to fleet operators.

Respondent argues that these requirements are merely incremental in nature since any given sales transaction requires a small additional amount of money and it is possible to enter on a shoestring if one is willing to do so. This may be so, but the most important customers are the large motor common carriers and truck-leasing companies who buy in large lots—often a hundred or several hundred units at a time. Only a few trailer manufacturers, led by Fruehauf and Trailmobile, have had the facilities to deal with these fleet operators who prefer to place their orders with manufacturers who can accept trade-ins on a large scale and extend favorable financing terms.

Lest there be any misunderstanding, we do not suggest as does the

Initial Decision, that the superior ability of the larger trailer manufacturers to offer services and financing is an unfair advantage that is somehow anticompetitive. The advantages are ones that basically arise out of firm size and, although in part may be caused by imperfections in the capital market, are nevertheless beneficial to the customers who are served thereby. They should therefore, be viewed as providing real, and not simply pecuniary, economies.

The ALJ found that the trailer manufacturing industry is highly profitable. However there is little concrete evidence in the record in the form of actual profit data. Although Gindy in the year preceding the acquisition had been highly profitable (this fact quickened Budd's interest in acquiring it), little information is revealed by the profit and loss statements of the top firms since for the most part they are parts of conglomerate corporations which do not report profits and losses on a product-line basis.[2] There was much testimony to the effect that the industry is at least *regarded* by both insiders and outsiders as a low-profit industry. A number of firms have exited from the industry in recent years because of losses, including Highway Trailer Company, which in 1968 ranked number six in the van trailer market.

The record indicates that from 1966 onward van trailer prices have not risen at a pace commensurate with increases in cost of labor and material. Prices even declined to below 1966 levels from 1967 through 1969. . . .

The foregoing suggests that despite the degree of concentration evidenced by the market share figures, the market may have been performing in a manner that has yielded prices and profits at a competitive or near-competitive level. The Commission has taken this into account in evaluating complaint counsel's argument that the loss of Budd as a grassroots entrant was an important loss to the market.

IV. Budd as a Potential Entrant

The Administrative Law Judge found that since at least 1956 Budd has been a potential entrant into the manufacture and sale of van trailers and containers and chassis and that by acquiring Gindy, Budd removed itself as an actual future entrant in these markets either by entry de novo[3] or by acquisition of a small company. In addition he found that Budd was perceived by firms in the market as a potential entrant and loss of its presence at the edge of the market removed any disciplining effects that would have ensued from its continued presence as a perceived potential entrant . . .

On the question of whether Budd was a perceived potential entrant, we

---

[2] By 1968, Fruehauf was a large diversified corporation. In terms of assets it exceeded Budd in size and ranked as the 234th largest industrial corporation in the country. Trailmobile was owned by the Pullman Company which was the 149th largest corporation. Until December 1968 Strick was a subsidiary of Penn Central. Brown Trailers was a division of the Clark Equipment Company, the 193rd largest corporation in terms of sales. Great Dane Trailers was a subsidiary of United States Freight Company.

[3] Italics missing from original document—editor's note.

disagree with the ALJ. A large number of industry witnesses testified in this proceeding and when asked whether they had viewed Budd as a potential entrant before the Gindy acquisition, the response was uniformly "no." . . .

. . . [E]xecutives from Miller, Dorsey, Theurer and Utility testified they did not perceive Budd as a potential entrant. . . . Prior to the time Budd acquired Gindy, these and the other trailer companies who appeared at the hearing did not take Budd into account in formulating competitive practices and prices. . . . Nor is there any reason to believe that had the Gindy acquisition not taken place Budd's continued presence outside the market would have influenced industry prices. Numerous industry witnesses, including representatives from the market leaders, identified other firms and types of firms they considered more likely to enter the truck trailer industry than Budd. These included automobile manufacturers. . . . truck tractor manufacturers . . . and truck body manufacturers. . . . No witness testified that their prices or practices were affected by these firms. The only conclusion that can be reasonably drawn from the evidence is that there is no basis upon which to believe that Budd's continued presence at the edge of the market would have any greater effect on market performance.

We are left then with the argument that Budd was a likely actual entrant which would have entered the market at some time in the future by means other than the Gindy acquisition. . . . We find it unneccessary, however, to review the lengthy arguments that have been presented on this issue.

Although the ALJ found that Budd was an actual potential entrant into the van and container markets, we think he jumped too quickly to the conclusion that entry by way of acquiring Gindy was anticompetitive. Insufficient attention was paid to whether Gindy should be viewed as a toehold or foothold firm, acquisition of which would lead to improved competition against dominant market leaders. As the Commission observed in *Bendix Corporation*, . . . 77 F.T.C. [731] at 818–19 (1970); "[I]n a highly concentrated, sluggish market, the acquisition of a small industry member by a powerful, innovative firm which, by building upon the base of the smaller firm can pose a more effective competitive challenge to the industry giants [may promote competition]. Such procompetitive mergers are not only not forbidden by Section 7, they are positively encouraged." "[T]he threat of a toehold merger by a powerful firm may often serve as a much greater incentive to competitive performance in the affected market than the prospect of more costly and slower internal, *de novo* expansion." id, at 819.[4]

---

[4] See also *Brown Shoe Co.* v. *United States*, 370 U.S. 294, 319: "When concern as to the Act's breadth [amended Section 7] was expressed, supporters of the amendments indicated that it would not impede, for example, a merger between two small companies to enable the combination to compete more effectively with larger corporations dominating the relevant market. . ."

In the *Bendix* case the Commission struck down the acquisition by Bendix of the third-ranking firm (Fram) which had 17.2 percent of the market. However it characterized as a toehold firm that could lawfully have been acquired by Bendix, fourth-ranking Wix Manufacturing Company which had 9.5 percent of the market and was not shown to be technologically inferior. Similarly, the Ajax Company, recognized as a permissible toehold or foothold candidate in *Stanley Words,* 78 F.T.C. 1023, 1072 (1971) . . . ranked third in the market with a share of about 8 percent. As we recently noted, the Commission has generally considered "firms having market shares below 10 percent as toehold companies, acquisition of which would have been procompetitive" *Beatrice Foods Company,* Dkt. 8864 (July 1, 1975, slip opinion p. 17 n. 8).

V. Gindy's Position in the Industry

Market share data set forth *supra,* show that Gindy ranked considerably below Fruehauf, Trailmobile, and Strick. In the overall trailer market Gindy's share fluctuated between 4.9 percent and 6.5 percent during the three years prior to the merger. In the van-trailer market, where Gindy's share was highest, it never rose appreciably above 7 to 8 percent as compared to Fruehauf's 27 percent and Trailmobile's 17 percent. Gindy's market position in 1968 was much closer to firms ranking below it, such as Brown Trailer (6.6 percent of the van-trailer market in 1968), Highway (5.5 percent), and Great Dane (5.1 percent). Complaint counsel in fact characterize Highway and Great Dane as available toehold firms. In the container-and-chassis market, Gindy ranked number 6 with only 3.8 percent of the market.

At the time of acquisition, Gindy's principal manufacturing plant was located in Eagle, Pennsylvania, in addition to which it had a manufacturing plant located in Lebanon, Pennsylvania, and in Martinsville, Virginia; [sic] and a relatively small production facility in St. Louis, Missouri, which was later closed down as obsolete. Gindy was described by numerous industry witnesses as being a regional producer. Ninety-five percent of its sales were made in the eastern part of the United States. In contrast, Fruehauf and Trailmobile were viewed by industry witnesses as the national companies and for many years have dominated the industry. . . .

Fruehauf, Trailmobile, and Strick had their own finance divisions, which because of their leverage in the money market, were able to offer financing on better terms than were generally available from banks. Prior to the merger, Gindy depended upon credit arrangements with several banks and an insurance company. . . .

The Administrative Law Judge, in holding that Gindy could not be viewed as a toehold or foothold acquisition candidate, relied on the fact that Gindy's shares in the alleged submarket, closed-top freight vans, exceeded 10 percent in 1968 and 1969. . . . However, as we have held, this is not a meaningful economic market or submarket, and Gindy's shares varied from 3 percent to 8 percent in the relevant markets during the years immediately prior to the merger.

We believe it to be desirable to observe a general rule in potential competition cases that firms possessing no more than 10 percent in a target market (where, as here, the four-firm concentration is approximately 60 percent or more) should ordinarily be presumed to be toehold or foothold firms. This presumption by no means is conclusive, and the inference of lack of anticompetitive effects flowing from acquisition of such a firm can be rebutted in particular cases. . . . The 10 percent demarcation is supported by the prior Commission cases, as noted, and is not inconsistent with the Department of Justice Merger Guidelines. . . .

In this case, the presumption is supported by the record which shows that the acquisition of Gindy by Budd engendered increased capacity and other procompetitive forces, the very effects the toehold doctrine was designed to elicit.

The record shows that to compete optimally in this industry, a producer of trailers must have a network of plants and sales and service facilities geographically dispersed throughout the country, a broad line of truck trailer products, and capability to provide financing customers' purchases of trailers on competitive terms. . . . Geographic dispersion of plants and outlets is required for several reasons. Customers of trailer manufacturers have been getting larger and so have the size of their orders. Freight costs of delivering are substantial, and it is difficult to compete in states which are far distant from a manufacturing plant. . . . Branch factories and outlets provide greater capacity to fill large orders, take trades, and provide service and repair facilities. . . .

We have already noted that at the time of acquisition Fruehauf and Trailmobile were the only producers of trailers and containers that operated on a nationwide basis. Their product lines were far broader than other producers of van trailers and chassis. . . . Fruehauf, Trailmobile, and Strick were offering more attractive finance terms than Gindy was able to obtain or offer.

In the opinion of Gindy officials, without the financial assistance Budd made available to Gindy subsequent to the acquisition, it is doubtful that Gindy would have substantially augmented its preacquisition level of operations. . . . Budd officials viewed Gindy as undercapitalized in comparison to Fruehauf and other major trailer companies, and that with Budd's help it could grow to become a more effective competitor, particularly in the area of financing trailer sales, and could be expanded from a regional to a national competitor. . . .

Subsequent to the acquisition, Budd established a financial corporation to help finance the van trailers sold by Gindy as well as sales by other Budd divisions. By virtue of this finance subsidiary, Gindy was able to finance trailer sales on more competitive terms. Furthermore, for the first time it was able to provide customer finance on container sales, which theretofore had been considered too risky by commercial banks. This enabled Gindy to compete in container sales and financing with Fruehauf and Trailmobile. . . .

In addition, Budd enlarged Gindy's Eagle plant and increased its capacity by 40 percent at a cost to Budd of $1.75 million. An addition to the Lebanon plant was made by Budd and a cost to it of $500,000. The record supports the ALJ's finding that these alterations made Gindy by 1971 "a more efficient van trailer producer than it was at the time of acquisition." . . .

The law judge, relying on the foregoing and other post-acquisition changes made by Budd in the Gindy Company, concluded that the acquisition also violated Section 7 because it entrenched Gindy and raised entry barriers. Contrary to the conclusions reached by the ALJ, there is nothing in the record to support the view that the acquisition has raised existing entry barriers or has otherwise entrenched Gindy. Between 1968 and 1972 Gindy's dollar sales of trailers increased from $35.7 million to $56.5 million, its share of that market increasing from 6.01 percent to 7.07 percent. But it appears that Gindy's gain was Furehauf's loss. Fruehauf's market share dropped during the same period of time from 28.88 percent to 23.28 percent. (The aggregate share of the three leading firms also declined, from 52.47 percent to 47.61 percent). [sic] Representatives of smaller firms testified that they did not believe the acquisition had made it more difficult for them to grow. For the most part the smaller trailer manufacturers increased their respective shares of the market after 1968. . . . Although these postacquisition data do not conclusively settle the question, clearly these are not the trends of a less competitive market.

In view of our finding that the acquisition did not lessen competition, *the initial decision will be vacated and the complaint dismissed.*

DISSENTING STATEMENT OF COMMISSIONER DIXON

By Commissioner DIXON: My reading of the record in this matter convinces me that Budd was an actual potential entrant into the markets found relevant by the administrative law judge,[5] and that Budd's entry

---

[5] Based on the finding that closed-top dry freight trailers and open-top van trailers could be manufactured by the same machinery and distributed through the same channels, the majority concluded that these two products should not be viewed as comprising distinct submarkets. Although cross-elasticity of production and distribution is determinative when considering the outer boundaries of a market, such cross-elasticity is the only one of the factors to be considered when drawing submarkets. My reading of the record comports with that of the administrative law judge insofar as he finds that these closed- and open-top van trailers are sufficiently distinct to warrant the finding that each should be considered a relevant submarket. Particularly persuasive in this connection is the administrative law judge's finding that these two products are sold to different customers because their end uses are distinct and the finding that there is no cross-elasticity as to price between them. It may be, as an example, that peanut butter and peanut oil are produced by the same machines and distributed by the same wholesalers. Yet we would not conclude from their cross-elasticity

through Gindy was anticompetitive as it did not come about through internal expansion or by acquisition of a toehold firm. I cannot accept the majority's holding that Gindy was a toehold firm. It is my understanding that a firm cannot qualify as a toehold if it is already a significant competitive factor in the relevant markets, or is likely to achieve that status without the infusion of capital from the acquiring firm. Assuming, *arguendo,* that Gindy became significant only after the challenged acquisition, . . . the manner in which it achieved this position demonstrates that Gindy was capable of ascending to such a position in the relevant markets on its own, and that it was likely to do so. There is no dispute that Budd's investment of a few million dollars increased Gindy's production capacity and geographical distribution and was all that was required to bring Gindy into more direct competition with the industry giants. In brief, it was well within the capacity of Gindy to become, through internal expansion, a significant competitor of Fruehauf, Strick, and Trailmobile, if it was not already at the time of the acquisition. Since this prospect was obviated by the Budd acquisition, as was the potential for Budd to become a significant competitor through internal expansion or acquisition of one of the smaller firms in the relevant markets, the acquisition should not be permitted to stand.

DISSENTING STATEMENT OF
COMMISSIONER HANFORD

By Commissioner HANFORD: I agree with Commissioner Dixon that open-top van trailers and closed-top dry freight vans are distinct product submarkets, and that the submarket which the majority has defined as encompassing both types of trailers fails to reflect economic reality. Accordingly, I find I am unable to agree with the majority's conclusion that Budd's purchase of Gindy constitutes entry by toehold acquisition. . . .

What we have here is a situation in which Budd was, prior to the acquisition, an actual potential entrant into markets which are characterized by high concentration and substantial barriers to effective competition. Moreover, it was one of the few most likely potential entrants into these markets. Budd could have entered these markets by toehold acquisition or *de novo* through internal expansion. It had the capacity to do so. Had it entered in either of these two ways, it would have been a direct competitor of Gindy, which at the time of the acquisition was ranked number two in the production of open-top van trailers. In addition, the other leading firms in this market would have had to contend with aggressive new competition from Budd as well as the existing competition from Gindy. . . .

of production and distribution that each does not comprise a separate product market. That one can be substituted for the other by the end user, and that there is no price cross-elasticity between them would be determinative. So it should be with open- and closed-top van trailers.

United States v. Falstaff Brewing Corp.
410 U.S. 526 (1973)

. . . . .

MR. JUSTICE WHITE delivered the opinion of the Court. . . .

As stipulated by the parties, the relevant product market is the production and sale of beer, and the six New England States[1] compose the geographic market. While beer sales in New England increased approximately 9.5% in the four years preceding the acquisition, the eight largest sellers increased their share of these sales from approximately 74% to 81.2%. In 1960, approximately 50% of the sales were made by the four largest sellers; by 1964, their share of the market was 54%; and by 1965, the year of acquisition, their share was 61.3%. The number of brewers operating plants in the geographic market decreased from 32 in 1935, to 11 in 1957, to six in 1964.[2]

Of the Nation's 10 largest brewers in 1964, only Falstaff and two others did not sell beer in New England; Falstaff was the largest of the three and had the closest brewery.[3] In relation to the New England market, Falstaff sold its product in western Ohio, to the west and in Washington, D.C., to the south.

The acquired firm, Narragansett, was the largest seller of beer in New England at the time of its acquisition, with approximately 20% of the market; had been the largest seller for the five preceding years; had constantly expanded its brewery capacity between 1960 and 1965; and had acquired either the assets or the trademarks of several smaller brewers in and around the geographic market.

The fourth largest producer of beer in the United States at the time of acquisition, Falstaff was a regional brewer[4] with 5.9% of the nation's production in 1964, having grown steadily since its beginning as a brewer in 1933 through acquisition and expansion of other breweries. As of January 1965, Falstaff sold beer in 32 states, but did not sell in the Northeast, an area composed of New England and states such as New York and New Jersey; the area being the highest beer consumption region in the United States. . . .

Falstaff met increasingly strong competition in the 1960s from four brewers who sold in all of the significant markets. National brewers pos-

---

[1] Maine, New Hampshire, Vermont, Massachusetts, Connecticut, and Rhode Island.

[2] Nationally, the number of brewers decreased from 663 in 1935 to 140 in 1965.

[3] Of the three "top ten" brewers that were not selling in New England, Falstaff ranked fourth nationally, the other two ranking eighth and ninth. From Boston, Massachusetts, the distance to Falstaff's closest brewery was 844 miles, while the distance to the eighth and ninth largest sellers' breweries was 1,385 and 2,000 miles respectively.

[4] A "regional," as contrasted with a "national" brewer, is one that is not selling in all the significant national markets.

sess competitive advantages since they are able to advertise on a nation-wide basis, their beers have greater prestige than regional or local beers, and they are less affected by the weather or labor problems in a particular region. Thus Falstaff concluded that it must convert from "regional" to "national" status, if it was to compete effectively with the national producers.[5] . . .

Before the acquisition was accomplished, the United States brought suit . . . alleging that the acquisition would violate §7 because its effect may be to substantially lessen competition in the production and sale of beer in the New England market. This contention was based on two grounds: because Falstaff was a potential entrant and because the acquisition eliminated competition that would have existed had Falstaff entered the market *de novo* or by acquisition and expansion of a smaller firm, a so-called toehold acquisition.[6] . . .

After a trial on the merits, the District Court found that the geographic market was highly competitive; that Falstaff was desirous of becoming a national brewer by entering the Northeast; that its management was committed against *de novo* entry; and that competition had not diminished since the acquisition. . . .

Also finding that the Government had failed to establish that the acquisition would result in a substantial lessening of competition, the District Court entered judgment for Falstaff and dismissed the complaint.

I

Section 7 of the Clayton Act forbids mergers in any line of commerce where the effect may be substantially to lessen competition or tend to create a monopoly. The section proscribes many mergers between competitors in a market . . . ; it also bars certain acquisitions of a market competitor by a noncompetitor, such as a merger by an entrant who threatens to dominate the market or otherwise upset market conditions to the detriment of competition. . . . Suspect also is the acquisition by a company not competing in the market but so situated as to be a potential competitor and likely to exercise substantial influence on market behavior. Entry through merger by such a company, although its competitive conduct in the market may be the mirror image of that of the acquired company, may nevertheless violate §7 because the entry eliminates a potential competitor exercising present influence on the market. . . .

In the case before us, Falstaff was not a competitor in the New England market, nor is it contended that its merger with Narragansett represented an entry by a dominant market force. It was urged, however, that Falstaff

---

[5] In 1958, Falstaff commissioned a study of actions it should take to maximize profits. The study recommended, *inter alia,* that Falstaff become a national brewer by entering those areas where it was not then marketing its product, especially the Northeast, and that Falstaff should build a brewery on the East Coast rather than buy.

[6] Hereinafter, reference to *de novo* entry includes toehold acquisition as well.

was a potential competitor so situated that its entry by merger rather than *de novo* violated §7. The District Court, however, relying heavily on testimony of Falstaff officers, concluded that the company had no intent to enter the New England market except through acquisition and that it therefore could not be considered a potential competitor in that market. Having put aside Falstaff as a potential *de novo* competitor, it followed for the District Court that entry by a merger would not adversely affect competition in New England.

The District Court erred as a matter of law. The error lay in the assumption that because Falstaff, as a matter of fact, would never have entered the market *de novo,* it could in no sense be considered a potential competitor. More specifically, the District Court failed to give separate consideration to whether Falstaff was a potential competitor in the sense that it was so positioned on the edge of the market that it exerted beneficial influence on competitive conditions in that market. . . .

The specific question with respect to this phase of the case is not what Falstaff's internal company decisions were but whether, given its financial capabilities and conditions in the New England market, it would be reasonable to consider it a potential entrant into that market. Surely, it could not be said on this record that Falstaff's general interest in the New England market was unknown; . . . and if it would appear to rational beer merchants in New England that Falstaff might well build a new brewery to supply the northeastern market then its entry by merger becomes suspect under §7. The District Court should therefore have appraised the economic facts about Falstaff and the New England market in order to determine whether in any realistic sense Falstaff could be said to be a potential competitor on the fringe of the market with likely influence on existing competition.[7] This does not mean that the testimony of company officials about actual intentions of the company is irrelevant or is to be looked upon with suspicion; but it does mean that theirs is not necessarily the last word in arriving at a conclusion about how Falstaff should be considered in terms of its status as a potential entrant into the market in issue.

Since it appears that the District Court entertained too narrow a view of Falstaff as a potential competitor and since it appears that the District Court's conclusion that the merger posed no probable threat to competition followed automatically from the finding that Falstaff had no intent to

---

[7] . . . Nor was there any lack of circumstantial evidence of Falstaff's on-the-fringe competitive impact. As the record shows, Falstaff was in the relevant line of commerce, was admittedly interested in entering the Northeast, and had, among other ways . . . made its interest known by prior-acquisition discussions. Moreover, there were, as my Brother MARSHALL would put it, objective economic facts as to Falstaff's capability to enter the New England market; and the same facts which he would have the District Court look to in determining whether the particular theory of potential competition we do not reach has been violated, would be probative of violation of §7 through loss of a procompetitive on-the-fringe influence. . . .

enter *de novo,* we remand this case for the District Court to make the proper assessment of Falstaff as a potential competitor.

II

Because we remand for proper assessment of Falstaff as an on-the-fringe potential competitor, it is not necessary to reach the question of whether §7 bars a market-extension merger by a company whose entry into the market would have no influence whatsoever on the present state of competition in the market—that is, the entrant will not be a dominant force in the market and has no current influence in the marketplace. We leave for another day the question of the applicability of §7 to a merger that will leave competition in the marketplace exactly as it was, neither hurt nor helped, and that it is challengeable under §7 only on grounds that the company could, but did not, enter *de novo* or through toehold acquisition and that there is less competition than there would have been had entry been in such a manner. . . .

The judgment of the District Court dismissing the complaint against Falstaff is reversed, and the case is remanded for further proceedings consistent with this opinion.

So ordered.

*   *   *   *   *

MR. JUSTICE MARSHALL, concurring in the result.

. . . I would hold that where, as here, strong objective evidence indicates that a firm is a potential entrant into a market, it is error for the trial judge to rely solely on the firm's subjective prediction of its own future conduct. While such subjective evidence is probative on the issue of potential entry, it is inherently unreliable and must be used with great care. Ordinarily, the district court should presume that objectively measurable market forces will govern a firm's future conduct. Only when there is a compelling demonstration that a firm will not follow its economic self-interest may the district court consider subjective evidence in predicting that conduct. Even then, subjective evidence should be preferred only when the objective evidence is weak or contradictory. Because the District Court failed to apply these standards, I would remand the case for further consideration.

I

[In this section, MR. JUSTICE MARSHALL presents a detailed discussion of the nature of the relevant product and geographic markets, the structure of the beer industry, and the salient characteristics of Falstaff and Narragansett.]

II

[After discussing the factual background MR. JUSTICE MARSHALL turns to a discussion of the appropriate legal standards to be applied in this case.]

A. The Purposes of §7

As is clear from its face, §7 was designed to deal with the anticompetitive effects of excessive industrial concentration caused by the corporate marriage of two competitors. "It is the basic premise of [§7] that competition will be most vital 'when there are many sellers, none of which has any significant market share.'" *United States* v. *Aluminum Co. of America,* 377 U.S., at 280.

But §7 does more than prohibit mergers with immediate anticompetitive effects. The Act by its terms prohibits acquisitions which "may . . . substantially . . . lessen competition, or . . . tend to create a monopoly." The use of the subjunctive indicates that Congress was concerned with the *potential* effects of mergers even though, at the time they occur, they may cause no present anticompetitive consequences. See, *e.g., FTC* v. *Procter & Gamble Co.,* 386 U.S. 568, 577 (1967). . . .

B. Modes of Potential Competition

Since 1950, we have repeatedly applied §7 to cases where the merging firms competed in the same line of commerce, and we have been willing to define the line of commerce liberally so as to reach anticompetitive practices in their "incipiency." . . . But in keeping with the spirit of the Celler-Kefauver Amendment, we have also applied §7 to cases where the acquiring firm is outside the market in which the acquired firm competes. These cases fall into three broad categories which, while frequently overlapping, can be dealt with separately for analytical purposes.

1. The Dominant Entrant. In some situations, a firm outside the market may have overpowering resources which, if brought to bear within the market, could ultimately have a substantial anticompetitive effect. If such a firm were to acquire a company within the relevant market, it might drive other marginal companies out of business, thus creating an oligopoly, or it might raise entry barriers to such an extent that potential new entrants would be discouraged from entering the market. Cf. *Ford Motor Co.* v. *United States,* 405 U.S. 562, 567–568 (1972); *FTC* v. *Procter & Gamble Co.,* 386 U.S., at 575.[8] Such a danger is especially intense

---

[8] To be sure, in terms of anticompetitive effects, the dominant firm's acquisition of another firm within the market might be functionally indistinguishable from a *de novo* entry, which §7 does not forbid. But "surely one premise of an antimerger statute such as §7 is that corporate growth by internal expansion is socially preferable to growth by acquisition." *United States* v. *Philadelphia National Bank,* 374 U.S. 321, 370 (1963). Moreover, entry by acquisition has the added evil of eliminating one firm in the market and thus increasing the burden on the remaining firms which must compete with the dominant entering firm.

when the market is already highly concentrated or entry barriers are already unusually high before the dominant firm enters the market.

2.   *The Perceived Potential Entrant.*   Even if the entry of a firm does not upset the competitive balance within the market, it may be that the removal of the firm from the fringe of the market has a present anticompetitive effect. In a concentrated oligopolistic market, the presence of a large potential competitor on the edge of the market, apparently ready to enter if entry barriers are lowered, may deter anticompetitive conduct within the market. . . . When the lingering firm enters the market by acquisition, the competitive influence exerted by the firm is lost with no offsetting gain through an increase in the number of companies seeking a share of the relevant market. The result is a net decrease in competitive pressure.[9] . . .

3.   *The Actual Potential Entrant.*   Since the effect of a perceived potential entrant depends upon the perception of those already in the market, it may in some cases be difficult to prove. Moreover, in a market which is already competitive, the existence of a perceived potential entrant will have no present effect at all.[10] The entry by acquisition of such a firm may nonetheless have an anticompetitive effect by eliminating an actual potential competitor. When a firm enters the market by acquiring a strong company within the market, it merely assumes the position of that company without necessarily increasing competitive pressures. Had such a firm not entered by acquisition, it might at some point have entered *de novo.* An entry *de novo* would increase competitive pressures within the market, and an entry by acquisition eliminates the possibility that such an increase will take place in the future. Thus, even if a firm at the fringe of the market exerts no present procompetitive effect, its entry by acquisition may end for all time the promise of more effective competition at some future date.

Obviously, the anticompetitive effect of such an acquisition depends on the possibility that the firm would have entered *de novo* had it not

---

[9] Thus, whereas the practical difference between entry by acquisition and entry *de novo* may be marginal in the case of a dominant entrant, . . . it is crucial in the case of a perceived potential entrant. If the perceived potential entrant enters *de novo,* its deterrent effect on anticompetitive practices remains and the total number of firms competing for market shares increases. But when such a firm enters by acquisition, it merely steps into the shoes of the acquired firm. The result is no net increase in the actual competition for market shares and the removal of a threat exerting procompetitive influence from outside the market.

[10] Still, even if the market is presently competitive, it is possible that it might grow less competitive in the future. For example, a market might be so concentrated that even though it is presently competitive, there is a serious risk that parallel pricing policies might emerge sometime in the near future. In such a situation, an effective competitor lingering on the fringe of the market—what might be called a *potential* perceived potential entrant—could exert a deterrent force when anticompetitive conduct is about to emerge. As its very name suggests, however, such a firm would be still a further step removed from the exertion of actual, present competitive influence, and the problems of proof are compounded accordingly—particularly in light of the showing of reasonable probability required under §7.

entered by acquisition. If the company would have remained outside the market but for the possibility of entry by acquisition, and if it is exerting no influence as a perceived potential entrant, then there will normally be no competitive loss when it enters by acquisition. Indeed, there may even be a competitive gain to the extent that it strengthens the market position of the acquired firm.[11] Thus, mere entry by acquisition would not prima facie establish a firm's status as an actual potential entrant. For example, a firm, although able to enter the market by acquisition, might, because of inability to shoulder the *de novo* start-up costs, be unable to enter *de novo*. But where a powerful firm is engaging in a related line of commerce at the fringe of the relevant market, where it has a strong incentive to enter the market *de novo,* and where it has the financial capabilities to do so, we have not hesitated to ascribe to it the role of an actual potential entrant. In such cases, we have held that §7 prohibits an entry by acquisition since such an entry eliminates the possibility of future actual competition which would occur if there were an entry *de novo. . . .*

C.   Problems of Proof—The Role of Subjective Evidence

. . . The unavoidable problems of proof are compounded in some cases by the relevance of subjective statements of future intent by the managers of the acquiring firm. Although not susceptible of precise analysis, the objective conditions of the market may at least be measured and quantified. But there exists no very good way of evaluating a subjective statement by the manager of a firm that the firm does or does not intend to enter a given market at some future date.

Fortunately, in two of the three forms of potential competition, such subjective evidence has no role to play. Clearly, in the case of a dominant entrant, the only issue is whether the firm's entry by acquisition will so upset objective market forces as to substantially reduce future competition. Since the firm will have already taken steps to enter the market by the time a §7 action is filed, its statements of subjective intent are irrelevant.

Similarly, when the Government proceeds on the theory that the acquiring firm is a perceived potential entrant, testimony as to the subjective intent of the acquiring firm is not probative. The perceived potential entrant exerts a procompetitive effect because companies in the market *perceive* it as a potential entrant. The companies in the market may entertain this perception whether the perceived potential entrant is *in fact* a potential entrant or not. Thus, a firm on the fringe of the market may exert a procompetitive effect even if it has no intention of entering the market, so long as it seems to those within the market that it may have such an

---

[11] However, if the acquired firm is strengthened to such an extent that it upsets the market balance and drives its competitors out of the market, the acquiring firm takes on the characteristics of a dominant entrant, and the merger may therefore violate §7 under that theory. . . .

intention. . . . It follows that subjective testimony by the managers of the perceived potential entrant is irrelevant.[12]

However, subjective statements of management are probative in cases where the acquiring firm is alleged to be an actual potential entrant. First, management's statements that it does not intend to make a *de novo* market entry, together with its associated reasons, provide an expert judgment on the conclusions to be drawn by the trier of fact from the objective market forces. Just as the Government may introduce expert testimony to inform and guide the trial court with respect to the appropriate business judgments to be derived from the objective data, so too the defendant is entitled to present the evaluation of its own "experts" who may include its management personnel. Although such evidence from management is obviously biased and self-serving, it is nonetheless admissible to prove that the objective market pressures do not favor a *de novo* entry.

More significantly, management's statement of subjective intent, if believed, affects the firm's status as an actual potential entrant. As indicated above, the actual potential entrant's entry by acquisition is anticompetitive only if it eliminates some future possibility that it might have entered *de novo*. An unequivocal statement by management that it has absolutely no intention of entering the market *de novo* at any time in the future is relevant to the issue of whether the possibility of such an entry exists. After all, the character of management is itself essentially an objective factor in determining whether the acquiring firm is an actual potential entrant.

But although subjective evidence is probative and admissible in actual potential-entry cases, its utility is sharply limited. We have certainly never suggested that subjective evidence of likely future entry is *required* to make out a §7 case. . . .

Nor do our prior cases hold that the district courts are bound by subjective statements of company officials that they have no intention of making a *de novo* entry. We have emphasized that the decision whether the acquiring firm is an actual potential entrant is, in the last analysis, an independent one to be made by the trial court on the basis of all relevant evidence properly weighted according to its credibility. . . .

. . . [S]ubjective evidence has, at best, only a marginal role to play in actual potential-entry cases. In order to make out a prima facie case, the Government need only show that objectively measurable market data favor a *de novo* entry and that the alleged potential entrant has the economic capability to make such an entry. To be sure, the defendant may

---

[12] Public statements by management that the firm does not intend to enter the market may be relevant. To the extent that such statements are believed by the firms within the market, they affect their perception of the firm outside the market as a potential entrant. But in that event, the statements of intent are admissible, not to show subjective state of mind, but, rather, as one of the objective factors controlling the perception of the firms within the market.

then introduce subjective testimony in rebuttal, and in the rare case where the objective evidence is evenly divided, it is conceivable that extremely credible subjective evidence might tip the balance. But where objectively measurable market forces make clear that it is in a firm's economic self-interest to make a *de novo* entry and that the firm has the economic capability to do so, I would hold that it is error for the District Court to conclude that the firm is not an actual potential entrant on the basis of testimony by company officials as to the firm's future intent.[13]

. . . [A]ny statement of future intent will be inherently self-serving. A defendant in a §7 case such as this wishes to enter the market by acquisition and its managers know that its ability to do so depends upon whether it can convince a court that it would not have entered *de novo* if entry by acquisition were prevented. It is thus strongly in management's interest to represent that it has no intention of entering *de novo*—a representation which is not subject to external verification and which is so speculative in nature that it could virtually never serve as the predicate for a perjury charge.

Moreover, in a case where the objective evidence strongly favors entry *de novo,* a firm which asks us to believe that it does not intend to enter *de novo* by implication asks us to believe that it does not intend to act in its own economic self-interest. But corporations are, after all, profit-making institutions, and, absent special circumstances, they can be expected to follow courses of action most likely to maximize profits. . . . The trier of fact should, therefore, look with great suspicion upon a suggestion that a company with an opportunity to expand its market and the means to seize upon that opportunity will follow a deliberate policy of self-abnegation if the route of expansion first selected is legally foreclosed to it. . . .

III

. . . The objective evidence in the record strongly suggests that Falstaff had both the capability and the incentive to enter the New England market *de novo*. It is undisputed that it was in Falstaff's interest to gain the status of a national brewer in the near future and that New

---

[13] It might be argued that economic decisions are "inherently subjective" and that any attempt to derive objective conclusions from economic data is futile. If this observation means that different people reach different conclusions from the same objective data, then the point must, of course, be conceded. Similarly, if the point is that economic predictions are difficult and fraught with uncertainty, it is well taken. . . . But although the factual controversies in §7 cases may prove difficult to resolve, the statutory scheme clearly demands their resolution. . . . Section 7 by its terms requires the trial judge to make a prediction, and it is entirely possible that others may reasonably disagree with the conclusion he reaches. . . . While it may be true that different people see economic facts in different light, §7 gives federal judges and juries the responsibility to reach *their* conclusions as to the economic facts. And "[i]f justice requires the fact to be ascertained, the difficulty of doing so is no ground for refusing to try." O. Holmes, *The Common Law* 48.

England was a logical area to begin its expansion. Indeed, Falstaff's own actions in entering the New England market support this conclusion. Nor can it be doubted that Falstaff had the economic capability to enter New England. Falstaff is the Nation's fourth largest brewer and the largest still outside of New England. It has been consistently profitable in recent years, has an excellent credit rating, and had, in 1964, enough excess capital to finance a 10-year, $35 million expansion project. . . .

To be sure, Falstaff introduced a great deal of evidence tending to show that entry *de novo* would have been less profitable for it than entry by acquisition. I have no doubt that this is true. Indeed, if it can be assumed that Falstaff is a rational, profit-maximizing corporation, its own decision offers strong proof that entry by acquisition was the preferable alternative. But the test in §7 cases is not whether anticompetitive conduct is profit maximizing. The very purpose of §7 is to direct the profit incentive into channels which are procompetitive. Thus, the proper test is whether Falstaff would have entered the market *de novo* if the preferable alternative of entry by acquisition had been denied it. The objective evidence strongly suggests that such an entry would have occurred. . . .

MR. JUSTICE REHNQUIST, with whom MR. JUSTICE STEWART concurs, dissenting.

. . . Although agreeing with my Brother MARSHALL'S criticism of the Court's reason for remanding this case, I cannot agree with his grounds for remanding to the District Court for reconsideration. That theory is based, erroneously I believe, on the notion that there is an identifiable difference between "objective" and "subjective" evidence in an antitrust case such as this. My Brother MARSHALL would have the District Court weigh "objective" evidence more heavily than "subjective" evidence. In the field of economic forecasting in general, and in the area of potential competition in particular, however, the distinction between "objective" and "subjective" evidence is largely illusory. It is, I believe, incorrect to state that a trier of fact can determine "objectively" what "is in a firm's economic self-interest." Such a determination is guesswork. The term "economic self-interest" is a convenient shorthand for describing the economic decision reached by an individual or firm, but does not connote some simple, mechanical formula which determines the input values, or their assigned weight, in the process of economic decision-making. The simple fact is that any economic decision is largely subjective. In the instant case, Falstaff sought to prove why it was not in the "economic self-interest" of that firm to enter a new geographic market without an established distribution system. Its explanation is as "objective" as any of the evidence offered by the Government to show why a hypothetical Falstaff should enter the market. The question of who is an "actual potential competitor" is entirely factual. In deciding questions of fact, it is the province of the trier to weigh all of the evidence; but it is peculiarly his province to determine questions of credibility. . . .

United States v. Marine Bancorporation, Inc., et al.

418 U.S. 602 (1974)

MR. JUSTICE POWELL delivered the opinion of the Court.

The United States brought this civil antitrust action under §7 of the Clayton Act . . . to challenge a proposed merger between two commercial banks. The acquiring bank is a large, nationally chartered bank based in Seattle, Washington, and the acquired bank is a medium-size, state-chartered bank located at the opposite end of the State in Spokane. The banks are not direct competitors to any significant degree in Spokane or any other part of the State. They have no banking offices in each other's home cities. The merger agreement would substitute the acquiring bank for the acquired bank in Spokane and would permit the former for the first time to operate as a direct participant in the Spokane market.

The proposed merger would have no effect on the number of banks in Spokane. The United States bases its case exclusively on the potential-competition doctrine under §7 of the Clayton Act. It contends that if the merger is prohibited, the acquiring bank would find an alternate and more competitive means for entering the Spokane area and that the acquired bank would ultimately develop by internal expansion or mergers with smaller banks into an actual competitor of the acquiring bank and other large banks in sections of the State outside Spokane. The Government further submits that the merger would terminate the alleged procompetitive influence that the acquiring bank presently exerts over Spokane banks due to the potential for its entry into that market.

After a full trial, the District Court held against the Government on all aspects of the case. We affirm that court's judgment. We hold that in applying the potential-competition doctrine to commercial banking, courts must take into account the extensive federal and state regulation of banks, particularly the legal restraints on entry unique to this line of commerce. The legal barriers to entry in the instant case, notably state-law prohibitions against *de novo* branching, against branching from a branch office, and against multibank holding companies, compel us to conclude that the challenged merger is not in violation of §7.

I. BACKGROUND

A. Facts

The acquiring bank, National Bank of Commerce (NBC), is a national banking association with its principal office in Seattle, Washington. Located in the northwest corner of the State, Seattle is the largest city in Washington. NBC is a wholly owned subsidiary of a registered bank holding company, Marine Bancorporation, Inc. (Marine), and in terms of assets, deposits, and loans is the second largest banking organization with headquarters in the State of Washington. At the end of 1971, NBC had total assets of $1.8 billion, total deposits of $1.6 billion, and total loans of $881.3 million.[1] It operates 107 branch banking offices within the state, 59 of which are located in the Seattle metropolitan area and 31 of which are in lesser developed sections of eastern Washington. In order of population, the four major metropolitan areas in Washington are Seattle, Tacoma, Spokane, and Everett. NBC has no branch offices in the latter three areas.

The target bank, Washington Trust Bank (WTB), founded in 1902, is a state bank with headquarters in Spokane. Spokane is located in the extreme eastern part of the State, approximately 280 road miles from Seattle. . . . NBC, the acquiring bank, has had a longstanding interest in securing entry into Spokane.

WTB has seven branch offices, six in the city of Spokane and one in Opportunity, a Spokane suburb. WTB is the eighth largest banking organization with headquarters in Washington and the ninth largest banking organization in the State. At the end of 1971, it had assets of $112 million, total deposits of $95.6 million, and loans of $57.6 million. It controls 17.4 percent of the 46 commercial banking offices in the Spokane metropolitan area. . . .

WTB is well managed and profitable. From December 31, 1966, to June 30, 1972, it increased its percentage of total deposits held by banking organizations in the Spokane metropolitan area from 16.6 percent to 18.6 percent. . . .

As of June 30, 1972, there were 91 national and state banking organizations in Washington. The five largest in the State held 74.3 percent of the State's total commercial bank deposits and operated 61.3 percent of its banking offices. At that time, the two largest in the State, Seattle-First National Bank and NBC, held 51.3 percent of total deposits and operated 36.5 percent of the banking offices in Washington.[2] There are six banking organizations operating in the Spokane metropolitan area. One organization, Washington Bancshares, Inc., controls two separate banks and their respective branch offices. As of midyear 1972, this organization in the

---

[1] By comparison, the largest banking organization with headquarters in Washington, Seattle-First National Bank, at the same time had assets of $2.8 billion, deposits of $2.5 billion, and loans of $1.4 billion.

[2] . . . The degree of concentration in commercial banking in Washington has not increased significantly in the last decade. For the 12-year period ending December 31, 1971, the 10 largest banking organizations increased their aggregate share of total deposits by a single percentage point. WTB's percentage of total deposits in the State was essentially stable for this period, decreasing from 1.5 percent to 1.4 percent. From 1960 to 1971 the number of commercial banks in Washington increased by five.

aggregate held 42.1 percent of total deposits in the area. Seattle-First National Bank, by comparison, held 31.6 percent. The target bank held 18.6 percent of total deposits at that time, placing it third in the Spokane area behind Washington Bancshares, Inc., and Seattle-First National Bank. Thus, taken together, Washington Bancshares, Seattle-First National Bank, and WTB hold approximately 92 percent of total deposits in the Spokane area. None of the remaining three commercial banks in Spokane holds a market share larger than 3.1 percent. . . . One of these banks, Farmers & Merchants Bank, has offices only in a Spokane suburb.

The degree of concentration of the commercial banking business in Spokane may well reflect the severity of Washington's statutory restraints on *de novo* geographic expansion by banks. Although Washington permits branching, the restrictions placed on that method of internal growth are stringent. . . . Since federal law subjects nationally chartered banks to the branching limitations imposed on their state counterparts, . . . national and state banks in Washington are restricted to mergers or acquisitions in order to expand into cities and towns with preexisting banking organizations.

The ability to acquire existing banks is also limited by a provision of state law requiring that banks incorporating in Washington include in their articles of incorporation a clause forbidding a new bank from merging with or permitting its assets to be acquired by another bank for a period of at least ten years, without the consent of the state supervisor of banking. . . . [O]nce a bank acquires or takes over one of the banks operating in a city or town other than the acquiring bank's principal place of business, it cannot branch from the acquired bank. . . . Thus, an acquiring bank that enters a new city or town containing banks other than the acquired bank is restricted to the number of bank offices obtained at the time of the acquisition. Moreover, multibank holding companies are prohibited in Washington. . . . Accordingly, it is not possible in Washington to achieve the rough equivalent of free branching by aggregating a number of unit banks under a bank holding company.[3]

B. The Proceedings

In February 1971, Marine, NBC, and WTB agreed to merge the latter into NBC. NBC, as the surviving bank, would operate all eight banking

---

[3] The wisdom of inflexible limitations on *de novo* bank expansion like those in force in Washington has been questioned. . . . They inhibit growth by internal expansion and compel banks to resort to mergers and acquisitions in order to enter many new markets. Although other reasons no doubt exist, these limitations ostensibly are designed to prevent banks from encountering financial difficulties through overextending themselves, and they often date from the period of bank failures in the 1930s. If bank safety is their purpose, such restrictions may deserve reconsideration today in light of the extensive range of regulatory controls that otherwise exist, including federal and state supervision of the issuance of new bank charters, controls on interest rates and investments, deposit insurance, and regular, intensive bank inspections. Whatever their efficacy, a question that is not ours to resolve, such barriers to new entry are a fact of banking life in Washington.

offices of WTB as branches of NBC. In March 1971, NBC and WTB applied to the Comptroller of the Currency pursuant to the Bank Merger Act of 1966 for approval of the merger. . . .

The Comptroller approved the merger in a report issued September 24, 1971. He concluded that state law precluded NBC from branching in Spokane and "effectively prevented" NBC from causing a new Spokane bank to be formed which could later be treated as a merger partner. . . . The Comptroller relied heavily on the view that the merger would contribute to the convenience and needs of bank customers in Spokane by bringing to them services not previously provided by WTB.

Acting within the 30-day limitation period set out in the Bank Merger Act of 1966, . . . the United States then commenced this action in the United States District Court for the Western District of Washington, challenging the legality of the merger under §7 of the Clayton Act. . . .

. . . The United States sought to establish that the merger "may . . . substantially . . . lessen competition" within the meaning of §7 in three ways: by eliminating the prospect that NBC, absent acquisition of the market share represented by WTB, would enter Spokane *de novo* or through acquisition of a smaller bank and thus would assist in deconcentrating that market over the long run; by ending present procompetitive effects allegedly produced in Spokane by NBC's perceived presence on the fringe of the Spokane market; and by terminating the alleged probability that WTB as an independent entity would develop through internal growth or through mergers with other medium-size banks into a regional or ultimately statewide counterweight to the market power of the State's largest banks. . . .

At the close of final oral argument following a week-long trial, the District Judge ruled for the defendants from the bench. . . . The court found that the merger would "substantially" increase competition in commercial banking in the Spokane metropolitan area and would have "no inherent anticompetitive effect. . . ." . . . In light of the legal and economic barriers to any other method of entry, the court further found "no reasonable probability" that, absent the challenged merger, NBC would enter the Spokane market in the "reasonably foreseeable future." . . .

. . . The Government thereupon brought this direct appeal. . . . We noted probable jurisdiction. . . .

II. THE RELEVANT MARKETS

Determination of the relevant product and geographic markets is "a necessary predicate" to deciding whether a merger contravenes the Clayton Act. . . . The District Court found that the relevant product market "within which the competitive effect of the merger is to be judged" is the "business of commercial banking (and the cluster of products and services denoted thereby). . . ." . . . The parties do not dispute this finding. . . .

The District Court found that the relevant geographic market is the Spokane metropolitan area, "consisting of the City of Spokane and the populated areas immediately adjacent thereto, including the area extending easterly through the suburb of Opportunity toward the Idaho border. . . ." . . . It contains all eight of the target bank's offices. On the basis of the record, we have no reason to doubt that it constitutes a reasonable approximation of the "localized" banking market in which Spokane banks offer the major part of their services and to which local consumers can practicably turn for alternatives. . . . It is also the area where "the effect of the merger on competition will be direct and immediate. . . ," which as this Court had held is the appropriate "section of the country" for purposes of §7. . . . Accordingly, we affirm the District Court's holding that the Spokane metropolitan area is the appropriate geographic market for determining the legality of the merger. . . .

. . . [T]he Government contends that the entire state is also an appropriate "section of the country" in this case. It is conceded that the state is not a banking market. But the Government asserts that the state is an economically differentiated region, because its boundaries delineate an area within which Washington banks are insulated from most forms of competition by out-of-state banking organizations. The Government further argues that this merger, and others it allegedly will trigger, may lead eventually to the domination of all banking in the state by a few large banks, facing each other in a network of local, oligopolistic banking markets. This assumed eventual statewide linkage of local markets, it is argued, will enhance statewide the possibility of parallel, standardized, anticompetitive behavior. . . .

The Government's proposed reading of the "any section of the country" phrase of §7 is at variance with this Court's §7 cases, and we reject it. Without exception the Court has treated "section of the country" and "relevant geographic market" as identical, . . . and it had defined the latter concept as the area in which the goods or services at issue are marketed to a significant degree by the acquired firm. . . .[4] In cases in which the acquired firm markets its products or services on a local, regional, and national basis, the Court has acknowledged the existence of more than one relevant geographic market.[5] But in no previous §7 case has the Court determined the legality of a merger by measuring its effects

---

[4] If a challenged combination takes the form of a joint venture by which two firms plan to enter a new area simultaneously, the relevant geographic market is the section of the country in which the newly formed enterprise will market its goods. . . .

[5] See, *e.g.*, *United States* v. *Pabst Brewing Co.*, 384 U.S. 546 (1966). Some of the Court's language in *Pabst* suggests that the Government may challenge a merger under §7 without establishing any relevant geographic market. . . . [W]hile *Pabst* stands for the proposition that there may be more than one relevant geographic market, it did not abandon the traditional view that for purposes of §7 "section of the country" means "relevant geographic market" and the latter concept means the area in which the relevant product is in fact marketed by the acquired firm.

on areas where the acquired firm is not a direct competitor. . . . We hold that in a potential-competition case like this one, the relevant geographic market or appropriate section of the country is the area in which the acquired firm is an actual, direct competitor.

Apart from the fact that the Government's statewide approach is not supported by the precedents, it is simply too speculative on this record. There has been no persuasive showing that the effect of the merger on a statewide basis "may be substantially to lessen competition" within the meaning of §7. . . . [I]t is to be remembered that §7 deals in "probabilities," not "ephemeral possibilities." . . . The Government's underlying concern for a linkage or network of statewide oligopolistic banking markets is, on this record at least, considerably closer to "ephemeral possibilities" than to "probabilities." To assume, on the basis of essentially no evidence, that the challenged merger will tend to produce a statewide linkage of oligopolies is to espouse a per se rule against geographic market extension mergers like the one at issue here. No §7 case from this Court has gone that far,[6] and we do not do so today. For the purpose of this case, the appropriate "section of the country" and the "relevant geographic market" are the same—the Spokane metropolitan area.

III. POTENTIAL-COMPETITION DOCTRINE

The term *potential competitor* appeared for the first item in a §7 opinion of this Court in *United States* v. *El Paso Natural Gas Co.*, 376 U.S. 651, 659 (1964). *El Paso* was in reality, however, an actual-competition rather than a potential-competition case. . . . The potential-competition doctrine has been defined in major part by subsequent cases, particularly *United States* v. *Falstaff Brewing Corp.*, 410 U.S. 526 (1973) . . . . Unequivocal proof that an acquiring firm actually would have entered *de novo* but for a merger is rarely available. Thus, as *Falstaff* indicates, the principal focus of the doctrine is on the likely effects of the premerger position of the acquiring firm on the fringe of the target market. In developing and applying the doctrine, the Court has recognized that a market extension merger may be unlawful if the target market is substantially concentrated, if the acquiring firm has the characteristics, capabilities, and economic incentive to render it a perceived potential *de novo* entrant, and if the acquiring firm's premerger presence on the fringe of the target market in fact tempered oligopolistic behavior on the part of existing participants in that market. In other words, the Court has interpreted §7 as encompassing what is commonly known as the "wings ef-

---

[6] We put aside cases where an acquiring firm's market power, existing capabilities, and proposed merger partner are such that the merger would produce an enterprise likely to dominate the target market (a concept known as entrenchment). See *FTC* v. *Procter & Gamble Co.*, 386 U.S. 568 (1967). . . . There is no allegation that the instant merger would produce entrenchment in the Spokane market.

fect"—the probability that the acquiring firm prompted premerger pro-competitive effects within the target market by being perceived by the existing firms in that market as likely to enter *de novo*. . . . The elimination of such present procompetitive effects may render a merger unlawful under §7.

Although the concept of perceived potential entry has been accepted in the Court's prior §7 cases, the potential-competition theory upon which the Government places principal reliance in the instant case has not. The Court has not previously resolved whether the potential-competition doctrine proscribes a market extension merger solely on the ground that such a merger eliminates the prospect for long-term deconcentration of an oligopolistic market that in theory might result if the acquiring firm were forbidden to enter except through a *de novo* undertaking or through the acquisition of a small existing entrant (a so-called foothold or toehold acquisition). *Falstaff* expressly reserved this issue. . . .

The Government's potential-competition argument in the instant case proceeds in five steps. First, it argues that the potential-competition doctrine applies with full force to commercial banks. Second, it submits that the Spokane commercial banking market is sufficiently concentrated to invoke that doctrine. Third, it urges us to resolve in its favor the question left open in *Falstaff*. Fourth, it contends that without regard to the possibility of future deconcentration of the Spokane market, the challenged merger is illegal under established doctrine because it eliminates NBC as a perceived potential entrant. Finally, it asserts that the merger will eliminate WTB's potential for growth outside Spokane. We shall address those points in the order presented.

A. Application of the Doctrine to Commercial Banks

Since *United States* v. *Philadelphia National Bank,* 374 U.S. 321 (1963), the Court has taken the view that, as a general rule, standard §7 principles applicable to unregulated industries apply as well to mergers between commercial banks. . . .

Although the Court's prior bank merger cases have involved combinations between actual competitors operating in the same geographic markets, an element that distinguishes them factually from this case, they nevertheless are strong precedents for the view that §7 doctrines are applicable to commercial banking. In accord with the general principles of those cases, we hold that geographic market extension mergers by commercial banks must pass muster under the potential-competition doctrine. We further hold, however, that the application of the doctrine to commercial banking must take into account the unique federal and state regulatory restraints on entry into that line of commerce. Failure to do so would produce misconceptions that go to the heart of the doctrine itself . . . .

. . . The conceptual difficulty with the Government's approach . . . is that it fails to accord full weight to the extensive federal and regulatory barriers to entry into commercial banking. . . . This omission is of great importance, because ease of entry on the part of the acquiring firm is a central premise of the potential-competition doctrine.[7]

Unlike, for example, the beer industry, see *Falstaff Brewing Corp., supra,* entry of new competitors into the commercial banking field is "wholly a matter of governmental grace. . ." and "far from easy.". . . Beer manufacturers are free to base their decisions regarding entry and the scale of entry into a new geographic market on nonregulatory considerations, including their own financial capabilities, their long-range goals as to markets, the cost of creating new production and distribution facilities, and above all the profit prospects in the target market. They need give no thought to public needs and convenience. No comparable freedom exists for commercial banks. Ease of entry into a market presumes ease of exit—that is, the withdrawal or financial collapse of a certain number of participants in that market. Reflecting this country's bitter experience of four decades ago that "[a] bank failure is a community disaster . . . ,"[8] entry into and exit from the commercial banking business have been extensively regulated by the Federal and State Governments. . . .

In *Philadelphia National Bank, supra,* the Court relied on regulatory barriers to entry to support its conclusion that mergers between banks in direct competition in the same market must be scrutinized with particular care under §7. . . . But the same restrictions on new entry render it difficult to hold that a geographic market extension merger by a commercial bank is unlawful under the potential-competition doctrine. Such limitations often significantly reduce, if they do not eliminate, the likelihood that the acquiring bank is either a perceived potential *de novo* entrant or a source of future competitive benefits through *de novo* or foothold entry. . . . In this case. . . . there are serious questions whether an "alternative to the merger route" through branching or a functional equivalent is a legal or feasible method of entry by NBC into the Spokane market.

B.   Structure of the Spokane Market

Since the legality of the challenged merger must be judged by its effects on the relevant product and geographic markets, commercial banking in

---

[7] This Court's potential-competition cases have repeatedly noted this factor. *E.g., FTC* v. *Procter & Gamble Co.,* 386 U.S. at 580; *United States* v. *Continental Can Co.,* 378 U.S., at 464–465. See J. Bain, *Industrial Organization* 8 (2d ed. 1968): "The condition of entry . . . determines the relative force of potential competition as an influence or regulator on the conduct and performance of sellers already established in a market." See P. Areeda, Antitrust Analysis 517 (1967): "The sight of a particular firm 'waiting at the market's edge' may emphasize the entry threat, but it is ease of entry, not necessarily an identifiable potential entrant, that limits present market power by reminding existing firms that high profits will attract outsiders."

[8] *Philadelphia National Bank,* 374 U.S., at 375 (HARLAN, J., dissenting).

the Spokane metropolitan area, it is imperative to determine the competitive characteristics of commercial banking in that section of the country. The potential-competition doctrine has meaning only as applied to concentrated markets. That is, the doctrine comes into play only where there are dominant participants in the target market engaging in interdependent or parallel behavior and with the capacity effectively to determine price and total output of goods or services. If the target market performs as a competitive market in traditional antitrust terms, the participants in the market will have no occasion to fashion their behavior to take into account the presence of a potential entrant. The present procompetitive effects that a perceived potential entrant may produce in an oligopolistic market will already have been accomplished if the target market is performing competitively. Likewise, there would be no need for concern about the prospects of long-term deconcentration of a market which is in fact genuinely competitive.

In an effort to establish that the Spokane commercial banking market is oligopolistic, the Government relied primarily on concentration ratios indicating that three banking organizations (including WTB) control approximately 92 percent of total deposits in Spokane. . . . The record indicates that neither the Government nor the appellees undertook any significant study of the performance, as compared to the structure, of the commercial banking market in Spokane.

We conclude that by introducing evidence of concentration ratios of the magnitude of those present here the Government established a prima facie case that the Spokane market was a candidate for the potential-competition doctrine. On this aspect of the case, the burden was then upon appellees to show that the concentration ratios, which can be unreliable indicators of actual market behavior, see *United States* v. *General Dynamics Corp.,* 415 U.S. 486 (1974), did not accurately depict the economic characteristics of the Spokane market. In our view, appellees did not carry this burden. . . . Appellees introduced no significant evidence of the absence of parallel behavior in the pricing or provision of commercial bank services in Spokane.[9]

We note that it is hardly surprising that the Spokane commercial banking market is structurally concentrated. . . . This is so because as a

---

[9] The marketing of many forms of commercial bank services is controlled by government regulation. For example, regulation, not concentration in a banking market, produces parallelism with respect to such important elements of the banking business as interest allowed on savings accounts and interest charged on home mortgage loans. There are also many individualized judgments in the banking business, such as the decision whether to extend credit in various cases, that are not prone to parallel behavior regardless of the concentration of a market. Nevertheless, unfettered competition among banks does exist in a number of areas important to the public, as evidenced by the much-advertised differences in various forms of services offered by banks within the same geographic market. It is with regard to the latter economic activity that actual market behavior, and especially the presence or absence of significant parallel conduct, becomes relevant in this type of case.

country we have made the policy judgment to restrict entry into commercial banking in order to promote bank safety. Thus, most banking markets in theory will be subject to the potential-competition doctrine. But the same factor that usually renders such markets concentrated and theoretical prospects for potential-competition §7 cases—regulatory barriers to new entry—will also make it difficult to establish that the doctrine invalidates a particular geographic market extension merger.

C.   *Potential* De Novo *or Foothold Entry*

. . . The Government contends that the challenged merger violates §7 because it eliminates the alleged likelihood that, but for the merger, NBC would enter Spokane *de novo* or through a foothold acquisition. Utilization of one of these methods of entry, it is argued, would be likely to produce deconcentration of the Spokane market over the long run or other procompetitive effects, because NBC would be required to compete vigorously to expand its initially insignificant market share.

Two essential preconditions must exist before it is possible to resolve whether the Government's theory, if proved, establishes a violation of §7. It must be determined: (1)   that in fact NBC has available feasible means for entering the Spokane market other than by acquiring WTB; and (2)   that those means offer a substantial likelihood of ultimately producing deconcentration of that market or other significant procompetitive effects. . . .

It is undisputed that under state law NBC cannot establish *de novo* branches in Spokane and that its parent holding company cannot hold more than 25 percent of the stock of any other bank. Entry for NBC into Spokane therefore must be by acquisition of an existing bank. The Government contends that NBC has two distinct alternatives for acquisition of banks smaller than WTB and that either alternative would be likely to benefit the Spokane commercial banking market.

First, the Government contends that NBC could arrange for the formation of a new bank (a concept known as sponsorship), insure that the stock for such a new bank is placed in friendly hands, and then ultimately acquire that bank. Appellees respond that this approach would violate the spirit if not the letter of state law restrictions on bank branching. . . .

. . . Although we note that the intricate procedure for entry by sponsorship espoused by the Government can scarcely be compared to the *de novo* entry opportunities available to unregulated enterprises such as beer producers, see *Falstaff, supra,* we will assume, *arguendo,* that NBC conceivably could succeed in sponsoring and then acquiring a new bank in Spokane at some indefinite time in the future. It does not follow from this assumption, however, that this method of entry would be reasonably likely to produce any significant procompetitive benefits in the Spokane commercial banking market. To the contrary, it appears likely that such a method of entry would not significantly affect that market.

State law would not allow NBC to branch from a sponsored bank after it was acquired. NBC's entry into Spokane therefore would be frozen at the level of its initial acquisition. Thus, if NBC were to enter Spokane by sponsoring and acquiring a small bank, it would be trapped into a position of operating a single branch office in a large metropolitan area with no reasonable likelihood of developing a significant share of that market. . . . This assumed method of entry therefore would offer little realistic hope of ultimately producing deconcentration of the Spokane market. Moreover, it is unlikely that a single new bank in Spokane with a small market share, and forbidden to branch, would have any other significant procompetitive effect on that market. . . . Since there is no substantial likelihood of procompetitive loss if the challenged merger is undertaken in place of the Government's sponsorship theory, we are unable to conclude that the effect of the former "may be substantially to lessen competition" within the meaning of the Clayton Act.

As a second alternative method of entry, the Government proposed that NBC could enter by a foothold acquisition of one of two small, state-chartered commercial banks that operate in the Spokane metropolitan area.[10] Appellees reply that one of those banks is located in a suburb and has no offices in the city of Spokane, that after an acquisition NBC under state law could not branch from the suburb into the city, and that such a peripheral foothold cannot be viewed as an economically feasible method of entry into the relevant market. . . .

Granting the Government the benefit of the doubt that these two small banks were available merger partners for NBC, or were available at some not too distant time, it again does not follow that an acquisition of either would produce the long-term market-structure benefits predicted by the Government. Once NBC acquired either of these banks, it could not branch from the acquired bank. This limitation strongly suggests that NBC would not develop into a significant participant in the Spokane market. . . .

In sum, with regard to either of its proposed alternative methods of entry, the Government has offered an unpersuasive case on the first precondition of the question reserved in *Falstaff*—that feasible alternative methods of entry in fact existed. Putting these difficulties aside, the Government simply did not establish the second precondition. It failed to demonstrate that the alternative means offer a reasonable prospect of long-term structural improvement or other benefits in the target market. In fact, insofar as competitive benefits are concerned, the Government is in the anomalous position of opposing a geographic market extension merger that will introduce a third full-service banking organization to the

---

[10] . . . The Government presses its foothold-acquisition approach with considerably less vigor than its sponsorship theory, which may reflect the fact that under the former approach the total number of banking organizations in Spokane would remain the same.

Spokane market, where only two are now operating, in reliance on alternative means of entry that appear unlikely to have any significant pro-competitive effect. . . . Accordingly, we cannot hold for the Government on its principal potential-competition theory. . . .

D.   Perceived Potential Entry

The Government's failure to establish that NBC has alternative methods of entry that offer a reasonable likelihood of producing procompetitive effects is determinative of the fourth step of its argument. Rational commercial bankers in Spokane, it must be assumed, are aware of the regulatory barriers that render NBC an unlikely or an insignificant potential entrant except by merger with WTB. In light of those barriers, it is improbable that NBC exerts any meaningful procompetitive influence over Spokane banks by standing "in the wings.". . .

E.   Elimination of WTB

In the final step of its argument, the Government challenges the merger on the ground that it will eliminate the prospect that WTB may expand outside its base in Spokane and eventually develop into a direct competitor with large Washington banks in other areas of the State. The District Court found, however, that the Government had "failed to establish. . . . that there is any reasonable probability that WTB will expand into other banking markets. . . ." . . . The record amply supports this finding. At no time in its 70-year history has WTB established branches outside the Spokane metropolitan area. Nor has it ever acquired another bank . . . or received a merger offer other than the one at issue here. . . . In sum, the Government's argument about the elimination of WTB's potential for expansion outside Spokane is little more than speculation. . . .

IV.   CONCLUSION

In applying the doctrine of potential competition to commercial banking, courts must, as we have noted, take into account the extensive federal and state regulation of banks. Our affirmance of the District Court's judgment in this case rests primarily on state statutory barriers to *de novo* entry and to expansion following entry into a new geographic market. In states where such stringent barriers exist and in the absence of a likelihood of entrenchment, the potential-competition doctrine—grounded as it is on relative freedom of entry on the part of the acquiring firm—will seldom bar a geographic market extension merger by a commercial bank. In states that permit free branching or multibank holding companies, courts hearing cases involving such mergers should take into account all relevant factors, including the barriers to entry created by state and federal control over the issuance of new bank charters. . . . If regulatory restraints are not determinative, courts should consider the factors that are pertinent to any potential-competition case, including the economic feasibility and likelihood of *de novo* entry, the capabilities and expansion history of the acquiring firm, and the performance as well as the structural characteristics of the target market.

The judgment is *affirmed*.

MR. JUSTICE DOUGLAS took no part in the decision of this case.

. . . . .

MR. JUSTICE WHITE, with whom MR. JUSTICE BRENNAN and MR. JUSTICE MARSHALL join, dissenting.

For the second time this Term, the Court's new antitrust majority has chipped away at the policies of §7 of the Clayton Act. In *United States* v. *General Dynamics Corp.*, 415 U.S. 486 (1974), the majority sustained the failing-company defense in a new guise. Here, it redefines the elements of potential competition and dramatically escalates the burden of proving that a merger "may be substantially to lessen competition" within the meaning of §7.

That we are dealing with a severely concentrated commercial banking market in the Spokane metropolitan area is conceded. The Court also proceeds on the basis that it was open to the Government to make its case by proving that the NBC-WTB merger would probably cause a substantial lessening of competition in either one of two ways. First, it could be proved that NBC, with the resources and desire to enter the Spokane market, would probably have entered the market either by acquiring one of the small Spokane banks or by sponsoring a new bank and ultimately acquiring it. The merger thus deprived the Spokane market of a new competitor, and produced the requisite anticompetitive effect. Second, it could be shown that NBC's resources and interest in entering the Spokane market were so obvious to or recognized by those already in the market that, as a potential competitor waiting in the wings, NBC very probably exercised a restraining influence on anticompetitive practices in the concentrated Spokane banking market.

The majority does not quibble about the fact of NBC's resources and its incentive to extend its banking activities into Spokane. . . . Given the opportunity, NBC would obviously enter Spokane. Under Washington law, it could not branch there; but it was free to acquire another bank, given consent of banking authorities. That consent was obtained for the acquisition involved in this case, and it may fairly be assumed that it could have been obtained for the acquisition, not of a major competitor contributing to the concentration in the Spokane market, but of one of the smaller banks—a so-called toehold position in the market.

Another mode of entry into Spokane was also available to NBC. It could have been instrumental in forming a new bank in that market and in due course have merged with the "sponsored" institution. It is argued that this route was all but legally unavailable to NBC, . . . but the sponsored-bank method of expansion has occurred frequently in the State of Washington. The District Court did not hold sponsorship barred by state law. This Court also refrains from so holding and proceeds on the assumption that the sponsored-bank route was available to NBC. . . .

Thus, although branching into Spokane was not legally feasible, there were other modes of entry no less attractive or less feasible than entering by establishing a new branch. It is incredible that if branching into Spokane had been allowable NBC would not have entered in this way. It is equally unlikely that absent the understandably attractive merger with WTB, NBC would not have proceeded to acquire a smaller bank or to be instrumental in forming a new sponsored bank.

The Court apparently assumes this to be the case, but goes on to hold that the Government's proof failed because neither a small new bank nor one of the existing small banks, if acquired, had a realistic chance of deconcentrating the Spokane market to any substantial extent. Also, absent the capability of making substantial inroads on the market shares of the principal banks, it is said that those banks had nothing to fear from NBC as a potential competitor and that NBC therefore had no current influence on competitive practices in the Spokane market.

I part company with the majority at this point. The Spokane market was highly concentrated. NBC had the resources and the desire to enter the market. There were no impenetrable legal or economic barriers to its doing so; and it is sufficiently plain from the record that absent merger with WTB, NBC could and would either have made a toehold entry or been instrumental in establishing a sponsored bank in Spokane. But NBC chose to merge with a larger bank and to deprive the market of the competition it would have offered had it entered in either of two other ways. In my opinion, this made out a sufficient prima facie case under §7 which, absent effective rebuttal, entitled the United States to judgment.

The Court's sole answer to the Government's proof is that even if NBC would have entered by acquisition or *de novo* through a sponsored bank, it would have "little realistic hope of ultimately producing deconcentration of the Spokane market." This was because under Washington law after acquiring an existing or newly formed bank, NBC could not branch from that institution but would be confined to the banking offices which it acquired at the time of the merger. In the Court's opinion, NBC, without branching, would have "no reasonable likelihood of developing a significant share of that market," and the Government's case therefore failed.

I cannot accept the per se view that, without branching, an able and willing newcomer to the banking market cannot be considered a sufficiently substantial competitive influence, immediately or in the foreseeable future, so that its loss to the market would warrant application of §7. This is particularly true if the putative entrant is a large and successful banking organization with wide experience in developing new markets.

Small banks can be profitable, and they can grow rapidly. The experience of the three small banks in Spokane proves this. Each of them is a profitable bank. . . . The deposits of each of the three small banks have grown. . . . Spokane would not appear to be a stagnant banking market, and it provides opportunities for smaller banking concerns. . . . Their market share, although remaining relatively small, increased from 3.9 percent to 7.8 percent. Of course, deposits in the three large banking organizations also grew. Two of them increased their market shares very slightly, but the third lost ground from 38.3 percent to 31.6 percent for a combined decline of the three from 96 percent to 92.3 percent. The small banks thus more than held their own in the Spokane market. This showing of the smaller banks hardly indicates such impotence on the part of small competitors that a new entrant in the market should necessarily be deemed to be without influence in the market and to be beyond recognition under §7. . . .

The details on the relative size of individual bank branches in Spokane or elsewhere in metropolitan areas of the State are not in the record; but it is unbelievable that there are no branches that have started very small and grown very large. New branches must make their way, often in head-to-head competition with other banks. Some are more successful than others, and I cannot accept, as a per se legal rule, the notion that a new bank sponsored by NBC in downtown Spokane or elsewhere in the city must be forever deemed to be without substantial competitive impact on the banking community.[11] It is incredible to me that the presence of a major Seattle bank like NBC in downtown Spokane could or would be ignored by the entrenched banking powers or should be ignored for the purposes of applying §7 of the Clayton Act. . . .

. . . NBC is a major financial institution with large lending limits and offering a full line of commercial banking services. It is obviously equipped to penetrate and compete vigorously in the Spokane lending market wholly aside from how fast deposits might grow in a newly established or acquired Spokane bank. It is quite untenable to assert that the competition that might be offered in the Spokane lending market by a new bank formed by this obviously vigorous competitor is too insignificant to warrant the protections of §7.[12]

-----

[11] Evidence introduced by the Government as to the ability of banks in the other major metropolitan banking markets of Washington—Seattle, Tacoma, and Everett—totally undercuts the Court's assumption that a bank with only one office cannot acquire a substantial enough market share to effect deconcentration. . . .

[12] As the majority recognizes, the relevant product market in this case is the cluster of services offered by commercial banks. A main component of that cluster, and one which determines profits, is the ability to provide loans, and it seems to me that a prospect of

The availability of branching is, of course, an important competitive consideration, but it should not be forgotten that American Commercial Bank, headquartered in downtown Spokane, has four branches and if acquired by NBC would give that bank a substantial operating capacity in Spokane. The majority, nevertheless, even assuming the acquisition of this bank by NBC, insists on its own view of competitive reality and holds that the loss of NBC as a competitor in place of American must be deemed an insignificant loss to competition. . . .

It is also true that if NBC entered in Spokane by sponsoring a new bank, the new bank itself could legally branch and create the necessary branch infrastructure for as long as it was not acquired by NBC or another outsider. The majority states that this is "probably unrealistic" and that it would "multiply the problems" of obtaining approval of sponsorship from bank regulatory agencies. But this is sheer speculation; the Court simply has no idea what the attitude of regulatory officials would be in this regard. . . .

Viewed in this light, the Court's per se rule becomes threadbare indeed when applied to NBC entering by acquisition into the Spokane market. The three existing smaller banks in Spokane have been successful and profitable and have even increased their share of the market in six years. Furthermore, Seattle-First National cannot legally go beyond its present seven branches in the Spokane market, and its share of the market has declined. It is quite unreasonable to think that NBC, if it acquired American Commercial, with its four branches could not be an effective competitor at least against Seattle-First National in Spokane, with its seven branches, or against WTB with its eight.

The Court also errs in holding that NBC, an obvious potential competitor, cannot be deemed to have exercised substantial influence on the Spokane market and that its entry by merger with a major Spokane bank therefore represents no probable injury to competition in that market. To the extent that the Court's holding on this branch of the case rests on its notion that no bank, without branching, can make substantial inroads on the Spokane market, I disagree for reasons already stated. Beyond that, however, the waiting-in-the-wings approach to potential competition rests on what objective factors indicate the perception of the reasonably minded competitor in the Spokane market might be of the likelihood and impact of an entry by NBC, either *de novo* or by acquisition of a small bank. Predictions of market behavior and competitive success are just not

---

competition for loans, whether based on deposits garnered in Spokane or elsewhere, has a substantial possibility of effecting deconcentration in at least one segment of the banking business. The fact that profitability and number of offices are not highly correlated is supported by comparing the experience of Washington Bancshares and Seattle-First National Bank. In 1971, the former had 23 offices and a net income of $2.2 million. The latter, with only seven offices, had a net income of $3.5 million. In that same year, although Washington Bancshares had $45.6 million more in deposits than did Seattle-First National, the latter had an edge of $7.2 million in commercial and industrial loans.

as certain or uniformly held as the Court makes them out to be. . . . The majority would have one believe that even if NBC was interested, no one in the market would take it seriously enough to restrain anticompetitive practices. It is certainly possible, however, that even if bankers in the market doubted that NBC would actually be successful in acquiring a significant market share, if they entered the market, the *possibility* of entry and the *possibility* of competition following entry were sufficiently strong to restrain anticompetitive practices. If bankers thought that there was a probability of entry, which there surely was, but that their losses from such entry could be substantial, if NBC, once in the market, competed more effectively than anticipated, they would take countermeasures and make entry less attractive by refraining from engaging in anticompetitive practices.

In the last analysis, one's view of this case, and the rules one devises for assessing whether this merger should be barred, turns on the policy of §7 of the Clayton Act to bar mergers which may contribute to further concentration in the structure of American business. . . .

With respect to whether depriving the market of the competition offered by a new entrant violates §7, it is not enough under the Court's view that the newcomer has itself found the market sufficiently attractive to enter and to assume all the start-up costs and risks attendant to a new business undertaking. The Court is willing also to assume that the new business will be profitable and long-lived, for under the approach taken today, it is not enough to show the loss of one or more profitable but small businesses. Apparently, it cannot be assumed that a small business, even when backed by a major enterprise, can or will be successful in competing against the entrenched powers in the market.

This thesis erects formidable barriers to the application of the potential-competition doctrine not only in the banking business but in other lines of commerce.[13] To show that the potential entrant, waiting in the wings, is exercising a present influence on the market, or that its loss as a *de novo* or toehold entrant may be a substantial injury to competition, it will not be enough to prove ability and willingness to enter, along with the probability, or even certainty, of entry. Nor will it suffice to prove that the potential or actual entrant would be a profitable concern and successfully prevent the major figures in the market from increasing their market shares. The courts must also examine conditions in the market and con-

---

[13] The Court professes to limit its per se rule to "an industry in which new entry is extensively regulated by the State and Federal Governments." The case, as decided, however, does not turn on barriers to entry, but barriers to effective competition, once entry is effected, and barriers to effective competition are not easily limited to regulated industries. The Court lays itself open for arguments that economic, as well as legal, barriers exist for new competitors. At least it is difficult to see why one should be more controlling than another; in fact, the Court inself blurs the two.

clude for themselves that there is a realistic expectation that the new entrant will appropriate for itself a substantial part of the business of the major competitors in the market.

The Court then delivers the *coup de grace* by imposing its own visions of reality in commercial banking markets: without unlimited branching authority in the market involved, no newcomer to the market can be sufficiently successful against others, who have the authority, to be a substantial competitor and to merit recognition under doctrines of potential competition. No new entrant can attain, let us say, 15 or 20 percent of the banking business in the Spokane area unless it has branching authority. The Court apparently insists this will be true no matter where the new banking office is located and no matter who and how well equipped and financed and new entrant may be. This is claiming a prescience that I doubt the Court has and is a view of the effectiveness and worth of competition, though having modest beginnings, that I do not share. . . .

7

Joint Ventures—
A Form of Merger

Joint ventures can be defined as the creation of new, jointly owned business enterprises by two or more corporations. Such ventures provide especially formidable problems for students of antitrust because of their potential for both good and evil. On the one hand, they provide a means by which resources can be pooled and risks shared; this often makes possible the completion of projects which, but for the joint venture, would not have been undertaken. On the other hand, the fact that potential competitors choose to operate jointly, rather than as rivals, is disturbing. The courts, in apparent recognition of the potential of joint ventures for increasing competition in some instances and diminishing it in others, have adopted a relatively flexible position toward them. In the *Terminal Railroad* decision, the Supreme Court recognized the value of the venture itself, yet sought to mitigate its anticompetitive consequences through the requirement of fair and equal access. In the *Penn-Olin* case the Court sought to extend and refine its analysis of joint ventures, particularly as it related to the question of potential competition.[1]

United States v. *Terminal Railroad Association of St. Louis*
224 U.S. 383 (1912)
MR. JUSTICE LURTON delivered the opinion of the Court.

The United States filed this bill to enforce the provisions of the Sherman Act of July 2, 1890 . . . against thirty-eight corporate and individual defendants . . . as a combination in restraint of interstate commerce and as a monopoly forbidden by that law. . . .

The principal defendant is the Terminal Railroad Association of St.

---

[1] In this regard see especially Section 8 of the decision, wherein JUSTICE CLARK attempts to define a series of rules for evaluating the consequences of joint ventures.

Louis, hereinafter designated as the Terminal Company. It is a corporation of the State of Missouri, and was organized under an agreement made in 1889 between Mr. Jay Gould and a number of the defendant railroad companies for the express purpose of acquiring the properties of several independent terminal companies at St. Louis with a view to combining and operating them as a unitary system.

. . . These properties included the great union station, the only existing railroad bridge—the Eads or St. Louis Bridge—and every connecting or terminal company by means of which that bridge could be used by railroads terminating on either side of the river. . . .

. . . [F]or a time, there existed three independent methods by which connection was maintained between railroads terminating on either side of the river at St. Louis: first, the original Wiggins Ferry Company, and its railway terminal connections; second, the Eads Railroad Bridge and the several terminal companies by means of which railroads terminating at St. Louis were able to use that bridge and connect with one another, constituting the system controlled by the Terminal Company, and, third, [t]he Merchants' Bridge and terminal facilities owned and operated by companies in connection therewith.

This resulted in some cases in an unnecessary duplication of facilities, but it at least gave to carriers and shippers some choice, a condition which, if it does not lead to competition in charges, does insure competition in service. Important as were the considerations mentioned, their independence of one another served to keep open the means for the entrance of new lines to the city, and was an obstacle to united opposition from existing lines. The importance of this will be more clearly seen when we come to consider the topographical conditions of the situation.

That the promoters of the Terminal Company designed to obtain the control of every feasible means of railroad access to St. Louis, or means of connecting the lines of railway entering on opposite sides of the river, is manifested by the declarations of the original agreement, as well as by the successive steps which followed. . . .

We come, then, to the question upon which the case must turn: Has the unification of substantially every terminal facility by which the traffic of St. Louis is served resulted in a combination which is in restraint of trade within the meaning and purpose of the Anti-trust Act?

It is not contended that the unification of the terminal facilities of a great city where many railroad systems center is, under all circumstances and conditions, a combination in restraint of trade or commerce. Whether it is a facility in aid of interstate commerce or an unreasonable restraint forbidden by the act of Congress . . . will depend upon the intent to be inferred from the extent of the control thereby secured over instrumentalities which such commerce is under compulsion to use, the method by which such control has been brought about and the manner in which that control has been exerted.

The consequence to interstate commerce of this combination cannot be appreciated without a consideration of natural conditions greatly affecting the railroad situation at St. Louis. Though twenty-four lines of railway converge at St. Louis, not one of them passes through. About one-half of these lines have their termini on the Illinois side of the river. The others, coming from the west and north, have their termini either in the city or on its northern edge. . . . The cost of construction and maintenance of railroad bridges over so great a river makes it impractical for every road desiring to enter or pass through the city to have its own bridge. The obvious solution is the maintenance of toll bridges open to the use of any and all lines upon identical terms. . . . The first bridge, called the Eads Bridge, was, and is, a toll bridge. Any carrier may use it on equal terms. But to use it there must be access over rails connecting the bridge and the railway. On the St. Louis side the bridge terminates at the foot of the great hills upon which the city is built; on the Illinois side it ends in the low and wide valley of the Mississippi. This condition resulted in the organization of independent companies which undertook to connect the bridge on each side with the various railroad termini. . . . Thus, though the bridge might be used by all upon equal terms, it was accessible only by means of the several terminal companies operating lines connecting it with the railroad termini.

This brought about a condition which led to the construction of the second bridge, the Merchants' Bridge. This, too, was, and is, a toll bridge, and may be used by all upon equal terms. . . . But this Merchants' Bridge, like the Eads Bridge, had no rail connections with any of the existing railroad systems, and these facilities, as in the case of the Eads Bridge, were supplied by a number of independent railway companies who undertook to fill in the gaps between the bridge ends and the termini of railroads on both sides of the river. . . . Now, it is evident that these lines connecting railroad termini with the railroad bridges dominated the situation. They stood, as it were, just outside the gateway, and none could enter, though the gate stood open, who did not comply with their terms. . . .

The result of the geographical and topographical situation is that it is, as a practical matter, impossible for any railroad company to pass through, or even enter St. Louis, so as to be within reach of its industries or commerce, without using the facilities entirely controlled by the Terminal Company. . . . Nor is this effect denied, for the learned counsel representing the proprietary companies, as well as the Terminal Company, say in their filed brief: "There indeed is compulsion, but it is inherent in the situation. The other companies use the terminal properties because it is not possible to acquire adequate facilities for themselves. The cost to any one company is prohibitive." Obviously, this was not true before the consolidation of the systems of the Wiggins Ferry Company and the Merchants' Bridge Company with the system theretofore controlled by the Terminal Company. That the nonproprietary companies might have been compelled to use the instrumentalities of one or the other of the three systems then available, and that the advantages secured might not have been so great as those offered by the unified system now operated by the Terminal Company, must be admitted. But that there existed before the three terminal systems were combined a considerable measure of competition for the business of the other companies, and a larger power of competition, is undeniable. . . . The independent existence of these three terminal systems was, therefore, a menace to complete domination as keeping open the way for greater competition. Only by their absorption or some equivalent arrangement was it possible to exclude from independent entrance . . . any . . . company which might desire its own terminals. . . .

The physical conditions which compel the use of the combined system by every road which desires to cross the river, either to serve the commerce of the city or to connect with lines separated by the river, is the factor which gives greatest color to the unlawfulness of the combination as now controlled and operated. If the Terminal Company was in law and fact the agent of all, the mere unification which has occurred would take on quite a different aspect. It becomes, therefore, of the utmost importance to know the character and purpose of the corporation. . . . The fact that the Terminal Company is not an independent corporation at all is of the utmost significance. There are twenty-four railroads converging at St. Louis. The relation of the Terminal Company is not one of impartiality to each of them. It was organized in 1889, at the instance of six of these railroad companies, for the purpose of acquiring all existing terminal instrumentalities for the benefit of the combination, and such other companies as they might thereafter admit to joint ownership by unanimous consent, and upon a consideration to be agreed upon. . . .

That these facilities were not to be acquired for the benefit of any railroad company which might desire a joint use thereof was made plain by a provision in the contract [of 1889] . . . which stipulated that other railroad companies not named therein as proprietary companies might only be admitted "to joint use of said terminal system on unanimous consent, but not otherwise, of the directors of the first party, and on payment of such a consideration as they may determine, and on signing this agreement," etc. Inasmuch as the directors of the Terminal Company consisted of one representative of each of the proprietary companies, selected by itself, it is plain that each of said companies had and still has a veto upon any joint use or control of terminals by any non-proprietary company. . . .

We fail to find . . . any provision abrogating the requirement of unanimous consent to the admission of other companies to the ownership of the Terminal Company, though counsel say that no such company will now find itself excluded from joint use or ownership upon application. . . .

By still another clause in the agreement the proprietary companies obligate themselves to forever use the facilities of the Terminal Company for all business destined to cross the river. This would seem to guarantee against any competitive system, since the companies to the agreement now control about one-third of the railroad mileage of the United States. . . .

That through their ownership and exclusive control they are in possession of advantages in respect to the enormous traffic which must use the St. Louis gateway, is undeniable. That the proprietary companies have not availed themselves of the full measure of their power to impede free competition of outside companies, may be true. Aside from their power under all of the conditions to exclude independent entrance to the city by any outside company, their control has resulted in certain methods which are not consistent with freedom of competition. . . .

We are not unmindful of the essential difference between terminal systems properly so described and railroad transportation companies. The first are but instrumentalities which assist the latter in the transfer of traffic between different lines, and in the collection and distribution of traffic. They are a modern evolution in the doing of railroad business, and are of the greatest public utility. They, under proper conditions, do not restrain, but promote commerce. . . .

While, therefore, the mere combining of several independent terminal systems into one may not operate as a restraint upon the interstate commerce which must use them, yet there may be conditions which will bring such a combination under the prohibition of the Sherman Act. . . .

It cannot be controverted that, in ordinary circumstances, a number of independent companies might combine for the purpose of controlling or acquiring terminals for their common but exclusive use. In such cases other companies might be admitted upon terms or excluded altogether. If such terms were too onerous, there would ordinarily remain the right and power to construct their own terminals. But the situation at St. Louis is most extraordinary, and we base our conclusion in this case, in a large measure, upon that fact. The "physical or topographical condition peculiar to the locality," which is advanced as a prime justification for a unified system of terminals, constitutes a most obvious reason why such a unified system is an obstacle, a hindrance and a restriction upon interstate commerce, unless it is the impartial agent of all who, owing to conditions, are under such compulsion, as here exists, to use its facilities. The witness upon whom the defendants chiefly rely to uphold the advantages of the unified system which has been constructed, Mr. Albert L. Perkins, gives this as his unqualified judgment. . . . The witness, however, points out that such a terminal company should be the agent of every company and, furthermore, that its service should not be for profit or gain. In short, that every railroad using the service should be a joint owner and equally interested in the control and management. . . .

The terminal properties in question are not so controlled and managed, in view of the inherent local conditions, as to escape condemnation as a restraint upon commerce. They are not under a common control and ownership. Nor can this be brought about unless the prohibition against the admission of other companies to such control is stricken out and provision made for the admission of any company to an equal control and management upon an equal basis with the present proprietary companies. . . .

We come now to the remedy. . . . If, as we have already said, the combination of two or more mere terminal companies into a single system does not violate the prohibition of the statute against contracts and combinations in restraint of interstate commerce, it is because such a combination may be of the greatest public utility. But when, as here, the inherent conditions are such as to prohibit any other reasonable means of entering the city, the combination of every such facility under the exclusive ownership and control of less than all of the companies under compulsion to use them violates both the first and second sections of the act, in that it constitutes a contract or combination in restraint of commerce among the States and an attempt to monopolize commerce among the States which must pass through the gateway of St. Louis. . . .

Plainly the combination which has occurred would not be an illegal restraint under the terms of the statute if it were what is claimed for it, a proper terminal association acting as the impartial agent of every line which is under compulsion to use its instrumentalities. If, as we have pointed out, the violation of the statute, in view of the inherent physical conditions, grows out of administrative conditions which may be eliminated and the obvious advantages of unification preserved, such a modification of the agreement between the Terminal Company and the proprietary companies as shall constitute the former the *bona fide* agent and servant of every railroad line which shall use its facilities, and an inhibition of certain methods of administration to which we have referred, will amply vindicate the wise purpose of the statute, and will preserve to the public a system of great public advantage.

These considerations lead to a reversal of the decree dismissing the bill. This is accordingly adjudged and the case is remanded to the District Court, with directions that a decree be there entered directing the parties to submit to the court, within ninety days after receipt of mandate, a plan for the reorganization of the contract between the fourteen defendant railroad companies and the Terminal Company, which we have pointed out as bringing the combination within the inhibition of the statute.

First. By providing for the admission of any existing or future railroad to joint ownership and control of the combined terminal properties, upon such just and reasonable terms as shall place such applying company upon a plane of equality in respect of benefits and burdens with the present proprietary companies.

Second. Such plan of reorganization must also provide definitely for the use of terminal facilities by any other railroad not electing to become a joint owner, upon such just and reasonable terms and regulations as will, in respect of use, character and cost of service, place every such company upon as nearly an equal plane as may be with respect to expenses and charges as that occupied by the proprietary companies. . . .

Reversed and remanded accordingly.

United States v. Penn-Olin Chemical Co.

378 U.S. 158 (1964)

MR. JUSTICE CLARK delivered the opinion of the Court.

Pennsalt Chemicals Corporation and Olin Mathieson Chemical Corporation jointly formed Penn-Olin Chemical Company to produce and sell sodium chlorate in the southeastern United States. The Government seeks to dissolve this joint venture as violative of both Section 7 of the Clayton Act and Section 1 of the Sherman Act. This direct appeal . . . from the United States District Court for the District of Delaware, raises two questions. First, whether Section 7 of the Clayton Act is applicable where two corporations form a third to engage in a new enterprise; and, second, if this question is answered in the affirmative, whether there is a violation of Section 1 or Section 7 under the facts of this case. The trial court found that the joint venture, on this record, violated neither of these sections and found it unnecessary to reach the first question. . . . In view of the importance of each of these questions in the administration of the antitrust laws, we noted probable jurisdiction. . . . We have concluded that a joint venture as organized here would be subject to the regulation of Section 7 of the Clayton Act and, reaching the merits, we hold that while on the present record there is no violation of Section 1 of the Sherman Act, the District Court erred in dismissing the complaint as to Section 7 of the Clayton Act. Accordingly, the judgment is vacated and remanded for further consideration.

1. LINE OF COMMERCE, RELEVANT MARKET, ETC.

At the outset it is well to note that some of the troublesome questions ordinarily found in antitrust cases have been eliminated by the parties. First, the line of commerce is a chemical known as sodium chlorate. . . . All sodium chlorate of like purity is usable interchangeably and is used primarily in the pulp and paper industry to bleach the pulp, making for a brighter and higher quality paper. . . . The pulp and paper industry consumes about 64% of total production of sodium chlorate. The chemical is also employed in the production of herbicides, agricultural chemicals and in certain derivatives, such as ammonium perchlorate. Next, the relevant market is not disputed. It is the southeastern part of the United States. Nor is the fact that Olin has never engaged in the commercial production of sodium chlorate contested. It has purchased and does purchase amounts of the chemical for internal consumption and has acted as sales agent for Pennsalt in the southeastern territory under contracts dated in December 1957 and February 1958. Olin also owns a patented process for bleaching pulp with chlorine dioxide. This process requires sodium chlorate and has been widely used by paper manufacturers under royalty-free licenses. . . .

2. THE COMPANIES INVOLVED

Pennsalt is engaged solely in the production and sale of chemicals and chemical products throughout the United States. Its assets are around a hundred million dollars and its sales are about the same amount. Its sodium chlorate production is located at Portland, Oregon, with a capacity of some 15,000 tons as of 1959. It occupied 57.8% of the market west of the Rocky Mountains. It has marketed sodium chlorate in the southeastern United States to some extent since 1957. Its shipments into that territory in 1960 were 4,186 tons of which Olin sold 3,202 tons on its sales agency contract.

Olin is a large diversified corporation, the result of a merger of Olin Industries, Inc., and Mathieson Chemical Corporation in 1954. One of its seven divisions operates plants in 15 States and produces a wide range of chemicals and chemical products accounting for about 30% of Olin's revenues. Olin's sales in 1960 grossed some $690,000,000 and its total assets were $860,000,000.

Penn-Olin was organized in 1960 as a joint venture of Olin and Pennsalt. Each owns 50% of its stock and the officers and directors are divided equally between the parents. Its plant at Calvert City, Kentucky, was built by equal contribution of the two parents and cost $6,500,000. It has a capacity to produce 26,500 tons of sodium chlorate annually and began operations in 1961. Pennsalt operates the plant and Olin handles the sales. Penn-Olin deals in no other chemicals.

3. BACKGROUND AND STATISTICS OF THE INDUSTRY

Prior to 1961 the sodium chlorate industry in the United States was made up of three producing companies. The largest producer, Hooker Chemical Corporation, entered the industry in 1956 when it acquired Oldbury Electro Chemical Company, which had been producing sodium chlorate for over half a century. Hooker now has two plants, one in the relevant marketing area at Columbus, Mississippi, which orginally had a capacity of 16,000 tons but which was doubled in 1962. The other plant is at Niagara Falls, New York, with a capacity of 18,000 tons. Hooker has assets of almost $200,000,000. American Potash & Chemical Corporation entered the industry in 1955 by the acquisition of Western Electro Chemical Company. American Potash also has two plants, one located at Henderson, Nevada, with a 27,000-ton capacity and the other at Aberdeen, Mississippi (built in 1957), the capacity of which was 15,000 tons. Its assets are almost $100,000,000. The trial court found that these two corporations "had a virtual monopoly" in the relevant southeast market, holding over 90% of the market.

A third company in the industry was Pennsalt which had a 15,392-ton plant at Portland, Oregon. It entered seriously into the relevant marketing area through a sales arrangement with Olin dated December 1957 and finalized in 1958, which was aimed at testing the availability of the southeastern market. Olin as an exclusive seller was to undertake the sale of 2,000 tons of sodium chlorate per year to pulp and paper mills in the southeast (except for Buckeye Cellulose Co., at Foley, Florida, which Pennsalt reserved to serve directly). In 1960, 4,186 tons of sodium chlorate were marketed in the relevant market with the aid of this agreement. This accounted for 8.9% of the sales in that market.

During the previous decade no new firms had entered the sodium chlorate industry, and little effort had been made by existing companies to expand their facilities prior to 1957. In 1953 Olin had made available to Pennsalt its Mathieson patented process for bleaching pulp with chlorine dioxide and the latter had installed it 100% in all of the western paper mills. This process uses sodium chlorate. At about the same time the process was likewise made available, royalty free, to the entire pulp and paper industry. By 1960 most of the chlorine dioxide generated by paper manufacturers was being produced under the Olin controlled process. This created an expanding demand for sodium chlorate and by 1960 the heaviest concentration of purchasers was located in the relevant southeastern territory. By 1957 Hooker began increasing the capacity of its Columbus plant and by 1960 it had been almost doubled. American Potash sensed the need of a plant in Mississippi to compete with Hooker and began its Aberdeen plant in 1957. It was completed to a 15,000-ton capacity in 1959, and this capacity was expanded 50% by 1961.

The sales arrangement between Pennsalt and Olin, previously mentioned, was superseded by the joint venture agreement on February 11, 1960, and the Penn-Olin plant operations at Calvert City, Kentucky, began in 1961. In the same year Pittsburgh Plate Glass Company announced that it would build a plant at Lake Charles, Louisiana, with a capacity of 15,000 tons. Pittsburgh Plate Glass had operated a sodium chlorate plant in Canada.

As a result of these expansions and new entries into the southeastern market, the projected production of sodium chlorate there more than doubled. . . . Penn-Olin's share of the expanded relevant market was about 27.6%. . . .

4. THE SETTING FROM WHICH THE JOINT VENTURE EMERGED

As early as 1951 Pennsalt had considered building a plant at Calvert City and starting in 1955 it initiated several cost and market studies for a sodium chlorate plant in the southeast. Three different proposals from within its own organization were rejected prior to 1957, apparently because the rate of return was so unattractive that "the expense of refining these figures further would be unwarranted." When Hooker announced in December 1956 that it was going to increase the capacity of its Columbus plant, the interest of Pennsalt management was reactivated. It appointed a "task force" to evaluate the company's future in the eastern market; it retained management consultants to study that market and its chief engineer prepared cost estimates. However, in December 1957 the management decided that the estimated rate of return was unattractive and considered it "unlikely" that Pennsalt would go it alone. It was suggested that Olin would be a "logical partner" in a joint venture and might in the interim be interested in distributing in the East 2,000 tons of the Portland sodium chlorate production. The sales agreement with Olin, heretofore mentioned, was eventually made. In the final draft the parties agreed that "neither . . . should move in the chlorate or perchlorate field without keeping the other party informed . . ." and that one would "bring to the attention of the other any unusual aspects of this business which might make it desirable to proceed further with production plans." Pennsalt claims that it finally decided, prior to this agreement, that it should not build a plant iself and that this decision was never reconsidered or changed. But the District Court found to the contrary.

During this same period—beginning slightly earlier— Olin began investigating the possibility of entering the sodium chlorate industry. It had never produced sodium chlorate commercially, although its predecessor had done so years before. However, the electrolytic process used in making sodium chlorate is intimately related to other operations of Olin and required the same general knowledge. Olin also possessed extensive experience in the technical aspects of bleaching pulp and paper and was intimate with the pulp and paper mills of the southeast. In April 1958 Olin's chemical division wrote and circulated to the management a "Whither Report" which stated in part:

> We have an unparalleled opportunity to move sodium chlorate into the paper industry as the result of our work on the installation of chlorine dioxide generators. We have a captive consumption for sodium chlorate.

And Olin's engineering supervisor concluded that entry into sodium chlorate production was "an attractive venture" since it "represents a logical expansion of the product line of the Industrial Chemicals Division . . ." with respect to "one of the major markets, pulp and paper bleaching, [with which] we have a favorable marketing position, particularly in the southeast.

The staff, however, did not agree with the engineering supervisor or the "Whither Report." . . . But, as the trial court found, the testimony indicated that Olin's decision to enter the joint venture was made without determining that Olin could not or would not be an independent competitor. That question, the president of Penn-Olin testified, "never reached the point of final decision."

This led the District Court to find that "[t]he possibility of individual entry into the southeastern market had not been completely rejected by either Pennsalt or Olin before they decided upon the joint venture." . . .

5. SECTION 7 OF THE CLAYTON ACT APPLIES TO "JOINT VENTURES"

Appellees argue that Section 7 applies only where the acquired company is "engaged" in commerce and that it would not apply to a newly formed corporation, such as Penn-Olin. The test, they say, is whether the enterprise to be acquired is engaged in commerce—not whether a corporation formed as the instrumentality for the acquisition is itself engaged in commerce at the moment of its formation. We believe that this logic fails in the light of the wording of the section and its legislative background. The test of the section is the effect of the acquisition. Certainly the formation of a joint venture and purchase by the organizers of its stock would substantially lessen competition—indeed foreclose it—as between them, both being engaged in commerce. This would be true whether they were in actual or potential competition with each other and even though the new corporation was formed to create a wholly new enterprise. Realistically, the parents would not compete with their progeny. Moreover, in this case the progeny was organized to further the business of its parents, already in commerce, and the fact that it was organized specifically to engage in commerce should bring it within the coverage of Section 7. In addition, long prior to trial Penn-Olin was actually engaged in commerce. To hold that it was not "would be illogical and disrespectful of the plain congressional purpose in amending Section 7 . . . [for] it would create a large loophole in a statute designed to close a loophole." *United States* v. *Philadelphia National Bank* . . . (1963). In any event, Penn-Olin was engaged in commerce at the time of suit and the economic effects of an acquisition are to be measured at that point rather than at the time of acquisition. *United States* v. *E. I. duPont de Nemours & Co.* . . . (1957). The technicality could, therefore, be averted by merely refiling an amended complaint at the time of trial. This would be a useless requirement.

6. THE APPLICATION OF THE MERGER DOCTRINE

This is the first case reaching this Court and on which we have written that directly involves the validity under Section 7 of the joint participation of two corporations in the creation of a third as a new domestic producing organization.[1] We are, therefore, plowing new ground. If it is true, however, that some aspects of the problem might be found in *United States* v. *Terminal R. Assn.*, 224 U.S. 383 (1912), and *Associated Press* v. *United States*, 326 U.S. 1 (1945), where joint ventures with great market power were subjected to control, even prior to the amendment to Section 7.

. . . Their [joint ventures] economic significance has grown tremendously in the last score of years, having been spurred on by the need for speed and size in fashioning a war machine during the early forties. Postwar use of joint subsidiaries and joint projects led to the spawning of thousands of such ventures in an effort to perform the commercial tasks confronting an expanding economy.

The joint venture, like the "merger" and the "conglomeration," often creates anticompetitive dangers. It is the chosen competitive instrument of two or more corporations previously acting independently and usually competitively with one another. The result is "a triumvirate of associated corporations."[2] If the parent companies are in competition, or might compete absent the joint venture, it may be assumed that neither will compete with the progeny in its line of commerce. Inevitably, the operations of the joint venture will be frozen to those lines of commerce which will not bring it into competition with the parents, and the latter, by the same token will be foreclosed from the joint venture's market.

This is not to say that the joint venture is controlled by the same criteria as the merger or conglomeration. The merger eliminates one of the participating corporations from the market while a joint venture creates a new competitive force therein. . . .

Overall, the same considerations apply to joint ventures as to mergers, for in each instance we are but expounding a national policy enunciated by the Congress to preserve and promote a free competitive economy. In furtherance of that policy, now entering upon its 75th year, this Court has formulated appropriate criteria, first under the Sherman Act and now, also, under the Clayton Act and other antitrust legislation. The Celler-Kefauver Amendment to Section 7, with which we now deal, was the answer of the Congress to a loophole found to exist in the original enactment. . . . The grand design of the original Section 7, as to stock acquisitions, as well as the Celler-Kefauver Amendment, as to the acquisition of assets, was to arrest incipient threats to competition which the Sherman Act did not ordinarily reach. It follows that actual restraints need not be proved. The requirements of the amendment are satisfied when a "tendency" toward monopoly or the "reasonable likelihood" of a substantial lessening of competition in the relevant market is shown. Con-

---

[1] For a discussion of the problem, see Kaysen & Turner, *Antitrust Policy*, 136–141 (1959).

[2] See Note, "Applicability of Section 7 to a Joint Venture," 11 *U.C.L.A. L. Rev.* 393, 396.

gress made it plain that the validity of such arrangements was to be gauged on a broader scale by using the words "may be substantially to lessen competition" which "indicate that its concern was with probabilities, not certainties." . . .

7. THE CRITERIA GOVERNING SECTION 7 CASES

We apply the light of these considerations in the merger cases to the problem confronting us here. The District Court found that "Pennsalt and Olin each possessed the resources and general capability needed to build its own plant in the southeast and to compete with Hooker and [American Potash] in that market. Each could have done so if it had wished." . . .[3] In addition, the District Court found that, contrary to the position of the management of Olin and Pennsalt, "the forecasts of each company indicated that a plant could be operated with profit." . . .

The District Court held, however, that these considerations had no controlling significance, except "as a factor in determining whether as a matter of probability *both* companies would have entered the market as individual competitors if Penn-Olin had not been formed. Only in this event would potential competition between the two companies have been foreclosed by the joint venture." . . . In this regard the court found it "impossible to conclude that as a matter of reasonable probability *both* Pennsalt and Olin would have built plants in the southeast if Penn-Olin had not been created." . . . The court made no decision concerning the probability that one would have built "while the other continued to ponder." It found that this "hypothesized situation affords no basis for concluding that Penn-Olin had the effect of substantially lessening competition." . . . That would depend, the court said, "upon the competitive impact which Penn-Olin will have as against that which might have resulted in Pennsalt or Olin had been an individual market entrant." . . . The court found that this impact could not be determined from the record in this case. "Solely as a matter of theory," it said, ". . . no reason exists to suppose that Penn-Olin will be a less effective competitor than Pennsalt or Olin would have been. The contrary conclusion is the more reasonable." . . .

---

[3] The court explained further: "At the time when the joint venture was agreed upon Pennsalt and Olin each had an extensive background in sodium chlorate. Pennsalt had years of experience in manufacturing and selling it. Although Olin had never been a commercial manufacturer, it possessed a substantially developed manufacturing technique of its own, and also had available to it a process developed by Vickers-Krebs with whom it had been negotiating to construct a plant. Olin had contracts among the southeastern pulp and paper mills which Pennsalt lacked, but Pennsalt's own estimates indicate that in a reasonable time it would develop adequate business to support a plant if it decided to build. A suitable location for a plant was available to each company—Calvert City, Kentucky for Pennsalt, and the TVA area around Chattanooga, Tennessee for Olin. The financing required would not have been a problem for either company." . . .

We believe that the court erred in this regard. Certainly the sole test would not be the probability that *both* companies would have entered the market. Nor would the consideration be limited to the probability that one entered alone. There still remained for consideration the fact that Penn-Olin eliminated the potential competition of the corporation that might have remained at the edge of the market, continually threatening to enter. Just as a merger eliminates actual competition, this joint venture may well foreclose any prospect of competition between Olin and Pennsalt in the relevant sodium chlorate market. The difference, of course, is that the merger's foreclosure is present while the joint venture's is prospective. Nevertheless, "[p]otential competition . . . as a substitute for . . . [actual competition] may restrain producers from overcharging those to whom they sell or underpaying those from whom they buy. . . . Potential competition, insofar as the threat survives [as it would have here in the absence of Penn-Olin], may compensate in part for the imperfection characteristic of actual competition in the great majority of competitive markets." Wilcox, *Competition and Monopoly in American Industry*, TNEC Monograph No. 21 (1940) 7–8. Potential competition cannot be put to a subjective test. It is not "susceptible of a ready and precise answer." . . . The existence of an aggressive, well equipped and well financed corporation engaged in the same or related lines of commerce waiting anxiously to enter an oligopolistic market would be a substantial incentive to competition which cannot be underestimated. Witness the expansion undertaken by Hooker and American Potash as soon as they heard of the interest of Olin Mathieson and of Pennsalt in southeast territory. This same situation might well have come about had either Olin or Pennsalt entered the relevant market alone and the other remained aloof watching developments.

8.   THE PROBLEM OF PROOF

Here the evidence shows beyond question that the industry was rapidly expanding; the relevant southeast market was requiring about one-half of the national production of sodium chlorate; few corporations had the inclination, resources and know-how to enter this market; both parent corporations of Penn-Olin had great resources; each had long been identified with the industry, one owning valuable patent rights while the other had engaged in sodium chlorate production for years; each had other chemicals, the production of which required the use of sodium chlorate; right up to the creation of Penn-Olin, each had evidenced a long-sustained and strong interest in entering the relevant market area; each enjoyed good reputation and business connections with the major consumers of sodium chlorate in the relevant market, *i.e.*, the pulp and paper mills; and finally, each had the know-how and the capacity to enter that market and could have done so individually at a reasonable profit. Moreover, each company had compelling reasons for entering the southeast market. Pennsalt needed to expand its sales to the southeast, which it could not do economically without a plant in that area. Olin was motivated by "the fact that [it was] already buying and using a fair quantity [of sodium chlorate] for the production of sodium chlorite and that [it was] promoting the Mathieson process of the generation of chlorine dioxide which uses sodium chlorate." Unless we are going to require subjective evidence, this array of probability certainly reaches the prima facie stage. As we have indicated, to require more would be to read the statutory requirement of reasonable probability into a requirement of certainty. This we will not do.

However, despite these strong circumstances, we are not disposed to disturb the court's finding that there was not a reasonable probability that both Pennsalt and Olin would have built a plant in the relevant market area. But we have concluded that a finding should have been made as to the reasonable probability that either one of the corporations would have entered the market by building a plant, while the other would have remained a significant potential competitor. The trial court said that this question "need not be decided." . . . [W]e prefer that the trial court pass upon this question and we venture no opinion thereon. Since the trial court might have been concerned over whether there was evidence on this point,[4] we reiterate that it is impossible to demonstrate the *precise* competitive effects of the elimination of either Pennsalt or Olin as a potential competitor. . . . There being no proof of specific intent to use Penn-Olin as a vehicle to eliminate competition, nor evidence of collateral restrictive agreements between the joint venturers, we put those situations to one side. We note generally the following criteria which the trial court might take into account in assessing the probability of a substantial lessening of competition: the number and power of the competitors in the relevant market; the background of their growth; the power of the joint venturers; the relationship of their lines of commerce; the competition existing between them and the power of each in dealing with the competitors of the other; the setting in which the joint venture was created; the reasons and necessities for its existence, the joint venture's line of commerce and the relationship thereof to that of its parents; the adaptability of its line of commerce to noncompetitive practices; the potential power of the joint venture in the relevant market; an appraisal of what the competition in the relevant market would have been if one of the joint venturers had entered it alone instead of through Penn-Olin; the effect, in the event of this occurrence, of the other joint venturer's potential competition; and such other factors as might indicate potential risk to competition in the relevant

---

[4] In this regard, the court should, of course, open the record for further testimony if the parties so desire.

market. In weighing these factors the court should remember that the mandate of the Congress is in terms of the probability of a lessening of substantial competition, not in terms of tangible present restraint.

The judgment is therefore vacated and the case is remanded for further proceedings in conformity with this opinion.

Vacated and remanded.

MR. JUSTICE WHITE dissents.

MR. JUSTICE DOUGLAS with whom MR. JUSTICE BLACK agrees, dissenting.

Agreements among competitors to divide markets are *per se* violations of the Sherman Act.[5] The most detailed, grandiose scheme of that kind is disclosed in *Addyston Pipe & Steel Co.* v. *United States,* 175 U.S. 211, where industrialists, acting like commissars in modern communist countries, determined what tonnage should be produced by each company and what territory was "free" and what was "bonus." . . .

In *United States* v. *National Lead Co.* . . . . a Sherman Act violation resulted from a division of world markets for titanium pigments, the key being allocation of territories through patent license agreements. A similar arrangement was struck down in *Timken Co.* v. *United States* . . . where world trade territories were allocated among an American, a British, and a French company through intercorporate arrangements called a "joint venture." *Nationwide Trailer Rental System, Inc.* v. *United States,* 355 U.S. 10 (affirming 156 F. Supp. 800), held violative of the antitrust laws an agreement establishing exclusive territories for each member of an organization set up to regulate the one-way trailer rental industry and empowering a member to prevent any other operator from becoming a member in his area.

In the late 1950s the only producers of sodium chlorate in the United States were Pennsalt, one of the appellees in this case, Hooker Chemical Corporation, and American Potash and Chemical Corporation. No new firms had entered the industry for a decade. Prices seemed to be stable and little effort had been made to expand existing uses or to develop new ones. But during the 1950s the sodium chlorate market began to grow, chiefly on account of the adoption of chlorine dioxide bleaching in the pulp industry. Domestic production more than quadrupled between 1950 and 1960. The growth was the most pronounced in the southeast. By 1960 the southeast had the heaviest concentration of sodium chlorate buyers, the largest being the pulp and paper mills; and nearly half the national

---

[5] See Oppenheim, "Antitrust Booms and Boomerangs," *59 Nw· U L. Rev.* 33, 35 (1964).

sodium chlorate productive capacity. In 1960 the southeast market was divided among the three producers as follows: Hooker, 49.5%, American Potash, 41.6%, Pennsalt, 8.9%.

Pennsalt, whose only sodium chlorate plant was at Portland, Oregon, became interested in establishing a plant in the rapidly growing southeast sodium chlorate market. It made cost studies as early as 1951 for such a project; and from 1955 on it gave the matter almost continuous consideration. . . .

In the early 1950s Olin too was investigating the possibilities of entering the southeast industry. It took various steps looking toward establishment of a production plant in the southeastern United States. . . .

During the years when Pennsalt and Olin were considering independent entry into the southeast market, they were also discussing joint entry. In order to test the southeast market the two agreed in December of 1957 that Pennsalt would make available to Olin, as exclusive seller, 2,000 tons of sodium chlorate per year for two or three years, Olin agreeing to sell the chemical only to pulp and paper companies in the southeast, except for one company which Pennsalt reserved the right to serve directly. Another agreement entered into in February 1958 provided that neither of the two companies would "move in the chlorate or perchlorate field without keeping the other party informed." And each by the agreement bound itself "to bring to the attention of the other any unusual aspects of this business which might make it desirable to proceed further with production plans." The purpose of this latter agreement, it was found, was to assure that each party would advise the other of any plans independently to enter the market before it would take any definite action on its own.

So what we have in substance is two major companies who on the eve of competitive projects in the southeastern market join forces. In principle the case is no different from one where Pennsalt and Olin decide to divide the southeastern market as was done in *Addyston Pipe* and in the other division-of-markets cases already summarized. Through the "joint venture" they do indeed divide it fifty-fifty. That division through the device of the "joint venture" is as plain and precise as though made in more formal agreements. As we saw in the *Timken* case, "agreements between legally separate persons and companies to suppress competition among themselves and others" cannot be justified "by labeling the project a 'joint venture.'" . . . And we added, "Perhaps every agreement and combination to restrain trade could be so labeled." . . . What may not be done by two companies who decide to divide a market surely cannot be done by the convenient creation of a legal umbrella—whether joint venture or common ownership and control . . . —under which they achieve the same objective by moving in unison.

An actual division of the market through the device of "joint venture" has, I think, the effect "substantially to lessen competition" within the meaning of Section 7 of the Clayton Act. . . .

We do not, of course, know for certain what would have happened if the "joint venture" had not materialized. But we do know that Section 7 deals only with probabilities, not certainties. We know that the interest of each company in the project was lively, that one if not both of them would probably have entered that market, and that even if only one had entered at the beginning the presence of the other on the periphery would in all likelihood have been a potent competitive factor. Cf. *United States* v. *El Paso Natural Gas Co.* . . . . We also know that as between Pennsalt and Olin the "joint venture" foreclosed all future competition by dividing the market fifty-fifty. That could not have been done consistently with our decisions had the "joint venture" been created after Pennsalt and Olin had entered the market or after either had done so. To allow the joint venture to obtain antitrust immunity because it was launched at the very threshold of the entry of two potential competitors into a territory is to let Section 7 be avoided by sophisticated devices.

There is no need to remand this case for a finding "as to the reasonable probability that either one of the corporations would have entered the market by building a plant, while the other would have remained a significant potential competitor." . . . This case—now almost three years in litigation—has already produced a trial extending over a 23-day period, the introduction of approximately 450 exhibits, and a 1,600-page record. We should not require the investment of additional time, money, and effort where, as here, a case turns on one crucial finding and the record is sufficient to enable this Court—which is as competent in this regard as the District Court—to supply it.

MR. JUSTICE HARLAN, dissenting.

I can see no purpose to be served by this remand except to give the Government an opportunity to retrieve an antitrust case which it has lost, and properly so. Believing that this Court should not lend itself to such a course, I would affirm the judgment of the District Court.

Note: On remand, the District Court found no reasonable probability that either company would have entered unilaterally [246 F. Supp. 917 (D. Del. 1965)]. This was ultimately affirmed by an equally divided Supreme Court [389 U.S. 308 (1967)].

PART FOUR

Trade Practices

8

Price Discrimination

Few issues in antitrust enforcement have engendered as much controversy as have efforts to enforce the Robinson-Patman Act. Underlying much of this controversy is the feeling by many economists and lawyers that the Act was designed to protect competitors rather than competition—a distinction others feel is a false one. Clearly, price discrimination may have the effect of promoting competition (e.g., by increasing the ability of new firms to break into established markets), or it may lessen competition by permitting a powerful competitor to "sharp-shoot" against more localized rivals. As a consequence, it is often difficult to determine the purpose or probable effect of discriminatory pricing.

This fundamental perplexity is compounded by several subordinate issues. First, there is the question, discussed in the *Morton Salt, Utah Pie,* and *American Excelsior* decisions, of the extent to which the Federal Trade Commission must go to prove that a given discrimination *may* injure competition.

The second, and perhaps more complex issue, concerns the so-called good faith defense and is discussed in the *Standard of Indiana* and *A&P* cases. In the former proceeding the Federal Trade Commission challenged the absolute character of the good faith defense, arguing that a showing of competitive injury removes the need to consider whether or not a seller met competition. In its 1951 decision the Court expressed a contrary view, holding the good faith defense to be absolute; it then upheld, some years later, the adequacy of the evidence of good faith offered by the company.

In *A&P,* the Court explicitly permitted its use on the seller side of the market to enable a large buyer to prevail against a charge of buyer-induced price discrimination (proscribed under Section 2(f) of the Act). As *U.S. Gypsum* illustrates, however (see Chapter 2 above), the defense apparently cannot be used to cloak patently illegal behavior.

Finally, the *Borden* case illustrates the problems that emerge in trying to lend economic content to legal phraseology, in this case, in determining whether two products are of like grade and quality within the meaning of the Robinson-Patman Act.

Federal Trade Commission v. Morton Salt Company

334 U.S. 37 (1948)

MR. JUSTICE BLACK delivered the opinion of the Court.

The Federal Trade Commission, after a hearing, found that the respondent, which manufacturers and sells table salt in interstate commerce, had disciminated in price between different purchasers of like grades and qualities, and concluded that such discriminations were in violation of Section 2 of the Clayton Act . . . as amended by the Robinson-Patman Act. . . . It accordingly issued a cease and desist order. . . . Upon petition of the respondent the Circuit Court of Appeals, wilth one judge dissenting, set aside the Commission's findings and order, directed the Commission to dismiss its complaint against respondent, and denied a cross petition of the Commission for enforcement of its order. 162 F.2d 949. The Court's judgment rested on its construction of the Act, its holding that crucial findings of the Commission were either not supported by evidence or were contrary to the evidence, and its conclusion that the Commission's order was too broad. Since questions of importance in the construction and administration of the Act were presented, we granted certiorari. . . .

Respondent manufactures several different brands of table salt and sells them directly to (1) wholesalers or jobbers, who in turn resell to the retail trade, and (2) large retailers, including chain store retailers. Respondent sells its finest brand of table salt, known as Blue Label, on what it terms a standard quantity discount system available to all customers. Under this system the purchasers pay a delivered price and the cost to both wholesale and retail purchasers of this brand differs according to the quantities bought. These prices are as follows, after making allowance for rebates and discounts:

	Per Case
Less-than-carload purchases	$1.60
Carload purchases	1.50
5,000-case purchases in any consecutive 12 months	1.40
50,000-case purchases in any consecutive 12 months	1.35

Only five companies have ever bought sufficient quantities of respondent's salt to obtain the $1.35 per case price. These companies could buy in such quantities because they operate large chains of retail stores in various parts of the country. As a result of this low price these five companies have been able to sell Blue Label salt at retail cheaper than wholesale purchasers from respondent could reasonably sell the same brand of salt to independently operated retail stores, many of whom competed with the local outlets of the five chain stores. . . .

In addition to these standard quantity discounts, special allowances were granted certain favored customers who competed with other customers to whom they were denied.

First.   Respondent's basic contention, which it argues this case hinges upon, is that its "standard quantity discounts, available to all on equal terms, as contrasted, for example, to hidden or special rebates, allowances, prices or discounts, are not discriminatory within the meaning of the Robinson-Patman Act." Theoretically, these discounts are equally available to all, but functionally they are not. For as the record indicates (if reference to it on this point were necessary) no single independent retail grocery store, and probably no single wholesaler, bought as many as 50,000 cases or as much as $50,000 worth of table salt in one year. Furthermore, the record shows that, while certain purchasers were enjoying one or more of respondent's standard quantity discounts, some of their competitors made purchases in such small quantities that they could not qualify for any of respondent's discounts, even those based on carload shipments. The legislative history of the Robinson-Patman Act makes it abundantly clear that Congress considered it to be an evil that a large buyer could secure a competitive advantage over a small buyer solely because of the large buyer's quantity purchasing ability. The Robinson-Patman Act was passed to deprive a large buyer of such advantages except to the extent that a lower price could be justified by reason of a seller's diminished costs due to quantity manufacture, delivery or sale, or by reason of the seller's good faith effort to meet a competitor's equally low price.

Section 2 of the original Clayton Act had included a proviso that nothing contained in it should prevent "discrimination in price . . . on account of differences in the grade, quality, or quantity of the commodity sold, or that makes only due allowance for difference in the cost of selling or transportation. . . ." That section has been construed as permitting quantity discounts, such as those here, without regard to the amount of the seller's actual savings in cost attributable to quantity sales or quantity deliveries. . . . The House Committee Report on the Robinson-Patman Act considered that the Clayton Act's proviso allowing quantity discounts so weakened Section 2 "as to render it inadequate, if not almost a nullity." . . . And it was . . . to protect competition from all price differentials except those based in full on cost savings that Section 2(a) of the amendment provided "That nothing herein contained shall prevent differentials which make only due allowance for differences in the cost of manufacture, sale, or delivery resulting from the differing methods or quantities in which such commodities are to such purchasers sold or delivered."

The foregoing references, without regard to others which could be mentioned, establish that respondent's standard quantity discounts are discriminatory within the meaning of the Act, and are prohibited by it whenever they have the defined effect on competition. . . .

302

Second. The Government interprets the opinion of the Circuit Court of Appeals as having held that in order to establish "discrimination in price" under the Act the burden rested on the Commission to prove that respondent's quantity discount differentials were not justified by its cost savings. Respondent does not so understand the Court of Appeals decision, and furthermore admits that no such burden rests on the Commission. We agree that it does not. . . . [S]ection 2(b) of the Act specifically imposes the burden of showing justification upon one who is shown to have discriminated in prices. . . .

Third. It is argued that the findings fail to show that respondent's discriminatory discounts had in fact caused injury to competition. There are specific findings that such injuries had resulted from respondent's discounts, although the statute does not require the Commission to find that injury has actually resulted. The statute requires no more than that the effect of the prohibited price discriminations "may be substantially to lessen competition . . . or to injure, destroy, or prevent competition." After a careful consideration of this provision of the Robinson-Patman Act, we have said that "the statute does not require that the discriminations must in fact have harmed competition, but only that there is a reasonable possibility that they 'may' have such an effect." *Corn Products Co.* v. *Federal Trade Comm'n,* 324 U.S. 726, 742. Here the Commission found what would appear to be obvious, that the competitive opportunities of certain merchants were injured when they had to pay respondent substantially more for their goods than their competitors had to pay. The findings are adequate.

Fourth. It is urged that the evidence is inadequate to support the Commission's findings of injury to competition. As we have pointed out, however, the Commission is authorized by the Act to bar discriminatory prices upon the "reasonable possibility" that different prices for like goods to competing purchasers may have the defined effect on competition. That respondent's quantity discounts did result in price differentials between competing purchasers sufficient in amount to influence their resale prices of salt was shown by evidence. This showing in itself is adequate to support the Commission's appropriate findings that the effect of such price discriminations "may be substantially to lessen competition . . . and to injure, destroy, and prevent competition."

The adequacy of the evidence to support the Commission's findings of reasonably possible injury to competition from respondent's price differentials between competing carload and less-than-carload purchasers is singled out for special attacks here. . . . The argument is that there is an obvious saving to a seller who delivers goods in carload lots. Assuming this to be true, that fact would not tend to disprove injury to the merchant compelled to pay the less-than-carload price. For a ten-cent carload price differential against a merchant would injure him competitively just as much as a ten-cent differential under any other name. However relevant the separate carload argument might be to the question of justifying a differential by cost savings, it has no relevancy in determining whether the differential works an injury to a competitor. Since Congress has not seen fit to give carload discounts any favored classification we cannot do so. Such discounts, like all others, can be justified by a seller who proves that the full amount of the discount is based on his actual savings in cost. The trouble with this phase of respondent's case is that it has thus far failed to make such proof.

It is also argued that respondent's less-than-carload sales are very small in comparison with the total volume of its business and for that reason we should reject the Commission's finding that the effect of the carload discrimination may substantially lessen competition and may injure competition between purchasers who are granted and those who are denied this discriminatory discount. To support this argument, reference is made to the fact that salt is a small item in most wholesale and retail businesses and in consumers' budgets. For several reasons we cannot accept this contention.

There are many articles in a grocery store that, considered separately, are comparatively small parts of a merchant's stock. Congress intended to protect a merchant from competitive injury attributable to discriminatory prices on any or all goods sold in interstate commerce, whether the particular goods constituted a major or minor portion of his stock. Since a grocery store consists of many comparatively small articles, there is no possible way effectively to protect a grocer from discriminatory prices except by applying the prohibitions of the Act to each individual article in the store.

Furthermore, in enacting the Robinson-Patman Act, Congress was especially concerned with protecting small businesses which were unable to buy in quantities, such as the merchants here who purchased in less-than-carload lots. To this end it undertook to strengthen this very phase of the old Clayton Act. . . . Since there was evidence sufficient to show that the less-than-carload purchasers might have been handicapped in competing with the more favored carload purchasers by the differential in price established by respondent, the Commission was justified in finding that competition might have thereby been substantially lessened or have been injured within the meaning of the Act.

Apprehension is expressed in this Court that enforcement of the Commission's order against respondent's continued violations of the Robinson-Patman Act might lead respondent to raise table salt prices to its carload purchasers. Such a conceivable, though, we think, highly improbable, contingency, could afford us no reason for upsetting the Commission's findings and declining to direct compliance with a statute passed by Congress.

The Commission here went much further in receiving evidence than the statute requires. It heard testimony from many witnesses in various parts of the country to show that they had suffered actual financial losses on account of respondent's discriminatory prices. Experts were offered to prove the tendency of injury from such prices. The evidence covers about two thousand pages, largely devoted to this single issue—injury to competition. It would greatly handicap effective enforcement of the Act to require testimony to show that which we believe to be self-evident, namely, that there is a "reasonable possibility" that competition may be adversely affected by a practice under which manufacturers and producers sell their goods to some customers substantially cheaper than they sell like goods to the competitors of these customers. This showing in itself is sufficient to justify our conclusion that the Commission's findings of injury to competition were adequately supported by evidence.

Fifth. The Circuit Court of Appeals held, and respondent here contends, that the order was too sweeping. . . .

. . . True, the Commission did not merely prohibit future discounts, rebates, and allowances in the exact mathematical percentages previously utilized by respondent. Had the order done no more than that, respondent could have continued substantially the same unlawful practices despite the order by simply altering the discount percentages and the quantities of salt to which the percentages applied. . . .

The judgment of the Circuit Court of Appeals is reversed and the proceedings are remanded to that court to be disposed of in conformity with this opinion.

Reversed.

[MR. JUSTICE JACKSON with whom MR. JUSTICE FRANKFURTER jointed, dissented in part.]

Standard Oil Company (of Indiana) v. Federal Trade Commission

340 U.S. 231 (1951)

MR. JUSTICE BURTON delivered the opinion of the Court.

In this case the Federal Trade Commission challenged the right of the Standard Oil Company, under the Robinson-Patman Act, to sell gasoline to four comparatively large "jobber" customers in Detroit as a less price per gallon than it sold like gasoline to many comparatively small service station customers in the same area. The Company's defenses were that (1) the sales involved were not in interstate commerce and (2) its lower price to the jobbers was justified because it was made to retain them as customers and in good faith to meet an equally low price of a competitor. The

Commission, with one member dissenting, ordered the company to cease and desist from making such a price differential. 43 F.T.C. 56. The Court of Appeals slightly modified the order and required its enforcement as modified. 173 F.2d 210. We granted certiorari on petition of the company because the case presents an important issue under the Robinson-Patman Act which has not been settled by this Court. . . .

For the reasons hereinafter stated, we agree with the court below that the sales were made in interstate commerce but we agree with petitioner that, under the Act, the lower price to the jobbers was justified if it was made to retain each of them as a customer and in good faith to meet an equally low price of a competitor.

. . . [T]he material facts are summarized here on the basis of the Commission's findings. The sales described are those of Red Crown gasoline because those sales raise all of the material issues and constitute about 90% of petitioner's sales in the Detroit area.

Since the effective data of the Robinson-Patman Act, June 19, 1936, petitioner has sold its Red Crown gasoline to its "jobber" customers at its tank-car prices. Those prices have been 1½¢ per gallon less than its tank-wagon prices to service station customers for identical gasoline in the same area. In practice, the service stations have resold the gasoline at the prevailing retail service station prices. Each of petitioner's so-called "jobber" customers has been free to resell its gasoline at retail or wholesale. Each, at some time, has resold some of it at retail. One now resells it only at retail. The others now resell it largely at wholesale. As to resale prices, two of the "jobbers" have resold their gasoline only at the prevailing wholesale or retail rates. The other two, however, have reflected, in varying degrees, petitioner's reductions in the cost of the gasoline to them by reducing their resale prices of that gasoline below the prevailing rates. The effect of these reductions has thus reached competing retail service stations in part through retail stations operated by the "jobbers" and in part through retail stations which purchased gasoline from the "jobbers" at less than the prevailing tank-wagon prices. The Commission found that such reduced resale prices "have resulted in injuring, destroying, and preventing competition between said favored dealers and retail dealers in respondent's [petitioner's] gasoline and other major brands of gasoline. . . ." . . . The distinctive characteristics of these "jobbers" are that each (1) maintains sufficient bulk storage to take delivery of gasoline in tank-car quantities (of 8,000 to 12,000 gallons) rather than in tank-wagon quantities (or 700 to 800 gallons) as is customary for service stations; (2) owns and operates tank wagons and other facilities for delivery of gasoline to service stations; (3) has an established business sufficient to insure purchases of from one to two million gallons a year; and (4) has adequate credit responsibility. While the cost of petitioner's sales and deliveries of gasoline to each of these four "jobbers" is no doubt less, per gallon, than the cost of its sales and deliveries of like gasoline to its service station customers in the same area, there is no finding that such difference accounts for the entire reduction in price made by petitioner to these "jobbers," and we proceed on the assumption that it does not entirely account for that difference.

Petitioner placed its reliance upon evidence offered to show that its lower price to each jobber was made in order to retain that jobber as a customer and in good faith to meet an equally low price offered by one or more competitors. The Commission, however, treated such evidence as not relevant. . . .

[The Commission stated:]

> . . . [E]ven though the lower prices in question may have been made by respondent in good faith to meet the lower prices of competitors, this does not constitute a defense in the face of affirmative proof that the effect of the discrimination was to injure, destroy and prevent competition with the retail stations operated by the said named dealers and with stations operated by their retailer-customers. . . .

. . . In its opinion in the instant case, the Commission recognizes that it is an absolute defense to a charge of price discrimination for a seller to prove, under Section 2(a) that its price differential makes only due allowances for differences in cost or for price changes made in response to changing market conditions. 41 F.T.C. at 283. Each of these three defenses is introduced by the same phrase "nothing . . . shall prevent," and all are embraced in the same word "justification" in the first sentence of Section 2(b). It is natural, therefore, to conclude that each of these defenses is entitled to the same effect, without regard to whether there also appears an affirmative showing of actual or potential injury to competition at the same or a lower level traceable to the price differential made by the seller. The Commission says, however, that the proviso in Section 2(b) as to a seller meeting in good faith a lower competitive price is not an absolute defense if an injury to competition may result from such price reduction. We find no basis for such a distinction between the defense in Section 2(a) and (b).

The defense in subsection (b), now before us, is limited to a price reduction made to meet in good faith an equally low price of a competitor. . . . [But] the actual core of the defense . . . still consists of the provision that wherever a lawful lower price of a competitor threatens to deprive a seller of a customer, the seller, to retain that customer, may in good faith meet that lower price. Actual competition, at least in this elemental form, is thus preserved. . . .

This right of a seller, under Section 2(b), to meet in good faith an equally low price of a competitor has been considered here before. Both in *Corn Products Refining Co.* v. *Federal Trade Comm'n*, 324 U.S. 726, and in *Federal Trade Comm'n* v. *Staley Mfg. Co.*, 324 U.S. 746, evidence in support of this defense was reviewed at length. There would have been no occasion thus to review it under the theory now contended for by the Commission. While this Court did not sustain the seller's defense in either case, it did unquestionably recognize the relevance of the evidence in support of that defense. The decision in each case was based upon the insufficiency of the seller's evidence to establish its defense, not upon the inadequacy of its defense as a matter of law. . . .

In the Staley case . . . most of the Court's opinion is devoted to the consideration of the evidence introduced in support of the seller's defense under Section 2(*b*). The discussion proceeds upon the assumption, applicable here, that if a competitor's "lower price" is a lawful individual price offered to any of the seller's customers, then the seller is protected, under Section 2(*b*), in making a counteroffer provided the seller proves that its counteroffer is made to meet in good faith its competitor's equally low price. . . .

. . . All that petitioner asks in the instant case is that its evidence be considered and that findings be made by the Commission as to the sufficiency of that evidence to support petitioner's defense under Section 2(*b*).

In addition, there has been widepsread understanding that, under the Robinson-Patman Act, it is a complete defense to a charge of price discrimination for the seller to show that its price differential has been made in good faith to meet a lawful and equally low price of a competitor. This understanding is reflected in actions and statements of members and counsel of the Federal Trade Commission. Representatives of the Department of Justice have testified to the effectiveness and value of the defense under the Robinson-Patman Act. We see no reason to depart now from that interpretation.

The heart of our national economic policy long has been faith in the value of competition. In the Sherman and Clayton Acts, as well as in the Robinson-Patman Act, "Congress was dealing with competition, which it sought to protect, and monopoly, which it sought to prevent." . . . We need not now reconcile, in its entirety, the economic theory which underlies the Robinson-Patman Act with that of the Sherman and Clayton Acts. It is enough to say that Congress did not seek by the Robinson-Patman Act either to abolish competition or so radically to curtail it that a seller would have no substantial right of self-defense against a price raid by a competitor. . . . There is . . . plain language and established practice which permits a seller, through Section 2(*b*), to retain a customer by realistically meeting in good faith the price offered to that customer, without necessarily changing the seller's price to its other customers.

In a case where a seller sustains the burden of proof placed upon it to establish its defense under Section 2(*b*), we find no reason to destroy that defense indirectly, merely because it also appears that the beneficiaries of the seller's price reductions may derive a competitive advantage from them or may, in a natural course of events, reduce their own resale prices to their customers. It must have been obvious to Congress that any price reduction to any dealer may always affect competition at that dealer's level as well as at the dealer's resale level, whether or not the reduction to the dealer is discriminatory. Likewise, it must have been obvious to Congress that any price reductions initiated by a seller's competitor would, if not met by the seller, affect competition at the beneficiary's level or among the beneficiary's customers just as much as if those reductions had been met by the seller. The proviso in Section 2(b), as interpreted by the Commission, would not be available when there was or might be an injury to competition at a resale level. So interpreted, the proviso would have such little, if any, applicability as to be practically meaningless. We may, therefore, conclude that Congress meant to permit the natural consequences to follow the seller's action in meeting in good faith a lawful and equally low price of its competitor.

In its argument here, the Commission suggests that there may be some situations in which it might recognize the proviso in Section 2(b) as a complete defense, even though the seller's differential in price did injure competition. In suport of this, the Commission indicates that in each case it must weigh the potentially injurious effect of a seller's price reduction upon competition at all lower levels against its beneficial effect in permitting the seller to meet competition at its own level. In the absence of more explicit requirements and more specific standards of comparison than we have here, it is difficult to see how an injury to competition at a level below that of the seller can thus be balanced fairly against a justification for meeting the competition at the seller's level. We hesitate to accept Section 2(b) as establishing such a dubious defense. . . .

The judgment of the Court of Appeals, accordingly, is reversed and the case is remanded to that court with instructions to remand it to the Federal Trade Commission to make finding in conformity with this opinion.

It is so ordered.

[MR. JUSTICE MINTON took no part in the consideration or decision of this case. MR. JUSTICE REED, joined by THE CHIEF JUSTICE and MR. JUSTICE BLACK, dissented.]

Note: In the proceedings following the remand, the Commission held that Standard did *not* act in good faith because its reduced prices were made pursuant to a price *system* rather than being "the result of departures from a nondiscrimiantory price scale." 49 F.T.C. 923, 954. The Court of Appeals found no basis in the 8-volume, 5,500-page record for such a conclusion, and reversed. 233 F.2d 649. The Supreme Court, in this decision next abstracted, affirmed the lower court view.

Federal Trade Commission v. Standard Oil Company (of Indiana)

355 U.S. 396 (1958)

MR. JUSTICE CLARK delivered the opinion of the Court.

This case is a sequel to *Standard Oil Co.* v. *Federal Trade Comm'n,* 340 U.S. 231 (1951), wherein the Court held that Section 2(b) of the Clayton Act . . . as amended by the Robinson-Patman Act . . . afforded a seller a complete defense to a charge of price discimination if its lower price was "made in good faith to meet a lawful and equally low price of a competitor." . . . We remanded the case with instructions that the Federal Trade Commission make findings on Standard's contention that its discriminatory prices were so made. The subsequent findings are not altogether clear. The Commission, acting on the same record, seemingly does not contest the fact that Standard's deductions were made to meet the equally low prices of its competitors. However, Standard was held not to have acted in good faith, and the Section 2(b) defense precluded, because of the Commission's determination that Standard's reduced prices were made pursuant to a price system rather than being "the result of departures from a nondiscriminatory price scale." . . . The Court of Appeals found no basis in the record for such a finding and vacated the order of the Commission, holding that Standard's "'good faith' defense was firmly established." . . . In view of our former opinion and the importance of bringing an end to this protracted litigation, we granted certiorari. . . . Having concluded that the case turns on a factual issue, decided by the Court of Appeals upon a fair assessment of the record, we affirm the decision below.

The long history of this 17-year-old case may be found both in the original opinion of the Court of Appeals . . . and in the original opinion of this Court, *supra.* . . .

The Commission urges us to examine its 8-volume record of over 5,500 pages and determine if its finding that Standard reduced prices to four "jobbers" pursuant to a pricing system was erroneous, as held by the Court of Appeals. The Commission contends that a Section 2(b) defense is precluded if the reductions were so made. If wrong in this, it maintains that the "good faith" element of a Section 2(b) defense is not made out by showing that competitors employ such a pricing system, and in any event is negatived by Standard's failure to make a bona fide effort to review its pricing system upon passage of the Robinson-Patman Act.

On the present posture of the case we believe that further review of the evidence is unwarranted. . . . [I]t now appears that "[p]roper decision of the controversy depends upon a question of fact," and therefore "we adhere to the usual rule of non-interference where conclusions of Circuit Courts of Appeals depend on appreciation of circumstances which admit of different interpretations." . . . We do no more on the issue of insubstantiality than decide that the Court of Appeals has made a "fair assessment" of the record. That conclusion is strengthened by the fact that the finding made by the Court of Appeals accords with that of the trial examiner, two dissenting members of the Commission, and another panel of the Court of Appeals when the case was first before that court in 1949, all of them being agreed that the prices were reduced in good faith to meet offers of competitors.

Both parties acknowledge that discrimination pursuant to a price system would preclude a finding of "good faith." *Federal Trade Comm'n* v. *A. E. Staley Mfg. Co. . . . ; Federal Trade Comm'n* v. *Cement Institute . . . ; Federal Trade Comm'n* v. *National Lead Co. . . .* The sole question then is one of fact: were Standard's reduced prices to four "jobber" buyers—Citrin-Kolb, Stikeman, Wayne, and Ned's—made pursuant to a pricing system rather than to meet individual competitive situations? . . .

It appears to us that the crucial inquiry is not why reduced prices were first granted to Citrin-Kolb, Stikeman, and Wayne, but rather why the reduced price was continued subsequent to passage of the Act in 1936. The findings show that both major and local suppliers made numerous attempts in the 1936–1941 period to lure these "jobbers" away from Standard with cut-rate prices, oftentimes much lower than the one-and-one-half-cent reduction Standard was giving them.[1] It is uncontradicted, as pointed out in one of the Commission dissents, that Standard lost three of its seven "jobbers" by not meeting compeitors' pirating offers in 1933–1934. All of this occurred in the context of a major gasoline price war in the Detroit area, created by an extreme overabundance of supply—a setting most unlikely to lend itself to general pricing policies. . . .

The findings as to Ned's, the only one of the "jobbers" initially to receive the tank-car price *post* Robinson-Patman, are highly significant. After a prolonged period of haggling, during which Ned's pressured Standard with information as to numerous more attractive price offers made by other suppliers, Standard responded to an ultimatum from Ned's in 1936 with a half-cent-per-gallon reduction from the tank-wagon price. The Commission concedes that this first reduction occurred at a time when Ned's did not meet the criteria normally insisted upon by Standard before giving any reduction. Two years later, after a still further period of haggling[2] and another Ned's ultimatum, Standard gave a second reduction of still another cent.

---

[1] The Commission places great importance on the fact that only one of these offers was a standing offer. This is not a situation involving only one or two competitive raids; however, continuation of reductions once granted is warranted by Section 2(b) when competitors' reduced price offers are recurring again and again in a cutthroat market.

[2] The findings indicate that similar haggling over an extended period of time occurred before each of the other "jobbers" obtained a reduced price. The great time consumed in the

In determining that Standard's prices to these four "jobbers" were reduced as a response to individual competitive situations rather than pursuant to a pricing system, the Court of Appeals considered the factors just mentioned, all of which weigh heavily against the Commission's position. The Commission's own findings thus afford ample witness that a "fair assessment" of the record has been made. Standard's use here of two prices, the lower of which could be obtained under the spur of threats to switch to pirating competitors, is a competitive deterrent far short of the discriminatory pricing of *Staley, Cement,* and *National Lead, supra,* and one which we believe within the sanction of Section 2(b) of the Robinson-Patman Act.

Affirmed.

MR. JUSTICE DOUGLAS, with whom THE CHIEF JUSTICE, MR. JUSTICE BLACK and MR. JUSTICE BRENNAN concur, dissenting.

The Court today cripples the enforcement of the Robinson-Patman Act . . . in an important area. . . .

First.   Standard admitted that it gave reduced prices to some retailers and refused those reduced prices to other retailers. Before granting these retailers the reduced prices Standard classified them as "jobbers." Standard's definition of a "jobber" took into account the volume of sales of the "jobber," his bulk storage facilities, his delivery equipment, and his credit rating. If Standard's tests were met, the "retailer" became a "jobber" even though he continued to sell at retail. Moreover, Standard's test of who was a "jobber" did not take into account the cost to Standard of making these sales. So Standard's definition of "jobber" was arbitrary, both as respects the matter of *costs* and the matter of *function.* It comes down to this: a big retailer gets one price; a small retailer gets another price. And this occurs at the *ipse dixit* of Standard, not because the cost of serving the big retailer is less nor because the big retailer, as respects the sales in question, performs a function different from any other retailer. . . .

Second.   It is argued, however, that the discrimination in favor of the big retailers and against the small ones is justified on the ground that Standard did no more than meet competition. . . .

If a seller offers a reduced price for no other reason than to meet the lawful low price of a competitor, then the seller's otherwise unlawful price falls within the protection of Section 2(b). But where, as here, a seller establishes a discriminatory pricing *system,* this system does not acquire

---

haggling process tends to negate any idea that the participants were only deciding whether a given purchaser met Standard's four well-defined "jobber" criteria—annual volume of one to two million gallons, own delivery facilities, bulk storage capable of taking tank-car delivery, and responsible credit rating.

the protection of Section 2(b) simply because in fact use of the system holds a customer against a competitive offer. In other words, a discriminatory pricing system which in fact meets competition is not a good-faith meeting of competition within the meaning of the Act. The effectiveness of the system does not demonstrate the good faith of its initiator.

Third. The mere fact that a competitor offered the lower price does not mean that Standard can lawfully meet it. Standard's system of price discrimination, shown not to be in "good faith," cannot be justified by showing that competitors were using the same system. "This startling conclusion is admissible only upon the assumption that the statute permits a seller to maintain an otherwise unlawful system of discriminatory prices, merely because he had adopted it in its entirely, as a means of securing the benefits of a like unlawful system maintained by his competitors." *Federal Trade Comm'n* v. *Staley Co., supra.* . . . See also *Federal Trade Comm'n* v. *Cement Institute, supra.* . . .

. . . It is only a *lawful* lower price that may be met. Were it otherwise then the law to govern is not the Robinson-Patman Act but the law of the jungle. . . .

When we let Standard classify a "retailer" as a "jobber" and grant a discriminatory price pursuant to arbitrary requirements merely because a competitor employs the same system, we make this provision of the Robinson-Patman Act ineffective. We should read the Act in a more hospitable way and allow Standard to maintain its discriminatory price schedule for retailers if and only if it can show

(a)   that that price was justified on the basis of costs or function, or

(b)   that it was in good faith meeting the *lawful* offer of a competitor, rather than merely matching a predatory price system, or meeting a competitor's "pirating" offers, to use the Court's word, with a "pirating" system of its own.

I would reverse this judgment and direct enforcement of the Commission's order.

Federal Trade Commission v. *Borden Company*

383 U.S. 637 (1966), *reconsidered,*
391 F.2d 175 (5th Cir. 1967)

MR. JUSTICE WHITE delivered the opinion of the Court.

The Borden Company, respondent here, produces and sells evaporated milk under the Borden name, a nationally advertised brand. At the same time Borden packs and markets evaporated milk under various private brands owned by its customers. This milk is physically and chemically identical with the milk it distributes under its own brand but is sold at both the wholesale and retail level at prices regularly below those obtained for the Borden brand milk. The Federal Trade Commission found the milk sold under the Borden and the private labels to be of like grade and quality as required for the applicability of §2(a) of the Robinson-Patman Act, held the price differential to be discriminatory within the meaning of the section, ascertained the requisite adverse effect on commerce, rejected Borden's claim of cost justification and consequently issued a cease-and-desist order. The Court of Appeals set aside the Commission's order on the sole ground that as a matter of law, the customer label milk was not of the same grade and quality as the milk sold under the Borden brand. . . . We now reverse the decision of the Court of Appeals and remand the case to that court for the determination of the remaining issues raised by respondent Borden in that court. . . .

The position of Borden and of the Court of Appeals is that the determination of like grade and quality, which is a threshold finding essential to the applicability of §2(a), may not be based solely on the physical properties of the products without regard to the brand names they bear and the relative public acceptance these brands enjoy—"consideration should be given to all commercially significant distinctions which affect market value, whether they be physical or promotional." 339 F.2d, at 137. Here, because the milk bearing the Borden brand regularly sold at a higher price than did the milk with a buyer's label, the court considered the products to be "commercially" different and hence of different "grade" for the purposes of §2(a), even though they were physically identical and of equal quality. Although a mere difference in brand would not in itself demonstrate a difference in grade, decided consumer preference for one brand over another, reflected in the willingness to pay a higher price for the well known brand, was, in the view of the Court of Appeals, sufficient to differentiate chemically identical products and to place the price differential beyond the reach of §2(a).

We reject this construction of §2(a), as did both the examiner and the Commission in this case. The Commission's view is that labels do not differentiate products for the purpose of determining grade or quality, even though the one label may have more customer appeal and command a higher price in the marketplace from a substantial segment of the public. That this is the Commission's long-standing interpretation of the present Act, as well as of §2 of the Clayton Act before its amendment by the Robinson-Patman Act,[1] may be gathered from the Commission's decisions dating back to 1936. . . . These views of the agency are entitled to respect . . . and represent a more reasonable construction of the statute than that offered by the Court of Appeals.

Obviously there is nothing in the language of the statute indicating that

---

[1] A proviso to §2 of the original Clayton Act expected price discrimination "on account of differences in the grade, quality, or quantity of the commodity sold. . . ." 38 Stat. 730 (1914).

grade, as distinguished from quality, is not to be determined by the characteristics of the product itself, but by consumer preferences, brand acceptability or what customers think of it and are willing to pay for it. Moreover, what legislative history there is concerning this question supports the Commission's construction of the statute rather than that of the Court of Appeals.

[For example:] During the 1936 hearings on the proposed amendments to Section 2 of the Clayton Act, the attention of the Congress was specifically called to the question of the applicability of §2 to the practice of a manufacturer selling his product under his nationally advertised brand at a different price than he charged when the product was sold under a private label. Because it was feared that the Act would require the elimination of such price differentials . . . and because private brands "would [thus] be put out of business by the nationally advertised brands," it was suggested that the proposed §2(a) be amended so as to apply only to sales of commodities of "like grade, quality and *brand*." (Emphasis added.) *Id.*, at 421. There was strong objection to the amendment and it was not adopted by the Committee. . . .

The Commission's construction of the statute also appears to us to further the purpose and policy of the Robinson-Patman Act. Subject to specified exceptions and defenses, §2(a) proscribes unequal treatment of different customers in comparable transactions, but only if there is the requisite effect upon competition, actual or potential. But if the transactions are deemed to involve goods of disparate grade or quality, the section has no application at all and the Commission never reaches either the issue of discrimination or that of anticompetitive impact. We doubt that Congress intended to foreclose these inquiries in situations where a single seller markets the identical product under several different brands, whether his own, his customers' or both. Such transactions are too laden with potential discrimination and adverse competitive effect to be excluded from the reach of §2(a) by permitting a difference in grade to be established by the label alone or by the label and its consumer appeal.[2]

If two products, physically identical but differently branded, are to be deemed of different grade because the seller regularly and successfully markets some quantity of both at different prices, the seller could, as far as §2(a) is concerned, make either product available to some customers and deny it to others, however discriminatory this might be and however damaging to competition. Those who were offered only one of the two

---

[2] Borden argues that it spends large sums to insure the high quality of its Borden brand milk on customers' shelves, inferring that there really is a difference between its own milk and the milk sold under private labels, at least by the time it reaches the consumer. Of course, if Borden could prove this difference, it is unlikely that the case would be here. The findings are to the contrary in this case and we write on the premise that the two products are physically the same at the time of consumer purchase. Borden's extra expenses in connection with its own milk are more relevant to the cost justification issue than to the question we have before us.

products would be barred from competing for those customers who want or might buy the other. The retailer who was permitted to buy and sell only the more expensive brand would have no chance to sell to those who always buy the cheaper product or to convince others, by experience or otherwise, of the fact which he and all other dealers already know—that the cheaper product is actually identical with that carrying the more expensive label.

The seller, to escape the Act, would have only to succeed in selling some unspecified amount of each product to some unspecified portion of his customers, however large or small the price differential might be. The seller's pricing and branding policy, by being successful, would apparently validate itself by creating a difference in "grade" and thus taking itself beyond the purview of the Act.[3]

Our holding neither ignores the economic realities of the marketplace nor denies that some labels will command a higher price than others, at least from some portion of the public. But it does mean that "the economic factors inherent in brand names and national advertising should not be considered in the jurisdictional inquiry under the statutory 'like grade and quality' tests." Report of the Attorney General's National Committee to Study the Antitust Laws 158 (1955). And it does mean that transactions like those involved in this case may be examined by the Commission under §2(a). The Commission will determine, subject to judicial review, whether the differential under attack is discriminatory within the meaning of the Act, whether competition may be injured, and whether the differential is cost-justified or is defensible as a good-faith effort to meet the

---

[3] The market acceptability test would hardly stop with insulating from inquiry the price differential between proprietary and private label sales. That test would also immunize from the Act sales at different prices of the same product under two different producer-owned labels, the one being less advertised and having less market acceptability than the other. And if it is "consumer preferences," . . . which create the difference in grade or quality, why should not Borden be able to discriminate between two purchasers or private label milk, as long as one label commands a higher price from consumers than the other and hence is of a different grade and quality? In this context perhaps the market acceptability test would be refined to preclude this differential on the grounds that Borden's customer, as distinguished from the consumer, will not pay more than his competitor for private label milk and therefore the milk sold by Borden under one private brand is really of the same grade and quality as the milk sold under the other brand even though ultimate consumers will pay more for one than the other. Taking this approach, if Borden packed for one wholesale customer under two private labels, one having more consumer appeal than the other because of the customer's own advertising program, Borden must sell both brands at the same price it charges other private label customers because all such milk is of the same grade and quality. At the same time, the customer buying from Borden under two labels could himself sell one label at a reduced price without inquiry under §2(a) because the milk in one container is no longer of the same grade and quality as that in the other, although both the milk and the containers came from Borden. Such an approach would obviously focus not on consumer preference as determinative of grade and quality but on who spent the advertising money that created the preference—Borden's customer, not Borden, created the preference and hence the milk is of the same grade and quality in Borden's hands but not in its customer's. The dissent would exempt the effective advertiser from the Act. We think Congress intended to remit him to his defense under the Act, including that of cost justification.

price of a competitor. "[T]angible consumer preferences as between branded and unbranded commodities should receive due legal recognition in the more flexible 'injury' and 'cost justification' provisions of the statute." *Id.*, at 159. This, we think, is precisely what Congress intended. The arguments for exempting private brand selling from §2(a) are, therefore, more appropriately addressed to the Congress than to this Court. . . .

. . . The judgment of the Court of Appeals is reversed and the case is remanded for further proceedings consistent with this opinion.

It is so ordered.

MR. JUSTICE STEWART, with whom MR. JUSTICE HARLAN joins, dissenting.

I cannot agree that mere physical or chemical identity between premium and private label brands is, without more, a sufficient basis for a finding of "like grade and quality" within the meaning of §2(a) of the Robinson-Patman Act. The conclusion that a product that travels at a premium in the marketplace is of "like grade and quality" with products of inferior commercial value is not required by the language of the Robinson-Patman Act, by its logic, or by its legislative history.

It is undisputed that the physical attributes and chemical constituents of Borden's premium and private label brands of evaporated milk are identical. It is also undisputed that the premium and private label brands are not competitive at the same price, and that if the private label milk is to be sold at all, it must be sold at prices substantially below the price commanded by Borden's premium brand. This simple market fact no more than reflects the obvious economic reality that consumer preferences can and do create significant commercial distinctions between otherwise similar products. By pursuing product comparison only so far as the result of laboratory analysis, the Court ignores a most relevant aspect of the inquiry into the question of "like grade and quality" under §2(a): Whether the products are different in the eyes of the consumer.[4]

There is nothing intrinsic to the concepts of grade and quality that requires exclusion of the commercial attributes of a product from their definition. The product purchased by a consumer includes not only the chemical components that any competent laboratory can itemize, but also a host of commercial intangibles that distinguish the product in the market

---

[4] No suggestion is made that any of the private label brands involved in this case show significant commercial differentiation from one another. It is possible, of course, that by extensive promotion private label brands could achieve consumer acceptance equivalent to that of a premium brand. In that situation, the products would still be economically different under the market test of §2(a) elucidated in this opinion, since the relevant comparison would exclude promotional efforts by persons other than the producer of the premium brand. Thus, promotional activities by customers of Borden in the present case could not affect the determination of "like grade and quality" with regard to sales by Borden. . . .

place.[5] The premium paid for Borden brand milk reflects the consumer's awareness, promoted through advertising, that these commercial attributes are part and parcel of the premium product he is purchasing. The record in the present case indicates that wholesale purchasers of Borden's private label brands continued to purchase the premium brand in undiminished quantities. The record also indicates that retail purchasers who bought the premium brand did so with the specific expectation of acquiring a product of premium quality. Contrary to the Court's suggestion . . . this consumer expectation cannot accurately be characterized as a misapprehension. Borden took extensive precautions to insure that a flawed product did not reach the consumer.[6] None of these precautions was taken for the private brand milk packed by Borden.[7] An important ingredient of the premium brand inheres in the consumer's belief, measured by past satisfaction and the market reputation established by Borden for its products, that tomorrow's can will contain the same premium product as that purchased today. To say, as the Court does, that these and other intangibles, which comprise an important part of the commercial value of a product, are not sufficient to confer on Borden's premium brand a "grade" or "quality" different from that of private label brands is to ignore the obvious market acceptance of that difference. . . .

The spare legislative history of the Robinson-Patman Act is in no way inconsistent with a construction of §2(a) that includes market acceptance in the test of "like grade and quality." That history establishes no more than that mere differences in brand or design, unaccompanied by any

---

[5] Cf. Chamberlain, *The Theory of Monopolistic Competition,* 56 (8th ed. 1962):

"A general class of product is differentiated if any significant basis exists for distinguishing the goods (or services) of one seller from those of another. Such a basis may be real or fancied, so long as it is of any importance whatever to buyers, and leads to a preference for one variety of the product over another. Where such differentiation exists, even though it be slight, buyers will be paired with sellers, not by chance and at random (as under pure competition), but according to their preferences.

"Differentiation may be based upon certain characteristics of the product itself, such as exclusive patented features; trade-marks; trade names; peculiarities of the package or container, if any; or singularity in quality, design, color, or style. . . . In so far as these and other intangible factors vary from seller to seller, the 'product' in each case is different, for buyers take them into account, more or less, and may be regarded as purchasing them along with the commodity itself." . . .

[6] Borden's Food Products Division maintained a staff of field representatives who inspected code-datings on cans of Borden brand milk in retail stores, in order to insure that older milk was sold first off the retailer's shelves. A witness for Borden testified that the principal dangers of long storage were discoloration of the milk, precipitation of calcium and other minerals, and separation and hardening of fat from the milk. As a further precaution against sales of defective milk, Borden dispatched its milk to wholesalers and retailers under a first-packed, first-shipped rotation plan that occasionally involved high-cost shipments from distant plants or warehouses. In addition, before shipment from a cold storage warehouse, Borden "tempered" its premium brand milk in order to prevent condensation on the cans, which might have resulted in rust to the cans and damage to the labels.

[7] As counsel for the respondent candidly stated on oral argument to the Court, "The difference as to the private label brand packed by Borden is that, as to that product, the Borden Company washes its hands of it at the factory door."

genuine physical, chemical, or market distinction, are insufficient to negate a finding of "like grade and quality" under §2(a).[8] Nothing that I have found in the legislative history speaks with precision to the sole issue before us here, the application of §2(a) to physically or chemically identical products that are in fact differentiated by substantial market factors.[9]

[By rejecting] . . . the proposal to add "and brands" to the "like grade and quality" provision in the bill . . . it can be inferred only that Congress contemplated "no *blanket* exemption . . . for 'like' products which differed *only* in brand . . . , leaving open the application of the Act to differentiated products reflecting more than a nominal or superficial variation." Rowe, *Price Discrimination under the Robinson-Patman Act,* 65 (1962). . . .

The other administrative precedents relied on by the Court also fail to establish any consistently settled interpretation by the Federal Trade Commission that physical identity is the sole touchstone of "like grade and quality." Those decisions singularly fail to focus on the significance of consumer preference as a relevant factor in the test of grade and quality. Moreover, the Commission has itself explicitly resorted to consumer preference or marketability to resolve the issue of "like grade and quality" in cases where minor physical variations accompany a difference in product brand. The caprice of the Commission's present distinction thus invites Borden to incorporate slight tangible variations in its private label products, in order to bring itself within the Commission's current practice of considering market preferences in such cases.

The Commission's determination of "like grade and quality" under §2(a) in this case is seriously inconsistent with the position it has taken under §2(b) in cases where a seller has presented the defense that he is in good faith meeting the equally low price of a competitor. The Commission decisions are clear that the "meeting competition" defense is not available to a seller who reduces the price of his premium product to the level of nonpremium products sold by his competitors. The Commission decisions

---

[8] The Court's suggestion, *ante,* p. 644, that a difference in label alone would exclude the reach of §2(a) if a market test were accepted for "like grade and quality" is no part of the present case and has never been offered as a serious interpretation of §2(a). Nor is there any issue raised here as to whether, under a market test of §2(a), a dubious pricing and branding policy adopted by a seller could "validate itself" and escape the Act by creating precarious distinctions in grade or quality. The price differential between Borden's premium and private label brands is concededly grounded upon a legitimate and stable market preference for the premium product. . . .

[9] Certain general language in the congressional reports may be taken, however, as supporting the interpretation that market factors are relevant in the construction of §2(a). The Report of the House Committee on the Judiciary stated that the general object of the bill was "to amend section 2 of the Clayton Act so as to suppress more effectually discriminations between customers of the same seller *not supported by sound economic differences in their business positions.* . . ." H.R. Rep. No. 2287, 74th Cong., 2d Sess., p. 7. (Emphasis added.) The Report of the Senate Committee on the Judiciary is phrased in substantially the same language. S.R. Rep. No. 1502, 74th Cong., 2d Sess., p. 3.

under §2(b) emphasize that market preference must be considered in determining whether a competitor is "meeting" rather than "beating" competition. In *Standard Oil Co.,* 49 F.T.C. 923, 952, the Commission put it baldly:

> [I]n the retail distribution of gasoline public acceptance rather than chemical analysis of the product is the important competitive factor.[10]

· · · · ·

The Court gives no substantial economic justification for its construction of §2(a). The principal rationale of the restriction of that section to commodities of "like grade and quality" is simply that it is not feasible to measure discrimination and injury to competition where different products are involved. That rationale is as valid for economic as for physical variation between products. Once a substantial economic difference between products is found, therefore, the inquiry of the Commission should be ended, just as it is ended when a substantial physical difference is found. . . .

The potential economic impact of Borden's distribution of private label brands on secondary line competition is . . . ambiguous. It is true that a market test of "like grade and quality" would enable Borden, so far as §2(a) is concerned, to make private label brands selectively available to customers of its premium brand. Not all wholesale and retail dealers who carry Borden's premium brand would be able, as of right, to take advantage of Borden's private label production. . . .

[It is also true that under] the Court's view of §2(a), Borden must now make private label milk available to all customers of its premium brand.[11] But that interpretation of §2(a) is hardly calculated to speed private label brands to the shelves of retailers. To avoid supplying a private label brand to a premium brand customer, Borden need only forego further sales of its premium brand to that customer. It is, therefore, not unlikely that the Court's decision will foster a discrimination greater than that which it purports to eliminate, since retailers previously able to obtain the premium Borden brand but not a private label brand, may now find their access to the premium brand foreclosed as well.

In *Automatic Canteen Co.* v. *FTC,* 346 U.S. 61, 63, this Court cautioned against construction of the Robinson-Patman Act in a manner that might "give rise to a price uniformity and rigidity in open conflict

---

[10] See also . . . *Callaway Mills Co., sub nom. Bigelow-Sanford Carpet Co.,* CCH Trade Reg. Rep. Transfer Binder, 1963–1965, ¶16,800, at p. 21755 (F.T.C. Dkt. 7634, Feb. 10, 1964): "Both the courts and the Commission have consistently denied the shelter of the [meeting competition] defense to sellers whose product, because of . . . intense public demand, normally commands a price higher than that usually received by sellers of competitive goods." . . .

[11] The Commission concedes that there is no evidence in the record that Borden refused to sell private label milk to any customer who specifically requested it. . . .

with the purposes of other antitrust legislation." Today that warning goes unheeded. In the guise of protecting producers and purchasers from discriminatory price competition, the Court ignores legitimate market preferences and endows the Federal Trade Commission with authority to disrupt price relationships between products whose identity has been measured in the laboratory but rejected in the market place. I do not believe that any such power was conferred upon the Commission by Congress, and I would, therefore, affirm the judgment of the Court of Appeals.

Utah Pie Co. v. Continental Baking Co.
386 U.S. 685 (1967)

MR. JUSTICE WHITE delivered the opinion of the Court.

This suit for treble damages and injunction under §§4 and 16 of the Clayton Act . . . was brought by petitioner, Utah Pie Company, against respondents, Continental Baking Company, Carnation Company and Pet Milk Company. The complaint charged a conspiracy under §§1 and 2 of the Sherman Act . . . and violations by each respondent of §2(a) of the Clayton Act as amended by the Robinson-Patman Act. . . . The jury found for respondents on the conspiracy charge and for petitioner on the price discrimination charge. . . . The Court of Appeals reversed, addressing itself to the single issue of whether the evidence against each of the respondents was sufficient to support a finding of probable injury to competition within the meaning of §2(a) and holding that it was not. 349 F.2d 122. We granted certiorari. . . . We reverse.

The product involved is frozen dessert pies—apple, cherry, boysenberry, peach, pumpkin, and mince. The period covered by the suit comprised the years 1958, 1959, and 1960 and the first eight months of 1961. Petitioner is a Utah corporation which for 30 years has been baking pies in its plant in Salt Lake City and selling them in Utah and surrounding States. It entered the frozen pie business in late 1957. It was immediately successful with its new line and built a new plant in Salt Lake City in 1958. The frozen pie market was a rapidly expanding one: 57,060 dozen frozen pies were sold in the Salt Lake City market in 1958, 111,729 dozen in 1959, 184,569 dozen in 1960, and 266,908 dozen in 1961. Utah Pie's share of this market in those years was 66.5%, 34.3%, 45.5%, and 45.3% respectively, its sales volume steadily increasing over the four years. Its financial position also improved. Petitioner is not, however, a large company. . . .

Each of the respondents is a large company and each of them is a major factor in the frozen pie market in one or more regions of the country. Each entered the Salt Lake City frozen pie market before petitioner began freezing dessert pies. None of them had a plant in Utah. . . . The Salt Lake City market was supplied by respondents chiefly from their California operations. They sold primarily on a delivered price basis.

The "Utah" label was petitioner's proprietary brand. Beginning in 1960, it also sold pies of like grade and quality under the controlled label "Frost 'N' Flame" to Associated Grocers and in 1961 it began selling to American Food Stores under the "Mayfresh" label. It also, on a seasonal basis, sold pumpkin and mince frozen pies to Safeway under Safeway's own "Bel-air" label.

The major competitive weapon in the Utah market was price. The location of petitioner's plant gave it natural advantages in the Salt Lake City marketing area and it entered the market at a price below the then going prices for respondents' comparable pies. For most of the period involved here its prices were the lowest in the Salt Lake City market. It was, however, challenged by each of the respondents at one time or another and for varying periods. There was ample evidence to show that each of the respondents contributed to what proved to be a deteriorating price structure over the period covered by this suit, and each of the respondents in the course of the ongoing price competition sold frozen pies in the Salt Lake market at prices lower than it sold pies of like grade and quality in other markets considerably closer to its plants. Utah Pie, which entered the market at a price of $4.15 per dozen at the beginning of the relevant period, was selling "Utah" and "Frost 'N' Flame" pies for $2.75 per dozen when the instant suit was filed some 44 months later. Pet, which was offering pies at $4.92 per dozen in February 1958, was offering "Pet-Ritz" and "Bel-air" pies at $3.56 and $3.46 per dozen respectively in March and April 1961. Carnation's price in early 1958 was $4.82 per dozen but it was selling at $3.46 per dozen at the conclusion of the period, meanwhile having been down as low as $3.30 per dozen. The price range experienced by Continental during the period covered by this suit ran from a 1958 high of over $5 per dozen to a 1961 low of $2.85 per dozen.

I

We deal first with petitioner's case against the Pet Milk Company. . . . Pet's initial emphasis was on quality, but in the face of competition from regional and local companies and in an expanding market where price proved to be a crucial factor, Pet was forced to take steps to reduce the price of its pies to the ultimate consumer. These developments had consequences in the Salt Lake City market which are the substance of petitioner's case against Pet.

First, Pet successfully concluded an arrangement with Safeway, which is one of the three largest customers for frozen pies in the Salt Lake market, whereby it would sell frozen pies to Safeway under the latter's own "Bel-air" label at a price significantly lower than it was selling its comparable "Pet-Ritz" brand in the same Salt Lake market and else-where. . . .

Second, it introduced a 20-ounce economy pie under the "Swiss Miss" label and began selling the new pie in the Salt Lake market in August 1960 at prices ranging from $3.25 to $3.30 for the remainder of the period. This pie was at times sold at a lower price in the Salt Lake City market than it was sold in other markets.

Third, Pet became more competitive with respect to the prices for its "Pet-Ritz" proprietary label. . . . According to the Court of Appeals, in seven of the 44 months Pet's prices in Salt Lake were lower than prices charged in the California markets. This was true although selling in Salt Lake involved a 30- to 35-cent freight cost.

The Court of Appeals first concluded that Pet's price differential on sales to Safeway must be put aside in considering injury to competition because in its view of the evidence the differential had been completely cost justified and because Utah would not in any event have been able to enjoy the Safeway custom. Second, it comcluded that the remaining dis-criminations on "Pet-Ritz" and "Swiss Miss" pies were an insufficient predicate on which the jury could have found a reasonably possible injury either to Utah Pie as a competitive force or to competition generally.

We disagree with the Court of Appeals in several respects. First, there was evidence from which the jury could have found considerably more price discrimination by Pet with respect to "Pet-Ritz" and "Swiss Miss" pies than was considered by the Court of Appeals. In addition to the seven months during which Pet's prices in Salt Lake were lower than prices in the California markets, there was evidence from which the jury could reasonably have found that in 10 additional months the Salt Lake City prices for "Pet-Ritz" pies were discriminatory as compared with sales in western markets other than California. Likewise, with respect to "Swiss Miss" pies, there was evidence in the record from which the jury could have found that in five of the 13 months during which the "Swiss Miss" pies were sold prior to the filing of this suit, prices in Salt Lake City were lower than those charged by Pet in either California or some other western market.

Second, with respect to Pet's Safeway business, the burden of proving cost justification was on Pet and, in our view, reasonable men could have found that Pet's lower priced, "Bel-air" sales to Safeway were not cost justified in their entirety. Pet introduced cost data for 1961 indicating a cost saving on the Safeway business greater than the price advantage extended to that customer. These statistics were not particularized for the Salt Lake market, but assuming that they were adequate to justify the 1961 sales, they related to only 24% of the Safeway sales over the relevant period. The evidence concerning the remaining 76% was at best incom-plete and inferential. It was insufficient to take the defense of cost justifi-cation from the jury, which reasonably could have found a greater incidence of unjustified price discrimination than that allowed by the Court of Appeals' view of the evidence.[1]

With respect to whether Utah would have enjoyed Safeway's business absent the Pet contract with Safeway, it seems clear that whatever the fact is in this regard, it is not determinative of the impact of that contract on competitors other than Utah and on competition generally. There were other companies seeking the Safeway business, including Continental and Carnation, whose pies may have been excluded from the Safeway shelves by what the jury could have found to be discriminatory sales to Safeway. What is more, Pet's evidence that Utah's unwillingness to install quality control equipment prevented Utah from enjoying Safeway's private label business is not the only evidence in the record relevant to that question. There was other evidence to the contrary. The jury would not have been compelled to find that Utah Pie could not have gained more of the Safeway business.

Third, the Court of Appeals almost entirely ignored other evidence which provides material support for the jury's conclusion that Pet's behavior satisfied the statutory test regarding competitive injury. This evidence bore on the issue of Pet's predatory intent to injure Utah Pie.[2] As an initial matter, the jury could have concluded that Pet's discriminatory pricing was aimed at Utah Pie; Pet's own management, as early as 1959, identified Utah Pie as an "unfavorable factor," one which "d[u]g holes in our operation" and posed a constant "check" on Pet's performance in the Salt Lake City market. Moreover, Pet candidly admitted that during the period when it was establishing its relationship with Safeway, it sent into Utah Pie's plant an industrial spy to seek information that would be of use to Pet in convincing Safeway that Utah Pie was not worthy of its custom. . . . Finally, Pet does not deny that the evidence showed it suffered substantial losses on its frozen pie sales during the greater part of time involved in this suit, and there was evidence from which the jury could have concluded that the losses Pet sustained in Salt Lake City were

---

[1] . . . Pet admitted that its cost-justification figures were drawn from past performance, so even crediting the data accompanying the 1960 contract regarding cost differences, Pet's additional evidence would bring under the justification umbrella only the 1959 sales. Thus, at the least, the jury was free to consider the 1960 Safeway sales as inadequately cost justified. Those sales accounted for 12.3% of the entire Salt Lake City market in that year. In the context of this case, the sales to Safeway are particularly relevant since there was evidence that private label sales influenced the general market, in this case depressing overall market prices.

[2] . . . [In] *Anheuser-Busch, Inc.* v. *F.T.C.*, 289 F.2d 835 . . . the court went so far as to suggest that: "If . . . the projection [to ascertain the future effect of price discrimination] is based upon predatoriness or buccaneering, it can reasonably be forecast that an adverse effect on competition *may* occur. In that event, the discriminations in their incipiency are such that they *may* have the prescribed effect to establish a violation of §2(a). If one engages in the latter type of pricing activity, a reasonable probability may be inferred that its willful misconduct may substantially lessen, injure, destroy or prevent competition." 289 F.2d, at 843. . . .

greater than those incurred elsewhere. It would not have been an irrational step if the jury concluded that there was a relationship between price and the losses.

It seems clear to us that the jury heard adequate evidence from which it could have concluded that Pet had engaged in predatory tactics in waging competitive warfare in the Salt Lake City market. Coupled with the incidence of price discrimination attributable to Pet, the evidence as a whole established, rather than negated, the reasonable possibility that Pet's behavior produced a lessening of competition proscribed by the Act.

II

Petitioner's case against Continental is not complicated. Continental was a substantial factor in the market in 1957. But its sales of frozen 22-ounce dessert pies, sold under the "Morton" brand, amounted to only 1.3% of the market in 1958, 2.9% in 1959, and 1.8% in 1960. Its problems were primarily that of cost and in turn that of price, the controlling factor in the market. In late 1960 it worked out a co-packing arrangement in California by which fruit would be processed directly from the trees into the finished pies without large intermediate packing, storing, and shipping expenses. Having improved its position, it attempted to increase its share of the Salt Lake City market by utilizing a local broker and offering short-term price concessions in varying amounts. Its efforts for seven months were not spectacularly successful. Then in June 1961, it took the steps which are the heart of petitioner's complaint against it. Effective for the last two weeks of June it offered its 22-ounce frozen apple pies in the Utah area at $2.85 per dozen. It was then selling the same pies at substantially higher prices in other markets. The Salt Lake City price was less than its direct cost plus an allocation for overhead. . . . Utah's response was immediate. It reduced its price on all of its apple pies to $2.75 per dozen. . . . Continental's total sales of frozen pies increased from 3,350 dozen in 1960 to 18,800 dozen in 1961. Its market share increased from 1.8% in 1960 to 8.3% in 1961. The Court of Appeals concluded that Continental's conduct had had only minimal effect, that it had not injured or weakened Utah Pie as a competitor, that it had not substantially lessened competition and that there was no reasonable possibility that it would do so in the future.

We again differ with the Court of Appeals. Its opinion that Utah was not damaged as a competitive force apparently rested on the fact that Utah's sales volume continued to climb in 1961 and on the court's own factual conclusion that Utah was not deprived of any pie business which it otherwise might have had. But this retrospective assessment fails to note that Continental's discriminatory below-cost price caused Utah Pie to reduce its price to $2.75. The jury was entitled to consider the potential impact of Continental's price reduction absent any responsive price cut by Utah Pie. Price was a major factor in the Salt Lake City market. Safeway, which had been buying Utah brand pies, immediately reacted and purchased a five-week supply of frozen pies from Continental, thereby temporarily foreclosing the proprietary brands of Utah and other firms from the Salt Lake City Safeway market. The jury could rationally have concluded that had Utah not lowered its price, Continental, which repeated its offer once, would have continued it, that Safeway would have continued to buy from Continental and that other buyers, large as well as small, would have followed suit. It could also have reasonably concluded that a competitor who is forced to reduce his price to a new all-time low in a market of declining prices will in time feel the financial pinch and will be a less effective competitive force.

Even if the impact on Utah Pie as a competitor was negligible, there remain the consequences to others in the market who had to compete not only with Continental's 22-ounce pie at $2.85 but with Utah's even lower price of $2.75 per dozen for both its proprietary and controlled labels. . . . The evidence was that there were nine other sellers in 1960 who sold 23,473 dozen pies, 12.7% of the total market. In 1961 there were eight other sellers who sold less than the year before—18,565 dozen or 8.2% of the total—although the total market had expanded from 184,569 dozen to 226,908 dozen. We think there was sufficient evidence from which the jury could find a violation of §2(a) by Continental.

III

The Carnation Company entered the frozen dessert pie business in 1955 through the acquisition of "Mrs. Lee's Pies" which was then engaged in manufacturing and selling frozen pies in Utah and elsewhere under the "Simple Simon" label. Carnation also quickly found the market extremely sensitive to price. Carnation decided, however, not to enter an economy product in the market, and during the period covered by this suit it offered only its quality "Simple Simon" brand. Its primary method of meeting competition in its markets was to offer a variety of discounts and other reductions, and the technique was not unsuccessful. . . .

. . . After Carnation's temporary setback in 1959 it instituted a new pricing policy to regain business in the Salt Lake City market. The new policy involved a slash in price of 60¢ per dozen pies, which brought Carnation's price to a level admittedly well below its costs, and well below the other prices prevailing in the market. The impact of the move was felt immediately, and the two other major sellers in the market reduced their prices. Carnation's banner year, 1960, in the end involved eight months during which the prices in Salt Lake City were lower than prices charged in other markets. The trend continued during the eight months in 1961 that preceded the filing of the complaint in this case. In each of those months the Salt Lake City prices charged by Carnation were well below prices charged in other markets, and in all but August 1961 the Salt Lake City delivered price was 20¢ to 50¢ lower than the prices charged in distant San

Francisco. The Court of Appeals held that only the early 1960 prices could be found to have been below cost. That holding, however, simply overlooks evidence from which the jury could have concluded that throughout 1961 Carnation maintained a below-cost price structure and that Carnation's discriminatory pricing, no less than that of Pet and Continental, had an important effect on the Salt Lake City market. We cannot say that the evidence precluded the jury from finding it reasonably possible that Carnation's conduct would injure competition.

IV

Section 2(a) does not forbid price competition which will probably injure or lessen competition by eliminating competitors, discouraging entry into the market or enhancing the market shares of the dominant sellers. But Congress has established some ground rules for the game. Sellers may not sell like goods to different purchasers at different prices if the result may be to injure competition to either the sellers' or the buyers' market unless such discriminations are justified as permitted by the Act. This case concerns the sellers' market. In this context, the Court of Appeals placed heavy emphasis on the fact that Utah Pie constantly increased its sales volume and continued to make a profit. But we disagree with its apparent view that there is no reasonably possible injury to competition as long as the volume of sales in a particular market is expanding and at least some of the competitors in the market continue to operate at a profit. Nor do we think that the Act only comes into play to regulate the conduct of price discriminators when their discriminatory prices consistently undercut other competitors. . . . In this case there was some evidence of predatory intent with respect to each of these respondents.[3] There was also other evidence upon which the jury could rationally find the requisite injury to competition. The frozen pie market in Salt Lake City was highly competitive. At times Utah Pie was a leader in moving the general level of prices down, and at other times each of the respondents also bore responsibility for the downward pressure on the price structure. We believe that the Act reaches price discrimination that erodes competition as much as it does price discrimination that is intended to have immediate destructive impact. In this case, the evidence shows a drastically declining price structure which the jury could rationally attribute to continued or sporadic price discrimination. The jury was entitled to conclude that "the effect of such discrimination," by each of these respondents, "may be substantially to lessen competition. . . . or to injure, destroy, or prevent

---

[3] It might be argued that the respondents' conduct displayed only fierce competitive instincts. Actual intent to injure another competitor does not, however, fall into that category, and neither, when viewed in the context of the Robinson-Patman Act, do persistent sales below cost and radical price cuts which are themselves discriminatory. Nor does the fact that a local competitor has a major share of the market make him fair game for discriminatory price cutting free of Robinson-Patman Act proscriptions. . . .

competition with any person who either grants or knowingly receives the benefit of such discrimination. . . ." The statutory test is one that necessarily looks forward on the basis of proven conduct in the past. Proper application of that standard here requires reversal of the judgment of the Court of Appeals.[4]

It is so ordered.

THE CHIEF JUSTICE took no part in the decision of this case.

MR. JUSTICE STEWART, with whom MR. JUSTICE HARLAN joins, dissenting.

I would affirm the judgment, agreeing substantially with the reasoning of the Court of Appeals as expressed in the thorough and conscientious opinion of Judge Phillips.

There is only one issue on this case in its present posture: . . . [D]id the respondents' actions have the anticompetitive effect required by the statute as an element of a cause of action?

The Court's own description of the Salt Lake City frozen pie market from 1958 through 1961, shows that the answer to that question must be no. In 1958 Utah Pie had a quasi-monopolistic 66.5% of the market. In 1961—after the alleged predations of the respondents—Utah Pie still had a commanding 45.3%, Pet had 29.4%, and the remainder of the market was divided almost equally between Continental, Carnation, and other, small local bakers. Unless we disregard the lessons so laboriously learned in scores of Sherman and Clayton Act cases, the 1961 situation has to be considered more competitive than that of 1958. Thus, if we assume that the price discrimination proven against the respondents had any effect on competition, that effect must have been beneficient.

That the Court has fallen into the error of reading the Robinson-Patman Act as protecting competitors, instead of competition, can be seen from its unsuccessful attempt to distinguish cases relied upon by the respondents. Those cases are said to be inapposite because they involved "no general decline in price structure," and no "lasting impact upon prices." But lower prices are the hallmark of intensified competition. . . .

---

[4] Each respondent argues here that prior price discrimination cases in the courts and before the Federal Trade Commission, in which no primary line injury to competition was found, establish a standard which compels affirmance of the Court of Appeals' holding. But the cases upon which the respondents rely are readily distinguishable. In *Anheuser-Busch, Inc.* v. *F.T.C.*, 289 F.2d 835, 839, there was no general decline in price structure attributable to the defendant's price discriminations, nor was there any evidence that the price discriminations were "a single lethal weapon aimed at a victim for a predatory purpose." *Id.*, at 842. In *Borden Co.* v. *F.T.C.*, 339 F.2d 953, the court reversed the Commission's decision on price discrimination in one market for want of sufficient interstate connection, and the Commission's charge regarding the other market failed to show any lasting impact upon prices caused by the single, isolated incident of price discrimination proved. . . .

I cannot hold that Utah Pie's monopolistic position was protected by the federal antitrust laws from effective price competition, and I therefore respectfully dissent.

International Air Industries, Inc., et al. v. *American Excelsior Company*
517 F.2d 714 (1975)
cert. denied
424 U.S. 943 (1975)

LEWIS R. MORGAN, Circuit Judge.

Appellants Vebco, Inc., and International Air Industries, Inc.,[1] filed a complaint . . . charging AMXCO, Inc.,[2] with a violation of the antitrust laws. A lengthy, complex and seemingly disorganized jury trial was held, resulting in a verdict in AMXCO's favor. Vebco appeals, alleging at least 20 substantive trial errors. We affirm the judgment below.

I

The facts in this case are heatedly contested. Since the trial below resulted in AMXCO's favor, we consider the facts in a light most favorable to it.

Vebco, Inc., is a New Mexico corporation with its principal place of business in El Paso, Texas. It was incorporated in 1959. Vebco is primarily a distributor of heating and air conditioning equipment, although it does manufacture some products, including handmade evaporative cooler pads. It sells its pads primarily in Arizona, New Mexico, and West Texas. . . .

AMXCO, a subsidiary of Texstar Company, has its principal place of business in Arlington, Texas. It maintains a branch office in El Paso, Texas, and manufactures evaporative cooler pads which it sells throughout the southwestern and far western parts of the United States.

The source of the controversy in this case is the cooler pad, an object made of aspen wood shavings covered with crinoline cloth, used in evaporative air conditioners. Such pads have historically been made by hand, but around 1960 AMXCO achieved a breakthrough in the field and began to produce a machine-made pad. Hand- and machine-made pads

---

[1] Although Vebco and International were nominally separate business entities, they operated as one business. . . . Therefore, "Vebco" will hereinafter refer to both plaintiffs, unless otherwise indicated.

[2] American Excelsior Company was the named defendant in the district court, but during the course of discovery Vebco realized that AMXCO, Inc., was the corporate successor to that company. The defendant-appellant will therefore hereinafter be referred to as "AMXCO."

are interchangeable in use, but the latter can be produced, transported, and stored more cheaply. Through its technological success and business expansion AMXCO became the world's largest producer of cooler pads.

Vebco and AMXCO have enjoyed a lengthy business relationship. The founder of Vebco, Vernon Britt, began to distribute pads for AMXCO in 1953. Until 1969, with only one short exception, the only pads Vebco distributed were manufactured by AMXCO. By selling AMXCO's pads, Vebco developed a highly successful business and gradually expanded its operations to include a complete line of heating and cooling implements.

Except for direct sales to "national accounts," AMXCO marketed all of its cooler pads through independent distributors such as Vebco. Vebco's primary customers in the El Paso-Las Cruces trade area were discount stores. The only large discount store in the area to which Vebco did not sell cooler pads was K Mart, serviced by Passage Supply, an independent distributor for AMXCO.

Prior to 1969, AMXCO favored its El Paso distributors over its Arizona distributors in freight policy: AMXCO paid freight costs of its El Paso distributors to their customers in Arizona but did not pay the freight costs of distributors in Arizona to their customers in El Paso and Las Cruces. In order to rectify this competitive inequity, AMXCO decided to eliminate the freight prepayment for its El Paso distributors. When AMXCO adopted a uniform freight policy, Vebco decided to set up its own manufacturing plant for cooler pads. With the aid of three former employees of AMXCO, the owners of Vebco formed a corporation and built a plant to manufacture cooler pads by hand in 1969. Vebco then entered the market as a manufacturer and successfully competed with AMXCO. Later that same year, Southwest Industries was formed. Like AMXCO, Southwest manufactured and marketed machine-made cooler pads. There were also numerous small-scale handmade pad manufacturers in the market.

When AMXCO learned that Vebco was manufacturing its own cooler pads, AMXCO terminated its distribution relationship with Vebco. Although it lost customers to Vebco in 1969, AMXCO took no action in regard to price. . . .

In late January, 1971, Vebco dropped its price to discount houses 5 percent below the price currently being quoted by both AMXCO and Vebco. . .—to a 14.5 percent discount below list price. This price cut brought Vebco considerable business, including the very lucrative K Mart account which had previously been serviced by AMXCO's distributor, Passage Supply. The record indicates that AMXCO's distributors complained that they could not effectively compete with Vebco, because the latter manufactured its own pads for distribution. . . .

Based on previous public bids by Vebco and Southwest, and on information received from customers, AMXCO determined that a 25 percent discount would be competitive in the market. AMXCO then contacted its old customer, K Mart, and at least one other discount house offering the 25 percent discount. However, AMXCO salesmen made no sales at the 25 percent discount, because, unknown to them, Vebco had verified their price and had notified its customers that it, too, would give the 25 percent discount. Because of the lack of sales at the 25 percent discount, and because at least one potential customer had reported that Vebco was selling at near a 50 percent discount, AMXCO again lowered its price, offering a 32.5 percent discount. Again, Vebco verified and met this price on March 15, 1971, and AMXCO made no substantial sales. . . .

During this intense period of competition, AMXCO delegated price-setting responsibility in the El Paso market to two of its local employees, Wendell Johnson and June Morris. Carl Gillespie, AMXCO's division manager, continued to make recommendations, and on March 16, 1971, he prepared a memorandum suggesting ways to compete with Vebco and Southwest, which included, as one possible alternative, the option of offering prices in El Paso low enough to insure that Vebco would not profit from competitive sales. On March 17, Gillespie also wrote Morris a letter which contained the statement:

> [I]f we are committed to a program of stunting the possible growth of Vebco and keeping our foot in this quite seizeable [sic] cooler pad market, then the real question we have here is just what price do we need to determine as our lowest price level.

Vebco had a great deal of difficulty sustaining a 32.5 percent discount, and on March 29, 1971, Vebco announced to its customers that it would return to the 25 percent discount. AMXCO subsequently made one sale to K Mart, its prior customer at a 39 percent discount. After the 1971 season, AMXCO raised its prices, offering discounts from 19 to 25 percent for the 1972 season.

On May 28, 1971, Vebco initiated this suit, charging AMXCO with a violation of Section 2(a) of the Clayton Act, as amended by the Robinson-Patman Act. . . . The complaint was amended on July 28, 1972, to charge, additionally, a violation of §2 of the Sherman Act. . . . The gravamen of the complaint is that AMXCO unlawfully discriminated in price from 1968 through 1971 and attempted to monopolize the El Paso-Las Cruces cooler pad market, as well as that of the southwestern United States, during the same period. . . . Vebco subsequently supplemented its complaint to include the 1972 cooler pad season. . . .

The record indicates that the dollar value of Vebco's cooler pad sales has increased every year since 1968, with the exception of a slight decline in 1972.[3] Conversely, AMXCO's share of the national cooler pad market has declined steadily since 1969. Vebco conceded at trial that it claimed

---

[3] Vebco's share of the El Paso cooler pad market also showed a steady increase from 1968 through 1971, the only years for which market figure percentages were introduced below.

only lost profits, presumably from keen price competition, rather than lost sales for the years prior to 1971. . . . [I]ndeed, only Vebco's markup on pads decreased.[4] . . .

All in all, the record before us reveals that since 1968, the cooler pad market in El Paso has been extremely competitive. The sales season for cooler pads is quite short and manufacturers must necessarily process orders early. On the other hand, the record indicates that customers intentionally quote lower prices to distributors and manufacturers than have actually been offered by a competitor in the hopes of securing a lucrative offer. Vebco, AMXCO, Southwest, and one other manufacturer continue to vigorously compete in the El Paso market.

II

Vebco's primary argument on appeal is that the district court erred in refusing to direct a verdict in Vebco's favor on the Robinson-Patman charge. . . . [W]e find that the trial court was correct in refusing to direct a verdict in Vebco's favor.

Section 2(a) prohibits price discrimination between different purchasers of commodities of like grade and quality "where the effect of such discrimination may be substantially to lessen competition or tend to create a monopoly in any line of commerce or to injure, destroy, or prevent competition."[5] The Act was primarily aimed at national chains that enter a locality and crush a more efficient local concern by cutting prices below cost and subsidizing local losses with excessive profits gleaned in a noncompetitive area. . . . However, Congress did not intend to abolish competition "or so radically to curtail it that a seller would have no substantial right of self-defense against a price raid by a competitor." . . . Thus our goal in applying the Robinson-Patman Act is to maintain active competition—including price rivalry—among the members of the business community.

Encouraging competition while at the same time forbidding anticompetitive behavior calls for considerable care in this case. The facts before us reveal a large entrenched firm with a dominant market share confronted by a fledgling company attempting to enter the same market. Such a situation necessitates the greatest scrutiny on our part, for anticompetitive price cuts by the monopolist could be directed toward driving the new competitor out of the market or disciplining it in order to force it to follow the monopolist's price leadership. On the other hand, we believe that

---

[4] Vebco's markup percentage or "gross margin" (retail price minus the cost divided by the retail price) for cooler pads in the years 1968 through 1972 inclusive, was 12, 17, 22, 13, and 18 percent respectively.

[5] The Act is concerned with competitive injury to three groups: competitors of the price discriminator ("primary line"), customers of the price discriminator ("secondary line"), customers of the price discriminator's customers ("tertiary line"). Only a primary line injury is alleged in this case, and our comments and conclusions therefore pertain only to such injury.

neither the Act nor any social value compels the sheltering of an individual competitor, at the expense of the public interest, from the competitive process. . . .

Vebco claims that AMXCO violated the Act when it sold cooler pads to El Paso customers at prices lower than it sold its pads elsewhere. A price discrimination difference, . . . but price discrimination is not illegal per se. . . . In order to meet the requirement of an adverse effect upon competition, Vebco claimed that there was considerable diversion of business from Vebco to AMXCO in 1971, and, additionally, that Vebco suffered a reduction in its profit margin because it had to compete with AMXCO.

It is settled law that a mere diversion of business from one competitor to another does not signify detriment to competition on the seller level. . . .

> The Act is really referring to the effect upon competition and not merely upon competitors. In this respect §2(a) must be read in conformity with the public policy of preserving competition, but it is not concerned with mere shifts of business between competitors. It is concerned with substantial impairment of the vigor or health of the contest for business, regardless of which competitor wins or loses. . . . *Anheuser-Busch, Inc.* v. *FTC*, 289 F.2d 835, 840 (7th Cir. [1961] 1971) (citations omitted). . . .

Mere loss of profits shows no more than that Vebco was forced to charge a competitive price because it faced competition. Similarly, the large size of the discriminator and even the fact that its sales increased during the period of discrimination would not necessarily make out a case.[6] . . . It is possible for damage to a single competitor to meet statutory requirements, . . . but a showing of more than competitive pricing and a shift of customers is necessary. Evidence of certain types of predatory conduct, we feel, would fulfill the requirements. . . .

Coupled with its claims of lost profits and diversion of business, Vebco introduced evidence purporting to show AMXCO's predatory intent in order to satisfy the statutory requirements. Of the actions which Vebco alleges evinced AMXCO's predatory intent, the only one meriting extensive comment is the Gillespie memo of March 17, 1971, which Vebco claims was conclusive proof of AMXCO's predatory intent. . . .

Judicial use of the term *predatory intent* is troublesome. Several cases hold that from a finding of certain actions, the trier of fact may infer predatory intent, and from this inference the proscribed inimical effects upon competition in turn may be inferred. . . . However, application of

---

[6] We do not intimate that all of these criteria necessarily apply to the case before us. For example, the record shows that AMXCO's percentage of the market declined during the relevant period.

these principles is particularly difficult, for predatory intent has never been clearly defined. Its appearance has been characterized by phrases such as "putting a crimp" into one's competitors, . . . punitively or destructively attacking other firms, . . . and acting vindictively with punitive effect. . . . But any price decrease by a legitimately competitive firm will necessarily have a nonremunerative effect upon other firms in the market, if only by decreasing their profit margins. It is therefore important to clearly indicate the types of business behavior which violate the Act. . . .

It is possible, of course, for a plaintiff to present evidence of predation sufficient to warrant a directed verdict, but quoting out of context segments of internal company memoranda is simply insufficient. Gillespie's memorandum reveals that AMXCO acted as any legitimately competitive and rational firm would; Gillespie considered Vebco's potential for growth and enumerated several alternatives which AMXCO officials could consider in meeting the new competitive challenge. In order to require a court to direct a verdict, Vebco must adduce evidence of what AMXCO did; at best, it showed only what AMXCO might have done. . . .

Since the allegedly harmful actions in this case involve pricing, we must examine the relationship between AMXCO's prices and costs in order to determine whether their price behavior was predatory.[7] By *predatory* we mean that AMXCO must have at least sacrificed present revenues for the purpose of driving Vebco out of the market with the hope of recouping the losses through subsequent higher prices.

When a firm sets its price equal to its average cost, its total revenues cover total costs, including normal returns on investment.[8] If a monopolist[9] is selling at a price at or above average cost, but could earn higher profits at a higher price, it may be attempting to deter entry into the field. Likewise a monopolist may attempt to drive out existing competition by temporarily lowering price to average cost. In either case, we believe that a price above cost is a fairly competitive price for it is profitable to the monopolist if not to its rivals; in effect, the price excludes only less efficient firms. Areeda and Turner, *supra,* . . . at 706–707.

In the case before us, the entry of Vebco and Southwest created excess

---

[7] We therefore do not consider other conceivably predatory behavior such as predatory investment or promotional spending.

[8] See Areeda and Turner, . . . ["Predatory Practices Under Section 2 of the Sherman Act," *88 Harv. L. Rev.* 697, 704 (1975)]; P. Samuelson, *Economics,* 447–48 (8th ed. 1970). Much of our discussion in the next few paragraphs is based upon accepted economic analysis. See e.g., P. Samuelson, *supra* at 428–510.

[9] For the purposes of this discussion a monopolist is one who has captured a sufficiently large part of a market to be able to determine market price by varying its output. . . . We do not use the term to indicate that the firm is a monopolist under the language of the Sherman Act and hence violating the law by its very existence.

manufacturing capacity in the cooler pad market.[10] Therefore, AMXCO's marginal cost was almost certainly below its average cost.[11] In such situations we do not believe that the monopolist's pricing behavior could be deemed anticompetitive unless the monopolist set a price below its own marginal cost—since any sale at or above marginal cost does not decrease short-run net returns.[12] It may be theoretically possible for a reduction of price to marginal cost by a monopolist to drive out an equally but not more efficient competitor. Id. at 711. However, establishing a price floor above marginal cost would permit the survival of far less efficient firms. Certainly, forcing a monopolist to charge a price higher than marginal cost could reduce industry output and waste economic resources in the short run.[13]

It is frequently quite difficult to calculate the incremental cost of making and selling the last unit (i.e., marginal cost) from a conventional business account. . . . Id. at 716. Consequently, the firm's average variable cost[14] may be effectively substituted for marginal cost in a predatory pricing analysis. Id. at 717–18. Thus a firm's pricing behavior can be considered anticompetitive when it sells at a price below its average variable cost.[15]

When price discrimination exists—as in the case before us—we see no reason to depart from the average variable cost test for predation unless it can be shown that there are significant barriers of entry into the relevant market. Thus, even if a monopolist is price discriminating, we will not infer damage to competition as a matter of law if the firm is charging a short-run, profit-maximizing price (above average variable cost) in the

---

[10]The record shows that Vebco and Southwest both built factories during the years at issue in this suit. The fact that this new production created excess capacity is also evidenced by an AMXCO memorandum which indicated that every sale Vebco made increased AMXCO's unit costs by idling some of its production facilities.

[11] Id. at 710. If AMXCO's production facilities had been producing beyond the output at which they function most efficiently, AMXCO's marginal costs, the cost of the last unit produced, would exceed its average cost. In such a situation, a reduction of price to marginal cost would still cover all of the company's expenses (fixed as well as variable), and equally efficient competitors would make substantial profits by restricting their output to efficient levels. See Areeda and Turner, *supra* . . . at 709–710.

[12] If AMXCO set its price below average cost yet above marginal cost, it might not be profit maximizing. However, prohibiting such behavior could have undesirable effects, for it may not be possible to make a long run profit in the market and a price equal to marginal cost would be loss-minimizing.

[13] There would also be insurmountable problems in the enforcement of a prohibition against marginal cost pricing. . . .

[14] Average variable cost is the costs that vary with changes in output divided by the output.

[15] It is conceivable that marginal cost would exceed average variable cost when a firm's output nears its optimum. When this is the case, using the latter as a surrogate for the former enables a firm to sell below marginal cost. However, this exception is justified because when the firm's capacity is strained, predation is especially unlikely. See id. at 718.

market in which it faces competition. And, even if its price is below this level, we will not infer damage to competition if the firm's price discrimination has beneficial effects or insignificant effects in the competitive market.[16] In short, in order to prevail as a matter of law,[17] a plaintiff must at least show that either (1) a competitor is charging a price below his average variable cost in the competitive market or (2) the competitor is charging a price below its short-run, profit-maximizing price and barriers to entry are great enough to enable the discriminator to reap the benefits of predation before new entry is possible.[18]

It is therefore important to look to price discriminator's costs, rather than his competitor's costs, to determine whether the price discrimination was anticompetitive. If a discriminator's price in the competitive market increases his net revenues in the short run, he will have no need to subsidize losses in the competitive market with the profits from his other markets.[19]

Evidence of AMXCO's costs was not cogently presented at trial, apparently because neither side considered it important. However, upon exhaustively searching the record, we find that the judge had much of the relevant data before him and we conclude from his data that the court properly denied Vebco's motion. The record indicates that AMXCO's manufacturing division charged its sales division a price for cooler pads which covered total costs, freight charges, and a "slight profit." Its sales division then resold the goods to distributors at a price based upon the distributors' bargaining power and competition in the area. . . . AMXCO's largest discount of 39.25 percent (at which only one sale was made) produced a profit to the sales division alone of nearly 15¢ a

---

[16] Since AMXCO has considerable market power we need not deal with various procompetitive justifications, such as promotional pricing, that a firm with considerably less market power might reasonably employ when charging a price below average variable cost.

[17] Much of what we say here should be relevant to the requisite elements of a prima facie Robinson-Patman case. Indeed, in *Utah Pie Co.* v. *Continental Baking Co.*, 386 U.S. 685, 696, n. 12, 702, n. 14 . . . (1967) the Supreme Court indicated that price below "cost" is perhaps, a necessary element of a prima facie case. However, because the Court repeatedly referred to "deteriorating price structure," the opinion may hold that it is not necessary to show a price below marginal cost in order to make out a prima facie case. To the extent that the opinion stands for the latter proposition, we limit our discussion to the elements necessary to sustain a motion for directed verdict.

[18] We employ the profit maximizing standard only because of our deference to a situation in which a monopolist could drive a slightly less efficient firm out of the market by charging a price above its own average cost, but then charge a very high price because of the difficulty of new entry. This standard should be applied only when the barriers to entry are extremely high. The lower the barriers to entry in a market, the closer to marginal cost a monopolist would have to set its price in order for a plaintiff to prevail as a matter of law, for we see no social utility in insuring the survival of inefficient firms where a new entry is possible.

[19] The absence of aid from other markets is a determinative factor in evaluating allegedly predatory conduct and, hence, in determining whether a statutory violation has occurred. . . .

pad. Thus, not only was the manufacturing division operating at a profit, but the sales division had a gross margin of around 33 percent. It would appear that AMXCO was selling its cooler pad at a price far above even its average cost.

Moreover, the record indicates that barriers to entry in the cooler pad market were virtually nonexistent.[20] Neighborhood hardware store operators could—and did—purchase excelsior wood and hand make their own pads for retail sale. Indeed, the total costs of entering the market on a scale large enough to supply the entire southwestern and far western United States has less than $300,000. The condition of the market and AMXCO's financial data therefore indicate that the price rivalry in the cooler pad market could reasonably be considered procompetitive and the judge properly denied Vebco's motion. . . .

Finally, we note that, in addition to believing the evidence rebutting Vebco's prima facie case, the jury could reasonably have found that AMXCO established one of the statute's affirmative defenses. The statute provides that even where price discrimination occurs, a discriminator may not be held liable for a violation of the Act if "his lower price . . . was made in good faith to meet an equally low price of a competitor. . . ." . . . In order to avail itself of this defense, AMXCO need only have shown that its pricing system was a reasonable method of meeting Vebco's lower price. . . . AMXCO need not have shown that its prices were in fact equal to those of Vebco, "but must only [have shown] facts which would lead a 'reasonable and prudent person' to believe that the granting of the lower prices would in fact meet the equally low price of a competitor." . . .

The facts of this case would enable a jury to believe that AMXCO set its price as a reasonable and prudent firm would, to meet Vebco's lower price. As the facts indicate, the cooler pad market was very competitive and buyers often misinformed a manufacturer of a competitor's price in order to induce a larger disco[u]nt. When AMXCO learned that Vebco had lowered its price, it responded with a price cut which had no result. It then cut its price a second time in order to regain its lost business. Because of the uncertain and competitive nature of the market, the jury could find that AMXCO met its burden under the affirmative defense of meeting competition.

* * * * *

Affirmed.

---

[20] We are considerably oversimplifying the barrier to entry discussion. . . . However, all of the relevant data, including a low minimum efficient scale of operation, significant ability to attract customers of other manufacturers, availability of raw materials, etc., suggest a very low barrier entry in the cooler pad market.

Great Atlantic & Pacific Tea Co., Inc.
v. Federal Trade Commission

440 U.S. 69 (1979)

MR. JUSTICE STEWART delivered the opinion of the Court.

The question presented in this case is whether the petitioner, the Great Atlantic and Pacific Tea Company (A&P), violated §2(f) of the Robinson-Patman Act, as amended, 15 U.S.C. §13(f), . . . by knowingly inducing or receiving illegal price discriminations from the Borden Company (Borden).

The alleged violation was reflected in a 1965 agreement between A&P and Borden under which Borden undertood to supply private-label milk to more than 200 A&P stores in a Chicago area that included portions of Illinois and Indiana. This agreement resulted from an effort by A&P to achieve cost savings by switching from the sale of brand-label milk (milk sold under the brand name of the supplying dairy) to the sale of private-label milk (milk sold under the A&P label).

To implement this plan, A&P asked Borden, its longtime supplier, to submit an offer to supply under private label certain of A&P's milk and other dairy product requirements. After prolonged negotiations, Borden offered to grant A&P a discount for switching to private-label milk provided A&P would accept limited delivery service. Borden claimed that this offer would save A&P $410,000 a year compared to what it had been paying for its dairy products. A&P, however, was not satisfied with this offer and solicited offers from other dairies. A competitor of Borden, Bowman Dairy, then submitted an offer which was lower than Borden's.[1]

At this point, A&P's Chicago buyer contacted Borden's chain store sales manager and stated, "I have a bid in my pocket. You [Borden] people are so far out of line it is not even funny. You are not even in the ball park." When the Borden representative asked for more details, he was told nothing except that a $50,000 improvement in Borden's bid "would not be a drop in the bucket."

Borden was thus faced with the problem of deciding whether to rebid. A&P at the time was one of Borden's largest customers in the Chicago area. Moreover, Borden had just invested more than $5 million in a new dairy facility in Illinois. The loss of the A&P account would result in underutilization of this new plant. Under these circumstances, Borden decided to submit a new bid which doubled the estimated annual savings to A&P, from $410,000 to $820,000. In presenting its offer, Borden em-

---

[1] The Bowman bid would have produced estimated annual savings of approximately $737,000 for A&P as compared with the first Borden bid, which would have produced estimated annual savings of $410,000.

phasized to A&P that it needed to keep A&P's business and was making the new offer in order to meet Bowman's bid. A&P then accepted Borden's bid after concluding that it was substantially better than Bowman's.

I

Based on these facts, the Federal Trade Commission filed a three-count complaint against A&P. Count I charged that A&P had violated §5 of the Federal Trade Commission Act by misleading Borden in the course of negotiations for the private-label contract, in that A&P had failed to inform Borden that its second offer was better than the Bowman bid. . . . Count II, involving the same conduct, charged that A&P had violated §2(f) of the Robinson-Patman Act by knowingly inducing or receiving price discriminations from Borden. Count III charged that Borden and A&P had violated §5 of the Federal Trade Commission Act by combining to stabilize and maintain the retail and wholesale prices of milk and other dairy products.

An Administrative Law Judge found, after extended discovery and a hearing that lasted over 110 days, that A&P had acted unfairly and deceptively in accepting the second offer from Borden and had therefore violated §5 of the Federal Trade Commission Act as charged in Count I. The Administrative Law Judge similarly found that this same conduct had violated §2(f) of the Robinson-Patman Act. Finally, he dismissed Count III on the ground that the Commission had not satisfied its burden of proof.

On review, the Commission reversed the Administrative Law Judge's finding as to Count I. Pointing out that the question at issue was what amount of disclosure is required of the buyer during contract negotiations, the Commission held that the imposition of a duty of affirmative disclosure would be "contrary to normal business practice and, we think, contrary to the public interest." Despite this ruling, however, the Commission held as to Count II that the identical conduct on the part of A&P had violated §2(f) of the Robinson-Patman Act, finding that Borden had discriminated in price between A&P and its competitors, that the discrimination had been injurious to competition, and that A&P had known or should have known that it was the beneficiary of unlawful price discrimination. . . . The Commission rejected A&P's defenses that the Borden bid had been made to meet competition and was cost justified.[2]

---

[2] Under §§2(a) and (b) of the Act, a seller who can establish either that a price differential was cost justified or offered in good faith to meet competition has a complete defense to a charge of price discrimination under the Act. . . .

With respect to the meeting-competition defense, the Commission stated that even though Borden as the seller might have had a meeting-competition defense, A&P as the buyer did not have such a defense because it knew that the bid offered was, in fact, better than the Bowman bid. With respect to the cost justification defense, the Commission found that Commission counsel had met the initial burden of going forward as required by this court's decision in *Automatic Canteen Co. of America* v. *FTC*, 346 U.S. 61, and that A&P

A&P filed a petition for review of the Commission's order in the Court of Appeals for the Second Circuit. The court held that substantial evidence supported the findings of the Commission, and that as a matter of law A&P could not successfully assert a meeting-competition defense because it, unlike Borden, had known that Borden's offer was better than Bowman's. . . . Finally, the court held that the Commission had correctly determined that A&P had no cost justification defense. 557 F.2d 971. Because the judgment of the Court of Appeals raises important issues of federal law, we granted certiorari. . . .

II

The Robinson-Patman Act was passed in response to the problem perceived in the increased market power and coercive practices of chain stores and other big buyers that threatened the existence of small independent retailers. Notwithstanding this concern with buyers, however, the emphasis of the Act is in §2(a), which prohibits price discriminations by sellers. Indeed, the original Patman Bill, as reported by Committees of both Houses, prohibited only seller activity, with no mention of buyer liability. . . . Section 2(f) of the Act, making buyers liable for inducing or receiving price discriminations by sellers, was the product of a belated floor amendment near the conclusion of the Senate debates. . . .

As finally enacted, §2(f) provides:

> That it shall be unlawful for any person engaged in commerce, in the course of such commerce, knowingly to induce or receive a discrimination in price *which is prohibited by this section.* (Emphasis added.)

Liability under §2(f) thus is limited to situations where the price discrimination is one "which is prohibited by this section." While the phrase "this section" refers to the entire §2 of the Act, only subsections (a) and (b) dealing with seller liability involve discriminations in price. Under the plain meaning of §2(f), therefore, a buyer cannot be liable if a prima facie case could not be established against a seller, or if the seller has an affirmative defense. In either situation, there is no price discrimination "prohibited by this section." . . . This legislative history of §2(f) fully confirms the conclusion that buyer liability under §2(f) is dependent on seller liability under §2(a).[3]

The derivative nature of liability under §2(f) was recognized by this Court in *Automatic Canteen Co. of America* v. *FTC,* 346 U.S. 61. In that

---

had not then satisfied its burden of showing that the prices were cost justified, or that it did not know that they were not.

The Commission upheld the Administrative Law Judge's dismissal of Count III of the complaint.

[3] In presenting the Conference Report to the House, Representative Utterback summarized the meaning of §2(f) by stating that "This paragraph makes the buyer liable for knowingly inducing or receiving any discrimination in price which is unlawful under the first paragraph [§2(a)] of the amendment." *80 Cong. Rec.* 9419 (1936).

case, the Court stated that even if the Commission has established a prima facie case of price discrimination, a buyer does not violate §2(f) if the lower prices received are either within one of the seller's defenses, or not known by him not to be within one of those defenses. . . .

III

The petitioner, relying on this plain meaning of §2(f) and the teaching of the *Automatic Canteen* case, argues that it cannot be liable under §2(f) if Borden had a valid meeting-competition defense. The respondent, on the other hand, argues that the petitioner may be liable even assuming that Borden had such a defense. The meeting-competition defense, the respondent contends, must in these circumstances be judged from the point of view of the buyer. Since A&P knew for a fact that the final Borden bid beat the Bowman bid, it was not entitled to assert the meeting-competition defense even though Borden may have honestly believed that it was simply meeting competition. Recognition of a meeting-competition defense for the buyer in this situation, the respondent argues, would be contrary to the basic purpose of the Robinson-Patman Act to curtail abuses by large buyers.

A

The short answer to these contentions of the respondent is that Congress did not provide in §2(f) that a buyer can be liable even if the seller has a valid defense. The clear language of §2(f) states that a buyer can be liable only if he receives a price discrimination "prohibited by this section." If a seller has a valid meeting-competition defense, there is simply no prohibited price discrimination. . . .

B

In the *Automatic Canteen* case, the Court warned against interpretations of the Robinson-Patman Act which "extend beyond the prohibitions of the Act and, in so doing, help give rise to a price uniformity and rigidity in open conflict with the purposes of other antitrust legislation." 343 U.S., at 63. Imposition of §2(f) liability on the petitioner in this case would lead to just such price uniformity and rigidity.[4]

In a competitive market, uncertainty among sellers will cause them to compete for business by offering buyers lower prices. Because of the evils of collusive action, the Court has held that the exchange of price information by competitors violates the Sherman Act. *United States* v. *Container Corp.*, 393 U.S. 333. Under the view advanced by the respondent, however, a buyer, to avoid liability, must either refuse a seller's bid or at least

---

[4] More than once the Court has stated that the Robinson-Patman Act should be construed consistently with broader policies of the antitrust laws. *United States* v. *United States Gypsum Co.* [438] U.S. [422]; *Automatic Canteen Co.* v. *FTC, supra,* at 74.

inform him that his bid has beaten competition. Such a duty of affirmative disclosure would almost inevitably frustrate competitive bidding and, by reducing uncertainty, lead to price matching and anticompetitive cooperation among sellers.[5]

Ironically, the Commission itself, in dismissing the charge under §5 of the Federal Trade Commission Act in this case, recognized the dangers inherent in a duty of affirmative disclosure:

> The imposition of a duty of affirmative disclosure, applicable to a buyer whenever a seller states that his offer is intended to meet competition, is contrary to normal business practice and, we think, contrary to the public interest.
>
> *   *   *   *   *
>
> We fear a scenario where the seller automatically attaches a meeting-competition caveat to every bid. The buyer would then state whether such bid meets, beats, or loses to another bid. The seller would then submit a second, a third, and perhaps a fourth bid until finally he is able to ascertain his competitor's bid.

The effect of the finding that the same conduct of the petitioner violated §2(f), however, is to impose the same duty of affirmative disclosure which the Commission condemned as anticompetitive, "contrary to the public interest," and "contrary to normal business practice," in dismissing the charge under §5 of the Federal Trade Commission Act. Neither the Commission nor the Court of Appeals offered any explanation for this apparent anomaly.

As in the *Automatic Canteen* case, we decline to adopt a construction of §2(f) that is contrary to its plain meaning and would lead to anticompetitive results. Accordingly, we hold that a buyer who has done no more than accept the lower of two prices competitively offered does not violate §2(f) provided the seller has a meeting-competition defense.[6]

---

[5] A duty of affirmative disclosure might also be difficult to enforce. In cases where a seller offers differing quantities or a different quality product, or offers to serve the buyer in a different manner, it might be difficult for the buyer to determine when disclosure is required.

[6] In *Kroger Co.* v. *FTC*, . . . [488 F.2d 1378 (6th Cir. 1971)], the Court of Appeals for the Sixth Circuit held that a buyer who induced price concessions by a seller by making deliberate misrepresentations could be liable under §2(f) even if the seller has a meeting competition defense.

This case does not involve a "lying buyer" situation. The complaint issued by the FTC alleged that A&P accepted Borden's offer knowing that Borden had granted a substantially lower price than the only other competitive bidder without notifying Borden of this fact." The complaint did not allege that Borden's second bid was induced by any misrepresentation. The Court of Appeals recognized that the *Kroger* case involved a "lying buyer" but stated that there was no meaningful distinction between the situation where "the buyer lies or merely keeps quiet about the nature of the competing bid." 557 F.2d, at 883. . . .

Because A&P was not a "lying buyer," we need not decide whether such a buyer could be liable under §2(f) even if the seller has a meeting-competition defense.

IV

Because both the Commission and the Court of Appeals proceeded on the assumption that a buyer who accepts the lower of two competitive bids can be liable under §2(f) even if the seller has a meeting-competition defense, there was not a specific finding that Borden did in fact have such a defense. But it quite clearly did.

A

The test for determining when a seller has a valid meeting competition defense is whether a seller can "show the existence of facts which would lead a reasonable and prudent person to believe that the granting of a lower price would in fact meet the equally low price of a competitor." *FTC* v. *AE Staley Manufacturing Co.*, 324 U.S. 746, 759–760. "A good faith belief, rather than absolute certainty, that a price concession is being offered to meet an equally low price offered by a competitor is sufficient to satisfy the Robinson-Patman's §2(b) defense." *United States* v. *United States Gypsum Co.*, [438] U.S. [422, 453].[7] Since good faith, rather than absolute certainty, is the touchstone of the meeting-competition defense, a seller can assert the defense even if it has unknowingly made a bid that in fact not only met but beat his competition. . . .

B

Under the circumstances of this case, Borden did act reasonably and in good faith when it made its second bid. The petitioner, despite its longstanding relationship with Borden, was dissatisfied with Borden's first bid and solicited offers from other dairies. . . .

. . . Borden was informed by the petitioner that it was in danger of losing its A&P business in the Chicago area unless it came up with a better offer. It was told that its first offer was "not even in the ball park" and that a $50,000 improvement "would not be a drop in the pocket [sic]." In light of Borden's established business relationship with the petitioner, Borden could justifiably conclude that A&P's statements were reliable and that it was necessary to make another bid offering substantial concessions to avoid losing its account with the petitioner.

Borden was unable to ascertain the details of the Bowman bid. It requested more information about the bid from the petitioner, but this request was refused. It could not then attempt to verify the existence and terms of the competing offer from Bowman without risking Sherman Act liability. . . . Faced with a substantial loss of business and unable to find out the precise details of the competing bid, Borden made another offer stating that it was doing so in order to meet competition. Under these

---

[7] Recognition of the right of a seller to meet a lower competitive price in good faith may be the primary means of reconciling the Robinson-Patman Act with the more general purposes of the antitrust laws of encouraging competition between sellers. . . .

circumstances, the conclusion is virtually inescapable that in making that offer Borden acted in a reasonable and good-faith effort to meet its competition, and therefore was entitled to a meeting-competition defense. . . .

Since Borden had a meeting-competition defense and thus could not be liable under §2(b) the petitioner who did no more than accept that offer cannot be liable under §2(f). . . .

Accordingly, the judgment is *reversed.*

It is so ordered.

MR. JUSTICE STEVENS took no part in the consideration or decision of this case.

[MR. JUSTICE WHITE concurred in part and dissented in part.]

MR. JUSTICE MARSHALL, dissenting in part:

I agree with the Court that the Federal Trade Commission and the Court of Appeals applied the wrong legal standard in assessing A&P's liability under the Robinson-Patman Act. However, I cannot join the Court's interpretation of §2(f) as precluding buyer liability under this Act unless the seller could also be found liable for price discrimination. Neither the language nor the sparse legislative history of §2(f) justifies this enervating standard for the determination of buyer liability. To the contrary, the Court's construction disregards the congressional purpose to curtail the coercive practices of chain stores and other large buyers. . . .

I

Section 2(f) provides that "[i]t shall be unlawful for any person . . . knowingly to induce or receive a discrimination in price *which is prohibited by this section.*" (Emphasis added.) The Court interprets the italicized language as "plainly meaning" that a buyer can be found liable for knowingly inducing price discrimination only if his seller is first proved liable under §§2(a) and 2(b). . . . Under this construction, proceedings involving only the Commission and a buyer will turn upon proof of a seller's liability, and whenever a seller could successfully claim the meeting-competition defense, the buyer must be exonerated.

In my view, the language of §2(f) does not compel this circuitous method of establishing buyer liability. Sections 2(a) and 2(b) of the Act define the elements of price discrimination and the affirmative defenses available to sellers. When Congress extended liability to buyers who encourage price discrimination, a ready means of defining the prohibition was to rely on the elements and defenses already delineated in §§2(a) and

2(b). Thus, the phrase "which is prohibited by this section" in §2(f) incorporates these elements and defenses by reference, making them applicable to buyers. So construed, §2(f) simply means that the same elements of a prima facie case must be established and the same basic affirmative defenses available, whether buyer or seller liability is in issue. The section does not require that another party actually satisfy all of the conditions of §§2(a) and 2(b) before buyer liability can even be considered. Determining buyer and seller liability independently, I believe, places less strain on the "plain meaning" of the language of §2(f) than does the absolutely derivative standard the majority announces today.

In construing §2(f), the Court relies on Congress' delay in adding the section to the final bill and on a remark by Representative Utterback during the legislative debates. *Ante*, at 5–7, and n. 10. The delay provides little logical justification for the Court's interpretation; rather, it more likely reflects Congress' late realization that halting the abusive practices of buyers . . . could not be accomplished solely through imposition of liability on sellers. Representative Utterback's statement, *80 Cong. Rec.* 9419 (1936), amounts to a slight paraphrase of §2(f) and in no way supports the Court's derivative standard.

I agree with the Court's suggestion . . . that we must resolve the dilemma confronting a buyer who properly invites a seller to meet a competitor's price and then fortuitously obtains a lower bid. Congress could not have expected the buyer to choose between asking the seller to increase the bid to a specific price or accepting the lower bid and facing liability under §2(f). Rather, it must have intended some accommodation for buyers who act in good faith yet receive bids that beat competition. This does not mean, however, that a buyer should be liable under §2(f) only if his seller also would be liable. That solution to the buyer's dilemma would enable him to manufacture his own defense by misrepresenting to a seller the response needed to meet a competitor's bid and then allowing the seller to rely in good faith on incorrect information. The Court purports to reserve this "lying buyer" issue, . . . but the derivative standard it adopts today belies the reservation. It "prohibited by this section" means that a buyer's liability depends on that of the seller, then absent seller liability, the buyer's conduct and bad faith are necessarily irrelevant.

I would hold that under §2(f), the Robinson-Patman Act defenses must be available to buyers on the same basic terms as they are to sellers. To be sure, some differences in the nature of the defenses would obtain because of the different bargaining positions of sellers and buyers. With respect to the meeting-competition defense at issue here, a seller can justify a price discrimination by showing that his lower price was offered in good faith to meet that of a competitor. . . . In my view a buyer should be able to claim that defense—independently of the seller—if he acted in good faith to induce the seller to meet a competitor's price, regardless of whether the seller's price happens to beat the competitor's. But a buyer who induces the lower bid by misrepresentation should not escape Robinson-Patman Act liability. . . . This definition of the meeting-competition defense both extricates buyers from an impossible dilemma and respects the congressional intent to prevent buyers from abusing their market power to gain competitive advantage. . . .

II

In my judgment, the numerous ambiguities in the record dictate that this case be remanded to the Commission. The Court, however, avoids a remand by concluding in the first instance that A&P's seller necessarily had a meeting-competition defense. . . . In so doing, the Court usurps the factfinding function best performed by the Commission.[8] . . .

Accordingly, I dissent from the Court's adoption of a derivative standard for determining buyer liability and its resolution of disputed factual issues without a remand.

---

[8] Considering the recent admonition in *United States Gypsum, supra,* at 456 n. 31, that "[t]he case by case interpretation and elaboration of the §2(b) defense is properly left to the other federal courts and the FTC in the context of concrete factual situations," the Court's action is particularly inappropriate. . . .

9

Tying Devices

The Supreme Court noted in the *Standard Stations* case (see Chapter 10) that, "tying agreements serve hardly any purpose beyond the suppression of competition." Yet, because of the possibility that such agreements might under some circumstances be economically justified and legally unexceptionable, the courts have hesitated to declare them unlawful per se. Once again, it becomes necessary to examine a trade practice—in this instance tying devices—on a case-by-case basis. The decisions presented below indicate that the crucial test in these cases is whether the tie-in involves one product or service in which the company enjoys substantial market power. In other words, the courts attempt to discover whether the tie-in represents an attempt by a firm to exert leverage so that its monopoly power in one area may be extended into another. In the *Northern Pacific* case the Court concluded that Northern Pacific's dominance of strategically situated landholdings in the Pacific Northwest was being used as a lever with which to induce purchasers and lessees of such landholdings to use its freight transportation facilities to the exclusion of competitors. Thus, the "preferential routing" clauses contained in its purchase and rental contracts constituted an illegal tying arrangement. In the *Jerrold* case, on the other hand, the Court recognized that under certain conditions tying contracts may result in positive economic benefits. Accordingly, if refused to strike down an arrangement whereby Jerrold, a new entrant, sold electronic equipment to community antenna television companies only on a full system basis and in conjunction with a service contract.

However, as the *Fortner* case clearly indicates, the Supreme Court still takes a relatively dim view of tying devices. This opinion might profitably be read in connection with the *International Salt* case presented in Chapter 13.

346

Northern Pacific Railway Company v. United States

356 U.S. 1 (1958)

MR. JUSTICE BLACK delivered the opinion of the Court.

In 1864 and 1870 Congress granted the predecessor of the Northern Pacific Railway Company approximately forty million acres of land in several Northwestern States and Territories to facilitate its construction of a railroad line from Lake Superior to Puget Sound. In general terms, this grant consisted of every alternate section of land in a belt 20 miles wide on each side of the track through States and 40 miles wide through Territories. The granted lands were of various kinds; some contained great stands of timber, some iron ore or other valuable mineral deposits, some oil or natural gas, while still other sections were useful for agriculture, grazing or industrial purposes. By 1949 the Railroad had sold about 37,000,000 acres of its holdings, but had reserved mineral rights in 6,500,000 of those acres. Most of the unsold land was leased for one purpose or another. In a large number of its sales contracts and most of its lease agreements the Railroad had inserted "preferential routing" clauses which compelled the grantee or lessee to ship over its lines all commodities produced or manufactured on the land, provided that its rates (and in some instances its service) were equal to those of competing carriers. Since many of the goods produced on the lands subject to these "preferential routing" provisions are shipped from one State to another the actual and potential amount of interstate commerce affected is substantial. Alternative means of transportation exist for a large portion of these shipments including the facilities of two other major railroad systems.

In 1949 the Government filed suit under Section 4 of the Sherman Act seeking a declaration that the defendant's "preferential routing" agreements were unlawful as unreasonable restraints of trade under Section 1 of that Act. After various pretrial proceedings the Government moved for summary judgment contending that on the undisputed facts it was entitled, as a matter of law, to the relief demanded. The district judge made numerous findings, as set forth in substance in the preceding paragraph, based on the voluminous pleadings, stipulations, depositions and answers to interrogatories filed in the case, and then granted the Government's motion (with an exception not relevant here). 142 F. Supp. 679. He issued an order enjoining the defendant from enforcing the existing "preferential routing" clauses or from entering into any future agreements containing them. The defendant took a direct appeal to this Court. . . .

The Sherman Act was designed to be a comprehensive charter of economic liberty aimed at preserving free and unfettered competition as the rule of trade. It rests on the premise that the unrestrained interaction of competitive forces will yield the best allocation of our economic resources, the lowest prices, the highest quality and the greatest material progress, while at the same time providing an environment conducive to the preservation of our democratic political and social institutions. But even were that premise open to question, the policy unequivocally laid down by the Act is competition. And to this end it prohibits "Every contract, combination . . . or conspiracy, in restraint of trade or commerce among the several States." Although this prohibition is literally all-encompassing, the courts have construed it as precluding only those contracts or combinations which "unreasonably" restrain competition. . . .

However, there are certain agreements or practices which because of their pernicious effect on competition and lack of any redeeming virtue are conclusively presumed to be unreasonable and therefore illegal without elaborate inquiry as to the precise harm they have caused or the business excuse for their use. This principle of *per se* unreasonableness not only makes the type of restraints which are proscribed by the Sherman Act more certain to the benefit of everyone concerned, but it also avoids the necessity for an incredibly complicated and prolonged economic investigation into the entire history of the industry involved, as well as related industries, in an effort to determine at large whether a particular restraint has been unreasonable—an inquiry so often wholly fruitless when undertaken. Among the practices which the courts have heretofore deemed to be unlawful in and of themselves are price fixing, *United States* v. *Socony-Vacuum Oil Co.* . . . ; division of markets, *United States* v. *Addyston Pipe & Steel Co.* . . . ; group boycotts, *Fashion Originators' Guild* v. *Federal Trade Comm'n* . . . ; and tying arrangements, *International Salt Co.* v. *United States*. . . .

For our purposes a tying arrangement may be defined as an agreement by a party to sell one product but only on the condition that the buyer also purchases a different (or tied) product, or at least agrees that he will not purchase that product from any other supplier. Where such conditions are successfully exacted competition on the merits with respect to the tied product is inevitably curbed. Indeed "tying agreements serve hardly any purpose beyond the suppression of competition." *Standard Oil Co. of California* v. *United States*. . . . They deny competitors free access to the market for the tied product, not because the party imposing the tying requirements has a better product or a lower price but because of his power or leverage in another market. At the same time buyers are forced to forego their free choice between competing products. For these reasons "tying agreements fare harshly under the laws forbidding restraints of trade." *Times-Picayune Publishing Co.* v. *United States*. . . . They are unreasonable in and of themselves whenever a party has sufficient economic power with respect to the tying product to appreciably restrain free competition in the market for the tied product and a "not insubstantial" amount of interstate commerce is affected. *Interna-*

tional Salt Co. v. *United States.* . . . Cf. *United States* v. *Paramount Pictures.* . . . Of course where the seller has no control or dominance over the tying product so that it does not represent an effectual weapon to pressure buyers into taking the tied item any restraint of trade attributable to such tying arrangements would obviously be insignificant at most. . . .

In this case we believe the district judge was clearly correct in entering summary judgment declaring the defendant's "preferential routing" clauses unlawful restraints of trade. We wholly agree that the undisputed facts established beyond any genuine question that the defendant possessed substantial economic power by virtue of its extensive landholdings which it used as leverage to induce large numbers of purchasers and lessees to give it preference, to the exclusion of its competitors, in carrying goods or produce from the land transferred to them. Nor can there be any real doubt that a "not insubstantial" amount of interstate commerce was and is affected by these restrictive provisions.

As pointed out before, the defendant was initially granted large acreages by Congress in the several northwestern states through which its lines now run. This land was strategically located in checkerboard fashion amid private holdings and within economic distance of transportation facilities. Not only the testimony of various witnesses but common sense makes it evident that this particular land was often prized by those who purchased or leased it and was frequently essential to their business activities. In disposing of its holdings the defendant entered into contracts of sale or lease covering at least several million acres of land which included "preferential routing" clauses. The very existence of this host of tying arrangements is itself compelling evidence of the defendant's great power, at least where, as here, no other explanation has been offered for the existence of these restraints. The "preferential routing" clauses conferred no benefit on the purchasers or lessees. While they got the land they wanted by yielding their freedom to deal with competing carriers, the defendant makes no claim that it came any cheaper than if the restrictive clauses had been omitted. In fact any such price reduction in return for rail shipments would have quite plainly constituted an unlawful rebate to the shipper. So far as the Railroad was concerned its purpose obviously was to fence out competitors, to stifle competition. While this may have been exceedingly beneficial to its business, it is the very type of thing the Sherman Act condemns. In short, we are convinced that the essential prerequisites for treating the defendant's tying arrangements as unreasonable *"per se"* were conclusively established below and that the defendant has offered to prove nothing there or here which would alter this conclusion.

In our view *International Salt Co.* v. *United States,* . . . which has been unqualifiedly approved by subsequent decisions, is ample authority for affirming the judgment below. . . .

The defendant attempts to evade the force of *International Salt* on the ground that the tying product there was patented while here it is not. But we do not believe this dinstinction has, or should have, any significance. In arriving at its decision in *International Salt* the Court placed no reliance on the fact that a patent was involved nor did it give the slightest intimation that the outcome would have been any different if that had not been the case. If anything, the Court held the challenged tying arrangements unlawful *despite* the fact that the tying item was patented, not because of it. . . .

The defendant argues that the holding in *International Salt* was limited by the decision in *Times-Picayune Publishing Co.* v. *United States*. . . . There the Court held that a unit system of advertising in two local newspapers did not violate Section 1 of the Sherman Act. . . . But the Court was extremely careful to confine its decision to the narrow record before it. . . .

While there is some language in the *Times-Picayune* opinion which speaks of "monopoly power" or "dominance" over the tying product as a necessary precondition for application of the rule of *per se* unreasonableness to tying arrangements, we do not construe this general language as requiring anything more than sufficient economic power to impose an appreciable restraint on free competition in the tied product (assuming all the time, of course, that a "not insubstantial" amount of interstate commerce is affected). . . . *Times-Picayune* . . . makes clear . . . that the vice of tying arrangements lies in the use of economic power in one market to restrict competition on the merits in another, regardless of the source from which the power is derived and whether the power takes the form of a monopoly or not.

The defendant contends that its "preferential routing" clauses are subject to so many exceptions and have been administered so leniently that they do not significantly restrain competition. . . . [I]f these restrictive provisions are merely harmless sieves with no tendency to restrain competition, as the defendant's argument seems to imply, it is hard to understand why it has expended so much effort in obtaining them in vast numbers and upholding their validity, or how they are of any benefit to anyone, even the defendant. But however that may be, the essential fact remains that these agreements are binding obligations held over the heads of vendees which deny defendant's competitors access to the fenced-off market on the same terms as the defendant. . . . All of this is only aggravated, of course, here in the regulated transportation industry where there is frequently no real rate competition at all and such effective competition as actually thrives takes other forms.

Affirmed.

[MR. JUSTICE CLARK took no part in the consideration or decision of this case. MR. JUSTICE HARLAN, whom MR. JUSTICE FRANKFURTER and MR. JUSTICE WHITTAKER joined, dissented.]

Fortner Enterprises, Inc. v. *United States Steel Corp.*

394 U.S. 495 (1969)

MR. JUSTICE BLACK delivered the opinion of the Court [on a motion for summary judgment].

. . . Petitioner, Fortner Enterprises, Inc., filed this suit seeking treble damages and an injunction against alleged violations of §§1 and 2 of the Sherman Act. . . . The complaint charged that respondents, United States Steel Corp. and its wholly owned subsidiary, the United States Steel Homes Credit Corp., had engaged in a contract, combination, and conspiracy to restrain trade and to monopolize trade in the sale of prefabricated houses. It alleged that there was a continuing agreement between respondents "to force corporations and individuals, including the plaintiff, as a condition to availing themselves of the services of United States Steel Homes Credit Corporation, to purchase at artifically high prices only United States Steel Homes. . . ." Specifically, petitioner claimed that in order to obtain loans totaling over $2,000,000 from the Credit Corp. for the purchase and development of certain land in the Louisville, Kentucky, area, it had been required to agree, as a condition of the loans, to erect a prefabricated house manufactured by U.S. Steel on each of the lots purchased with the loan proceeds. Petitioner claimed that the prefabricated materials were then supplied by U.S. Steel at unreasonably high prices and proved to be defective and unusable, thus requiring the expenditure of additional sums and delaying the completion date for the development. Petitioner sought treble damages for the profits thus lost, along with a decree enjoining respondents from enforcing the requirement of the loan agreement that petitioner use only houses manufactured by U.S. Steel.

. . . Noting that the agreement involved here was essentially a tying arrangement, under which the purchaser was required to take a tied product—here prefabricated homes—as a condition of being allowed to purchase the tying product—here credit, the District Judge held that petitioner had failed to establish the prerequisites of illegality under our tying cases, namely sufficient market power over the tying product and foreclosure of a substantial volume of commerce in the tied product. . . . Since we find no basis for sustaining this summary judgment, we reverse and order that the case proceed to trial.

We agree with the District Court that the conduct challenged here primarily involves a tying arrangement of the traditional kind. The Credit Corp. sold its credit only on the condition that petitioner purchase a certain number of prefabricated houses from the Homes Division of U.S. Steel. Our cases have made clear that, at least when certain prerequisites are met, arrangements of this kind are illegal in and of themselves, and no specific showing of unreasonable competitive effect is required. The discussion in *Northern Pacific R. Co.* v. *United States* . . . is dispositive of this question:

> . . . They are unreasonable in and of themselves whenever a party has sufficient economic power with respect to the tying product to appreciably restrain free competition in the market for the tied product and a 'not insubstantial' amount of interstate commerce is affected. *International Salt Co.* v. *United States.* . . .

Despite its recognition of this strict standard, the District Court held that petitioner had not even made out a case for the jury. The court held that respondents did not have "sufficient economic power" over credit, the tying product here, because although the Credit Corp.'s terms evidently made the loans uniquely attractive to petitioner, petitioner had not proved that the Credit Corp. enjoyed the same unique attractiveness or economic control with respect to buyers generally. The court also held that the amount of interstate commerce affected was "insubstantial because only a very small percentage of the land available for development in the area was foreclosed to competing sellers of prefabricated houses by the contract with petitioner.["] We think it plain that the District Court misunderstood the two controlling standards and misconceived the extent of its authority to evaluate the evidence in ruling on this motion for summary judgment. . . .

. . . [I]t is clear that petitioner raised questions of fact which, if proved at trial, would bring this tying arrangement within the scope of the *per se* doctrine. The requirement that a "not insubstantial" amount of commerce be involved makes no reference to the scope of any particular market or to the share of that market foreclosed by the tie, and hence we could not approve of the trial judge's conclusions on this issue even if we agreed that his definition of the relevant market was the proper one.[1] An analysis of market shares might become relevant if it were alleged that an apparently small dollar-volume of business actually represented a substantial part of the sales for which competitors were bidding. But normally

---

[1] Since the loan agreements obligated petitioner to erect houses manufactured by U.S. Steel on the land acquired, the trial judge thought the relevant foreclosure was the percentage of the undeveloped land in the county that was no longer open for sites on which homes made by competing producers could be built. This apparently was an insignificant .00032%. But of course the availability of numerous vacant lots on which houses might legally be erected would be small consolation to competing producers once the economic demand for houses had been pre-empted by respondents. It seems plain that the most significant percentage figure with reference to the tied product is the percentage of annual sales of houses, or prefabricated houses, in the area that was foreclosed to other competitors by the tying arrangement.

the controlling consideration is simply whether a total amount of business, substantial enough in terms of dollar-volume so as not to be merely *de minimis*, is foreclosed to competitors by the tie, for as we said in *International Salt*, it is "unreasonable, *per se*, to foreclose competitors from any substantial market" by a tying arrangement. . . .

The complaint and affidavits filed here leave no room for doubt that the volume of commerce allegedly foreclosed was substantial. . . . [W]e cannot agree with respondents that a sum of almost $200,000 is paltry or "insubstantial." . . . For purposes of determining whether the amount of commerce foreclosed is too insubstantial to warrant prohibition of the practice, therefore, the relevant figure is the total volume of sales tied by the sales policy under challenge, not the portion of this total accounted for by the particular plaintiff who brings suit. . . . In the present case, the annual sales allegedly foreclosed by respondents' tying arrangements throughout the country totaled almost $4,000,000 in 1960, more than $2,800,000 in 1961, and almost $2,300,000 in 1962. These amounts could scarcely be regarded as insubstantial.

The standard of "sufficient economic power" does not, as the District Court held, require that the defendant have a monopoly or even a dominant position throughout the market for the tying product. Our tie-in cases have made unmistakably clear that the economic power over the tying product can be sufficient even though the power falls far short of dominance and even though the power exists only with respect to some of the buyers in the market. . . .

These decisions rejecting the need for proof of truly dominant power over the tying product have all been based on a recognition that because tying arrangements generally serve no legitimate business purpose that cannot be achieved in some less restrictive way, the presence of any appreciable restraint on competition provides a sufficient reason for invalidating the tie. Such appreciable restraint results whenever the seller can exert some power over some of the buyers in the market, even if his power is not complete over them and over all other buyers in the market. In fact, complete dominance throughout the market, the concept that the District Court apparently had in mind, would never exist even under a pure monopoly. Market power is usually stated to be the ability of a single seller to raise price and restrict output, for reduced output is the almost inevitable result of higher prices. Even a complete monopolist can seldom raise his price without losing some sales; many buyers will cease to buy the product, or buy less, as the price rises. Market power is therefore a source of serious concern for essentially the same reason, regardless of whether the seller has the greatest economic power possible or merely some lesser degree of appreciable economic power. In both instances, despite the freedom of some or many buyers from the seller's power, other buyers—whether few or many, whether scattered throughout the market or part of some group within the market—can be forced to accept the higher price because of their stronger preferences for the product, and the seller could therefore choose instead to force them to accept a tying arrangement that would prevent free competition for their patronage in the market for the tied product. Accordingly, the proper focus of concern is whether the seller has the power to raise prices, or impose other burdensome terms such as a tie-in, with respect to any appreciable number of buyers within the market.

The affidavits put forward by petitioner clearly entitle it to its day in court under this standard. A construction company president stated that competitors of U.S. Steel sold prefabricated houses and built conventional homes for at least $400 less than U.S. Steel's price for comparable models. Since in a freely competitive situation buyers would not accept a tying arrangement obligating them to buy a tied product at a price higher than the going market rate, this substantial price differential with respect to the tied product (prefabricated houses) in itself may suggest that respondents had some special economic power in the credit market. In addition, petitioner's president, A. B. Fortner, stated that he accepted the tying condition on respondents' loan solely because the offer to provide 100% financing, lending an amount equal to the full purchase price of the land to be acquired, was unusually and uniquely advantageous to him. He found that no such financing was available to his corporation on any such cheap terms from any other source during the 1959–1962 period. . . .

We do not mean to accept petitioner's apparent argument that market power can be inferred simply because the kind of financing terms offered by a lending company are "unique and unusual." We do mean, however, that uniquely and unusually advantageous terms can reflect a creditor's unique economic advantages over his competitors.[2] Since summary judgment in antitrust cases is disfavored, *Poller, supra,* the claims of uniqueness in this case should be read in the light most favorable to petitioner. They could well mean that U.S. Steel's subsidiary Credit Corp. had a unique economic ability to provide 100% financing at cheap rates . . . because of economies resulting from the nationwide character of its operations. In addition, potential competitors such as banks and savings and loan associations may have been prohibited from offering 100% financing by state or federal law. . . .

Brief consideration should also be given to respondents' additional argument that even if their unique kind of financing reflected economic power in the credit market, and even if a substantial volume of commerce

---

[2] Uniqueness confers economic power only when other competitors are in some way prevented from offering the distinctive product themselves. Such barriers may be legal, as in the case of patented and copyrighted products, *e.g., International Salt; Loew's,* or physical, as when the product is land, *e.g., Northern Pacific.* It is true that the barriers may also be economic, as when competitors are simply unable to produce the distinctive product profitably, but the uniqueness test in such situations is somewhat confusing since the real source of economic power is not the product itself but rather the seller's cost advantage in producing it.

was affected, the arrangement involving credit should not be held illegal under normal tie-in principles. In support of this, respondents suggest that every sale on credit in effect involves a tie. They argue that the offering of favorable credit terms is simply a form of price competition equivalent to the offering of a comparable reduction in the cash price of the tied product. Consumers should not, they say, be deprived of such advantageous services, and they suffer no harm because they can buy the tangible product with credit obtained elsewhere if the combined price of the seller's credit-product package is less favorable than the cost of purchasing the components separately.

All of respondents' arguments amount essentially to the same claim— namely, that this opinion will somehow prevent those who manufacture goods from ever selling them on credit. But our holding in this case will have no such effect. There is, at the outset of every tie-in case, including the familiar cases involving physical goods, the problem of determining whether two separate products are in fact involved. In the usual sale on credit the seller, a single individual or corporation, simply makes an agreement determining when and how much he will be paid for his product. In such a sale the credit may constitute such an inseparable part of the purchase price for the item that the entire transaction could be considered to involve only a single product. It will be time enough to pass on the issue of credit sales when a case involving it actually arises. Sales such as that are a far cry from the arrangement involved here, where the credit is provided by one corporation on condition that a product be purchased from a separate corporation, and where the borrower contracts to obtain a large sum of money over and above that needed to pay the seller for the physical products purchased. Whatever the standards for determining exactly when a transaction involves only a "single product," we cannot see how an arrangement such as that present in this case could ever be said to involve only a single product.

Nor does anything in respondents' arguments serve to distinguish credit from other kinds of goods and services, all of which may, when used as tying products, extend the seller's economic power to new markets and foreclose competition in the tied product. The asserted business justifications for a tie of credit are not essentially different from the justifications that can be advanced when the tying product is some other service or commodity. Although advantageous credit terms may be viewed as a form of price competition in the tied product, so is the offer of any other tying product on advantageous terms. In both instances, the seller can achieve his alleged purpose, without extending his economic power, by simply reducing the price of the tied product itself.[3]

The potential harm is also essentially the same when the tying product

---

[3] Where price reductions on the tied product are made difficult in practice by the structure of that market, the seller can still achieve his alleged objective by offering other kinds of fringe benefits over which he has no economic power.

is credit. The buyer may have the choice of buying the tangible commodity separately, but as in other cases the seller can use his power over the tying product to win customers that would otherwise have constituted a market available to competing producers of the tied product. "[C]ompetition on the merits with respect to the tied product is inevitably curbed." *Northern Pacific*, 356 U.S., at 6. Nor can it be assumed that because the product involved is money needed to finance a purchase, the buyer would not have been able to purchase from anyone else without the seller's attractive credit. A buyer might have a strong preference for a seller's credit because it would eliminate the need for him to lay out personal funds, borrow from relatives, put up additional collateral, or obtain guarantors, but any of these expedients might have been chosen to finance a purchase from a competing producer if the seller had not captured the sale by means of his tying arrangement.

In addition, barriers to entry in the market for the tied product are raised since, in order to sell to certain buyers, a new company not only must be able to manufacture the tied product but also must have sufficient financial strength to offer credit comparable to that provided by larger competitors under tying arrangements. If the larger companies have achieved economies of scale in their credit operations, they can of course exploit these economies legitimately by lowering their credit charges to consumers who purchase credit only, but economies in financing should not, any more than economies in other lines of business, be used to exert economic power over other products that the company produces no more efficiently than its competitors.

For all these reasons we can find no basis for treating credit differently in principle from other goods and services. Although money is a fungible commodity—like wheat or, for that matter, unfinished steel—credit markets, like other markets, are often imperfect, and it is easy to see how a big company with vast sums of money in its treasury could wield very substantial power in a credit market. Where this is true, tie-ins involving credit can cause all the evils that the antitrust laws have always been intended to prevent, crippling other companies that are equally, if not more, efficient in producing their own products. Therefore, the same inquiries must be made as to economic power over the tying product and substantial effect in the tied market, but where these factors are present no special treatment can be justified solely because credit, rather than some other product, is the source of the tying leverage used to restrain competition.

The judgment of the Court of Appeals is reversed, and the case is remanded with directions to let this suit proceed to trial.

Reversed and remanded.

MR. JUSTICE WHITE, with whom MR. JUSTICE HARLAN joins, dissenting.

The Court does not purport to abandon the general rule that some market power in the tying product is essential to a §1 violation. But it applies the rule to permit proscription of a seller's extension of favorable credit terms conditioned on the purchase of an agreed quantity of the seller's product without any offer of proof that the seller has any market power in the credit market itself. . . . Proscription of the sale of goods on easy credit terms as an illegal tie without proof of market power in credit not only departs from established doctrine but also in my view should not be outlawed as *per se* illegal under the Sherman Act. Provision of favorable credit terms may be nothing more or less than vigorous competition in the tied product, on a basis very nearly approaching the price competition which it has always been the policy of the Sherman Act to encourage. Moreover, it is far from clear that, absent power in the credit market, credit financing of purchases should be regarded as a tie of two distinct products any more than a commodity should be viewed as tied to its own price. Since provision of credit by sellers may facilitate competition, since it may provide essential risk or working capital to entrepreneurs or businessmen, and since the logic of the majority's opinion does away in practice with the requirement of showing market power in the tying product while retaining that requirement in form, the majority's *per se* rule is inappropriate. I dissent.

In this case there is no offer to prove monopoly or dominance in the tying product—money. And in no sense is the money provided to petitioner unique, even though the terms on which it was furnished and was to be repaid may have been advantageous, and indeed the money itself available from no other source on equally good terms. United States Steel was principally interested in the sales of houses, and petitioner in the economical development of its housing project. Before concluding that the financing arrangements on which U.S. Steel sold its houses amounted to anything more than a price reduction on the houses, or that easy financing terms show that their provider has market power in the money market, the Court should have in mind the rationale on which the illegality of tying arrangements is based.

There is general agreement in the cases and among commentators[4] that the fundamental restraint against which the tying proscription is meant to guard is the use of power over one product to attain power over another, or otherwise to distort freedom of trade and competition in the second product. This distortion injures the buyers of the second product, who because of their preference for the seller's brand of the first are artificially forced to make a less than optimal choice in the second. And even if the

---

[4] *E.g.*, Report of the Attorney General's National Committee to Study the Antitrust Laws 145 (1955); Austin, "The Tying Arrangement: A Critique and Some New Thoughts," *1967 Wis. L. Rev.* 88; Bowman, "Tying Arrangements and the Leverage Problem," *67 Yale L. J.* 19 (1957); Day, "Exclusive Dealing, Tying and Reciprocity—A Reappraisal," *29 Ohio St. L. J.* 539, 540–541 (1968); Turner, "The Validity of Tying Arrangements Under the Antitrust Laws," *72 Harv. L. Rev.* 50, 60–61 (1958).

customer is indifferent among brands of the second product and therefore loses nothing by agreeing to use the seller's brand of the second in order to get his brand of the first,[5] such tying agreements may work significant restraints on competition in the tied product. The tying seller may be working toward a monopoly position in the tied product[6] and, even if he is not, the practice of tying forecloses other sellers of the tied product and makes it more difficult for new firms to enter that market. They must be prepared not only to match existing sellers of the tied product in price and quality, but to offset the attraction of the tying product itself. Even if this is possible through simultaneous entry into production of the tying product, entry into both markets is significantly more expensive than simple entry into the tied market, and shifting buying habits in the tied product is considerably more cumbersome and less responsive to variations in competitive offers.[7] In addition to these anticompetitive effects in the tied product, tying arrangements may be used to evade price control in the tying product through clandestine transfer of the profit to the tied product; they may be used as a counting device to effect price discrimination; and they may be used to force a full line of products on the customer so as to extract more easily from him a monopoly return on one unique product in the line.[8]

---

[5] Theoretically, the tie may do the tier little good unless the buyer is in that position. Even if the seller has a complete monopoly in the tying product, this is the case. The monopolist can exact the maximum price which people are willing to pay for his product. By definition, if his price went up he would lose customers. If he then refuses to sell the tying product without the tied product, and raises the price of the tied product above market, he will also lose customers. The tying link works no magic. However, difficulty in extracting the full monopoly profit without the tie, Burstein, "A Theory of Full-Line Forcing," 55 *Nw. U. L. Rev.* 62 (1960), or the marginal advantage of a guaranteed first refusal from otherwise indifferent customers of the tied product, or other advantages mentioned in the text, may make the tie beneficial to its originator.

[6] If the monopolist uses his monopoly profits in the first market to underwrite sales below market price in the second, his monopoly business becomes less profitable. There remains an incentive to do so nonetheless when he thinks he can obtain a monopoly in the tied product as well, permitting him later to raise prices without fear of entry to recoup the monopoly profit he has forgone. But just as the firm whose deep pocket stems from monopoly profits in the tying product may make this takeover, so may anyone else with a deep pocket, from whatever source.

[7] Even when the terms of the tie allow a competitor to obtain the business in the tied product simply by offering a price lower than, rather than equal to, the tier's the Court has found sufficient restriction in the tied product, as in the *Northern Pacific* case.

[8] Tie-ins may also at times be beneficial to the economy. Apart from the justifications discussed in the text are the following. They may facilitate new entry into fields where established sellers have wedded their customers to them by ties of habit and custom. . . . They may permit clandestine price cutting in products which otherwise would have no price competition at all because of fear of retaliation from the few other producers dealing in the market. They may protect the reputation of the tying product if failure to use the tied product in conjunction with it may cause it to misfunction. . . . And, if the tied and tying products are functionally related, they may reduce costs through economies of joint production and distribution. These benefits which may flow from tie-ins, though perhaps in some cases a potential basis for an affirmative defense, were not sufficient to avoid the imposition of a *per se* proscription, once market power has been demonstrated. But in

All of these distortions depend upon the existence of some market power in the tying product quite apart from any relationship which it might bear to the tied product. In this case, what proof of any market power in the tying product has been alleged? Only that the tying product—money—was not available elsewhere on equally good terms, and perhaps not at all. Let us consider these possibilities in turn.

First, if enough money to proceed was available elsewhere and U.S. Steel was simply offering credit at a lower price, in terms of risk of loss, repayment terms, and interest rate, surely this does not establish that U.S. Steel had market power by any measure in the money market. There was nothing unique about U.S. Steel's money except its low cost to petitioner. A low price on a product is ordinarily no reflection of market power. It proves neither the existence of such power nor its absence, although absence of power may be the more reasonable inference. One who has such power benefits from it precisely because it allows him to raise prices, not lower them, and ordinarily he does so.

A low price in the tying product—money, the most fungible item of trade since it is by definition an economic counter—is especially poor proof of market power when untied credit is available elsewhere. In that case, the low price of credit is functionally equivalent to a reduction in the price of the houses sold. Since the buyer has untied credit available elsewhere, he can compare the houses-credit package of U.S. Steel as competitive with the price of the untied credit plus the cost of houses from another source. By cutting the price of his houses, a competitor of U.S. Steel can compete with U.S. Steel houses on equal terms since U.S. Steel's money is no more desirable to the purchaser than money from another source except in point of price. The same money which U.S. Steel is willing to risk or forgo by providing better credit terms it could sacrifice by cutting the price of houses. There is no good reason why U.S. Steel should always be required to make the price cut in one form rather than another, which its purchaser prefers.

Provision of credit financing by the seller of a commodity to its buyer is a very common event in the American economy. Often the seller is not willing to supply credit generally for the business and personal needs of the public at large, but restricts his credit to the purchasers of the commodity which he is principally in the business of selling. In all such cases, the commodity may be viewed as tied to the credit. In all such cases, the money itself is no more desirable from one source than from another. But in all such cases, under the majority opinion, the mere fact that the credit is offered on uniquely advantageous terms makes the transaction a *per se* violation of §1 of the Sherman Act. And so long as the buyer has chosen to

---

determining whether even the market-power requirement should be eliminated, as the logic of the majority opinion would do, extending the *per se* rule to absolute dimensions, the fact that tie-ins are not entirely unmitigated evils should be borne in mind.

accept the seller's credit terms over any others available to him, the buyer, like petitioner here, must have viewed them as uniquely advantageous to him. The logic of the majority opinion, then, casts great doubt on credit financing by sellers. . . .

Second, adopting the other asumption, that sufficient credit to go forward with the enterprise was simply unavailable to petitioner from any other source at all, the result in this case is even worse. Were it not for the credit extended by U.S. Steel, petitioner would have been unable to carry out its development. U.S. Steel would not have foreclosed anyone from selling houses to petitioner since no one would have sold any houses to petitioner. A seller who is willing to take credit risks which no one else finds acceptable is simply engaging in the hard and risky competition which it is the policy of the Sherman Act to encourage. And if he may not do so, then those businesses and entrepreneurs who depend for their survival and growth or for the initiation of new enterprises on the availability of credit financing from sellers may well fail for lack of credit availability from other sources. Of course, if the credit was unavailable elsewhere because U.S. Steel was a monopolist of credit in a relevant market—which petitioner does not assert—the tie would be illegal. But here it was evidently unavailable elsewhere simply because others were not willing to match U.S. Steel's relatively low price for acceptance of high risk.

. . . Where the seller exercises no market power in the tying item but buyers prefer the tie-in because the seller offers the tying product on favorable terms—where the price is unusually low or where the seller gives the product away conditioned on buying other merchandise—the seller in effect is merely competing in the tied product market. Buyers are not burdened. They may buy both tied and tying products elsewhere on normal terms. Nor are the seller's competitors restrained. The economic advantage of the tie-in to buyers can be matched by other sellers of the tied product by offering lower prices on that product. Promotional tie-ins effected by underpricing the tying product do not themselves prove there is any market power to exercise in that product market, unless the economic resources to withstand lower profit margins and the willingness to compete in this manner are themselves suspect. . . .

The principal evil at which the proscription of tying aims is the use of power in one market to acquire power in, or otherwise distort, a second market. This evil simply does not exist if there is no power in the first market. The first market here is money, a completely fungible item. I would not apply a *per se* rule here without independent proof of market power. Cutting prices in the credit market is more likely to reflect a competitive attempt to offset the market power of others in the tied product than it is to reflect existing market power in the credit market. Those with real power do not offer uniquely advantageous deals to their customers; they raise prices.

. . . I do not consider petitioner's allegations that U.S. Steel lowered its price of credit sufficient to establish market power in credit and I can find no offer by petitioner of the necessary supplementary proof.

MR. JUSTICE FORTAS, with whom MR. JUSTICE STEWART joins, dissenting.

I share my Brother WHITE'S inability to agree with the majority in this case, and, in general, I subscribe to his opinion. I add this separate statement of the reasons for my dissent.

The facts of this case are materially different from any tying case that this Court has heretofore decided. The tying doctrine originated in situations where the seller of product A offers it for sale only on the condition that the buyer also agree to buy product B from the seller. . . .

. . . But, here, U.S. Steel is not selling or leasing land subject to an agreement that its prefabricated houses be used thereon. If these were the facts, and if U.S. Steel controlled enough land within an economically demarcated area or "market," however defined, the case might well be governed by *Northern Pacific*. But, here, U.S. Steel is not selling or providing land. It is selling prefabricated steel houses to be erected in a subdivision and it is providing financing for the land acquisition, improvement, development, and erection costs. Most of the financing is related not to the land cost but to the purchase and installation of the houses.

U.S. Steel neither owned nor controlled any of the land involved in the venture. On the contrary, the building lots constituting the subdivision on which the houses were to be built were owned by another company of which the principal owner was Mr. Fortner, who owned the petitioner. Nor is U.S. Steel selling credit in any general sense. The financing which it agrees to provide is solely and entirely ancillary to its sale of houses. . . .

. . . This is a sale of a single product with the incidental provision of financing. It is not a sale of one product on condition that the buyer will not deal with competitors for another product or will buy the other product exclusively from the seller.

As my Brother WHITE shows, to treat the financing of the housing development as a "tying" product for the houses is to distort the doctrine and to depart from the reason for its existence. Such an extension of the tying doctrine entirely departs from the factual pattern which is described in §3 of the Clayton Act and which has been the basis of this Court's extension of the doctrine to the Sherman Act and its development of the rule that such tying arrangements are illegal on a *per se* basis—*i.e.*, without any showing that they constitute an unreasonable restraint of trade or tend to create a monopoly. The Court has established this rule because the kind of tying arrangement at issue in prior cases involved the use of a leverage position in the tying product—the patented machine, the copyrighted film, the unique land—to force the buyer to purchase the tied product. To apply this rule to a situation where the only "leverage" is a lower price for the article sold or more advantageous financing or credit terms for the article sold and for ancillary costs connected with the sale is to distort the doctrine, and indeed, to convert it into an instrument which penalizes price competition for the article that is sold. . . .

The effect of this novel extension—this distortion, as I view it—of the tying doctrine may be vast and destructive. It is common in our economy for a seller to extend financing to a distributor or franchisee to enable him to purchase and handle the seller's goods at retail, to rent retail facilities, to acquire fixtures or machinery for service to customers in connection with distribution of the seller's goods, or, as here, to prepare the land for and to acquire and erect the seller's houses for sale to the public. . . . Arrangements of this sort run throughout the economy. They frequently, and perhaps characteristically, represent an indispensable method of financing distributive and service trades, and not until today has it been held that they are tying arrangements and therefore *per se* unlawful. . . .

. . . Almost all modern selling involves providing some ancillary services in connection with making the sale—delivery, installation, supplying fixtures, servicing, training of the customer's personnel in use of the material sold, furnishing display material and sales aids, extension of credit. Customarily—indeed almost invariably—the seller offers these ancillary services only in connection with the sale of his own products, and they are often offered without cost or at bargain rates. It is possible that in some situations, such arrangements could be used to restrain competition or might have that effect, but to condemn them out-of-hand under the "tying" rubric, is, I suggest, to use the antitrust laws themselves as an instrument in restraint of competition.

For these reasons, I dissent.

Note: On remand, the District Court directed a verdict in favor of Fortner, on the ground that U.S. Steel possessed sufficient economic power in the credit market. The Court of Appeals reversed and remanded for a new trial by the District Court, which again found for Fortner. This time, the Court of Appeals affirmed, only to have the Supreme Court, in 1977, find for U.S. Steel *(Fortner II),* on the grounds that it did *not* possess the requisite economic power.

United States v. *Jerrold Electronics Corporation*

187 F. Supp. 545 (E.D.Pa. 1960),
affirmed per curiam 365 U.S. 567 (1961)

VAN DUSEN, District Judge.

This action was commenced with the filing of a complaint on February 15, 1957, charging Jerrold Electronics Corporation, its president, Milton

Jerrold Shapp, and five of its corporate subsidiaries with being parties to a conspiracy and contracts in unreasonable restraint of trade and commerce in community television antenna equipment in violation of Section 1 of the Sherman Act . . . ; with being parties to a conspiracy and attempting to monopolize trade and commerce in community television antenna equipment in violation of Section 2 of the Sherman Act . . . ; and with contracting to sell and making sales upon unlawful conditions in violation of Section 3 of the Clayton Act. . . .

· · · · ·

II. BACKGROUND

Jerrold Electronics Corporation (hereinafter "Jerrold") was incorporated under the laws of Pennsylvania in March 1948 by Milton Shapp to engage in the sale of a television booster developed by one of his friends. This device was designed to improve television reception in fringe areas by amplifying the weak signals available there. At Shapp's request, his friend began working on the development of master antenna equipment. The purpose of this equipment was to enable a single antenna to serve a number of television receivers. . . .

Jerrold installed the first operational master antenna system for Montgomery Ward in Baltimore during the summer of 1949. The success of this system resulted in a number of orders from other dealers. At first, this master antenna equipment was sold through the distributors who were handling Jerrold's booster. This proved unsatisfactory, however, because these distributors and their customers lacked the technical training and experience with respect to master antenna systems which was necessary to install and maintain them properly. . . .

In October 1950, Shapp was approached by a group of men from Lansford, Pennsylvania, who were interested in bringing television into their community. The people of Lansford were unable to receive any television signals through the use of conventional equipment because of the town's location. It was possible to receive a signal on a hilltop approximately a mile outside of town, however. They wanted to set up an antenna at this site and hook it up with receivers in the town. Subscribers to their service would pay a connection fee and monthly service charge. . . . It was . . . apparent to . . . [Shapp] that this was a natural and promising area for Jerrold to enter, since there were many communities which, because of distance or topographical features, were in the same predicament as Lansford and had no immediate hope of obtaining television from any other source because of the freeze on the licensing of new television stations in effect at that time.

Shapp and the Lansford group finally worked out a mutually satisfactory arrangement. Jerrold was to install a system using its standard equipment, which the Lansford people would purchase. Jerrold was to use the system as an on-the-spot laboratory to work on the problems it anticipated, discover new problems, and develop the equipment necessary to eliminate them. . . . A few days later, a similar arrangement was made with a group from Mahanoy City, Pennsylvania. . . .

The Lansford system was "turned on" in mid-December 1950 and the Mahonoy City system went into operation in January 1951. . . . The initial results were deemed successful and the systems received considerable publicity, including articles in the *Wall Street Journal* and *Newsweek* magazine, since they were the first significant operational systems of this kind. As a result of the publicity, Shapp was approached by people from hundreds of communities interested in community antenna systems, both as a means of bringing television into their homes and as a profitable investment. These people came from all walks of life. Many of them had little or no technical background or knowledge. Furthermore, the system that went into operation in Lansford in December 1950 was only connected to a few showrooms. With the extension and continual operation of the system, the anticipated problems began to arise. They were of such a magnitude that Shapp's organization was completely tied up analyzing them and designing new equipment to cope with them. Also, there were several instances in which aspiring community system operators had obtained Jerrold's standard equipment through its distributors and attempted to install systems with unsatisfactory results. Under these circumstances, it was decided that no Jerrold equipment would be sold for community purposes until gear adequate to the task had been developed.

Some acquaintance with the technical aspects of a community television antenna system is essential to a full understanding of the contentions of both parties in this matter. This seems to be the most appropriate point to digress from the narrative to describe the nature of such a system and some of the particular problems which faced Jerrold and other companies which entered this field.

There are four parts to a community television antenna system. The first is the antenna site, referred to in the trade as the "head end." The second is the apparatus which carries the signal from the antenna into the community, known as the "run to town." The third is the "skeleton system " that is constructed through the town to carry the television signals to the extremities of the area to be covered. Finally, there is the "tap-off" from the skeleton system which carries the signal to the home of each subscriber to the service. . . .

The installation of a successful community television antenna system involves more than simply purchasing certain items of equipment and hooking them together. Each system presents different problems giving rise to different equipment needs because of variations in the frequency, quantity and quality of the signals available at the antenna site, the length of the run to town, and the layout of the town itself. Proper planning is necessary to keep equipment costs at a minimum and, at the same time, produce a saleable picture in town. In the first place, the best antenna site must be determined considering the signals present and the distance from town. The run to town must be set up keeping in mind future maintenance problems. Similarly, the most efficient routing of the lines in town must be determined. In this connection, there arises a special problem of negotiating with the utility companies for the use of their poles. This aspect is important, both in terms of costs and acceptability to the community, since there may be an adverse reaction to the erection of additional poles and wires. Then there is the problem of selecting equipment of the proper specifications, including antennas and cable, as well as electronic gear. Finally, it is essential that the equipment be properly spaced along the line so that the input signal is at a proper level.

III. TIE-IN SALES

By the spring of 1951, the Jerrold people felt they were prepared to start selling equipment for community television antenna purposes. As a result of their work in Lansford and Mahanoy City, they had developed a new line of equipment for community antenna systems designated "W" equipment. After consulting with his engineers and several of Jerrold's commission salesmen who dealt with the distributors, Shapp decided that the W equipment should only be sold with engineering services to insure that the system would function properly. A general policy, therefore, was established of selling electronic equipment to community antenna companies only on a full system basis and in conjunction with a service contract which provided for technical services with respect to the layout, installation and operation of the system.

The first of the service contracts employed by Jerrold in executing this policy was designated Form 103. . . . Paragraph 8 . . . provided:

> 8. That in the event Antenna Company desires to receive and distribute the signals of any television stations other than those being received and distributed at the time of the initial installation of the System, Antenna Company agrees to purchase, at the then prevailing prices, whatever additional Jerrold Equipment may be necessary to receive and distribute the desired signals throughout the System, and it is understood that a maximum of three (3) television channels can be so received and distributed in the presently designed System.

Paragraph 12 of the contract provided:

> 12. That Antenna Company agrees that it will not install, as part of the System, any Equipment or attachments which in the opinion of Jerrold will impair the operation of the System or impair the quality of television reception and signal distribution capabilities of the System, or that might cause damage to or impair the efficiency of any of the Equipment comprising the System.

· · · · ·

In October 1953, the Form 103A and 103B service contracts were replaced by the WK–1 Form. . . . The new contract was generally the same as its predecessors. A few changes were made in some of the provisions relevant to the case at bar. The provision contained in paragraph 8 of the earlier contracts was eliminated. Also, the language formerly appearing in paragraph 12 now appeared in paragraph 8 and was revised to read as follows:

> VIII. Since the parties acknowledge that Jerrold cannot reasonably be required to perform its obligations hereunder if the System comprises electronic equipment other than that manufactured by Jerrold Electronics Corporation, Antenna Company agrees that it will not install, as a part of the System any equipment or attachments which, in the opinion of Jerrold, will impair the quality of television reception and signal distribution capabilities of the System, or which might cause damage to, or impair the efficiency of, any of the Equipment comprising the System.

Finally, the duration of the contract was reduced from five to two and one-half years.

On March 16, 1954, Jerrold offered its cusomers two more service contracts designated SP–1 . . . and SP–2. . . . The period of their use overlapped that of the WK–1 contract. The SP–1 contract was designed to accompany the sale of new systems and was of six months' duration. The SP–2 contract was designed to make Jerrold service available to existing systems and was of one year's duration. Each of these contracts contained the following provision, similar to those in the earlier contracts:

> Since we cannot reasonably be required to perform our obligations as enumerated in this letter if the system contains electronic equipment other than that manufactured by Jerrold Electronics Corporation, you agree not to install, as part of the system, any equipment or attachments which, in our opinion, will impair the quality of television reception and signal distribution capabilities of the system, or which might cause damage to, or impair the efficiency of, any of the equipment comprising the System.

The Government contends that Jerrold's policy and practice of selling on a system basis only and of making sales only in conjunction with a service contract constituted unlawful tie-ins in violation of Section 1 of the Sherman Act . . . and Section 3 of the Clayton Act. . . . It also asserts that the provision in the 103 series contracts for the exclusive use of Jerrold equipment for the addition of extra channels to the system, and the provision in all of the contracts not to install unapproved, non-Jerrold equipment, violated these sections of the anti-trust laws.

III-A. Service Contracts

. . . . .

The Government concedes that Section 3 of the Clayton Act does not apply to . . . tie-ins involving services. The government asserts, however, that sales upon the condition that the purchaser subscribe to the services of the vendor constitute an unreasonable restraint of trade in violation of Section 1 of the Sherman Act. The defendants claim that this requirement was reasonable and offered evidence on this point, which was received over the objection of the Government which maintained that the contracts were unreasonable *per se* under the decision in *Northern Pacific Railway Co.* v. *United States*. . . .

It is clear from the amount of service rendered by Jerrold under its compulsory service contracts that a "not insubstantial" amount of interstate commerce was affected, particularly in view of the relatively limited market. . . .

A more difficult question is presented by the second requirement that Jerrold be shown to have sufficient economic power with respect to its equipment to appreciably restrain free competition in the market for the services it rendered. The minimum amount of economic power required is by no means clear. Fortunately, the facts of this case obviate the necessity of ascertaining that standard. In resolving this matter, the first task is to determine the relevant market in which to measure Jerrold's power. Since in this aspect of the case we are only concerned with power which will appreciably restrain competition in the market for the services of installing, maintaining and operating community antenna systems, we are necessarily only interested in power over equipment used in community systems. Jerrold admits that, as to the sale of complete community television antenna systems, it was an undoubted leader up until mid-1954, and more than a majority of the new systems from 1950 to mid-1954 were purchased from it. Indeed, Jerrold consistently advertised throughout this period that at least 75% of the community systems in the United States were "Jerrold systems." Economic power over a product can be inferred from sales leadership. . . . The Supreme Court also stated in the *Northern Pacific* case that the requisite economic power can be inferred from the very existence of the tying clauses where no other explanation for their use is offered. The majority of the court appears to feel that this explanation must include a showing of some benefit conferred upon the purchasers in return for their sacrifice of a free choice of alternatives, but also considered the seller's motive. This is an extremely difficult burden to meet and, in the opinion of this court, it has not been satisfied by the evidence offered by the defendants in the case at bar. Another fact from which economic power can be inferred is the desirability of the tying product to the purchaser. *Northern Pacific Railway Co.* v. *United States, supra* . . . (dissent). Mr. Shapp has stated that Jerrold's highly specialized head end equipment was the only equipment available which was designed to meet all of the varying problems arising at the antenna site. It was thus in great demand by system operators. This placed Jerrold in a strategic position and gave it the leverage necessary to persuade customers to agree to its service contracts. This leverage constitutes "economic power" sufficient to invoke the doctrine of *per se* unreasonableness.

While the trial judge is of the opinion that the Government has established both of the prerequisites necessary for treating Jerrold's policy and practice of selling its community equipment only in conjunction with a service contract as unreasonable, *per se,* under the *Northern Pacific* decision, he does not believe that the inquiry must end there in view of the rather unique circumstances involved in this particular case. Any judicially, as opposed to legislatively, declared *per se* rule is not conclusively binding on this court as to any set of facts not basically the same as those in the cases in which the rule was applied. In laying down such a rule, a court would be, in effect, stating that in all the possible situations it can think of, it is unable to see any redeeming virtue in tying arrangements which would make them reasonable. The Supreme Court of the United States did not purport in the *Northern Pacific* case to anticipate all of the possible circumstances under which a tying arrangement might be used. Therefore, while the *per se* rule should be followed in almost all cases, the court must always be conscious of the fact that a case might arise in which the facts indicate that an injustice would be done by blindly accepting the *per se* rule. In this case, the court felt that the facts asserted by the defendants in their pre-trial statement and trial brief warranted hearing their testimony and argument on the issue of reasonableness. It was partly influenced in this decision by the fact that the history of the industry was brief, and the position of the defendants did not seem to require a prolonged economic investigation—factors which the Supreme Court felt justified the *per se* rule.

When Jerrold was ready to place its W equipment on the market in May 1950, it was confronted with a rather unique situation. In the first place, while it was convinced that its equipment would work, Jerrold recognized that it was sensitive and unstable. Consequently, modifications were still being made. . . . Secondly, as has already been noted, there were hundreds of people anxious to set up community antenna systems. Most of these people had no technical background at all. None of them had any experience with community systems since, at that time, there was only one other operating system in the country besides the Jerrold systems in Lansford and Mahanoy City.[1] In addition, many of these people did not have solid or extensive financing to back their proposed venture. Finally, Jerrold had directed most of its resources towards the development of its community equipment. It was of utmost importance to it that its investment prove successful.

Shapp, his engineers and salesmen, envisioned widespread chaos if Jerrold simply sold its community equipment to anyone who wanted it.

---

[1] This was an experimental system of R.C.A.'s in Pottsville, Pa.

This fear was based on more than mere speculation. . . . The amount of capital necessary to start a system was substantial. Interest would wane rapidly if the systems installed did not consistently produce satisfactory results. Not only Jerrold's reputation but the growth of the entire industry was at stake during the development period. In addition to its reputation, Jerrold was also dependent upon successful system operation for payment. Many operators were not in a position to pay cash for the necessary equipment and the risks were such that outside financing could not be obtained. Therefore, payment was often contingent on the success of the system. It appeared that it was cheaper and more practical to insure that a system was properly installed in the first place than to attempt to get it operating once it was strung up. Furthermore, as has already been noted, use of existing utility poles was an important cost and public relations factor. The utility companies were reluctant to have men of unknown ability working on their poles. Therefore, it was desirable that the system be installed under the supervision of men whose ability was known to the utility companies through other dealings. For these reasons, it was decided that community equipment should be sold with engineering services in order to foster the orderly growth of the industry on which the future of Jerrold depended.

The Government does not dispute the reasonableness of the contracts for services but objects to the fact that they were compulsory. The crucial question, therefore, is whether Jerrold could have accomplished the ends it sought without requiring the contracts. It has been suggested that Jerrold could have accomplished the same results by addressing the persuasive argument it made to this court to its customers and leaving use of the contracts on a voluntary basis. . . . This argument assumes that Jerrold and the industry could survive the "transitory disloyalties" this approach would entail. Jerrold's service was costly and many operators, because of their limited finances, preferred to do-it-themselves and save the expense. . . . If Jerrold's equipment was available without a contract, many impatient operators probably would have attempted to install their systems without assistance. . . . Jerrold's supply of equipment was limited. Unrestricted sales would have resulted in much of this equipment going into systems where prospects of success were at best extremely doubtful. Jerrold's short and long-term well-being depended on the success of these first systems. It could not afford to permit some of its limited equipment to be used in such a way that it would work against its interests. A wave of system failures at the start would have greatly retarded, if not destroyed, this new industry and would have been disastrous for Jerrold, who, unlike others experimenting in this field such as R.C.A. and Philco, did not have a diversified business to fall back on but had put most of its eggs in one precarious basket in an all out effort to open up this new field. . . . For these reasons, this court concludes that Jerrold's policy and practice of selling its community equipment only in conjunction with a service contract was reasonable and not in violation of Section 1 of the Sherman Act at the time of its inception. . . .

The court's conclusion is based primarily on the fact that the tie-in was instituted in the launching of a new business with a highly uncertain future. As the industry took root and grew, the reasons for the blanket insistence on a service contract disappeared. The development of the community antenna industry throughout the country was not uniform. It advanced and became established most rapidly in the East, particularly in Pennsylvania. Progress was slower in the Northwest and Southwest. Thus, when the reasons for this policy ceased to exist in the East, there were still good reasons for its continuance in other areas. Oral reports of successful systems 3,000 miles away are not as convincing as a number of failures nearby. Jerrold recognized this fact and abandoned its policy gradually. In March 1954, it dropped the policy as a general rule and thereafter applied it on an area-by-area and case-by-case basis.[2] Mr. Shapp candidly admits that he can "not make the assertion that in each stage of this evolution our timing has been exactly correct." . . . [W]hile Jerrold has satisfied this court that its policy was reasonable at its inception, it has failed to satisfy us that it remained reasonable throughout the period of its use,[3] even allowing it a reasonable time to recognize and adjust its policies to changing conditions. Accordingly, the court concludes that the defendants' refusal to sell Jerrold equipment except in conjunction with a service contract violated Section 1 of the Sherman Act during part of the time this policy was in effect.

III-B.   Full System Sales

Jerrold also admits that it was its policy and practice from May 1951 to March 1954 not to sell its various items of equipment designed for community antenna systems separately, but only to sell them as components of a complete system. As a result of this program, individual pieces of Jerrold equipment were unavailable for both new systems and existing non-Jerrold systems. The government contends that this too constitutes an unlawful tie-in because Jerrold is driving competitors from the field by

---

[2] The Government contends that Jerrold abandoned this policy because of the threat of Government antitrust action. The court finds to the contrary. It is clear that Jerrold persisted in this policy in some areas of the country after it was aware of the Government's interest in the matter. It would, therefore, seem that the Government's activity was not a motivating factor.

[3] In addition to changes in the condition of the industry, it is also noted that there is some indication in the record that in some areas of the country Jerrold was unable to give the service it felt was necessary to install a successful system. Nevertheless, a contract was required. While this court feels that Jerrold was hopeful that the service would be adequate, it feels that it was unreasonable to make sales on this condition when it could not meet its obligations. The proper course would have been to make sales free of any contract requirement or refuse to make any sales at all, as it had done between January and May 1951.

using its market power with respect to some of its equipment to induce the purchase of other equipment it manufactures.

Since this aspect of Jerrold's activity involves the tying of goods to goods, Section 3 of the Clayton Act, as well as Section 1 of the Sherman Act, is applicable. . . . The court's determination of the relevant market and finding as to Jerrold's position in that market when considering the engineering service contract requirement are equally applicable to this aspect of the case. The record also makes it clear that a not insubstantial amount of commerce was affected.

[Judge Van Deusen then rejected Jerrold's contention that its antenna system was a single product, and hence concluded that its method of selling did constitute a tying arrangement.]

Balancing these considerations only, the defendants' position would seem to be highly questionable. . . . There is a further factor, however, which, in the court's opinion, makes Jerrold's decision to sell only full systems reasonable. There was a sound business reason for Jerrold to adopt this policy. Jerrold's decision was intimately associated with its belief that a service contract was essential. This court has already determined that, in view of the condition of Jerrold, the equipment, and the potential customers, the defendants' policy of insisting on a service contract was reasonable at its inception. Jerrold could not render the service it promised and deemed necessary if the customer could purchase any kind of equipment he desired. The limited knowledge and instability of equipment made specifications an impractical, if not impossible, alternative. Furthermore, Jerrold's policy could not have been carried out if separate items of its equipment were made available to existing systems or any other customer because the demand was so great that this equipment would find its way to a new system.[4] Thus, the court concludes that Jerrold's policy of full system sales was a necessary adjunct to its policy of compulsory service and was reasonably regarded as a product as long as the conditions which dictated the use of the service contract continued to exist.[5] As the circumstances changed and the need for compulsory service contracts disappeared, the economic reasons for exclusively selling complete systems were eliminated. Absent these economic reasons, the court feels that a full system was not an appropriate sales unit. . . .

The defendants also assert a further justification for its policy insofar as it applied to systems using a large quantity of non-Jerrold equipment.

---

[4] There are numerous references in the record to cases where Jerrold's equipment was discovered in non-Jerrold systems; it was procured from system operators as second-hand and excess equipment and from Jerrold distributors in violations of their authority from Jerrold.

[5] Jerrold's argument that it was selling a legitimate single product and that no tying was involved would also apply to the installation aspect of the service contracts, since this covers the assembly of the components into the marketed product.

Jerrold spent considerable time and effort in developing its head end equipment. As a result, its equipment was considered the best available and an asset to any system, since it affected the quality of the initial signal which would be transmitted through the rest of the system. The head end equipment, while intricate, did not represent a large portion of the investment in a system because only a few items were involved. The real profit in a system came from the sale of the amplifiers, since a large number were involved. Jerrold felt that other companies who had not invested time and money into the development of satisfactory head end equipment sought to take advantage of it by competing with it as to the amplifiers, but relying on Jerrold's head end equipment to make the system successful. Shapp resented these other companies "picking our brains" and competing for the real source of profit. Jerrold, therefore, felt justified in recovering its substantial investment in the development of superior head end equipment by using it to preserve for itself a share of the more lucrative market for amplifiers. While the court is sympathetic with Jerrold's predicament, it does not feel that it provides sufficient justification for the use of a tying arrangement. If the demand for Jerrold's equipment was so great, it could recover its investment by raising its prices. Admittedly, the return would not be as great, but it provides sufficient protection to serve as a more reasonable and less restrictive alternative to a tying arrangement.

The court concludes that the defendants' policy of selling full systems only was lawful at its inception but constituted a violation of Section 1 of the Sherman Act and Section 3 of the Clayton Act during part of the time it was in effect.

III-C. The Veto Provisions

In addition to initially selling its equipment only on a full system basis, Jerrold also imposed certain limitations on the equipment that could be added to the system in the future by means of certain provisions in its service contracts. One of these is the provision appearing in all of the contracts to the effect that the operator shall not install any unapproved, non-Jerrold equipment. The Government contends that these clauses prohibit the use of competitive equipment. It is apparent that these clauses do not absolutely require the use of Jerrold equipment. . . . Equipment approved by Jerrold was also permitted. . . .

. . . An examination of the record discloses uncontradicted testimony concerning numerous systems which used non-Jerrold equipment without objection, although this fact was known to the defendants. On the other hand, no instances were brought to the court's attention in which it is clear that an operator considered himself unable to obtain non-Jerrold equipment because of the veto clause. The court finds that these provisions were not intended, and were not used, to prevent the use of competitive equipment in systems covered by a service contract.

The veto provisions were necessary to protect Jerrold in view of its maintenance obligations under the contracts and its financial interest in the success of the systems. Reasonable restraints are permissible for such purposes. *International Salt Co., Inc.* v. *United States, supra.* The restraint imposed by the requirement that Jerrold approve all equipment other than that it manufactured is reasonable in view of the meaning given to this provision as evidenced by Jerrold's conduct with respect to it. It must also be noted that, because of the instability of the equipment and rapid growth of the industry, the use of pre-determined specifications, rather than the more flexible approval approach, would probably have been more restrictive if Jerrold was to be afforded the protection to which it was entitled.

III-D. The Additional Channels Provision

The Government also challenges the provision appearing in the 103 series contracts which requires operators to purchase from Jerrold the equipment necessary to receive any stations in addition to those received at the time of the initial installation. . . . The defendants argue that this provision was justified because "it would be a business folly to try to fit someone else's equipment into the actual spaces provided for additional channels." They also urge that these provisions are consistent with its policy of full system sales.

The court agrees with the Government that these provisions constitute unlawful tie-ins in violation of Section 1 of the Sherman Act and Section 3 of the Clayton Act, regardless of the defendants' actual motives. It can discover no reasons which justify this absolute restriction on the operator's choice of equipment which are not served by the "veto provision." . . .

IV.   CORPORATE ACQUISITIONS

[In a lengthy section of its decision the court found that the effect of a series of acquisitions by Jerrold of CATV systems "is to foreclose competitors . . . from a share of the market in community television antenna system equipment." Additional acquisitions were barred for three years.]

V.   CONSPIRACY AND ATTEMPT TO MONOPOLIZE

.   .   .   .   .

The trial judge finds that Jerrold's policy of selling its equipment exclusively on a full system basis and in conjunction with a service contract, while not shown to be reasonable at all times in which it was in effect, was never intended by the defendants to drive competitors from the business of supplying equipment for community television antenna systems and to achieve a monopoly in this field for Jerrold. Among other things, it must be kept in mind that this policy was evolved and put into effect when

Jerrold first marketed community antenna equipment. At that time, both R.C.A. and Philco were entering the business. Furthermore, the future of this brand new field was quite uncertain. It is highly unlikely that the most ambitious businessman would enter this business from the beginning with a policy intended to force such formidable competitors as these from the field and acquire the power to control prices or foreclose access to this market. . . .

FINAL JUDGMENT

. . . . .

The defendants are enjoined and restrained from, directly or indirectly:

(A) Selling or offering to sell equipment on the condition or understanding that the purchaser thereof purchase services from the defendants;

(B) Furnishing or offering to furnish services on the condition or understanding that the recipient thereof purchase any Jerrold equipment;

(C) Selling or offering to sell any item of Jerrold equipment on the condition or understanding that the purchaser thereof buy or use any other Jerrold equipment;

(D) Selling or offering to sell any equipment on the condition or understanding that the purchaser thereof will not purchase or use equipment manufactured or sold by any other person; provided, however, this subsection (D) shall not prohibit defendants from electing to sell or offer for sale Jerrold equipment upon the condition or understanding that defendants will not guarantee, warrant or, in any manner, be responsible for, the operation or efficiency of such equipment, or the system in which the same may be installed or used, if the purchaser thereof installs, as a part of such system, any equipment or attachments manufactured by any other person which, in defendants' opinion, might either (a) impair the quality of television reception or signal distribution capability of the system, or (b) cause damage to, or impair the operation or efficiency of, any of the Jerrold equipment sold or offered for sale. . . .

10

Exclusive Dealing Arrangements

The problems involved in exclusive dealing cases are several. First and foremost is that of separating those arrangements which improve the workability of competition from those which foreclose competitors from a substantial market. Subsidiary to this is the problem of determining just what constitutes a substantial market. It may safely be said that what the Court attempts to do in these cases is to strike down exclusive arrangements which, resulting from the exercise of appreciable market power, tend to exclude competitors from a substantial market, while sanctioning those exclusive dealing arrangements which were freely entered into by both parties to serve a legitimate economic need.

The *Standard Fashion* case sets forth the Court's view that the qualifying clause of Sections 2 and 3 of the Clayton Act ("where the effect . . . may be to substantially lessen competition or tend to . . . create a monopoly. . .") is satisfied when it is shown that a contract would *probably* lessen competition. In the later *Standard Stations* decision, the Court explicitly refused to consider the possible economic justifications of California Standard's exclusive dealing and full requirements contracts. That the Court did not outlaw all exclusive dealing, however, is shown by the later *Tampa Electric* decision—in which Nashville Coal's long-term contract was upheld as a necessary business arrangement which had not produced demonstrably deleterious effects on competition.

A fuller understanding of these cases will follow from reading them in conjunction with those presented in Chapters 9 and 11.

Standard Fashion Company v. Magrane-Houston Company

258 U.S. 346 (1922)

MR. JUSTICE DAY delivered the opinion of the Court.

. . . . .

Petitioner is a New York corporation engaged in the manufacture and distribution of patterns. Respondent conducted a retail dry goods business . . . in the City of Boston. On November 25, 1914, the parties entered into a contract by which the petitioner granted to the respondent an agency for the sale of Standard patterns at respondent's store, for a term of two years from the date of the contract, and from term to term thereafter until the agreement should be terminated as thereinafter provided. Petitioner agreed to sell to respondent Standard Patterns at a discount of 50 percent from retail prices, with advertising matter and publications upon terms stated. . . . Respondent agreed not to assign or transfer the agency, or to remove it from its original location without the written consent of the petitioner, and not to sell or permit to be sold on its premises during the term of the contract any other make of patterns, and not to sell Standard Patterns except at label prices. . . .

The principal question in the case, and the one upon which the writ of certiorari was granted involves the construction of Section 3 of the Clayton Act. . . .

. . . The real question is: Does the contract of sale come within the third section of the Clayton Act, because the [effect of the] covenant not to sell the patterns of others "may be to substantially lessen competition or tend to create a monopoly."

The Clayton Act, as its title and the history of its enactment disclose, was intended to supplement the purpose and effect of other anti-trust legislation, principally the Sherman Act of 1980. . . .

The Clayton Act sought to reach the agreements embraced within its sphere in their incipiency, and in the section under consideration to determine their legality by specific tests of its own which declared illegal contracts of sale made upon the agreement or understanding that the purchaser shall not deal in the goods of a competitor or competitors of the seller, which may "substantially lessen competition or tend to create a monopoly." . . .

Section 3 condemns sales or agreements where the effect of such sale or contract of sale "may" be to substantially lessen competition or tend to create a monopoly. It thus deals with consequences to follow the making of the restrictive covenant limiting the right of the purchaser to deal in the goods of the seller only. But we do not think that the purpose in using the word "may" was to prohibit the mere possibility of the consequences described. It was intended to prevent such agreements as would under the circumstances disclosed probably lessen competition, or create an actual tendency to monopoly. That it was not intended to reach every remote lessening of competition is shown in the requirement that such lessening must be substantial.

Both courts below found that the contract interpreted in the light of the circumstances surrounding the making of it was within the provisions of the Clayton Act as one which substantially lessened competition and tended to create monopoly. These courts put special stress upon the fact found that, of 52,000 so-called pattern agencies in the entire country, the petitioner, or a holding company controlling it and two other pattern companies, approximately controlled two-fifths of such agencies. As the Circuit Court of Appeals summarizing the matter, pertinently observed:

> The restriction of each merchant to one pattern manufacturer must in hundreds, perhaps in thousands, of small communities amount to giving such single pattern manufacturer a monopoly of the business in such community. Even in the larger cities, to limit to a single pattern maker the pattern business of dealers most resorted to by customers whose purchases tend to give fashions their vogue, may tend to facilitate further combinations; so that the plaintiff, or some other aggressive concern, instead of controlling two-fifths, will shortly have almost, if not quite, all the pattern business.

We agree with these conclusions, and have no doubt that the contract, properly interpreted, with restrictive covenant, brings it fairly within the section of the Clayton Act under consideration.

Affirmed.

Standard Oil Company of California (and Standard Stations, Inc.) v. United States
337 U.S. 293 (1949)
MR. JUSTICE FRANKFURTER delivered the opinion of the Court.

This is an appeal to review a decree enjoining the Standard Oil Company of California and its wholly-owned subsidiary, Standard Stations, Inc., from enforcing or entering into exclusive supply contracts with any independent dealer in petroleum products and automobile accessories. . . . The use of such contracts was successfully assailed by the United States as violative of Section 1 of the Sherman Act and Section 3 of the Clayton Act.

The Standard Oil Company of California . . . owns petroleum-producing resources and refining plants in California and sells petroleum products in what has been termed in these proceedings the "Western area". . . . It sells through its own service stations, to the operators of independent service stations, and to industrial users. It is the largest seller of gasoline in the area. In 1946 its combined sales amounted to 23% of the total taxable gallonage sold there in that year: sales by company-owned service stations constituted 6.8% of the total, sales under exclusive dealing contracts with independent service stations, 6.7% of the total; the remainder were sales to industrial users. Retail service-station sales by Standard's six leading competitors absorbed 42.5% of the total taxable gallonage; the remaining retail sales were divided between more than seventy small companies. It is undisputed that Standard's major competitors employ similar exclusive dealing arrangements. In 1948 only 1.6% of retail outlets were what is known as "split-pump" stations, that is, sold the gasoline of more than one supplier.

Exclusive supply contracts with Standard had been entered into, as of March 12, 1947, by the operators of 5,937 independent stations, or 16% of the retail gasoline outlets in the Western area, which purchased from Standard in 1947, $57,646,233 worth of gasoline and $8,200,089.21 worth of other products. Some outlets are covered by more than one contract so that in all about 8,000 exclusive supply contracts are here in issue. These are of several types, but a feature common to each is the dealer's undertaking to purchase from Standard all his requirements of one or more products. Two types, covering 2,777 outlets, bind the dealer to purchase of Standard all his requirements of gasoline and other petroleum products as well as tires, tubes, and batteries. The remaining written agreements, 4,368 in number, bind the dealer to purchase of Standard all his requirements of petroleum products only. It was also found that independent dealers had entered 742 oral contracts by which they agreed to sell only Standard's gasoline. . . .

Between 1936 and 1946 Standard's sales of gasoline through independent dealers remained at a practically constant proportion of the area's total sales; its sales of lubricating oil declined slightly during that period from 6.2% to 5% of the total. Its proportionate sales of tires and batteries for 1946 were slightly higher than they were in 1936, though somewhat lower than for some intervening years; they have never, as to either of these products, exceeded 2% of the total sales in the Western area.

Since Section 3 of the Clayton Act was directed to prohibiting specific practices even though not covered by the broad terms of the Sherman Act, it is appropriate to consider first whether the enjoined contracts fall within the prohibition of the narrower Act. . . .

The District Court held that the requirement of showing an actual or potential lessening of competition or a tendency to establish monopoly was adequately met by proof that the contracts covered "a substantial number of outlets and a substantial amount of products, whether considered comparatively or not." . . . Given such quantitative substantiality, the substantial lessening of competition—so the court reasoned—is an automatic result, for the very existence of such contracts denies dealers opportunity to deal in the products of competing suppliers and excludes supplies from access to the outlets controlled by those dealers. . . .

The issue before us, therefore, is whether the requirement of showing that the effect of the agreements "may be to substantially lessen competition" may be met simply by proof that a substantial portion of commerce is affected or whether it must also be demonstrated that competitive activity has actually diminished or probably will diminish. . . .

It is . . . apparent that none of these [earlier] cases[1] controls the disposition of the present appeal, for Standard's share of the retail market for gasoline, even including sales through company-owned stations, is hardly large enough to conclude as a matter of law that it occupies a dominant position, nor did the trial court so find. The cases do indicate, however, that some sort of showing as to the actual or probable economic consequences of the agreements, if only the inferences to be drawn from the fact of dominant power, is important, and to that extent they tend to support appellant's position.

Two of the three cases decided by this Court which have held Section 3 inapplicable also lend support to the view that such a showing is necessary. These are, *Federal Trade Comm'n* v. *Sinclair Co.,* 261 U.S. 463, and *Pick Mfg. Co.* v. *General Motors Corp.,* 299 U.S. 3. The third . . . is of no present relevance. . . .

But then came *International Salt Co.* v. *United States,* 332 U.S. 392. That decision, at least as to contracts tying the sale of a nonpatented to a patented product, rejected the necessity of demonstrating economic consequences once it has been established that "the volume of business affected" is not "insignificant or insubstantial" and that the effect of the contracts is to "foreclose competitors from [a] substantial market." . . . Upon that basis we affirmed a summary judgment granting an injunction against the leasing of machines for the utilization of salt products on the condition that the lessee use in them only salt supplied by defendant. . . . It is clear, therefore, that unless a distinction is to be drawn for purposes of the applicability of Section 3 between requirements contracts and contracts tying the sale of a nonpatented to a patented product, the showing that Standard's requirements contracts affected a gross business of $58,000,000 comprising 6.7% of the total in the area goes far toward supporting the inference that competition has been or probably will be substantially lessened.

In favor of confining the standard laid down by the *International Salt* case to tying agreements, important economic differences may be noted.

---

[1] The Court had summarized its opinions in the five earlier cases in which it had found violations of Section 3. These were: *United Shoe Machinery Corp.* v. *United States,* 258 U.S. 451; *International Business Machines Corp.* v. *United States,* 298 U.S. 131; *International Salt Company* v. *United States,* 332 U.S. 392; *Standard Fashion Co.* v. *Magrane-Houston Co.,* 258 U.S. 364; and *Fashion Originators' Guild* v. *Federal Trade Commission,* 312 U.S. 457. IMS.

Tying agreements serve hardly any purpose beyond the suppression of competition. The justification most often advanced in their defense—the protection of the good will of the manufacturer of the tying device—fails in the usual situation because specification of the type and quality of the product to be used in connection with the tying device is protection enough. If the manufacturer's brand of the tied product is in fact superior to that of competitors, the buyer will presumably choose it anyway. The only situation, indeed, in which the protection of good will may necessitate the use of tying clauses is where specifications for a substitute would be so detailed that they could not practicably be supplied. In the usual case only the prospect of reducing competition would persuade a seller to adopt such a contract and only his control of the supply of the tying device, whether conferred by patent monopoly or otherwise obtained, could induce a buyer to enter one. . . . The existence of market control of the tying device, therefore, affords a strong foundation for the presumption that it has been or probably will be used to limit competition in the tied product also.

Requirements contracts, on the other hand, may well be of economic advantage to buyers as well as to sellers, and thus indirectly of advantage to the consuming public. In the case of the buyer, they may assure supply, afford protection against rises in price, enable long-term planning on the basis of known costs, and obviate the expense and risk of storage in the quantity necessary for a commodity having a fluctuating demand. From the seller's point of view, requirements contracts may make possible the substantial reduction of selling expenses, give protection against price fluctuations, and—of particular advantage to a newcomer to the field to whom it is important to know what capital expenditures are justified— offer the possibility of a predictable market. . . . They may be useful, moreover, to a seller trying to establish a foothold against the counterattacks of entrenched competitors. . . . Since these advantages of requirements contracts may often be sufficient to account for their use, the coverage by such contracts of a substantial amount of business affords a weaker basis for the inference that competition may be lessened than would similar coverage by tying clauses, especially where use of the latter is combined with market control of the tying device. A patent, moreover, although in fact there may be many competing substitutes for the patented article, is at least *prima facie* evidence of such control. And so we could not dispose of this case merely by citing *International Salt Co.* v. *United States*. . . .

Thus, even though the qualifying clause of Section 3 is appended without distinction of terms equally to the prohibition of tying clauses and of requirements contracts, pertinent considerations support, certainly as a matter of economic reasoning, varying standards as to each for the proof necessary to fulfill the conditions of that clause. If this distinction were accepted, various tests of the economic usefulness or restrictive effect of requirements contracts would become relevant. Among them would be evidence that competition has flourished despite use of the contracts, and under this test much of the evidence tendered by appellant in this case would be important. . . . Likewise bearing on whether or not the contracts were being used to suppress competition, would be the conformity of the length of their term to the reasonable requirements of the field of commerce in which they were used. . . . Still another test would be the status of the defendant as a struggling newcomer or an established competitor. Perhaps most important, however, would be the defendant's degree of market control, for the greater the dominance of his position, the stronger the inference that an important factor in attaining and maintaining that position had been the use of requirements contracts to stifle competition rather than to serve legitimate economic needs. . . .

Yet serious difficulties would attend the attempt to apply these tests. We may assume, as did the court below, that no improvement of Standard's competitive position has coincided with the period during which the requirements-contract system of distribution has been in effect. We may assume further that the duration of the contracts is not excessive and that Standard does not by itself dominate the market. But Standard was a major competitor when the present system was adopted, and it is possible that its position would have deteriorated but for the adoption of that system. When it is remembered that all the other major suppliers have also been using requirements contracts, and when it is noted that the relative share of the business which fell to each has remained about the same during the period of their use, it would not be farfetched to infer that their effect has been to enable the established suppliers individually to maintain their own standing and at the same time collectively, even though not collusively, to prevent a late arrival from wresting away more than an insignificant portion of the market. If, indeed, this were a result of the system, it would seem unimportant that a short-run by-product of stability may have been greater efficiency and lower costs, for it is the theory of the antitrust laws that the long-run advantage of the community depends upon the removal of restraints upon competition. . . .

Moreover, to demand that bare inference be supported by evidence as to what would have happened but for the adoption of the practice that was in fact adopted or to require firm prediction of an increase of competition as a probable result of ordering the abandonment of the practice, would be a standard of proof, if not virtually impossible to meet, at least most ill-suited for ascertainment by courts. . . .

. . . Though it may be that such an alternative to the present system as buying out independent dealers and making them dependent employees of Standard Stations, Inc., would be a greater detriment to the public interest than perpetuation of the system, this is an issue, like the choice between greater efficiency and freer competition, that has not been submitted to our decision. We are faced, not with a broadly phrased expression of general policy, but merely a broadly phrased qualification of an otherwise narrowly directed statutory provision. . . .

We conclude, therefore, that the qualifying clause of Section 3 is satisfied by proof that competition has been foreclosed in a substantial share of the line of commerce affected. It cannot be gainsaid that observance by a dealer of his requirements contract with Standard does effectively foreclose whatever opportunity there might be for competing suppliers to attract his patronage, and it is clear that the affected proportion of retail sales of petroleum products is substantial. In view of the widespread adoption of such contracts by Standard's competitors and the availability of alternative ways of obtaining an assured market, evidence that competitive activity has not actually declined is inconclusive. Standard's use of the contracts creates just such a potential clog on competition as it was the purpose of Section 3 to remove wherever, were it to become actual, it would impede a substantial amount of competitive activity.

Since the decree below is sustained by our interpretation of Section 3 of the Clayton Act, we need not go on to consider whether it might also be sustained by Section 1 of the Sherman Act. . . .

The judgment below is Affirmed.

[MR. JUSTICE JACKSON, with whom THE CHIEF JUSTICE and MR. JUSTICE BURTON joined, dissented. MR. JUSTICE DOUGLAS separately dissented.]

Tampa Electric Co. v. Nashville Coal Co.

365 U.S. 320 (1961)

MR. JUSTICE CLARK delivered the opinion of the Court.

We granted certiorari to review a declaratory judgment holding illegal under Section 3 of the Clayton Act a requirements contract between the parties providing for the purchase by petitioner of all the coal it would require as boiler fuel at its Gannon Station in Tampa, Florida, over a 20-year period. . . . Both the District Court . . . and the Court of Appeals, . . . Judge Weick dissenting, agreed with respondents that the contract fell within the proscription of Section 3 and therefore was illegal and unenforceable. We cannot agree that the contract suffers the claimed antitrust illegality[1] and, therefore, do not find it necessary to consider respondents' additional argument that such illegality is a defense to the action and a bar to enforceability.

---

[1] In addition to their claim under Section 3 of the Clayton Act, respondents argue the contract is illegal under the Sherman Act, 15 U.S.C. Sections 1-2.

THE FACTS

Petitioner Tampa Electric Company is a public utility located in Tampa, Florida. It produces and sells electric energy to a service area, including the city, extending from Tampa Bay eastward 60 miles to the center of the State, and some 30 miles in width. As of 1954 petitioner operated two electrical generating plants comprising a total of 11 individual generating units, all of which consumed oil in their burners. In 1955 Tampa Electric decided to expand its facilities by the construction of an additional generating plant to be comprised ultimately of six generating units, and to be known as the "Francis J. Gannon Station." Although every electrical generating plant in peninsular Florida burned oil at that time, Tampa Electric decided to try coal as boiler fuel in the first two units constructed at the Gannon Station. Accordingly, it contracted with the respondents[2] to furnish the expected coal requirements for the units. The agreement, dated May 23, 1955, embraced Tampa Electric's "total requirements of fuel . . . for the operation of its first two units to be installed at the Gannon Station . . . not less than 225,000 tons of coal per unit per year," for a period of 20 years. The contract further provided that "if during the first 10 years of the term . . . the Buyer constructs additional units [at Gannon] in which coal is used as the fuel, it shall give the Seller notice thereof two years prior to the completion of such unit or units and upon completion of same the fuel requirements thereof shall be added to this contract." It was understood and agreed, however, that "the Buyer has the option to be exercised two years prior to completion of said unit or units of determining whether coal or some other fuel shall be used in same." Tampa Electric had the further option of reducing, up to 15%, the amount of its coal purchases covered by the contract after giving six months' notice of an intention to use as fuel a by-product of any of its local customers. The minimum price was set at $6.40 per ton delivered, subject to an escalation clause based on labor cost and other factors. Deliveries were originally expected to begin in March 1957, for the first unit, and for the second unit at the completion of its construction.

In April 1957, soon before the first coal was actually to be delivered and after Tampa Electric, in order to equip its first two Gannon units for the use of coal, had expended some $3,000,000 more than the cost of constructing oil-burning units, and after respondents had expended approximately $7,500,000 readying themselves to perform the contract, the latter advised petitioner that the contract was illegal under the antitrust laws, would therefore not be performed, and no coal would be delivered. This turn of events required Tampa Electric to look elsewhere for its coal

---

[2] The original contract was with Potter Towing Company, and by subsequent agreements with Tampa Electric responsibility thereunder was assumed by respondent West Kentucky Coal Company.

requirements. The first unit at Gannon began operating August 1, 1957, using coal purchased on a temporary basis, but on December 23, 1957, a purchase order contract for the total coal requirements of the Gannon Station was made with Love and Amos Coal Company. It was for an indefinite period cancellable on 12 months' notice by either party, or immediately upon tender of performance by respondents under the contract sued upon here. The maximum price was $8.80 per ton, depending upon the freight rate. In its purchase order to the Love and Amos Company, Tampa estimated that its requirements at the Gannon Station would be 350,000 tons in 1958; 700,000 tons in 1959 and 1960; 1,000,000 tons in 1961; and would increase thereafter, as required, to "about 2,250,000 tons per year." The second unit at Gannon Station commenced operation 14 months after the first, *i.e.,* October 1958. Construction of a third unit, the coal for which was to have been provided under the original contract, was also begun.

The record indicates that the total consumption of coal in peninsular Florida, as of 1958, aside from Gannon Station, was approximately 700,000 tons annually. It further shows that there were some 700 coal suppliers in the producing area where respondents operated, and that Tampa Electric's anticipated maximum requirements at Gannon Station, *i.e.,* 2,250,000 tons annually, would approximate 1% of the total coal of the same type produced and marketed from respondents' producing area.

Petitioner brought this suit in the District Court pursuant to 28 U.S.C. Section 2201, for a declaration that its contract with respondents was valid, and for enforcement according to its terms. In addition to its Clayton Act defense, respondents contended that the contract violated both Sections 1 and 2 of the Sherman Act which, it claimed, likewise precluded its enforcement. The District Court, however, granted respondents' motion for summary judgment on the sole ground that the undisputed facts, recited above showed the contract to be a violation of Section 3 of the Clayton Act. The Court of Appeals agreed. Neither court found it necessary to consider the applicability of the Sherman Act.

DECISIONS OF DISTRICT COURT
AND COURT OF APPEALS

Both courts admitted that the contract "does not expressly contain the 'condition'" that Tampa Electric would not use or deal in the coal of respondents' competitors. Nonetheless, they reasoned, the "total requirements" provision had the same practical effect, for it prevented Tampa Electric for a period of 20 years from buying coal from any other source for use at that station. Each court cast aside as "irrelevant" arguments citing the use of oil as boiler fuel by Tampa Electric as its other stations, and by other utilities in peninsular Florida, because oil was not in fact used at Gannon Station, and the possibility of exercise by Tampa Electric of the option reserved to it to build oil-burning units at Gannon was too remote. Found to be equally remote was the possibility of Tampa's conversion of existing oil-burning units at its other stations to the use of coal which would not be covered by the contract with respondents. It followed, both courts found, that the "line of commerce" on which the restraint was to be tested was coal—not boiler fuels. Both courts compared the estimated coal tonnage as to which the contract pre-empted competition for 20 years, namely 1,000,000 tons a year in 1961, with the previous annual consumption of peninsular Florida, 700,000 tons. Emphasizing that fact as well as the contract value of the coal covered by the 20-year term, *i.e.*, $128,000,000, they held that such volume was not "insignificant or insubstantial" and that the effect of the contract would "be to substantially lessen competition," in violation of the Act. Both courts were of the opinion that in view of the executory nature of the contract, judicial enforcement of any portion of it could not be granted without directing a violation of the Act itself, and enforcement was, therefore, denied.

APPLICATION OF SECTION 3 OF THE CLAYTON ACT

In the almost half century since Congress adopted the Clayton Act, this Court has been called upon 10 times, including the present, to pass upon questions arising under Section 3.[3] . . .

In practical application, even though a contract is found to be an exclusive dealing arrangement, it does not violate the section unless the court believes it probable that performance of the contract will foreclose competition in a substantial share of the line of commerce affected. Following the guidelines of earlier decisions, certain considerations must be taken. *First*, the line of commerce, i.e., the type of goods, wares, or merchandise, etc., involved must be determined, where it is in controversy, on the basis of the facts peculiar to the case. *Second*, the area of effective competition in the known line of commerce must be charted by careful selection of the market area in which the seller operates, and to which the purchaser can practicably turn for supplies. In short, the threatened foreclosure of competition must be in relation to the market affected. . . .

Third, and last, the competition foreclosed by the contract must be found to constitute a substantial share of the relevant market. That is to say, the opportunities for other traders to enter into or remain in that market must be significantly limited. . . .

To determine substantiality in a given case, it is necessary to weight the probable effect of the contract on the relevant area of effective competition, taking into account the relative strength of the parties, the proportionate volume of commerce involved in relation to the total volume of

---

[3] A detailed discussion of the *Standard Fashion, United Shoe, International Salt* and *Standard Oil of California* cases followed. IMS.

commerce in the relevant market area, and the probable immediate and future effects which pre-emption of that share of the market might have on effective competition therein. It follows that a mere showing that the contract itself involves a substantial number of dollars is ordinarily of little consequence.

THE APPLICATION OF SECTION 3 HERE

In applying these considerations to the facts of the case before us, it appears clear that both the Court of Appeals and the District Court have not given the required effect to a controlling factor in the case—the relevant competitive market area. This omission, by itself, requires reversal, for, as we have pointed out, the relevant market is the prime factor in relation to which the ultimate question, whether the contract forecloses competition in a substantial share of the line of commerce involved, must be decided. For the purposes of this case, therefore, we need not decide two threshold questions passed by Tampa Electric. They are whether the contract in fact satisfies the initial requirement of Section 3, *i.e.*, whether it is truly an exclusive-dealing one, and, secondly, whether the line of commerce is boiler fuels, including coal, oil and gas, rather than coal alone.[4] We, therefore, for the purposes of this case, assume, but do not decide, that the contract is an exclusive-dealing arrangement within the compass of Section 3, and that the line of commerce is bituminous coal.

RELEVANT MARKET OF EFFECTIVE COMPETITION

Neither the Court of Appeals nor the District Court considered in detail the question of the relevant market. They do seem, however, to have been satisfied with inquiring only as to competition within "Peninsular Florida." It was noted that the total consumption of peninsular Florida was 700,000 tons of coal per year, about equal to the estimated 1959 requirements of Tampa Electric. It was also pointed out that coal accounted for less than 6% of the fuel consumed in the entire State.[5] The District Court concluded that though the respondents were only one of 700 coal producers who could serve the same market, peninsular Florida, the contract for a period of 20 years excluded competitors from a substantial amount of trade. Respondents contend that the coal tonnage covered by the contract must be weighed against either the total consumption of coal in peninsular Florida, or all of Florida, or the Bituminous

---

[4] In support of these contentions petitioner urges us to consider that it remains free to convert existing oil-burning units at its other plants to coal-burning units, the fuel for which it would be free to purchase from any seller in the market; also that just as it is permitted to use oil at its other plants, so, too it may construct all future Gannon units as oil burners; and that in any event it is free to draw a maximum of 15% of its Gannon fuel requirements from by-products of local customers. Petitioner further argues that its novel reliance upon coal in fact created new fuel competition in an area that theretofore relied almost exclusively upon oil and, to a lesser extent, upon natural gas.

[5] Oil and, to a lesser extent, natural gas are the primary fuels consumed in Florida.

Coal Act area comprising peninsular Florida and the Georgia "finger," or, at most, all of Florida and Georgia. If the latter area were considered the relevant market, Tampa Electric's proposed requirements would be 18% of the tonnage sold therein. Tampa Electric says that both courts and respondents are in error, because the "700 coal producers who could serve" it, as recognized by the trial court and admitted by respondents, operated in the Appalachian coal area and that its contract requirements were less than 1% of the total marketed production of these producers; that the relevant effective area of competition was the area in which these producers operated, and in which they were willing to compete for the consumer potential.

We are persuaded that on the record in this case, neither peninsular Florida, nor the entire State of Florida, nor Florida and Georgia combined constituted the relevant market of effective competition. We do not believe that the pie will slice so thinly. By far the bulk of the overwhelming tonnage marketed from the same producing area as serves Tampa is sold outside of Georgia and Florida, and the producers were "eager" to sell more coal in those States.[6] While the relevant competitive market is not ordinarily susceptible to a "metes and bounds" definition, cf. *Times-Picayune Pub. Co.* v. *United States,* 345 U.S. 594, 611, it is of course the area in which respondents and the other 700 producers effectively compete. . . . The record shows that, like the respondents, they sold bituminous coal "suitable for [Tampa's] requirements," mined in parts of Pennsylvania, Virginia, West Virginia, Kentucky, Tennessee, Alabama, Ohio and Illinois. We take notice of the fact that the approximate total bituminous coal (and lignite) product in the year 1954 from the districts in which these 700 producers are located was 359,289,000 tons, of which some 290,567,000 tons were sold on the open market. Of the latter amount some 78,716,000 tons were sold to electric utilities. We also note that in 1954 Florida and Georgia combined consumed at least 2,304,000 tons, 1,100,000 of which were used by electric utilities, and the sources of which were mines located in no less than seven States. We take further notice that the production and marketing of bituminous coal (and lignite) from the same districts, and assumedly equally available to Tampa on a commercially feasible basis, is currently on a par with prior years. In point of statistical fact, coal consumption in the combined Florida-Georgia area has increased significanlty since 1954. In 1959 more than 3,775,000 tons were there consumed, 2,913,000 being used by electric utilities including, presumably, the coal used by the petitioner. The coal continued to come from at least seven States. From these statistics it clearly appears that the proportionate volume of the total relevant coal

---

[6] Peabody Coal Company offered to supply petitioner with coal from its mines in western Kentucky, for use in the units at another of its Florida stations, and that offer prompted a renegotiation of the price petitioner was paying for the oil then being consumed at that station.

product as to which the challenged contract pre-empted competition, less than 1%, is, conservatively speaking, quite insubstantial. A more accurate figure, even assuming pre-emption to the extent of the maximum anticipated total requirements, 2,250,000 tons a year, would be .77%.

EFFECT ON COMPETITION IN
THE RELEVANT MARKET

It may well be that in the context of antitrust legislation protracted requirements contracts are suspect, but they have not been declared illegal *per se*. Even though a single contract between single traders may fall within the initial broad proscription of the section, it must also suffer the qualifying disability, tendency to work a substantial—not remote—lessening of competition in the relevant competitive market. It is urged that the present contract pre-empts competition to the extent of purchases worth perhaps $128,000,000 and that this "is, of course, not insignificant or insubstantial." While $128,000,000 is a considerable sum of money, even in these days, the dollar volume, by itself, is not the test, as we have already pointed out.

The remaining determination, therefore, is whether the pre-emption of competition to the extent of the tonnage involved tends to substantially foreclose competition in the relevant coal market. We think not. That market sees an annual trade in excess of 250,000,000 tons of coal and over a billion dollars—multiplied by 20 years it runs into astronomical figures. There is here neither a seller with a dominant position in the market as in *Standard Fashions, supra;* nor myriad outlets with substantial sales volume, coupled with an industry-wide practice of relying upon exclusive contracts, as in *Standard Oil, supra;* nor a plainly restrictive tying arrangement as in *International Salt, supra.* On the contrary, we seem to have only that type of contract which "may well be of economic advantage to buyers as well as to sellers." *Standard Oil Co.* v. *United States, supra.* . . . In the case of the buyer it "may assure supply," while on the part of the seller it "may make possible the substantial reduction of selling expenses, give protection against price fluctuations, and . . . offer the possibility of a predictable market." *Id.* . . . The 20-year period of the contract is singled out as the principal vice, but at least in the case of public utilities the assurance of a steady and ample supply of fuel is necessary in the public interest. Otherwise consumers are left unprotected against service failures owing to shutdowns; and increasingly unjustified costs might result in more burdensome rate structures eventually to be reflected in the consumer's bill. The compelling validity of such considerations has been recognized fully in the natural gas public utility field. This is not to say that utilities are immunized from Clayton Act proscriptions, but merely that, in judging the term of a requirements contract in relation to the substantiality of the foreclosure of competition, particularized considerations of the parties' operations are not irrelevant.

In weighing the various factors, we have decided that in the competitive bituminous coal marketing area involved here the contract sued upon does not tend to foreclose a substantial volume of competition.

We need not discuss the respondents' further contention that the contract also violates Section 1 and Section 2 of the Sherman Act, for if it does not fall within the broader proscription of Section 3 of the Clayton Act it follows that it is not forbidden by those of the former. *Times-Picayune Pub.* Co. v. *United States.* . . .

The judgment is reversed and the case remanded to the District Court for further proceedings not inconsistent with this opinion.

It is so ordered.

MR. JUSTICE BLACK and MR. JUSTICE DOUGLAS are of the opinion that the District Court and the Court of Appeals correctly decided this case and would therefore affirm their judgments.

11

Other Vertical Restrictions

As the chapter's title implies, the cases included herein have involved practices whose effects cannot neatly be categorized. In the *General Motors, Schwinn, Topco,* and *GTE Sylvania* cases, the courts have sought to define the limits which suppliers can impose upon their customers. Until recently (per *Schwinn*), once title to the product passed from the hands of the seller to the buyer, the courts took a very dim view of the imposition of restrictions on the buyer's freedom to dispose of the product as he saw fit. However, in *GTE Sylvania,* the Supreme Court explicitly rejected this position, holding instead that, absent pricing restrictions, vertical restrictions henceforth will be subject to a rule-of-reason analysis, with its attendant evaluation of relative costs and benefits.

The *Chicken Delight* case typifies the continuing controversy surrounding the practice of franchising. Again, the courts appear to be seeking a means by which to strike a balance between the right of the franchisor to protect the economic integrity of his franchise, and the freedom of the franchisee to operate in his own best interests.

United States v. *General Motors Corporation*

384 U.S. 127 (1966)

MR. JUSTICE FORTAS delivered the opinion of the Court.

This is a civil action brought by the United States to enjoin the appellees from participating in an alleged conspiracy to restrain trade in violation of §1 of the Sherman Act. The United States District Court for the Southern District of California concluded that the proof failed to establish the alleged violation, and entered judgment for the defendants. . . . We reverse.

I

The appellees are the General Motors Corporation, which manufactures, among other things, the Chevrolet line of cars and trucks, and three associations of Chevrolet dealers in and around Los Angeles, California. All of the Chevrolet dealers in the area belong to one or more of the appellee associations.

Chevrolets are ordinarily distributed by dealers operating under a franchise from General Motors. The dealers purchase the cars from the manufacturer, and then retail them to the public. The relationship between manufacturer and dealer is incorporated in a comprehensive uniform Dealer Selling Agreement. This agreement does not restrict or define those to whom the dealer may sell. Nor are there limitations as to the territory within which the dealer may sell. Compare *White Motor Co.* v. *United States,* 372 U.S. 253. The franchise agreement does, however, contain a clause (hereinafter referred to as the "location clause") which prohibits a dealer from moving to or establishing "a new or different location, branch sales office, branch service station, or place of business including any used car lot or location without the prior written approval of Chevrolet."

Beginning in the late 1950s, "discount houses" engaged in retailing consumer goods in the Los Angeles area and "referral services" began offering to sell new cars to the public at allegedly bargain prices. Their sources of supply were the franchised dealers. By 1960 a number of individual Chevrolet dealers, without authorization from General Motors, had developed working relationships with these establishments. A customer would enter one of these establishments and examine the literature and price lists for automobiles produced by several manufacturers. In some instances, floor models were available for inspection. Some of the establishments negotiated with the customer for a trade-in of his old car, and provided financing for his new-car purchase.

The relationship with the franchised dealer took various forms. One arrangement was for the discounter to refer the customer to the dealer. The car would then be offered to him by the dealer at a price previously agreed upon between the dealer and the discounter. In 1960, a typical referral agreement concerning Chevrolets provided that the price to the customer was not to exceed $250 over the dealer's invoiced cost. For its part in supplying the customer, the discounter received $50 per sale.

Another common arrangement was for the discounter itself to negotiate the sale, the dealer's role being to furnish the car and to transfer title to the customer at the direction of the discounter. One dealer furnished Chevrolets under such an arrangement, charging the discounter $85 over its invoiced cost, with the discounter getting the best price it could from its customer.

These were the principal forms of trading involved in this case, although within each there were variations, and there were schemes which fit neither pattern.[1] By 1960 these methods for retailing new cars had reached considerable dimensions. Of the 100,000 new Chevrolets sold in the Los Angeles area in that year, some 2,000 represented discount house or referral sales. One Chevrolet dealer attributed as much as 25% of its annual sales to participation in these arrangements, while another accounted for between 400 and 525 referral sales in a single year.

Approximately a dozen of the 85 Chevrolet dealers in the Los Angeles area were furnishing cars to discounters in 1960. As the volume of these sales grew, the nonparticipating Chevrolet dealers located near one or more of the discount outlets began to feel the pinch. Dealers lost sales because potential customers received, or thought they would receive,[2] a more attractive deal from a discounter who obtained his Chevrolets from a distant dealer. The discounters vigorously advertised Chevrolets for sale, with alluring statements as to price savings. The discounters also advertised that all Chevrolet dealers were obligated to honor the new-car warranty and to provide the free services contemplated therein; and General Motors does indeed require Chevrolet dealers to service Chevrolet cars, wherever purchased, pursuant to the new-car warranty and service agreement. Accordingly, nonparticipating dealers were increasingly called upon to service, without compensation, Chevrolets purchased through discounters. Perhaps what grated most was the demand that they "precondition" cars so purchased—make the hopefully minor adjustments and do the body and paint work necessary to render a factory-fresh car both customer- and road-worthy.

On June 28, 1960, at a regular meeting of the appellee Losor Chevrolet Dealers Association, member dealers discussed the problem and resolved to bring it to the attention of the Chevrolet Division's Los Angeles zone manager, Robert O'Connor. . . . O'Connor promised he would speak to the offending dealers. When no help was forthcoming . . . [t]he member

---

[1] At least one discount house actually purchased its cars from cooperative dealers, then resold them to its customers. In this situation, which in the trade is referred to as "bootlegging," the customer does not receive a new-car warranty. General Motors, while disapproving of the practice, does not assert that it violates the "location clause." In those arrangements against which General Motors and the associations did direct their efforts, title to the new car passed directly from dealer to retail customer, who thus obtained a new-car warranty and service agreement.

There must also be distinguished the ubiquitous practice of using "bird dogs"—informal sources who steer occasional customers toward a particular dealer, in return for relatively small fees—often a bottle of liquor. This practice is not only deemed by General Motors not to violate the "location clause," but has the corporation's endorsement as a desirable sales device.

[2] There is evidence in the record that discount sales undercut the prices at which franchised dealers were able to, or chose to compete. . . . Moreover, the discounters advertised and actually provided auto loans at interest rates substantially lower than those offered by G.M.A.C., General Motors' financing subsidiary. . . .

dealers . . . agreed . . . to flood General Motors and the Chevrolet Division with letters and telegrams asking for help. Salesmen, too, were to write.

Hundreds of letters and wires descended upon Detroit—with telling effect. Within a week Chevrolet's O'Connor was directed to furnish his superiors in Detroit with "a detailed report of the discount house operations . . . as well as what action we in the Zone are taking to curb such sales."

By mid-December General Motors had formulated its response. . . .

General Motors personnel proceeded to telephone all area dealers, both to identify those associated with the discounters and to advise non-participants that General Motors had entered the lists. The principal offenders were treated to unprecendented individual confrontations with [Roy] Cash, the regional manager [of the Chevrolet Division]. These brief meetings were wholly successful in obtaining from each dealer his agreement to abandon the practices in question. Some capitulated during the course of the four- or five-minute meeting, or immediately thereafter. One dealer, who met not with Cash but with the city sales manager for Chevrolet, put off decision for a week "to make sure that the other dealers, or most of them, had stopped their business dealings with the discount houses."[3]

There is evidence that unanimity was not obtained without reference to the ultimate power of General Motors. . . .

By mid-January General Motors had elicited from each dealer a promise not to do business with the discounters. But such agreements would require policing—a fact which had been anticipated. General Motors earlier had initiated contacts with firms capable of performing such a function. This plan, unilaterally to police the agreements, was displaced, however, in favor of a joint effort between General Motors, the three appellee associations, and a number of individual dealers.

. . . Early in 1961, the three associations agreed jointly to finance the "shopping" of the discounters to assure that no Chevrolet dealer continued to supply them with cars. Each of the associations contributed $5,000, and a professional investigator was hired. He was instructed to try to

---

[3] According to Francis Bruder, a dealer who had been doing business with the discounters since 1957, "Cash told me that he felt certain that the other dealers would discontinue dealing with discount houses and referral services as well. I left this meeting with the impression that every dealer who had been doing business with a discount house or referral service would soon quit."

This was precisely the impression General Motors had intended to implant. As was explained in an inter-office memorandum to the general sales manager of General Motors' Chevrolet Division, "[All dealers were talked to] in order that every dealer with whom the subject was discussed would know that a similar discussion was being held with all other dealers so that, if certain dealers should elect to discontinue their cooperation with a discount house, we might be able to discourage some other dealer who might be solicited from starting the practice."

purchase new Chevrolets from the proscribed outlets, to tape-record the transactions, if any, and to gather all the necessary documentary evidence—which the associations would then lay "at the doorstep of Chevrolet." These joint associational activities were both preceded and supplemented by similar "shopping" activities by individual dealers and by appellee Losor Chevrolet Dealers Association.

General Motors collaborated with these policing activities. There is evidence that zone manager O'Connor and a subordinate, Jere Faust, actively solicited the help of individual dealers in uncovering violations. . . .

By the spring of 1961, the campaign to eliminate the discounters from commerce in new Chevrolet cars was a success. Sales through the discount outlets seem to have come to a halt. Not until a federal grand jury commenced an inquiry into the matters which we have sketched does it appear that any Chevrolet dealer resumed its business association with the discounters.

II

On these basic facts, the Government first proceeded criminally. A federal grand jury in the Southern District of California returned an indictment. After trial, the defendants were found not guilty. The present civil action, filed shortly after return of the indictment, was then brought to trial.

Both the government and the appellees urge the importance, for purposes of decision, of the "location clause" in the Dealer Selling Agreement which prohibits a franchised dealer from moving to or establishing "a new or different location, branch sales office, branch service station, or place of business . . . without the prior written approval of Chevrolet." . . .

We need not reach . . . questions concerning the meaning, effect, or validity of the "location clause" or of any other provision in the Dealer Selling Agreement, and we do not. We do not decide whether the "location clause" may be construed to prohibit a dealer, party to it, from selling through discounters, or whether General Motors could by unilateral action enforce the clause, so construed. We have here a classic conspiracy in restraint of trade: joint, collaborative action by dealers, the appellee associations, and General Motors to eliminate a class of competitors by terminating business dealings between them and a minority of Chevrolet dealers and to deprive franchised dealers of their freedom to deal through discounters if they so choose. Against this fact of unlawful combination, the "location clause" is of no avail. . . .

The District Court decided otherwise. It concluded that the described events did not add up to a combination or conspiracy violative of the antitrust laws. . . .

The trial court attempted to justify its conclusion on the following reasoning: That each defendant and alleged co-conspirator acted to promote its own self-interest; that General Motors, as well as the defendant associations and their members, has a lawful interest in securing compliance with the "location clause" and in thus protecting the franchise system of distributing automobiles—business arrangements which the court deemed lawful and proper; and that in seeking to vindicate these interests the defendants and their alleged co-conspirators entered into no "agreements" among themselves, although they may have engaged in "parallel action."

These factors do not justify the result reached. It is of no consequence, for purposes of determining whether there has been a combination or conspiracy under §1 of the Sherman Act, that each party acted in its own lawful interest. . . . [I]t has long been settled that explicit agreement is not a necessary part of a Sherman Act conspiracy—certainly not where, as here, joint and collaborative action was pervasive in the initiation, execution, and fulfillment of the plan. *United States* v. *Parke, Davis & Co., supra*, at 43; *United States* v. *Bausch & Lomb Optical Co.*, 321 U.S. 707, 722–723; *Federal Trade Comm'n* v. *Beech-Nut Packing Co.*, 257 U.S. 441, 455.

Neither individual dealers nor the associations acted independently or separately. The dealers collaborated, through the associations and otherwise, among themselves and with General Motors, both to enlist the aid of General Motors and to enforce the dealers' promises to forsake the discounters. The associations explicitly entered into a joint venture to assist General Motors in policing the dealers' promises, and their joint proffer of aid was accepted and utilized by General Motors.

As Parke Davis had done, General Motors sought to elicit from all the dealers' agreements, substantially interrelated and interdependent, that none of them would do business with the discounters. These agreements were hammered out in meetings between nonconforming dealers and officials of General Motors' Chevrolet Division, and in telephone conversations with other dealers. It was acknowledged from the beginning that substantial unanimity would be essential if the agreements were to be forthcoming. And once the agreements were secured, General Motors both solicited and employed the assistance of its alleged co-conspirators in helping to police them. What resulted was a fabric interwoven by many strands of joint action to eliminate the discounters from participation in the market, to inhibit the free choice of franchised dealers to select their own methods of trade and to provide multilateral surveillance and enforcement. This process for achieving and enforcing the desired objective can by no stretch of the imagination be described as "unilateral" or merely "parallel." . . .

There can be no doubt that the effect of the combination or conspiracy here was to restrain trade and commerce within the meaning of the Sherman Act. Elimination, by joint collaborative action, of discounters from access to the market is a *per se* violation of the Act.

. . . This [is] . . . not new doctrine, for it [has] . . . long been recognized that "there are certain agreements or practices which because of their pernicious effect on competition and lack of any redeeming virtue are conclusively presumed to be unreasonable and therefore illegal without elaborate inquiry as to the precise harm they have caused or the business excuse for their use," and that group boycotts are of this character. *Northern Pac. R. Co.* v. *United States*, 356 U.S. 1, 5. See also *Fashion Originators' Guild of America, Inc.* v. *Federal Trade Comm'n*, 312 U.S. 457, and *Eastern States Retail Lumber Dealers' Assn.* v. *United States*, 234 U.S. 600, 613–614, neither of which involved price-fixing.

The principle of these cases is that where businessmen concert their actions in order to deprive others of access to merchandise which the latter wish to sell to the public, we need not inquire into the economic motivation underlying their conduct. . . . Exclusion of traders from the market by means of combination or conspiracy is so inconsistent with the free-market principles embodied in the Sherman Act that it is not to be saved by reference to the need for preserving the collaborators' profit margins or their system for distributing automobiles, any more than by reference to the allegedly tortious conduct against which a combination or conspiracy may be directed—as in *Fashion Originators' Guild of America, Inc.* v. *Federal Trade Comm'n, supra,* at 468.

We note, moreover, that inherent in the success of the combination in this case was a substantial restraint upon price competition—a goal unlawful *per se* when sought to be effected by combination or conspiracy. *E.g., United States* v. *Parke, Davis & Co.,* 362 U.S. 29, 47; *United States* v. *Socony-Vacuum Oil Co.,* 310 U.S. 150, 223. And the *per se* rule applies even when the effect upon prices is indirect. *Simpson* v. *Union Oil Co.,* 377 U.S. 13, 16–22; *Socony-Vacuum Oil Co., supra.*

There is in the record ample evidence that one of the purposes behind the concerted effort to eliminate sales of new Chevrolet cars by discounters was to protect franchised dealers from real or apparent price competition. The discounters advertised price savings. . . . Some purchasers found and others believed that discount prices were lower than those available through the franchised dealers. . . . Certainly, complaints about price competition were prominent in the letters and telegrams with which the individual dealers and salesmen bombarded General Motors in November 1960. . . . And although the District Court found to the contrary, there is evidence in the record that General Motors itself was not unconcerned about the effect of discount sales upon general price levels.[4]

---

[4] In an inter-office memorandum, circulated among General Motors officials immediately prior to formulation of corporate policy *vis-à-vis* the discounters, it was stated that "It would appear that one of the real hazards of condoning this type of operation is that discounted prices are freely quoted to a large portion of the public." Moreover, we note that some discounters advertised that they would finance new-car purchases at an interest rate of 5½%, a rate substantially lower than that available at franchised Chevrolet dealers through G.M.A.C., a subsidiary of General Motors Corporation. . . . Finally, it is conceded that

The protection of price competition from conspiratorial restraint is an object of special solicitude under the antitrust laws. We cannot respect that solicitude by closing our eyes to the effect upon price competition of the removal from the market, by combination or conspiracy, of a class of traders. Nor do we propose to construe the Sherman Act to prohibit conspiracies to fix prices at which competitors may sell, but to allow conspiracies or combinations to put competitors out of business entirely.

Accordingly, we reverse and remand to the United States District Court for the Southern District of California in order that it may fashion appropriate equitable relief. . . .

It is so ordered.

United States v. Arnold, Schwinn & Co.

388 U.S. 365 (1967)

MR. JUSTICE FORTAS delivered the opinion of the Court.

The United States brought this appeal to review the judgment of the District Court in a civil antitrust case alleging violations of §1 of the Sherman Act. . . . The complaint charged a continuing conspiracy since 1952 between defendants and other alleged co-conspirators involving price fixing, allocation of exclusive territories to wholesalers and jobbers, and confinement of merchandise to franchised dealers. Named as defendants were Arnold, Schwinn & Company ("Schwinn"), the Schwinn Cycle Distributors Association ("SCDA"), and B. F. Goodrich Company ("B. F. Goodrich").[1] . . .

Appellee Schwinn is a family-owned business which for many years has been engaged in the manufacture and sale of bicycles and some limited bicycle parts and accessories. Appellee SCDA is an association of distributors handling Schwinn bicycles and other products. The challenged marketing program was instituted in 1952. In 1951 Schwinn had the largest single share of the United States bicycle market—22.5%. In 1961 Schwinn's share of market had fallen to 12.8% although its dollar and unit sales had risen substantially. In the same period, a competitor, Murray Ohio Manufacturing Company, which is now the leading United States bicycle producer, increased its market share from 11.6% in 1951 to 22.8% in 1961. Murray sells primarily to Sears, Roebuck & Company and other mass merchandisers. By 1962 there were nine bicycle producers in the

---

General Motors is intensely concerned that each of its dealers has an adequate "profit opportunity" . . . , a concern which necessarily involves consideration of the price realized by dealers.

[1] B. F. Goodrich negotiated a consent decree with the Government prior to trial, and dropped out of the case.

Nation, operating 11 plants. Imports of bicycles amounted to 29.7% of sales in 1961. . . .

Schwinn sells its products primarily to or through 22 wholesale distributors, with sales to the public being made by a large number of retailers. In addition, it sells about 11% of its total to B. F. Goodrich for resale in B. F. Goodrich retail or franchised stores. There are about 5,000 to 6,000 retail dealers in the United States which are bicycle specialty shops, generally also providing servicing. About 84% of Schwinn's sales are through such specialized dealers. Schwinn sells only under the Schwinn label, never under private label, while about 64% of all bicycles are sold under private label. Distributors and retailers handling Schwinn bicycles are not restricted to the handling of that brand. They may and ordinarily do sell a variety of brands.

The United States does not contend that there is in this case any restraint on interbrand competition, nor does it attempt to sustain its charge by reference to the market for bicycles as a whole. Instead, it invites us to confine our attention to the intrabrand effect of the contested restrictions. It urges us to declare that the method of distribution of a single brand of bicycles, amounting to less than one-seventh of the market, constitutes an unreasonable restraint of trade or commerce among the several States.

Schwinn's principal methods of selling its bicycles are as follows: (1) sales to distributors, primarily cycle distributors, B. F. Goodrich and hardware jobbers; (2) sales to retailers by means of consignment or agency arrangements with distributors; and (3) sales to retailers under the so-called Schwinn Plan which involves direct shipment by Schwinn to the retailer with Schwinn invoicing the dealers, extending credit, and paying a commission to the distributor taking the order. . . . During the 1952–1962 period, as the District Court found, "well over half of the bicycles sold by Schwinn have been sold direct to the retail dealer (not to a cycle distributor) by means of Schwinn Plan sales and consignment and agency sales." Less than half were sold to distributors.

After World War II, Schwinn had begun studying and revamping its distribution pattern. As of 1951–1952, it had reduced its mailing list from about 15,000 retail outlets to about 5,500. It instituted the practice of franchising approved retail outlets. The franchise did not prevent the retailer from handling other brands, but it did require the retailer to promote Schwinn bicycles and to give them at least equal prominence with competing brands. The number of franchised dealers in any area was limited, and a retailer was franchised only as to a designated location or locations. Each franchised dealer was to purchase only from or through the distributor authorized to serve that particular area. He was authorized to sell only to consumers, and not to unfranchised retailers. . . .

Schwinn assigned specific territories to each of its 22 wholesale cycle distributors. These distributors were instructed to sell only to franchised

Schwinn accounts and only in their respective territories which were specifically described and allocated on an exclusive basis. The District Court found "that certain cycle distributors have in fact not competed with each other . . . and that in so doing they have conspired with Schwinn to unreasonably restrain competition contrary to the provisions of Section 1 of the Sherman Act." The court, however, restricted this finding and its consequent order to transactions in which the distributor *purchased* the bicycles from Schwinn for resale, as distinguished from sales by the distributor as agent or consignee of Schwinn or on the Schwinn Plan. The United States urges that this Court should require revision of the decree in this respect to forbid territorial exclusivity regardless of the technical form by which the products are transferred from Schwinn to the retailer or consumer. . . .

We come, then, to the legal issues in this case. We are here confronted with challenged vertical restrictions as to territory and dealers. The source of the restrictions is the manufacturer. These are not horizontal restraints, in which the actors are distributors with or without the manufacturer's participation. We have held in such a case, where the purpose was to prevent the distribution of automobiles to or by "discounters," that a "classic conspiracy in restraint of trade" results. . . . Nor is this a case of territorial or dealer restrictions accompanied by price fixing, for here the issue of unlawful price fixing was tendered, litigated, decided against the appellant, and appellant has not appealed. If it were otherwise—if there were here a finding that the restrictions were part of a scheme involving unlawful price fixing, the result would be a *per se* violation of the Sherman Act. . . . The Government does not contend that a *per se* violation of the Sherman Act is presented by the practices which are involved in this appeal. . . . Accordingly, we are remitted to an appraisal of the market impact of these practices.

In *White Motor Co.* v. *United States,* 372 U.S. 253 (1963), this Court refused to affirm summary judgment against the manufacturer even though there were not only vertical restrictions as to territory and customer selection but also unlawful price fixing. The Court held that there was no showing that the price fixing was "an integral part of the whole distribution system" and accordingly it declined to outlaw the system because of the possibility that a trial laying bare "the economic and business stuff out of which these arrangements emerge" might demonstrate their reasonableness. *Id.,* at 263. So here we must look to the specifics of the challenged practices and their impact upon the marketplace in order to make a judgment as to whether the restraint is or is not "reasonable" in the special sense in which §1 of the Sherman Act must be read for purposes of this type of inquiry. . . .

We first observe that the facts of this case do not come within the specific illustrations which the Court in *White Motor* articulated as possible factors relevant to a showing that the challenged vertical restraint is sheltered by the rule of reason because it is not anticompetitive. Schwinn was not a newcomer, seeking to break into or stay in the bicycle business. It was not a "failing company." On the contrary, at the initiation of these practices, it was the leading bicycle producer in the Nation. Schwinn contends, however, and the trial court found, that the reasons which induced it to adopt the challenged distribution program were to enable it and the small, independent merchants that made up its chain of distribution to compete more effectively in the marketplace. Schwinn sought a better way of distributing its product: a method which would promote sales, increase stability of its distributor and dealer outlets, and augment profits. But this argument, appealing as it is, is not enough to avoid the Sherman Act proscription; because, in a sense, every restrictive practice is designed to augment the profit and competitive position of its participants. Price fixing does so, for example, and so may a well-calculated division of territories. . . . The antitrust outcome does not turn merely on the presence of sound business reason or motive. Here, for example, if the test of reasonableness were merely whether Schwinn's restrictive distribution program and practices were adopted "for good business reasons" and not merely to injure competitors, or if the answer turned upon whether it was indeed "good business practice," we should not quarrel with Schwinn's eloquent submission or the finding of the trial court. But our inquiry cannot stop at that point. Our inquiry is whether, assuming nonpredatory motives and business purposes and the incentive of profit and volume considerations, the effect upon competition in the marketplace is substantially adverse. The promotion of self-interest alone does not invoke the rule of reason to immunize otherwise illegal conduct. It is only if the conduct is not unlawful in its impact in the marketplace or if the self-interest coincides with the statutory concern with the preservation and promotion of competition that protection is achieved. . . .

On this basis, restraints as to territory or customers, vertical or horizontal, are unlawful if they are "ancillary to the price-fixing" (*White Motor Co.* v. *United States, supra,* at 260) or if the price fixing is "an integral part of the whole distribution system." . . . [*United States* v. *Bausch & Lomb Optical Co.,* 321 U.S. 707 (1944) at 720.] In those situations, it is needless to inquire further into competitive effects because it is established doctrine that, unless permitted by statute, the fixing of prices at which others may sell is anticompetitive, and the unlawfulness of the price fixing infects the distribution restrictions. . . . At the other extreme, a manufacturer of a product, other and equivalent brands of which are readily available in the market, may select his customers, and for this purpose he may "franchise" certain dealers to whom, alone, he will sell his goods. Cf. *United States* v. *Colgate & Co.,* 250 U.S. 300 (1919). If the restraint stops at that point—if nothing more is involved than vertical "confinement" of the manufacturer's own sales of the merchandise to selected dealers, and if competitive products are readily available to others, the restriction, on these facts alone, would not violate the Sherman Act. It is within these boundary lines that we must analyze the present case.

The District Court here enjoined appellees from limiting the territory within which any wholesaler or jobber may sell any Schwinn product which it has purchased. It held that these are agreements to divide territory and, as such, are *per se* violations of §1 of the Sherman Act. The court made clear that it confined its order to transactions in which the distributor *purchases* from Schwinn. As to consignment, agency and Schwinn Plan transactions, the court held that, in these instances, "Schwinn has a right to allocate its agents or salesmen to a particular territory." The court also held that the franchising of retailers was reasonable in view of the competitive problem presented by "giant" bicycle retailers such as Sears and Ward and by other mass merchandisers, and it declined to enjoin appellees' practices with respect to confinement of sale by distributors or Schwinn to franchised retailers, or to forbid Schwinn and its distributors from continuing to prohibit franchised retailers from selling to discount houses or other unfranchised retailers for resale to the public.

As noted above, appellees have not appealed from the District Court's order, and, accordingly, we have before us only the Government's pleas: (1) that the decree should not be confined to *sale* transactions between Schwinn and wholesalers but should reach territorial restrictions upon distributors whether they are incident to sale and resale transactions or to consignment, agency or Schwinn-Plan relationship between Schwinn and the distributors; (2) that agreements requiring distributors to limit their distribution to only such retailers as are franchised should be enjoined; and (3) that arrangements preventing franchised retailers from supplying non-franchised retailers, including discount stores, should also be forbidden.

As to point (2), the Government argues that it is illogical and inconsistent to forbid territorial limitations on resales by distributors where the distributor owns the goods, having bought them from Schwinn, and, at the same time, to exonerate arrangements which require distributors to confine resales of the goods they have bought to "franchised" retailers. It argues that requiring distributors, once they have purchased the product, to confine sales to franchised retailers is indistinguishable in law and principle from the division of territory which the decree condemns. Both, the Government argues, are in the nature of restraints upon alienation which are beyond the power of the manufacturer to impose upon it vendees and which, since the nature of the transaction includes an agreement, combination or understanding, are violations of §1 of the Sherman Act. . . . We agree, and upon remand, the decree should be revised to enjoin any limitation upon the freedom of distributors to dispose of the Schwinn products, which they have bought from Schwinn, where and to whomever they choose. The principle is, of course, equally applicable to sales to retailers, and the decree should similarly enjoin the making of any sales to retailers upon any condition, agreement or understanding limiting the retailer's freedom as to where and to whom it will resell the products.

The appellant vigorously argues that, since this remedy is confined to situations where the distributor and retailer acquire title to the bicycles, it will provide only partial relief; that to prevent the allocation of territories and confinement to franchised retail dealers, the decree can and should be enlarged to forbid these practices, however effected—whether by sale and resale or by agency, consignment, or the Schwinn Plan. But we are dealing here with a vertical restraint embodying the unilateral program of a single manufacturer . . . raising the fundamental question of the degree to which a manufacturer may not only select the customers to whom he will sell, but also allocate territories for resale and confine access to his product to selected, or franchised, retailers. We conclude that the proper application of §1 of the Sherman Act to this problem requires differentiation between the situation where the manufacturer parts with title, dominion, or risk with respect to the article, and where he completely retains ownership and risk of loss.

As the District Court held, where a manufacturer *sells* products to his distributor subject to territorial restrictions upon resale, a *per se* violation of the Sherman Act results. And, as we have held, the same principle applies to restrictions of outlets with which the distributors may deal and to restraints upon retailers to whom the goods are sold. . . . On the other hand, as indicated in *White Motor*, we are not prepared to introduce the inflexibility which a *per se* rule might bring if it were applied to prohibit all vertical restrictions of territory and all franchising, in the sense of designating specified distributors and retailers as the chosen instruments through which the manufacturer, retaining ownership of the goods, will distribute them to the public. Such a rule might severely hamper smaller enterprises resorting to reasonable methods of meeting the competition of giants and of merchandising through independent dealers, and it might sharply accelerate the trend towards vertical integration of the distribution process. . . .

The Government does not here contend for a *per se* rule as to agency, consignment, or Schwinn-Plan transactions even though these may be used—as they are here—to implement a scheme of confining distribution outlets as in this case. Where the manufacturer retains title, dominion, and risk with respect to the product and the position and function of the dealer in question are, in fact, indistinguishable from those of an agent or salesman of the manufacturer, it is only if the impact of the confinement is "unreasonably" restrictive of competition that a violation of §1 results from such confinement, unencumbered by culpable price fixing. . . . As the District Court found, Schwinn adopted the challenged distribution programs in a competitive situation dominated by mass merchandisers which command access to large-scale advertising and promotion, choice of retail outlets, both owned and franchised, and adequate sources of supply. It is not claimed that Schwinn's practices or other circumstances resulted in an inadequate competitive situation with respect to the bicycle market; and there is nothing in this record . . . to lead us to conclude that Schwinn's program exceeded the limits reasonably necessary to meet the competitive problems posed by its more powerful competitors. In these circumstances, the rule of reason is satisfied.

We do not suggest that the unilateral adoption by a single manufacturer of an agency or consignment pattern and the Schwinn type of restrictive distribution system would be justified in any and all circumstances by the presence of the competition of mass merchandisers and by the demonstrated need of the franchise system to meet that competition. But certainly, in such circumstances, the vertically imposed distribution restraints—*absent* price fixing and in the presence of adequate sources of alternative products to meet the needs of the unfranchised—may not be held to be *per se* violations of the Sherman Act. . . .

. . . Critical in this . . . [case] are the facts: (1) that other competitive bicycles are available to distributors and retailers in the marketplace, and there is no showing that they are not in all respects reasonably interchangeable as articles of competitive commerce with the Schwinn product,[2] (2) that Schwinn distributors and retailers handle other brands of bicycles as well as Schwinn's; (3) in the present posture of the case we cannot rule that the vertical restraints are unreasonable because of their intermixture with price fixing; and (4) we cannot disagree with the findings of the trial court that competition made necessary the challenged program; that it was justified by, and went no further than required by, competitive pressures; and that its net effect is to preserve and not to damage competition in the bicycle market. Application of the rule of reason here cannot be confined to intrabrand competition. When we look to the product market as a whole, we cannot conclude that Schwinn's franchise system with respect to products as to which it retains ownership and risk constitutes an unreasonable restraint of trade. . . .

Accordingly, the judgment of the District Court is reversed and the cause remanded for the entry of a decree in accordance with this question.

It is so ordered.

MR. JUSTICE CLARK and MR. JUSTICE WHITE took no part in the decision of this case.

MR. JUSTICE STEWART, whom MR. JUSTICE HARLAN joins, concurring in part and dissenting in part.

I agree with the Court's basic determination that Schwinn's marketing system is, under the rule of reason, entirely consonant with the antitrust

---

[2] We do not regard Schwinn's claim of product excellence as establishing the contrary.

laws. But I cannot understand how that marketing system becomes *per se* unreasonable and illegal in those instances where it is effectuated through sales to wholesalers and dealers. . . .

Schwinn's selective distribution policy may be said to embody restraints on trade. As such, it is subject to antitrust scrutiny, but the scrutiny does not stop with the label "restraint." The words written by MR. JUSTICE BRANDEIS for a unanimous Court in *Chicago Board of Trade* v. *United States*, 246 U.S. 231, 238, bear repeating:

> Every agreement concerning trade, every regulation of trade, restrains. To bind, to restrain, is of their very essence. The true test of legality is whether the restraint imposed is such as merely regulates and perhaps thereby promotes competition or whether it is such as may suppress or even destroy competition. To determine that question the court must ordinarily consider the facts peculiar to the business to which the restraint is applied; its condition before and after the restraint was imposed; the nature of the restraint and its effect, actual or probable. The history of the restraint, the evil believed to exist, the reason for adopting the particular remedy, the purpose or end sought to be attained, are all relevant facts.

. . . It is worth emphasizing that the justifications for Schwinn's franchising policy rest not only on the facts of this particular record, but on larger issues of social and economic policy. This Court has recognized Congress' concern with the disappearance of the small independent merchant in the face of competition from vertically integrated giants. . . . This trend in many cases reflects the inexorable economic realities of modern marketing. But franchising promises to provide the independent merchant with the means to become an efficient and effective competitor of large integrated firms. Through various forms of franchising, the manufacturer is assured qualified and effective outlets for his products, and the franchisee enjoys backing in the form of know-how and financial assistance. These franchise arrangements also make significant social and economic contributions of importance to the whole society. . . .

Indiscriminate invalidation of franchising arrangements would eliminate their creative contributions to competition and force "suppliers to abandon franchising and integrate forward to the detriment of small business. In other words, we may inadvertently compel concentration" by misguided zealousness.[3] . . .

For these reasons I completely agree with the Court's basic approach to this case. . . . It upholds the legality of the Schwinn Plan, which is the heart of Schwinn's marketing system, now accounting for 75% of the distribution of Schwinn's products. It also upholds the legality of Schwinn's agency and consignment arrangements.

But the Court inexplicably turns its back on the values of competition by independent merchants and the flexible wisdom of the rule of reason

---

[3] Wilson, "Some Problems Relative to Franchise Arrangements," 11 *Antitrust Bull.* 473, 488. It should be noted that since the start of this litigation, Schwinn has taken over 30% of the wholesaling of its products by vertical integration.

when dealing with distribution effected through sales to wholesalers. In Schwinn's particular marketing system, this mode of distribution plays a subsidiary role, serving to meet "fill-in" orders by dealers, whose basic stock is obtained through the Schwinn Plan. Without considering its function, purpose or effect, the Court declares this aspect of Schwinn's program to be *per se* invalid. It likewise applies the same automatic rule of illegality to strike down Schwinn's policy of ensuring that franchised dealers do not resell to unfranchised retailers and thus subvert the whole distributional scheme.

Despite the Government's concession that the rule of reason applies to all aspects of Schwinn's distribution system, the Court nevertheless reaches out to adopt a potent *per se* rule. No previous antitrust decision of this Court justifies this action. Instead, it completely repudiates the only case in point, *White Motor*. . . . The Court today is unable to give any reasons why, only four years later, this precedent should be overruled. . . . And I am completely at a loss to fathom how the Court can adopt its *per se* rule concerning distributional sales and yet uphold identical restrictions in Schwinn's marketing scheme when distribution takes the form of consignment or Schwinn Plan deliveries. It does not demonstrate that these restrictions are in their actual operation somehow more anticompetitive or less justifiable merely because the contractual relations between Schwinn and its jobbers and dealers bear the label "sale" rather than "agency" or "consignment." Such irrelevant formulae are false guides to sound adjudication in the antitrust field. . . .

The Court advances two justifications for its new *per se* rule. I do not find either persuasive. First, the Court correctly observes that the District Court invalidated territorial limitations on the resale activities of Schwinn's wholesalers. . . . But the Court completely overlooks the fact that the territorial limitations invalidated by the District Court were the product of a horizontal conspiracy between the wholesalers. . . . In striking down this horizontal division of markets between competing distributors, the District Court was simply following familiar precedent. . . . By contrast, the restrictions involved in the franchising methods now before us are quite different in nature, as the Court points out elsewhere in its opinion. . . . As the Court also emphasizes, the legal principles applicable to horizontal and vertical restrictions are quite different.[4] Thus, applying the rule of reason to the vertical restraints now in issue is not at all "illogical and inconsistent" with *per se* invalidation of the wholesalers' horizontal division of markets.

---

[4] One difference between a horizontal conspiracy and vertical restraints imposed by the manufacturer is that there is often serious question whether the latter conduct involves the "contract, combination . . . or conspiracy" required by §1 of the Sherman Act. . . . The District Judge in this case refused to find that the relevant conduct of Schwinn and its distributors amounted to a "contract," "combination" or "conspiracy." Instead, he stated that "the Schwinn franchising program was conceived, hatched and born into life . . . in the minds of the Schwinn officials," and agreed that "the action was unilateral in nature." . . .

The Court's second justification for its new *per se* doctrine is the "ancient rule against restraints on alienation." . . . But it is hardly the practice of this Court to embrace a rule of law merely on grounds of its antiquity. Moreover, the common-law doctrine of restraints on alienation is not nearly so rigid as the Court implies. The original rule concerned itself with arbitrary and severe restrictions on alienation, such as total prohibition of resale. As early as 1711 it was recognized that only *unreasonable* restraints should be proscribed, and that partial restrictions could be justified when ancillary to a legitimate business purpose and not unduly anticompetitive in effect. . . .

Centuries ago, it could perhaps be assumed that a manufacturer had no legitimate interest in what happened to his products once he had sold them to a middleman and they had started on their way down the channel of distribution. But this assumption no longer holds true in a day of sophisiticated marketing policies, mass advertising, and vertically integrated manufacturer-distributors. Restrictions like those involved in a franchising program should accordingly be able to claim justification under the ancillary restraints doctrine. . . .

. . . Moreover, the Court's answer makes everything turn on whether the arrangement between a manufacturer and his distributor is denominated a "sale" or "agency." Such a rule ignores and conceals the "economic and business stuff out of which" a sound answer should be fashioned. *White Motor Co.* v. *United States, supra,* at 263. The Court has emphasized in the past that these differences in form often do not represent "differences in substance." *Simpson* v. *Union Oil Co.,* 377 U.S. 13, 22. Draftsmen may cast business arrangements in different legal molds for purposes of commercial law, but these arrangements may operate identically in terms of economic function and competitive effect. It is the latter factors which are the concern of the antitrust laws. The record does not show that the purposes of Schwinn's franchising program and the competitive consequences of its implementation differed, depending on whether Schwinn sold its products to wholesalers or resorted to the agency, consignment, or Schwinn Plan methods of distribution. And there is no reason generally to suppose that variations in the formal legal packaging of franchising programs produce differences in their actual impact in the marketplace. Our experience is to the contrary. As stated in *United States* v. *Masonite Corp.,* 316 U.S. 265, 278, 280:

> [T]his Court has quite consistently refused to allow the form into which the parties chose to cast the transaction to govern.

> . . . . .

> So far as the Sherman Act is concerned, the result must turn not on the skill with which counsel has manipulated the concepts of 'sale' and 'agency' but on the significance of the business practices in terms of restraint of trade.

. . .

In view of the commendably careful and realistic approach the Court has taken in analyzing the basic structure of Schwinn's marketing program, it is particularly disappointing to see the Court balk at the label "sale," and turn from reasoned response to a wooden and irrelevant formula.

United States v. Topco Associates, Inc.

405 U.S. 596 (1972)

MR. JUSTICE MARSHALL delivered the opinion of the Court. . . .

I

Topco is a cooperative association of approximately 25 small and medium-sized regional supermarket chains that operate stores in some 33 States.[1] Each of the member chains operates independently; there is no pooling of earnings, profits, capital, management, or advertising resources. No grocery business is conducted under the Topco name. Its basic function is to serve as a purchasing agent for its members.[2] In this capacity, it procures and distributes to the members more than 1,000 different food and related nonfood items, most of which are distributed under brand names owned by Topco. The association does not itself own any manufacturing, processing, or warehousing facilities, and the items that it procures for members are usually shipped directly from the packer or manufacturer to the members. Payment is made either to Topco or directly to the manufacturer at a cost that is virtually the same for the members as for Topco itself. . . .

Topco was founded in the 1940s by a group of small, local grocery chains, independently owned and operated, that desired to cooperate to obtain high quality merchandise under private labels in order to compete more effectively with larger national and regional chains.[3] . . . By 1964,

---

[1] Topco, which is referred to at times in this opinion as the "association," is actually composed of 23 chains of supermarket retailers and two retailer-owned cooperative wholesalers.

[2] In addition to purchasing various items for its members, Topco performs other related functions: *e.g.,* it insures that there is adequate quality control on the products that it purchases; it assists members in developing specifications on certain types of products (*e.g.,* equipment and supplies); and it also aids the members in purchasing goods through other sources.

[3] The founding members of Topco were having difficulty competing with larger chains. This difficulty was attributable in some degree to the fact that the larger chains were capable of developing their own private-label programs.

Private-label products differ from other brand-name products in that they are sold at a limited number of easily ascertainable stores. A&P, for example, was a pioneer in developing a series of products that were sold under an A&P label and that were only available in A&P stores. It is obvious that by using private-label products, a chain can achieve significant cost economies in purchasing, transportation, warehousing, promotion, and advertis-

Topco's members had combined retail sales of more than $2 billion; by 1967, their sales totaled more than $2.3 billion, a figure exceeded by only three national grocery chains.[4]

Members of the association vary in the degree of market share that they possess in their respective areas. The range is from 1.5% to 16%, with the average being approximately 6%. While it is difficult to compare these figures with the market shares of larger regional and national chains because of the absence in the record of accurate statistics for these chains, there is much evidence in the record that Topco members are frequently in as strong a competitive position in their respective areas as any other chain. The strength of this competitive position is due, in some measure, to the success of Topco-brand products. Although only 10% of the total goods sold by Topco members bear the association's brand names, the profit on these goods is substantial and their very existence has improved the competitive potential of Topco members with respect to other large and powerful chains.

It is apparent that from meager beginnings approximately a quarter of a century ago, Topco has developed into a purchasing association wholly owned and operated by member chains, which possess much economic muscle, individually as well as cooperatively.

II

. . . The United States charged that, beginning at least as early as 1960 and continuing up to the time that the complaint was filed, Topco had combined and conspired with its members to violate §1 . . . in two respects. First, the Government alleged that there existed:

> a continuing agreement, understanding and concert of action among the co-conspirator member firms acting through Topco, the substantial terms of which have been and are that each co-conspirator member firm will sell Topco-controlled brands only within the marketing territory allocated to it, and will refrain from selling Topco-controlled brands outside such marketing territory.

The division of marketing territories to which the complaint refers consists of a number of practices by the association.

---

ing. These economies may afford the chain opportunities for offering private-label products at lower prices than other brand-name products. This, in turn, provides many advantages of which some of the more important are: a store can offer national-brand products at the same price as other stores, while simultaneously offering a desirable, lower priced alternative; or, if the profit margin is sufficiently high on private-brand goods, national-brand products may be sold at reduced price. Other advantages include: enabling a chain to bargain more favorably with national-brand manufacturers by creating a broader supply base of manufacturers, thereby decreasing dependence on a few, large national-brand manufacturers; enabling a chain to create a "price-mix" whereby prices on special items can be lowered to attract customers while profits are maintained on other items; and creation of general goodwill by offering lower priced, higher quality goods.

[4] The three largest chains are A&P, Safeway, and Kroger.

Article IX, §2, of the Topco bylaws establishes three categories of territorial licenses that members may secure from the association:

> (a) *Exclusive*—An exclusive territory is one in which the member is licensed to sell all products bearing specified trademarks of the Association, to the exclusion of all other persons.
>
> (b) *Non-exclusive*—A non-exclusive territory is one in which a member is licensed to sell all products bearing specified trademarks of the Association, but not to the exclusion of others who may also be licensed to sell products bearing the same trademarks of the Association in the same territory.
>
> (c) *Coextensive*—A coextensive territory is one in which two (2) or more members are licensed to sell all products bearing specified trademarks of the Association to the exclusion of all other persons. . . .

When applying for membership, a chain must designate the type of license that it desires. Membership must first be approved by the board of directors, and thereafter by an affirmative vote of 75% of the association's members. If, however, the member whose operations are closest to those of the applicant, or any member whose operations are located within 100 miles of the applicant, votes against approval, an affirmative vote of 85% of the members is required for approval. Bylaws, Art. I, §5. Because, as indicated by the record, members cooperate in accommodating each other's wishes, the procedure for approval provides, in essence, that members have a veto of sorts over actual or potential competition in the territorial areas in which they are concerned.

Following approval, each new member signs an agreement with Topco designating the territory in which that member may sell Topco-brand products. No member may sell these products outside the territory in which it is licensed. Most licenses are exclusive, and even those denominated "coextensive" or "non-exclusive" prove to be *de facto* exclusive. Exclusive territorial areas are often allocated to members who do no actual business in those areas on the theory that they may wish to expand at some indefinite future time and that expansion would likely be in the direction of the allocated territory. When combined with each member's veto power over new members, provisions for exclusivity work effectively to insulate members from competition in Topco-brand goods. Should a member violate its license agreement and sell in areas other than those in which it is licensed, its membership can be terminated under Art. IV, §§2 (a) and 2(b) of the bylaws. Once a territory is classified as exclusive, either formally or *de facto*, it is extremely unlikely that the classification will ever be changed. See Bylaws, Art. IX.

The Government maintains that this scheme of dividing markets violates the Sherman Act because it operates to prohibit competition in Topco-brand products among grocery chains engaged in retail operations. The Government also makes a subsidiary challenge to Topco's practices regarding licensing members to sell at wholesale. . . .

From the inception of this lawsuit, Topco accepted as true most of the Government's allegations regarding territorial divisions and restrictions on wholesaling, although it differed greatly with the Government on the conclusions, both factual and legal, to be drawn from these facts.

Topco's answer to the complaint is illustrative of its posture in the District Court and before this Court:

> Private label merchandising is a way of economic life in the food retailing industry, and exclusivity is the essence of a private label program; without exclusivity, a private label would not be private. Each national and large regional chain has its own exclusive private label products in addition to the nationally advertised brands which all chains sell. Each such chain relies upon the exclusivity of its own private label line to differentiate its private label products from those of its competitors and to attract and retain the repeat business and loyalty of consumers. Smaller retail grocery stores and chains are unable to compete effectively with the national and large regional chains without also offering their own exclusive private label products.
>
> . . . . .
>
> The only feasible method by which Topco can procure private label products and assure the exclusivity thereof is through trademark licenses specifying the territory in which each member may sell such trademarked products. Answer, App. 11.

Topco essentially maintains that it needs territorial divisions to compete with larger chains; that the association could not exist if the territorial divisions were anything but exclusive; and that by restricting competition in the sale of Topco-brand goods, the association actually increases competition by enabling its members to compete successfully with larger regional and national chains. . . .

III

On its face, §1 of the Sherman Act appears to bar any combination of entrepreneurs so long as it is "in restraint of trade." Theoretically, all manufacturers, distributors, merchants, sellers, and buyers could be considered as potential competitors of each other. Were §1 to be read in the narrowest possible way, any commercial contract could be deemed to violate it. *Chicago Board of Trade* v. *United States*, 246 U.S. 231, 238 (1918) (Brandeis, J.) The history underlying the formulation of the antitrust laws led this Court to conclude, however, that Congress did not intend to prohibit all contracts, nor even all contracts that might in some insignificant degree or attenuated sense restrain trade or competition. In lieu of the narrowest possible reading of §1, the Court adopted a "rule of reason" analysis for determining whether most business combinations or contracts violate the prohibitions of the Sherman Act. *Standard Oil Co.* v. *United States*, 221 U.S. 1 (1911). An analysis of the reasonableness of particular restraints includes consideration of the facts peculiar to the business in which the restraint is applied, the nature of the restraint and its effects, and the history of the restraint and the reasons for its adoption. *Chicago Board of Trade* v. *United States, supra,* at 238.

While the Court has utilized the "rule of reason" in evaluating the legality of most restraints alleged to be violative of the Sherman Act, it has also developed the doctrine that certain business relationships are *per se* violations of the Act without regard to a consideration of their reasonableness. . . .

It is only after considerable experience with certain business relationships that courts classify them as *per se* violations of the Sherman Act. . . . One of the classic examples of a *per se* violation of §1 is an agreement between competitors at the same level of the market structure to allocate territories in order to minimize competition. Such concerted action is usually termed a "horizontal" restraint, in contradistinction to combinations of persons at different levels of the market structure, *e.g.*, manufacturers and distributors, which are termed "vertical" restraints. This Court has reiterated time and time again that "[h]orizontal territorial limitations . . . are naked restraints of trade with no purpose except stifling of competition." *White Motor Co.* v. *United States,* 372 U.S. 253, 263 (1963). Such limitations are *per se* violations of the Sherman Act. . . .

We think that it is clear that the restraint in this case is a horizontal one, and, therefore, a *per se* violation of §1. The District Court failed to make any determination as to whether there were *per se* horizontal territorial restraints in this case and simply applied a rule of reason in reaching its conclusions that the restraints were not illegal. . . . In so doing, the District Court erred. . . .

Whether or not we would decide this case the same way under the rule of reason used by the District Court is irrelevant to the issue before us. The fact is that courts are of limited utility in examining difficult economic problems.[5] Our inability to weigh, in any meaningful sense, destruction of competition in one sector of the economy against promotion of competition in another sector is one important reason we have formulated *per se* rules.

In applying these rigid rules, the Court has consistently rejected the notion that naked restraints of trade are to be tolerated because they are well intended or because they are allegedly developed to increase competition. . . .

Antitrust laws in general, and the Sherman Act in particular, are the

---

[5] . . . Without the *per se* rules, businessmen would be left with little to aid them in predicting in any particular case what courts will find to be legal and illegal under the Sherman Act. Should Congress ultimately determine that predictability is unimportant in this area of the law, it can, of course, make *per se* rules inapplicable in some or all cases, and leave courts free to ramble through the wilds of economic theory in order to maintain a flexible approach.

Magna Carta of free enterprise. They are as important to the preservation of economic freedom and our free-enterprise system as the Bill of Rights is to the protection of our fundamental personal freedoms. And the freedom guaranteed each and every business, no matter how small, is the freedom to compete—to assert with vigor, imagination, devotion, and ingenuity whatever economic muscle it can muster. Implicit in such freedom is the notion that it cannot be foreclosed with respect to one sector of the economy because certain private citizens or groups believe that such foreclosure might promote greater competition in a more important sector of the economy. . . .

The District Court determined that by limiting the freedom of its individual members to compete with each other, Topco was doing a greater good by fostering competition between members and other large supermarket chains. But, the fallacy in this is that Topco has no authority under the Sherman Act to determine the respective values of competition in various sectors of the economy. On the contrary, the Sherman Act gives to each Topco member and to each prospective member the right to ascertain for itself whether or not competition with other supermarket chains is more desirable than competition in the sale of Topco-brand products. Without territorial restrictions, Topco members may indeed "[cut] each other's throats." Cf. *White Motor Co., supra,* at 278 (CLARK, J., dissenting). But, we have never found this possibility sufficient to warrant condoning horizontal restraints of trade. . . .

There have been tremendous departures from the notion of a free-enterprise system as it was originally conceived in this country. These departures have been the product of congressional action and the will of the people. If a decision is to be made to sacrifice competition in one portion of the economy for greater competition in another portion, this too is a decision that must be made by Congress and not by private forces or by the courts. Private forces are too keenly aware of their own interests in making such decisions and courts are ill-equipped and ill-situated for such decision-making. To analyze, interpret, and evaluate the myriad of competing interests and the endless data that would surely be brought to bear on such decisions, and to make the delicate judgment on the relative values to society of competitive areas of the economy, the judgment of the elected representatives of the people is required.

Just as the territorial restrictions on retailing Topco-brand products must fall, so must the territorial restrictions on wholesaling. The considerations are the same, and the Sherman Act requires identical results. . . .

We reverse the judgment of the District Court and remand the case for entry of an appropriate decree.

It is so ordered.

MR. CHIEF JUSTICE BURGER, dissenting.

This case does not involve restraints on interbrand competition or an allocation of markets by an association with monopoly or near-monopoly control of the sources of supply of one or more varieties of staple goods. Rather, we have here an agreement among several small grocery chains to join in a cooperative endeavor that, in my view, has an unquestionably lawful principal purpose; in pursuit of that purpose they have mutually agreed to certain minimal ancillary restraints that are fully reasonable in view of the principal purpose and that have never before today been held by this Court to be *per se* violations of the Sherman Act.

In joining in this cooperative endeavor, these small chains did not agree to the restraints here at issue in order to make it possible for them to exploit an already established line of products through noncompetitive pricing. There was no such thing as a Topco line of products until this cooperative was formed. The restraints to which the cooperative's members have agreed deal only with the marketing of the products in the Topco line, and the only function of those restraints is to permit each member chain to establish, within its own geographical area and through its own local advertising and marketing efforts, a local consumer awareness of the trademarked family of products as that member's "private-label" line. The goal sought was the enhancement of the individual members' abilities to compete, albeit to a modest degree, with the large national chains which had been successfully marketing private-label lines for several years. The sole reason for a cooperative endeavor was to make economically feasible such things as quality control, large quantity purchases at bulk prices, the development of attractively printed labels, and the ability to offer a number of different lines of trademarked products. All these things, of course, are feasible for the large national chains operating individually, but they are beyond the reach of the small operators proceeding alone.[6]

After a careful review of the economic considerations bearing upon this case, the District Court determined that "the relief which the government here seeks would not increase competition in Topco private label brands"; on the contrary, such relief "would substantially diminish competition in the supermarket field." 319 F. Supp. 1031, 1043. This Court has not today determined, on the basis of an examination of the underlying economic realities, that the District Court's conclusions are incorrect. Rather, the majority holds that the District Court had no business examining Topco's practices under the "rule of reason"; it should

---

[6] The District Court's findings of fact include the following: "33. A competitively effective private label program to be independently undertaken by a single retailer or chain would require an annual sales volume of $250 million or more and in order to achieve optimum efficiency, the volume required would probably have to be twice that amount." 319 F. Supp. 1031, 1036.

not have sought to determine whether Topco's practices did in fact restrain trade or commerce within the meaning of §1 of the Sherman Act; it should have found no more than that those practices involve a "horizontal division of markets" and are, by that very fact, *per se* violations of the Act.

I do not believe that our prior decisions justify the result reached by the majority. Nor do I believe that a new *per se* rule should be established in disposing of this case, for the judicial convenience and ready predictability that are made possible by *per se* rules are not such overriding considerations in antitrust law as to justify their promulgation without careful prior consideration of the relevant economic realities in the light of the basic policy and goals of the Sherman Act.

I

[In this section MR. CHIEF JUSTICE BURGER sought to distinguish the various cases relied upon by the majority.]

II

. . . In the face of the District Court's well supported findings that the effects of . . . a [*per se*] rule in this case will be adverse to the public welfare,[7] the Court lays down that rule without regard to the impact that the condemned practices may have on competition. In doing so, the Court virtually invites Congress to undertake to determine that impact. . . . I question whether the Court is fulfilling the role assigned to it under the statute when it declines to make this determination; in any event, if the Court is unwilling on this record to assess the economic impact, it surely should not proceed to make a new rule to govern the economic activity. . . .

With all respect, I believe that there are two basic fallacies in the Court's approach here. First, while I would not characterize our role under the Sherman Act as one of "rambl[ing] through the wilds," it is indeed one that requires our "examin[ation of] difficult economic problems." We can undoubtedly ease our task, but we should not abdicate that role by formulation of *per se* rules with no justification other than the enhancement of predictability and the reduction of judicial investigation. Second, from the general proposition that *per se* rules play a necessary

---

[7] Among the facts found by the District Court are the following: private-label brand merchandising, which is beyond the reach of the small chains acting independently and which by definition depends upon local exclusivity, permits the merchandiser to offer the public "lower consumer prices on products of high quality" and "to bargain more favorably with national brand manufacturers"; such merchandising fosters "the establishment of a broader supply base of manufacturers, thereby decreasing dependence upon a relatively few, large national brand manufacturers"; it also enables "[s]maller manufacturers, the most common source of private label products, who are generally unable to develop national brand name recognition for their products, [to] benefit . . . by the assurance of a substantial market for their products. . . ." 319 F. Supp., at 1035.

role in antitrust law, it does not follow that the particular *per se* rule promulgated today is an appropriate one. Although it might well be desirable in a proper case for this Court to formulate a *per se* rule dealing with horizontal territorial limitations, it would not necessarily be appropriate for such a rule to amount to a blanket prohibition against all such limitations. More specifically, it is far from clear to me why such a rule should cover those division-of-market agreements that involve no price fixing and which are concerned only with trademarked products that are not in a monopoly or near-monopoly position with respect to competing brands. The instant case presents such an agreement; I would not decide it upon the basis of a *per se* rule.[8]

The District Court specifically found that the horizontal restraints involved here tend positively to promote competition in the supermarket field and to produce lower costs for the consumer. The Court seems implicitly to accept this determination, but says that the Sherman Act does not give Topco the authority to determine for itself "whether or not competition with other supermarket chains is more desirable than competition in the sale of Topco-brand products." . . . But the majority overlooks a further specific determination of the District Court, namely, that the invalidation of the restraints here at issue "would not increase competition in Topco private label brands." 319 F. Supp., at 1043. Indeed, the District Court seemed to believe that it would, on the contrary, lead to the likely demise of those brands in time. And the evidence before the District Court would appear to justify that conclusion.

There is no national demand for Topco brands, nor has there ever been any national advertising of those brands. It would be impracticable for Topco, with its limited financial resources, to convert itself into a national brand distributor in competition with distributors of existing national brands. Furthermore, without the right to grant exclusive licenses, it could not attract and hold new members as replacements for those of its present members who, following the pattern of the past, eventually grow sufficiently in size to be able to leave the cooperative organization and develop their own individual private-label brands. Moreover, Topco's present members, once today's decision has had its full impact over the course of time, will have no more reason to promote Topco products

---

[8] The national chains market their own private-label products, and these products are available nowhere else than in the stores of those chains. The stores of any one chain, of course, do not engage in price competition with each other with respect to their chain's private-label brands, and no serious suggestion could be made that the Sherman Act requires otherwise. I fail to see any difference whatsoever in the economic effect of the Topco arrangement for the marketing of Topco-brand products and the methods used by the national chains in marketing their private-label brands. True, the Topco arrangement involves a "combination," while each of the national chains is a single integrated corporation. The controlling consideration, however, should be that in neither case is the policy of the Sherman Act offended, for the practices in both cases work to the benefit, and not to the detriment, of the consuming public.

through local advertising and merchandising efforts than they will have such reason to promote any other generally available brands.

The issues presented by the antitrust cases reaching this Court are rarely simple to resolve under the rule of reason; they do indeed frequently require us to make difficult economic determinations. We should not for that reason alone, however, be overly zealous in formulating new *per se* rules, for an excess of zeal in that regard is both contrary to the policy of the Sherman Act and detrimental to the welfare of consumers generally. Indeed, the economic effect of the new rule laid down by the Court today seems clear: unless Congress intervenes, grocery staples marketed under private-label brands with their lower consumer prices will soon be available only to those who patronize the large national chains.

Continental T.V., Inc., et al. v. *GTE Sylvania Inc.*

433 U.S. 36 (1977)

MR. JUSTICE POWELL delivered the opinion of the Court.

Franchise agreements between manufacturers and retailers frequently include provisions barring the retailers from selling franchised products from locations other than those specified in the agreements. This case presents important questions concerning the appropriate antitrust analysis of these restrictions under §1 of the Sherman Act, . . . and the Court's decision in *United States* v. *Arnold, Schwinn & Co.*, 388 U.S. 365 (1967).

I

Respondent GTE Sylvania Inc. (Sylvania) manufactures and sells television sets through its Home Entertainment Products Division. Prior to 1962, like most other television manufacturers, Sylvania sold its televisions to independent or company-owned distributors who in turn resold to a large and diverse group of retailers. Prompted by a decline in its market share to a relatively insignificant 1 percent to 2 percent of national television sales,[1] Sylvania conducted an intensive reassessment of its marketing strategy, and in 1962 adopted the franchise plan challenged here. Sylvania phased out its wholesale distributors and began to sell its televisions directly to a smaller and more select group of franchised retailers. An acknowledged purpose of the change was to decrease the number of competing Sylvania retailers in the hope of attracting the more aggressive and competent retailers thought necessary to the improvement of the company's market position. . . . To this end, Sylvania limited the number of franchises granted for any given area and required each fran-

---

[1] RCA at that time was the dominant firm with as much as 60 percent to 70 percent of national television sales in an industry with more than 100 manufacturers.

chisee to sell his Sylvania products only from the location or locations at which he was franchised.[2] A franchise did not constitute an exclusive territory, and Sylvania retained sole discretion to increase the number of retailers in an area in light of the success or failure of existing retailers in developing their market. The revised marketing strategy appears to have been successful during the period at issue here, for by 1965 Sylvania's share of national television sales had increased to approximately 5 percent, and the company ranked as the Nation's eighth largest manufacturer of color television sets.

This suit is the result of the rupture of a franchiser-franchisee relationship that had previously prospered under the revised Sylvania plan. Dissatisfied with its sales in the city of San Francisco,[3] Sylvania decided in the spring of 1965 to franchise Young Brothers, an established San Francisco retailer of televisions, as an additional San Francisco retailer. The proposed location of the new franchise was approximately a mile from a retail outlet operated by petitioner Continental T.V., Inc. (Continental), one of the most successful Sylvania franchisees. . . . Continental protested that the location of the new franchise violated Sylvania's marketing policy, but Sylvania persisted in its plans. . . .

During this same period, Continental expressed a desire to open a store in Sacramento, California, a desire Sylvania attributed at least in part to Continental's displeasure over the Young Brothers decision. Sylvania believed that the Sacramento market was adequately served by the existing Sylvania retailers and denied the request.[4] In the face of this denial, Continental advised Sylvania in early September 1965, that it was in the process of moving Sylvania merchandise from its San Jose, California warehouse to a new retail location that it had leased in Sacramento. . . . Shortly thereafter, Sylvania terminated Continental's franchises. . . .

The antitrust issues before us originated in cross-claims brought by Continental against Sylvania and Maguire [a finance company that handled the credit arrangements between Sylvania and its retailers]. Most important for our purposes was the claim that Sylvania had violated §1 of the Sherman Act by entering into and enforcing franchise agreements that prohibited the sale of Sylvania products other than from specified locations.[5] . . . Relying on this Court's decision in *United States* v. *Arnold, Schwinn & Co., supra,* the District Court . . . [gave the jury the following instruction]:

---

[2] Sylvania imposed no restrictions on the right of the franchisee to sell the products of competing manufacturers.

[3] Sylvania's market share in San Francisco was approximately 2.5 percent—half its national and northern California average.

[4] Sylvania had achieved exceptional results in Sacramento, where its market share exceeded 15 percent in 1965.

[5] Although Sylvania contended in the District Court that its policy was unilaterally enforced, it now concedes that its location restriction involved understandings or agreements with the retailers.

Therefore, if you find by a preponderance of the evidence that Sylvania entered into a contract, combination or conspiracy with one or more of its dealers pursuant to which Sylvania exercised dominion or control over the products sold to the dealer, after having parted with title and risk to the products, you must find any effort thereafter to restrict outlets or store locations from which its dealers resold the merchandise which they had purchased from Sylvania to be a violation of Section 1 of the Sherman Act, regardless of the reasonableness of the location restrictions.

In answers to special interrogatories, the jury found that Sylvania had engaged "in a contract, combination or conspiracy in restraint of trade in violation of the antitrust laws with respect to location restrictions alone." . . .

On appeal, the Court of Appeals for the Ninth Circuit, sitting en banc, reversed by a divided vote. The court acknowledged that there is language in *Schwinn* that could be read to support the District Court's instruction but concluded that *Schwinn* was distinguishable on several grounds. Contrasting the nature of the restrictions, their competitive impact, and the market shares of the franchisers in the two cases, the court concluded that Sylvania's location restriction had less potential for competitive harm than the restrictions invalidated in *Schwinn* and thus should be judged under the "rule of reason" rather than the per se rule stated in *Schwinn*. . . .

We granted Continental's petition for certiorari to resolve this important question of antitrust law.

II

A

We turn first to Continental's contention that Sylvania's restriction on retail locations is a per se violation of §1 of the Sherman Act as interpreted in *Schwinn*. The restrictions at issue in *Schwinn* were part of a three-tier distribution system comprising, in addition to Arnold, Schwinn & Co. (Schwinn), 22 intermediate distributors and a network of franchised retailers. Each distributor had a defined geographic area in which it had the exclusive right to supply franchised retailers. Sales to the public were made only through franchised retailers, who were authorized to sell Schwinn bicycles only from specified locations. In support of this limitation, Schwinn prohibited both distributors and retailers from selling Schwinn bicycles to nonfranchised retailers. At the retail level, therefore, Schwinn was able to control the number of retailers of its bicycles in any given area according to its view of the needs of that market.

The Court . . . [on appeal by the United States] stated that the resolution of the case would require an examination of "the specifics of the challenged practices and their impact upon the marketplace in order to make a judgment as to whether the restraint is or is not 'reasonable' in the special sense in which §1 of the Sherman Act must be read for purposes of this type of inquiry." . . . Despite this description of its task, the Court proceeded to articulate the following "bright line" per se rule of illegality for vertical restrictions: "Under the Sherman Act, it is unreasonable without more for a manufacturer to seek to restrict and confine areas or persons with whom an article may be traded after the manufacturer has parted with dominion over it." . . . But the Court expressly stated that the rule of reason governs when "the manufacturer retains title, dominion, and risk with respect to the product and the position and function of the dealer in question are, in fact, indistinguishable from those of an agent or salesman of the manufacturer." . . .

B

In the present case, it is undisputed that title to the televisions passed from Sylvania to Continental. Thus, the *Schwinn* per se rule applies unless Sylvania's restriction on locations falls outside *Schwinn's* prohibition against a manufacturer's attempting to restrict a "retailer's freedom as to where and to whom it will resell the products." . . . As the Court of Appeals conceded, the language of *Schwinn* is clearly broad enough to apply to the present case. Unlike the Court of Appeals, however, we are unable to find a principled basis for distinguishing *Schwinn* from the case now before us.

Both Schwinn and Sylvania sought to reduce but not to eliminate competition among their respective retailers through the adoption of a franchise system. . . . These restrictions allowed Schwinn and Sylvania to regulate the amount of competition among their retailers by preventing a franchisee from selling franchised products from outlets other than the one covered by the franchise agreement. To exactly the same end, the Schwinn franchise plan included a companion restriction, apparently not found in the Sylvania plan, that prohibited franchised retailers from selling Schwinn products to nonfranchised retailers. In *Schwinn* the Court expressly held that this restriction was impermissible under the broad principle stated there. In intent and competitive impact, the retail-customer restriction in *Schwinn* is indistinguishable from the location restriction in the present case. In both cases the restrictions limited the freedom of the retailer to dispose of the purchased products as he desired. The fact that one restriction was addressed to territory and the other to customers is irrelevant to functional antitrust analysis and, indeed, to the language and broad thrust of the opinion in *Schwinn*.[6] As MR. CHIEF JUSTICE HUGHES stated in *Appalachian Coals, Inc.* v. *United States,*

---

[6] The distinctions drawn by the Court of Appeals and endorsed in MR. JUSTICE WHITE's separate opinion have no basis in *Schwinn*. The intrabrand competitive impact of the restrictions at issue in *Schwinn* ranged from complete elimination to mere reduction; yet, the Court did not even hint at any distinction on this ground. Similarly, there is no suggestion that the per se rule was applied because of Schwinn's prominent position in its industry. . . . Although Schwinn did hint at preferential treatment for new entrants and failing firms, the District Court below did not even submit Sylvania's claim that it was failing to the jury. . . .

288 U.S. 344, 360, 377 (1933): "Realities must dominate the judgment. . . . The Antitrust Act aims at substance."

III

Sylvania argues that if *Schwinn* cannot be distinguished, it should be reconsidered. Although *Schwinn* is supported by the principle of *stare decisis,* . . . we are convinced that the need for clarification of the law in this area justifies reconsideration. *Schwinn* itself was an abrupt and largely unexplained departure from *White Motor Co.* v. *United States,* 372 U.S. 253 (1963), where only four years earlier the Court had refused to endorse a per se rule for vertical restrictions. Since its announcement, *Schwinn* has been the subject of continuing controversy and confusion, both in the scholarly journals and in the federal courts. The great weight of scholarly opinion has been critical of the decision,[7] and a number of the federal courts confronted with analogous vertical restrictions have sought to limit its reach.[8] In our view, the experience of the past ten years should be brought to bear on this subject of considerable commercial importance.

The traditional framework of analysis under §1 of the Sherman Act is familiar and does not require extended discussion. Section 1 prohibits "[e]very contract, combination. . . , or conspiracy, in restraint of trade or commerce." Since the early years of this century a judicial gloss on this statutory language has established the "rule of reason" as the prevailing standard of analysis. . . . Under this rule, the factfinder weighs all of the circumstances of a case in deciding whether a restrictive practice should be prohibited as imposing an unreasonable restraint on competition.[9] Per se rules of illegality are appropriate only when they relate to conduct that is manifestly anticompetitive. As the Court explained in *Northern Pac. R. Co.* v. *United States,* 356 U.S. 1, 5 (1958), "there are certain agreements or practices which because of their pernicious effect on competition and lack of any redeeming virtue are conclusively presumed to be unreason-

---

[7] A former assistant attorney general in charge of the Antitrust Division has described *Schwinn* as "an exercise in barren formalism" that is "artificial and unresponsive to the competitive needs of the real world." Baker, "Vertical Restraints in Times of Change: From *White* to *Schwinn* to Where?," *44 Antitrust L. J.* 537 (1975). . . .

[8] Indeed, as one commentator has observed, many courts "have struggled to distinguish or limit *Schwinn* in ways that are a tribute to judicial ingenuity." Robinson . . . ["Recent Antitrust Developments: 1974," 75 *Colum. L. Rev.* 243 (1975)], n. 13, at 272. . . .

[9] One of the most frequently cited statements of the rule of reason is that of JUSTICE BRANDEIS in *Chicago Board of Trade* v. *United States* 246 U.S. 231, 238 (1918):

"The true test of legality is whether the restraint imposed is such as merely regulates and perhaps thereby promotes competition or whether it is such as may suppress or even destroy competition. To determine that question the court must ordinarily consider the facts peculiar to the business to which the restraint is applied; its condition before and after the restraint was imposed; the nature of the restraint and its effect, actual or probable. The history of the restraint, the evil believed to exist, the reason for adopting the particular remedy, the purpose or end sought to be attained, are all relevant facts. This is not because a good intention will save an otherwise objectionable regulation or the reverse; but because knowledge of the intent may help the court to interpret facts and to predict consequences."

able and therefore illegal without elaborate inquiry as to the precise harm they have caused or the business excuse for their use.''[10]

In essence, the issue before us is whether *Schwinn's* per se rule can be justified under the demanding standards of *Northern Pac. R. Co.* The Court's refusal to endorse a per se rule in *White Motor Co.* was based on its uncertainty as to whether vertical restrictions satisfied those standards. Addressing this question for the first time, the Court stated:

> We need to know more than we do about the actual impact of these arrangements on competition to decide whether they have such a "pernicious effect on competition and lack . . . any redeeming virtue" . . . and therefore should be classified as *per se* violations of the Sherman Act 372 U.S., at 263.

Only four years later the Court in *Schwinn* announced its sweeping per se rule without even a reference to *Northern Pac. R. Co.* and with no explanation of its sudden change in position.[11] We turn now to consider *Schwinn* in light of *Northern Pac. R. Co.*

The market impact of vertical restrictions[12] is complex because of their potential for a simultaneous reduction of intrabrand competition and stimulation of interbrand competition.[13] Significantly, the Court in

---

[10] Per se rules thus require the Court to make broad generalizations about the social utility of particular commercial practices. The probability that anticompetitive consequences will result from a practice and the severity of those consequences must be balanced against its procompetitive consequences. Cases that do not fit the generalization may arise, but a per se rule reflects the judgment that such cases are not sufficiently common or important to justify the time and expense necessary to identify them. Once established, per se rules tend to provide guidance to the business community and to minimize the burdens on litigants and the judicial system of the more complex rule of reason trials . . . but those advantages are not sufficient in themselves to justify the creation of per se rules. If it were otherwise, all of antitrust law would be reduced to per se rules, thus introducing an unintended and undesirable rigidity in the law.

[11] After *White Motor Co.*, the courts of appeals continued to evaluate territorial restrictions according to the rule of reason . . .

[12] As in *Schwinn*, we are concerned here only with nonprice vertical restrictions. The per se illegality of price restrictions has been established firmly for many years and involves significantly different questions of analysis and policy. As MR. JUSTICE WHITE notes, post, . . . some commentators have argued that the manufacturer's motivation for imposing vertical price restrictions may be the same as for nonprice restrictions. There are, however, significant differences that could easily justify different treatment. In his concurring opinion in *White Motor Co.*, MR. JUSTICE BRENNAN noted that, unlike nonprice restrictions, "[r]esale price maintenance is not designed to, but almost invariably does in fact, reduce price competition not only *among* sellers of the affected product, but quite as much *between* that product and competing brands." 372 U.S. at 268. . . . Furthermore, Congress recently has expressed its approval of a per se analysis of vertical price restrictions by repealing those provisions of the Miller-Tydings and McGuire Acts allowing fair trade pricing at the option of the individual States. . . . No similar expression of congressional intent exists for nonprice restrictions.

[13] Interbrand competition is the competition among the manufacturers of the same generic product—television sets in this case—and is the primary concern of antitrust law. The extreme example of a deficiency of interbrand competition is monopoly, where there is only one manufacturer. In contrast, intrabrand competition is the competition between the distributors—wholesale or retail—of the product of a particular manufacturer.

Schwinn did not distinguish among the challenged restrictions on the basis of their individual potential for intrabrand harm or interbrand benefit. Restrictions that completely eliminated intrabrand competition among Schwinn distributors were analyzed no differently from those that merely moderated intrabrand competition among retailers. The pivotal factor was the passage of title: all restrictions were held to be per se illegal where title had passed, and all were evaluated and sustained under the rule of reason where it had not. The location restriction at issue here would be subject to the same pattern of analysis under *Schwinn*.

It appears that this distinction between sale and nonsale transactions resulted from the Court's effort to accomodate the perceived intrabrand harm and interbrand benefit of vertical restrictions. The per se rule for sale transactions reflected the view that vertical restrictions are "so obviously destructive" of intrabrand competition . . . that their use would "open the door to exclusivity of outlets and limitation of territory further than prudence permits." . . .[14] Conversely, the continued adherence to the traditional rule of reason for nonsale transactions reflected the view that the restrictions have too great a potential for the promotion of interbrand competition to justify complete prohibition.[15] The Court's opinion

---

The degree of intrabrand competition is wholly independent of the level of interbrand competition confronting the manufacturer. Thus, there may be fierce intrabrand competition among the distributors of a product produced by a monopolist and no intrabrand competition among the distributors of a product produced by a firm in a highly competitive industry. But when interbrand competition exists, as it does among television manufacturers, it provides a significant check on the exploitation of intrabrand market power because of the ability of consumers to substitute a different brand of the same product.

[14] The Court also stated that to impose vertical restrictions in sale transactions would "violate the ancient rule against restraints on alienation." 388 U.S., at 380. This isolated reference has provoked sharp criticism from virtually all of the commentators on the decision, most of whom have regarded the Court's apparent reliance on the "ancient rule" as both a misreading of legal history and a perversion of antitrust analysis. . . .

We are similarly unable to accept Judge Browning's interpretation of *Schwinn*. In his dissent below he argued that the decision reflects the view that the Sherman Act was intended to prohibit restrictions on the autonomy of independent businessmen even though they have no impact on "price, quality, and quantity of goods and services." . . . This view is certainly not explicit in *Schwinn*, which purports to be based on an examination of the "impact [of the restrictions] upon the marketplace." . . . Competitive economies have social and political as well as economic advantages, . . . but an antitrust policy divorced from market considerations would lack any objective benchmarks. . . .

[15] In that regard, the Court specifically stated that a more complete prohibition "might severely hamper smaller enterprises resorting to reasonable methods of meeting the competition of giants and of merchandising through independent dealers." . . . The Court also broadly hinted that it would recognize additional exceptions to the per se rule for new entrants in an industry and for failing firms, both of which were mentioned in *White Motor* as candidates for such exceptions . . . The Court might have limited the exceptions to the per se rule to these situations, which present the strongest arguments for the sacrifice of intrabrand competition for interbrand competition. Significantly, it chose instead to create the more extensive exception for nonsale transactions which is available to all businesses, regardless of their size, financial health, or market share. This broader exception demonstrates even more clearly the Court's awareness of the "redeeming virtues" of vertical restrictions.

provides no analytical support for these contrasting positions. Nor is there even an assertion in the opinion that the competitive impact of vertical restrictions is significantly affected by the form of the transaction. Nonsale transactions appear to be excluded from the per se rule, not because of a greater danger of intrabrand harm or a greater promise of interbrand benefit, but rather because of the Court's unexplained belief that a complete per se prohibition would be too "inflexible." . . .

Vertical restrictions reduce intrabrand competition by limiting the number of sellers of a particular product competing for the business of a given group of buyers. Location restrictions have this effect because of practical constraints on the effective marketing area of retail outlets. Although intrabrand competition may be reduced, the ability of retailers to exploit the resulting market may be limited both by the ability of consumers to travel to other franchised locations and perhaps more importantly, to purchase the competing products of other manufacturers. None of these key variables, however, is affected by the form of the transaction by which a manufacturer conveys his products to the retailers.

Vertical restrictions promote interbrand competition by allowing the manufacturer to achieve certain efficiencies in the distribution of his products. These "redeeming virtues" are implicit in every decision sustaining vertical restrictions under the rule of reason. Economists have identified a number of ways in which manufacturers can use such restrictions to compete more effectively against other manufacturers. . . .[16] For example, new manufacturers and manufacturers entering new markets can use the restrictions in order to induce competent and aggressive retailers to make the kind of investment of capital and labor that is often required in the distribution of products unknown to the consumer. Established manufacturers can use them to induce retailers to engage in promotional activities or to provide service and repair facilities necessary to the efficient marketing of their products. Service and repair are vital for many products, such as automobiles and major household appliances. The availability and quality of such services affect a manufacturer's good will and competitiveness of his product. Because of market imperfections such as the so-called free-rider effect, these services might not be provided by retailers in a purely competitive situation, despite the fact that each retailer's benefit would be greater if all provided the services than if none did. . . .

Economists also have argued that manufacturers have an economic interest in maintaining as much intrabrand competition as is consistent

---

[16] Marketing efficiency is not the only legitimate reason for a manufacturer's desire to exert control over the manner in which his products are sold and serviced. As a result of statutory and common law developments, society increasingly demands that manufacturers assume direct responsibility for the safety and quality of their products. . . . The legitimacy of these concerns has been recognized in cases involving vertical restrictions. . . .

with the efficient distribution of their products. . . .[17] Although the view that the manufacturer's interest necessarily corresponds with that of the public is not universally shared, even the leading critic of vertical restrictions concedes that *Schwinn's* distinction between sale and nonsale transactions is essentially unrelated to any relevant economic impact. Comanor, "Vertical Territorial and Customer Restrictions: *White Motor* and Its Aftermath," *81 Harv. L. Rev.* 1419, 1422 (1968).[18] Indeed, to the extent that the form of the transaction is related to interbrand benefits, the Court's distinction is inconsistent with its articulated concern for the ability of smaller firms to compete effectively with larger ones. Capital requirements and administrative expenses may prevent smaller firms from using the exception for nonsale transactions. . . .[19]

We conclude that the distinction drawn in *Schwinn* between sale and nonsale transactions is not sufficient to justify the application of a per se rule in one situation and a rule of reason in the other. The question remains whether the per se rule stated in *Schwinn* should be expanded to include nonsale transactions or abandoned in favor of a return to the rule of reason. We have found no persuasive support for expanding the per se rule. . . .

We revert to the standard articulated in *Northern Pac. R. Co.*, and reiterated in *White Motor*, for determining whether vertical restrictions must be "conclusively presumed to be unreasonable and therefore illegal without elaborate inquiry as to the precise harm they have caused or the business excuse for their use." . . . Such restrictions, in varying forms, are widely used in our free market economy. As indicated above, there is substantial scholarly and judicial authority supporting their economic utility. There is relatively little authority to the contrary.[20] Certainly,

---

[17] "Generally a manufacturer would prefer the lowest retail price possible, once its price to dealers has been set, because a lower retail price means increased sales and higher manufacturer revenues." Note, *88 Harv. L. Rev.* 636, 641 (1975). In this context, a manufacturer is likely to view the difference between the price at which it sells to its retailers and their price to the consumer as its "cost of distribution," which it would prefer to minimize. . . .

[18] Professor Comanor argues that the promotional activities encouraged by vertical restrictions result in product differentiation and, therefore, a decrease in interbrand competition. This argument is flawed by its necessary assumption that a large part of the promotional efforts resulting from vertical restrictions will not convey socially desirable information about product availability, price, quality, and services. Nor is it clear that a per se rule would result in anything more than a shift to less efficient methods of obtaining the same promotional effects.

[19] We also note that per se rules in this area may work to the ultimate detriment of the small businessmen who operate as franchisees. To the extent that a per se rule prevents a firm from using the franchise system to achieve efficiencies that it perceives as important to its successful operation, the rule creates an incentive for vertical integration into the distribution system, thereby eliminating to that extent the role of independent businessmen. . . .

[20] There may be occasional problems in differentiating vertical restrictions from horizontal restrictions originating in agreements among the retailers. There is no doubt that restrictions in the latter category would be illegal per se, . . . but we do not regard the problems of proof as sufficiently great to justify a per se rule.

there has been no showing in this case, either generally or with respect to Sylvania's agreements, that vertical restrictions have or are likely to have a "pernicious effect on competition" or that they "lack . . . any redeeming virtue." . . .[21] Accordingly, we conclude that the per se rule stated in *Schwinn* must be overruled. . . . In so holding we do not foreclose the possibility that particular applications of vertical restrictions might justify per se prohibition under *Northern Pac. R. Co.* But we do make clear that departure from the rule-of-reason standard must be based upon demonstrable economic effect rather than—as in *Schwinn*—upon formalistic line drawing.

In sum, we conclude that the appropriate decision is to return to the rule of reason that governed vertical restrictions prior to *Schwinn*. When anticompetitive effects are shown to result from particular vertical restrictions they can be adequately policed under the rule of reason, the standard traditionally applied for the majority of anticompetitive practices challenged under §1 of the Act. Accordingly, the decision of the Court of Appeals is *affirmed*.

MR. JUSTICE REHNQUIST took no part in the consideration or decision of this case.

MR. JUSTICE WHITE, concurring in the judgment.

Although I agree with the majority that the location clause at issue in this case is not a per se violation of the Sherman Act and should be judged under the rule of reason, I cannot agree that this result requires the overruling of *United States* v. *Arnold, Schwinn & Co.*, 388 U.S. 365 (1967). In my view this case is distinguishable from *Schwinn* because there is less potential for restraint of intrabrand competition and more potential for stimulating interbrand competition. As to intrabrand competition, Sylvania, unlike Schwinn, did not restrict the customers to whom or the territories where its purchasers could sell. As to interbrand competition, Sylvania, unlike Schwinn, had an insignificant market share at the time it adopted its challenged distribution practice and enjoyed no consumer preference that would allow its retailers to charge a premium over other brands. . . . To reach out to overrule one of this Court's recent interpretations of the Sherman Act, after such a cursory examination of the necessity for doing so, is surely an affront to the principle that considera-

---

[21] The location restriction used by Sylvania was neither the least nor the most restrictive provision that it could have used. . . . But we agree with the implicit judgment in *Schwinn* that a per se rule based on the nature of the restriction is, in general, undesirable. Although distinctions can be drawn among the frequently used restrictions, we are inclined to view them as differences of degree and form. . . . We are unable to perceive significant social gain from channeling transactions into one form or another. Finally, we agree with the Court in *Schwinn* that the advantages of vertical restrictions should not be limited to the categories of new entrants and failing firms. Sylvania was faltering, if not failing, and we think it would be unduly artificial to deny it the use of valuable competitive tools.

tions of *stare decisis* are to be given particularly strong weight in the area of statutory construction. . . .

One element of the system of interrelated vertical restraints invalidated in *Schwinn* was a retail-customer restriction prohibiting franchised retailers from selling Schwinn products to nonfranchised retailers. The Court rests its inability to distinguish *Schwinn* entirely on this retail-customer restriction, finding it "[i]n intent and competitive impact . . . indistinguishable from the location restriction in the present case," because "[i]n both cases the restrictions limited the freedom of the retailer to dispose of the purchased products as he desired." . . . The customer restriction may well have, however, a very different "intent and competitive impact" than the location restriction: it prevents discount stores from getting the manufacturer's product and thus prevents intrabrand price competition. Suppose, for example, that interbrand competition is sufficiently weak that the franchised retailers are able to charge a price substantially above wholesale. Under a location restriction, these franchisers are free to sell to discount stores seeking to exploit the potential for sales at prices below the prevailing retail level. One of the franchised retailers may be tempted to lower its price and act in effect as a wholesaler for the discount house in order to share in the profits to be had from lowering prices and expanding volume. . . .

Under a retail customer restriction, on the other hand, the franchised dealers cannot sell to discounters, who are cut off altogether from the manufacturer's product and the opportunity for intrabrand price competition. This was precisely the theory on which the Government successfully challenged Schwinn's customer restrictions in this Court. . . .

It is true that, as the majority states, Sylvania's location restriction inhibited to some degree "the freedom of the retailer to dispose of the purchased products" by requiring the retailer to sell from one particular place of business. But the retailer is still free to sell to any type of customer—including discounters and other unfranchised dealers—from any area. I think this freedom implies a significant difference for the effect of a location clause on intrabrand competition. The District Court on remand in *Schwinn* evidently thought so as well, for after enjoining Schwinn's customer restrictions as directed by this Court it expressly sanctioned location clauses, permitting Schwinn to "designat[e] in its retailer franchise agreements the location of the place or places of business for which the franchise is issued." . . .

An additional basis for finding less restraint of intrabrand competition in this case, emphasized by the Ninth Circuit en banc, is that *Schwinn* involved [territorial] restrictions on competition among distributors at the wholesale level. . . . Moreover, like its franchised retailers, Schwinn's distributors were absolutely barred from selling to nonfranchised retailers, further limiting the possibilities of intrabrand price competition.

The majority apparently gives no weight to the Court of Appeals' reliance on the difference between the competitive effects of Sylvania's location clause and Schwinn's interlocking "system of vertical restraints affecting both wholesale and retail distribution." . . .

Just as there are significant differences between *Schwinn* and this case with respect to intrabrand competition, there are also significant differences with respect to interbrand competition. Unlike Schwinn, Sylvania clearly had no economic power in the generic product market. At the time they instituted their respective distribution policies, Schwinn was "the leading bicycle producer in the Nation," with a national market share of 22.5 percent, . . . whereas Sylvania was a "faltering, if not failing" producer of television sets, with "a relatively insignificant 1 percent to 2 percent" share of the national market in which the dominant manufacturer had a 60 percent to 70 percent share. . . . Moreover, the Schwinn brand name enjoyed superior consumer acceptance and commanded a premium price as, in the District Court's words, "the Cadillac of the bicycle industry." . . . This premium gave Schwinn dealers a margin of protection from interbrand competition and created the possibilities for price cutting by discounters that the Government argued were forestalled by Schwinn's customer restrictions. . . . Thus, judged by the criteria economists use to measure market power—product differentiation and market share . . . —Schwinn enjoyed a substantially stronger position in the bicycle market than did Sylvania in the television market. This Court relied on Schwinn's market position as one reason not to apply the rule of reason to the vertical restraints challenged there. "Schwinn was not a newcomer, seeking a break into or a stay in the bicycle business. It was not a 'failing company.' On the contrary, at the initiation of these practices, it was the leading bicycle producer in the Nation." . . . And the Court of Appeals below found "another significant distinction between our case and *Schwinn*" in Sylvania's "precarious market share," which "was so small when it adopted its locations practice that it was threatened with explusion from the television market." . . .

In my view there are at least two considerations, both relied upon by the majority to justify overruling *Schwinn,* that would provide a "principled basis" for instead refusing to extend *Schwinn* to a vertical restraint that is imposed by a "faltering" manufacturer with a "precarious" position in a generic product market dominated by another firm. The first is that, as the majority puts it, "when interbrand competition exists, as it does among television manufacturers, it provides a significant check on the exploitation of intrabrand market power because of the ability of consumers to substitute a different brand of the same product." . . . Second is the view, argued forcefully in the economic literature cited by the majority, that the potential benefits of vertical restraints in promoting interbrand competition are particularly strong where the manufacturer imposing the restraints is seeking to enter a new market or to expand a small market share. . . . The majority even recognizes that *Schwinn* "hinted" at an exception for new entrants and failing firms from its per se rule. . . .

In other areas of antitrust law, this Court has not hesitated to base its rules of per se illegality in part on the defendant's market power. . . . I see no doctrinal obstacle to excluding firms with such minimal market power as Sylvania's from the reach of the *Schwinn* rule.[22]

I have, moreover, substantial misgivings about the approach the majority takes to overruling *Schwinn*. The reason for the distinction in *Schwinn* between sale and nonsale transactions was not, as the majority would have it, "the Court's effort to accommodate the perceived intra-brand harm and interbrand benefit of vertical restrictions. . ." ; the reason was rather, as Judge Browning argued in dissent below, the notion in many of our cases involving vertical restraints that independent businessmen should have the freedom to dispose of the goods they own as they see fit. . . .

After summarily rejecting this concern, reflected in our interpretations of the Sherman Act for "the autonomy of independent businessmen," . . . the majority not suprisingly finds "no justification" for *Schwinn's* distinction between sale and nonsale transactions because the distinction is "essentially unrelated to any relevant economic impact." . . . But while according some weight to the businessman's interest in controlling the terms on which he trades in his own goods may be anathema to those who view the Sherman Act as directed solely to economic efficiency, . . . this principle is without question more deeply embedded in our cases than the notions of free-rider effects and distributional efficiencies borrowed by the majority from the "new economics of vertical relationships." . . . Perhaps the Court is right in partially abandoning this principle and in judging the instant nonprice vertical restraints solely by their "relevant economic impact"; but the precedents which reflect this principle should not be so lightly rejected by the Court. . . .

I have a further reservation about the majority's reliance on "relevant economic impact" as the test for retaining per se rules regarding vertical restraints. It is common ground among the leading advocates of a purely economic approach to the question of distribution restraints that the economic arguments in favor of allowing vertical nonprice restraints generally apply to vertical price restraints as well.[23] Although the majority

---

[22] . . . The majority's failure to use the market share of Schwinn and Sylvania as a basis for distinguishing these cases is the more anomalous for its reliance. . . . on the economic analysis of those who distinguish the anticompetitive effects of distribution restraints on the basis of the market shares of the distributors. . . .

[23] Professor Posner writes, for example: "There is no basis for choosing between [price fixing and market division] on social grounds. If resale price maintenance is like dealer price fixing, and therefore bad, a manufacturer's assignment of exclusive sales territories is like market division, and therefore bad too. . . .

asserts that "the per se illegality of price restrictions . . . involves significantly different questions of analysis and policy," . . . I suspect this purported distinction may be as difficult to justify as that of *Schwinn* under the terms of the majority's analysis. . . . Indeed, the Court has already recognized that resale price maintenance may increase output by inducing "demand-creating activity" by dealers (such as additional retail outlets, advertising and promotion, and product servicing) that outweighs the additional sales that would result from lower prices brought about by dealer price competition. . . . These same output-enhancing possibilities of nonprice vertical restraints are relied upon by the majority as evidence of their "social utility and economic soundness," . . . and as a justification for judging them under the rule of reason. The effect, if not the intention, of the Court's opinion is necessarily to call into question the firmly established per se rule against price restraints.

Although the case law in the area of distributional restraints has perhaps been less than satisfactory, the Court would do well to proceed more deliberately in attempting to improve it. . . . In order to decide this case, the Court need only hold that a location clause imposed by a manufacturer with negligible economic power in the product market has a competitive impact sufficiently less restrictive than the *Schwinn* restraints to justify a rule-of-reason standard, even if the same weight is given here as in *Schwinn* to dealer autonomy. I therefore concur in the judgment.

MR. JUSTICE BRENNAN, with whom MR. JUSTICE MARSHALL joins, dissenting.

I would not overrule the per se rule stated in *United States* v. *Arnold, Schwinn & Co.*, 388 U.S. 365 (1967), and would therefore reverse the decision of the Court of Appeals for the Ninth Circuit.

Siegel v. *Chicken Delight, Inc.*
448 F.2d 43 (9th Cir. 1971)
cert. denied 405 U.S. 955 (1972)

. . . . .

I. FACTUAL BACKGROUND

Over its eighteen years' existence, Chicken Delight has licensed several hundred franchisees to operate home delivery and pick-up food stores. It charged its franchisees no franchise fees or royalties. Instead, in exchange for the license granting the franchisees the right to assume its

---

"[If helping new entrants break into a market] is a good justification for exclusive territories, it is an equally good justification for resale price maintenance, which as we have seen is simply another method of dealing with the free-rider problem. . . . In fact, *any* argument that can be made on behalf of exclusive territories can also be made on behalf of resale price maintenance." Posner, *supra*, n. 7, at 292–293. (Footnote omitted.) . . .

identity and adopt its business methods and to prepare and market certain food products under its trade-mark, Chicken Delight required its franchisees to purchase a specified number of cookers and fryers and to purchase certain packaging supplies and mixes exclusively from Chicken Delight. . . . The prices fixed for these purchases were higher than, and included a percentage markup which exceeded that of, comparable products sold by competing suppliers.

II. THE EXISTENCE OF AN UNLAWFUL TYING ARRANGEMENT

. . . In order to establish that there exists an unlawful tying arrangement plaintiffs must demonstrate *First,* that the scheme in question involves two distinct items and provides that one (the tying product) may not be obtained unless the other (the tied product) is also purchased. . . . *Second,* that the tying product possesses sufficient economic power appreciably to restrain competition in the tied product market. . . . *Third,* that a "not insubstantial" amount of commerce is affected by the arrangement. . . . Chicken Delight concedes that the third requirement has been satisfied. It disputes the existence of the first two. Further it asserts that, even if plaintiffs should prevail with respect to the first two requirements, there is a *fourth* issue: whether there exists a special justification for the particular tying arrangement in question. . . .

A. Two Products

. . . The hallmark of a tie-in is that it denies competitors free access to the tied product market, not because the party imposing the arrangement has a superior product in that market, but because of the power or leverage exerted by the tying product. . . . Rules governing tying arrangements are designed to strike, not at the mere coupling of physically separable objects, but rather at the use of a dominant desired product to compel the purchase of a second, distinct commodity. . . . In effect, the forced purchase of the second, tied product is a price exacted for the purchase of the dominant, tying product. By shutting competitors out of the tied product market, tying arrangements serve hardly any purpose other than the suppression of competition. . . .

Chicken Delight urges us to hold that its trade-mark and franchise licenses are not items separate and distinct from the packaging, mixes, and equipment, which it says are essential components of the franchise system. . . . To treat the combined sale of all these items as a tie-in for antitrust purposes, Chicken Delight maintains, would be like applying the antitrust rules to the sale of a car with its tires or a left shoe with the right. Therefore, concludes Chicken Delight, the lawfulness of the arrangement should not be measured by the rules governing tie-ins. We disagree.

. . . In determining whether an aggregation of separable items should be regarded as one or more items for tie-in purposes in the normal cases of sales of products the courts must look to the function of the aggregation. . . . Consideration is given to such questions as whether the amalgamation of products resulted in cost savings apart from those reductions in sales expenses and the like normally attendant upon any tie-in, and whether the items are normally sold or used as a unit with fixed proportions.[1]

Where one of the products sold as part of an aggregation is a trademark or franchise license, new questions are injected. In determining whether the license and the remaining ("tied") items in the aggregation are to be regarded as distinct items which can be traded in distinct markets consideration must be given to the function of trade-marks.

The historical conception of a trade-mark as a strict emblem of source of the product to which it attaches has largely been abandoned. The burgeoning business of franchising has made trade-mark licensing a widespread commercial practice and has resulted in the development of a new rationale for trade-marks as representations of product quality. . . . This is particularly true in the case of a franchise system set up not to distribute the trade-marked goods of the franchisor, but, as here, to conduct a certain business under a common trade-mark or trade name. . . . Under such a type of franchise, the trade-mark simply reflects the goodwill and quality standards of the enterprise which it identifies. As long as the system of operation of the franchisees lives up to those quality standards and remains as represented by the mark so that the public is not misled, neither the protection afforded the trade-mark by law nor the value of the trade-mark to the licensee depends upon the source of the components.

This being so, it is apparent that the goodwill of the Chicken Delight trade-mark does not attach to the multitude of separate articles used in the operation of the licensed system or in the production of its end product. It is not what is used, but how it is used and what results that have given the system and its end product their entitlement to trade-mark protection. It is to the system and the end product that the public looks with the confidence that established goodwill has created.

. . . Thus, sale of a franchise license, with the attendant rights to operate a business in the prescribed manner and to benefit from the goodwill of the trade name, in no way requires the forced sale by the franchisor of some or all of the component articles. Just as the quality of a

---

[1] It should be readily apparent that, measured against these tests, the package sales here in question are quite different from the sale of an automobile and its tires or a left shoe and the right. In particular, there are several factors in this case which other courts have deemed sufficient to find a tie-in. Undisputed testimony at trial established that other franchisors in fast food businesses similar to that of Chicken Delight sold their licenses separate from the essential supplies. The various supplies sold here were sold individually and in differing amounts, rather than in a preassembled package, and the franchisees were billed accordingly. At no time were the franchisees required to purchase all their various supplies from Chicken Delight. Chicken Delight did not itself manufacture the tied items.

copyrighted creation cannot by a tie-in be appropriated by a creation to which the copyright does not relate, . . . so here attempts by tie-in to extend the trade-mark protection to common articles (which the public does not and has no reason to connect with the trade-mark) simply because they are said to be essential to production of that which is the subject of the trade-mark, cannot escape antitrust scrutiny.

. . . Chicken Delight's assertions that only a few essential items were involved in the arrangement does not give us cause to reach a different conclusion. The relevant question is not whether the items are essential to the franchise, but whether it is essential to the franchise that the items be purchased from Chicken Delight. This raises not the issue of whether there is a tie-in but rather the issue of whether the tie-in is justifiable, a subject to be discussed below.

We conclude that the District Court was not in error in ruling as matter of law that the arrangement involved distinct tying and tied products.

B. Economic Power

. . . Under the *per se* theory of illegality, plaintiffs are required to establish not only the existence of a tying arrangement but also that the tying product possesses sufficient economic power to appreciably restrain free competition in the tied product markets. . . .

Chicken Delight points out that while it was an early pioneer in the fast food franchising field, the record establishes that there has recently been a dramatic expansion in this area, with the advent of numerous firms, including many chicken franchising systems, all competing vigorously with each other. Under the circumstances, it contends that the existence of the requisite market dominance remained a jury question.

The District Court ruled, however, that Chicken Delight's unique registered trade-mark, in combination with its demonstrated power to impose a tie-in, established as matter of law the existence of sufficient market power to bring the case within the Sherman Act.

We agree. . . .

It can hardly be denied that the Chicken Delight trade-mark is distinctive; that it possesses goodwill and public acceptance unique to it and not enjoyed by other fast food chains.

. . . It is now clear that sufficient economic power is to be presumed where the tying product is patented or copyrighted. . . .

Just as the patent or copyright forecloses competitors from offering the distinctive product on the market, so the registered trade-mark presents a legal barrier against competition. It is not the nature of the public interest that has caused the legal barrier to be erected that is the basis for the presumption, but the fact that such a barrier does exist. Accordingly we see no reason why the presumption that exists in the case of the patent and copyright does not equally apply to the trade-mark. . . .

Thus we conclude that the District Court did not err in ruling as matter of law that the tying product—the license to use the Chicken Delight trade-mark—possessed sufficient market power to bring the case within the Sherman Act.

C. *Justification*

Chicken Delight maintains that, even if its contractual arrangements are held to constitute a tying arrangement, it was not an unreasonable restraint under the Sherman Act. Three different bases for justification are urged.

. . . First, Chicken Delight contends that the arrangement was a reasonable device for measuring and collecting revenue. There is no authority for justifying a tying arrangement on this ground. Unquestionably, there exist feasible alternative methods of compensation for the franchise licenses, including royalties based on sales volume or fees computed per unit of time, which would neither involve tie-ins nor have undesirable anticompetitive consequences.[2]

. . . Second, Chicken Delight advances as justification the fact that when it first entered the fast food field in 1952 it was a new business and was then entitled to the protection afforded by *United States* v. *Jerrold Electronics Corp.,* . . . 187 F. Supp. 545 (E.D. Pa. 1960). As to the period here involved—1963 to 1970—it contends that transition to a different arrangement would be difficult if not economically impossible.

We find no merit in this contention. Whatever claim Chicken Delight might have had to a new business defense in 1952—a question we need not decide—the defense cannot apply to the 1963–70 period. To accept Chicken Delight's argument would convert the new business justification into a perpetual license to operate in restraint of trade. *See* Id., 187 F. Supp. at 558, 561.

The third justification Chicken Delight offers is the "marketing identity" purpose, the franchisor's preservation of the distinctiveness, uniformity and quality of its product.

. . . In the case of a trade-mark this purpose cannot be lightly dismissed. Not only protection of the franchisor's goodwill is involved. The licensor owes an affirmative duty to the public to assure that in the hands of his licensee the trade-mark continues to represent that which it purports to represent. For a licensor, through relaxation of quality control, to permit inferior products to be presented to the public under his licensed mark might well constitute a misuse of the mark. . . .

However, to recognize that such a duty exists is not to say that every means of meeting it is justified. Restraint of trade can be justified only in the absence of less restrictive alternatives. In cases such as this, where the alternative of specification is available,[3] the language used in *Stan-*

---

[2] It bears noting that Chicken Delight's competitors in the fast food franchising business did not find it necessary to use tie-ins.

[3] There may, of course, be cases where some extraordinary condition forecloses specification, *e.g.*, where it would divulge a trade secret.

dard Oil Co. v. *United States,* . . . 337 U.S. at 306 (1949), . . . in our view states the proper test, applicable in the case of trade-marks as well as in other cases:

> . . . the protection of the good will of the manufacturer of the tying device—fails in the usual situation because specification of the type and quality of the product to be used in connection with the tying device is protection enough. . . . The only situation, indeed, in which the protection of good will may necessitate the use of tying clauses is where specifications for a substitute would be so detailed that they could not practicably be supplied. . . .

The District Court found factual issues to exist as to whether effective quality control could be achieved by specification in the case of the cooking machinery and the dip and spice mixes. These questions were given to the jury under instructions; and the jury, in response to special interrogatories, found against Chicken Delight. . . .

As to the paper packaging, the court ruled as matter of law that no justification existed. It stated, 311 F. Supp. at page 851:

> Defendants' showing on paper packaging is nothing more than a recitation of the need for distinctive packaging to be used uniformly by all franchisees in identifying the hot foods. This was not contested. However, the admissions in evidence clearly demonstrate that the tied packaging was easily specifiable. In fact, the only specifications required were printing and color. Moreover, defendants have admitted that any competent manufacturer of like products could consistently and satisfactorily manufacture the packaging products if defendants furnished specifications. Those suppliers could have sold to the franchisees through normal channels of distribution.

We agree. One cannot immunize a tie-in from the antitrust laws by simply stamping a trade-mark symbol on the tied product—at least where the tied product is not itself the product represented by the mark.

We conclude that the District Court was not in error in holding as matter of law (and upon the limited jury verdict) that Chicken Delight's contractual requirements constituted a tying arrangement in violation of §1 of the Sherman Act. Upon this aspect of the case, judgment is affirmed. . . .

PART FIVE

Antitrust and Regulation

12

Does Regulation Make
a Difference?

The cases presented in this chapter serve two purposes. First, they supplement the recent merger decisions set forth in Chapter 5 and are of interest as merger cases alone. Second, they illustrate a development in antitrust which continues to generate a substantial amount of controversy among both students and policymakers—attempts to reconcile the methods used by regulators with those favored by antitrust enforcement officials.

Parker v. *Brown*

338 U.S. 341 (1943)

MR. CHIEF JUSTICE STONE delivered the opinion of the Court.

The questions for our consideration are whether the marketing program adopted for the 1940 raisin crop under the California Agricultural Prorate Act is rendered invalid (1) by the Sherman Act, or (2) by the Agricultural Marketing Agreement Act of 1937, as amended, . . . or (3) by the Commerce Clause of the Constitution.[1]

Appellee, a producer and packer of raisins in California brought this suit in the district court to enjoin appellants—the State Director of Agriculture, Raisin Proration Zone No. 1, the members of the State Agricultural Prorate Advisory Commission and of the Program Committee for Zone No. 1, and others charged by the statute with the administration of the Prorate Act—from enforcing, as to appellee, a program for marketing the 1940 crop of raisins produced in "Raisin Proration Zone No. 1." . . .

As appears from the evidence and from the findings of the district

---

[1] We include here only that portion of the opinion relating to (1). IMS.

court, almost all of the raisins consumed in the United States, and nearly one-half of the world crop, are produced in Raisin Proration Zone No. 1. Between 90 and 95 percent of the raisins grown in California are ultimately shipped in interstate or foreign commerce. . . .

The California Agricultural Prorate Act authorizes the establishment, through action of state officials, of programs for the marketing of agricultural commodities produced in the state, so as to restrict competition among the growers and maintain prices in the distribution of their commodities to packers. The declared purpose of the Act is to "conserve the agricultural wealth of the State" and to "prevent economic waste in the marketing of agricultural products" of the state. . . .

Upon the petition of ten producers for the establishment of a prorate marketing plan for any commodity within a defined production zone . . . , and after a public hearing . . . , and after making prescribed economic findings . . . showing that the institution of a program for the proposed zone will prevent agricultural waste and conserve agricultural wealth of the state without permitting unreasonable profits to producers, the Commission is authorized to grant the petition. The Director, with the approval of the Commission, is then required to select a program committee from among nominees chosen by the qualified producers within the zone, to which he may add not more than two handlers or packers who receive the regulated commodity from producers for marketing. . . .

The program committee is required . . . to formulate a proration marketing program for the commodity produced in the zone, which the Commission is authorized to approve after a public hearing and a "finding that the program is reasonably calculated to carry out the objectives of the Act." The Commission may, if so advised, modify the program and approve it as modified. If the proposed program, as approved by the Commission, is consented to by 65 percent in number of producers in the zone owning 51 percent of the acreage devoted to production of the regulated crop, the Director is required to declare the program instituted. . . .

Authority to administer the program, subject to the approval of the Director of Agriculture, is conferred on the program committee. . . . Section 22.5 declares that it shall be a misdemeanor . . . for any producer to sell or any handler to receive or possess without proper authority any commodity for which a proration program has been instituted. . . . Section 25 imposes a civil liability of $500 "for each and every violation" of any provision of a proration program.

The seasonal proration marketing program for raisins, with which we are now concerned, became effective on September 7, 1940. This provided that the program committee should classify raisins as "standard," "substandard," and "inferior"; "inferior" raisins are those which are unfit for human consumption, as defined in the Federal Food, Drug and Cosmetic Act. . . . The committee is required to establish receiving stations within the zone to which every producer must deliver all raisins which he desires to market. The raisins are graded at these stations. All inferior raisins are to be placed in the "inferior raisin pool," to be disposed of by the committee "only for assured by-product and other diversion purposes." All substandard raisins, and at least 20 percent of the total standard and substandard raisins produced, must be placed in a "surplus pool." Raisins in this pool may also be disposed of only for "assured by-product and other diversion purposes," except that under certain circumstances the program committee may transfer standard raisins from the surplus pool to the stabilization pool. Fifty percent of the crop must be placed in a "stabilization pool."

Under the program the producer is permitted to sell the remaining 30 percent of his standard raisins, denominated "free tonnage," through ordinary commercial channels, subject to the requirement that he obtain a "secondary certificate" authorizing such marketing and pay a certificate fee of $2.50 for each ton covered by the certificate. Certification is stated to be a device for controlling "the time and volume of movement" of free tonnage into such ordinary commercial channels. Raisins in the stabilization pool are to be disposed of by the committee "in such manner as to obtain stability in the market and to dispose of such raisins," but no raisins (other than those subject to special lending or pooling arrangements of the Federal Government) can be sold by the committee at less than the prevailing market price for raisins of the same variety and grade on the date of sale. . . .

Appellee's bill of complaint challenges the validity of the proration program as in violation of the Commerce Clause and the Sherman Act; in support of the decree of the district court he also urges that it conflicts with and is superseded by the Federal Agricultural Marketing Agreement Act of 1937. The complaint alleges that he is engaged within the marketing zone both in producing and in purchasing and packing raisins for sale and shipment interstate; that before the adoption of the program he had entered into contracts for the sale of 1940 crop raisins; that, unless enjoined, appellants will enforce the program against appellee by criminal prosecutions and will prevent him from marketing his 1940 crop, from fulfilling his sales contracts, and from purchasing for sale and selling in interstate commerce raisins of that crop. . . .

VALIDITY OF THE PRORATE PROGRAM UNDER THE SHERMAN ACT

Section 1 of the Sherman Act, 15 U.S.C. §1, makes unlawful "every contract, combination . . or conspiracy, in restraint of trade or commerce among the several States." And, 15 U.S.C. §2, makes it unlawful to "monopolize, or attempt to monopolize, or combine or conspire with any other person or persons, to monopolize any part of the trade or commerce among the several States." We may assume for present purposes that the California prorate program would violate the Sherman Act if it were organized and made effective solely by virtue of a contract, combination or conspiracy of private persons, individual or corporate. . . .

But it is plain that the prorate program here was never intended to operate by force of individual agreement or combination. It derived its authority and its efficacy from the legislative command of the state and was not intended to operate or become effective without that command. We find nothing in the language of the Sherman Act or in its history which suggests that its purpose was to restrain a state or its officers or agents from activities directed by its legislature. In a dual system of government in which, under the Constitution, the states are sovereign, save only as Congress may constitutionally subtract from their authority, an unexpressed purpose to nullify a state's control over its officers and agents is not lightly to be attributed to Congress.

The Sherman Act makes no mention of the state as such, and gives no hint that it was intended to restrain state action or official action directed by a state. The Act is applicable to "persons' including corporations . . . , and it authorizes suits under it by persons and corporations. . . .

There is no suggestion of a purpose to restrain state action in the Act's legislative history. The sponsor of the bill which was ultimately enacted as the Sherman Act declared that it prevented only "business combinations." . . . That its purpose was to suppress combinations to restrain competition and attempts to monopolize by individuals and corporations, abundantly appears from its legislative history. . . .

True, a state does not give immunity to those who violate the Sherman Act by authorizing them to violate it, or by declaring that their action is lawful, . . . and we have no question of the state or its municipality becoming a participant in a private agreement or combination by others for restraint of trade. . . . Here the state command to the Commission and to the program committee of the California Prorate Act is not rendered unlawful by the Sherman Act since, in view of the latter's words and history, it must be taken to be a prohibition of individual and not state action. It is the state which has created the machinery for establishing the prorate program. Although the organization of a prorate zone is proposed by producers, and a prorate program, approved by the Commission, must also be approved by referendum of producers, it is the state, acting through the Commission, which adopts the program and which enforces it with penal sanctions, in the execution of a governmental policy. The prerequisite approval of the program upon referendum by a prescribed number of producers is not the imposition by them of their will upon the minority by force of agreement or combination which the Sherman Act prohibits. The state itself exercises its legislative authority in making the regulation and in prescribing the conditions of its application. The required vote on the referendum is one of these conditions. . . .

The state in adopting and enforcing the prorate program made no contract or agreement and entered into no conspiracy in restraint of trade or to establish monopoly but, as sovereign, imposed the restraint as an act of government which the Sherman Act did not undertake to prohibit. . . .

Reversed.

      ᵻ • • ᵻ ᵻ

Note: In two subsequent cases, *Washington Gas Light Co.* v. *Virginia Electric and Power Co.*, 438 F.2d 248 (4th Cir. 1971) and *Gas Light Co. of Columbus* v. *Georgia Power Co.*, 440 F.2d 1135 (5th Cir. 1971), the courts have held that promotional practices of electric utilities which have been approved (either expressly or tacitly) by state regulatory commissions are entitled to antitrust immunity under the *Parker* rule. The former was settled out of court; the latter was denied certiorari by the Supreme Court.

Cantor v. *Detroit Edison Co.*

428 U.S. 579 (1976)

MR. JUSTICE STEVENS delivered the opinion of the Court.[1]

In *Parker* v. *Brown*, 317 U.S. 341, the Court held that the Sherman Act was not violated by state action displacing competition in the marketing of raisins. In this case we must decide whether the *Parker* rationale immunizes private action which has been approved by a state and which must be continued while the state approval remains effective.

The Michigan Public Service Commission pervasively regulates the distribution of electricity within the State and also has given its approval to a marketing practice which has a substantial impact on the otherwise unregulated business of distributing electric light bulbs. Assuming, *arguendo,* that the approved practice has unreasonably restrained trade in the light-bulb market, the District Court . . . and the Court of Appeals . . . . held, on the authority of *Parker,* that the Commission's approval exempted the practice from the federal antitrust laws. . . . We now reverse.

Petitioner, a retail druggist selling light bulbs, claims that respondent is using its monopoly power in the distribution of electricity to restrain competition in the sale of bulbs in violation of the Sherman Act. . . . We state only the facts pertinent to that issue and assume, without opining, that without such approval an antitrust violation would exist. To the extent that the facts are disputed, we must resolve doubts in favor of the petitioner since summary judgment was entered against him. We first

---

[1] Parts II and IV of this opinion are joined only by MR. JUSTICE BRENNAN, MR. JUSTICE WHITE, and MR. JUSTICE MARSHALL.

describe respondent's "lamp-exchange program," we next discuss the holding in *Parker* v. *Brown,* and then we consider whether that holding should be extended to cover this case. . . .

I

Respondent, the Detroit Edison Co., distributes electricity and electric light bulbs to about five million people in southeastern Michigan. In this marketing area, respondent is the sole supplier of electricity, and supplies consumers with almost 50 percent of the standard-size light bulbs they use most frequently.[2] Customers are billed for the electricity they consume, but pay no separate charge for light bulbs. Respondent's rates, including the omission of any separate charge for bulbs, have been approved by the Michigan Public Service Commission and may not be changed without the Commission's approval. Respondent must, therefore, continue its lamp-exchange program until it files a new tariff and that new tariff is approved by the Commission.

Respondent, or a predecessor, has been following the practice of providing limited amounts of light bulbs to its customers without additional charge since 1886.[3] . . . In 1916 the Michigan Public Service Commission first approved a tariff filed by respondent setting forth the lamp-supply program. Thereafter, the Commission's approval of respondent's tariffs has included implicit approval of the lamp-exchange program. . . .

In 1972 respondent provided its residential customers with 18,564,381 bulbs at a cost of $2,835,000. . . . In its accounting to the Michigan Public Service Commission, respondent included this amount as a portion of its cost of providing service to its customers. Respondent's accounting records reflect no direct profit as a result of the distribution of bulbs. The purpose of the program, according to respondent's executives, is to increase the consumption of electricity. The effect of the program, according to petitioner, is to foreclose competition in a substantial segment of the light-bulb market. . . .

The distribution of electricity in Michigan is pervasively regulated by the Michigan Public Service Commission. . . . The statute confers express power on the Commission "to regulate all rates, fares, fees, charges, services, rules, conditions of service, and all other matters pertaining to the formation, operation, or direction of such public utilities." . . .

---

[2] Respondent does not distribute florescent lights or high-intensity discharge lamps; if bulbs of those types were included, respondent's share of the market would only be about 23 percent.

[3] Under respondent's practice, new residential customers are provided with bulbs in "such quantities as may be needed" for all of their permanent fixtures; thereafter, respondent replaces residential customers' burned-out light bulbs in proportion to their estimated use of electricity for lighting. The customer incurs no direct charge for such bulbs at the time they are furnished to him but normally turns in any burned-out bulbs to obtain a new supply.

The distribution of electric light bulbs in Michigan is unregulated. The statute creating the Commission contains no direct reference to light bulbs. Nor, as far as we have been advised, does any other Michigan statute authorize the regulation of that business. Neither the Michigan Legislature, nor the Commission, has ever made any specific investigation of the desirability of a lamp-exchange program or of its possible effect on competition in the light-bulb market. Other utilities regulated by the Michigan Public Service Commission do not follow the practice of providing bulbs to their customers at no additional charge. The Commission's approval of respondent's decision to maintain such a program does not, therefore, implement any statewide policy relating to light bulbs. We infer that the state's policy is neutral on the question whether a utility should, or should not, have such a program.

Although there is no statute, Commission rule, or policy which would prevent respondent from abandoning the program merely by filing a new tariff providing for a proper adjustment in its rates, it is nevertheless apparent that while the existing tariff remains in effect, respondent may not abandon the program without violating a Commission order, and therefore without violating state law. . . .

II

In *Parker* v. *Brown* the Court considered whether the Sherman Act applied to state action. The way the Sherman Act question was presented and argued in that case sheds significant light on the character of the state-action concept embraced by the *Parker* holding.

The plaintiff, Brown, was a producer and packer of raisins; the defendants were the California Director of Agriculture and other public officials charged by California statute with responsibility for administering a program for the marketing of the 1940 crop of raisins. The express purpose of the program was to restrict competition among the growers and maintain prices in the distribution of raisins to packers. . . . Nevertheless, in the District Court, Brown did not argue that the defendants had violated the Sherman Act. He sought an injunction against the enforcement of the program on the theory that it interfered with his constitutional right to engage in interstate commerce. . . . With one judge dissenting, the District Court held that the program violated the Commerce Clause and granted injunctive relief. . . .

The defendant state officials took a direct appeal to this Court. Probable jurisdiction was noted on April 6, 1942, and the court heard oral argument on the Commerce Clause issue on May 5, 1942. In the meantime, on April 27, 1942, the Court held that the State of Georgia is a "person" within the meaning of §7 of the Sherman Act and therefore entitled to maintain an action for treble damages. . . .

Presumably because the Court was then concerned with the relationship between the sovereign states and the antitrust laws, it immediately set *Parker* v. *Brown* for reargument . . . and, on its own motion requested the Solicitor General of the United States to file a brief as *amicus curiae* and directed the parties to discuss the question whether the California statute was rendered invalid by the Sherman Act. . . .

This Court set aside the injunction entered by the District Court. . . . The Court held that even though comparable programs organized by private persons would be illegal, the action taken by state officials pursuant to express legislative command did not violate the Sherman Act. . . .

This narrow holding . . . avoided any question about the applicability of the antitrust laws to private action taken under color of state law.

Unquestionably the term *state action* may be used broadly to encompass individual action supported to some extent by state law or custom. Such a broad use of the term, which is familiar in civil rights litigation, . . . is not, however, what MR. CHIEF JUSTICE STONE described in his *Parker* opinion. He carefully selected language which plainly limited the Court's holding to official action taken by state officials. . . .

In this case, unlike *Parker,* the only defendant is a private utility. No public officials or agencies are named as parties and there is no claim that any state action violated the antitrust laws. Conversely, in *Parker* there was no claim that any private citizen or company had violated the law. The only Sherman Act issue decided was whether the sovereign State itself, which had been held to be a person within the meaning of §7 of the statute, was also subject to its prohibitions. Since the case now before us does not call into question the legality of any act of the State of Michigan or any of its officials or agents, it is not controlled by the *Parker* decision.

III

In this case we are asked to hold that private conduct required by state law is exempt from the Sherman Act. Two quite different reasons might support such a rule. First, if a private citizen has done nothing more than obey the command of his state sovereign, it would be unjust to conclude that he has thereby offended federal law. Second, if the state is already regulating an area of the economy, it is arguable that Congress did not intend to superimpose the antitrust laws as an additional, and perhaps conflicting, regulatory mechanism. We consider these two reasons separately.

We may assume, *arguendo,* that it would be unacceptable ever to impose statutory liability on a party who had done nothing more than obey a state command. Such an assumption would not decide this case, if, indeed, it would decide any actual case. For typically cases of this kind involve a blend of private and public decisionmaking. . . . The Court has already decided that state authorization, . . . approval, . . . encouragement, . . . or participation . . . in restrictive private conduct confers on antitrust immunity. And in *Schwegmann Bros.* v. *Calvert*

Corp., 341 U.S. 384, the Court invalidated the plaintiff's entire resale price maintenance program even though it was effective throughout the State only because the Louisiana statute imposed a direct restraint on retailers who had not signed fair trade agreements.[4] . . .

The case before us also discloses a program which is the product of a decision in which both the respondent and the Commission participated. Respondent could not maintain the lamp-exchange program without the approval of the Commission, and now may not abandon it without such approval. Nevertheless, there can be no doubt that the option to have, or not to have, such a program is primarily respondent's, not the Commission's. . . . Indeed, respondent initiated the program years before the regulatory agency was even created. There is nothing unjust in the conclusion that respondent's participation in the decision is sufficiently significant to require that its conduct implementing the decision, like comparable conduct by unregulated businesses, conform to applicable federal law.[5] Accordingly, even though there may be cases in which the state's participation in a decision is so dominant that it would be unfair to hold a private party responsible for his conduct in implementing it, this record discloses no such unfairness.

Apart from the question of fairness to the individual who must conform not only to state regulation but to the federal antitrust laws as well, we must consider whether Congress intended to superimpose antitrust standards on conduct already being regulated under a different standard. *Amici curiae* forcefully contend that the competitive standard imposed by antitrust legislation is fundamentally inconsistent with the "public interest" standard widely enforced by regulatory agencies, and that the essential teaching of *Parker* v. *Brown* is that the federal antitrust laws should not be applied in areas of the economy pervasively regulated by state agencies.

There are at least three reasons why this argument is unacceptable. First, merely because certain conduct may be subject both to state regulation and to the federal antitrust laws does not necessarily mean that it must satisfy inconsistent standards; second, even assuming inconsistency, we could not accept the view that the federal interest must inevita-

---

[4] Thus, although the private decision to enforce a statewide fair trade program was not only approved by the State, but actually would have been ineffective without the statutory command to nonsigners to adhere to the prices set by the plaintiff, the rationale of *Parker* v. *Brown* did not immunize the restraint. Quite the contrary, in his opinion for the Court MR. JUSTICE DOUGLAS cited *Parker* for the proposition that private conduct was forbidden by the Sherman Act even though the State had compelled retailers to follow a parallel price policy. He said: "Therefore, when a state compels retailers to follow a parallel price policy, it demands private conduct which the Sherman Act forbids." . . .

[5] Nor is such a conclusion even arguably inconsistent with the underlying rationale of *Parker* v. *Brown*. For in that case California required every raisin producer in the State to comply with the proration program, whereas Michigan has never required any utility to adopt a lamp-exchange program.

bly be subordinated to state's; and finally, even if we were to assume that Congress did not intend the antitrust laws to apply to areas of the economy primarily regulated by a state, that assumption would not foreclose the enforcement of the antitrust laws in an essentially unregulated area such as the market for electric light bulbs.

Unquestionably there are examples of economic regulation in which the very purpose of the government control is to avoid the consequences of unrestrained competition. Agricultural marketing programs, such as that involved in *Parker* were of that character. But all economic regulation does not necessarily suppress competition. On the contrary, public utility regulation typically assumes that the private firm is a natural monopoly and that public controls are necessary to protect the consumer from exploitation. . . . There is no logical inconsistency between requiring such a firm to meet regulatory criteria insofar as it is exercising its natural monopoly powers and also to comply with antitrust standards to the extent that it engages in business activity in competitive areas of the economy. . . . Thus, Michigan's regulation of respondent's distribution of electricity poses no necessary conflict with a federal requirement that respondent's activities in competitive markets satisfy antitrust standards. . . .

The Court has consistently refused to find that regulation gave rise to an implied exemption without first determining that exemption was necessary in order to make the regulatory act work, "and even then only to the minimum extent necessary." . . .

The application of that standard to this case inexorably requires rejection of respondent's claim. For Michigan's regulatory scheme does not conflict with federal antitrust policy and, conversely, if the federal antitrust laws should be construed to outlaw respondent's light-bulb exchange program, there is no reason to believe that Michigan's regulation of its electric utilities will no longer be able to function effectively. Regardless of the outcome of this case, Michigan's interest in regulating its utilities' distribution of electricity will be almost entirely unimpaired.

We conclude that neither Michigan's approval of the tariff filed by respondent, nor the fact that the lamp-exchange program may not be terminated until a new tariff is filed, is a sufficient basis for implying an exemption from the federal antitrust laws for that program.[6]

IV

. . .

Since the District Court has not yet addressed the question whether the

---

[6] Of course, the absence of an exemption from the antitrust laws does not mean that those laws have been violated.

complaint alleged a violation of the antitrust laws, the case is remanded for a determination of that question and for such other proceedings as may be appropriate.

Reversed and remanded.

MR. CHIEF JUSTICE BERGER, concurring in the judgment and in all except Parts II and IV of the Court's opinion.

MR. JUSTICE BLACKMUN, concurring in the judgment.

I agree with the Court insofar as it holds that the fact that anticompetitive conduct is sanctioned, or even required, by state law does not of itself put that conduct beyond the reach of the Sherman Act. Since the opposite proposition is the ground on which the Court of Appeals affirmed the dismissal of this suit, I also agree that its judgment must be reversed. My approach, however, is somewhat different from that of the Court.

I

Our question in this case is one that the Sherman Act's framers did not directly confront or explicitly address: what was to be the result if the expanding ambit of the Sherman Act should bring it into conflict with inconsistent state law? But it seems to me that this bridge . . . has been crossed. In *Schwegmann Bros.* v. *Calvert Distillers Corp.*, 341 U.S. 384 (1951), the issue was whether the Sherman Act permitted enforcement of a Louisiana statute requiring compliance by liquor retailers with resale price agreements to which they were not parties, but which had been entered into by other retailers with their wholesale suppliers. The Court held the Louisiana statute unenforceable; there is no plausible reading of that decision other than that the statute was pre-empted by the Sherman Act. . . .

Congress itself has given support to the view that inconsistent state laws are preempted by the Sherman Act. Were it the case that state statutes held complete sway, Congress would not have found it necessary in 1937 to pass the Miller-Tydings Fair Trade Act . . . amending the Sherman Act, specifically exempting from the latter's operation certain price maintenance agreements sanctioned by state law. . . . There are other instances of Congress' acting to protect state-sanctioned anticompetitive schemes from the Sherman Act. . . . These express grants of Sherman Act immunity seem significant to me. As the Court stated in *United States* v. *Borden Co.*, 308 U.S. 188, 201 (1939), construing the immunity granted to certain agreements by the Agricultural Marketing Agreement Act of 1937, "[i]f Congress has desired to grant any further immunity, Congress doubtless would have said so."

II

I also agree with MR. JUSTICE STEVENS that the particular anticompetitive scheme attacked in this case must fall despite the imprimatur it claims to have received from the State of Michigan. To say, as I have, that the Sherman Act generally preempts inconsistent state laws is not to answer the much more difficult question as to which such laws are preempted and to what extent. I fear there are no easy solutions, though several suggest themselves. . . .

. . . The balancing of harm and benefit is, in general, a process with which federal courts are well acquainted in the antitrust field. The special problem of assessing state interests to determine whether they are strong enough to prevail against supreme federal dictates is also a familiar one to the federal courts. Indeed, a state action that interferes with competition not only among its own citizens but also among the states is already subject under the Commerce Clause to much the same searching review of state justifications as is proposed here. . . .

III

By these standards the present case does not seem a difficult one. The light-bulb tie-in presents the usual dangers of such a scheme, principally that respondent will extend its monopoly from the sale of electric power into that of light bulbs, not because it sells better light bulbs, but because its light bulbs are the ones customers must pay for if they are to have light at all. . . . On the record before us the scheme appears to be unjustified. No doubt it originated as a means to promote electric power use, but it is difficult to see why a tie-in (rather than an optional, promotional light-bulb sale) was necessary to that end even in the 19th century, laying aside the question whether the promotion of greater electric power use remains today a plausible public goal. Respondent would justify the scheme on the ground of consumer savings, its light bulbs assertedly being cheaper and better than those commercially available. . . . But again, a tie-in is not necessary to pass along these savings. A tie-in is only necessary in order to force consumers to pay for light bulbs from Detroit Edison rather than someone else. But there is no indication that one light bulb does not fit the socket as well as another, or that the sale of light bulbs is in any way crucial to respondent's successful operation. Conceivably, Michigan's aim is the very extension of the monopoly, born of a preference for having light bulbs supplied by one whose prices are already regulated. But ending competition in the light-bulb market cannot be accepted as an adequate state objective without some evidence—of which there is not the least hint in this record—that such competition is in some way ineffective. For all that appears, light-bulb marketing, unlike electric power production, is not a natural monopoly, nor does it implicate health or safety, nor is it beset with problems of instability or other flaws in the competitive market. This is what I take it the Court means when it says the electric light-bulb market is "essentially unregulated," and on that understanding I agree with its conclusion. . . .

MR. JUSTICE STEWART, with whom MR. JUSTICE POWELL and MR. JUSTICE REHNQUIST join, dissenting.

The Court today holds that a public utility company, pervasively regulated by a state utility commission, may be held liable for treble damages under the Sherman Act for engaging in conduct which, under the requirements of its tariff, it is obligated to perform. I respectfully dissent from this unprecedented application of the federal antitrust laws, which will surely result in disruption of the operation of every state-regulated public utility company in the nation and in the creation of "the prospect of massive treble damage liabilities"[7] payable ultimately by the companies' customers.

The starting point in analyzing this case is *Parker* v. *Brown* 317 U.S. 341. While *Parker* did not create the "so-called state-action exemption" . . . from the federal antitrust laws, . . . it is the case that is most frequently cited for the proposition that the "[Sherman] Act was intended to regulate private practices and not to prohibit a state from imposing a restraint as an act of government." *Goldfarb* v. *Virginia State Bar*, 421 U.S. 773, 788. The plurality opinion would hold that case decided only that "the sovereign state itself, ". . . could not be sued under the Sherman Act. This view of *Parker*, which would trivialize that case to the point of overruling it,[8] flies in the face of the decisions of this Court that have interpreted or applied *Parker's* "state action" doctrine and is unsupported by the sources on which the plurality relies. . . .

In *Eastern R. Conf.* v. *Noerr Motors*, 365 U.S. 127, for instance, the Court held that no violation of the Sherman Act could be predicated on the attempt by private persons to influence the passage or enforcement of state laws regulating competition in the trucking industry.[9] The Court took as its starting point the ruling in *Parker* v. *Brown* that where restraint upon trade or monopolization is the result of valid governmental action, as opposed to private action, no violation of the Act can be made out." . . . The Court viewed it as "equally clear that the Sherman Act

---

[7] Posner, "The Proper Relationship Between State Regulation and the Federal Antitrust Laws," *49 N.Y.U. L. Rev.* 693, 728 (1974).

[8] If *Parker* v. *Brown, supra*, could be circumvented by the simple expedient of suing the private party against whom the state's anticompetitive command runs, then that holding would become an empty formalism, standing for little more than the proposition that Porter Brown sued the wrong parties. . . .

[9] The only exception is where the attempt to influence state regulation is a "sham" aimed at "harass[ing] and deter[ring] . . . competitors from having 'free and unlimited access' to the agencies and courts. . . ." *California Motor Transport Co.* v. *Trucking Unlimited*, 404 U.S. 508, 515.

does not prohibit two or more persons from associating together in an attempt to persuade the legislature or the executive to take particular action with respect to a law that would produce a restraint or monopoly." . . . A contrary ruling, the Court held, "would substantially impair the power of government to take actions through its legislature and executive that operate to restrain trade." . . .

Litigation testing the limits of the state-action exemption has focused on whether alleged anticompetitive conduct by private parties is indeed "the result of" state action. Thus, in *Goldfarb* v. *Virginia State Bar*, 421 U.S. 773, the question was whether price fixing practiced by the respondents was "required by the State acting as sovereign. *Parker* v. *Brown*, 317 U.S., at 350–352. . . . "The Court held that the "so-called state-action exemption," id., at 788, did not protect the respondents because it "cannot fairly be said that the State of Virginia through its Supreme Court Rules required the anticompetitive activities of either respondent. . . . It is not enough that, as the County Bar puts it, anticompetitive conduct is 'prompted' by state action; rather, anticompetitive activities must be compelled by direction of the State acting as a sovereign." . . .

Parker, Noerr, and *Goldfarb* point unerringly to the proper disposition of this case. The regulatory process at issue has three principal stages. First, the utility company proposes a tariff. Second, the Michigan Public Service Commission investigates the proposed tariff and either approves it or rejects it. Third, if the tariff is approved, the utility company must, under command of state law, provide service in accord with its requirements until or unless the Commission approves a modification. The utility company thus engages in two distinct activities: it proposes a tariff and, if the tariff is approved, it obeys its terms. The first action cannot give rise to antitrust liability under *Noerr* and the second—compliance with the terms of the tariff under the command of state law—is immune from antitrust liability under *Parker* and *Goldfarb*. . . .

The plurality's contrary view would effectively overrule not only *Parker* but the entire body of post-*Parker* case law in this area, including *Noerr*. With the *Parker* holding reduced to the trivial proposition that the Sherman Act was not intended to run directly against state officials or governmental entities, the Court would fashion a new two-part test for determining whether state utility regulation creates immunity from the federal antitrust law. The first part of the test would focus on whether subjecting state-regulated utilities to antitrust liability would be "unjust." The second part of the test would look to whether the draftsmen of the Sherman Act intended to "superimpose" antitrust standards, and thus exposure to treble damages, on conduct compelled by state regulatory laws. . . .

With scarcely a backward glance at the *Noerr* case, the Court concludes that because the utility company's "participation" in the decision to incorporate the lamp-exchange program into the tariff was "sufficiently significant," there is nothing "unjust" in concluding that the company is required to conform its conduct to federal antitrust law "like comparable conduct by unregulated businesses. . . ." . . . This attempt to distinguish between the exemptive force of mandatory state rules adopted at the behest of private parties and those adopted pursuant to the state's unilateral decision is flatly inconsistent with the rationale of *Noerr.* . . .[10]

Today's holding will not only penalize the right to petition but may very well strike a crippling blow at state utility regulation. As the Court seems to acknowledge, such regulation is heavily dependent on the active participation of the regulated parties, who typically propose tariffs which are either adopted, rejected, or modified by utility commissions. But if a utility can escape the unpredictable consequences of the second arm of the Court's new test, see *infra,* this page, only by playing possum—by exercising no "option" in the Court's terminology, . . .—then it will surely be tempted to do just that, posing a serious threat to efficient and effective regulation. . . .

The Court's delineation of the second arm of the new test proceeds as follows. Apart from the "fairness" question, the Court states, there are "at least three reasons" why the light-bulb program should not enjoy Sherman Act immunity. . . . "First," the Court observes, "merely because certain conduct may be subject both to state regulation and to the federal antitrust laws does not necessarily mean that it must satisfy inconsistent standards. . . ." . . . That is true enough as an abstract proposition, but the very question is whether the utility's alleged "tie" of light-bulb sales to the provision of electric service is immune from antitrust liability, assuming it would constitute an antitrust violation in the absence of regulation. . . . Second, the Court states, "even assuming inconsistency, we could not accept the view that the federal interest must inevitably be subordinated to the State's. . . ."

The Court's analysis rests on a mistaken premise. The "implied immunity" doctrine employed by this Court to reconcile the federal antitrust laws and federal regulatory statutes cannot, rationally, be put to the use for which the Court would employ it. That doctrine, a species of the basic rule that repeals by implication are disfavored, comes into play only when two arguably inconsistent *federal* statutes are involved. "'Implied repeal,'" of federal antitrust laws by inconsistent state regulatory statutes is not only "'not favored,'" . . . it is impossible. See U.S. Const., Art. VI, cl. 2.

A closer scrutiny of the Court's holding reveals that its reference to the

---

[10] As the Court noted in *Noerr,* the scheme at issue in *Parker* required popular initiative. 365 U.S., at 137–138, n. 17. And as it further noted, *Parker* itself expressly rejected the argument that the necessity for private initiative affected the "program's validity under the Sherman Act. . . ." Id., at 137.

inapposite "implied repeal" doctrine is simply window dressing for a type of judicial review radically different from that engaged in by this Court in *Gordon* v. *New York Stock Exchange*, 422 U.S. 659, and *United States* v. *Philadelphia National Bank*, 374 U.S. 321. Those cases turned exclusively on issues of statutory construction and involved no judicial scrutiny of the abstract "necessity" or "centrality" of particular regulatory provisions. Instead, the federal regulatory statute was accepted as a given, as was the federal antitrust law. The Court's interpretative effort was aimed at accommodating these arguably inconsistent bodies of law, not at second-guessing legislative judgments concerning the "necessity" for including particular provisions in the regulatory statute.

The Court's approach here is qualitatively different. The State of Michigan, through its Public Service Commission, has decided that requiring Detroit Edison to provide free light bulbs as a term and condition of service is in the public interest. Yet the Court is prepared to set aside that policy determination: "The lamp-supply program is by no means . . . *imperative* in the continued effective functioning of Michigan's regulation of the utilities industry." . . . ([E]mphasis added.) Even "if the federal antitrust laws should be construed to outlaw respondent's light-bulb-exchange program, there is no reason to believe that Michigan's regulation of its electric utilities will no longer be able to *function effectively*. Regardless of the outcome of this case, Michigan's interest in regulating its utilities' distribution of electricity will be *almost entirely unimpaired*." . . . ([E]mphasis added.)

The emphasized language in these passages shows that the Court is adopting an interpretation of the Sherman Act which will allow the federal judiciary to substitute its judgment for that of state legislatures and administrative agencies with respect to whether particular anticompetitive regulatory provisions are "'sufficiently central,'" . . . to a judicial conception of the proper scope of state utility regulation. The content of those "'purposes,'" . . . which the Court will suffer the states to promote derives presumably from the mandate of the Sherman Act. On this assumption—and no other is plausible—it becomes apparent that the Court's second reason for extending the Sherman Act to cover the light-bulb program, when divested of inapposite references to the federal implied repeal doctrine, is merely a restatement of the third rationale, which the Court phrases as follows: "[F]inally, even if we were to assume that Congress did not intend the antitrust laws to apply to areas of the economy primarily regulated by a state, that assumption would not foreclose the enforcement of the antitrust laws in an essentially unregulated area such as the market for electric light bulbs." . . . This statement raises at last the only legitimate question, which is whether *Parker* erred in holding that Congress, in enacting the Sherman Act, did not intend to vitiate state regulation of the sort at issue here by creating treble-damages exposure for activities performed in compliance therewith.

The Court's rationale appears to be that the draftsmen of the Sherman Act intended to exempt state-regulated utilities from treble damages only to the extent those utilities are complying with state rules which narrowly reflect the "typica[l] assum[ption] that the [utility] is a natural monopoly" and which regulate the utility's "natural monopoly powers" as opposed to its "business activity in competitive areas of the economy." . . . Furthermore, such regulation must be "sufficiently central" to the regulation of natural monopoly powers if it is to shield the regulated party from antitrust liability. . . . This Delphic reading of the Sherman Act, which is unaided by any reference to the language or legislative history of that Act, is, of course, inconsistent with *Parker* v. *Brown*. *Parker* involved a state scheme aimed at artificially raising the market price of raisins. Raisin production is not a "natural monopoly." If the limits of the state-action exemption from the Sherman Act are congruent with the boundaries of "natural monopoly" power, then *Parker* was wrongly decided.

But the legislative history of the Sherman Act shows conclusively that *Parker* was correctly decided. The floor debates and the House Report on the proposed legislation clearly reveal, as at least one commentator has noted, that "Congress fully understood the narrow scope given to the commerce clause" in 1890. . . . This understanding is, in many ways, of historic interest only, because subsequent decisions of this Court have "permitted the reach of the Sherman Act to expand along with expanding notions of congressional power." . . . But the narrow view taken by the Members of Congress in 1890 remains relevant for the limited purpose of assessing their intention regarding the interaction of the Sherman Act and state economic regulation. . . .

The Court's opinion simply ignores the clear evidence of congressional intent and substitutes its own policy judgment about the desirability of disregarding any facet of state economic regulation that it thinks unwise or of no great importance. In adopting this freewheeling approach to the language of the Sherman Act the Court creates a statutory simulacrum of the substantive due process doctrine I thought had been put to rest long ago. . . . For the Court's approach contemplates the selective interdiction of those anticompetitive state regulatory measures that are deemed not "central" to the limited range of regulatory goals considered "imperative" by the federal judiciary.

Henceforth, a state-regulated public utility company must at its peril successfully divine which of its countless and interrelated tariff provisions a federal court will ultimately consider "central" or "imperative." If it guesses wrong, it may be subjected to treble damages as a penalty for its compliance with state law.

United States v. Philadelphia National Bank
374 U.S. 321 (1963)

MR. JUSTICE BRENNAN delivered the opinion of the Court.

The United States, appellant here, brought this civil action . . . to enjoin a proposed merger of The Philadelphia National Bank (PNB) and Girard Trust Corn Exchange Bank (Girard), appellees here. The complaint charged violations of Section 1 of the Sherman Act, . . . and Section 7 of the Clayton Act. . . . From a judgment for appellees after trial . . . the United States appealed to this Court. . . . We reverse the judgment of the District Court. We hold that the merger of appellees is forbidden by Section 7 of the Clayton Act and so must be enjoined; we need not, and therefore do not, reach the further question of alleged violation of Section 1 of the Sherman Act.

I. THE FACTS AND PROCEEDINGS BELOW

A. The Background: Commercial Banking in the United States

Because this is the first case which has required this Court to consider the application of the antitrust laws to the commercial banking industry, and because aspects of the industry and of the degree of governmental regulation of it will recur throughout our discussion, we deem it appropriate to begin with a brief background description.[1]

Commercial banking in this country is primarily unit banking. That is, control of commercial banking is diffused throughout a very large number of independent, local banks—13,460 of them in 1960—rather than concentrated in a handful of nationwide banks, as, for example, in England and Germany. There are, to be sure, in addition to the independent banks, some 10,000 branch banks; but branching, which is controlled largely by state law—and prohibited altogether by some States—enables a bank to extend itself only to state lines and often not that far. It is also the case, of course, that many banks place loans and solicit deposits outside their home area. But with these qualifications, it remains true that ours is essentially a decentralized system of community banks. Recent years, however, have witnessed a definite trend toward concentration. Thus, during the decade ending in 1960 the number of commercial banks in the United States declined by 714, despite the chartering of 887 new banks and a very substantial increase in the Nation's credit needs during the period. Of the 1,601 independent banks which thus disappeared, 1,503, with combined total resources of well over $25,000,000,000, disappeared as the result of mergers.

---

[1] The discussion of this portion of the opinion draws upon undisputed evidence of record in the case, supplemented by pertinent reference materials. (The interested reader is referred to the footnotes in the original decision for a lengthy reading list.) IMS.

Commercial banks are unique among financial institutions in that they alone are permitted by law to accept demand deposits. This distinctive power gives commercial banking a key role in the national economy. For banks do not merely deal in, but are actually a source of, money and credit; when a bank makes a loan by crediting the borrower's demand deposit account, it augments the Nation's credit supply.[2] Furthermore, the power to accept demand deposits makes banks the intermediaries in most financial transactions (since transfers of substantial moneys are almost always by check rather than by cash) and, concomitantly, the repositories of very substantial individual and corporate funds. The banks' use of these funds is conditioned by the fact that their working capital consists very largely of demand deposits, which makes liquidity the guiding principle of bank lending and investing policies; thus it is that banks are the chief source of the country's short-term business credit.

Banking operations are varied and complex; "commercial banking" describes a congeries of services and credit devices. But among them the creation of additional money and credit, the management of the checking-account system, and the furnishing of short-term business loans would appear to be the most important. For the proper discharge of these functions is indispensable to a healthy national economy, as the role of bank failures in depression periods attests. It is therefore not surprising that commercial banking in the United States is subject to a variety of governmental controls, state and federal. Federal regulation is the more extensive, and our focus will be upon it. It extends not only to the national banks, *i.e.*, banks chartered under federal law and supervised by the Comptroller of the Currency. . . . For many state banks . . . as well as virtually all the national banks . . . are members of the Federal Reserve System (FRS), and more than 95% of all banks . . . are insured by the Federal Deposit Insurance Corporation (FDIC). State member and non-member insured banks are subject to a federal regulatory scheme almost as elaborate as that which governs the national banks. . . .

But perhaps the most effective weapon of federal regulation of banking is the broad visitatorial power of federal bank examiners. Whenever the agencies deem it necessary, they may order "a thorough examination of all the affairs of the bank," whether it be a member of the FRS or a non-member insured bank. . . . Such examinations are frequent and intensive. In addition, the banks are required to furnish detailed periodic reports of their operations to the supervisory agencies. . . . In this way the agencies maintain virtually a day-to-day surveillance of the American banking system. . . .

Federal supervision of banking has been called "[p]robably the out-

---

[2] Such creation is not, to be sure, pure sleight of hand. A bank may not make a loan without adequate reserves. Nevertheless, the element of bank money creation is real. *E.g.*, Samuelson, *Economics* (5th ed. 1961), 331–343.

standing example in the federal government of regulation of an entire industry through methods of supervision. . . . The system may be one of the most successful [systems of economic regulation], if not the most successful." . . . To the efficacy of this system we may owe, in part, the virtual disappearance of bank failures from the American economic scene.

B. The Proposed Merger of PNB and Girard

The Philadelphia National Bank and Girard Trust Corn Exchange Bank are, respectively, the second and third largest of the 42 commercial banks with head offices in the Philadelphia metropolitan area, which consists of the City of Philadelphia and its three contiguous counties in Pennsylvania. The home county of both banks is the city itself; Pennsylvania law, however, permits branching into the counties contiguous to the home county, . . . and both banks have offices throughout the four-county area. PNB, a national bank, has assets of over $1,000,000,000, making it (as of 1959) the twenty-first largest bank in the Nation. Girard, a state bank, is a member of the FRS and is insured by the FDIC; it has assets of about $750,000,000. Were the proposed merger to be consummated, the resulting bank would be the largest in the four-county area, with (approximately) 36% of the area banks' total assets, 36% of deposits, and 34% of net loans. It and the second largest (First Pennsylvania Bank and Trust Company, now the largest) would have between them 59% of the total assets, 58% of deposits, and 58% of the net loans, while after the merger the four largest banks in the area would have 78% of total assets, 77% of deposits, and 78% of net loans.

The present size of both PNB and Girard is in part the result of mergers. Indeed, the trend toward concentration is noticeable in the Philadelphia area generally, in which the number of commercial banks has declined from 108 in 1947 to the present 42. Since 1950, PNB has acquired nine formerly independent banks and Girard six; and these acquisitions have accounted for 59% and 85% of the respective banks' asset growth during the period, 63% and 91% of their deposit growth, and 12% and 37% of their loan growth. During this period, the seven largest banks in the area increased their combined share of the area's total commercial bank resources from about 61% to about 90%.

In November 1960 the boards of directors of the two banks approved a proposed agreement for their consolidation under the PNB charter. . . . Such a consolidation is authorized, subject to the approval of the Comptroller of the Currency. . . . But under the Bank Merger Act of 1960 . . . the Comptroller may not give his approval until he has received reports from the other two banking agencies and the Attorney General respecting the probable effects of the proposed transaction on competition. All three reports advised that the proposed merger would have substantial anticompetitive effects in the Philadelphia metropolitan area. However, on February 24, 1961, the Comptroller approved the merger. No opinion was rendered at that time. But as required . . . , the Comptroller explained the basis for his decision to approve the merger in a statement to be included in his annual report to Congress. As to effect upon competition, he reasoned that "[s]ince there will remain an adequate number of alternative sources of banking service in Philadelphia, and in view of the beneficial effects of this consolidation upon international and national competition it was concluded that the over-all effect upon competition would not be unfavorable." He also stated that the consolidated bank "would be far better able to serve the convenience and needs of its community by being of material assistance to its city and state in their efforts to attract new industry and to retain existing industry." The day after the Comptroller approved the merger, the United States commenced the present action. No steps have been taken to consummate the merger pending the outcome of this litigation.

.   .   .   .   .

II.   THE APPLICABILITY OF SECTION 7 OF THE CLAYTON ACT TO BANK MERGERS

A.   The Original Section and the 1950 Amendment

.   .   .   .   .

Fourth.   It is settled law that "[i]mmunity from the antitrust laws is not lightly implied." . . . This canon of construction, which reflects the felt indispensable role of antitrust policy in the maintenance of a free economy, is controlling here. For there is no indication in the legislative history to the 1950 amendment of Section 7 that Congress wished to confer a special dispensation upon the banking industry; if Congress had so wished, moreover, surely it would have exempted the industry from the stock-acquisition as well as the assets-acquisition provision.

Of course, our construction of the amended Section 7 is not foreclosed because, after the passage of the amendment, some members of Congress, and for a time the Justice Department, voiced the view that bank mergers were still beyond the reach of the section. "[T]he views of a subsequent Congress form a hazardous basis for inferring the intent of an earlier one." . . . This holds true even though misunderstanding of the scope of Section 7 may have played some part in the passage of the Bank Merger Act of 1960. . . . The design fashioned in the Bank Merger Act was predicated upon uncertainty as to the scope of Section 7, and we do no violence to that design by dispelling the uncertainty.

B.   The Effect of the Bank Merger Act of 1960

Appellees contended below that the Bank Merger Act, by directing the banking agencies to consider competitive factors before approving mergers . . . immunizes approved mergers from challenge under the federal antitrust laws. We think the District Court was correct in rejecting this contention. No express immunity is conferred by the Act.[3] Repeals of the antitrust laws by implication from a regulatory statute are strongly disfavored, and have only been found in cases of plain repugnancy between the antitrust and regulatory provisions. . . .

In the *California [El Paso]* case . . . the Court held that the FPC's approval of a merger did not confer immunity from Section 7 of the Clayton Act, even though, as in the instant case, the agency had taken the competitive factor into account in passing upon the merger application. . . . We think *California* is controlling here. Although the Comptroller was required to consider effect upon competition in passing upon appellees' merger application, he was not requried to give this factor any particular weight; he was not even required to (and did not) hold a hearing before approving the application; and there is no specific provision for judicial review of his decision. . . .

Nor did Congress, in passing the Bank Merger Act, embrace the view that federal regulation of banking is so comprehensive that enforcement of the antitrust laws would be either unnecessary, in light of the completeness of the regulatory structure, or disruptive of that structure. On the contrary, the legislative history of the Act seems clearly to refute any suggestion that applicability of the antitrust laws was to be affected. Both the House and Senate Committee Reports stated that the Act would not affect in any way the applicability of the antitrust laws to bank acquisitions. . . . Moreover, bank regulation is in most respects less complete than public utility regulation, to which interstate rail and air carriers, among others, are subject. Rate regulation in the banking industry is limited and largely indirect . . . ; banks are under no duty not to discriminate in their services; and though the location of bank offices is regulated, banks may do business—place loans and solicit deposits—where they please. The fact that the banking agencies maintain a close surveillance of the industry with a view toward preventing unsound practices that might impair liquidity or lead to insolvency does not make federal banking regulation all-pervasive, although it does minimize the hazards of intense competition. Indeed, that there are so many direct public controls over unsound competitive practices in the industry refutes the argument that private controls of competition are necessary in the public interest and ought therefore to be immune from scrutiny under the antitrust laws. Cf. Kaysen and Turner, *Antitrust Policy* (1959), 206. . . .

It should be unnecessary to add that in holding as we do that the Bank Merger Act of 1960 does not preclude application of Section 7 of the Clayton Act to bank mergers, we deprive the later statute of none of its

---

[3] Contrast this with the express exemption provisions of, *e.g.*, the Federal Aviation Act . . . ; Federal Communications Act . . . ; Interstate Commerce Act . . . ; Shipping Act . . . ; Webb-Pomerene Act . . . ; and the Clayton Act itself. . . .

intended force. Congress plainly did not intend the 1960 Act to extinguish other sources of federal restraint of bank acquisitions having anticompetitive effects. . . .

III. THE LAWFULNESS OF THE PROPOSED MERGER UNDER SECTION 7

The statutory test is whether the effect of the merger "may be substantially to lessen competition" "in any line of commerce in any section of the country." We analyzed the test in detail in *Brown Shoe Co.* v. *United States*, . . . and that analysis need not be repeated or extended here, for the instant case presents only a straightforward problem of application to particular facts.

We have no difficulty in determining the "line of commerce" (relevant product or services market) and "section of the country" (relevant geographical market) in which to appraise the probable competitive effects of appellees' proposed merger. We agree with the District Court that the cluster of products (various kinds of credit) and services (such as checking accounts and trust administration) denoted by the term "commercial banking," . . . composes a distinct line of commerce. Some commercial banking products or services are so distinctive that they are entirely free of effective competition from products or services of other financial institutions; the checking account is in this category. Others enjoy such cost advantages as to be insulated within a broad range from substitutes furnished by other institutions. For example, commercial banks compete with small-loan companies in the personal-loan market; but the small-loan companies' rates are invariably much higher than the banks', in part, it seems, because the companies' working capital consists in substantial part of bank loans.[4] Finally, there are banking facilities which, although in terms of cost and price they are freely competitive with the facilities provided by other financial institutions, nevertheless enjoy a settled consumer preference, insulating them, to a marked degree, from competition; this seems to be the case with savings deposits. In sum, it is clear that

---

[4] Cf. *United States* v. *Aluminum Co. of America,* 148 F.2d 416, 425 (C.A. 2d Cir. 1945). In the instant case, unlike *Aluminum Co.,* there is virtually no time lag between the banks' furnishing competing financial institutions (small-loan companies, for example) with the raw material, *i.e.,* money, and the institutions' selling the finished product, *i.e.,* loans; hence the instant case, compared with *Aluminum Co.* in this respect, is *a fortiori.* As one banker testified quite frankly in the instant case in response to the question: "Do you feel that you are in substantial competition with these institutions [personal-finance and sales-finance companies] that you lend . . . such money to for loans that you want to make?"—"Oh, no, we definitely do not. If we did, we would stop making the loans to them." (R. 298.) The reason for the competitive disadvantage of most lending institutions *vis-à-vis* banks is that only banks obtain the bulk of their working capital without having to pay interest or comparable charges thereon, by virtue of their unique power to accept demand deposits. The critical area of short-term commercial credit . . . appears to be one in which banks have little effective competition, save in the case of very large companies which can meet their financing needs from retained earnings or from issuing securities or paper.

commercial banking is a market "sufficiently inclusive to be meaningful in terms of trade realities." *Crown Zellerbach Corp.* v. *Federal Trade Comm'n,* 296 F. 2d 800, 811 (C.A. 9th Cir. 1961).

We part company with the District Court on the determination of the appropriate "section of the country." The proper question to be asked in this case is not where the parties to the merger do business or even where they compete, but where, within the area of competitive overlap, the effect of the merger on competition will be direct and immediate. See Bock, *Mergers and Markets* (1960), 42. This depends upon "the geographic structure of supplier-consumer relations." Kaysen and Turner, *Antitrust Policy* (1959), 102. In banking, as in most service industries, convenience of location is essential to effective competition. Individuals and corporations typically confer the bulk of their patronage on banks in their local community; they find it impractical to conduct their banking business at a distance. . . . The factor of inconvenience localizes banking competition as effectively as high transportation costs in other industries. . . . Therefore, since, as we recently said in a related context, the "area of effective competition in the known line of commerce must be charted by careful selection of the market area in which the seller operates, *and to which the purchaser can practicably turn for supplies,*" *Tampa Elec. Co.* v. *Nashville Coal Co.,* 365 U.S. 320, 327 (emphasis supplied); see *Standard Oil Co.* v. *United States,* 337 U.S. 293, 299 and 300, n. 5, the four-county area in which appellees' offices are located would seem to be the relevant geographical market. Cf. *Brown Shoe Co., supra,* at 338–339. In fact, the vast bulk of appellees' business originates in the four-county area.[5] Theoretically, we should be concerned with the possibility that bank offices on the perimeter of the area may be in effective competition with bank offices within; actually, this seems to be a factor of little significance.[6]

---

[5] The figures for PNB and Girard respectively are: 54% and 63% of the dollar volume of their commercial and industrial loans originate in the four-county area; 75% and 70%, personal loans; 74% and 84%, real estate loans; 41% and 62%, lines of credit; 94% and 72%, personal trusts, 81% and 94%, time and savings deposits; 56% and 77%, demand deposits; 93% and 87%, demand deposits of individuals. Actually, these figures may be too low. . . .

[6] Appellees suggest not that bank offices skirting the four-county area provide meaningful alternatives to bank customers within the area, but that such alternatives are provided by large banks, from New York and elsewhere, which solicit business in the Philadelphia area. There is no evidence of the amount of business done in the area by banks with offices outside the area; it may be that such figures are unobtainable. In any event, it would seem from the local orientation of banking insofar as smaller customers are concerned . . . that competition from outside the area would only be important to the larger borrowers and depositors. If so, the four-county area remains a valid geographical market in which to assess the anticompetitive effect of the proposed merger upon the banking facilities available to the smaller customer—a perfectly good "line of commerce," in light of Congress' evident concern, in enacting the 1950 amendments to Section 7, with preserving small business. See *Brown Shoe Co., supra,* at 315–316. As a practical matter the small businessman can only satisfy his credit needs at local banks. To be sure, there is still some artificiality in deeming the

We recognize that the area in which appellees have their offices does not delineate with perfect accuracy an appropriate "section of the country" in which to appraise the effect of the merger upon competition. Large borrowers and large depositors, the record shows, may find it practical to do a large part of their banking business outside their home community; very small borrowers and depositors may, as a practical matter, be confined to bank offices in their immediate neighborhood; and customers of intermediate size, it would appear, deal with banks within an area intermediate between these extremes. . . . [See notes 5 and 6, *supra.*] So also, some banking services are evidently more local in nature than others. But that in banking the relevant geographical market is a function of each separate customer's economic scale means simply that a workable compromise must be found: some fair intermediate delineation which avoids the indefensible extremes of drawing the market either so expansively as to make the effect of the merger upon competition seem insignificant, because only the very largest bank customers are taken into account in defining the market, or so narrowly as to place appellees in different markets, because only the smallest customers are considered. We think that the four-county Philadelphia metropolitan area, which state law apparently recognizes as a meaningful banking community in allowing Philadelphia banks to branch within it, and which would seem roughly to delineate the area in which bank customers that are neither very large nor very small find it practical to do their banking business, is a more appropriate "section of the country" in which to appraise the instant merger than any larger or smaller or different area. Cf. Hale and Hale, *Market Power: Size and Shape Under the Sherman Act* (1958), 119. We are helped to this conclusion by the fact that the three federal banking agencies regard the area in which banks have their offices as an "area of effective competition." . . .

Having determined the relevant market, we come to the ultimate question under Section 7: whether the effect of the merger "may be substantially to lessen competition" in the relevant market. Clearly, this is not the kind of question which is susceptible of a ready and precise answer in most cases. It requires not merely an appraisal of the immediate impact of the merger upon competition, but a prediction of its impact upon competitive conditions in the future; this is what is meant when it is said that the amended Section 7 was intended to arrest anticompetitive tendencies in their "incipiency." See *Brown Shoe Co.* . . . Such a prediction is

---

four-county area the relevant "section of the country" so far as businessmen located near the perimeter are concerned. But such fuzziness would seem inherent in any attempt to delineate the relevant geographical market. Note, *52 Col. L. Rev.* 766, 778–779, n. 77 (1952). And it is notable that outside the four-county area, appellees' business rapidly thins out. Thus, the other six counties of the Delaware Valley account for only 2% of appellees' combined individual demand deposits; 4%, demand deposits of partnerships and corporations; 7%, loans; 2%, savings deposits; 4%, business time deposits.

sound only if it is based upon a firm understanding of the structure of the relevant market; yet the relevant economic data are both complex and elusive. . . . And unless businessmen can assess the legal consequences of a merger with some confidence, sound business planning is retarded. . . . So also, we must be alert to the danger of subverting congressional intent by permitting a too-broad economic investigation. . . . And so in any case in which it is possible, without doing violence to the congressional objective embodied in Section 7, to simplify the test of illegality, the courts ought to do so in the interest of sound and practical judicial administration. . . . This is such a case.

We noted in *Brown Shoe Co.* . . . that "[t]he dominant theme pervading congressional consideration of the 1950 amendments [to Section 7] was a fear of what was considered to be a rising tide of economic concentration in the American economy." This intense congressional concern with the trend toward concentration warrants dispensing, in certain cases, with elaborate proof of market structure, market behavior, or probable anticompetitive effects. Specifically, we think that a merger which produces a firm controlling an undue percentage share of the relevant market, and results in a significant increase in the concentration of firms in that market, is so inherently likely to lessen competition substantially that it must be enjoined in the absence of evidence clearly showing that the merger is not likely to have such anticompetitive effects. . . .

Such a test lightens the burden of proving illegality only with respect to mergers whose size makes them inherently suspect in light of Congress' design in Section 7 to prevent undue concentration. Furthermore, the test is fully consonant with economic theory. That "[c]ompetition is likely to be greatest when there are many sellers, none of which has any significant market share,"[7] is common ground among most economists, and was undoubtedly a premise of congressional reasoning about the antimerger statute.

The merger of appellees will result in a single bank's controlling at least 30% of the commercial banking business in the four-county Philadelphia metropolitan area.[8] Without attempting to specify the smallest market share which would still be considered to threaten undue concentration,

---

[7] Comment, "Substantially to Lessen Competition . . .": "Current Problems of Horizontal Mergers," 68 *Yale L.J.* 1627, 1638–1639 (1959). . . .

[8] . . . We note three factors that cause us to shade the percentages given earlier in this opinion, in seeking to calculate market share. (1) The percentages took no account of banks which do business in the four-county area but have no offices there; however, this seems to be a factor of little importance, at least insofar as smaller customers are concerned, see note [6], *supra*. (2) The percentages took no account of banks which have offices in the four-county area but not their home offices there; however, there seem to be only two such offices and appellees in this Court make no reference to this omission. (3) There are no percentages for the amount of business of banks located in the area, other than appellees, which originates in the area. Appellees contend that since most of the 40 other banks are smaller, they do a more concentratedly local business than appellees, and hence account for a relatively larger proportion of such business. If so, we doubt much correction is needed.

we are clear that 30% presents that threat.[9] Further, whereas presently the two largest banks in the area (First Pennsylvania and PNB) control between them approximately 44% of the area's commercial banking business, the two largest after the merger (PNB-Girard and First Pennsylvania) will control 59%. Plainly, we think, this increase of more than 33% in concentration must be regarded as significant.

Our conclusion that these percentages raise an inference that the effect of the contemplated merger of appellees may be substantially to lessen competition is not an arbitrary one, although neither the terms of Section 7 nor the legislative history suggests that any particular percentage share was deemed critical. . . .

There is nothing in the record of this case to rebut the inherently anticompetitive tendency manifested by these percentages. There was, to be sure, testimony by bank officers to the effect that competition among banks in Philadelphia was virogous and would continue to be vigorous after the merger. We think, however, that the District Court's reliance on such evidence was misplaced. This lay evidence on so complex an economic-legal problem as the substantiality of the effect of this merger upon competition was entitled to little weight, in view of the witnesses' failure to give concrete reasons for their conclusions.[10]

Of equally little value, we think, are the assurances offered by appellees' witnesses that customers dissatisfied with the services of the resulting bank may readily turn to the 40 other banks in the Philadelphia area. In every case short of outright monopoly, the disgruntled customer has alternatives; even in tightly oligopolistic markets, there may be small firms

---

The five largest banks in the four-county area at present control some 78% of the area banks' assets. Thus, even if the small banks have a somewhat different pattern of business, it is difficult to see how that would substantially diminish the appellees' share of the local banking business.

No evidence was introduced as to the quantitative significance of these three factors, and appellees do not contend that as a practical matter such evidence could have been obtained. Under the circumstances, we think a downward correction of the percentages to 30% produces a conservative estimate of appellees' market share.

[9] Kaysen and Turner, *supra,* . . . suggest that 20% should be the line of prima facie unlawfulness; Stigler suggests that any acquisition by a firm controlling 20% of the market after the merger is presumptively unlawful; Markham mentions 25%. Bok's principal test is increase in market concentration, and he suggests a figure of 7% or 8%. . . . We intimate no view on the validity of such tests for we have no need to consider percentages smaller than those in the case at bar, but we note that such tests are more rigorous than is required to dispose of the instant case. Needless to say, the fact that a merger results in a less-than-30% market share, or in a less substantial increase in concentration than in the instant case, does not raise an inference that the merger is *not* violative of Section 7. See, *e.g., Brown Shoe Co.* . . .

[10] The fact that some of the bank officers who testified represented small banks in competition with appellees does not substantially enhance the probative value of their testimony. The test of a competitive market is not only whether small competitors flourish but also whether consumers are well served. . . . In an oligopolistic market, small companies may be perfectly content to follow the high prices set by the dominant firms, yet the market may be profoundly anticompetitive.

operating. A fundamental purpose of amending Section 7 was to arrest the trend toward concentration, the *tendency* to monopoly, before the consumer's alternatives disappeared through merger, and that purpose would be ill-served if the law stayed its hand until 10, or 20, or 30 more Philadelphia banks were absorbed. This is not a fanciful eventuality, in view of the strong trend toward mergers evident in the area . . . and we might note also that entry of new competitors into the banking field is far from easy.[11]

So also, we reject the position that commercial banking, because it is subject to a high degree of governmental regulation, or because it deals in the intangibles of credit and services rather than in the manufacture or sale of tangible commodities, is somehow immune from the anticompetitive effects of undue concentration. Competition among banks exists at every level—price, variety of credit arrangements, convenience of location, attractiveness of physical surroundings, credit information, investment advice, service charges, personal accommodations, advertising, miscellaneous special and extra services—and it is keen; on this appellees' own witnesses were emphatic. There is no reason to think that concentration is less inimical to the free play of competition in banking than in other service industries. On the contrary, it is in all probability more inimical. For example, banks compete to fill the credit needs of businessmen. Small businessmen especially are, as a practical matter, confined to their locality for the satisfaction of their credit needs. . . . If the number of banks in the locality is reduced, the vigor of competition for filling the marginal small business borrower's needs is likely to diminish. At the same time, his concomitantly greater difficulty in obtaining credit is likely to put him at a disadvantage *vis-à-vis* larger businesses with which he competes. In this fashion, concentration in banking accelerates concentration generally.

We turn now to three affirmative justifications which appellees offer for the proposed merger. The first is that only through mergers can banks follow their customers to the suburbs and retain their business. This justification does not seem particularly related to the instant merger, but in any event it has no merit. There is an alternative to the merger route: the opening of new branches in the areas to which the customers have moved—so-called *de novo* branching. Appellees do not contend that they are unable to expand thus, by opening new offices rather than acquiring existing ones, and surely one premise of an antimerger statute such as Section 7 is that corporate growth by internal expansion is socially preferable to growth by acquisition.

Second, it is suggested that the increased lending limit of the resulting

---

[11] Entry is, of course, wholly a matter of governmental grace. . . . In the 10-year period ending in 1961, only one new bank opened in the Philadelphia four-county area. That was in 1951. At the end of 10 years, the new bank controlled only one-third of 1% of the area's deposits.

bank will enable it to compete with the large out-of-state banks, particularly the New York banks, for very large loans. We reject this application of the concept of "countervailing power." Cf. *Kiefer-Stewart Co.* v. *Joseph E. Seagram & Sons*, 340 U.S. 211. If anticompetitive effects in one market could be justified by procompetitive consequences in another, the logical upshot would be that every firm in an industry could, without violating Section 7, embark on a series of mergers that would make it in the end as large as the industry leader. For if all the commercial banks in the Philadelphia area merged into one, it would be smaller than the largest bank in New York City. This is not a case, plainly, where two small firms in a market propose to merge in order to be able to compete more successfully with the leading firms in that market. Nor is it a case in which lack of adequate banking facilities is causing hardships to individuals or businesses in the community. The present two largest banks in Philadelphia have lending limits of $8,000,000 each. The only businesses located in the Philadelphia area which find such limits inadequate are large enough readily to obtain bank credit in other cities.

This brings us to appellees' final contention, that Philadelphia needs a bank larger than it now has in order to bring business to the area and stimulate its economic development. . . . We are clear, however, that a merger the effect of which "may be substantially to lessen competition" is not saved because, on some ultimate reckoning of social or economic debits and credits, it may be deemed beneficial. A value choice of such magnitude is beyond the ordinary limits of judicial competence, and in any event has been made for us already, by Congress when it enacted the amended Section 7. Congress determined to preserve our traditionally competitive economy. It therefore proscribed anticompetitive mergers, the benign and the malignant alike, fully aware, we must assume, that some price might have to be paid.

In holding as we do that the merger of appellees would violate Section 7 and must therefore be enjoined, we reject appellees' pervasive suggestion that application of the procompetitive policy of Section 7 to the banking industry will have dire, although unspecified, consequences for the national economy. Concededly, PNB and Girard and healthy and strong; they are not undercapitalized or overloaned; they have no management problems; the Philadelphia area is not overbanked; ruinous competition is not in the offing. Section 7 does not mandate cutthroat competition in the banking industry, and does not exclude defenses based on dangers to liquidity or solvency, if to avert them a merger is necessary. It does require, however, that the forces of competition be allowed to operate within the broad framework of governmental regulation of the industry. The fact that banking is a highly regulated industry critical to the Nation's welfare makes the play of competition not less important but more so. At the price of some repetition, we note that if the businessman is denied credit because his banking alternatives have been eliminated by mergers, the whole edifice of an entrepreneurial system is threatened; if the costs of banking services and credit are allowed to become excessive by the absence of competitive pressures, virtually all costs, in our credit economy, will be affected; and unless competition is allowed to fulfill its role as an economic regulator in the banking industry, the result may well be even more governmental regulation. Subject to narrow qualifications, it is surely the case that competition is our fundamental national economic policy, offering as it does the only alternative to the cartelization or governmental regimentation of large portions of the economy. . . . There is no warrant for declining to enforce it in the instant case.

The judgment of the District Court is reversed and the case remanded with direction to enter judgment enjoining the proposed merger.

It is so ordered.

MR. JUSTICE WHITE took no part in the consideration or decision of this case.

MR. JUSTICE HARLAN, whom MR. JUSTICE STEWART joins, dissenting.

I suspect that no one will be more surprised than the Government to find that the Clayton Act has carried the day for its case in this Court.

In response to an apparently accelerating trend toward concentration in the commercial banking system in this country, a trend which existing laws were evidently ill-suited to control, numerous bills were introduced in Congress from 1955 to 1960. During this period, the Department of Justice and the federal banking agencies advocated divergent methods of dealing with the competitive aspects of bank mergers, the former urging the extension of Section 7 of the Clayton Act to cover such mergers and the latter supporting a regulatory scheme under which the effect of a bank merger on competition would be only one of the factors to be considered in determining whether the merger would be in the public interest. The Justice Department's proposals were repeatedly rejected by Congress, and the regulatory approach of the banking agencies was adopted in the Bank Merger Act of 1960. . . .

Sweeping aside the "design fashioned in the Bank Merger Act" as "predicated upon uncertainty as to the scope of Section 7" of the Clayton Act . . . , the Court today holds Section 7 to be applicable to bank mergers and concludes that it has been violated in this case. I respectfully submit that this holding, which sanctions a remedy regarded by Congress as inimical to the best interests of the banking industry and the public, and which will in large measure serve to frustrate the objectives of the Bank

Merger Act, finds no justification in either the terms of the 1950 amendment of the Clayton Act or the history of the statute.

I

The key to this case is found in the special position occupied by commercial banking in the economy of this country. With respect to both the nature of the operations performed and the degree of governmental supervision involved, it is fundamentally different from ordinary manufacturing and mercantile businesses.

The unique powers of commercial banks to accept demand deposits, provide checking account services, and lend against fractional reserves permit the banking system as a whole to create a supply of "money," a function which is indispensable to the maintenance of the structure of our national economy. . . .

Deposit banking operations affect not only the volume of money and credit, but also the value of the dollar and the stability of the currency system. In this field, considerations other than simply the preservation of competition are relevant. Moreover, commercial banks are entrusted with the safekeeping of large amounts of funds belonging to individuals and corporations. Unlike the ordinary investor, these depositors do not regard their funds as subject to a risk of loss and, at least in the case of demand depositors, they do not receive a return for taking such a risk. A bank failure is a community disaster; its impact first strikes the bank's depositors most heavily, and then spreads throughout the economic life of the community. Safety and soundness of banking practices are thus critical factors in any banking system.

The extensive blanket of state and federal regulation of commercial banking, much of which is aimed at limiting competition, reflects these factors. Since the Court's opinion describes, at some length, aspects of the supervision exercised by the federal banking agencies . . . , I do no more here than point out that, in my opinion, such regulation evidences a plain design grounded on solid economic considerations to deal with banking as a specialized field.

This view is confirmed by the Bank Merger Act of 1960 and its history. . . .

Indeed the inapplicability to bank mergers of Section 7 of the Clayton Act, even after it was amended in 1950, was, for a time, an explicit premise on which the Department of Justice performed its antitrust duties. . . .

The inapplicability of Section 7 to bank mergers was also an explicit basis on which Congress acted in passing the Bank Merger Act of 1960. . . .

But instead of extending the scope of Section 7 to cover bank mergers, as numerous proposed amendments to that section were designed to accomplish, Congress made the deliberate policy judgment that "it is impossible to subject bank mergers to the simple rule of Section 7 of the Clayton Act. Under that act, a merger would be barred if it might tend substantially to lessen competition, regardless of the effects on the public interest." . . . Because of the peculiar nature of the commercial banking industry, its crucial role in the economy, and its intimate connection with the fiscal and monetary operations of the Government, Congress rejected the notion that the general economic and business premises of the Clayton Act should be the only considerations applicable to this field. Unrestricted bank competition was thought to have been a major cause of the panic of 1907 and of the bank failures of the 1930s, and was regarded as a highly undesirable condition to impose on banks in the future. . . .

Thus the Committee on Banking and Currency recommended "continuance of the existing exemption from Section 7 of the Clayton Act." . . . Congress accepted this recommendation; it decided to handle the problem of concentration in commercial banking "through banking laws, specially framed to fit the particular needs of the field. . . ." . . . As finally enacted in 1960, the Bank Merger Act embodies the regulatory approach advocated by the banking agencies, vesting in them responsibility for its administration and placing the scheme within the framework of existing banking laws. . . .

The congressional purpose clearly emerges from the terms of the statute and from the committee reports, hearings, and floor debates on the bills. Time and again it was repeated that effect on competition was *not to be the controlling factor* in determining whether to approve a bank merger, that a merger could be approved as being in the public interest even though it would cause a substantial lessening of competition. . . . [I]t was the congressional intention to place the responsibility for approval squarely on the banking agencies; the report of the Attorney General on the competitive aspects of a merger was to be advisory only. And there was deliberately omitted any attempt to specify or restrict the kinds of circumstances in which the agencies might properly determine that a proposed merger would be in the public interest notwithstanding its adverse effect on competition.

What Congress has chosen to do about mergers and their effect on competition in the highly specialized field of commercial banking could not be more "crystal clear." . . . But in the face of overwhelming evidence to the contrary, the Court, with perfect equanimity, finds "uncertainty" in the foundations of the Bank Merger Act . . . and on this premise puts it aside as irrelevant to the task of construing the scope of Section 7 of the Clayton Act.

I am unable to conceive of a more inappropriate case in which to overturn the considered opinion of all concerned as to the reach of prior legislation. For 10 years everyone—the department responsible for antitrust law enforcement, the banking industry, the Congress, and the bar—proceeded on the assumption that the 1950 amendment of the Clayton Act did not affect bank mergers. This assumption provided a major impetus to the enactment of remedial legislation, and Congress, when it finally settled on what it thought was the solution to the problem at hand, emphatically rejected the remedy now brought to life by the Court.

The result is, of course, that the Bank Merger Act is almost completely nullified; its enactment turns out to have been an exorbitant waste of congressional time and energy. As the present case illustrates, the Attorney General's report to the designated banking agency is no longer truly advisory, for if the agency's decision is not satisfactory a Section 7 suit may be commenced immediately. The bank merger's legality will then be judged solely from its competitive aspects, unencumbered by any considerations peculiar to banking.[12] And if such a suit were deemed to lie after a bank merger has been consummated, there would then be introduced into this field, for the first time to any significant extent, the threat of divestiture of assets and all the complexities and disruption attendant upon the use of that sanction. The only vestige of the Bank Merger Act which remains is that the banking agencies will have an initial veto.

This frustration of a manifest congressional design is, in my view, a most unwarranted intrusion upon the legislative domain. I submit that *whatever* may have been the congressional purpose in 1950, Congress has now so plainly pronounced its current judgment that bank mergers are not within the reach of Section 7 that this Court is duty bound to effectuate its choice.

But I need not rest on this proposition, for, as will now be shown, there is nothing in the 1950 amendment to Section 7 or its legislative history to support the conclusion that Congress even then intended to subject bank mergers to this provision of the Clayton Act.

II

. . . . .

The legislative history of the 1950 amendment also unquestionably negates any inference that Congress intended to reach bank mergers. It is true that the purpose was "to plug a loophole" in Section 7. . . . But simply to state this broad proposition does not answer the precise questions presented here: what was the nature of the loophole sought to be closed; what were the means chosen to close it?

The answer to the latter question is unmistakably indicated by the

---

[12] Indeed the Court has erected a simple yardstick in order to alleviate the agony of analyzing economic data—control of 30% of a commercial banking market is prohibited. . . .

relationship between the 1950 amendment and previous judicial decisions. . . .

. . . [T]he legislative history demonstrates that it was the asset-acquisition provision that was designed to plug the loophole created by *Thatcher, Swift,* and *Arrow*. . . .

I do not mean to suggest, of course, that Section 7 of the Clayton Act is thereby rendered applicable only to ordinary commercial and industrial corporations and not to firms in any "regulated" sector of the economy. . . . Rather, the absence of any mention of banks in the legislative history of the 1950 amendment, viewed in light of the prior congressional treatment of banking as a distinctive area with special characteristics and needs, compels the conclusion that bank mergers were simply not then regarded as part of the loophole to be plugged.

This conclusion is confirmed by a number of additional considerations. It was not until *after* the passage of the 1950 amendment of Section 7 that Representative Celler, its co-sponsor, requested the staff of the Antitrust Subcommittee of the House Committee on the Judiciary "to prepare a report indicating the concentration existing in our banking system."
. . . It is also worth noting that in 1956 Representative Celler himself introduced another amendment to Section 7, explaining that "all the bill [H. R. 5948] does is plug a loophole in the present law dealing with bank mergers. . . . This loophole exists because Section 7 of the Clayton Act prohibits bank mergers . . . only if such mergers are accomplished by stock acquisition." . . . The amendment passed the House but was defeated in the Senate.

For all these reasons, I think the conclusion is inescapable that Section 7 of the Clayton Act does not apply to the PNB-Girard merger. The Court's contrary conclusion seems to me little better than a *tour de force*.[13]

Memorandum of MR. JUSTICE GOLDBERG.

I agree fully with my Brother HARLAN that Section 7 of the Clayton Act has no application to bank mergers of the type involved here, and I therefore join in the conclusions expressed in his opinion on that point. However, while I thus dissent from the Court's holding with respect to the applicability of the Clayton Act to this merger, I wish to make clear that I do not necessarily dissent from its judgment invalidating the merger. To do so would require me to conclude in addition that on the record as it stands the government has failed to prove a violation of the Sherman Act, which is fully applicable to the commercial banking business. In my opinion there is a substantial Sherman Act issue in this case, but since the

---

[13] Since the Court does not reach the Sherman Act aspect of this case, it would serve no useful purpose for me to do so.

Court does not reach it and since my views relative thereto would be superfluous in light of today's disposition of the case, I express no ultimate conclusion concerning it. . . .

Note: In the case of *United States* v. *Phillipsburg National Bank and Trust Co.,* 399 U.S. 350 (1970), the principles set forth above were emphatically reaffirmed. Indeed, in a lengthy dissent, Justice Harlan declared that "[a]fter today's opinion the legality of every merger of two directly competing banks—no matter how small—is placed in doubt. . . ." (*Id.* at p. 374.) However, cf. *United States* v. *Marine Bancorporation, Inc.,* 418 U.S. 602 (1974).

Otter Tail Power Co. v. United States
410 U.S. 366 (1973)

. . . . .

MR. JUSTICE DOUGLAS delivered the opinion of the Court.

In this civil antitrust suit brought by appellee against Otter Tail Power Co. (Otter Tail), an electric utility company, the District Court found that Otter Tail had attempted to monopolize and had monopolized the retail distribution of electric power in its service area in violation of §2 of the Sherman Act. . . . The District Court found that Otter Tail had attempted to prevent communities in which its retail distribution franchise had expired from replacing it with a municipal distribution system. The principal means employed were (1) refusals to sell power at wholesale to proposed municipal systems in the communities where it had been retailing power; (2) refusals to "wheel" power to such systems, that is to say, to transfer by direct transmission or displacement electric power from one utility to another over the facilities of an intermediate utility; (3) the institution and support of litigation designed to prevent or delay establishment of those systems; and (4) the invocation of provisions in its transmission contracts with several other power suppliers for the purpose of denying the municipal systems access to other suppliers by means of Otter Tail's transmission systems.

Otter Tail sells electric power at retail in 465 towns in Minnesota, North Dakota, and South Dakota. The District Court's decree enjoins it from refusing to sell electric power at wholesale to existing or proposed municipal electric power systems in the areas serviced by Otter Tail, from refusing to wheel electric power over the lines from the electric power suppliers to existing or proposed municipal systems in the area, from entering into or enforcing any contract which prohibits use of Otter Tail's lines to wheel electric power to municipal electric power systems, or from entering into or enforcing any contract which limits the customers to whom and areas in which Otter Tail or any other electric power company may sell electric power.

The decree also enjoins Otter Tail from instituting, supporting, or engaging in litigation, directly or indirectly, against municipalities and their officials who have voted to establish municipal electric power systems for the purpose of delaying, preventing, or interfering with the establishment of a municipal electric power system. . . .

In towns where Otter Tail distributes at retail, it operates under municipally granted franchises which are limited from 10 to 20 years. Each town in Otter Tail's service area generally can accommodate only one distribution system, making each town a natural monopoly market for the distribution and sale of electric power at retail. The aggregate of towns in Otter Tail's service area is the geographic market in which Otter Tail competes for the right to serve the towns at retail.[1] That competition is generally for the right to serve the entire retail market within the composite limits of a town, and that competition is generally between Otter Tail and a prospective or existing municipal system. These towns number 510 and of those Otter Tail serves 91%, or 465.

Otter Tail's policy is to acquire, when it can, existing municipal systems within its service areas. It has acquired six since 1947. . . . Proposed municipal systems have great obstacles; they must purchase the electric power at wholesale. To do so they must have access to existing transmission lines. The only ones available[2] belong to Otter Tail. . . .

The antitrust charge against Otter Tail does not involve the lawfulness of its retail outlets, but only its methods of preventing the towns it served from establishing their own municipal systems when Otter Tail's franchises expired. The critical events centered largely in four towns—Elbow Lake, Minnesota; Hankinson, North Dakota; Colman, South Dakota; and Aurora, South Dakota. When Otter Tail's franchise in each of these towns terminated, the citizens voted to establish a municipal distribution system. Otter Tail refused to sell the new systems energy at wholesale and refused to agree to wheel power from other suppliers of wholesale energy.

Colman and Aurora had access to other transmission. Against them, Otter Tail used the weapon of litigation.

---

[1] Northern States Power Co. also supplies some towns in Otter Tail's area with electric power at retail. But the District Court excluded these towns from Otter Tail's area because the two companies do not compete in the towns served by each other. Of the 615 remaining towns in the area, 465 are served at retail by Otter Tail, 45 by municipal systems, and 105 by rural electric cooperatives. The cooperatives are barred by §4 of the Rural Electrification Act of 1936, 49 Stat. 1365, as amended, 7 U.S.C. §904, from borrowing federal funds to provide power to towns already receiving central station service. For this and related reasons, the District Court excluded the rural cooperatives from the relevant market.

[2] Subtransmission lines, with voltages from 34.5 kv to 69 kv are used for moving power from the bulk supply lines to points of local distribution. Of Otter Tail's basic subtransmission system in this area, two-thirds of those lines are 41.6 kv subtransmission lines.

As respects Elbow Lake and Hankinson, Otter Tail simply refused to deal, although according to the findings it had the ability to do so. Elbow Lake, cut off from all sources of wholesale power, constructed its own generating plant. Both Elbow Lake and Hankinson requested the Bureau of Reclamation and various cooperatives to furnish them with wholesale power; they were willing to supply it if Otter Tail would wheel it. But Otter Tail refused, relying on provisions in its contracts which barred the use of its lines for wheeling power to towns which it had served at retail. Elbow Lake after completing its plant asked the Federal Power Commission, under §202(b) of the Federal Power Act . . . to require Otter Tail to interconnect with the town and sell it power at wholesale. The Federal Power Commission ordered first a temporary . . . and then a permanent connection. . . . Hankinson tried unsuccessfully to get relief from the North Dakota Commission and then filed a complaint with the federal commission seeking an order to compel Otter Tail to wheel. While the application was pending, the town council voted to withdraw it and subsequently renewed Otter Tail's franchise.

It was found that Otter Tail instituted or sponsored litigation involving four towns in its service area which had the effect of halting or delaying efforts to establish municipal systems. Municipal power systems are financed by the sale of electric revenue bonds. Before such bonds can be sold, the town's attorney must submit an opinion which includes a statement that there is no pending or threatened litigation which might impair the value or legality of the bonds. The record amply bears out the District Court's holding that Otter Tail's use of litigation halted or appreciably slowed the efforts for municipal ownership. . . .

I

Otter Tail contends that by reason of the Federal Power Act it is not subject to antitrust regulation with respect to its refusal to deal. We disagree with that position.

. . . Activities which come under the jurisdiction of a regulatory agency nevertheless may be subject to scrutiny under the antitrust laws. . . .

The District Court determined that Otter Tail's consistent refusals to wholesale or wheel power to its municipal customers constituted illegal monopolization. Otter Tail maintains here that its refusals to deal should be immune from antitrust prosecution because the Federal Power Commission has the authority to compel involuntary interconnections of power pursuant to §202(b) of the Federal Power Act. The essential thrust of §202, however, is to encourage voluntary interconnections of power. . . . Only if a power company refuses to interconnect voluntarily may the Federal Power Commission, subject to limitations unrelated to antitrust considerations, order the interconnection. The standard which governs its decision is whether such action is "necessary or appropriate in the public interest." Although antitrust considerations may be relevant, they are not determinative.

There is nothing in the legislative history which reveals a purpose to insulate electric power companies from the operation of the antitrust laws. . . .

Thus, there is no basis for concluding that the limited authority of the Federal Power Commission to order interconnections was intended to be a substitute for, or to immunize Otter Tail from, antitrust regulation for refusing to deal with municipal corporations.

II

The decree of the District Court enjoins Otter Tail from "[r]efusing to sell electric power at wholesale to existing or proposed municipal electric power systems in cities and towns located in [its service area]" and from refusing to wheel electric power over its transmission lines from other electric power lines to such cities and towns. But the decree goes on to provide:

> The defendant shall not be compelled by the Judgment in this case to furnish wholesale electric service or wheeling service to a municipality except at rates which are compensatory and under terms and conditions which are filed with and subject to approval by the Federal Power Commission.

So far as wheeling is concerned, there is no authority granted the Commission under Part II of the Federal Power Act to order it. . . . Insofar as the District Court ordered wheeling to correct anticompetitive and monopolistic practices of Otter Tail, there is no conflict with the authority of the Federal Power Commission.

As respects the ordering of interconnections, there is no conflict on the present record. Elbow Lake applied to the Federal Power Commission for an interconnection with Otter Tail and, as we have said, obtained it. Hankinson renewed Otter Tail's franchise. So the decree of the District Court, as far as the present record is concerned, presents no actual conflict between the federal judicial decree and an order of the Federal Power Commission. The argument concerning the pre-emption of the area by the Federal Power Commission concerns only instances which may arise in the future, if Otter Tail continues its hostile attitude and conduct against "existing or proposed municipal electric power systems." The decree of the District Court has an open end by which that court retains jurisdiction "necessary or appropriate" to carry out the decree or "for the modification of any of the provisions." It also contemplates that future disputes over interconnections and the terms and conditions governing those interconnections will be subject to Federal Power Commission perusal. It will be time enough to consider whether the antitrust remedy may override the power of the Commission under §202(b) as, if, and when the Commission denies the interconnection and the District Court nevertheless undertakes to direct it. At present, there is only a potential conflict, not a present concrete case or controversy concerning it.

III

The record makes abundantly clear that Otter Tail used its monopoly power in the towns in its service area to foreclose competition or gain a competitive advantage, or to destroy a competitor, all in violation of the antitrust laws. See *United States* v. *Griffith,* 334 U.S. 100, 107. The District Court determined that Otter Tail has "a strategic dominance in the transmission of power in most of its service area" and that it used this dominance to foreclose potential entrants into the retail area from obtaining electric power from outside sources of supply. 331 F. Supp., at 60. Use of monopoly power "to destroy threatened competition" is a violation of the "attempt to monopolize" clause of §2 of the Sherman Act. *Lorain Journal* v. *United States,* 342 U.S. 143, 154; *Eastman Kodak Co.* v. *Southern Photo Materials Co.,* 273 U.S. 359, 375. So are agreements not to compete, with the aim of preserving or extending a monopoly. *Schine Chain Theatres* v. *United States,* 334 U.S. 110, 119. In *Associated Press* v. *United States* 326 U.S. 1, a cooperative news association had bylaws that permitted member newspapers to bar competitors from joining the association. We held that that practice violated the Sherman Act, even though the transgressor "had not yet achieved a complete monopoly." *Id.,* at 13.

When a community serviced by Otter Tail decides not to renew Otter Tail's retail franchise when it expires, it may generate, transmit, and distribute its own electric power. We recently described the difficulties and problems of those isolated electric power systems. See *Gainesville Utilities* v. *Florida Power Corp.,* 402 U.S. 515, 517–520. Interconnection with other utilities is frequently the only solution. *Id.,* at 519 n. 3. That is what Elbow Lake in the present case did. There were no engineering factors that prevented Otter Tail from selling power at wholesale to those towns that wanted municipal plants or wheeling the power. The District Court found—and its findings are supported—that Otter Tail's refusals to sell at wholesale or to wheel were soley to prevent municipal power systems from eroding its monopolistic position.

Otter Tail relies on its wheeling contracts with the Bureau of Reclamation and with cooperatives which it says relieve it of any duty to wheel power to municipalities served at retail by Otter Tail at the time the contracts were made. The District Court held that these restrictive provisions were "in reality, territorial allocation schemes," 331 F. Supp., at 63, and were *per se* violations of the Sherman Act, citing *Northern Pacific R. Co.* v. *United States,* 356 U.S. 1. Like covenants were there held to "deny defendant's competitors access to the fenced-off market on the same terms as the defendant." *Id.,* at 12. We recently re-emphasized the vice under the Sherman Act of territorial restrictions among potential competitors. *United States* v. *Topco Associates*, 405 U.S. 596, 608. The fact that some of the restrictive provisions were contained in a contract with the Bureau of Reclamation is not material to our problem for, as the Solicitor General says, "government contracting officers do not have the power to grant immunity from the Sherman Act." Such contracts stand on their own footing and are valid or not, depending on the statutory framework within which the federal agency operates. The Solicitor General tells us that these restrictive provisions operate as a "hindrance" to the Bureau and were "agreed to by the Bureau only at Otter Tail's insistence," as the District Court found. The evidence supports that finding.

IV

The District Court found that the litigation sponsored by Otter Tail had the purpose of delaying and preventing the establishment of municipal electric systems "with the expectation that this would preserve its predominant position in the sale and transmission of electric power in the area." . . . 331 F. Supp., at 62. . . . On that phase of the order, we vacate and remand for consideration in light of our intervening decision in *California Motor Transport Co.*

V

Otter Tail argues that, without the weapons which it used, more and more municipalities will turn to public power and Otter Tail will go downhill. . . .

The . . . Sherman Act . . . assumes that an enterprise will protect itself against loss by operating with superior service, lower costs, and improved efficiency. Otter Tail's theory collided with the Sherman Act as it sought to substitute for competition anticompetitive uses of its dominant economic power.[3]

The fact that three municipalities which Otter Tail opposed finally got their municipal systems does not excuse Otter Tail's conduct. That fact does not condone the antitrust tactics which Otter Tail sought to impose. Moreover, the District Court repeated what we said in *FTC* v. *National Lead Co.*, 352 U.S. 419, 431, "those caught violating the Act must expect some fencing in." The proclivity for predatory practices has always been a consideration for the District Court in fashioning its antitrust decree. See *United States* v. *Crescent Amusement Co.*, 323 U.S. 173, 190.

We do not suggest, however, that the District Court, concluding that Otter Tail violated the antitrust laws, should be impervious to Otter Tail's

---

[3] The Federal Power Commission said in *Elbow Lake* v. *Otter Tail Power Co.*, 46 F.P.C., at 678:

"The public interest is far broader than the economic interest of a particular power supplier. . . . The private company's lack of enthusiasm for the arrangement cannot deter us, so long as the public interest requires it."

assertion that compulsory interconnection or wheeling will erode its integrated system and threaten its capacity to serve adequately the public. As the dissent properly notes, the Commission may not order interconnection if to do so "would impair [the utility's] ability to render adequate service to its customers." 16 U.S.C. §824a(b). The District Court in this case found that the "pessimistic view" advanced in Otter Tail's "erosion study" "is not supported by the record." Furthermore, it concluded that "it does not appear that Bureau of Reclamation power is a serious threat to the defendant nor that it will be in the foreseeable future." Since the District Court has made future connections subject to Commission approval and in any event has retained jurisdiction to enable the parties to apply for "necessary or appropriate" relief and presumably will give effect to the policies embodied in the Federal Power Act, we cannot say under these circumstances that it has abused its discretion.

Except for the provision of the order discussed in part IV of this opinion, the judgment is

Affirmed.

MR. JUSTICE BLACKMUN and MR. JUSTICE POWELL took no part in the consideration or decision of this case.

MR. JUSTICE STEWART, with whom THE CHIEF JUSTICE and MR. JUSTICE REHNQUIST join, concurring in part and dissenting in part. . . .

The Court in this case has followed the District Court into a misapplication of the Sherman Act to a highly regulated, natural-monopoly industry wholly different from those that have given rise to ordinary antitrust principles. In my view, Otter Tail's refusal to wholesale power through interconnection or to perform wheeling services was conduct entailing no antitrust violation.

. . . The District Court . . . mechanically applied the familiar Sherman Act formula: since Otter Tail possessed monopoly power[4] and had acted to preserve that power, it was guilty of an antitrust violation. Nowhere did the District Court come to grips with the significance of the Federal Power Act, either in terms of the specific regulatory apparatus it

---

[4] The District Court looked to Otter Tail's service area, and measured market dominance in terms of the number of towns within that area served by Otter Tail. Computed this way, Otter Tail provides 91% of the retail market. 331 F. Supp. 54, 59. As the appellant points out, however, these towns vary in size from more than 29,000 to 20 inhabitants. If Otter Tail's size were measured by actual retail sales, its market share would be only 28.9% of the electricity sold at retail within its geographic market area. It is important to note that another reasonable geographical market unit might be each individual municipality. Viewed this way, whichever power company sells electricity at retail in a town has a complete monopoly. [Footnote relocated. IMS.]

established or the policy considerations that moved the Congress to enact it. Yet it seems to me that these concerns are central to the disposition of this case.

. . . In the face of natural monopolies at retail and similar economies of scale in the subtransmission of power, Congress was forced to address the very problem raised by this case—use of the lines of one company by another. One obvious solution would have been to impose the obligations of a common carrier upon power companies owning lines capable of the wholesale transmission of electricity. . . . Yet, after substantial debate . . . the Congress declined to follow this path. . . .

This legislative history, especially when viewed in the light of repeated subsequent congressional refusals to impose common carrier obligations in this area . . . indicates a clear congressional purpose to allow electric utilities to decide for themselves whether to wheel or sell at wholesale as they see fit. This freedom is qualified by a grant of authority to the Commission to order interconnection (but not wheeling) in certain circumstances. But the exercise of even that power is limited by a consideration of the ability of the regulated utility to function. The Commission may not order interconnection where this would entail an "undue burden" on the regulated utility. In addition, the Commission has

> no authority to compel the enlargement of generating facilities for such purposes, nor to compel such public utility to sell or exchange energy when to do so would impair its ability to render adequate service to its customers. 16 U.S.C. §824a(b).

As the District Court found, Otter Tail is a vertically integrated power company. But the bulk of its business—some 90% of its income—derives from sales of power at retail. Left to its own judgment in dealing with its customers, it seems entirely predictable that Otter Tail would decline wholesale dealing with towns in which it had previously done business at retail. If the purpose of the congressional scheme is to leave such decisions to the power companies in the absence of a contrary requirement imposed by the Commission, it would appear that Otter Tail's course of conduct in refusing to deal with the municipal system at Elbow Lake and in refusing to promise to deal with the proposed system at Hankinson, was forseeably within the zone of freedom specifically created by the statutory scheme.[5] As a retailer of power, Otter Tail asserted a legitimate

---

[5] The District Court was persuaded that the restrictions on wheeling contained in Otter Tail's contracts with the Bureau of Reclamation were "in reality, territorial allocation schemes." 331 F. Supp., at 63. I think this finding was clearly erroneous. Territorial allocation arrangements that have run afoul of the antitrust laws have traditionally been horizontal, and have involved the elimination of competition between two enterprises that were similarly situated in the market. *United States* v. *Topco Associates,* 405 U.S. 596; *Timken Roller Bearing Co.* v. *United States,* 341 U.S. 593; cf. *White Motor Co.* v. *United States,* 372 U.S. 253, 261-264. Otter Tail and the Bureau of Reclamation stand in a vertical, not a horizontal, relationship. Furthermore, though Otter Tail refused to wheel power to towns

business interest in keeping its lines free for its own power sales and in refusing to lend a hand in its own demise by wheeling cheaper power from the Bureau of Reclamation to municipal consumers which might otherwise purchase power at retail from Otter Tail itself.

The opinion of the Court emphasizes that Otter Tail's actions were not simple refusals to deal—they resulted in Otter Tail's maintenance of monopoly control by hindering the emergence of municipal power companies . . . [But] a monopoly is sure to result either way. If the consumers of Elbow Lake receive their electric power from a municipally owned company or from Otter Tail, there will be a monopoly at the retail level, for there will in any event be only one supplier. The very reason for the regulation of private utility rates—by state bodies and by the Commission—is the inevitability of a monopoly that requires price control to take the place of price competition. Antitrust principles applicable to other industries cannot be blindly applied to a unilateral refusal to deal on the part of a power company, operating in a regime of rate regulation and licensed monopolies.

The Court's opinion scoffs at Otter Tail's defense of business justification. . . . This question-begging disregard of the economic health of Otter Tail is wholly at odds with the congressional purpose in specifying the conditions under which interconnections can be required.

This is not to say that Otter Tail's financial health is paramount in all instances, . . . or that the electric power industry as regulated by the Commission is *per se* exempt from the antitrust laws. In the absence of a specific statutory immunity, cf. *Hughes Tool Co.* v. *Trans World Airlines,* 409 U.S. 363, such exemptions are not lightly to be implied, *United States* v. *Philadelphia National Bank,* 374 U.S. 321. Furthermore, no sweeping antitrust exemption is warranted, as it has been in cases involving certain pervasively regulated industries, under the doctrine of "primary jurisdiction."[6] . . .

With respect to decisions by regulated electric utilities as to whether or not to provide nonretail services, I think that in the absence of horizontal conspiracy, the teaching of the "primary jurisdiction" cases argues for leaving governmental regulation to the Commission instead of the invari-

---

whose consumers it formerly served at retail, it did not exact from the Bureau a promise that the latter would not provide power to such towns by alternative means. Hence, I cannot see how these contracts operate as territorial-allocation schemes. If Otter Tail had demanded that the Bureau not sell to former Otter Tail customers, or if Otter Tail had combined with other retailers of electricity and undertaken mutual noncompetition agreements, this would be a different case.

[6] . . . [T]he considerable freedom allowed to electric utilities with respect to coordination of service persuades me that the antitrust laws apply to the extent they are not repugnant to specific features of the regulatory scheme. For this reason . . . a genuine territorial allocation agreement might be prohibited under the Sherman Act. . . . Were it not for the legislative history noted above, a consistent refusal to deal with municipally owned power companies might also be impermissible under the Sherman Act. For me, however, the legislative history with respect to wheeling and interconnection is dispositive.

ably less sensitive and less specifically expert process of antitrust litigation. I believe this is what Congress intended by declining to impose common carrier obligations on companies like Otter Tail, and by entrusting the Commission with the burden of "assuring an abundant supply of electric energy throughout the United States" and with the power to order interconnections when necessary in the public interest. This is an area where "sporadic action by federal courts" *can* "work mischief." Cf. *United States* v. *Radio Corp. of America,* 358 U.S., at 350. . . .

Both because I believe Otter Tail's refusal to wheel or wholesale power was conduct exempt from the antitrust laws and because I believe the District Court's decree improperly pre-empted the jurisdiction of the Federal Power Commission, I would reverse the judgment before us.

Silver v. New York Stock Exchange

373 U.S. 341 (1963)

MR. JUSTICE GOLDBERG delivered the opinion of the Court.

We deal here today with the question, of great importance to the public and the financial community, of whether and to what extent the federal antitrust laws apply to securities exchanges regulated by the Securities Exchange Act of 1934. More particularly, the question is whether the New York Stock Exchange is to be held liable to a nonmember broker-dealer under the antitrust laws or regarded as impliedly immune therefrom when, pursuant to rules the Exchange has adopted under the Securities Exchange Act of 1934, it orders a number of its members to remove private direct telephone wire connections previously in operation between their offices and those of the nonmember, without giving the nonmember notice, assigning him any reason for the action, or affording him an opportunity to be heard.

I

The facts material to resolution of this question are not in dispute. Harold J. Silver, who died during the pendency of this action, entered the securities business in Dallas, Texas, in 1955, by establishing the predecessor of petitioner Municipal Securities (Municipal) to deal primarily in municipal bonds. The business of Municipal having increased steadily, Silver, in June 1958, established petitioner Municipal Securities, Inc. (Municipal, Inc.), to trade in corporate over-the-counter securities. Both firms are registered broker-dealers and members of the National Association of Securities Dealers, Inc. (NASD); neither is a member of the respondent Exchange.

Instantaneous communication with firms in the mainstream of the securities business is of great significance to a broker-dealer not a member of the Exchange, and Silver took steps to see that this was established for his firms. Municipal obtained direct private telephone wire connections with the municipal bond departments of a number of securities firms (three of which were members of the Exchange) and banks, and Municipal, Inc., arranged for private wires to the corporate securities trading departments of ten member firms of the Exchange, as well as to the trading desks of a number of nonmember firms.

Pursuant to the requirements of the Exchange's rules, all but one of the member firms which had granted private wires to Municipal, Inc., applied to the Exchange for approval of the connections. . . . During the summer of 1958 the Exchange granted "temporary approval" for these, as well as for a direct teletype connection to a member firm in New York City and for stock ticker service to be furnished to petitioners directly from the floor of the Exchange.

On February 12, 1959, without prior notice to Silver, his firms, or anyone connected with them, the Exchange's Department of Member Firms decided to disapprove the private wire and related applications. Notice was sent to the member firms involved, instructing them to discontinue the wires, a directive with which compliance was required by the Exchange's Constitution and rules. These firms in turn notified Silver that the private wires would have to be discontinued, and the Exchange advised him directly of the discontinuance of the stock ticker service. The wires and ticker were all removed by the beginning of March. By telephone calls, letters, and a personal trip to New York, Silver sought an explanation from the Exchange of the reason for its decision but was repeatedly told it was the policy of the Exchange not to disclose the reasons for such action. . . .

Petitioners contend that their volume of business dropped substantially thereafter and that their profits fell, due to a combination of forces all stemming from the removal of the private wires—their consequent inability to obtain quotations quickly, the inconvenience to other traders in calling petitioners, and the stigma attaching to the disapproval. As a result of this change in fortunes, petitioners contend, Municipal, Inc., soon ceased functioning as an operating business organization, and Municipal has remained in business only on a greatly diminished scale. . . .

II

The fundamental issue confronting us is whether the Securities Exchange Act has created a duty of exchange self-regulation so pervasive as to constitute an implied repealer of our antitrust laws, thereby exempting the Exchange from liability in this and similar cases.

A

It is plain, to begin with, that removal of the wires by collective action of the Exchange and its members would, had it occurred in a context free from other federal regulation, constitute a per se violation of §1 of the

Sherman Act. The concerted action of the Exchange and its members here was, in simple terms, a group boycott depriving petitioners of a valuable business service which they needed in order to compete effectively as broker-dealers in the over-the-counter securities market. *Fashion Originators' Guild* v. *Federal Trade Comm'n,* 312 U.S. 457. . . . Unlike listed securities, there is no central trading place for securities traded over the counter. The market is established by traders in the numerous firms all over the country through a process of constant communication to one another of the latest offers to buy and sell. The private wire connection, which allows communication to occur with a flip of a switch, is an essential part of this process. Without the instantaneously available market information provided by private wire connections, an over-the-counter dealer is hampered substantially in his crucial endeavor—to buy, whether it be for customers or on his own account, at the lowest quoted price and sell at the highest quoted price. Without membership in the network of simultaneous communication, the over-the-counter dealer loses a significant volume of trading with other members of the network which would come to him as a result of his easy accessibility. These important business advantages were taken away from petitioners by the group action of the Exchange and its members. Such "concerted refusals by traders to deal with other traders . . . have long been held to be in the forbidden category," *Klor's, Inc.,* v. *Broadway-Hale Stores, Inc.,* 359 U.S., at 212, of restraints which "because of their inherent nature or effect . . . injuriously restrained trade," *United States* v. *American Tobacco Co.,* 221 U.S. 106, 179.[1] Hence, absent any justification derived from the policy of another statute or otherwise, the Exchange acted in violation of the Sherman Act. In this case, however, the presence of another statutory scheme, that of the Securities Exchange Act of 1934, means that such a conclusion is only the beginning, not the end, of inquiry.

B

The difficult problem here arises from the need to reconcile pursuit of the antitrust aim of eliminating restraints on competition with the effective operation of a public policy contemplating that securities exchanges will

---

[1] The fact that the consensus underlying the collective action was arrived at when the members bound themselves to comply with Exchange directives upon being admitted to membership rather than when the specific issue of Silver's qualifications arose does not diminish the collective nature of the action. A blanket subscription to possible future restraints does not excuse the restraints when they occur. . . . Nor does any excuse derive from the fact that the collective refusal to deal was only with reference to the private wires, the member firms remaining willing to deal with petitioners for the purchase and sale of securities. . . . A valuable service germane to petitioners' business and important to their effective competition with others was withheld from them by collective action. That is enough to create a violation of the Sherman Act. . . .

engage in self-regulation which may well have anticompetitive effects in general and in specific applications.

The need for statutory regulation of securities exchanges and the nature of the duty of self-regulation imposed by the Securities Exchange Act are properly understood in the context of a consideration of both the economic role played by exchanges and the historical setting of the Act. Stock exchanges perform an important function in the economic life of this country. They serve, first of all, as an indispensable mechanism through which corporate securities can be bought and sold. To corporate enterprise such a market mechanism is a fundamental element in facilitating the successful marshaling of large aggregations of funds that would otherwise be extremely difficult of access. To the public the exchanges are an investment channel which promises ready convertibility of stock holdings into cash. . . . Recognition of the importance of the exchanges' role led the House Committee on Interstate and Foreign Commerce to declare in its report preceding the enactment of the Securities Exchange Act of 1934 that "The great exchanges of this country upon which millions of dollars of securities are sold are affected with a public interest in the same degree as any other great utility." . . .

The exchanges are by their nature bodies with a limited number of members, each of which plays a certain role in the carrying out of an exchange's activities. The limited-entry feature of exchanges led historically to their being treated by the courts as private clubs . . . and to their being given great latitude by the courts in disciplining errant members. . . . As exchanges became a more and more important element in our Nation's economic and financial system, however, the private-club analogy became increasingly inapposite and the ungoverned self-regulation became more and more obviously inadequate, with acceleratingly grave consequences. This impotency ultimately led to the enactment of the 1934 Act. . . .

The pattern of governmental entry, however, was by no means one of total displacement of the exchanges' traditional process of self-regulation. The intention was rather, as MR. JUSTICE DOUGLAS said, while chairman of the S.E.C., one of "letting the exchanges take the leadership with Government playing a residual role. Government would keep the shotgun, so to speak, behind the door, loaded, well oiled, cleaned, ready for use but with the hope it would never have to be used." . . .

Thus arose the federally mandated duty of self-policing by exchanges. Instead of giving the Commission the power to curb specific instances of abuse, the Act placed in the exchanges a duty to register with the Commission . . . and decreed that registration could not be granted unless the exchange submitted copies of its rules . . . and unless such rules were "just and adequate to insure fair dealing and to protect investors,". . . . The general dimensions of the duty of self-regulation are suggested by §19(b) of the Act, . . . which gives the Commission power to order changes in exchange rules respecting a number of subjects. . . .

One aspect of the statutorily imposed duty of self-regulation is the obligation for formulate rules governing the conduct of exchange members. The Act specifically requires that registration cannot be granted "unless the rules of the exchange include provision for the expulsion, suspension, or disciplining of a member for conduct or proceeding inconsistent with just and equitable principles of trade . . . , "§6(b). . . . In addition, the general requirement of §6(d) that an exchange's rules be "just and adequate to insure fair dealing and to protect investors" has obvious relevance to the area of rules regulating the conduct of an exchange's members.

The §6(b) and §6(d) duties taken together have the broadest implications in relation to the present problem, for members inevitably trade on the over-the-counter market in addition to dealing in listed securities,[2] and such trading inexorably brings contact and dealings with nonmember firms which deal in or specialize in over-the-counter securities. It is no accident that the Exchange's Constitution and rules are permeated with instances of regulation of members' relationships with nonmembers including nonmember broker-dealers. . . . A member's purchase of unlisted securities for itself or on behalf of its customer from a boiler-shop operation[3] creates an obvious danger of loss to the principal in the transaction, and sale of securities to a nonmember insufficiently capitalized to protect customers' rights creates similar risks. In addition to the potential financial injury to the investing public and Exchange members that is inherent in these transactions as well as in dealings with nonmembers who are unreliable for any other reason, all such intercourse carries with it the gravest danger of engendering in the public a loss of confidence in the Exchange and its members, a kind of damage which can significantly impair fulfillment of the Exchange's function in our economy. Rules which regulate Exchange members' doing of business with nonmembers in the over-the-counter market are therefore very much pertinent to the aims of self-regulation under the 1934 Act. . . .

The Exchange's constitutional provision and rules relating to private

---

[2] Member firms of the New York Stock Exchange accounted for over half of the total dollar volume of over-the-counter business in fiscal 1961, Special Study, *op. cit., supra*, c. IB, pp. 17–18, and trading in over-the-counter stocks constituted 21.6 percent of the estimated gross income of member firms of the Exchange for the same period, id., c. I, Table I-12.

[3] In deposition, the assistant director of the Exchange's Department of Member Firms described a boiler shop as "usually a physically small operation which employs high pressure telephone salesmanship to oversell to the public by quantity, and in many cases by quality." He said that this kind of firm, as well as bucket shops, inadequately capitalized firms, and firms which might misrepresent or withhold material facts from customers, was among those which the Exchange seeks to prevent from having the use of its facilities.

wire connections . . . are unquestionably part of this fulfillment of the §6(b) and §6(d) duties, for such wires between members and nonmembers facilitate trading in the exchange of information about unlisted securities, and such contact with an unreliable nonmember not only may further his business undesirably, but may injure the member or the member's customer on whose behalf the contact is made and ultimately imperil the future status of the Exchange by sapping public confidence. . . . The sweeping of the nonmembers into the currents of the Exchange's process of self-regulation is therefore unavoidable; the case cannot be disposed of by holding as the district judge did that the substantive act of regulation engaged in here was outside the boundaries of the public policy established by the Securities Exchange Act of 1934.

C

But, it does not follow that the case can be disposed of, as the Court of Appeals did, by holding that since the Exchange has a general power to adopt rules governing its members' relations with nonmembers, particular applications of such rules are therefore outside the purview of the antitrust laws. Contrary to the conclusions reached by the courts below, the proper approach to this case, in our view, is an analysis which reconciles the operation of both statutory schemes with one another rather than holding one completely ousted.

The Securities Exchange Act contains no express exemption from the antitrust laws or, for that matter, from any other statute. This means that any repealer of the antitrust laws must be discerned as a matter of implication, and "[i]t is a cardinal principal of construction that repeals by implication are not favored." . . . Repeal is to be regarded as implied only if necessary to make the Securities Exchange Act work, and even then only to the minimum extent necessary. This is the guiding principal to reconciliation of the two statutory schemes.

Although the act gives to the Securities and Exchange Commission the power to request exchanges to make changes in their rules . . . and impliedly, therefore, to disapprove any rules adopted by an exchange, . . . it does not give the Commission jurisdiction to review particular instances of enforcement of exchange rules. . . . This aspect of the statute for one thing, obviates any need to consider whether petitioners were required to resort to the Commission for relief before coming into Court. . . . Moreover, the Commission's lack of jurisdiction over particular applications of exchange rules means that the question of antitrust exemption does not involve any problem of conflict or coextensiveness of coverage with the agency's regulatory power. . . .[4] The issue is

---

[4] Were there Commission jurisdiction and ensuing judicial review for scrutiny of a particular exchange ruling . . . a different case would arise concerning exemption from the operation of laws designed to prevent anticompetitive activity, an issue we do not decide today.

only that of the extent to which the character and objectives of the duty of exchange self-regulation contemplated by the Securities Exchange Act are incompatible with the maintenance of an antitrust action. . . .

The absence of Commission jurisdiction, besides defining the limits of the inquiry, contributes to its solution. There is nothing built into the regulatory scheme which performs the antitrust function of insuring that an exchange will not in some cases apply its rules so as to do injury to competition which cannot be justified as furthering legitimate self-regulative ends. . . . Enforcement of exchange rules, particularly those of the New York Stock Exchange with its immense economic power, may well, in given cases, result in competitive injury to an issuer, a nonmember broker-dealer or another when the imposition of such injury is not within the scope of the great purposes of the Securities Exchange Act. Such unjustified self-regulatory activity can only diminish public respect for and confidence in the integrity and efficacy of the exchange mechanism. Some form of review of exchange self-policing, whether by administrative agency or by the courts, is therefore not at all incompatible with the fulfillment of the aims of the Securities Exchange Act. . . . Since the antitrust laws serve, among other things, to protect competitive freedom, i.e., the freedom of individual business units to compete unhindered by the group action of others, it follows that the antitrust laws are peculiarly appropriate as a check upon anticompetitive acts of exchanges which conflict with their duty to keep their operations and those of their members honest and viable. Applicability of the antitrust laws, therefore, rests on the need for vindication of their positive aim of insuring competitive freedom. Denial of their applicability would defeat the congressional policy reflected in the antitrust laws without serving the policy of the Securities Exchange Act. . . .

Yet it is only frank to acknowledge that the absence of power in the Commission to review particular exchange exercises of self-regulation does create problems for the Exchange. The entire public policy of self-regulation, beginning with the idea that the Exchange may set up barriers to membership, contemplates that the Exchange will engage in restraints of trade which might well be unreasonable absent sanction by the Securities Exchange Act. Without the oversight of the Commission to elaborate from time to time on the propriety of various acts of self-regulation, the Exchange is left without guidance and without warning as to what regulative action would be viewed as excessive by an antitrust court possessing power to proceed based upon the considerations enumerated in the preceding paragraphs. But, under the aegis of the rule of reason, traditional antitrust concepts are flexible enough to permit the Exchange sufficient breathing space within which to carry out the mandate of the Securities Exchange Act. . . . Although, as we have seen, the statutory scheme of that Act is not sufficiently pervasive to create a total exemption from the antitrust laws . . . it is also true that particular instances of exchange self-regulation which fall within the scope and purposes of the Securities Exchange Act may be regarded as justified in answer to the assertion of an antitrust claim.

III

The final question here is, therefore, whether the act of self-regulation in this case was so justified. The answer to that question is that it was not, because the collective refusal to continue the private wires occurred under totally unjustifiable circumstances. Notwithstanding their prompt and repeated requests, petitioners were not informed of the changes underlying the decision to invoke the Exchange rules and were not afforded an appropriate opportunity to explain or refute the charges against them.

Given the principle that exchange self-regulation is to be regarded as justified in response to antitrust charges only to the extent necessary to protect the achievement of the aims of the Securities Exchange Act, it is clear that no justification can be offered for self-regulation conducted without provision for some method of telling a protesting nonmember why a rule is being invoked so as to harm him and allowing him to reply in explanation of his position. No policy reflected in the Securities Exchange Act is, to begin with, served by denial of notice and an opportunity for hearing. Indeed, the aims of the statutory scheme of self-policing—to protect investors and promote fair dealing—are defeated when an exchange exercises its tremendous economic power without explaining its basis for acting, for the absence of an obligation to give some form of notice and, if timely requested, a hearing creates a great danger of perpetration of injury that will damage public confidence in the exchanges. The requirement of such a hearing will, by contrast, help in effectuating antitrust policies by discouraging anticompetitive application of exchange rules which are not justifiable as within the scope of the purposes of the Securities Exchange Act. . . . And, given the possibility of antitrust liability for anticompetitive acts of self-regulation which fall too far outside the scope of Exchange Act, the utilization of a notice and hearing procedure with its inherent check upon unauthorized exchange action will diminish rather than enlarge the likelihood that such liability will be incurred and hence will not interfere with the Exchange's ability to engage efficaciously in legitimate substantive self-regulation. . . . Provision of such a hearing will, moreover, contribute to the effective functioning of the antitrust court, which would be severely impeded in providing the review of exchange action which we deem essential if the exchange could obscure rather than illuminate the circumstances under which it has acted. Hence the affording of procedural safeguards not only will substantively encourage the lessening of anticompetitive behavior outlawed by the Sherman Act but will allow the antitrust court to perform its function effectively. . . .

Our decision today recognizes that the action here taken by the Ex-

488

change would clearly be in violation of the Sherman Act unless justified by reference to the purposes of the Securities Exchange Act, and holds that that statute affords no justification for anticompetitive collective action taken without according fair procedures.[5] Congress in effecting a scheme of self-regulation designed to insure fair dealing cannot be thought to have sanctioned and protected self-regulative activity when carried out in a fundamentally unfair manner.[6] The point is not that the antitrust laws impose the requirement of notice and a hearing here, but rather that, in acting without according petitioners these safeguards in response to their request, the Exchange has plainly exceeded the scope of its authority under the Securities Exchange Act to engage in self-regulation and therefore has not even reached the threshold of justification under that statute for what would otherwise be an antitrust violation. . . . [I]t is perfectly clear that the Exchange can offer no justification under the Securities Exchange Act for its collective action in denying petitioners the private wire connections without notice and an opportunity for hearing, and . . . the Exchange has therefore violated §1 of the Sherman Act. . . . It requires but little appreciation of the extent of the Exchange's economic power and of what happened in this country during the 1920s and 1930s to realize how essential it is that the highest ethical standards prevail as to every aspect of the Exchange's activities. What is basically at issue here is whether the type of partnership between government and private enterprise that marks the design of the Securities Exchange Act of 1934 can operate effectively to insure the maintenance of such standards in the long run. We have today provided not a brake upon the private partner executing the public policy of self-regulation but a balance wheel to insure that it can perform this necessary activity in a setting compatible with the objectives of both the antitrust laws and the Securities Exchange Act.

The judgment is reversed and the case is remanded for further proceedings consistent with this opinion.

It is so ordered.

---

[5] It may be assumed that the Securities and Exchange Commission would have had the power, under §19(b) of the Exchange Act, . . . to direct the Exchange to adopt a general rule providing a hearing and attendant procedures to nonmembers. However, any rule that might be adopted by the Commission would, to be consonant with the antitrust laws, have to provide as a minimum the procedural safeguards which those laws make imperative in cases like this. Absent Commission adoption of a rule requiring fair procedure, and in light of both the utility of such a rule as an antitrust matter and its compatibility with securities-regulation principles, . . . no incompatibility with the Commission's power inheres in announcement by an antitrust court of the rule. . . .

[6] The basic nature of the rights which we hold to be required under the antitrust laws in the circumstances of today's decision is indicated by the fact that public agencies, labor unions, clubs, and other associations have, under various legal principles, all been required to afford notice, a hearing, and an opportunity to answer charges to one who is about to be denied a valuable right. . . .

MR. JUSTICE CLARK concurs in the result on the grounds stated in the opinion of the District Court, 196 F.Supp. 209, and the dissenting opinion in the Court of Appeals, 302 F.2d 714.

MR. JUSTICE STEWART, whom MR. JUSTICE HARLAN joins, dissenting.

The Court says that the fundamental question in this case is "whether and to what extent the federal antitrust laws apply to securities exchanges regulated by the Securities Exchange Act of 1934." I agree that this is the issue presented, but with all respect it seems to me that the answer which the Court has given is both unsatisfactory and incomplete.

The Court begins by pointing out, correctly, that removal of the petitioners' wire connections by collective action of the Exchange and its members would constitute a violation of the Sherman Act, had it occurred in an ordinary commercial context.[7] The Court then reviews at length the purpose, scope, and structure of the Securities Exchange Act and holds, again correctly I think, that the substantive act of regulation engaged in here was inside "the boundaries of the public policy" established by the Exchange Act. The Court next reminds us, correctly, that the Exchange Act contains no express exemption from the antitrust laws, and that a stock exchange or its members might in some cases "apply its rules so as to do injury to competition which cannot be justified as furthering legitimate self regulative ends."

So far, so good. The Court has fairly and thoroughly stated the competing considerations bearing upon the basic problem involved in this case. But then—in the last five pages of the Court's opinion—the nature of the problem seems suddenly to change. The case becomes one involving due process concepts of notice, confrontation, and hearing. . . .

The Court says that because of the failure to accord "procedural safeguards" to the petitioners, the respondent Exchange is ipso facto liable to them under the antitrust laws. This means that a bucket-shop operator who had been engaged in swindling the public could collect treble damages from a stock exchange which had denied him its wire connections without first according him notice and a hearing. For, as I understand the Court's opinion, the exchange would not be allowed to prove in this hypothetical antitrust case that the plaintiff *was* such a swindler, even though proof of that fact to an absolute certainty were available. This result seems to me completely to frustrate the purpose and policy of the Securities Exchange Act, and to bear no relevance to the purpose and policy of the antitrust laws. Even assuming that Congress

---

[7] . . . It may be assumed, I think, that almost every exercise of an exchange's statutory duty of self-regulation would involve an actual or threatened concerted refusal to deal—a "group boycott."

agreed with the Court's notions of the appropriate procedures under the Exchange Act, I cannot believe that Congress would have provided an antitrust forum and private treble damage liability to enforce them.

Whether there has been a violation of the antitrust laws depends not at all upon whether or not the defendants' conduct was arbitrary. As this Court has said, "the reasonableness of the methods pursued by the combination to accomplish its unlawful object is no more material than would be the reasonableness of the prices fixed by unlawful combination." *Fashion Originators' Guild* v. *Federal Trade Comm'n*, 312 U.S. 457, 468. . . . Yet the Court today says that because the Exchange did not accord the petitioners what the Court considers "fair procedures" under the Exchange Act, the Exchange has therefore violated §1 of the Sherman Act. . . .

The purpose of the self-regulation provisions of the Securities Exchange Act was to delegate governmental power to working institutions which would undertake, at their own initiative, to enforce compliance with ethical as well as legal standards in a complex and changing industry. This self-initiating process of regulation can work effectively only if the process itself is allowed to operate free from a constant threat of antitrust penalties. To achieve this end, I believe it must be held that the Securities Exchange Act removes antitrust liability for any action taken in good faith to effectuate an exchange's statutory duty of self-regulation. The inquiry in each case should be whether the conduct complained of was for this purpose. If it was, that should be the end of the matter so far as the antitrust laws are concerned—unless, of course, some antitrust violation other than the mere concerted action of an exchange and its members is alleged.[8]

I would vacate the judgment of the Court of Appeals and remand the case to the District Court for further proceedings consistent with the views expressed in this dissenting opinion.

Richard A. Gordon v. *New York Stock Exchange, Inc.*
422 U.S. 659 (1975)

. . . . .

MR. JUSTICE BLACKMUN delivered the opinion of the Court.

This case presents the problem of reconciliation of the antitrust laws with a federal regulatory scheme in the particular context of the practice

---

[8] For example, an exchange would be liable under the antitrust laws if it conspired with outsiders, or if it attempted to use its power to monopolize. . . . Furthermore, individual members of an exchange would be liable if it were shown that they had conspired to use the exchange's machinery for the purpose of suppressing competition. . . . Application of the antitrust laws to such conduct would rest on the presence of an independent violation, not, as the present case does, simply upon concerted activity by the exchange and its members.

of the securities exchanges and their members of using fixed rates of commission. The United States District Court for the Southern District of New York and the United States Court of Appeals for the Second Circuit concluded that fixed commission rates were immunized from antitrust attack because of the Securities and Exchange Commission's authority to approve or disapprove exchange commission rates and its exercise of that power.

I

In early 1971 petitioner Richard A. Gordon, individually and on behalf of an asserted class of small investors, filed this suit against the New York Stock Exchange, Inc. (NYSE), the American Stock Exchange, Inc. (Amex), and two member firms of the exchanges. . . . The complaint challenged a variety of exchange rules and practices and, in particular, claimed that the system of fixed commission rates, utilized by the exchanges at that time for transactions less than $500,000, violated §§1 and 2 of the Sherman Act, 15 U.S.C. §§1 and 2. . . .

Respondents moved for summary judgment on the ground that the challenged actions were subject to the overriding supervision of the Securities and Exchange Commission (SEC) under §19(b) of the Securities and Exchange Act of 1934, 15 U.S.C. §78s(b), and, therefore, were not subject to the strictures of the antitrust laws. The District Court granted respondents' motion as to all claims. 366 F. Supp. 1261 (1973). . . .

II

Resolution of the issue of antitrust immunity for fixed commission rates may be made adequately only upon a thorough investigation of the practice in the light of statutory restrictions and decided cases. We begin with a brief review of the history of commission rates in the securities industry.

Commission rates for transactions on the stock exchanges have been set by agreement since the establishment of the first exchange in this country. The New York Stock Exchange was formed with the Buttonwood Tree Agreement of 1792, and from the beginning minimum fees were set and observed by the members. . . . Successive constitutions of the NYSE have carried forward this basic provision. Similarly, when Amex emerged in 1908–1910, a pattern of fixed commission rates was adopted there. . . .

Despite the monopoly power of the few exchanges, exhibited not only in the area of commission rates but in a wide variety of other aspects, the exchanges remained essentially self-regulating and without significant supervision until the adoption of the Securities Exchange Act of 1934. . . .

As finally enacted, the Exchange Act . . . gave the SEC the power to fix and insure "reasonable" rates. Section 19(b) provided:

(b) *The Commission is further authorized, if* after making appropriate request in writing to a national securities exchange that such exchange effect on its own behalf specified changes in its rules and practices, and after appropriate notice and opportunity for hearing, *the Commission determines* that such exchange has not made the changes so requested, and that *such changes are necessary or appropriate for the protection of investors or to insure fair dealing in securities traded in* upon such exchange or to insure fair administration of such exchange, by rules or regulations or by order *to alter or supplement the rules of such exchange* (insofar as necessary or appropriate to effect such changes) *in respect of such matters as . . . (9) the fixing of reasonable rates of commission, interest, listing, and other charges.* (Emphasis added.)

This provision conformed to the Act's general policy of self-regulation by the exchanges coupled with oversight by the SEC. . . .

III

. . . [W]e turn to the actual post-1934 experience of commission rates on the NYSE and Amex. After these two exchanges had registered in 1934 under §6 of the Exchange Act, 15 U.S.C. §78f, both proceeded to prescribe minimum commission rates just as they had prior to the Act. . . . Although several rate changes appear to have been effectuated without comment by the SEC, in other instances the SEC thoroughly exercised its supervisory powers. Thus, for example, as early as 1958 a study of the NYSE commission rates to determine whether the rates were "reasonable and in accordance with the standards contemplated by applicable provisions of the Securities Exchange Act of 1934," was announced by the SEC. . . . App. A240. This study resulted in an agreement by the NYSE to reduce commission rates in certain transactions, to engage in further study of the rate structure by the NYSE in collaboration with the SEC, and to provide the SEC with greater advance notice of proposed rate changes. . . . The SEC specifically stated that it had undertaken the study "in view of the responsibilities and duties imposed upon the Commission by Section 19(b) . . . with respect to the rules of national securities exchanges, including rules relating to the fixing of commission rates." . . .

Under subsection (d) of §19 of the Act (which subsection was added in 1961) . . . the SEC was directed to investigate the adequacy of exchange rules for the protection of investors. Accordingly, the SEC began a detailed study of exchange rules in that year. In 1963 it released its conclusions in a six-volume study. SEC Report of Special Study of Securities Markets, H. Doc. No. 95, 88th Cong., 1st Sess. The Study, among other things, focused on problems of the structure of commission rates and procedures, and standards for setting and reviewing rate levels. . . . [W]hile the Study did not produce any major immediate changes in commission rate structure or levels, it did constitute a careful articulation of the problems in the structure and of the need for further studies that would be essential as a basis for future changes. . . .

In 1968, the SEC, while continuing the study started earlier in the decade, began to submit a series of specific proposals for change and to require their implementation by the exchanges. Through its Exchange Act Release No. 8324, May 28, 1968, App. A286, the SEC requested the NYSE to revise its commission rate schedule, including a reduction of rates for orders for round lots in excess of 400 shares or, alternatively, the elimination of minimum rate requirements for orders in excess of $50,000. These changes were viewed by the SEC as interim measures, to be pending further consideration "in the context of the Commission's responsibilities to consider the national policies embodied both in the securities laws and in the antitrust laws." Letter of May 28, 1968, from SEC Chairman Cohen to NYSE President Haack. . . .

In 1971 the SEC concluded its hearings begun in 1968. Finding that "minimum commissions on institutional size orders are neither necessary nor appropriate," the SEC announced that it would not object to competitive rates on portions of orders above a stated level. . . . Although at first supporting a $100,000 order as the cutoff below which fixed rates would be allowed, *ibid.*, the SEC later decided to permit use of $500,000 as the breakpoint. After a year's use of this figure, the SEC required the exchanges to reduce the cutoff point to $300,000 in April 1972. . . .

Further reduction followed relatively quickly. On January 16, 1973, the SEC announced it was considering requiring the reduction of the breakpoint on competitive rates to orders in excess of $100,000. . . . In June, the SEC began hearings on the rate schedules. . . . Three months later, after completion of the hearings, the SEC . . . announced . . . "It will act promptly to terminate the fixing of commission rates by stock exchanges after April 30, 1975, if the stock exchanges do not adopt rule changes achieving that result." . . .

Hearings on intramember commission rates began in April 1974. . . . The SEC concluded that intramember rates should not be fixed beyond April 30, 1975. . . .

Effective May 1, 1975, competitive rates were to be utilized by exchange members in transactions of all sizes for persons other than members of the exchanges. Effective May 1, 1976, competitive rates were to be mandatory in transactions for members as well, i.e., floor brokerage rates. Competition in floor brokerage rates was so deferred until 1976 in order to permit an orderly transition. . . .

During this period of concentrated study and action by the SEC, lasting more than a decade, various congressional committees undertook their own consideration of the matter of commission rates. . . .

In 1975 both Houses of the Congress did in fact enact legislation dealing directly with commission rates. Although the bills initially passed by each chamber differed somewhat, the Conference Committee compromised the differences. . . . The measure, as so compromised, was signed by the President on June 5, 1975.

The new legislation amends §19(b) of the Securities Exchange Act to substitute for the heretofore existing provision a scheme for SEC review of proposed rules and rule changes of the various self-regulatory organizations. Reference to commission rates is now found in the new §6(e), generally providing that after the date of enactment "no national securities exchange may impose any schedule or fix rates of commissions, allowances, discounts, or other fees to be charged by its members." An exception is made for floor brokerage rates which may be fixed by the exchanges until May 1, 1976. Further exceptions from the ban against fixed commissions are provided if approved by the SEC after certain findings. . . .

As of May 1, 1975, pursuant to order of the SEC, fixed commission rates were eliminated and competitive rates effectuated. . . .

This lengthy history can be summarized briefly: In enacting the Securities Exchange Act of 1934, the Congress gave clear authority to the SEC to supervise exchange self-regulation with respect to the "fixing of reasonable rates of commission." Upon SEC determination that exchange rules or practices regarding commission rates required change in order to protect investors or to insure fair dealing, the SEC was authorized to require adoption of such changes as were deemed necessary or appropriate. This legislative permission for the fixing of commission rates under the supervision of the SEC occurred seven years *after* this Court's decision in *United States* v. *Trenton Potteries Co.*, 273 U.S. 392 (1927), to the effect that price fixing was a *per se* violation of the Sherman Act. Since the Exchange Act's adoption, and primarily in the last 15 years, the SEC has been engaged in thorough review of exchange commission rate practices. The committees of the Congress, while recently expressing some dissatisfaction with the progress of the SEC in implementing competitive rates, have generally been content to allow the SEC to proceed without new legislation. As of May 1, 1975, the SEC, by order, has abolished fixed rates. And new legislation, enacted into law June 5, 1975, codifies this result, although still permitting the SEC some discretion to reimpose fixed rates if warranted.

IV

This Court has considered the issue of implied repeal of the antitrust laws in the context of a variety of regulatory schemes and procedures. Certain axioms of construction are now clearly established. Repeal of the antitrust laws by implication is not favored and not casually to be allowed. Only where there is a "plain repugnancy between the antitrust and regulatory provisions" will repeal be implied. . . .

The starting point for our consideration of the particular issue presented by this case, *viz.,* whether the antitrust laws are impliedly repealed or replaced as a result of the statutory provisions and administrative and congressional experience concerning fixed commission rates, of course, is our decision in *Silver*.[1] There the Court considered the relationship between the antitrust laws and the Securities Exchange Act. . . . Concluding that the proper approach . . . was to reconcile the operation of the antitrust laws with a regulatory scheme, the Court established a "guiding principle" for the achievement of this reconciliation. Under this principle, "[r]epeal is to be regarded as implied only if necessary to make the Securities Exchange Act work, and even then only to the minimum extent necessary." *Id.*, at 357. . . .

The Court . . . cautioned, however, that "[s]hould review of exchange self-regulation be provided through a vehicle other than antitrust laws, a different case as to antitrust exemption would be presented." 373 U.S., at 360. It amplified this statement in a footnote:

> Were there Commission jurisdiction and ensuing judicial review for scrutiny of a particular exchange ruling . . . a different case would arise concerning exemption from the operation of laws designed to prevent anticompetitive activity, an issue we do not decide today. 373 U.S., at 358 n. 12.

It is patent that the case presently at bar is, indeed, that "different case" to which the Court in *Silver* referred. In contrast to the circumstances of *Silver*, §19(b) gave the SEC direct regulatory power over exchange rules and practices with respect to "the fixing of reasonable rates of commission." Not only was the SEC authorized to disapprove rules and practices concerning commission rates, but the agency also was permitted to require alteration or supplementation of the rules and practices when "necessary or appropriate for the protection of investors or to insure fair dealings in securities traded in upon such exchange." Since 1934 all rate exchanges have been brought to the attention of the SEC, and it has taken an active role in review of proposed rate changes during the last 15 years. Thus, rather than presenting a case of SEC impotence to affect application of exchange rules in particular circumstances, this case involves explicit statutory authorization for SEC review of all exchange rules and practices dealing with rates of commission and resultant SEC continuing activity.

Having determined that this case is, in fact, the "different case," we must then make inquiry as to the proper reconciliation of the regulatory and antitrust statutes involved here, keeping in mind the principle that repeal of the antitrust laws will be "implied only if necessary to make the Securities Exchange Act work, and even then only to the minimum extent necessary." *Id.*, at 357. We hold that these requirements for implied repeal are clearly satisfied here. To permit operation of the antitrust laws with respect to commission rates, as urged by petitioner Gordon and the

---

[1] *Silver* v. *New York Stock Exchange*, 373 U.S. 341 (1963). IMS.

United States as *amicus curiae,* would unduly interfere, in our view, with the operation of the Securities Exchange Act. . . .

The United States appears to suggest that only if there is a pervasive regulatory scheme, as in the public utility area, can it be concluded that the regulatory scheme ousts the antitrust laws. . . . It is true that in some prior cases we have been concerned with the question of the pervasiveness of the regulatory scheme as a factor in determining whether there is an implied repeal of the antitrust laws. See, *e.g., Otter Tail Power Co.* v. *United States,* 410 U.S. 366, 373–375 (1973). In the present case, however, respondents do not claim that repeal should be implied because of a pervasive regulatory scheme, but because of the specific provision of §19 (b) (9) and the regulatory action thereunder. . . . Hence, whether the Exchange Act amounts to pervasive legislation ousting the antitrust acts is not a question before us.

We agree with the District Court and the Court of Appeals, and with respondents, that to deny antitrust immunity with respect to commission rates would be to subject the exchanges and their members of conflicting standards. . . . If antitrust courts were to impose different standards or requirements, the exchanges might find themselves unable to proceed without violation of the mandate of the courts or of the SEC. Such different standards are likely to result because the sole aim of antitrust legislation is to protect competition, whereas the SEC must consider, in addition, the economic health of the investors, the exchanges, and the securities industry. . . . Given the expertise of the SEC, the confidence the Congress has placed in the agency, and the active roles the SEC and the Congress have taken, permitting courts throughout the country to conduct their own antitrust proceedings would conflict with the regulatory scheme authorized by Congress rather than supplement that scheme. . . .

In sum, the statutory provision authorizing regulation, §19(b)(9), the long regulatory practice, and the continued congressional approval illustrated by the new legislation, point to one, and only one, conclusion. The Securities Exchange Act was intended by the Congress to leave the supervision of the fixing of reasonable rates of commission to the SEC. Interposition of the antitrust laws, which would bar fixed commission rates as *per se* violations of the Sherman Act, in the face of positive SEC action, would preclude and prevent the operation of the Exchange Act as intended by Congress and as effectuated through SEC regulatory activity. Implied repeal of the antitrust laws is, in fact, necessary to make the Exchange Act work as it was intended; failure to imply repeal would render nugatory the legislative provision for regulatory agency supervision of exchange commission rates.

Affirmed.

Goldfarb et ux. v. Virginia State Bar et al.

421 U.S. 773 (1975)

MR. CHIEF JUSTICE BURGER delivered the opinion of the Court.

We granted certiorari to decide whether a minimum-fee schedule for lawyers published by the Fairfax County Bar Association and enforced by the Virginia State Bar violates §1 of the Sherman Act. . . . The Court of Appeals held that, although the fee schedule and enforcement mechanism substantially restrained competition among lawyers, publication of the schedule by the County Bar was outside the scope of the act because the practice of law is not "trade or commerce," and enforcement of the schedule by the State Bar was exempt from the Sherman Act as state action as defined in *Parker* v. *Brown,* 317 U.S. 341 (1943).

I

In 1971 petitioners, husband and wife, contracted to buy a home in Fairfax County, Virginia. The financing agency required them to secure title insurance; this required a title examination, and only a member of the Virginia State Bar could legally perform that service. . . . Petitioners therefore contacted a lawyer who quoted them the precise fee suggested in a minimum-fee schedule published by respondent Fairfax County Bar Association; the lawyer told them that it was his policy to keep his charges in line with the minimum-fee schedule which provided for a fee of 1 percent of the value of the property involved. Petitioners then tried to find a lawyer who would examine the title for less than the fee fixed by the schedule. They sent letters to 36 other Fairfax County lawyers requesting their fees. Nineteen replied, and none indicated that he would charge less than the rate fixed by the schedule; several stated that they knew of no attorney who would do so.

The fee schedule the lawyers referred to is a list of recommended minimum prices for common legal services. Respondent Fairfax County Bar Association published the fee schedule although, as a purely voluntary association of attorneys, the County Bar has no formal power to enforce it. Enforcement has been provided by respondent Virginia State Bar which is the administrative agency . . . through which the Virginia Supreme Court regulates the practice of law in that state; membership in the State Bar is required in order to practice in Virginia. . . . Although the State Bar has never taken formal disciplinary action to compel adherence to any fee schedule, it has published reports . . . condoning fee schedules, and has issued two ethical opinions . . . indicating that fee schedules cannot be ignored. . . .[1]

Because petitioners could not find a lawyer willing to charge a fee

---

[1] . . . The parties stipulated that these opinions are a substantial influencing factor in lawyers' adherence to the fee schedules. . . .

lower than the schedule dictated, they had their title examined by the lawyer they had first contacted. They then brought this class action against the State Bar and the County Bar . . . alleging that the operation of the minimum-fee schedule, as applied to fees for legal services relating to residential real estate transactions, constitutes price fixing in violation of §1 of the Sherman Act. Petitioners sought both injunctive relief and damages.

After a trial solely on the issue of liability the District Court held that the minimum-fee schedule violated the Sherman Act. . . . The court viewed the fee-schedule system as a significant reason for petitioners' failure to obtain legal services for less than the minimum fee, and it rejected the County Bar's contention that as a "learned profession" the practice of law is exempt from the Sherman Act.

The Court of Appeals reversed as to liability. . . . Despite its conclusion that it "is abundantly clear from the record before us that the fee schedule and the enforcement mechanism supporting it act as a substantial restraint upon competition among attorneys practicing in Fairfax County," . . . the Court of Appeals held the State Bar immune under *Parker* v. *Brown, supra,* and held the County Bar immune because the practice of law is not "trade or commerce" under the Sherman Act. There has long been judicial recognition of a limited exclusion of "learned professions" from the scope of the antitrust laws, the court said; that exclusion is based upon the special form of regulation imposed upon the professions by the States, and the incompatibility of certain competitive practices with such professional regulation. It concluded that the promulgation of a minimum-fee schedule is one of "those matters with respect to which an accord must be reached between the necessities of professional regulation and the dictates of the antitrust laws." The accord reached by that court was to hold the practice of law exempt from the antitrust laws. . . .

We granted certiorari . . . and are thus confronted for the first time with the question of whether the Sherman Act applies to services performed by attorneys in examining titles in connection with financing the purchase of real estate.

II

Our inquiry can be divided into four steps: Did respondents engage in price fixing? If so, are their activities in interstate commerce or do they affect interstate commerce? If so, are the activities exempt from the Sherman Act because they involve a "learned profession?" If not, are the activities "state action" within the meaning of *Parker* v. *Brown,* 317 U.S. 341 (1943), and therefore exempt from the Sherman Act?

A

The County Bar argues that because the fee schedule is merely advisory, the schedule and its enforcement mechanism do not constitute price fixing. Its purpose, the argument continues, is only to provide legitimate information to aid member lawyers in complying with Virginia professional regulations. Moreover, the County Bar contends that in practice the schedule has not had the effect of producing fixed fees. The facts found by the trier belie these contentions, and nothing in the record suggests these findings lack support.

A purely advisory fee schedule issued to provide guidelines, or an exchange of price information without a showing of an actual restraint on trade, would present us with a different question. . . . The record here, however, reveals a situation quite different from what would occur under a purely advisory fee schedule. Here a fixed, rigid price floor arose from respondents' activities: every lawyer who responded to petitioners' inquiries adhered to the fee schedule, and no lawyer asked for additional information in order to set an individualized fee. The price information disseminated did not concern past standards, . . . but rather minimum fees to be charged in future transactions, and those minimum rates were increased over time. The fee schedule was enforced through the prospect of professional discipline from the State Bar, and the desire of attorneys to comply with announced professional norms . . . ; the motivation to conform was reinforced by the assurance that other lawyers would not compete by underbidding. This is not merely a case of an agreement that may be inferred from an exchange of price information, . . . for here a naked agreement was clearly shown, and the effect on prices is plain. . . .

Moreover, in terms of restraining competition and harming consumers like petitioners the price-fixing activities found here are usually damaging. A title examination is indispensable in the process of financing a real estate purchase, and since only an attorney licensed to practice in Virginia may legally examine a title, . . . consumers could not turn to alternative sources for the necessary service. All attorneys, of course, were practicing under the constraint of the fee schedule. . . . The County Bar makes much of the fact that it is a voluntary organization; however, the ethical opinions issued by the State Bar provide that any lawyer, whether or not a member of his county bar association, may be disciplined for "*habitually* charg[ing] less than the suggested minimum fee schedule adopted by his local bar [sic] Association. . . ." . . . These factors coalesced to create a pricing system that consumers could not realistically escape. On this record respondents' activities constitute a classic illustration of price fixing.

B

[In this Section, the Court found that the commerce at issue was sufficiently interstate in character to satisfy the jurisdictional requirements of the Sherman Act.]

C

The County Bar argues that Congress never intended to include the learned professions within the terms "trade or commerce" in §1 of the Sherman Act,[2] and therefore the sale of professional services is exempt from the Act. No explicit exemption or legislative history is provided to support this contention; rather, the existence of state regulation seems to be its primary basis. Also, the County Bar maintains that competition is inconsistent with the practice of a profession because enhancing profit is not the goal of professional activities; the goal is to provide services necessary to the community.[3] That, indeed, is the classic basis tradition-ally advanced to distinguish professions from trades, businesses, and other occupations, but it loses some of its force when used to support the fee control activities involved here.

In arguing that learned professions are not "trade or commerce" the County Bar seeks a total exclusion from antitrust regulation. Whether state regulation is active or dormant, real or theoretical, lawyers would be able to adopt anticompetitive practices with impunity. We cannot find support for the proposition that Congress intended any such sweeping exclusion. The nature of an occupation, standing alone, does not provide sanctuary from the Sherman Act, . . . nor is the public-service aspect of professional practice controlling in determining whether §1 includes pro-fessions. . . . Congress intended to strike as broadly as it could in §1 of the Sherman Act, and to read into it so wide an exemption as that urged on us would be at odds with that purpose.

The language of §1 of the Sherman Act, of course, contains no excep-tion. . . . And our cases have repeatedly established that there is a heavy presumption against implicit exemptions. . . . Indeed, our cases have specifically included the sale of services within §1. . . . Whatever else it may be, the examination of a land title is a service; the exchange of such a service for money is "commerce" in the most common usage of that word. It is no disparagement of the practice of law as a profession to acknowledge that it has this business aspect,[4] and §1 of the Sherman

---

[2] The County Bar cites phrases in several cases that implied the practice of a learned profession is not "trade or commerce" under the antitrust laws. . . . These citations are to passing references in cases concerned with other issues; and, more important, until the present case it is clear that we have not attempted to decide whether the practice of a learned profession falls within §1 of the Sherman Act. . . .

[3] The reason for adopting the fee schedule does not appear to have been wholly altruistic. The first sentence in respondent State Bar's 1962 Minimum Fee Schedule Report states: "The lawyers have slowly, but surely, been committing economic suicide as a profession." Virginia State Bar, Minimum Fee Schedule Report 1962, p. 3, App. 20.

[4] The fact that a restraint operates upon a profession as distinguished from a business is, of course, relevant in determining whether that particular restraint violates the Sherman Act. It would be unrealistic to view the practice of professions as interchangeable with other business activities, and automatically to apply to the professions antitrust concepts which

Act. . . . In the modern world it cannot be denied that the activities of lawyers play an important part in commercial intercourse, and that anticompetitive activities by lawyers may exert a restraint on commerce.

D

In *Parker* v. *Brown,* 317 U.S. 341 (1943), the Court held that an anticompetitive marketing program which "derived its authority and its efficacy from the legislative command of the state" was not a violation of the Sherman Act because the act was intended to regulate private practices and not to prohibit a State from imposing a restraint as an act of government. . . . Respondent State Bar and respondent County Bar both seek to avail themselves of this so-called state-action exemption.

Through its legislature Virginia has authorized its highest court to regulate the practice of law. . . . That court has adopted ethical codes which deal in part with fees, and far from exercising state power to authorize binding price fixing, explicitly directed lawyers not "to be controlled" by fee schedules. . . . The State Bar, a state agency by law, . . . argues that in issuing fee schedule reports and ethical opinions dealing with fee schedules it was merely implementing the fee provisions of the ethical codes. The County Bar, although it is a voluntary association and not a state agency, claims that the ethical codes and the activities of the State Bar "prompted" it to issue fee schedules and thus its actions, too, are state action for Sherman Act purposes.

The threshold inquiry in determining if an anticompetitive activity is state action of the type the Sherman Act was not meant to proscribe is whether the activity is required by the State acting as sovereign. . . . Here we need not inquire further into the state-action question because it cannot fairly be said that the State of Virginia through its Supreme Court Rules required the anticompetitive activities of either respondent. Respondents have pointed to no Virginia statute requiring their activities; state law simply does not refer to fees, leaving regulation of the profession to the Virginia Supreme Court; although the Supreme Court's ethical codes mention advisory fee schedules they do not direct either respondent to supply them, or require the type of price floor which arose from respondents' activities. Although the State Bar apparently has been granted the power to issue ethical opinions, there is no indication in this record that the Virginia Supreme Court approves the opinions. Respondents' arguments, at most, constitute the contention that their activities complemented the objective of the ethical codes. In our view that is not state action for Sherman Act purposes. It is not enough that, as the County Bar

---

originated in other areas. The public service aspect, and other features of the professions, may require that a particular practice, which could properly be viewed as a violation of the Sherman Act in another context, be treated differently. We intimate no view on any other situation than the one with which we are confronted today.

puts it, anticompetitive conduct is "prompted" by state action; rather, anticompetitive activities must be compelled by direction of the State acting as a sovereign.

The fact that the State Bar is a state agency for some limited purposes does not create an antitrust shield that allows it to foster anticompetitive practices for the benefit of its members. . . . The State Bar, by providing that deviation from County Bar minimum fees may lead to disciplinary action, has voluntarily joined in what is essentially a private anticompetitive activity, and in that posture cannot claim it is beyond the reach of the Sherman Act. . . . Its activities resulted in a rigid price floor from which petitioners, as consumers, could not escape if they wished to borrow money to buy a home.

III

We recognize that the states have a compelling interest in the practice of professions within their boundaries, and that as part of their power to protect the public health, safety, and other valid interests they have broad power to establish standards for licensing practitioners and regulating the practice of professions. We also recognize that in some instances the state may decide that "forms of competition usual in the business world may be demoralizing to the ethical standards of a profession." *United States* v. *Oregon State Medical Society,* 343 U.S. 326, 336 (1952). . . . The interest of the states in regulating lawyers is especially great since lawyers are essential to the primary governmental function of administering justice, and have historically been "officers of the courts." . . . In holding that certain anticompetitive conduct by lawyers is within the reach of the Sherman Act we intend no diminution of the authority of the state to regulate its professions.

The judgment of the Court of Appeals is reversed and the case is remanded to that court with orders to remand to the District Court for further proceedings consistent with this opinion.

Reversed and remanded.

MR. JUSTICE POWELL took no part in the consideration or decision of this case.

PART SIX

Legal Monopolies and Antitrust

13

Patents—The Right and Its Limits

Our patent laws are predicated upon the assumption that progress in the sciences and in the useful arts will best be promoted by granting to the inventor a legal monopoly of his discovery. Thus, in a sense, the patent laws may be viewed as exceptions to our antitrust policy of preserving competition. In another sense, however, the patent laws appear as instruments which are designed to accelerate technological progress by granting short-term monopoly privileges as offsets to the risks involved in introducing a new product or process; that is, they may stimulate competition in the long-run, Schumpeterian sense of that word. In any event, conflict between the patent and antitrust laws has arisen only when the holder of the patent right has been deemed to overstep the bounds of his lawful monopoly in an attempt to suppress competition. This may occur when, as in the *Hartford-Empire* case, patent cross-licensing is used, not to promote competition by making technological information more widely available in the industry, but to monopolize an entire industry. A patentee may also violate the antitrust laws when, as in the *International Salt* case, he uses the patent monopoly as a lever to gain dominance in another and totally different market.

Current trends appear to favor giving antitrust criteria greater weight than the standards of the patent statutes whenever the two conflict with one another. Thus, while the *General Electric* case held that a patentee could attach terms and conditions to the grant of a patent license, that right has since been significantly diluted. In *Hartford-Empire,* for example, the Supreme Court appeared to say that what a single patentee could do, two or more patentees, acting through a cross-licensing agreement, could not.

These cases provide at least a partial understanding of the varied and complex public policy issues involved in antitrust suits of this type. In addition, the *Hartford-Empire* case illustrates perhaps more clearly than any other in this general area the problem of framing an adequate decree—one which prevents future antitrust violations without unnecessarily impinging on the patent right.

United States v. General Electric Company
272 U.S. 476 (1926)
MR. CHIEF JUSTICE TAFT delivered the opinion of the Court.

This is a bill in equity brought by the United States in the District Court for the Northern District of Ohio to enjoin the General Electric Company, the Westinghouse Electric and Manufacturing Company, and the Westinghouse Lamp Company from further violation of the Anti-Trust Act of July 2, 1890. . . . The bill made two charges, one that the General Electric Company in its business of making and selling incandescent electric lights had devised and was carrying out a plan for their distribution throughout the United States by a number of so-called agents, exceeding 21,000, to restrain interstate trade in such lamps and to exercise a monopoly of the sale thereof; and, second, that it was achieving the same illegal purpose through a contract of license with the defendants, the Westinghouse Electric and Manufacturing Company and the Westinghouse Lamp Company.[1] . . .

The second question in the case involves the validity of a license granted March 1, 1912, by the Electric Company to the Westinghouse Company to make, use and sell lamps under the patents owned by the former. It was charged that the license in effect provided that the Westinghouse Company would follow prices and terms of sales from time to time fixed by the Electric Company and observed by it, and that the Westinghouse Company would, with regard to lamps manufactured by it under the license, adopt and maintain the same conditions of sale as observed by the Electric Company in the distribution of lamps manufactured by it. . . .

The Electric Company is the owner of . . . patents . . . [which] cover completely the making of the modern electric lights with the tungsten filaments, and secure to the Electric Company the monopoly of their making, using and vending.

The total business in electric lights for the year 1921 was $68,300,000, and the relative percentages of business done by the companies were, Electric, 69 percent, Westinghouse, 16 percent, other licensees, 8 percent, and manufacturers not licensed, 7 percent.

. . . . .

---

[1] For present purposes we focus upon the second of the two charges; the first raises issues that are peripheral to the subject of this chapter. IMS.

. . . Had the Electric Company, as the owner of the patents entirely controlling the manufacture, use and sale of the tungsten incandescent lamps, in its license to the Westinghouse Company, the right to impose the condition that its sales should be at prices fixed by the licensor and subject to change according to its discretion? . . .

The owner of a patent may assign it to another and convey, (1) the exclusive right to make, use and vend the invention throughout the United States, or, (2) an undivided part or share of that exclusive right, or (3) the exclusive right under the patent within and through a specific part of the United States. But any assignment or transfer short of one of these is a license, giving the licensee no title in the patent and no right to sue at law in his own name for an infringement. . . . Conveying less than title to the patent, or part of it, the patentee may grant a license to make, use and vend articles under the specifications of his patent for any royalty or upon any condition the performance of which is reasonably within the reward which the patentee by the grant of the patent is entitled to secure. It is well settled, . . . that where a patentee makes the patented article and sells it, he can exercise no future control over what the purchaser may wish to do with the article after his purchase. It has passed beyond the scope of the patentee's rights. . . . But the question is a different one which arises when we consider what a patentee who grants a license to one to make and vend the patented article may do in limiting the licensee in the exercise of the right to sell. The patentee may make and grant a license to another to make and use the patented articles, but withhold his right to sell them. The licensee in such a case acquires an interest in the articles made. He owns the material of them and may use them. But if he sells them, he infringes the right of the patentee, and may be held for damages and enjoined. If the patentee goes further, and licenses the selling of the articles, may he limit the selling by limiting the method of sale and the price? We think he may do so, provided the conditions of sale are normally and reasonably adapted to secure pecuniary reward for the patentee's monopoly. One of the valuable elements of the exclusive right of a patentee is to acquire profit by the price at which the article is sold. The higher the price, the greater the profit, unless it is prohibitory. When the patentee licenses another to make and vend, and retains the right to continue to make and vend on his own account, the price at which his licensee will sell will necessarily affect the price at which he can sell his own patented goods. It would seem entirely reasonable that he should say to the licensee, "Yes, you may make and sell articles under my patent, but not so as to destroy the profit that I wish to obtain by making them and selling them myself." He does not thereby sell outright to the licensee the articles the latter may make and sell, or vest absolute ownership in them. He restricts the property and interest the licensee has in the goods he makes and proposes to sell.

[MR. JUSTICE TAFT then reviewed several earlier cases, including those which involved the setting of prices of unpatented materials used in conjunction with a patented article. He concluded that they were not relevant to the present case since "[the] price at which a patented article sells is certainly a circumstance having a more direct relation, and is more germane to the rights of the patentee, than the unpatented material with which the patented article may be used. Indeed, . . . price fixing is usually the essence of that which secures proper reward to the patentee."]

Nor do we think that the decisions of this Court holding restrictions as to price of patented articles invalid, apply to a contract of license like the one in this case. . . . These cases really are only instances of the application of the principle of *Adams* v. *Burke,* 17 Wall. 453, 456, . . . that a patentee may not attach to the article made by him, or with his consent, a condition running with the article in the hands of purchasers, limiting the price at which one who becomes its owner for full consideration shall part with it. They do not consider or condemn a restriction put by a patentee upon his licenses as to the prices at which the latter shall sell articles which he makes and only can make legally under the license. . . .

For the reasons given, we sustain the validity of the license granted by the Electric Company to the Westinghouse Company. The decree of the District Court dismissing the bill is

Affirmed.

Note: In 1973, General Electric's agency marketing system was ajudged a *per se* violation of Section 1 of the Sherman Act on the grounds that the Company's patents were no longer controlling and, hence, no longer immune from the reach of the antitrust laws. *U.S.* v. *General Electric Company* 358 F. Supp. 731.

Hartford-Empire Company v. *United States*
323 U.S. 386 (1945)
MR. JUSTICE ROBERTS delivered the opinion of the Court.

These are appeals from a decree awarding an injunction against violations of Sections 1 and 2 of the Sherman Act, as amended, and Section 3 of the Clayton Act. Two questions are presented. Were violations proved? If so, are the provisions of the decree right?

The complaint named as defendants . . . the leaders in automatic glass-making machinery and in the glassware industry. The charge is that all the defendants agreed, conspired, and combined to monopolize, and did monopolize and restrain interstate and foreign commerce by acquiring patents covering the manufacture of glassmaking machinery, and by excluding others from a fair opportunity freely to engage in commerce in such machinery and in the manufacture and distribution of glass products. The gravamen of the case is that the defendants have cooperated in obtaining and licensing patents covering glassmaking machinery, have limited and restricted the use of the patented machinery by a network of agreements, and have maintained prices for unpatented glassware. . . .

In 1919 the Glass Container Association of America was formed. . . . The court below, on sufficient evidence, has found that the association, through its statistical committee, assigned production quotas to its members and that they and Hartford were zealous in seeing that these were observed.

In summary, the situation brought about in the glass industry, and existing in 1938, was this: Hartford, with the technical and financial aid of others in the conspiracy, had acquired, by issue to it or assignment from the owners, more than 600 patents. These, with over 100 Corning controlled patents, over 60 Owens patents, over 70 Hazel patents, and some 12 Lynch patents, had been, by cross-licensing agreements, merged into a pool which effactually controlled the industry. This control was exercised to allot production in Corning's field[1] to Corning, and that in restricted classes within the general container field to Owens, Hazel, Thatcher, Ball, and such other smaller manufacturers as the group agreed should be licensed. The result was that 94% of the glass containers manufactured in this country on feeders and formers were made on machinery licensed under the pooled patents.

The District Court found that invention of glassmaking machinery had been discouraged, that competition in the manufacture and sale or licensing of such machinery had been suppressed, and that the system of restricted licensing had been employed to suppress competition in the manufacture of unpatented glassware and to maintain prices of the manufactured product. The findings are full and adequate and are supported by evidence, much of it contemporary writings of corporate defendants or their officers and agents. . . .

We affirm the District Court's findings and conclusions that the corporate appellants combined in violation of the Sherman Act, that Hartford and Lynch contracted in violation of the Clayton Act, and that the individual appellants with exceptions to be noted participated in the violations in their capacities as officers and directors of the corporations. . . .

I.   Little need be said concerning the legal principles which vindicate the District Court's findings and conclusions. . . .

. . . It is clear that, by cooperative arrangements and binding agreements, the appellant corporations, over a period of years, regulated and suppressed competition in the use of glassmaking machinery and employed their joint patent position to allocate fields of manufacture and to maintain prices of unpatented glassware.

---

[1] The pressed and blown glass, or noncontainer field. IMS.

The explanations offered by the Appellants are unconvincing. It is said, on behalf of Hartford, that its business, in its inception, was lawful and within the patent laws; and that, in order to protect its legitimate interests as holder of patents for automatic glass machinery, it was justified in buying up and fencing off improvement patents, the grant of which, while leaving the fundamental inventions untouched, would hamper their use unless tribute were paid to the owners of the so-called improvements which, of themselves, had only a nuisance value.

The explanation fails to account for the offensive and defensive alliance of patent owners with its concomitant stifling of initiative, invention, and competition.

Nor can Owens' contention prevail that it long ago abandoned any cooperation with the other corporate defendants and has been free of any trammel to unrestricted competition either in the machinery or glass field. Owens remained active in the association. It remained dominant in the suction field. In continued in close touch with Hartford and with other large manufacturers of glassware who were parties to the conspiracy. The District Court was justified in finding that the mere cancellation of the written word was not enough, in the light of subsequent conduct, to acquit Owens of further participation in the conspiracy. . . .

II. The Government sought the dissolution of Hartford. The court, however, decided that a continuance of certain of Hartford's activities would be of advantage to the glass industry and denied, for the time being, that form of relief. The court was of opinion, however, that the long series of transactions and the persistent manifestations of a purpose to violate the antitrust statutes required the entry of a decree which would preclude the resumption of unlawful practices. It was faced, therefore, with the difficult problem of awarding an injunction which would insure the desired end without imposing punishments or other sanctions for past misconduct, a problem especially difficult in view of the status and relationship of the parties.

At the trial the Government stated that in this suit it was not attacking the validity of any patent or claiming any patent had been awarded an improper priority.

At the time of the District Court's decision, Hartford had reduced the royalties of all its licensees to its then schedule of standard royalties so that all stood on an equal basis so far as license fees were concerned. Government counsel did not assert, or attempt to prove, that these royalties were not reasonable in amount.

Owens, as respects suction invention licenses, had removed all restrictive clauses; Hartford had done the same with respect to all its glass machinery licenses and so had Hartford and Lynch with respect to forming machine licenses. . . .

The association had ceased to allot quotas amongst the glass manufacturers or to furnish advance information or make recommendations to its members. The licensing system of Hartford remained that of leasing machinery built for it embodying the patented inventions. Rentals consisted of standard royalties on production. Under this system Hartford rendered a service in the repair, maintenance, and protection of the machines, which is valuable, if not essential, to the users. This was the status with which the court had to deal.

The applicable principals are not doubtful. The Sherman Act provides criminal penalties for its violation, and authorizes the recovery of a penal sum in addition to damages in a civil suit by one injured by violation. It also authorizes an injunction to prevent continuing violations by those acting contrary to its proscriptions. The present suit is in the last named category and we may not impose penalties in the guise of preventing future violations. This is not to say that a decree need deal only with the exact type of acts found to have been committed or that the court should not, in framing its decree, resolve all doubts in favor of the Government, or may not prohibit acts which in another setting would be unobjectionable. But, even so, the court may not create, as to the defendants, new duties, prescription of which is the function of Congress, or place the defendants, for the future, "in a different class than other people," as the Government has suggested. The decree must not be "so vague as to put the whole conduct of the defendants' business at the peril of a summons for contempt"; enjoin "all possible breaches of the law"; or cause the defendants hereafter not "to be under the protection of the law of the land." With these principles in mind we proceed to examine the terms of the decree entered. . . .

The court appointed a receiver for Hartford *pendente lite*. By paragraphs 10 to 20 of the final decree it continued him in office and gave directions as to his administration of Hartford's affairs, including certain actions to be taken to effectuate features of the decree affecting Hartford's business and licenses, which will later be described, and meantime to continue the receipt of royalties under existing licenses, these to be repaid to the licensees on the decree becoming final. . . .

. . . [T]he receivership and the impounding of funds were not necessary to the prescription of appropriate relief. The receivership should be wound up and the business returned to Hartford. The royalties paid to the receiver by Hartford's lessees may, unless the District Court finds that Hartford has, since the entry of the receivership decree, violated the antitrust laws, or acted contrary to the terms of the final decree as modified by this opinion, be paid over to Hartford. . . .

Paragraphs 21, 22, and 23 . . . forbid any disposition or transfer of possession of such machinery by any means other than an outright sale, and require Hartford to offer in writing to sell each of the present lessees all the machinery now under lease to such lessee at a reasonable price. . . .

All of the appellants attack these provisions. . . .

. . . The Government replies that the injunction is intended only to prevent them from again setting up a patent pool and monopolizing the patented inventions. . . . But the decree as entered requires that each of the defendants must hereafter forever abstain from leasing a patented machine, no matter what the date of the invention, and compels each of them if he desires to distribute patented machinery to sell the machine which embodies the patent to everyone who applies, at a price to be fixed by the court. The injunction as drawn is not directed at any combination, agreement or conspiracy. It binds every defendant forever irrespective of his connection with any other or of the independence of his action. . . .

[Paragraph 24 requires defendants to license all present and future patents on a royalty-free basis.]

Since the provisions of paragraphs 21 to 24 inclusive, in effect confiscate considerable portions of the appellants' property we think they go beyond what is required to dissolve the combination and prevent future combinations of like character. It is to be borne in mind that the Government has not, in this litigation, attacked the validity of any patent or the priority ascribed to any by the Patent Office, nor has it attacked, as excessive or unreasonable, the standard royalties heretofore exacted by Hartford. Hartford has reduced all of its royalties to a uniform scale and has waived and abolished and agreed to waive and abolish all restrictions and limitations in its outstanding leases so that every licensee shall be at liberty to use the machinery for the manufacture of any kind of quantity of glassware comprehended within the decree. Moreover, if licenses or assignments by any one of the corporate defendants to any other still contain any offensive provision, such provision can, by appropriate injunction, be cancelled, so that the owner of each patent will have unrestricted freedom to use and to license, and every licensee equally with every other will be free of restriction as to the use of the leased or licensed machinery, method or process, or the articles manufactured thereon or thereunder.

It is suggested that there is not confiscation since Hartford might, with the later consent of the court, sell its patents. Under the decree as entered below nothing can be obtained by Hartford for the use of its patents and we cannot speculate as to what might be the ultimate adjustments made by the trial court in the decree.

If, as suggested, some of Hartford's patents were improperly obtained, or if some of them were awarded a priority to which the invention was not entitled, avenues are open to the Government to raise these questions and to have the patents cancelled. But if, as we must assume on this record, a defendant owns valid patents, it is difficult to say that, however much in the past such defendant has abused the rights thereby conferred, it must now dedicate them to the public.

That a patent is property, protected against appropriation both by individuals and by government, has long been settled. In recognition of this quality of a patent the courts, in enjoining violations of the Sherman Act arising from the use of patent licenses, agreements, and leases, have abstained from action which amounted to a forfeiture of the patents. . . .

Since paragraphs 21 to 24(a) inclusive are to be eliminated, this paragraph, which is ancillary to them, should also be deleted from the decree, but in view of the nature of the conspiracy found, an injunction should go against the further prosecution of all infringement suits pending at the date this suit was brought. Hartford and the other corporate defendants mentioned in paragraph 24 should be required to lease or license glass making machinery of the classes each now manufacturers to any who may desire to take licenses, (under patents on such machinery or on improvements, methods or processes applicable thereto), at standard royalties and without discrimination or restriction, and if at the time of entry of the decree there are any alleged infringers who are willing to take such licenses they should be released, and the patent owner deprived of all damages and profits which it might have claimed for past infringement. The decree should, however, be without prejudice to the future institution of any suit or suits for asserted infringements against persons refusing to take licenses under any of the presently licensed inventions arising out of their use after the date of the decree. The decree should not forbid any defendant from seeking recovery for infringement, occurring after the date of the final decree, of patents not covering feeders, formers, stackers, lehrs, or processes or methods applicable to any of them.

Paragraph 27 cancels all outstanding agreements between corporate appellants. . . .

In view of what we have already said about these earlier paragraphs, the license agreements as modified by the parties and in accordance with the views here expressed, should be allowed to stand. . . .

Paragraph 28 orders cancellation of all Hartford machinery leases now outstanding and requires that each lessee be offered a new license (without royalty, pursuant to paragraph 24) and offered the right to purchase all of the machinery now held under lease (as required by paragraph 23). In view of what has been said this provision should not stand.

Paragraph 29 enjoins the insertion or enforcement of any provision in any agreement heretofore or hereafter made by any of the appellants which (a) directly or indirectly limits or restricts (1) the type or kind of product, whether glassware or any other, which can be produced on machines or equipment or by processes embodying inventions licensed under patents or patent applications, (2) the use of the product so produced, (3) the character, weight, color, capacity, or composition of the product, (4) the quantity, (5) the market, either as to territory or customers in or to which the product may be sold or distributed, (6) the price or terms of sale or other disposition of the product, or (7) the use of the machinery or equipment distributed or the inventions licensed in connection with any other machinery or equipment, or the use of it in any specified plant or locality; *(b)* authorizes termination of the license for unauthorized use; *(c)* provides that the licensee shall not contest the validity of any patent or patents of the licensor; *(d)* provides that improvements by the licensee on machinery leased and sold shall become the property of the lessor; *(e)* provides that rights to improvements and inventions covering licensed machinery or processes or methods shall become the exclusive property of the lessor or vendor; or *(f)* grants to any licensee a preferential position by lower rates of royalty, by different provisions of licensing, leasing, or sale, by exclusive licensing, rebate, discounts or requiring a share in net or gross income, or by any other means.

The paragraph now covers every kind of invention and every patent, present or future, in any field if owned or controlled or distributed by an appellant.

The injunction will stop all inventions or acquirement of patents in any field by any appellant unless for its own use in its business, for it sets such limitations upon the reward of a patent as to make it practically worthless except for use by the owner. It is unlimited in time. It is not limited to any joint action or conspiracy violative of the antitrust laws; it covers inventions in every conceivable field.

The Government now agrees that this injunction should be limited to glassmaking machinery and glassware as defined in paragraph 1 of the decree of the District Court. . . .

Paragraph 31 requires court approval of "any agreement between any of the defendants" and "of any license agreement made pursuant to this judgment." This is too sweeping. The provision is without limit of time and not terminable upon fulfillment of any condition. . . . This paragraph, if retained, should be restricted in application to lease or license agreements and agreements respecting patents and trade practices, production and trade relations.

By paragraph 33 each of the individual defendants is enjoined from "holding, controlling, directly or indirectly, or through corporations, agents, trustees, representatives, or nominees, any of the issued and outstanding capital stock, bonds, or other evidences of indebtedness of more than one corporation engaged either in the manufacture and sale of glassware or in the manufacture or distribution of machinery used in the manufacture of glassware or in both. . . ." . . . The purpose of dealing with stock ownership is to prevent aggregation of control to the end of establishing a monopoly or stifling competition. The ownership of a few, or even a few hundred, shares of stock of a glass manufacturing company not in competition with the company of which a defendant happens to be a director of officer can have no tendency towards such a result. . . .

Moreover, the injunction is against ownership of bonds of any such company. It is difficult to see how such ownership in any reasonable amount by any of the individuals in question could tend towards a violation of the Sherman Act. . . .

The decree should be modified to prohibit acquisition of stocks or bonds of any corporate appellant by any other such appellant, and to prohibit only the acquisition of a measure of control through ownership of stocks or bonds or otherwise, by any individual in a company competing with that with which he is officially connected or a subsidiary or affiliate of such competing company. . . .

Paragraphs 37 to 39 are directed at the Glass Containers Association. . . .

The injunctions entered in paragraphs 37 to 39, inclusive, compel the association to abolish its statistical committee and to refrain from establishing any committee with similar functions. . . .

We think the injunction as respects the association, while leaving it in existence, practically destroys its functioning, even as an innocent trade association for what have been held lawful ends. The association has undoubtedly been an important instrument of restraint and monopoly. It may be made such again, and detection and prevention and punishment for such resumption of violations of law may be difficult if not impossible. In the light of the record, we think it better to order its dissolution, and to provide that the corporate defendants be restrained for a period of five years from forming or joining any such trade association. . . .

Paragraph 52 deals with the problem of suppressed or unworked patents. Much is said in the opinion below, and in the briefs, about the practice of the appellants in applying for patents to "block off" or "fence in" competing inventions. In the cooperative effort of certain of the appellants to obtain dominance in the field of patented glassmaking machinery, many patents were applied for to prevent others from obtaining patents on improvements which might, to some extent, limit the return in the way of royalty on original or fundamental inventions. The decree should restrain agreements and combinations with this object. But it is another matter to restrain every defendant, for the indefinite future, from attempting to patent improvements of machines or processes previously patented and then owned by such defendant. This paragraph is, in our judgment, too broad. In effect it prohibits several of the corporate defendants from applying for patents covering their own inventions in the art of glassmaking. For reasons elsewhere elaborated it cannot be sustained. . . .

A patent owner is not in the position of a quasi-trustee for the public or under any obligation to see that the public acquires the free right to use the invention. He has no obligation either to use it or to grant its use to others. If he discloses the invention in his application so that it will come into the public domain at the end of the 17-year period of exclusive right he has fulfilled the only obligation imposed by the statute. . . .

[The judgment of the District Court was reversed in part and affirmed in part, and the decree was vacated and remanded. JUSTICES DOUGLAS, MURPHY and JACKSON took no part in the consideration or decision of the case. JUSTICES BLACK and RUTLEDGE each separately dissented in part.]

International Salt Co., Inc. v. *United States*
332 U.S. 392 (1947)

MR. JUSTICE JACKSON delivered the opinion of the Court.

The Government brought this civil action to enjoin the International Salt Company, appellant here, from carrying out provisions of the leases of its patented machines to the effect that lessees would use therein only International's salt products. The restriction is alleged to violate Section 1 of the Sherman Act, and Section 3 of the Clayton Act. . . .

It was established . . . that the International Salt Company is engaged in interstate commerce in salt, of which it is the country's largest producer for industrial uses. It also owns patents on two machines for utilization of salt products. . . . The principal distribution of each of these machines is under leases which, among other things, require the lessees to purchase from appellant all unpatented salt and salt tablets consumed in the leased machines. . . .

. . . In 1944, appellant sold approximately 119,000 tons of salt, for about $500,000, for use in these machines.

The appellant's patents, confer a limited monopoly of the invention they reward. From them appellant derives a right to restrain others from making, vending or using the patented machines. But the patents confer no right to restrain use of, or trade in, unpatented salt. By contracting to close this market for salt against competition, International has engaged in a restraint of trade for which its patents afford no immunity from the antitrust laws. . . .

Appellant contends, however, that summary judgment was unauthorized becuase it precluded trial of alleged issues of fact as to whether the restraint was unreasonable within the Sherman Act or substantially lessened competition or tended to create a monopoly in salt within the Clayton Act. We think the admitted facts left no genuine issue. Not only is price-fixing unreasonable, *per se, United States* v. *Socony-Vacuum Oil Co.* . . . ; *United States* v. *Trenton Potteries Co.* . . . , but also it is unreasonable, *per se,* to foreclose competitors from any substantial market. . . . The volume of business affected by these contracts cannot be said to be insignificant or insubstantial and the tendency of the arrangement to accomplishment of monopoly seems obvious. Under the law, agreements are forbidden which "tend to create a monopoly," and it is immaterial that the tendency is a creeping one rather than one that proceeds at full gallop; nor does the law await arrival at the goal before condemning the direction of the movement. . . .

Appellant also urges that since under the leases it remained under an obligation to repair and maintain the machines, it was reasonable to confine their use to its own salt because its high quality assured satisfactory functioning and low maintenance cost. . . .

Of course, a lessor may impose on a lessee reasonable restrictions designed in good faith to minimize maintenance burdens and to assure satisfactory operation. . . . But it is not pleaded, nor is it argued, that the machine is allergic to salt of equal quality produced by anyone except International. If others cannot produce salt equal to reasonable specifications for machine use, it is one thing; but it is admitted that, at times, at least, competitors do offer such a product. They are, however, shut out of the market by a provision that limits it, not in terms of quality, but in terms of a particular vendor. Rules for use of leased machinery must not be disguised restraints of free competition, though they may set reasonable standards which all suppliers must meet. . . .

Judgment affirmed.

[MR. JUSTICE FRANKFURTER, joined by MR. JUSTICE REED and MR. JUSTICE BURTON, dissented in part.]

Appendix

Excerpts from Antitrust Statutes

SHERMAN ACT, 1890

Sec. 1. Every contract, combination in the form of trust or otherwise, or conspiracy, in restraint of trade or commerce among the several States, or with foreign nations, is hereby declared to be illegal. Every person who shall make any such contract or engage in any such combination or conspiracy, shall be deemed guilty of a misdemeanor, and, on conviction thereof, shall be punished by fine not exceeding $5,000, or by imprisonment not exceeding one year, or by both said punishments, in the discretion of the court.

Sec. 2. Every person who shall monopolize, or attempt to monopolize, or combine or conspire with any other person or persons, to monopolize any part of the trade or commerce among the several States, or with foreign nations, shall be deemed guilty of a misdemeanor, and, on conviction thereof, shall be punished by fine not exceeding $5,000, or by imprisonment not exceeding one year, or by both said punishments, in the discretion of the court.

ANTITRUST PROCEDURES AND PENALTIES ACT, 1974, AMENDING SECTIONS 1 AND 2 OF THE SHERMAN ACT

Sec. 1. Every contract, combination in the form of trust or otherwise, or conspiracy, in restraint of trade or commerce among the several States, or with foreign nations, is hereby declared to be illegal. Every person who shall make any contract or engage in any combination or conspiracy hereby declared to be illegal shall be deemed guilty of a felony and, on conviction thereof, shall be punished by fine not exceeding $1 million if a corporation, or, if any other person, $100,000, or by imprisonment not exceeding three years, or by both said punishments, in the discretion of the court.

Sec. 2. Every person who shall monopolize, or attempt to monopolize, or combine or conspire with any other person or persons, to

518

monopolize any part of the trade or commerce among the several States, or with foreign nations, shall be deemed guilty of a felony, and, on conviction thereof, shall be punished by fine not exceeding $1 million if a corporation, or, if any other person, $100,000, or by imprisonment not exceeding three years, or by both said punishments, in the discretion of the court.

CLAYTON ACT, 1914

Sec. 2. That it shall be unlawful for any person engaged in commerce, in the course of such commerce, either directly or indirectly, to discriminate in price between different purchasers of commodities, which commodities are sold for use, consumption, or resale within the United States or any Territory thereof or the District of Columbia or any insular possession or other place under the jurisdiction of the United States, where the effect of such discrimination may be to substantially lessen competition or tend to create a monopoly in any line of commerce: *Provided,* That nothing herein contained shall prevent discrimination in price between purchasers of commodities on account of differences in the grade, quality, or quantity of the commodity sold, or that makes only due allowance for differences in the cost of selling or transportation, or discrimination in price in the same or different communities made in good faith to meet competition: *And provided further,* That nothing herein contained shall prevent persons engaged in selling goods, wares, or merchandise in commerce from selecting their own customers in bona fide transactions and not in restraint of trade.

ROBINSON–PATMAN ACT, 1936, AMENDING SECTION 2 OF THE CLAYTON ACT

Sec. 2. *(a)* That it shall be unlawful for any person engaged in commerce, in the course of such commerce, either directly or indirectly, to discriminate in price between different purchasers of commodities of like grade and quality, where either or any of the purchases involved in such discrimination are in commerce, where such commodities are sold for use, consumption, or resale within the United States or any Territory thereof or the District of Columbia or any insular possession or other place under the jurisdiction of the United States, and where the effect of such discrimination may be substantially to lessen competition or tend to create a monopoly in any line of commerce, or to injure, destroy, or prevent competition with any person who either grants or knowingly receives the benefit cf such discrimination, or with customers of either of them: *Provided,* That nothing herein contained shall prevent differentials which make only due allowance for differences in the cost of manufacture, sale, or delivery resulting from the differing methods or quantities in which such commodities are to such purchasers sold or delivered: *Provided, however,* That the Federal Trade Commission may, after due investigation and hearing to all interested parties, fix and establish quantity limits, and revise the same as it finds necessary, as to particular commodities or classes of commodities, where it finds that available purchasers in greater quantities are so few as to render differentials on account thereof unjustly discriminatory or promotive of monopoly in any line of commerce; and the foregoing shall then not be construed to permit differentials based on differences in quantities greater than those so fixed and established: *And provided further,* That nothing herein contained shall prevent persons engaged in selling goods, wares, or merchandise in commerce from selecting their own customers in bona fide transactions and not in restraint of trade: *And provided further,* That nothing herein contained shall prevent price changes from time to time where in response to changing conditions affecting the market for or the marketability of the goods concerned, such as but not limited to actual or imminent deterioration of perishable goods, obsolescence of seasonal goods, distress sales under court process, or sales in good faith in discontinuance of business in the goods concerned.

(b) Upon proof being made, at any hearing on a complaint under this section, that there has been discrimination in price or services or facilities furnished, the burden of rebutting the prima-facie case thus made by showing justification shall be upon the person charged with a violation of this section, and unless justification shall be affirmatively shown, the Commission is authorized to issue an order terminating the discrimination: *Provided, however,* That nothing herein contained shall prevent a seller rebutting the prima-facie case thus made by showing that his lower price or the furnishing of services or facilities to any purchaser or purchasers was made in good faith to meet an equally low price of a competitor, or the services or facilities furnished by a competitor.

(c) That it shall be unlawful for any person engaged in commerce, in the course of such commerce, to pay or grant, or to receive or accept, anything of value as a commission, brokerage, or other compensation, or any allowance or discount in lieu thereof, except for services rendered in connection with the sale or purchase of goods, wares, or merchandise, either to the other party to such transaction or to an agent, representative, or other intermediary therein where such intermediary is acting in fact for or in behalf, or is subject to the direct or indirect control, of any party to such transactions other than the person by whom such compensation is so granted or paid.

(d) That it shall be unlawful for any person engaged in commerce to pay or contract for the payment of anything of value to or for the benefit of a customer of such person in the course of such commerce as compensation or in consideration for any services or facilities furnished by or through such customer in connection with the processing, handling, sale, or offering for sale of any products or commodities manufactured, sold, or

offered for sale by such person, unless such payment or consideration is available on proportionally equal terms to all other customers competing in the distribution of such products or commodities.

(e)   That it shall be unlawful for any person to discriminate in favor of one purchaser against another purchaser or purchasers of a commodity bought for resale, with or without processing, by contracting to furnish or furnishing, or by contributing to the furnishing of, any services or facilities connected with the processing, handling, sale, or offering for sale of such commodity so purchased upon terms not accorded to all purchasers on proportionally equal terms.

(f)   That it shall be unlawful for any person engaged in commerce, in the course of such commerce, knowingly to induce or receive a discrimination in price which is prohibited by this section.

CLAYTON ACT, 1914

Sec. 3.   That it shall be unlawful for any person engaged in commerce, in the course of such commerce, to lease or make a sale or contract for sale of goods, wares, merchandise, machinery, supplies, or other commodities, whether patented or unpatented, for use, consumption, or resale within the United States or any Territory thereof or the District of Columbia or any insular possession or other place under the jurisdiction of the United States, or fix a price charged therefor, or discount from, or rebate upon, such price, on the condition, agreement, or understanding that the lessee or purchaser thereof shall not use or deal in the goods, wares, merchandise, machinery, supplies, or other commodity of a competitor or competitors of the lessor seller, where the effect of such lease, sale, or contract for sale or such condition, agreement, or understanding may be to substantially lessen competition or tend to create a monopoly in any line of commerce.

FEDERAL TRADE COMMISSION ACT, 1914

Sec. 5.   That unfair methods of competition in commerce are hereby declared unlawful.

CLAYTON ACT, 1914

Sec. 7.   That no corporation engaged in commerce shall acquire, directly or indirectly, the whole or any part of the stock or other share capital of another corporation engaged also in commerce where the effect of such acquisition may be to substantially lessen competition between the corporation whose stock is so acquired and the corporation making the acquisition or to restrain such commerce in any section or community or tend to create a monopoly of any line of commerce.

No corporation shall acquire, directly or indirectly, the whole or any part of the stock or other share capital of two or more corporations engaged in commerce where the effect of such acquisition or the use of such stock by the voting or granting of proxies or otherwise may be to substantially lessen competition between such corporations, or any of them, whose stock or other share capital is so acquired, or to restrain such commerce in any section or community or tend to create a monopoly of any line of commerce.

CELLER–KEFAUVER ACT, 1950, AMENDING SECTION 7 OF THE CLAYTON ACT

Sec. 7. That no corporation engaged in commerce shall acquire, directly or indirectly, the whole or any part of the stock or other share capital and no corporation subject to the jurisdiction of the Federal Trade Commission shall acquire the whole or any part of the assets of another corporation engaged also in commerce, where in any line of commerce in any section of the country, the effect of such acquisition may be substantially to lessen competition, or to tend to create a monopoly.

Index of Cases

526